The New Penguin History of Scotland

R. A. HOUSTON AND W. W. J. KNOX

The New Penguin History of Scotland

From the Earliest Times to the Present Day

ALLEN LANE
THE PENGUIN PRESS
In association with the National Museums of Scotland

For Veena and Patty

ALLEN LANE
THE PENGUIN PRESS

Published by the Penguin Group
Penguin Books Ltd, 80 Strand, London WC2 0RL, England
Penguin Putnam Inc., 375 Hudson Street, New York, New York 10014, USA
Penguin Books Australia Ltd, 250 Camberwell Road, Camberwell, Victoria 3124, Australia
Penguin Books Canada Ltd, 10 Alcorn Avenue, Toronto, Ontario, Canada M4V 3B2
Penguin Books India (P) Ltd, 11, Community Centre, Panchsheel Park, New Delhi – 110 017, India
Penguin Books (NZ) Ltd, Cnr Rosedale and Airborne Roads, Albany, Auckland, New Zealand
Penguin Books (South Africa) (Pty) Ltd, 24 Sturdee Avenue, Rosebank 2196, South Africa

Penguin Books Ltd, Registered Offices: 80 Strand, London WC2 0RL, England

www.penguin.com

First published 2001
1

Copyright © R. A. Houston and W. W. J. Knox, 2001

Set in 11/14 pt Monotype Octavian
Typeset by Rowland Phototypesetting Ltd, Bury St Edmunds, Suffolk
Printed and bound in Great Britain by Butler and Tanner Ltd, Frome, Somerset

Cover repro and printing by Concise Cover Printers

A CIP catalogue record for this book is available from the British Library

ISBN 0-713-99187-9
ISBN US 0-140-26367-5

Contents

List of Illustrations

Picture research by Cecilia Mackay, with the kind assistance of Helen Nicoll at the National Museums of Scotland.

All photographs are copyright © Trustees of the National Museums of Scotland, except where indicated otherwise in parentheses.

Power, Authority and Status

1. Silver-gilt brooch, *c.* AD 700.
2. Regalia made for clan chieftains, third millennium BC to the seventh century AD.
3. Remains of Roman statue, *c.* AD 350.
4. Belt pistol.

Sacred Symbols and Messages

1. Carved female figure found at Ballachulish, dating from between 730 and 520 BC.
2. Silver plaques decorated with red enamel, AD 600–700.
3. An illumination from 'The Forman Armorial', late sixteenth century (copyright © Manuscripts Library, Trustees of the National Library of Scotland).
4. 'Luckenbooth' brooch.
5. Oak figure of St Andrew, *c.* 1500.

Scotland's Voice

1. *The Ballade . . . of Lord Barnard Stewart*, by William Dunbar, printed by Myllar and Chepman (copyright © Rare Books Library, the Trustees of the National Library of Scotland).

2. Ladies' fan decorated in support of the Act of Union, 1707.
3. Ladies' fan supporting the Jacobite cause, *c.* 1745.
4. Enamelled wineglass portraying the Young Pretender, late eighteenth century.
5. Silver quaich depicting the profile of Queen Anne.

Leisure and Play

1. Booklet of Border rugby fixtures, 1932–3. (Private collection, on loan to National Museums of Scotland.)
2. Slate gaming board, eleventh or twelfth century.
3. The Lewis chessmen, twelfth century.
4. Silver and purple chairs by Charles Rennie Mackintosh, 1903.
5. Irn-Bru (Irn-Bru is a registered trademark of A. G. Barr & Co.).

Turbulence and Unrest

1. Rowel spurs belonging to Auld Wat Scott, sixteenth century.
2. Folding camp-stool, said to have been thrown by Jenny Geddes at the Dean of St Giles' Kirk, 1637.
3. Soldier's knapsack from the 10th Regiment of North British Militia, 1798.

The Highlanders: Fighting Men

1. Portrait of William Cumming, piper to the Laid of Grant, by Richard Waitt, 1714.
2. Cast of a grave slab found at Finlaggan, mid sixteenth-century.
3. Highland dirks from the seventeenth and eighteenth centuries.

Spreading the Message of the Lord

1. Abraham's sacrifice of Isaac, from the ceiling of Dean House, Edinburgh, *c.* 1605–27.
2. Pewter communion plates and beakers, 1671.
3. Pebble marked with cross from St Ninian's Cave, Wigtownshire.
4. The Fetternear banner, *c.* 1520.
5. Mask and wig used by the seventeenth-century minister Alexander Peden.
6. Pictish cross slab, AD 700–900.

Trade, Commerce and Economic Expansion

1. Official seal of Crail, Fife.

2. Hand-held coin scale, 1773.
3. Early banknotes, 1723 and 1750.
4. Banner of St Cuthbert's Lodge of Free Gardeners, founded in 1843.

Signals and Connections

1. Baird television receiver, 1930.
2. Mirror galvanometer of Lord Kelvin.
3. LNER poster of the Forth Bridge, by H. G. Gawthorn, 1928 (copyright © National Railway Museum, York/Science & Society Picture Library).
4. Ticket for the Glasgow and Garnkirk railway, opened in 1831.
5. Medal commemorating the opening of the Forth Rail Bridge, 1890.

In a Foreign Land

1. Silver snuff-box, 1849.
2. Poster promoting emigration to the Colonies, Arbroath, 1882 (courtesy of DMC Ltd, Crieff/SCRAN).
3. Deerskin bag owned by Dr John Rae, nineteenth century (on loan to the National Museums of Scotland from the University of Edinburgh).

Acknowledgements

We are grateful to those invited to attend the September 1999 colloquium in the Parliament Hall of St Andrews University. We should like particularly to thank Professor Christopher Smout, who gave the opening address, and the commentators on the chapters – Professor James Campbell, Professor John Morrill, and Dr John Stevenson. The meeting was funded by the School of History, University of St Andrews. Among colleagues at St Andrews, Colin Martin and David Allan deserve special thanks. We are indebted to the contributors for their extensive, helpful and sometimes spirited comments on the Introduction. We both benefited from sabbatical leave from St Andrews at different points during the final editing process. Rab Houston would also like to acknowledge the additional semester's leave made possible for him by a grant from the Arts and Humanities Research Board, during which much of the time-consuming work of editing the typescripts was carried out.

RAH and WWJK

Introduction: Scots and their Histories

R. A. HOUSTON

W. W. J. KNOX

'If you know whence you came, there is really no limit to where you can go.' This was the conclusion the novelist James Baldwin reached after considering why the exclusion of the Afro-American from mainstream histories of the United States had created a sense of inferiority among black people there. His statement underlines how important history can be to a people and how knowledge of the past can empower and liberate. More than most Europeans, the Scots can identify with Baldwin's sentiments. A recent survey of Scotland's schoolchildren concluded that they had only a very limited knowledge of the Scottish past and much of what they knew was dependent on media representations of their history.

Whether this is truer of Scots than of others can be debated. However, the apparent lack of informed knowledge of Scotland's past is one of the inspirations for this volume. Its purpose is simple: that is, more fully and accurately to understand the place of Scotland and the Scots in time. All Scotland's peopled past has to be understood, from the first settlements of prehistory to the present day. This aims to be a history of the Scottish people as a whole, for one of the most exciting developments for the present generation of historians has been a growing interest in the lives of the neglected masses rather than simply in kings, bishops and battles.

Each chapter has an introduction and a varying number of sections devoted to political, social, cultural and economic developments during the period covered. While we have endeavoured to ensure thematic unity throughout the volume, the characteristic themes of each epoch will determine the approach. For example, issues concerned with the exercise of the king's power, or with the relationship between church and monarch, will figure prominently in any analysis of medieval and early modern Scottish politics. A discussion of the twentieth-century political scene in Scotland will involve party politics, mass participation and voting patterns. Surviving sources will also shape the sorts of questions that can be answered. Documentary sources do not exist before the first century. The wealthy and powerful left many more traces of their lives than did the poor, especially in written records of the distant past. Yet a history which concentrates on the well documented omits 90 per cent of males and virtually all females until very recently. Finally, authors have been encouraged to make a case for the importance of their era and to put their individual stamp on each period. There will be some chronological overlap as chapters pick up earlier themes and signpost later developments. Healthy disagreements – on issues like the role of conquest rather than peaceful assimilation in the spread of the Celtic language or the significance of the Union of Parliaments in 1707 – have been allowed to stand as examples of the productive tensions which drive advances in historical understanding.

This Introduction, however, takes a slightly different approach. It seeks to delineate central themes in the history of Scotland and to ask how these have fitted into the Scots' perceptions of themselves and their history. Furthermore, it investigates how certain aspects of Scottish history have assumed a central role at the expense of others in the making of identity. History makes a people. Yet it is also true that every nation makes its own history. In this process, some history is invented, and other aspects are forgotten or neglected. The myths created from a selective rendering of facts can perform powerful (and positive) functions, both in ensuring stability and in promoting change. Arguably a few myths about Scottish history may be even more important in shaping identity and in facilitating actions than any amount of historical 'fact'; but myth can also lead to self-delusion.

This is where the historian comes in, sifting the evidence and telling Scotland's story as closely as possible to 'the way it was'. Thus readers of this volume should not look for a tartan history. They should also abandon simple notions of linear progress. Scotland's history was one of trends, but these sometimes changed abruptly. It is more helpful to think of powerful continuities, cycles and occasional historical dead-ends when we study Scotland's history over the last 10,000 years. Before reading the detailed chapters, readers may ponder the following examples. Even in prehistory, the social ethos fluctuated between communal and hierarchical emphases, between socially inclusive and exclusive priorities. Similarly, the centre of political power, now so firmly in the east-central Lowlands, was at some periods in the far north, at others in the south-west, and at times in the west-central Lowlands. Land may have been used as extensively and populated as densely around 1000 BC as it was in 1300 AD. Population densities were sometimes as high in upland areas as in the central Lowlands. It is a commonplace that medieval people were generally shorter than modern, but Neolithic men and women may have been taller than their medieval successors. Scotland's economic powerhouse shifted from south to north and back, from one coast to the other and back, and within regions, through all its recorded history. A historical turning-point that seems inevitable in retrospect turns out on investigation to be only one of many possible outcomes. The sixteenth-century Reformation and the Glorious Revolution of 1688–90 are examples.

Moreover, what seem timeless values that have only recently changed may themselves have late origins. The idea that women should have an exclusively domestic role rather than a workplace and domestic one is historically specific to certain narrow social groups or to larger sections of society at certain times, notably in the nineteenth and the first half of the twentieth century. Modern Scots are urban-dwelling people, but towns may not have existed prior to the eleventh century and it was only 150 years ago that a majority of the population came to live in cities.

The search for what is distinctive to Scotland should not blind us to the European-wide processes in which Scotland shared. It experienced the price inflation of the sixteenth century and the population rise of the later eighteenth century, but the causes and implications of these phenomena were specific to Scotland. Urbanization came late to Scotland, but was more rapid and socially disturbing than in much of Europe. Other aspects too were distinctive. In the late medieval and early-modern period most of Scotland's cultural influences came from France and the Low Countries, while Ireland drew inspiration from the Mediterranean world, especially Spain; the English were highly eclectic; Wales was much more English-centred for both trade and culture than the other Celtic nations.

These paradoxes and discontinuities, similarities and differences, are as much the historian's business as is plotting 'progress'. This volume, therefore, hopes to give those who care about Scotland a fuller picture of its history. It will also bring to the attention of the Scottish and other peoples the rich variety and wide range of historical scholarship which has emerged in the last few decades. Scotland's story is powerful and instructive. It deserves to be discovered and then told. For Scotland's modern identity is tied up in its history, and especially in issues such as religion, education, politics, economic opportunity, lifestyle, and relationship between individuals and groups as well as with the environment.

Identities

The Scots are tall, rugged people who live in the mountain fastness of their native land, on a diet of oatmeal porridge and whisky. They wear kilts of a tartan weave, play a deafening musical instrument called the bagpipes, are immediately hospitable, but cautious with money . . . They are sparing with words, but when they speak they speak the truth. They have a hard and Spartan religious faith and regard virtually any activity on a Sunday as a grave sin. When they leave their native land, they immediately rise to the top in other peoples' industries and professions.

These are the words of the Glasgow journalist Clifford Hanley in his 1980 book, *The Scots*. His composite stereotype of the modern Scot points to the larger questions of Scottish identity. What are Scotland's claims to nationhood and how justified are they? Norman Stone, the historian and journalist, recently claimed that only Jerusalem had contributed more to world civilization than Scotland. In a less erudite (if no less evocative) manner, the ex-manager of the Scottish football team in the 1970s, Ally MacLeod, declared that Scotland was 'the best wee nation God ever put breath in'. More soberly, the Australian writer Robert Hughes has said that 'small nations should neither strut nor cringe'. Are the Scots simply a peripheral part of a larger north-European state, deluding themselves and the rest of the world with national pretensions? Or have they a legitimate right to consider themselves as more significant?

In answering this, it must be remembered that Scotland was a unified nation for only about four hundred years, maybe less, since Orkney and Shetland were only formally added in 1470. The man popularly thought of as the first king of Scotland, Cinaed mac Ailpín (Kenneth MacAlpine, who died in 848), is actually best seen as the founder of the dynasty of the kings of Scots. He ruled over a lesser Scotland made up of the former Pictland and Dál Riata, and covering the area between the Forth, Moray and the central Highlands. Scotland was thus, perhaps, a kingdom from 839–44, but it only became a unity that is close to the modern meaning of a state in the thirteenth century. The Highlands and Islands did not become integrated until the mid-eighteenth century.

This late unification is hardly surprising in view of the different forms of social organization which sprang from the ethnic diversity of the peoples who became the Scots and those who led them. There is no common ancestral or genetic heritage which links the peoples of Scotland. During the early Middle Ages Scotland was made up of five main linguistically separate groups. The Picts inhabited that part of Scotland from Caithness to the Forth – Fortriu, strictly a sub-kingdom of the king of the Picts, but the name may have become synonymous with the whole kingdom; the Britons (confusingly known as Welsh in the twelfth century) were found in parts of southern Scotland; the Gaels inhabited the kingdom of Dál Riata (roughly modern Argyllshire and the Isles); the Angles lived in Northumbria, Lothian, and Galloway; and the Vikings ruled Orkney and Shetland, the Western Isles and Caithness from *c.* 800. The term 'Scoti' was used from Roman times and into the early eighth century by the northern-English ecclesiastical chronicler Bede to describe both Scots and Irish Gaels. They shared a common culture. It was only from the tenth century that a clear distinction was made between the Gaels of Ireland and the Albanaig (men of Alba), and in that sense it was only then that singular 'Scots' can be identified.

The linguistic and ethnic mix was further complicated by the influx of Anglo-French during the reign of David I (1124–53), a development which had the effect of Normanizing the Scottish nobility and clergy. French was used by the aristocracy and clergy, Latin by the clergy. Through the development of chartered burghs, the speech of Lowlanders in general was also anglicized. In the late Middle Ages, Scots (a variant of English) was the tongue of the Germanic Angles of Lothian and elsewhere, and only expanded under Anglo-Norman influence because it became the language of commerce. Elsewhere, Gaelic was widely spoken, though there were also Norse dialects in the

Northern Isles. Gaelic speaking was at its height in the eleventh century, but it was never spoken by all. From *c.* 1350 onwards Scots expanded at the expense of Gaelic, which became identified principally with the Highlands and Islands.

Rulers mirrored the ethnic and linguistic mix of the population of Scotland. Many of the better-known Scottish kings and queens had only a tenuous family connection with the land they ultimately ruled. Queen Margaret, the wife of Malcolm III (1058–93) and Scotland's only canonized royal saint, spent part of her childhood in Hungary and knew no Gaelic; David I spent his adolescent years at the English court; Robert the Bruce (reigned 1306–29) was of Anglo-French descent, and he may have believed in the Irish and Scottish peoples 'stemming from one seed of birth'. Mary, Queen of Scots (1542–87) spent a quarter of her life in France, and it was her dying wish to be buried at Rheims with her Guise relatives. Even the great folk hero of Scotland, William Wallace (d. 1305), was descended from a Normanized Welshman (in the medieval sense of the Welsh), Richard le Walleys. The ethnic diversity of the aristocracy reflected the complex origins of the monarchy. Scottish nobles also held lands in England, Ireland and France.

There are two further considerations in charting the origins and development of a national identity. First, identity is never static and is always contested. There are local and regional identities which may overlie or be overlaid by national consciousness and which often compete with it. Instead of a single national community, there was a complex set of 'relative identities' which depended on circumstances. Second, the influence of other cultures has been powerful in shaping the national identity over time. Invading armies, military conquest and foreign settlers have all left their mark on Scotland's development, not only by assimilation but also by rejection. Indeed, as the political theorist Peter Sahlins put it, national identity is not only defined by the 'social or territorial boundaries drawn to distinguish the collective self', it is also defined by a relation with the 'other'. Being Scots means not being, for example, English or French.

Highland and Lowland

Both national and regional identities were complex and shifting. Nowhere is this better illustrated than in the changing relationship of Lowland Scotland with the Highlands. It was only at the end of the fourteenth century that the chronicler John of Fordun spoke of a Highland–Lowland divide for the first time. Such a distinction may have existed before this, but it is certain that by the time of James VI (1567–1625) a clear linguistic cleft had opened between Gaelic and Scots, Highlands and Lowlands: a divide defined by increasingly strong political and military antagonisms. The language, economy and social organization of the western Highlands were by then different from those of the Lowlands, though other parts of the northern uplands (like the north-western parts of Stirlingshire and Perthshire) are best seen as transitional zones. At James's court the

Highlands reached the ambiguous status of being both quaint and barbarous, and it was fashionable for courtiers to ridicule Gaelic culture, its legends and origins. The crown also instituted legislation (the 1609 Statutes of Iona) aimed among other things at feasting and fighting, which were at the heart of Highland society.

This political and cultural assault intensified during the seventeenth century as Highlanders came to be perceived as lawless and threatening by their Lowland neighbours, and governments continued to attempt pacification and integration. The massacre of MacDonalds by Campbells at Glencoe in 1692 (and the less well-known carnage on Eigg in 1690) were extreme examples of the strategy to bind the clan chiefs to the government by personal oath and, if necessary, fear. At the same time, the threat apparently posed by militant post- (or counter-) Reformation Catholicism abroad was passed on by association to Highlanders as a whole, though not all were Catholic. By 1800 Lowlanders easily referred to Highlanders as not only different, but also inferior, while the latter described the Lowlanders and English as 'sassenachs' or Saxons. This term, being the only one available to describe the English, had no pejorative meaning in Gaelic. It only acquired one when used in Scots. More value-loaded for Gaels was the word 'Gall', meaning a foreigner (plural 'Gaill').

State legislation banned the wearing of Highland dress and the carrying of bagpipes, except for Highland regiments abroad, after the 1745 Jacobite rebellion which marked the final, unsuccessful attempt by a Stewart claimant to oust the Hanoverians from the throne. The ban lasted until 1782. The view that civilization was founded on Protestantism and Lowland values was further promoted by the educational work of the Society in Scotland for the Propagation of Christian Knowledge in the eighteenth century. Yet at the same time the 'Romantic revival' of the late eighteenth and early nineteenth century made allegedly heathen Highlanders into heroes when associated with their military participation in the making of the British Empire. From the beginning of the Seven Years War (1756) to the end of the Napoleonic conflicts in 1815, nearly 50,000 Highlanders were recruited into British regiments. In 1822 George IV, dressed in tartan, processed triumphantly through an Edinburgh decked out with Highland symbols. The pageant had been masterminded by none other than the great Tory and monarchist, Sir Walter Scott. Queen Victoria (1837–1901) endorsed the monarchy's love of the Highlands by decking out the dining-room of Balmoral in tartan and singing Jacobite songs, such as 'Oh, wae's me for Prince Charlie'.

For the Lowland Scots this romanticism was short-lived. During the famine of the mid-1840s disdain for Highland life reached its height when the Lowland press alleged that the idleness and fatalism of the racially inferior (Catholic) Highlander was to blame for the catastrophe. Charitable giving for Highland causes there certainly was, but such press outbursts qualify the popular idea that 'Highlandism' had become, through Scott's influence, the dominant force in Scottish cultural life in the first half of the nineteenth century, even if it was a powerful strain. Material aspects of Highland life and regional identity – heather and thistles, bagpipes and tartan – have come to be included among the symbols of a construct called 'Scottishness'. Modern urban dwellers see nothing incongruous in wearing a kilt at weddings, or singing songs that represent a modern, romanticized sensibility about a very distant way of life.

After 1850 the distinctions between Highland and Lowland Scotland became increasingly blurred. The 1872 Education Act banned school lessons from being taught in Gaelic. Courts too refused to recognize Gaelic. As a result of these institutional changes and of emigration, the number of Gaelic speakers, declining for centuries because of proscription and because Highlanders saw the economic advantages of English, began to drop off dramatically. In 1689 some 25 to 30 per cent of the Scottish population could claim Gaelic as their first language; by 1806 the number had fallen to 19 per cent; in 1981 it was a mere 2 per cent. Currently there are more Gaelic speakers in Strathclyde than in the Western Isles, more in Glasgow than on Skye, and more in Nova Scotia than in either.

Language may be a component of national identity, but its significance has varied over time and place. From the twelfth century to the twentieth, the language of uniformity, integration and growing national identity was Scots or English. Gaelic was 'the other'. Taken together, *A Dictionary of the Older Scots Tongue from the Twelfth Century to the End of the Seventeenth* (begun by Sir William Craigie in 1931 and still in progress) and *The Scottish National Dictionary* (11 volumes, 1931–76), contain over 50,000 words particular to Scots. However, Scots has not formed a powerful focus for identity in modern Scotland. Indeed the shunning of certain words, such as clarty (dirty), hoose (house), mither (mother), as well as the levelling of accents, particularly among the better-off, has further anglicized and thus reduced the importance of language in shaping identity. Language remains an important part of national identity, but the language in question is now Gaelic. Its importance remains to be tested. Wales, which has long had a strong linguistic basis for its nationalism (including a full Welsh Bible two centuries before Scotland had a full Gaelic one), has a nationalist movement that finds less expression in political forms and separatist aspirations than is the case in Scotland. The first full Bible in Scots was not published until 1983.

External Influences

Gaelic speakers presently see English (and the English) as 'the other', and this negative or oppositional side seems a compelling and powerful force in shaping national identity. During the last millennium, the plural histories of the non-English component peoples of the modern British Isles reflect their struggles to retain an identity against the cultural pressure of the English. In the first millennium after Christ the forces shaping oneness were similar, but 'the other' with which it was compared was more cosmopolitan. Roman encounters with the peoples of southern Scotland were extensive. In addition to scores of semi-permanent garrisons at places like Ardoch near Crieff, another 200 temporary camps are recorded – the remnants of many military campaigns.

Nevertheless, the Romans were only brief settlers in northern Britain. They advanced and withdrew, imposing themselves on the landscape as a matter of policy. The archaeological record of the Romans is usually presented as vestiges of advanced civilization in an uncivilized land. However, some of their methods of 'civilizing' were questionable. The campaigns of Septimus Severus in the early third century AD against the Maeatae and the Caledonians of the eastern Lowlands involved armies of perhaps 50,000 men: numbers not exceeded before or since on British soil. Their genocidal scorched-earth policy is less notorious than that of Edward I more than a millennium later (or of Cromwell's invasion in the mid-seventeenth century), but the effect on Scotland's people and agriculture may have been even more devastating.

The mark of invaders is clearer in some areas than others. Some conquerors have left relatively little trace in the archaeological record. The Scandinavians or Vikings (the former an ethnic label, the latter an occupational one) are an example. Though the Hebrides were ruled by the Norse from the ninth until the thirteenth century, their settlement remains are elusive. Elsewhere the intangible but important residue of place-names demonstrates a clear Scandinavian influence. This is in contrast with the Outer Hebrides and the Northern Isles, and may show the limits of integration of parts of Scotland into a Scandinavian kingdom. The Vikings have had a much poorer press than the Romans, an image as mere rapists and pillagers that has only been challenged over the last generation.

That is not to say that outsiders came to Scotland with their swords sheathed. Half a millennium of interstitial violence characterized relations between Scotland and England. The Anglo-Scottish border, which until *c.* 1100 was a loose territorial convenience, became thereafter a focus for different allegiances and, ultimately, patterns of settlement and association as separate governmental forms developed on either side of the boundary. It was partly through repeated warfare with the English that the national consciousness was forged. In the wars of independence (variously dated, but probably best seen as 1286–1403), the modern nation was born. Moreover, the independence of nation and people became intertwined with that of the church. This was given symbolic significance when an Act of Parliament in 1385 commanded Scots soldiers to wear the blue and white cross of St Andrew – the saltire – rather than wrap themselves in the yellow and red of the lion rampant – the flag of the monarchy. The symbol itself was an international one, for the Burgundians carried the saltire when they occupied Paris in the fifteenth century.

Only slowly did there develop a less confrontational set of relationships, which culminated in the Union of the Crowns in 1603. This Act anticipated, but did not predetermine, the incorporating Union of Parliaments in 1707. A unitary British state emerged thereafter. Perhaps from 1603 but certainly from 1707, Scots adopted a dual nationality, Scottish and British – albeit with difficulty, as the Cromwellian occupation in the 1650s and the Jacobite risings of 1715 and 1745 show. Almost constant military conflict with France between 1688 and 1815 also tempered the 'auld alliance' and allowed a British identity to develop, partly against the French. With Scots and English reconciled, the concept of 'the other' found a new focus in overseas (imperial) enemies and in the large-scale immigration of the Catholic Irish. To be Scottish in the nineteenth century was at least partly not to be Irish.

Identity has always been tied up in oppositions. However, cultural developments are also dependent on the reception of outside influences. Foreign influence was sought out and welcomed as much as it was imposed and resisted. By the Middle Ages trading contacts had been established with a number of ports in the Baltic and in the Low Countries. Flemish settlers were important in the foundation of early burghs. Merchants from the Baltic and North Sea littoral are buried in the medieval and early modern churchyards of Scotland. Towns of the seventeenth century were keen to have skilled foreigners settle, notably those with expertise in metalworking and textile manufacture (including the Flemish and French Protestant refugees).

The effect on material culture has been enduring. Fife stone was brought in to build the original Scottish church at Rotterdam in 1643, while Dutch pantiles used for ballast became roofing on the Dutch-style crow-step gables of the East Neuk ports. The flow of trade was complemented by intellectual currents. Being a member of a universal church until the Reformation, Scotland was open to the international flow of philosophical and theological discourse. The Scottish church was mentioned in a papal bull of 1174 as a 'special daughter', and it is interesting that Macbeth (1040–57), the later much-despised but highly successful king of Scotland, made the first recorded pilgrimage by a king of Alba to the Threshold of the Apostle in Rome. The great statement of Scottish independence, the Declaration of Arbroath (1320), is addressed to Pope John XXII, although it is uncertain whether its contents were known outside church and court circles at the time. French influences were found at the court of Scotland, and France was the principal destination for travelling Scottish students until the late sixteenth century. Some of the medieval monasteries of Scotland were described as little parts of France.

That medieval Scotland was much influenced by France is a commonplace, but the cultural impact of the Low Countries was also strong in the early modern period. The sway of both parts of Europe is evident in church building and decoration. The revolutionary plan of Burntisland kirk compares with the Calvinist church at La Rochelle in western France, while Edinburgh's Tron kirk has Dutch parallels. Foreign influences in castles and aristocratic townhouses are mainly French until the seventeenth century – a reflection of aristocratic education. Italian trends are also apparent in the wing of Crichton Castle built after 1560. Thus between the fourteenth and the sixteenth century Scottish architecture was open to continental influence, but it also demonstrated an interest in developing the possibilities of earlier Scottish solutions to the problems of style and function in building. Scotland had followed English styles of 'polite' architecture rather closely between the eleventh and thirteenth centuries but diverged thereafter to adopt the Romanesque revival widespread on the continent. The houses of the nobles after 1603 assumed a greater importance than in other states, ignoring or even leading the royal taste rather than following it. Scots adopted and adapted the architecture of the Renaissance. It is fitting, then, that the new building for the Scottish parliament was designed by a Catalan.

In geographical location and cultural influences, Scotland can also be seen as a Scandinavian country. As well as impositions in the Viking age there were also shared forms which came from similarities in climate. As in Scandinavia, the Alps and the Pyrenees, 'shieling' or seasonal transhumance to fatten cattle was practised in the Highlands and Islands. Until the large-scale immigration of Irish after the end of the eighteenth century, Scots had generally been receptive to outside influences and assimilated newcomers in a way that never happened in Ireland. There are also more subtle interactions. To paraphrase the words of the historian Professor John Pocock, the peoples of the British Isles have, as a consequence of a shared polity, interacted so as to change the conditions of one another's development.

Oppositions, or 'the other'

In spite of this, we must return to oppositions. From the seventeenth century, the British state was avowedly Protestant. The presence of a Catholic minority both tested and reinforced that element of hostility. Anti-Catholic riots occurred in Scotland's major cities, notably in the late 1680s and late 1770s – the Union of 1707 repressed rather than suppressed sectarian conflict. On account of their ethnic origin and their religion (though not all were Catholic), the immigrant Irish tended either to be shunned or perceived as a threat. Anti-Irish societies, such as the Loyal Orange Order, flourished in the west of Scotland among the miners, shipbuilders, and other sections of labouring people. The Order itself was founded in response to disturbances in Ulster in the 1790s and to Irish Catholic emancipation. It grew in size and influence with the heavy flow of immigrants in the early nineteenth century and again after the Irish famines of the 1840s. By 1878 there were 100 Orange lodges in Glasgow alone and 15,000 members out of a British total of 90,000. This figure increased with the influx of Protestant Irish from what were then the most Orange counties of Ireland, such as Armagh. Later the Order became more overtly Conservative and Unionist. Modern Scotland currently has about 50,000 Orangemen, who equal in number the active membership of all other mainstream political parties nationally. Anti-Catholicism pervaded society in the late eighteenth and early nineteenth century. It proved enduring. Writing in the 1930s, Helen Crawfurd, daughter of a prosperous Glasgow baker, suffragette, member of the

Independent Labour Party (ILP), and a founder member of the British Communist Party, recalled of growing up 'that she looked upon the Fenian and Catholic Irish as sub-human'.

It was the inter-war period that marked the high point of tension between native Protestants and Irish Catholics. Extremist organizations, such as the Protestant Action Society (PAS), were active in Edinburgh and Glasgow, winning support in local elections. In Edinburgh, demonstrations and intimidation orchestrated by John Cormack, leader of the PAS, took place in the mid-1930s. Catholics literally feared for their lives. The Church of Scotland fuelled tensions by publishing a pamphlet in 1923 entitled *The Menace of the Irish Race to Our Scottish Nationality*, and the right wing of the Nationalist movement took up the old theme that the Irish were racially inferior. The aftermath of the Second World War saw relations between Catholics and Protestants improve. The older forms of discrimination in the labour market, in housing and in other aspects of social life have largely disappeared. The growth of ecumenism and the destruction of former industries and industrial communities in which sectarianism thrived has marginalized this enduring conflict. However, its vestiges are found in the chants and taunts of rival football supporters at Ibrox and Parkhead, and in the existence of separate Catholic schools.

With the decline of these religious tensions, the Scots have had to redefine themselves once more. The 'other' can also be applied to peoples from different ethnic origins. There were black Africans living and working as servants in Scotland during the eighteenth century; until *c.* 1800 they were formally slaves, most of whom had come to Britain via the Atlantic sugar and tobacco colonies. However, non-whites form a smaller percentage of the modern population north of the border than they do in England. Again there are variations. Whites made up 99 per cent of the population of Scotland's richest region (Grampian) in 1995. In contrast, one child in nine entering Glasgow's schools in 1999 was non-white. While colour is an obvious differentiator, other ethnic groups could be found in Scotland during the last hundred years. Immigration by eastern Europeans in the second half of the nineteenth century was stemmed by the restrictive Aliens Act of 1905. In spite of this, there were 9,000 Russian Jews living in the Gorbals in 1918 and a sizable Lithuanian community in and around Coatbridge. Some of the latter were deported during the First World War; between 1940 and 1945 Italian Scots were interned, even if many eventually re-entered a society which was more welcoming to wartime allies like the Poles. Racism certainly exists within modern Scottish society, though the extent of support for overtly racist groups such as the British National Party seems very limited.

The relative absence of 'others' has led to a rethinking or a reawakening of interest in the Union and the relationship of Scottish culture to the power lying south of Berwick-on-Tweed. Although Scots in the nineteenth and twentieth centuries stressed similarities between their society and countries in continental Europe, the ease with which Scots sought and found placement in England shows that in many ways their perceived internationalism has been less significant than access to and assimilation by England and its empire. An anonymous correspondent of the *Caledonian Mercury*, an Edinburgh newspaper, stated in 1786: 'We are not so different from the present English manners as they are from those of 1600 . . . the main influences on lowland culture since 1600 have either been directly derived from England or from experiences Scotland and England have undergone together.' There were more people of English than Irish birth in mid-nineteenth-century Edinburgh. However, modern Scots who identify themselves against an 'other' may do so by expressing vehement anti-English sentiments.

At one level it is not possible to speak of Scottish politics separately from British politics during the last 300 years. However, there were distinctive political values, like the enduring strength of Liberalism from 1832 to 1914 (England was more consistently Conservative). Additionally, the Union of 1707 allowed for Scottish control over the major institutions of civil society: the law, the church and education. These peculiarly Scottish institutions provided a continuing basis for national allegiances and this was strengthened in 1885 with the founding of the Scottish Office. Although initially in Whitehall rather than Edinburgh, the Scottish Office was relocated to St Andrews House, Edinburgh, in 1939. From that date, the Secretary of State for Scotland assumed greater control over all areas of Scottish economic and social life. The Scottish Office acted as a symbol of independent Scotland and this was reflected in the desire of some political parties for a form of home rule. From the late nineteenth century, both the Liberal and Labour Parties accepted and supported the idea of a federated empire in which Scotland and Ireland would run their own domestic affairs, while ceding to Westminster control of defence and foreign policy. In 1924 the Labour MP for Glasgow Gorbals, George Buchanan, introduced a Government of Scotland Bill which provided for the independence of Scotland within a federal Britain. In spite of the support enjoyed by Buchanan's bill among all Scottish Labour MPs, the Labour Prime Minister, Ramsay MacDonald, allowed the Tories to talk it out.

This was the climax of support for home rule before the present generation. By the late 1920s the whole mood was swinging away from nationalism as unemployment grew to mass levels. Some prominent Scots began to argue that the solution to the country's economic difficulties lay in a strong British state. For those on the left, the rise of fascism further discredited nationalism. The founding of the wartime welfare state and the large-scale programme of nationalization by the Labour government of 1945–50 saw national identity subsumed within a greater British consciousness. Nationalist politicians received minimal support from the Scottish electorate in the 1950s and early 1960s. However, the collapse of the empire, the decline in Protestant churchgoing, and the fall in the Tory vote fractured the Unionist constituency and laid the basis for a nationalist revival. This reached a peak in 1974 when the Scottish Nationalist Party (SNP) won eleven seats and 30 per cent of the vote. The SNP performed disastrously in 1979, but nationalism as a serious political alternative to Unionism did not go away. The contrast with the Conservatives is stark. Capable of winning half the votes cast in Scotland during the 1950s, the Unionists and their allies faded in the 1980s and 1990s to less than one fifth – and no parliamentary seats. The SNP became the recognized opposition to Labour.

The growth of the nationalist vote is a reflection of the increased sense of national awareness. The cultural renaissance that took place in Scotland in the arts, history and the media from the 1960s was partly responsible. Many Scots now see themselves as Scottish rather than British. However we understand them, powerful forces created a sense of identity. Just as nineteenth-century immigrants to Scotland came to see themselves as Scottish (or British) in time, modern English settlers in the Highlands and Islands seem determined to be more Scottish than the Scots. While for their part, Scots may like Americans and dislike the English, Americanization, if anything, currently exerts a greater influence on Scottish culture than anglicization.

Landscape and Economy

Identity is not constant over time because its social bases change. Furthermore, belonging and being different do not mean the same to everyone. There is, of course, a shared core of cultural and political experiences that makes up a common identity – at least at a simple level. Yet the different narratives which constitute our understanding of history tend to serve different ends. Thus Scottish identity is a chimera; it exists, but is not easily defined.

Identity is concerned with past memory, the environment as well as 'the other', and is sustained through powerful narratives and myths. Landscape is important to heritage constructs and to certain aspects of modern identity. Yet as peoples make their histories, they also form the land and the interaction of humans with nature significantly influences the sense of being. The changing Scottish landscape provides important clues to the development of national sentiments over the centuries. The physical geography of Scotland has undergone much change as it adapted to the imperatives of climatic shifts and economic development.

The last ice age, which ended 10,000 years ago, did much to shape the distinctive features of Scotland's visible geology. More recent changes have arguably had a greater impact on the countryside. Pollen analysis shows clearly that the arrival of people on Shetland around 5,000 years ago was associated with a sharp reduction in the number of trees (in what had been a heavily wooded landscape) in favour of heather and grasses. Indeed in some senses Scotland's landscape was modern at an early date. It is a myth that medieval (or even Dark Age) Scotland was heavily wooded: there was no 'forest of Caledon'. We assume also that heather is a timeless feature of the Scottish hillside; in fact it was only introduced to the Cheviots in the thirteenth and fourteenth centuries, and for the last 200 years it has been on the decline across Scotland thanks to sheep grazing. Moreover, as the climate became wetter and colder between *c.* 1550 and *c.* 1700, plots which were once cultivated in the Middle Ages were abandoned in favour of farming at lower altitudes. The distinctive field patterns of Galloway were created by cattle enclosures of the early eighteenth century. The apparently endless kilometres of dry stone walls in the Highlands and Southern Uplands were the result of sheep farming in the nineteenth century.

We also tend to assume that the landscape of Scotland was largely unchanging before the agricultural revolutions of the eighteenth and nineteenth centuries, and the sprawling urbanization of the twentieth century. This is quite wrong. The landscape may in fact have been more dynamic before the eighteenth century. Buildings were much flimsier before that time and the stone-built ones which survive (like the brochs of the north) represent only a fraction of those ever erected. Many urban buildings were made of wood before the seventeenth century; indeed, most of Scotland had few stone-built houses before 1500. Not surprisingly, rapid, destructive and terrifying fires were a fact of life, randomly razing buildings and requiring their renewal. Buildings were also a much less permanent feature than we might expect: some rural ones made of turf and thatched with straw or heather had to be rebuilt annually. Because they represented no real impediment, it was simple to rearrange whole land-holdings and settlements.

Documentary and archaeological evidence shows that the landscape was shaped by processes of change that were far from uniform or 'progressive'. Aggregation and fragmentation of holdings have occurred over the centuries. The landscape and agriculture of Scotland are thus far from timeless. Take runrig, a system of land distribution which is often seen as a constant feature of agriculture before what eighteenth-century writers termed 'Improvement'. As it appears to archaeologists, runrig was made up of parcels of arable and pastoral land. Documents confirm it was a flexible system of land allocation: it could have equal or unequal shares and it could have sub-tenancies too. In contractual terms, infield was that area assessed for rental; outfield was not assessed. Infield was normally arable but it could contain pastoral too, while some outfield might be temporarily cultivated. Runrig *may* have started in the twelfth and thirteenth centuries, though there is also evidence that it was a later development. The remains of enclosure banks within the pre-crofting rigs may indicate that runrig was imposed on a very different farming system as a way of adjusting to the population growth of the sixteenth century. Apparently 'archaic' forms which become visible at one point in time must be set against a history of constantly changing adaptations.

Large-scale changes in land usage were accomplished, albeit over long periods. Between the Middle Ages and the eighteenth century, the western half of the small Shetland island of Papa Stour was flayed of all turf, topsoil and peat, which was used to render the eastern part of the island more fertile. The peat was burned and in the mid-nineteenth century there were plans to evacuate the island because of the problem of fuel, but in the end the islanders got permission to dig peat on the Shetland mainland, and from another island sixty kilometres away. So the organization of farming was, in all likelihood, constantly changing. Furthermore, it became surprisingly modern in some parts at an early date. Factory farming is not an invention of the twentieth century, but its earlier existence is clear from the landscape and documentary record of East Lothian in the eighteenth century.

Although economic change has been the dynamo behind changes in the landscape, absence of dynamic economic development can also play an important part in shaping urban and rural scenery. Some landscapes became fossilized as economic change passed them by. This happened to the Glendevon estate in south-west Perthshire around 1780. The most scenic towns of modern Scotland are usually those which stopped developing long ago. Culross in Fife is a famous example, where changes in trade patterns left a backwater; Methil and Kirkcaldy, which enjoyed greater economic success in the nineteenth and early twentieth centuries, show the mixed blessings for the urban landscape of economic development. Across the central Lowlands, pit bings and worked-out mines, man-made waterways, polluted rivers and streams, discarded or working quarries and opencast mines all mark the landscape.

What applies to the landscape can equally apply to the plants and animals that fill it. Studies of certain types of fauna – sheep, deer, fish, and the midge – make it possible to chart the environmental impact of the human exploitation of natural resources. The interaction of people, nature and the land is shown in the advent of midges as a serious problem in the mid-nineteenth century. Climatic change and the introduction of large numbers of livestock to the Highlands created a habitat which turned midges from an occasional into a persistent nuisance. Over-fishing has denuded the stocks of fish so plentiful before the modern era. What it would have taken 9,000 sailing-boats to catch in the nineteenth century can now be taken from the sea by three dozen modern vessels. The fears engendered by exploitation have witnessed a sea-change in policies towards nature. Resource management has replaced resource exploitation. We now farm as well as catch fish, plant as well as cut down trees. We appreciate the delicate balance between the satisfaction of human needs and the preservation of the environment. Yet, as the last 5,000 years show, the environment and landscape have generally been sacrificed in the process of economic development.

Pre-industrial economies were far from simple or static. There existed an extensive trading network from medieval times – perhaps before this, as the Picts are thought to have had a large fleet. Close links with the sea are hardly surprising since no part of the country is more than 75 kilometres from the sea or a navigable waterway – and most Scots live within 20 kilometres of such. In the Dark Ages and the early Middle Ages, the Irish Sea was the principal trading zone. Later emphasis was on the North Sea. With a population of around 7,000 (large by contemporary standards),

Berwick-on-Tweed was Scotland's main medieval port until sacked by the English in 1296. Thereafter, Leith (Edinburgh's port), Aberdeen, Dundee, Perth and (for much of the fourteenth century) Linlithgow were the leading harbours. In the sixteenth and seventeenth centuries, now-quiet Fife havens such as Anstruther and Dysart bustled with shipping. Scotland looked to the south and to the North Sea and Baltic for trade. The main medieval European ports through which its exports flowed were Bruges, Middelburg and Veere, which are all on the Scheldt estuary. Scots traded with the eastern Baltic from the fourteenth century and by the seventeenth century many had settled in Poland and Sweden. Indeed, until the eighteenth century much of Scotland's trade was concentrated in the ports of the east coast, between the rivers Esk and Tweed, and it was not until the eighteenth century that the ports of the west attained their modern significance. Superficially at least, the return to a westerly focus is reminiscent of the early Middle Ages. Yet while trade with Ireland in coal and cattle remained, the change in focus was principally the result of growing commerce with the North American and Caribbean colonies. Glasgow was the prime beneficiary of the commerce in tobacco, sugar, and other raw materials.

The existence of extensive trading networks shows that Scotland was far from a purely agricultural economy before 1800. Some landowners had coal- and lead-mining interests in the seventeenth and eighteenth centuries. Substantial, concentrated enterprises were unusual, but examples include Bonawe ironworks near Taynuilt in Argyllshire (opened in 1753) and Leadhills in Lanarkshire. There was industry before industrialization. What distinguished it was the small-scale and largely domestic location of production. The fundamental brake on economic growth prior to *c.* 1800 had always been the organic basis of raw materials and energy. Industrial material came largely from the land in the form of wool, wood, and animal products. Energy too came from the land. The iron works at Bonawe needed one acre of well-managed coppice to make a ton of pig iron. Over a twenty-year growing cycle, the works would have required 10,000 acres of forest, located on Mull as well as the mainland. Virtually all production depended in some way on sun and soil. What broke the stop–start cycles of growth was the large-scale exploitation of coal for energy (harnessed through the new technology of steam), and the systematic mining of ores and minerals for metals and fertilizers.

New sources of energy and new raw materials allowed a dramatic increase in both production and consumption from the end of the eighteenth century. However, it was not just coal but also cotton that propelled the economy towards industrialization. Novel methods of organizing workers in cotton factories became the symbol of the new industrial era. By 1825 nine out of ten manufacturing workers in Scotland were employed in the textile industry. In spite of this, cotton's importance was as a foundation block, for the factory economy was not born until after 1840. Agriculture and domestic service were still the largest employers of labour at this time. Within fifty years agriculture employed only a fraction of those working in industry. The growth of the integrated industrial economy, based on iron, and later steel, shipbuilding, coal and engineering, turned Scotland into the workshop of the world. Scottish industries became world leaders in the production of iron and ships, chemicals and railway engines, and a host of other products. The mix of inventive genius and plentiful supplies of cheap labour, fuel and raw materials proved an irresistible combination.

The emphasis on heavy industry was to prove a disaster when it eventually collapsed. Even by 1914, the economy was running into difficulties from foreign competition and a failure to diversify into new product areas. After the First World War a brief manufacturing boom between 1918 and 1920 was followed by a general economic depression and unemployment on a wide scale. This intensified after the Wall Street crash of 1929 and unemployment soared to approximately one in four of the working population of Scotland. In spite of the decline of heavy industry, no one in Scotland saw modern consumer industries, such as aircraft, cars and electrical goods, as an attractive alternative to the reliance on heavy industry. The outbreak of the Second World War in September 1939, and the re-stocking boom that followed in 1945, provided a lifeline for the distressed Scottish economy. However, the expansion came to an end in the 1960s as heavy industry contracted in the face of foreign competition, mainly from the Far East. By 1990 job losses in the traditional industries had been so immense that the Association of University Teachers had more members in Scotland than the National Union of Mineworkers.

The collapse of heavy industry has been socially devastating for many Scots and unemployment has been higher than the United Kingdom average throughout the last four decades. Increasing numbers of Scots have found work in the service sector, and its share of employment and Gross Domestic Product has rocketed. This trend has been more pronounced among women than men, and work has increasingly been part-time rather than full-time. Men have suffered from higher levels of unemployment and households are becoming more and more dependent on women's earnings. This development has historical parallels: full-time employment for women was consistently higher than for men in nineteenth-century Dundee, thanks to the jute industry.

Living and Dying

The environment has always been an active partner in the process of economic and social change. Both consciously and unconsciously, the relationship between people and environment has been crucial in determining both the material conditions of life and the physical landscape in which Scots past and present have lived. This relationship between lifestyle, the physical world and social relationships is also exemplified in Scotland's demographic history.

Industrial expansion and population growth went hand-in-hand. Scotland's population more than doubled in the nineteenth century. Until the eighteenth century growth rates were generally slower, prone to sudden surges and equally sudden episodes of severe mortality. This does not mean that earlier centuries had not witnessed population growth. Demographic pressures became evident in the high Middle Ages, but were alleviated by the independent effect of deadly diseases, of which the plague ('Black Death') is the most notorious. Positive adjustments were also made by extending the amount of land under cultivation. The next major increase in numbers came in the sixteenth century. This time, Scotland's people dealt with the problem not by growing more food but by changing what they ate. Meat products became a luxury for ordinary Scots, who came to rely on grain for their calories. Widespread meat-eating did not resume until the eighteenth century when agrarian change improved living standards. The phrase 'creative adaptations', which is often used when discussing language and culture, applies equally well here.

In both the thirteenth and sixteenth centuries, and to a greater or lesser extent throughout all recent centuries, emigration helped to ease the demographic pressure. However, one apparently obvious adaptation that no Europeans seem to have used before the nineteenth century was contraception. Fertility was limited by delaying or even eschewing marriage, and by prolonging breast-feeding. Death also kept the population in check. Famine and plague could wipe out population gains, as in 1695 when around one-fifth of Scots perished through starvation. The disappearance of plague in the mid-seventeenth century and an end to widespread and deadly famines in the eighteenth century helped people to live longer, as did inoculation and, later, vaccination against smallpox, a less spectacular but more continually present killer than the plague. Aided by medical advances and the more benign side-effects of exponential economic growth, numbers grew almost continuously for more than a century from *c.* 1770. What was new about this modern rise was that it was sustained for generations at rates unprecedented in history. Growth rates slowed again in the twentieth century because individuals and societies chose to have fewer children rather than because of the largely autonomous forces which had driven demographics for centuries. While the population of England and Wales grew by 40 per cent between 1911 and 1988, that of Scotland grew by only 7 per cent.

Different chronologies of growth were paralleled by divergences in population structure. Infant mortality rates were probably higher in Scotland than England for much of the eighteenth and early nineteenth centuries; yet they were lower than in England and Wales between *c.* 1881 and *c.* 1911, and rose only slightly thereafter until rates converged in the 1970s. The timing of modern changes in mortality reflected changing social priorities (such as the provision of running water), but also medical developments. Maternal mortality was declining slowly in the nineteenth century but significant improvements were not seen until the 1920s and 1930s. Other demographic structures were very different from today. Scotland had many more young people in the past than it has now. Those aged sixty years and older made up less than a sixth of the population of eighteenth-century Scotland while those aged fifteen or younger comprised more than a third of her people. Currently there are more females over the age of sixty in Scotland than there are under the age of sixteen.

Population Movements

Emigration, mainly of younger Scots, has counterbalanced population growth. Scotland has always had a mobile population. The migratory hunter-gatherers who first peopled Scotland ultimately became settlers, but Scotland's people have always moved around within its frontiers and they have travelled, settled, and been themselves replenished by immigration over land and sea. Scotland may indeed have had one of the highest levels of emigration of any European society prior to the nineteenth century. Around 1300 there were whole streets of Scots in Paris. Medieval and early modern Scots (and the Swiss) were prominent as mercenaries – then an honourable profession. Importantly, the vast majority of single emigrants (who formed the bulk of movers until quite recent times) were males. A shortage of men may explain certain distinctive aspects of Scotland's pre-modern demography, including the high proportion of women who never married and the late age at first marriage. Especially in trading and fishing communities, prolonged absences by menfolk may have given women unusual independence.

Scots took their skills and their values with them. Indeed, until the coming of the telegraph in the nineteenth century, movements of ideas, techniques and technology were inextricable from that of people. In the nineteenth and twentieth centuries, Scottish law, medical expertise and its university system were all successfully exported to the wider world by missionaries and imperial bureaucrats. There are Scots kirks (as opposed to churches attended by expatriate Scots) in, for example, Adelaide, Lausanne, Lisbon, Paris, and Rotterdam. The last, founded in 1643, currently has approximately thirty nationalities among its worshippers. Scots were also prominent in Far Eastern trading companies.

In the late sixteenth and seventeenth century most movement was to Ireland, which had available land and higher wages for skilled craftsmen. In 1600, 2 per cent of the population of Ireland was of Scots or English descent (confusingly sometimes known together as 'New English'), but this had risen to 27 per cent by the early eighteenth century. This migration had profound implications both for early modern history and for the current political divide in Northern Ireland. Outflow to the Atlantic colonies took off dramatically in the late seventeenth century. From a mere trickle in the 1650s to about 10,000 a year in the early 1770s, at least 150,000 Scots had settled in America by 1785. Between 1815 and 1838, 15,000 Scots emigrated to Nova Scotia alone. Involuntary migration, in the form of the transportation of convicted criminals, added to the flow. Covenanters, Jacobites, and assorted rogues, whores and vagabonds were sent to the

American colonies and, after the American Declaration of Independence in 1776, to Australia. The pattern of voluntary emigration continued into the nineteenth and twentieth centuries. Between 1841 and 1931, two million Scots emigrated and a further 750,000 moved to other parts of the United Kingdom. Indeed, emigration was a bigger drain on population in the second decade of the twentieth century than the First World War. Between 1911 and 1921, 630,000 Scots left Scotland compared with the 150,000 Scots who died, including the few civilian casualties. After 1921 there was extensive emigration in every decade except the 1930s and 1940s, and Scotland suffered a fall in population in every year of the 1970s and 1980s, with the exception of 1973 and 1974.

Before assuming that emigration was always driven by poor prospects at home, we should note that the mid-nineteenth-century outflows coincided with rapid growth in productivity and earnings. Most emigration from Scottish shores has been voluntary, partly prompted by the perception of superior opportunities abroad. Both immigration and emigration have nevertheless long been emotive political issues as much as human stories. Nowhere is this more evident than in the history of the Highlands and Islands. Highland migrants have sometimes been described in a tone of patronizing compassion. Pride and choice have too often been ignored in the search for villains and their victims. Retrospective regret has caused us to assume experience and motivation rather than discovering it. Far from being reluctant cast-outs, at the time of the revolutionary and Napoleonic Wars, Highland tenants were anxious to leave and landlords wanted to stop them. Some 70,000 left the glens and islands between 1760 and the passing of the restrictive Passenger Vessels Act of 1803, most of them from the middling ranks of the 'tacksmen' (so called because they held a 'tack' or lease directly from the landowner). We should not gloss over the darker aspects of the past, but nor should we ever ignore the resilience of the tenants and cottars, and their role in shaping their own destiny.

The period between the 1810s and the 1880s saw the meaning of the term 'clearance' transformed. It began with landowners redistributing labour supply, and ended with them trying to solve the problems they had created early in the century by means of wholesale evictions, plantations in overcrowded and economically marginal fishing villages, and later by emigration schemes. Against a background of steady de-peopling, opposition to agrarian change actually grew. Indeed, falling numbers did not diminish protest and crofting wars broke out in the 1880s. The Napier Commission was established to investigate the causes of unrest and to find some solutions. The outcome of its recommendations was to provide the crofters with security of tenure, fair rents and other reforms, but it did nothing to stem the outflow of population from the Highlands. This was running at around 50,000 per decade in the last quarter of the nineteenth century.

Landlords also contributed to the net outflow of population by converting large tracts of Highland Scotland into a sporting playground for the rich. Deer forests were a factor in the unrest of the 1880s as local people objected to wild animals taking preference over them as occupants of the land. By 1900 forests accounted for a third of land in the crofting counties. People were not evicted to make way for deer, but the deer forests prevented the re-peopling of land originally cleared in the early and mid-nineteenth century for sheep. In 1811 there were 250,000 sheep in the Highlands; by the 1840s there were over a million. By 1884 deer forests covered two million acres (two-fifths of the area of Wales and one-tenth that of Scotland), mostly in the crofting counties. Those who left the Highlands showed little inclination to return when they had found a much better material life elsewhere. Land raids continued into the 1920s but against the agitation for more land, people continued to drift away in the inter-war years when holdings actually became more freely available. From 1931 old people outnumbered young children.

The experience of voluntary or forced mobility – we may even use the more loaded term 'dispossession' – has characterized rural Scots throughout the ages. There was almost certainly an increase in landlessness thanks to the population growth of the late thirteenth century; in the sixteenth century certain types of sitting tenant whose titles were insecure were removed to facilitate consolidation of holdings and re-letting on terms more advantageous to landlords. What is interesting is why a particular type of mobility in the nineteenth-century Highlands has left such bitter memories embedded in its oral culture. In contrast, in the Lowlands, which had every bit as much dislocation, it has not. Furthermore, the mass unemployment and displacements in Lowland industrial Scotland during the 1920s and 1930s affected a greater number and a higher proportion of people than had been the case in the nineteenth century.

One answer may be the existence of a widely held belief that land was a communal entity within a moral economy: the Gaelic idea of *dùthchas*, which had no real equivalent outside the Highland cultural zone. Those doing the evicting were held to have a moral responsibility towards those under them, including obligations based on real or notional kinship. Associated with this is the fact that the Gaels were subject to a cultural displacement that was more severe than for Lowlanders, who were more used to cities and commercialism. In short, the Highlands and Islands had a value system quite different from that of the Lowlands. The dissolving forces of political and cultural change which, in the memorable words of the geographer Professor Robert Dodgshon, turned landowners from chiefs into landlords during the eighteenth century had a profound impact on Gaelic society, also turning kinsmen into crofters.

Family

The modern Highlands and Islands are being re-peopled, marking a departure from at least 300 years of history. In other senses, the demographic patterns of the past survive into the present day. Both men and women marry well into their twenties and significant numbers never marry at all. What has changed dramatically has been the role (and perhaps the very definition) of the family. For centuries the family was the basis of ideology, politics, economics, residence, welfare, socialization and procreation. It was understood not simply as husband, wife and resident children (for this was the characteristic form for as long as we have reliable records), but as all those who lived in a household. That included servants, apprentices and any others, be they relations or lodgers.

This is not to say that there were no fractures in the edifice of the traditional family and community. From levels of just 3 or 4 per cent, illegitimacy ratios more than doubled in the late eighteenth and early nineteenth centuries. The trend continued in some parts of Scotland. In the Banffshire parish of Rothiemay, the illegitimacy ratio rose from 10 per cent in the 1830s to nearly 30 per cent in the 1870s. In this region, four-fifths of women marrying in the late nineteenth century had their first child before, or within three months after, marriage. These high levels were not equalled until the closing years of the twentieth century. In contrast, the peacetime ratio for the pre-1939 period was just one in twenty.

In the second half of the twentieth century the inclusive definition and extensive role of the family has rapidly been eroded. In the late 1980s one half of all women marrying under the age of thirty had cohabited prior to marriage compared with just 3 per cent in the 1960s. The year 1997 was the first when more than half of births in Dundee were to single mothers or to cohabiting but unmarried partners. At 1987 rates, one-third of marriages of the late 1970s will end in divorce, compared with just 7 per cent of marriages contracted in the early 1950s. The introduction of widespread knowledge and use of contraceptive techniques produced a pronounced fall in family size from the end of the nineteenth century. Two-fifths of marriages made in the 1870s produced more than six children compared with less than 2 per cent for 1920s marriages.

Accompanying the growth of population have been changes in lifestyles and in family structures. Younger readers will probably have spent more than half their teenage years at school, for growing up and being formally educated are now largely synonymous. Increasingly, young people are continuing with some form of further or higher education into their late teens and early twenties. Formal and informal learning was a central part of becoming an adult in former times, but the mechanisms were very different from those of today. From at least the Middle Ages, Scots who reached the age of fourteen or fifteen years (depending on the century, up to a third of those born might not live that long) spent the following decade of their lives working as servants in agriculture. Servants were principally employed in the fields and barns of Scotland. Towns were small and urban living was not a common experience until well into the eighteenth century. Yet, towns were big employers of both apprentices and domestics. In the 1690s, one in ten of all Scottish girls were in domestic service in one of the four largest burghs (Edinburgh, Glasgow, Aberdeen, Dundee).

Youth as a phase of modern life, characterized by prolonged education and the existence of a specific material culture, is a development of the last century and a half. Prior to that, the transition from child to adult happened at an early age. Boys could enter a late-medieval Scottish university as young as twelve, while the less fortunate, such as orphans, might find themselves begging for a living from the age of seven or eight. In industry, too, children worked from a young age until regulation was introduced in 1830. Nevertheless, as late as the 1900s school-age children could be found spending part of their day in class and the rest in a factory.

Before industrialization, youngsters entered the world of work as servants; service was the characteristic life experience of all young adults. For girls this continued until the early twentieth century. In that sense, there were considerable social continuities *despite* the massive economic changes in agriculture between *c.* 1770 and 1870. However, economic changes from the middle of the eighteenth century were altering the distribution of employment in profound and irreversible ways. There had been limited opportunities outside agriculture and domestic service for the majority of Scots, but industrial development created greater choice and opportunity for both men and women in the labour market. Initially these were in domestic industry as spinners and weavers, but later there were openings in factories, shipyards, coal mines, engineering and ironworks. The growth of the professions, particularly teaching and nursing, widened opportunities for middle-class females, as did the expansion of consumer services in the late nineteenth century. In spite of this, Scotland remained a patriarchal society. Outside cities like Dundee, the proportion of married women in full-time paid employment was much lower. Nor did work necessarily liberate women, since the workplace hierarchy tended to reflect that of the family.

Labour shortages following the Second World War, combined with the growth of consumerism and youth culture, altered the balance of power within the family. The sex, drugs and rock-'n'-roll culture led to a disaffection of youth from established patterns of authority. The massive increase in married women going out to work also fractured established roles in the family. Modern women laboured in the home and the workplace – as they had for centuries. In 1911 the typical female worker was a single young woman between the ages of thirteen and twenty; eighty years on, married women easily outnumbered single women in the labour market. The twentieth century has witnessed a diminution in the authority of the male breadwinner and a downgrading of his economic importance. Decline has been accompanied by major improvements in the social and economic position of women and young people. This does not mean that gender divisions have been bridged. Women are still paid on average around a third less than men and more are to be found in part-time work. However, the rigidly patriarchal society of former times has been replaced by more complex and accommodating relationships both in the family and the workplace.

Rich and Poor

Hierarchies of gender and status were closely tied to the levels of reward that people gained from their labour. The toil of countless generations of men, women and children transformed Scotland into an industrial powerhouse and world leader in the second half of the nineteenth century. But what rewards did this extraordinary achievement provide for the Scottish people? The short answer is: very little. In 1911 over half the Scottish population lived in one- or two-roomed houses, and in Glasgow and Dundee the figure was over 60 per cent. Overcrowding was the result, with nearly 56 per cent of Glaswegians living more than two to a room; fifty years later the figure was still over 50 per cent. In 1965 more than a third of Glasgow houses had no fixed toilet or bath. Part of the problem was poverty since, even in the prosperous nineteenth and twentieth centuries, Scots endured a standard of living far below that of their English neighbours. Again, modern conveniences which are now taken for granted only became (nearly) universal quite recently. Some 95 per cent of Glasgow houses had indoor sanitation in 1985. Most Scots are undoubtedly better off in material terms, as is plain in the rising ownership of homes, cars and consumer durables. Yet government figures showed that one in five primary school children in Scotland were entitled to free school meals in 1997. In Glasgow the figure was 40 per cent.

There is nothing particularly modern about the gulf between rich and poor. The Middle Ages had people with no land and a few who owned hundreds of square kilometres; it had prosperous and poor tenant farmers. Some 496 craftsmen paid tax in Edinburgh in 1583. Of these, 50 per cent paid a sixth of the total amount levied whereas the top 15 per cent paid 56 per cent of the levy. The American Benjamin Franklin was dismayed by the stark inequalities of Scottish society when he visited in the eighteenth century. The limits of egalitarianism are most evident in the distribution of poor relief. From the mid-eighteenth century until the 1920s, legal judgements generally found against any entitlement to long-term poor relief for the able-bodied unemployed. Indeed, Scotland's poor law was different from that of England until within living memory. Relief was discretionary and recipients had less clearly defined rights than in England; it was usually supplementary and therefore meagre; there were fewer institutions like workhouses, which existed mainly in some of the larger towns. The industrious poor were held in high regard while the idle able-bodied were regarded as undeserving.

Industrialization may have widened employment opportunities, but in its first phase it was dependent on inputs of cheap labour and thus did little to improve the standard of living of the majority of Scots. The economist Dudley Baxter's study of the distribution of income in 1867 showed that 70 per cent of 'productive persons' in Scotland earned less than thirty pounds per annum, while the top 10 per cent gobbled up half the national income. Wages in Scotland continued to lag behind English levels in many occupations in the later nineteenth century and this trend was maintained for most of the twentieth.

In Dundee in 1906 half the men earned less than a pound a week, when the social investigator Seebohm Rowntree's poverty line was drawn at £1. 1s. 8d. (108 pence) for a family of five. Moreover, Scots have had to endure higher levels of unemployment than the rest of the UK. This was the case in the economic depression of the 1920s and 1930s, but in the more prosperous 1950s and 1960s unemployment was still running at a far higher level north of the border. The persistence of these trends combined with the lower levels of earnings has made Scotland, particularly the west–central region, one of the poorest areas in Britain. Of course there are disparities even within Scotland. Glasgow and Dundee, overwhelmingly working-class cities, have been worse off than the more middle-class cities of Edinburgh and Aberdeen. Changes in demographic structure, combined with major shifts in the labour market, have created new opportunities for women and the young to participate in the public sphere. However, large numbers of poorer Scots remain excluded from the discourses of civil society.

Religion

Material inequality did not preclude a sense of spiritual egalitarianism. Material well-being can be associated with spiritual impoverishment. Regardless of its material associations, religion has for centuries provoked strong feelings about linkages with politics and society. Conventional wisdom has it that this is a development which emerged with the Protestant Reformation of the sixteenth century. However, this aspect of Scottish society has deep roots. The relationship between church and people, and between church and state, is one of the many dimensions of modern Scotland that cannot be understood without a long-term perspective.

Diversity in religion did not begin in the sixteenth century. As with many aspects of the pre-medieval period, we can make broad generalizations about 'the Celtic world' but can be much less specific about the territory now known as Scotland. There were clearly a large number of gods with various attributes, and very probably an organized pan-tribal priesthood (the druids) at least in Britain and Gaul in the last century BC. Pagan religions in prehistory were probably just as different from one another as any of them were from early Christianity. Furthermore, the nature of pagan religions probably changed dramatically through prehistory: their material expression certainly did. In immediately pre-Christian times, the only tangible evidence is that of Pictish burials (square barrow cemeteries) and, of course, symbol stones. Paganism had a longer history than Christianity, and with it some impressive monuments. Among them are tombs like Maes Howe on Orkney or the standing stones of Calanais on Lewis. Such building projects show the importance of belief systems to contemporaries; the sophisticated social organization necessary to complete such projects; and a long tradition of scholarship essential correctly to align the erections with significant solar turning-points. They also suggest an enduring association between religious and secular authorities throughout the pagan as well as the Christian era.

Christianity was, of course, found among the Romans who occupied Scotland in the early centuries AD, and was already present in the south-west by 500. It developed in connection with Whithorn and its bishop, Ninian. Roman and Celtic strands were woven into a distinctive expression of Christianity in the following centuries. Christianity spread more widely through Scotland in the fifth and sixth centuries and was already prevalent among noble Britons of southern Scotland and Gaels of the north-west by 600 AD. Pictland was largely converted by 700 AD. English Northumbria (including Lothian and Galloway) was vibrantly Christian by roughly the same date. St Columba (c. 521–97), the most famous of the early missionaries, was working in parts of Pictland which were already at least partly Christian, even if he and his successors considerably extended its influence. Seventh- and eighth-century influences on ecclesiastical development came principally from Northumbria.

Major developments occurred in the twelfth century, reflecting a fundamental reorganization of European Christendom imposed from above. Church government and liturgy were standardized, while the status of the clergy (celibate and in a separate hierarchy from the laity) was reformulated. The dating of Christian festivals was standardized, possibly by accommodation with the chronology of pre-Christian celebrations. Territorial organization was defined more clearly, whereas the early medieval church had revolved around centres like Whithorn and Dunkeld whose influence and relationship to each other was irregular.

Monasticism was also revived in the twelfth century to enhance the spiritual health of the kingdom by study and prayer. The consolidation of the Christian church proceeded, and with it some enduring structures and institutions. Church buildings are one example but the diocesan and parish structure, introduced in the twelfth century, is still with us in its essentials. The process threw up anomalies that sometimes took centuries to rectify. Lowland dioceses were claimed by the archbishopric of York until the thirteenth century, and Scotland did not secure its own province(s) until the creation of the archbishoprics of St Andrews and Glasgow in the fifteenth century. Galloway accepted York's jurisdiction until the fourteenth century, but most other Scottish sees were answerable directly to the papacy.

Deriving a picture of how people related to religion is much more difficult than charting changes in ecclesiastical organization. Ordinary people had more contact with clerics in minor orders than they did with parish priests: such clerics were church servants but were prominent in the religious experience of the laity. Friars, notably the Dominicans, were an important international influence in Scotland from the thirteenth century, preaching, teaching, and running 'hospitals' for pilgrims. Indeed, pilgrimages were an important focus of medieval piety. Most sites had local significance, but there were some like St Duthac's at Tain which had a national reputation, and others like

St Andrews whose standing was international. In the towns of the fourteenth and fifteenth centuries, confraternities flourished and also collegiate churches, of which the early fifteenth-century foundation of St Giles, Edinburgh, is perhaps the best known. One distinctive feature of medieval Scotland was the shortage of documented heresy. This may indicate the early existence of a society with an unusual degree of consensus (and one without the networks of small and medium-sized towns which provided a fertile breeding ground for dissent elsewhere in Europe). Alternatively, it may show the success of the church in suppressing dissent. In the long term, the (Lowland) church was able to impose its definition of marriage and legitimacy on the whole of Scotland, over that of a Gaelic culture which tolerated polygamy and the easier dissolution of relationships.

Medieval religion was nothing if not vital. However, the special relationship with the Church of Rome was severed by the Reformation in the second half of the sixteenth century. Protestantism ousted Catholicism in many parts of northern Europe, but Scotland's experience of this monumental religious change was distinctive. Where the Scandinavian and German lands espoused the word according to Martin Luther, Scotland followed the Swiss model of John Calvin which appealed to the northern Netherlands and certain parts of what is now France. England followed a middle path in which the influence of both Luther and Calvin is evident, along with that of Huldreich Zwingli.

The new Protestant faith which emerged in this period was welcomed by some, but imposed on others. Monasticism, one of the cornerstones of medieval Christianity, reached its high point in Scotland during the twelfth century. However, Scottish monasteries were not suppressed at the Reformation as happened in England. Already being bled before the Reformation, they simply withered through lack of recruitment; under criticism, they had been showing signs of a lack of vitality for many decades before 1560.

After that date, the process of conversion to Protestantism was completed rather quickly in many Lowland areas. In the diocese of Aberdeen, three-quarters of the 102 parishes had a Protestant incumbent by 1563 and all but seven by 1567. Yet the battle to win the hearts and minds of committed Christians to Protestantism may have taken longer. Catholic influence remained important in the north-east until at least 1638, the date of the signing of the National Covenant and of the beginning of serious protest against the religious innovations of Charles I. The region was a bastion of Episcopalianism in the eighteenth century, when it was an important recruiting ground for the Jacobite cause. Jesuit missions were sent to the Highlands during the seventeenth and early eighteenth centuries. Yet, as so often in Scottish history, the opponents came from within, not without. Struggles over religion between 1638 and 1690 were about whether church government and forms of worship should be Presbyterian or Episcopalian, not Protestant or Catholic. For their part, Scottish religious radicals were exiled in England, Ireland and the Netherlands in the late sixteenth and early seventeenth centuries: these men added to the Reformation there and returned with their Calvinist ideas honed. Nor should we ignore the powerful ties between Scottish Presbyterians and radical English Puritans in the period up to 1646.

The eighteenth century saw the development of further divisions. The Protestant faith was prone to schisms because of its emphasis on individual routes to salvation. Thus a variety of secession churches established themselves, the first in 1733. The divisions were, if anything, associated with a rise in religiosity rather than a decline towards the lukewarm and the secular. The early nineteenth century saw a wave of religious revival movements in the Highlands, coupled with a broadly based drift away from the established church because of opposition to patronage (appointment of clergy by other than the flock). This ended in the Disruption of 1843 and the establishment of the Free Church of Scotland.

Visitors to Scotland in the eighteenth century pondered on whether strict outward forms, like observance of the Sabbath, necessarily meant that the Scots were more deeply religious than other nations. Whatever was in their hearts and minds then, two parallel developments have occurred since. First, there has been a fragmentation and consolidation of churches. Second, church attendance has risen and fallen over time, but has recently become much less a central part of everyday life. This is not to say that church attendance was universal in the distant past. There were complaints about poor attendance both before and after the Reformation. However, the processes of industrialization and urbanization led to many hundreds of thousands of Scots becoming alienated from the established church. It was estimated that in the 1820s around two-thirds of the slum-dwellers of Glasgow and a third of the population of Edinburgh did not attend an established church. Floods of immigrants overwhelmed the capacity of churches to accommodate their numbers and of pastors to minister to their needs. What some less than charitable contemporaries called the 'godless poor' lost the habit of attendance and never regained it. Such moral judgements should not be taken at face value. Those criticized as 'godless', 'heathen', or 'superstitious' may simply have displayed their religiosity differently from their critics. There were many pathways to God.

Whatever the problems in meeting demand in the early nineteenth century, there was a surge in church and school building after the Disruption which equalled or even surpassed the great age of English church building in the late Middle Ages. Between 1850 and 1899 the Church of Scotland built 276 churches, the Free Church 215, and the United Presbyterian Church 161. Scotland had approximately 900 parishes at that time. The building programme, coupled with missionary initiatives after 1851, arrested the decline – at least among skilled workers and their families. Research into Glasgow between 1848 and 1865 has shown that skilled workers made up 69 per cent of Church of Scotland membership and 80 per cent of dissenting churches. The revival was also accompanied later in the century by a change in the social composition of the Scottish church. The dissenting churches were far more representative of the middle classes and the Highlands as pew rents became prohibitively high, and the level of voluntary offerings increased by 1891 to three times that of the Church of Scotland. A drift of the working classes back to the established church took place. Indeed, religious fragmentation may have been associated with a rise in church attendance, notably in the towns – which by some measures had higher levels of observance in 1851 than in rural Scotland. Certainly there was no overall fall in attendance, and the Roman Catholics saw an impressive increase in numbers as church building flourished in the second half of the nineteenth century.

The story of the twentieth century is similarly not a linear trend towards secularization, but a series of phases of growth and decline; and of a shift from a comprehensive religious culture to a society based on a variety of voluntary, but nevertheless strongly held, religious beliefs. Faced with a decline in both attendance and political influence, the Church of Scotland and the United Free Church reunited in 1929 behind an appeal to the rhetoric of a Christian commonwealth. Together they comprised 90 per cent of Presbyterian activists. In contrast with the inter-war years, during the 1940s and 1950s church involvement actually rose. As late as 1951, 59 per cent of adults in Scotland were said to be church members, compared with only 23 per cent in England and Wales. Indeed it is only in the last fifty years that the forces of secularization have firmly encompassed the prosperous middle classes. Church attendance and membership is only evident nowadays among an ever-decreasing older section of society. In 1984, it was estimated that only 9 per cent of the non-Catholic population attended church on Sundays, although in Catholic dioceses the figure was as high as 43 per cent. By comparison, in Ireland as a whole 65 per cent of parishioners attend Mass at least once a week (a generation ago it was over 90 per cent). The Church of Scotland had 660,000 communicant members in 1997, half the level of the 1930s.

Religion has declined as an organized force. Nevertheless, there remains a firmly perceived need for religion to solemnize life-cycle events, and churches continue occasionally to be heard on political and social issues. Indeed, the social legacy of religion for Scots is a powerful one. Religious education, although no longer confined solely to Christianity, remains compulsory in schools. Until the 1960s religion played an important role in shaping both class structure and the recreational habits of the Scots, as well as the urban and rural landscape. The shift of population after 1945 from the inner cities to peripheral working-class housing estates and middle-class suburbs saw the decay of many of the city churches built in the nineteenth century. Some were demolished; others survive as restaurants, pubs and nightclubs, serving Mammon rather than God.

Religious divisions intensified social splits. Diverging values and widening social differences were fragmenting Highland and Lowland society in the eighteenth and nineteenth centuries. The religious schism of 1843 was linked to emerging class differences, and theological disputes were taken very seriously by Scots in ways perhaps unthinkable to most of the population today. This is why the social tensions associated with religious change were so pronounced and why the geographical distribution of change was so complex. In Ross-shire and Lewis, clergy left the established church wholesale, but in Skye and Uist the ministry remained 'Moderate' while their flocks espoused 'popular' evangelicalism. Interestingly, although the Disruption of 1843 was one of the most significant social and cultural events of the nineteenth century, it has left little trace in the popular consciousness of Scottish history – other than for members of the Free Church.

If social divisions played a part in why the Disruption occurred, they were further widened by the attitudes of landowners to the supporters of the Free Church. Part of the struggle waged by the peasantry against the Highland landlords was religious. Landlords remained loyal to the Church of Scotland, but their tenants joined *en masse* the newly-formed Free Church. Some landowners refused to allow churches on their land. In one case, the tenants of Sir James Riddell of Ardnamurchan were constrained to worship on a boat moored at sea. In urban areas religion divided the population on sectarian lines, and a social history of Scottish municipal politics shows how church membership was associated with a person's party allegiance. In the nineteenth century the Church of Scotland was strongly Tory, while the non-established churches were Liberal, as were Roman Catholics.

As Scottish politics began to resemble the multi-party system of the present, the established church remained solidly Tory. Some of the dissenters moved towards the emerging Labour Party: there was not a great deal of difference between the latter's social programme and that of the United Free Church in the 1920s. In the decades following the end of the Second World War, religion still had an important influence on voting behaviour. As late as 1968, a study of Dundee showed that a working-class member of the Church of Scotland was far more likely to vote Tory than a working-class Catholic. Since then – and in line with the decline in church-going – religion has had a decreasing impact on voting, or on attitudes to politics. High-profile campaigns by the Church of Scotland against the poll tax and nuclear warfare in the 1980s had no appreciable independent influence.

Other legacies of Scotland's religious past have proved enduring. The power of Sabbatarianism, born in the age of the Covenants, was still strong in the eighteenth century and had a lasting impact on the Scottish Sunday. While in Rome, James Boswell prayed to God 'to drive away melancholy and keep clouds of Presbyterian Sundays from rendering the mind gloomy'. The Calvinist stress on hard work and prayer greatly influenced the social habits and pastimes of the Scottish people in ways which endured well into the post-1945 decades, even though the modern Sabbath is only strictly observed by a small minority of the population. More recent temperance campaigns, opposition to novel forms of enjoyment such as dog-racing, betting, cinema, football, bingo, rock-'n'-roll, and the Sunday opening of shops have ultimately failed. But for a time Protestant churches made sure that the 'dreich Scottish Sunday' was a reality one had to endure to understand, with only the homely values of the *Sunday Post* newspaper for comfort.

It may be difficult for modern readers to appreciate the pervasive power of the religious idiom for the people of the past. From the Dark Ages onwards, debates about tonsures, vestments, altars, or church government, which seem at best puzzling and at worst irrelevant to many modern readers, could fire the hearts and minds of those who lived through them. It was not until comparatively recently that diversity in religion was tolerated, and later still that agnosticism and even atheism could be greeted with anything other than horror.

Education

Until the nineteenth century, a measure of outward religious orthodoxy was essential to hold many administrative posts. Conformity in religion was a passport to social and political advancement. In modern Scotland, an individual's talent and the quality of his or her education generally count for much more. Indeed, education is a field in which Scotland has an international reputation and it is an important part of national identity. Once again, the origins of this reputation lie far in the medieval past. Monasteries had trained young men since at least the seventh century, though medieval friaries provided wider education. Monastic and urban schools are documented from the twelfth and thirteenth centuries in the Lowlands. The latter expanded in number in the thirteenth century, staffed increasingly by secular rather than regular clergy, and there is abundant evidence of schools in towns in the fourteenth and fifteenth centuries. Any burgh worth its salt had a (Latin) grammar school by 1500. Among these, the long-established Aberdeen grammar school was thriving in the early sixteenth century. Most schools had an ecclesiastical origin, staff and purpose, though secular and vocational training was also available, the latter mainly through apprenticeship. The civilizing and integrating potential of education is shown in an Act of 1496 which sought to compel major landowners to send their eldest sons to school and university. In the Highlands and Islands, often seen as educationally backward in the past, there was a Gaelic tradition of education in medicine, as well as bardic schools.

Thus the Protestant Reformation built on existing achievements while placing a renewed emphasis on literacy. *The First Book of Discipline* of 1560–61, the blueprint for a Reformation, had more to say about education than any other single topic. The aim of the church was to provide a school in every parish in Scotland and, after several attempts, this was established by Act of Parliament in 1696. As a result, on paper at least, Scotland had a national system of education long before England (even if the national reality fell short of the ideal for some time after 1696). Within a generation of the Act, the traveller and writer Daniel Defoe remarked that while his native land was 'full of ignorance', in Scotland the 'poorest people have their children taught and instructed'.

Whether Scots were any better at reading and writing than the English in the age of Defoe remains a subject of contention. Nevertheless, belief in the value of education pervaded society. While some eighteenth-century commentators and decision-makers south of the border argued that education was dangerous because it raised expectations in the educated that society could not meet, Scottish thinkers agreed that only through reading the Bible could the individual be put in touch with the word of God. As long as Scotland remained a predominantly rural society such an objective was achievable, but as more and more people moved to the towns looking for work the system broke down. Contemporary studies showed that large numbers of children in the first half of the nineteenth century were excluded from the educational system through the necessity of earning a living to help their impoverished families. Nineteenth-century surveys also showed that, while the majority of male adults could read, very few could write, and the proportion of women able to do so was even smaller. The children of Irish parents fared even worse, with only thirteen Catholic schools in Glasgow out of 213 in 1857 and an attendance rate of only a third of those of school age. As a contemporary, George Lewis, wrote in 1843, Scotland was 'a half-educated nation'.

Those fortunate enough to receive an education were faced with class sizes of sixty to seventy in state schools and 150 in Catholic schools (children of widely differing ages sat in the same class), as well as cold and draughty classrooms. Discipline was to the fore and children were schooled in rote learning of the 3Rs. As only boys were considered for higher education, girls received second-class schooling. Domestic training aimed to turn them into domestic servants and, later, into wives and mothers.

The situation was improved by the Education Act of 1872, which introduced a system of national compulsory schooling at elementary level run by the state and not the church, and made parents responsible for attendance. As a result truancy and illiteracy were much reduced. By 1910–11 Scotland had more children in the age group five to fourteen attending school than all other north-west European countries except France. These children were taught mainly in state schools, with only a minority being educated in the private sector. Scotland had 2,799 board schools and 353 voluntary schools (a ratio of approximately 8:1), whereas England had 5,878 board schools and 14,275 voluntary establishments (a ratio of 1:2.5).

The fact that a number of boys from humble backgrounds made it to university from these parish and burgh schools has led some academics to extol the educational system of Scotland for its democratic nature. All that was necessary north of the border for the 'lad o' pairts' to rise up the educational ladder was ability. This is part of the notion that Scots possess a 'democratic intellect' that derives from a social consensus based on Calvinism and which manifested itself in easy social mobility and social mixing. There is some foundation for this view. Scotland had five universities in 1600, though most of them contained only a few dozen students: St Andrews (founded in 1411/12); Glasgow (1450–51); King's College, Aberdeen (1495); Marischal College, Aberdeen (1593, and not amalgamated with King's to form the University of Aberdeen until 1860); and Edinburgh (1582). England had just Oxford and Cambridge. Scotland's medieval universities were part of an integrated European world of letters. Until the Reformation, the lack of confessional differences was one reason for easy mobility among both students and staff. Another is that teaching and learning in Scotland was in the international language of Latin (and continued to be until the eighteenth century). Thereafter, hardening political divisions and the growing variety of theological training available created barriers to mobility. After *c.* 1560 mobility declined and recruitment areas contracted to become much more local compared with those of the late Middle Ages. Academic peregrinations did not end, for Protestant universities like Leiden were soon founded to take over the advanced medical education which had been available at Padua or Paris. Universities became more nationalist, and with them the educational rhetoric embodied in, for example, *The First Book of Discipline*.

The idea of a democratic intellect has further elements of truth. By the First World War Scotland still had one university place for every 1,000 of the population, compared with one in 5,800 in England. The social distribution of university students was always broader in Scotland than in England. The Argyll Commission which looked into Scottish education in 1867 found that 19 per cent of matriculated students at the University of Glasgow in 1860 came from working-class backgrounds, many more than went to Oxford or Cambridge. However, the Commission also noted that a minister's son had a hundred times better chance of going to university than a miner's son, and very few students managed to get beyond the first-year Latin examinations. Furthermore, only a tiny percentage of working-class students could be found in the more prestigious law and medical faculties which gave the best opportunity for occupational mobility. The chances of a male from the lowest social class gaining a degree in law was one in 20,000 and in medicine one in 6,000.

The social limitations on educational opportunity are clear when we look at female experiences. Until 1893 no women were allowed to matriculate at any of Scotland's five universities. Even then, their progress in higher education came slowly and irregularly. Women were much more quickly integrated into the life of St Andrews University than was the case at Aberdeen. In 1895–6 fewer than 5 per cent of Aberdeen's matriculated students were women, compared with nearly 18 per cent at Scotland's oldest university. Yet it was not until 1964 that the first woman professor was appointed at the University of Aberdeen.

The quality of the education in some subjects was inferior to that of England's universities and some students from Scottish universities had to trek south or, while Latin was still the teaching language, go abroad to complete their studies. There was no university entrance examination in Scotland until the end of the nineteenth century. Indeed, in 1860, 29 per cent of the student population was in the age group 14–15 years, although the proportion declined sharply after 1880. The world-class reputation Scotland achieved in education is based principally on its achievements in medicine and science. Between 1750 and 1850 Oxford and Cambridge turned out 500 doctors, while the four Scottish universities trained 10,000. By the decade 1815–25, around 1,000 students a year were attending the medical faculty in Edinburgh and some 17,000 had passed through between 1760 and 1826. Scottish universities produced nine out of ten British medical graduates between 1750 and 1800.

The missionary impulse of the Protestant churches brought a Scottish version of Protestantism to the world, as did the role the Scots played both as administrators and soldiers in the service of the British imperial state. These expatriates extolled the virtues of Scottish education and thus quality became associated with a system which was arguably failing a large part of the population and continued to do so into the twentieth century. In spite of the educational reforms of the 1940s and the introduction of student grants, the number of university students from working-class backgrounds only amounted to a quarter of the total in 1961, whereas a hundred years earlier they accounted for one-sixth. In 1951, 87 per cent of young adults in Scotland in the age group 20–24 had left school at fifteen or younger. Further educational reforms in the 1960s, including the founding of new universities like Stirling, allowed growing numbers of young Scots into higher education. In 1970, 17 per cent of the 17–21 age group were in higher education. The trend was accelerated by a further broadening of the definition of higher education. In 1995–6 some 46 per cent of the age group 17–21 years attended a university or similar institution.

From Participation to Representation

Education is part of the image of the Scottish democratic intellect. For centuries the explicit purpose of education was the advancement of society rather than the individual. Political and ideological priorities were first and foremost the family and the community. Writing of the laws which dealt with the care of the mentally incapable, the noted eighteenth-century English lawyer William Blackstone criticized the definition of prodigality in Roman law as out of step with 'a free nation, who claim and exercise the liberty of using their own property as they pleased'. Individualism as we know it only emerged after the end of the eighteenth century.

Instruction in the interests of informed political participation is an even more recent development, for democracy too came late to Scotland. That much is true if we look at the proportion of those able to vote in parliamentary elections. Scotland had, of course, no parliament of its own after 1707, but it did have seats at Westminster. In the 1780s

Scotland had approximately 4,000 parliamentary electors in a population of perhaps 1.5 million (0.2 per cent), whereas the English electorate may have been as large as a third of a million in a population of about 7.5 million people (4 per cent). By this measure, England was twenty times more 'democratic' in the late eighteenth century (and probably had been for centuries before). In 1832, the year of the famous Parliamentary Reform Bill, the electorate comprised about 20 per cent of the male population of England compared with 13 per cent of that of Scotland. By 1867 the proportion of males enfranchised was approximately equal in Scotland and England at about one-third, and in 1884 the franchise was homogenized across Britain with two-thirds of males able to vote. The Scottish electorate nearly trebled after the passing of the Representation of the People Act in 1918. Women over the age of thirty were enfranchised and the abolition of certain residential qualifications led to a 50 per cent rise in the proportion of adult males with the vote. It was not until 1928 that women were given franchise rights equal to those of men.

Women only achieved the vote within living memory. The first woman MP in Scotland was Katherine Ramsay, the Duchess of Atholl, who served for Perth and Kinross between 1923 and 1938. Other groups were also excluded from formal participation in politics. The professions have, in many ways, been the leaders of political, intellectual and cultural developments in Scotland since the eighteenth century – and perhaps before. The Reformation took root and then became established in the cities thanks to the adherence to Protestantism of lawyers and merchants. The National Covenant of 1638 (designed to rally support for the Presbyterian opposition to Charles I's ecclesiastical policies) was written by a Fife minister, Alexander Henderson, and an Edinburgh advocate, Archibald Johnston. Yet until the nineteenth century, lawyers had no recognized place in the constitution or 'set' of the burgh of Edinburgh. They thus had no formal say in town government or in the election of an MP, for that was done by the town council.

The picture of pre-Victorian Scotland is not quite as 'undemocratic' as it perhaps appears to modern readers. As conceived by the crown (and perhaps sometimes by participants), the function of medieval and early modern parliaments was not to provide a vehicle for representation, but to register consent to legislation and taxation. Most parliamentary electors were landowners in the Middle Ages. Political power followed the primary source of wealth and it was not until the end of the fourteenth century that burgesses were regularly summoned to attend parliament. Town councils themselves had a growing importance. Between the late fifteenth and the early nineteenth century, some of their members were elected by the members of craft associations ('incorporations') and merchant guilds, giving adult males from the middle ranks of urban society a chance to politic or 'bustle'. The right of different types of craftsmen to elect a deacon or leader of their association was recognized in the early fifteenth century. Craftsmen later achieved a stronger identity and a formal place in burgh government. However, merchants, who were generally wealthier, dominated the oligarchies which ran Scotland's towns until the nineteenth century. From the fifteenth to the eighteenth century inclusive, and especially in the smaller towns, most adult males would have had some (often multiple and frequent) experience of local office-holding, secular or ecclesiastical, during their lives: for example, as a kirk session elder, deacon or treasurer of an incorporation or guild, or a court juror or official. Judged in this way, participation may have been more rather than less extensive than in the nineteenth and twentieth centuries.

At the same time, words like 'liberty' and 'democracy' did not have the same meanings as they did after the American and French revolutions of the late eighteenth century. Liberty tended to mean the freedom to own property without the fear of it being expropriated by the state – even if that property included the lives of black Africans, as it might until the 1800s. Understanding of political representation was also different. In the countryside and the towns, political theory had it that those who depended on someone above them in the hierarchy were represented by them, be they employees, women, servants, or children. Dark Age and medieval society functioned principally through the bonds of kinship, clientship and patronage: the latter essentially personal bonds of right and obligation based on service and protection. Until the nineteenth century, patronage, nepotism and the purchasing of positions were regarded as perfectly acceptable. Birth, connections, and even a person's legal status, whether bondman or free, were vital to their prospects in life.

The issue of participation can be seen more broadly still, for politics should not be understood simply as the actions of politicians and voters. Men and women could be politicized by involvement in many different fields of life. For example, medieval warfare against the English politicized those beneath the land-owning classes in two ways. The first influence was military recruitment, for Robert I's statute of 1318 sought to enlist the wealthy Scots peasantry. Second came taxation. Edward I requisitioned all Scottish wool, an act which hit at the same social group. Thus the wars of independence articulated opinion well beyond the land-owning class. This does not mean that we should exaggerate the sense of shared political identity in the Middle Ages. The notion of *communitas regni* – a 'community of the realm' – was certainly well established in the thirteenth century, but it was a rhetorical device as much as a real statement of consensus. Nevertheless, it may be that involvement in warfare helped to politicize important sections of the population in this and in other ages. The Covenanting wars of the mid-seventeenth century were another politico-religious melting pot, while the radicalization of soldiers returning from the First and Second World Wars is a more modern example.

For women, involvement in seventeenth-century taxation and anti-Catholic protests, or in eighteenth-century food and conscription riots, created and reinforced a broadly political viewpoint. Such issues brought men, women and children on to the streets in protest. Riots were the response of a disenfranchised and, at times, desperate people.

Recourse to riot, however, seems to have been less common in Scotland than in England. There was no Scottish equivalent of the Peasants' Revolt of 1381 or of the famous early-nineteenth-century 'Captain Swing' riots in southern England. Most documented riots in Scotland were urban rather than rural. However, before the reforms of parliamentary franchise in the nineteenth century, discontented urban-dwellers tended to use the courts rather than the streets as their preferred arena for solving grievances.

Unusual as violent protest was, there were armed rebellions and even full-scale 'wars': for example, the Covenanting struggles of the seventeenth century, the Jacobite risings of the eighteenth century, and the Highland land conflicts during the 1880s. And there were larger-scale popular protests, such as those of the Galloway 'Levellers' in the 1720s against cattle enclosures. In the eighteenth century the king's birthday was generally seen by the lower orders as an excuse for riot and mayhem, in which lampooning of one's social superiors was an accepted part of the celebrations. These challenges to the image of an ordered and deferential society only died out in the mid-nineteenth century. Other means of expressing dissatisfaction, or even of articulating alternative political viewpoints, were available. In *The History of the Sufferings of the Church of Scotland from the Restoration to the Revolution* (1721–2) the eminent Presbyterian minister Robert Wodrow drew on oral traditions of the Covenanters of the 1670s and 1680s which preserved an approved image of protest against Charles II. Particularly in rural areas a strong oral tradition persisted deep into the nineteenth century. Because it was so much harder to censor than what was written or printed, talking could give power to the formally powerless. 'Waulking' songs sung by women who prepared cloth might tell of an unhappy marriage or an exploitative employer, though they might equally praise a prominent nobleman. Bothy ballads of the north-east Lowlands could be used to criticize a greedy or unkind employer. An apparently passive form of protest, song and story could exert a powerful influence on public opinion and could therefore be an effective form of 'political' protest.

However we understand it, the relative lack of popular protest in the pre-modern era should not automatically be seen as proof of shared values across the society. There were very tangible inequalities in power which can also help to explain the apparent quiescence. To take just one example, supporters of French revolutionary ideas were ruthlessly suppressed by the courts in the 1790s, while the lack of owner-occupiers and the acute dependence of agricultural labour on employers in much of the Lowlands made workers think twice about rioting. There was also a philosophical dimension. The radical working and middle classes were much influenced by the ideas presented to them by the Scottish Enlightenment. These stressed the importance of reason and argument over violence and irrationality. A shared faith in the value of education (whatever its actual achievements) and in the improvability of civil society made Scotland's people more interested in treading a positive and peaceful path towards betterment. Protest was to be ordered and non-violent, which is perhaps why in the nineteenth century the movement by workers to secure the vote in Scotland (Chartism) generally used peaceful action rather than physical force.

Scotland's reputation for political radicalism in the twentieth century is thus a rather new departure. The image of a radical people is a powerful one and it has some substance. Red Clydeside was born in the industrial and anti-war struggles of the First World War. Since then, west-central Scotland has remained a principal theatre of industrial conflict in the UK. It has always been close to, or at the top of, the league table of working days lost to strikes in industry throughout the twentieth century. But for all the images of Red Clydeside, the roots of radicalism may lie elsewhere in very traditional, religiously inspired concepts. Alongside reason and enlightenment there ran older currents of political thought which interpreted theology in practical social terms. In the words of the writer Tom Nairn, 'Scotland's gritty sense of equality derives from the old theocracy, not from Jacobinism or Bolshevism'.

In the twentieth century this tradition has been transformed into Labourism, defined as a commitment to some form of state control of industry and social welfare. Extreme political opinion has existed on both left and right, albeit only on the margins. Communism, the doctrine of a small minority of Scottish radicals, has only achieved electoral success in West Fife, where Willie Gallacher held the seat from 1935 to 1951. No Communist has ever been elected MP for Glasgow or held a seat on the city council. Not all political developments evinced this sense of primitive egalitarianism or mature socialism. The Scottish headquarters of the British Union of Fascists was at Dalbeattie, and the notorious 'black shirt' Sir Oswald Mosley's first meeting in Scotland was held in Dumfries. Moreover, the Conservative and Unionist Party has dominated Scotland politically for most of the twentieth century, even holding power in working-class constituencies such as Glasgow Govan. Since then it has been increasingly marginalized.

The arrival and development of mass democracies has empowered large swathes of Scottish society. Direct participation in political decision-making was denied to the vast majority of Scotland's people until very recently. Indeed, the social bases of political power were extremely narrow. The following section considers those bases, examines the nature of governance in historic Scotland, and explores the experience which ordinary men and women had of being governed.

State and Society

Relations between people are only partly mediated through participation in politics. They are also embedded in the social structure and represented as class or status-group interests. A person's position in the social structure may also generate a sense of separateness and a set of values in opposition to other social classes. All societies exhibit these social characteristics and in this sense Scotland is no different. Indeed, the fundamentals of the social structure remained superficially much the same for centuries. Most people lived on the land and depended utterly on its products for their livelihood. Crucially, for much of Scotland's history the land did not belong to those who worked it, or at least not in a modern 'freehold' sense.

Dark Age land-holding seems to have been by a group or by a chief on behalf of a tribe. This does not mean that individuals or families had equal shares or that there was uncertainty about their entitlement. What may have been lacking until much later was the right to a settled and demarcated plot of land. While the nature of land-holding prior to the early Middle Ages is unclear, a major change seems to have occurred in the twelfth century. Gradually, 'customary', kin-based land ownership began to mutate into a more individual, charter-based system. This development is commonly associated with the introduction of Anglo-Norman feudalism in the twelfth century. However, this created parallel ties to existing 'tribal' holding, for feudalism was a contractual form of land-holding. The subsequent development of feudalism in Scotland involved adjustments between the Anglo-Norman model and the indigenous land-holding and social structures which produced a distinctive and enduring system. This ultimately allowed a complete reorganization of land-holding by the crown along lines which cut across traditional Celtic tribal structures and kinship ties, and which subordinated all holders to the king. Yet the Scottish version of feudalism spread slowly and it did not obtain in all of its lands. The penetration of feudalism into the western Highlands and Islands may have been slight and its influence confined to landowners and their immediate sub-tenants, even in the late fourteenth century. Scots feudal land law was not imposed on Orkney until the sixteenth century.

Anglo-Norman feudal influence was not the only major development in land tenure. Another important landmark in reducing the overwhelming concentration of land ownership came in the fifteenth and sixteenth centuries, when the church and aristocratic landowners initiated a development called 'feuing'. A feu allowed the feuer rights to the land in perpetuity in exchange for a single lump sum and a small annual fee. Rents had simply involved an annual payment in return for short-term renewal of rights to property which was not owned. Feuing created a class of middling landowners, later known as 'lairds', who were approximately equivalent to English freeholders.

Feu duties were still being widely paid into the 1970s, when a commutation act allowed a one-off payment to terminate them. Feudal 'superiors' still have to be consulted about major changes in land use. Feudal law is still with us, even if at the time of writing it is scheduled for abolition by the Scottish parliament. 'Feudal' itself has become a pejorative term, yet concentration of land ownership made possible the pleasing Palladian regularity of the Georgian townscapes which characterize parts of Edinburgh, Glasgow and Perth.

The church was an important source of feued land. This and the story of education, which we told earlier in this introduction, remind us that, both before and after the

Reformation, the Christian church had a significance which far exceeded religion. If any medieval 'institution' had a bureaucracy, it was the church rather than the crown. Cistercian monasteries of the high Middle Ages were important in extending the farming of marginal upland areas. The medieval church was also an important political force. The bedding-down of Christianity in the eighth and ninth centuries produced an alliance between church and nobility which, among other things, revolutionized the nature of Pictish kingship. Cross slabs of the period demonstrate this very clearly and mark out the differing relationships between church and society in the east of Scotland from those prevalent in the west. Links between church and crown were strengthened with the creation of the kingdom of Alba: bishops legitimized kings and gave them administrators, while monarchs protected the church, its mission, and its property, continuing the symbiosis between secular and religious power which had existed since the Neolithic period. Aristocracy and clerical élites were also linked by ties of kinship and land ownership. By the twelfth century the Scottish church had become an important symbol of national identity. The parochial and episcopal structure systematized by David I remains essentially the same at the present day. At times during the Middle Ages the strength of the alliance between church and crown fluctuated, but the clerical élite remained politically significant. Clergymen like George Wishart, bishop of Glasgow, were called 'Guardians of the Realm' during the wars of independence, and the Declaration of Arbroath was drawn up by churchmen.

The nature of the relationship between church and state changed again at the Reformation, but the need for political alliances and accommodations remained. Through its influence, the post-Reformation kirk was able to turn certain sins like adultery into crimes punished by public humiliation, imprisonment, or even death. The Church of Scotland enjoyed quasi-political status into the nineteenth century. At the local level, too, the church permeated all aspects of life, including the administration of poor relief. The elders and ministers who made up kirk sessions, and who supervised the behaviour of every person in the parish, were the nearest thing to a police force that most Scots knew until the eighteenth century. Certain 'private' areas of life were the concern of church and secular authorities. Both before and after the Reformation, ecclesiastical authorities took a keen interest in moral as well as theological matters, though the concern of post-Reformation kirk sessions with sexual misdemeanours was unusual both historically and in comparison with other parts of Europe. And in small, tightly-knit communities the power of public opinion should not be underestimated. For example, it was not until well into the nineteenth century that illegitimacy became mainly a personal concern rather than a church and community issue in some rural parts of Scotland.

Church influence on cultural forms was similarly profound. The spread of written charters granting title to land and other privileges did not come until the thirteenth century. Before then (and in their symbolic aspects until much later), land transfers were conducted through spoken words and public gestures. Handing over a clod of earth had as much significance as signing or sealing a written title. The advent of such titles as the norm arose from the interests of a church which had both the bureaucratic need and the literate servants to create such forms. Indeed, medieval literacy was largely the preserve of merchants and of 'professional' scribes employed in the service of lords and the church. In medieval England, and in sixteenth- and seventeenth-century Scotland, written forms had been driven by the need of the crown for permanent records.

It is conventionally assumed that Scotland in the Middle Ages had a weak crown – the result of a succession of minorities – and an ineffectual government. In truth, the state was probably more governed in the Middle Ages than appears from the surviving documentation. That governance was devolved and lacked English levels of centralization. However, this should not prevent us from suggesting that Lowland Scots had as much experience of the state as their continental counterparts. Indeed, given its compact size and relatively homogeneous population, Scotland may have been more closely governed than, for example, the kingdom of France.

The crown certainly had officials (sheriffs, introduced in the twelfth century, were well established by the late thirteenth century; customs officials became entrenched in the next century), but it had also to devolve authority to the aristocracy. In 1300 three-quarters of the stone castles in the kingdom belonged to subjects rather than to the crown. The devolved nature of local government in early modern Scotland was a function of the relative weakness of the crown compared with that of England, which in turn arose from the parallel rather than opposing growth of royal and noble power during the later Middle Ages. The political and social importance of the church is therefore only one example of the many focuses of power which existed before the modern age. Governance took many forms. Burghs chartered from the twelfth century onwards were not simply trading towns, but also had fiscal and administrative functions. Decision-making was thus highly decentralized for much of Scotland's history.

Until united with England, the Scottish crown was poor; in a European context the British crown remained so during the seventeenth and eighteenth centuries. While prepared to spend astronomical sums on warfare from *c*. 1690 onwards, neither the crown nor the state it headed was willing centrally to fund social infrastructures which modern readers take for granted. In so far as they used 'public' money at all, pre-nineteenth-century schools were based on local initiatives and local taxation. Certain other forms of public welfare provision were similarly organized on a local rather than national basis, using private and voluntary charity rather than taxation. Lunatic asylums are an example. Certain types of 'social' taxation were strenuously and successfully resisted for centuries by landowners. Because state demand for regular taxation came much later to Scottish communities than to English, and because the control of central institutions like the Privy Council remained weak until the 1660s, Scotland's parishes never developed the same range of civil functions as in England.

It was not until 1598 that the Scottish parliament made justice into a state concern.

Until the sixteenth and seventeenth centuries, Scottish kings and governments (in striking contrast with those of England) did not attack the practice of blood feud, as they appreciated both their own weakness and the value of the feud in the preservation of local order. Local courts of 'barony' and 'regality', the latter with extensive criminal jurisdiction, run by members of the landed classes persisted until the mid-eighteenth century. Towns too could have regality jurisdictions, including Melrose and Glasgow. Recognizing until well into the eighteenth century the continuing power of kinship groups in a closely-knit society, criminal justice stressed reconciliation and restitution rather than simple retribution. Even the place of the ruler in the hierarchy of violence was very different in earlier times. Kingship in Alba (and elsewhere in Europe) had a turbulent history between 850 and 1100 – and beyond. Violence was perpetrated by kings, but it was directed against them more commonly than was later to be the case.

Pre-modern times are indeed often referred to as violent – with some justification. Martial symbolism is strongly represented in the later Bronze Age. Defensive architecture remained common in the Lowlands and the Southern Uplands into the seventeenth century, thanks to continued raiding both by the inhabitants of those regions and by Highlanders and Borderers. However, that does not make all pre-modern ages 'violent'. For one thing, Scotland's peopled past is punctuated by long periods of peace. For another, the use of force was for centuries regarded as quite legitimate. Perhaps as much as the Vikings who succeeded them, the Picts operated an economy of plunder. While they existed as a separate people, they were the most enduringly successful parasites in Dark Age Europe. Like other predatory peoples (including the Romans), they kept and traded slaves. Raiding seems to have been a commonplace feature of clan society. Norms of behaviour for individuals and groups were very different from the modern West.

On closer observation, other signs of apparent social fracture turn out to be more complex. Phenomena such as the blood feud of the sixteenth century, with its apparently brutal connotations, was in fact a way of structuring and therefore controlling disruptive conflict. Hostile propaganda labelled Highlanders as particularly warlike, but while their social organization may have contained a strong martial tradition, a threatening edge evident in traditions such as 'sorning' (eliciting hospitality by threat of force), and prominent elements of feuding (and feasting), there is no clear evidence of their being particularly violent. Furthermore, another way of looking at the issue of violence is to suggest that the seventeenth century saw a curbing of private violence, but that this was replaced in the eighteenth century by public violence (warfare) on an unprecedented scale, conducted from the mid-eighteenth century outside rather than within Britain.

For most purposes, the lords' criminal jurisdictions ran parallel with those of royal courts such as the civil Court of Session (founded in 1532) and the criminal Court of Justiciary (reorganized into its modern form in 1672). It was not until 1748 that criminal courts belonging to feudal lords rather than the crown ceased to exist, meaning that all justice henceforth was royal justice. Justices or Commissioners of the Peace, the cornerstone of English local government, were not introduced into Scotland until 1609 and never achieved the same significance as south of the border, even when their role was expanded in the eighteenth century.

The comparative weakness of the state until a late date had some negative implications for social policy. The absence of civil registration of births in Scotland until 1855 made it difficult to apply the Factory Acts in order to restrict child labour. Landowners blocked plans for county asylums in the early nineteenth century, leading the reformer Dr Andrew Halliday to conclude that 'the swine in Germany are better cared for' than the mad in Scotland. Publicly funded asylums existed in Aberdeen, Dundee, Edinburgh, Glasgow, and Montrose by the end of 1820, but they housed only a few hundred lunatics and the real period of growth came from the 1840s.

The Factory Acts of the first half of the nineteenth century were the first major breach with laissez-faire, followed by reform of the old Scots poor law in 1845, then elementary education which was placed under state control from 1872. There was also legislation governing transport and many other facets of social and economic life. The establishment of mass democracies created pressures for social reform, and political parties competed with each other to satisfy the growing list of demands from the electorate.

The involvement of the state in the personal and public lives of Scots and other citizens of the United Kingdom has increased enormously in the twentieth century. But Scotland was also the birthplace of the great exponent of free market economics – Adam Smith – and its economy until very recently was based on these economic values. The country's social policies and the attitudes of the middle classes towards the recipients of poor relief reflected these values. In the workplace, Scottish industrialists were seen by the Fabian socialists Sydney and Beatrice Webb as 'captains of industry' *par excellence*, managing their concerns as they saw fit. But in the course of the nineteenth and twentieth centuries Scotland became numerically a working-class society. Through the rise of the mass electorate, it has been the aspirations and interests of this class that have come to dominate the political agenda. Although this is always a contested agenda, the Scottish people have come to see the state as the best guarantor of civil and social rights. Two centuries ago the same role might have been performed by a landlord, two millennia ago by a warlord.

Discovering Scotland's History

We have looked so far at topics which have shaped modern and historic Scottish identities. We have tried to show how very different the past was, not only the material environment in which people lived, but also their mental world, their approach to family and community, and their understanding of politics. Scotland's history is worth studying for what it tells us about ourselves and our place in time. But it is also interesting and important in itself. Just as other cultures have to be understood in their own terms in the modern world, so have the lives of the people of the past.

If we were to consult the products of the heritage industry and the 400 or so museums in Scotland, we would have a very different perspective from that offered by historians. These institutions mostly emphasize the colourful over the mundane, the great over the humble, the martial over the peaceful. Robert Burns (1759–96) has more museums devoted to him than any other Scot. From this we might conclude that the character and aspirations of the Scottish people are found in the national bard's poetry and prose. We might legitimately argue from Burns's works that the Scots are a radical and democratic people. However, countering the humanist and republican appeal of his poem 'A Man's a Man for a' That' is Burns's equally powerful attachment to royalty and the pomp and ceremony that surrounded it. Whatever his republican sympathies, Burns was a member of the King and Country loyalist volunteers formed to maintain the political *status quo* in the 1790s. Like Burns, modern museum-goers seem to be mildly enthusiastic royalists whose perception of history shades towards the Jacobite end of the spectrum. It could be argued that clans and clansmen are celebrated beyond their historical importance. Queen Victoria might indeed have approved. Interestingly, while there are many Jacobite museums, there is no heritage centre solely dedicated to the Highland Clearances or the Covenanters – even if both appear as displays in other generalist museums. There is only one (the St Mungo Museum of Religious Life and Art in Glasgow) devoted exclusively to religion. World-class engineers and scientists seem to be largely ignored, even such household names as John Logie Baird or Sir Alexander Fleming.

The perceptions provided by the heritage industry are episodic and selective, as well as misleading. Along with the cinema and the media in general, it has constructed a national stereotype which has been sold to the world. Scots are portrayed as practical and, at the same time, as romantic. Cinema has projected an image of the subservient practical Scot, personified by the characters played in countless films by the actor Gordon Jackson, almost invariably uttering the immortal words, 'Aye, sir.' Such is the power of this perception that even in the modern television science fiction series 'Star Trek', the Scottish chief engineer is represented in the same way. Ealing and Hollywood also provided a romantic image of Scotland as a land of hills, mists and passions in the film musical 'Brigadoon' and in many other treatments of Scottish historical fiction, such as *Kidnapped*, *Rob Roy*, and *The Master of Ballantrae*. The 1990s film 'Braveheart', which won several Oscars, is also in the romantic vein, although this time with a pronounced nationalist message. It is set in the Highlands, whereas Wallace was a Lowlander. These representations have their roots in the romantic view of Scottish history found in the novels of Sir Walter Scott, but it is a past which is tartan and Highland-centred, a past which relies on myth rather than historical evidence. As R. B. Cunninghame-Graham put it in *The Ipane*: 'Scott arose and threw a glamour over

Scotland which was nearly all his own. True we were poor, but then our poverty was so romantic.' This is an over-simplification, for Scott's novels have strong elements of realism (including historical accuracy in *The Heart of Midlothian*). But story-telling can never be a substitute for a history that is based on evidence and shows a willingness to confront the unpalatable realities of the Scottish past.

History is not (and should not be) exclusively the preserve of academic historians. All of us can discover Scottish history for ourselves, and by finding our place in time we can help to make our future. The tradition of local history in Scotland has in some regards lagged behind that in England, even if journals like the *Transactions of the Dumfries and Galloway Archaeological and Natural History Society* have been published since 1876. As late as 1964 it could be said that the history of Scotland from 1707 was less studied than that of Yorkshire in terms of the volume of scholarly publications. This has since changed dramatically and there are flourishing local history societies, notably in the south-west, which are producing respectable research that transcends traditional legend, anecdote, trivia and genealogy.

The sources for Scottish history exist in abundance. Censuses and parish registers in New Register House provide (quite literally) tonnes of material for family history, but there are also the massive resources of the National Archives of Scotland and original documents in many local libraries and museums. The spoken memories of older people, written down or recorded and transcribed by oral historians, are invaluable repositories of information about, for example, folk culture and the experience of childhood. Film archives, moving and still, are another under-exploited source for the last four generations or so.

Of course, the further back in time we go, the harder it is to find documentation. Historians of Dark Age and early medieval Scotland have few sources to work on and those they have are frequently contradictory. There are English and Irish annals, a Scottish chronicle and the 'Prophecy of Berchán', poetry, hagiography, place-names, questionable king lists and genealogies. Most documentary sources which survive were written for a purpose: to persuade, to celebrate, to create a particular version of the past. For example, the story of the Scots' migration into Argyll in the fifth century may have been invented for political purposes. Archaeology can help enormously to redress both the lack of written accounts and, where they exist, their bias towards the interests of the powerful and the wealthy. For example, sculptured stones are a rich source of information about society, politics and warfare – some of it admittedly more propaganda than objective account. The Dark Ages are so called only because of the paucity and problematic nature of historical sources. There was nothing particularly dismal about the art of the period, which included the magnificent Sueno's Stone near Forres.

Archaeology's contribution is not confined to the period before the widespread keeping of written records – indeed the discipline is at its most powerful when it is integrated with documentary material, the one approach complementing and illuminating the other. This is especially true of the investigation of past landscapes, whether industrial, urban, or rural. Over the past half-century, aerial photography has added a revolutionary dimension, making an apparently quiet, empty landscape seem full of the works of people: cairns, ploughed-out ditches, earthworks, burial grounds and field patterns. These and other normally invisible manifestations of former human activity are revealed by the differential growth and colour of crops ripening above them. Archaeology has revealed an Iron Age landscape containing thousands of farmsteads, as well as field systems, paddocks and droving roads. Upland areas sometimes show, picked out in low winter light or by wind-blown snow, palimpsests of landscape evolution which can often be measured in millennia. Environmental history, and the associated scientific disciplines by which former climatic patterns and biological regimes can be reconstructed (notably palynology or the science of pollen analysis), provides another avenue of inquiry with a potential as yet only dimly appreciated. Through these still nascent approaches we are beginning to see how Scotland's varied landscapes changed through time, and how they influenced, and were influenced by, the people who inhabited them.

Excavations are necessarily limited in space and time, but if driven by carefully articulated research they can add significantly to the wider picture. Urban archaeology in towns like Perth has provided intimate snapshots of domestic life, industry, trade, and even recreation, particularly for the medieval period. Of the discipline's most recent developments, underwater archaeology may perhaps be singled out as having the greatest unrealized potential. Shipwrecks litter Scotland's coastal margins, a testimony both to the country's stormy waters and the intensity of traffic which has plied them since earliest times. Historical wreck sites are quite literally time-capsules, and although the few discovered so far are all early modern there is no reason to suppose that other periods are not represented too. The many submerged crannogs (artificial islands) in Scottish lochs, dating from prehistory to the seventeenth century, represent another rich resource for future archaeologists, historians and environmentalists. Their inhospitable waterlogged environments mean that air, a prime destroyer of organic material, is excluded and materials like wood and leather survive much better than they do in other contexts. Since past material cultures were overwhelmingly organic in nature, such sites hold the key to redressing a major imbalance in the historical record.

In short, those who seek to understand Scotland's past are faced with a mass of original documents and artefacts, not to mention a rich and varied landscape. In the archives, on the ground and under the sea, the sources of Scotland's history beckon us.

Note on the Text

In Chapter 2 Gaelic and Scots forms of personal names are given together, reflecting the transitional period before the high Middle Ages, when (as seen in Chapter 3) Scots forms came to dominate. In Chapter 2 the use of an asterisk before a word indicates that we do not actually have this form of the word preserved in this way in a source, and that the form is a reconstructed one.

Until 1971 imperial weights and pre-decimal currency were in use. Metric measurements are used throughout, except in quotations, where equivalents are given. Currencies have been rendered as used in the period under discussion. The decimal equivalents are: one old penny (1*d*.) equals approximately two-fifths of a new penny; one old shilling (1*s*. or 1/–) equals exactly five new pence (5p), and 20 old shillings equal one pound (£1). For example, £5.55p was rendered as £5 11*s*. 0*d*. Other currency units were used until the late eighteenth century, notably the 'merk' or mark, which was two-thirds of one pound (13*s*. 4*d*., or approximately 66 new pence). These are sterling equivalents. During the seventeenth and eighteenth centuries the Scottish pound was a separate currency. In the eighteenth century £1 sterling was worth approximately £12 Scots.

Throughout the relevant chapters, the surname of Scotland's medieval and early modern royal house has been rendered as 'Stewart'. Until the sixteenth century, its members called themselves Stewart and it was Queen Mary who started signing herself Stuart; after 1603 that became the convention in England. In Scotland, however, both forms were used.

1

Prehistory

IAN ARMIT

Prologue

In the late summer of AD 83 the farms and fields of fertile Strathmore lay abandoned and untended, the crops scavenged, and the food stores stripped bare. Through this deserted landscape passed a military force greater than anything ever before seen in Scotland. The Roman army of invasion, more than 20,000 strong, stretched for nearly twenty miles as it marched, preceded by its scouts, guides and interpreters, and shadowed by its fleet, harrying the coasts, plundering supplies, and spreading chaos among the coastal farms and villages.

For some time, the disparate and fractious Caledonian tribes had been holding assemblies, cementing their uneasy alliances, and preparing themselves for war. Through a skilful combination of force and threat, bribery and promise, the Roman governor, Gnaeus Julius Agricola, had subdued their neighbours, the Votadini, and the other tribes who lived to the south, across the Forth and Clyde. Now, as his biographer and son-in-law Tacitus tells us in the first written account of Scotland's past, Agricola's sights were set on Caledonia, and the final conquest of Britain. For more than a generation the Roman Empire had been expanding ever closer, swallowing up the independent tribes and petty kingdoms that lay to the south, beyond the Cheviots. News of each conquest filtered northwards with the defeated and the disaffected. It also came through merchants, adventurers, and ambassadors, and from those among the Caledonians who had travelled south and seen the Roman province at first hand.

This was no 'national' struggle. For some, Rome was a source of great opportunity: a powerful friend to help quash one's troublesome neighbours; a source of rare exotic goods with which to display one's prestige; a market for surplus produce. For the tribes of northern Scotland, however, as for many others throughout the Empire, Rome threatened to destroy the *status quo*, to bring down native leaders, and to destroy the complex web of kinship, alliance, and obligation that held their societies together. The campaign was to end at Mons Graupius, somewhere in the north-east, where up to 10,000 Caledonians died in a courageous but doomed stand against the Roman advance. The devastation of the countryside wrought by the Roman army probably ensured that as many again died of famine and disease in the winter which followed. Scotland's first flirtation with written history has the familiar ring of glorious defeat.

Archaeology and Scotland's History

For many people, Scottish history starts with the Romans. Anything before comes under the general heading of 'misty origins', a Celtic netherworld of ill-understood peoples and obscure, unwritten events. Yet although Agricola's campaigns marked the start of 300 or so years of contact, the Roman encounter with Scotland ultimately amounted to little more than a sporadic series of military episodes. The political will to incorporate the whole of Britain within the empire was never sustained long enough to see the job done. More pressing concerns along existing frontiers always took precedence in an empire which stretched from Scotland to Egypt, Portugal, and Mesopotamia. In terms of Scotland's human history, the Romans arrived late and stayed only briefly.

Indeed, the lands through which the legions passed had already been moulded and shaped by over 8,000 years of human occupation. The forests which developed after the last glaciation had long since been cleared by countless generations of farmers. The last major pockets of woodland in the Cheviots had been removed in the centuries just prior to the Roman invasion, a culmination of four millennia of human expansion. In parts of upland Perthshire and Sutherland, Bronze Age farmers, a thousand years before the Romans, had pushed the limits of cultivation beyond anything later attempted until soil exhaustion finally forced them back down to the crowded valleys. The worn-down circular banks that mark the remains of their once substantial roundhouses, the grassed-over field banks and clearance cairns, had all lain abandoned for a thousand years before the Roman incursions. They remain visible today, in the glens around Lairg in Sutherland, in Strathtay and Strathardle in Perthshire, and in many other now desolate locations, above the high tide-mark of medieval upland agriculture.

Even before the Bronze Age, complex societies had grown, flourished and disappeared; the stone circles and related 'henge' monuments (large circular enclosures named after Stonehenge, but generally without a stone circle) across the whole of the country reflect a highly developed yet wholly unfamiliar culture, in which social and political power derived from control over religious life and social ritual, and which shared in cultural developments across the whole of Britain and beyond. Yet the lack of written records of even the most basic kind shuts off these first eight millennia of human occupation from conventional written history. Instead we are forced to rely more or less exclusively on the evidence of archaeology, and related sciences such as palynology (or pollen analysis).

This presents problems for the integration of the prehistoric period into narrative accounts of Scottish history. The nature of the evidence dictates that archaeologists ask different questions from those posed by historians. The names of individuals and peoples are rarely, if ever, recoverable, and attempts to understand the fine detail of political motivation or social history without the benefit of written documents are invariably doomed to failure or fantasy.

This does not mean that the events and processes of prehistory are wholly lost to us. The material remains of Scotland's prehistory are extraordinarily rich, and archaeology's technical and theoretical tool-kit continues to evolve new ways of recovering and explaining them. But the questions which archaeologists address must inevitably be broader in scale than those of documentary historians. Developments in aspects of human life such as social organization, religious practice, land-holding, and technology can all be studied through archaeology, but the scale of analysis will generally relate to change over centuries or even millennia rather than decades or years.

Since archaeological data and archaeological questions are different, archaeological writing is also necessarily different from historical writing. This is partly why the prehistoric preambles of books primarily devoted to documentary history often seem rather awkward and unsatisfactory. This chapter does not, therefore, attempt to provide a potted archaeology of Scotland. Instead it seeks to survey some of the main themes of Scottish prehistory, in order to put the history of the last two millennia into a longer perspective. Examples have been drawn from the mass of archaeological data to highlight these themes, but there has been no attempt to be comprehensive in coverage or to engage in the minutiae of archaeological debate on the many contentious areas of the discipline. That would require a book in itself, and one quite different in scope and approach. None the less, the reader should remember that for every general statement or sweeping assertion which follows, innumerable exceptions or points of contention are to be found in the voluminous archaeological literature.

Economy and Technology

Archaeology is very good at documenting changes in economy and technology, many of which can be traced relatively uncontroversially from the discarded debris found on archaeological sites, and from the evidence of environmental change studied through pollen analysis and related sciences. It is in the area of technology that we see the closest approximation to a 'steady march of progress'. Although economic advances are less easy to define or to identify, there can be little doubt that the development of new tools and technologies over the millennia gradually expanded the subsistence opportunities open to prehistoric communities: for example, new, less amenable soils became available for cultivation as metal agricultural implements replaced those made of stone.

Indeed the popular, and to a lesser degree academic, perception of prehistory continues to be structured with reference to technological change, that is, the Stone Age (in its Palaeolithic, Mesolithic and Neolithic flavours), the Bronze Age and the Iron Age. These labels are retained by most archaeologists as terms of convenience, although they are no longer seen as marking major cultural or social revolutions. Nevertheless, the development of economy and technology provides a convenient means by which to construct a chronological overview of Scottish prehistory which will form a backdrop to the subsequent thematic discussion.

We have no idea when Scotland was first occupied, and indeed are never likely to know. There was human occupation at least in southern Britain around 500,000 years ago, but the ice sheets and climatic upheavals of successive glaciations effectively wiped the slate clean in the north, making it extremely difficult to trace any human activity before about 7500 BC. As elsewhere in the temperate forested lands of northern and western Europe, the first settlers were hunter-gatherers, and generally highly mobile, exploiting a wide range of natural resources in the course of their seasonal round. As such, each community ranged over large tracts of land and a variety of ecological zones, from coastal to riverine to upland. In this way, over many generations, groups from the south and east expanded into what is now Scotland. Population densities were capped by the availability of natural foodstuffs: plant foods such as fruit, nuts, seeds and roots; wild animals such as red deer, boar and small mammals; birds and fish. Conventionally the period remains known as the Mesolithic (or Middle Stone Age).

These communities, although made up of fully modern humans with complex social behaviour, did not require substantial or permanent homes, and do not seem to have built monuments for their dead. Since their wood, leather, basketry and other perishable products have long since decayed, we are generally left with little more than their tools of stone and bone, and the occasional slight remains of transient houses and work-sites. The flint and bone-work which survives is sufficient to indicate highly developed technologies in those materials which reflect basic subsistence needs (such as hunting, hide preparation and the processing of plant foods), yet it also shows marked changes over time in response to stylistic and cultural preference. Little modification of the environment was practised, although the deliberate use of fire to create clearings, giving high-quality grazing, seems to have been a familiar strategy for attracting and concentrating game.

By 3500 BC the landscapes of Scotland were changing quite significantly. For the first time, communities began to adopt a farming way of life. Over several millennia, knowledge of farming techniques had spread across Europe from Asia, where the wild ancestors of the early domesticated animals and cultivated plants are found. The rapid spread of farming over much of the continent suggests that colonists were on the move, clearing land and establishing new settlements. But this 'wave of advance' stalled well before it reached Scotland. Around the north and west fringes of Europe, hunter-gatherer

4

societies were well established and highly successful. Only gradually did they adopt the new techniques and technologies of their farming neighbours.

It was from communities such as these that hunter-gatherers in Scotland first acquired domestic animals and plants, and husbandry skills, although some colonists from the continent probably also came directly to establish their own settlements. The adoption of farming seems to have been rather piecemeal, however, proceeding at different rates in different places. None the less, by around 3500 BC the characteristic settlements throughout Scotland were probably small, permanent farms. Since the application of more labour could increase the agricultural productivity of the land, there was now a positive economic incentive to increase family size, while the availability of animal milk made earlier weaning of infants and an increased birth-rate possible. It seems that the density of population thus began to increase markedly. While the adoption of agriculture created the conditions necessary to enable populations to rise, the resultant increase in population itself created pressure for the expansion of farming into new areas.

The tool-kits used by these farming communities differed in crucial ways from what had gone before, although stone remained the key material for tool-making. While flint production continued, the products were often of lesser quality and complexity than before. The characteristic tool of the period is probably the polished stone axe head, originally hafted in a wooden shaft. Innumerable examples of these have been found across Britain and Ireland. They were used for a range of tasks, including the felling of trees to clear farmland, and day-to-day wood-working. These axe heads could be made of exotic materials, and some were traded over considerable distances. Examples from a production centre, or 'axe factory', at Craig na Cailleach, above the north shore of Loch Tay, have been found as far afield as Derbyshire. Similarly, axe heads from County Antrim are to be found in the Northern and Western Isles. In many cases, the more exotic products were probably symbols of status and social connections rather than practical tools. Stone ard points (for an early form of plough which broke the soil but did not turn it) and simple 'saddle' querns, in which grain was ground for flour, add to the repertoire of tools which commonly survive from this period.

There remains some dispute as to quite how settled these first farming communities were. Some have argued that the change from hunter-gatherer behaviour to farming was less of a radical transformation than archaeologists have traditionally believed. Parallels with societies from other times and places suggest that communities may have flirted with agriculture, settling to tend crops for a few years, before re-embarking on the traditional seasonal round of their ancestors, or perhaps adopting some minor element of stock-rearing within an essentially mobile economy.

Early settlers may have had strong social and cultural reasons for the ways in which they acquired and used different foods. Social sanctions may have both prevented the uptake of farming in some areas, and encouraged it in others, for example where the desire to build a food surplus for gift-giving and conspicuous consumption led people to intensify production. Once populations began to rise, however, it soon became impractical to return to a hunting and gathering way of life. By 2000 BC there is little doubt that communities in most parts of Scotland were fully settled and devoted most of their labour to the management of stock and the cultivation of fields. As far north as Orkney and Shetland enhanced soils were already being deliberately and laboriously created by the admixture of manure and turf to add to the fertility and stability of arable fields, for instance on the Orcadian island of Sanday; a prime example of the commitment of early farming communities to the land they farmed.

The introduction of bronze in the centuries prior to 2000 BC did not lead to any immediately perceptible shift in prehistoric economies. The new metal, knowledge of which was introduced through contacts with southern Britain or Ireland, was at first used predominantly for objects of personal adornment, although simple flat axes also appeared early on. As casting techniques evolved, more sophisticated tools were made, although time and skill was expended on the production of ever more efficient weapons than on the mundane tools for agricultural and craft work.

How much access the majority of the population had to these items is unknown, and we may be dealing principally with the status symbols of the élite rather than the tools of subsistence farmers. Copper and tin, the constituents of bronze, are seldom found together, and thus the growth of a bronze 'industry' presupposes extensive contacts across wide geographical areas. Tin from Cornwall and Brittany, for example, was traded as far afield as the Mediterranean. The earlier contacts discerned through the movement of polished stone axe heads grew enormously during the Bronze Age, with 'style zones' of similar artefacts and decorative motifs linking areas as distant from one another as Britain, Ireland, Scandinavia and Spain in the centuries around 1000 BC. Considerable wealth was accumulated through the control of the trade networks associated with bronze, but what relevance this had for most people is hard to gauge. Aside from the disappearance of stone axes, the tool-kit of saddle querns and stone ard points survived essentially unchanged for many centuries after the first appearance of bronze.

Whatever the role of the metal itself, however, the Bronze Age, and in particular the second millennium BC, was a period of enormous agricultural expansion in many parts of Scotland. It was a period of a more gentle, warmer climate; this, together with the population growth which had been an increasing factor since the adoption of a more settled way of life, seems to have encouraged farming communities to establish new settlements on previously uncultivated ground in the uplands. In parts of Perthshire and Sutherland farming landscapes were established at altitudes well in excess of 300 metres above sea-level. These comprised scattered but substantial timber roundhouses which probably each held an extended family (judging from the large floor space of the buildings), set within large areas of sprawling fields defined by banks and clearance cairns.

The very existence of these upland settlements must imply that the more favourable lower ground was fully utilized during this period. Although much lower-lying land was unavailable for arable agriculture before post-medieval and early modern land drainage operations, vast tracts of lowland Scotland were densely occupied and heavily exploited throughout prehistory, and in the Bronze Age they were presumably peopled to capacity. Only the massive funerary monuments which were built during the Neolithic and Bronze Age periods, great mounds of earth and stone, have survived as (largely) immovable islands in the arable deserts that have engulfed these areas since the intensification of agriculture over the past two or three centuries. The houses, fields and enclosures survive only in the uplands.

Wheeled vehicles were certainly available by the end of the Bronze Age to improve the efficiency of transport both within the farm and between communities, although most journeys by land would inevitably have been on foot or horseback (as was the case indeed until the eighteenth century in Scotland). A solid wooden wheel from Blair Drummond Moss in Stirlingshire has recently been radiocarbon dated to around 1000 BC. Wooden trackways across low-lying wetlands were almost certainly in use, as they were in Ireland and England (where the earliest example, from the Somerset Levels, is Neolithic in date), although the known Scottish examples, including one close to Blair Drummond Moss itself, are not securely dated as yet.

The Bronze Age push into the uplands was relatively short-lived and many such outposts were probably abandoned after a few generations, the areas returning to seasonal grazing and secondary woodland. In many cases, as in parts of Sutherland, over-ambitious agriculture was at least partly to blame. Soil exhaustion and erosion, the latter caused by removal of trees and ground disturbance by ploughing and over-grazing, rendered many upland areas unviable for arable agriculture. A general climatic downturn in the latter part of the second millennium BC added to the problems of upland farmers, increasing wetness and shortening the growing season. Climatic disruptions caused by dust clouds issuing from volcanic eruptions in Iceland may also have had a damaging effect. Although short-term in themselves, such events could have had long-term consequences for marginal areas, as particles deposited through rainfall increased the acidity of soils; perhaps enough to tip the balance in favour of abandonment. This period also saw the initiation or acceleration of peat growth in many areas.

This extraordinary episode of precocious upland farming, with all its implications for the scale of population and social organization in uplands and lowlands alike, remains to be fully explored and explained. Its apparent correspondence with the general widening of social and economic contacts under the auspices of the trade in bronze, however, suggests that major social developments must have been under way in the second millennium BC. The landscapes of Scotland must be envisaged as heavily settled, albeit with few large agglomerations of population.

The retreat from the uplands seems to have been under way by the early part of the first millennium BC, and the collapse of the bronze industry was to follow close behind. The introduction of iron technology, again ultimately from southern Europe, was radically to alter the basis of subsistence technology, essentially by democratizing it. Whereas the raw materials of bronze, copper and tin had to be brought together by a complex process of inter-communal negotiation and gift-giving, sometimes over large distances, iron ores were relatively commonplace. The need for extensive contacts and the ability to generate wealth by controlling these contacts crumbled as knowledge of iron-working slowly spread.

It was during the Iron Age, from around 700 BC onwards, that metal technology made real inroads into the basic subsistence economies of most people living in what was to become Scotland. From the middle of the millennium the last stone ard points disappear from the archaeological record in the far north of Scotland, indicating by proxy the adoption of iron-tipped implements for agriculture (although the iron objects themselves survive very poorly in the generally acid soils of Scotland, and are thus rarely found). A further major innovation of the Iron Age, which probably spread to Scotland from central Europe sometime after 400 BC, was the rotary quern, a small, hand-turned stone mill used for the domestic grinding of grain. This was substantially more efficient than the older saddle quern, and seems to coincide with a major arable expansion at least in certain parts of Scotland.

In the closing centuries BC, the south of Scotland once more saw a major push of agricultural settlement into the uplands. Whole valley systems in the Cheviots were entirely cleared of trees in this period, as thinly-settled areas were brought firmly into agricultural use. Miles-long systems of linear earthworks, for example in Roxburghshire, signal the division of much of the southern uplands, apparently for stock farming, while similar land boundaries, possibly for large mixed farms, have been detected as ploughed-out 'crop-marks' in the lowlands. This development of an apparent specialization between stock farming and arable farming hints at the emergence of a more integrated economy in which communities might concentrate on the production of a narrower range of resources, obtaining others by trade or exchange. North of the Forth and Clyde the closing centuries BC also witness the emergence of large semi-subterranean grain stores, known as 'souterrains' (literally 'undergrounds'), which seem to have been part of the standard layout of prosperous farms in the region. As with the extensification of agricultural activity in southern Scotland, this development in the north-east hints at a widespread intensification of arable production.

The Roman army therefore did not march into a landscape of economic stagnation, and still less into a forested wasteland occupied by primitive 'Celtic cowboys' (to use the late Professor Stuart Piggott's memorable phrase). Instead it entered regions largely cleared of woodland, though still containing extensive bogs and marshlands. Farming communities in the south were seemingly already tending towards specialization in either stock farming or arable, while those elsewhere practised mixed farming with the emphasis on stock or arable largely dependent on environmental constraints and social preferences.

Landscape and Boundaries

It is of course largely meaningless to speak about 'Scotland' in prehistory. The geographical boundaries of the nation as we perceive them now were utterly without relevance until well into the period of documentary history. In prehistory, boundaries of all kinds, physical, environmental, social and economic, created divisions between communities in different parts of Scotland which were at least as great as those which separated them from neighbours in England, Ireland, and the mainland of northern Europe.

Scotland's most obvious internal boundaries are between the north and west, and the south and east. The north and west, with its fragmented landscapes broken by long sea lochs and fractured into innumerable archipelagos, has generally limited agricultural potential, and this has imposed strict limits on economic growth in recent centuries. Whether such factors were as relevant in earlier millennia is open to doubt, although the environmentally imposed difficulties in generating an agricultural surplus and the impracticality of sustaining major centres of population must have been perennially limiting factors which prevented some of the economic developments seen in south and east Scotland. Yet complex societies could and did emerge in the north and west during prehistory (as they did much later, with the Lordship of the Isles), as the extraordinary flowering of Neolithic society in Orkney, with its monumental funerary architecture, eloquently demonstrates. Iron Age broch architecture shows that, even in later prehistory, the area could support relatively dense populations with sufficient surplus labour to engage in monumental building and the ostentatious display of status.

Other internal boundaries mattered far more in prehistory than now, when modern communications routes cut across former barriers to land transport. The 'waist' formed by the Firths of Forth and Clyde, with the intervening morass of the Upper Forth Valley, made a virtual island of the north. Significant differences in material culture, perhaps reflecting deep-rooted cultural, linguistic and ethnic differences, characterize the areas north and south of the Forth and Tay from as early as the Neolithic period. In Roman times the division was still clearly marked, with Caledonia, and later the Pictish kingdom, occupying the lands north of the firths. Northwards again, the Mounth was another major marker, dividing the north-east into two distinct zones which repeatedly found reflection in the distribution of cultural attributes.

While natural boundaries always acted to structure social and economic territories to some degree, they provided no absolute barrier to communication or expansion. Just as the post-Roman Gaelic kingdom of Dál Riata held sway over both Argyll and parts of Ulster, and its contemporary Northumbria extended from modern Yorkshire to Lothian, political entities of the prehistoric period variously straddled modern borders. It is probably safe to say that none will ever have approached the territorial extent of the medieval Scottish nation-state, although there is no reason, other than conventional prehistorian's conservatism, why certain Bronze Age polities need have been smaller than those of the post-Roman period.

Not only are the modern borders of Scotland essentially arbitrary, but even its very geography has undergone massive changes since the first human occupation. A graphic illustration is the land bridge which once linked the east of Scotland to the land mass that became Denmark. By the end of the Mesolithic period 'Doggerland', as it is aptly and evocatively known (after Dogger Bank), had been partially engulfed by the rising waters of the North Sea, but was none the less still an immense and populated island, and home to countless generations of hunter-gatherers. This near neighbour only finally disappeared during the Neolithic period, and its existence must be taken into account in studies of the movement of agricultural ideas and technologies into Britain.

The severance and final drowning of 'Doggerland' was accompanied by numerous other alterations to the coastlines of Britain. During the last glaciation, the weight of the ice sheets depressed the land mass of Scotland, and when this ice finally melted, the newly-uncovered land itself began to rise. At the same time, the unlocking of water from the ice caps caused sea-levels to rise, and the interplay between these twin processes caused considerable fluctuations in relative sea-levels around the Scottish coast. This has led to the drowning of former Mesolithic and Neolithic coastlines in the Western Isles, where sea-level rise has outstripped the rise of the land surface, but also to the preservation of contemporary coastlines as raised beaches, high above the modern sea-level on the west mainland, for example around Oban. When relative sea-levels were at their highest, around 5500 BC, the inland penetration of the rivers Forth and Tay was such that only a land bridge some 12 kilometres wide joined the northern and southern halves of the country. The well-known discoveries of whale bones in the Carse clays near Stirling give some indication of the degree to which the shape of the land mass has changed since this Mesolithic high-water mark.

Since the Neolithic period such broad-scale environmental shifts have been less marked and the most obvious landscape changes have been the result of human activity. The wholesale clearance of forests that occurred from the Neolithic to the Iron Age radically altered the environment of Scotland. As rainwater passed more quickly through the newly-exposed soils, stream and river flows increased markedly, generating major processes of soil erosion and redeposition. The sediment washed into upland watercourses was deposited downstream to create deep blankets of colluvium and alluvial fans. Such apparently 'natural' features of the landscape can often be the direct result of ancient human land management, as in the Cheviots, for example. The deforested soils were also prone to loss of nutrients and to alterations in soil structure. Thus early agriculture created the conditions which determine the character and vegetation cover of many Scottish upland landscapes even today.

Contacts and Communications

The fractured coastlines of the north and west more or less dictated that travel by sea would be the primary means of communication along Scotland's Atlantic coasts throughout prehistory. From the beginnings of the Neolithic, if not earlier, zones of contact can be discerned that link Scotland's Atlantic façade, through the Irish Sea, to the Atlantic sea-ways of Europe. Megalithic tombs, their burial chambers built of massive blocks of stone, occur in a series of variously defined and overlapping regional groups along this geographical zone during the Neolithic. The so-called Clyde tombs of south-west Scotland, for example, seem closer in form to those of the northern half of Ireland than they do to other parts of Scotland.

The south and east of Scotland, however, looked more to the North Sea basin. Contacts between Scotland and northern Europe did not disappear with 'Doggerland'. One of the earliest known farming settlements, and certainly the most extraordinary, is that excavated at Balbridie in Aberdeenshire. This was a truly massive timber-framed building dating to around 3600 BC. Not only was it around 24 metres long (a modern 'semi' might be 8 or 9 metres), but it was 10 metres across, suggesting a pitched roof well over 6 metres above the floor. This monumental piece of timber architecture quickly dispels any notion of primitive farmers struggling to scrape a living from the soil. The closest known parallels for the Balbridie longhouse come not from southern Scotland or England, as we might expect, but from Germany and the Netherlands. The impression of direct contact, whether by colonizing settlement or close social ties, is compelling.

The average prehistoric farmer, however, is unlikely to have appreciated the nature and extent of the links which so excite modern archaeologists. Those ploughing the upland fields of Perthshire or Sutherland in the late second millennium BC are unlikely ever to have travelled more than a few miles from their homes; indeed they were far less mobile than their hunter-gatherer ancestors who travelled routinely over significant distances to exploit a wide range of natural resources. Some people almost certainly did make significant journeys, particularly those concerned with the trade in metal ores and the manufacture and disposal of bronze objects. The close similarities in styles of bronze-work across northern Europe reflects a vast and complex web of contacts, but probably one that involved only a tiny and rather privileged proportion of the population. Even here there is a problem, for how can we say whether a given bronze ornament passed from, say, southern Ireland to Aberdeenshire as a direct gift from one wealthy chief to another, or through perhaps twenty transactions between manufacturers, traders, chiefs and dependants, perhaps over several generations?

The movement of individuals, groups and, indeed, whole populations remains crucial in understanding the nature of Scottish (and European) prehistory. It is not too long since nearly all significant changes in technology, language, or cultural traits were seen as reflecting invasion and colonization; the movement of people (generally from the south) displacing or subjugating native peoples. Thus the first farmers, the 'beaker folk', the Celts, and numerous other groups were thought to represent successive waves of ethnic replacement. This 'invasionist' view of prehistory is one which has proved remarkably difficult to shake off, and still finds its way into numerous textbooks and popular accounts. Cultural changes, however, take place in innumerable ways, few of which require substantial movements of people (although actual or threatened violence, whether between individuals or communities, should not be underplayed as a mechanism of social change). Indeed, major infusions of population are exceptionally difficult to document throughout Scottish, and indeed British, prehistory.

The first occupants of Scotland were the descendants of communities who had preyed on herds of large mammals in the glacial tundra on the fringes of the ice sheets. As the climate changed they adapted to forest conditions and exploited a wider range of resources. As the animals and plants on which they depended colonized the northern lands released by the melting ice sheets, hunter-gatherer bands followed them into empty and uncontested territory. We have also already considered how early farmers, equipped with a radically new technology and in a rapidly growing population, could expand quickly northwards and westwards across Europe into under-used lands, along deep river valleys, as each generation sent splinters of population to clear and farm virgin lands. However, even this most blatant episode of colonization stalled when it ran into lands occupied by successful and established hunter-gatherers around the northern and western coasts of Europe. For subsequent cultural changes in Scotland's prehistory, it is impossible to document any large-scale immigration of people, even though we must surmise that individuals and small groups must frequently have moved. Two examples can suffice: the 'beaker folk' and the Celts.

A new and distinctive style of ceramics, known as beaker pottery, came to prominence across much of Europe at more or less the same time as the adoption of bronze, in the centuries before 2000 BC. These were usually small, fine drinking vessels, elaborately decorated in a range of styles that recur from Spain to the Netherlands and the Western Isles of Scotland. Characteristically, beakers are found as grave goods, and they are often associated with items of jewellery, weapons, and the accoutrements of archery. For many years the spread of this distinctive pottery was seen as a direct reflection of population movement. These 'beaker folk', archers and horsemen, were thought to have swept across much of Europe, imposing themselves as rulers over the native inhabitants. More recent work has shown little evidence for this. The manifest continuity in virtually all aspects of society other than burial practice renders it much more likely that what spread was not 'a people' but a set of ideas. It has been plausibly suggested that the collection of drinking equipment which recurs in graves reflects the religious significance attached to the consumption of alcohol, which itself may have been first introduced at this time. Analysis suggests that at least some Scottish beakers held mead or beer for the deceased to quaff in the afterlife. This early association of drink and religion has a peculiar Scottish resonance.

The Celts are an altogether thornier issue, made more so by their invocation as spiritual fathers of a whole range of present-day cultural phenomena, from New Age religion to fiddle music. Since the eighteenth century it has become common to think of communities in Scotland, Ireland, Wales, Cornwall and Brittany as representing a Celtic fringe; surviving remnants of the peoples who inhabited a much wider 'Celtic Europe' before the expansion of the Roman Empire.

Linguistically, it seems unarguable that the languages spoken in these areas, for example Gaelic and Breton, are closely related, and derive from the language groups spoken across Europe in the first millennium BC. This language family has been termed 'Celtic' after the Iron Age people described by Roman and Greek authors as Celtae, Keltoi or similar, and the classical accounts are full of colourful descriptions of the exploits and behaviour of these societies. In fact these people represent only one group within a rather wider zone of what we would now recognize as Celtic-speaking communities, most of whom would not have recognized themselves as Celts in any sense. Indeed none of the classical authors ever referred to the indigenous peoples of Britain or Ireland as Celts. Apart from speaking a related language, we should not assume, therefore, that these communities necessarily had much in common with the Celts as described by Caesar and others.

During the nineteenth century, the recognition of widespread Iron Age art styles, known as Hallstatt and La Tene, led continental scholars to believe that they had found the historical Celts. The spread of these art styles was seen to represent the expansion of the Celts themselves, through invasion and colonization, into the far reaches of northern and western Europe in the last few centuries BC. However, the identification of this art style with the Celtic language, despite its prevalence even today, is no more than assumption and does not accord well with the evidence from classical authors, such as Caesar. Like beaker pottery 2,000 years earlier, the spread of these art styles is more consistent with trade, gift-giving and social aspiration among a network of well-connected and wealthy members of European Iron Age societies.

Celtic languages need not have arrived with an incoming people. Colonization is only one possible means of language change, and not necessarily a particularly common one. Processes such as the emulation of a dominant social group (talking 'properly'), the impact of arcane or religious languages (for example, Latin in medieval Europe) can be equally, if not more important. In the absence of literacy, centralized education, and bureaucracy, prehistoric Europe would have been linguistically untidy. Innumerable related languages and dialects would have co-existed, requiring many people to be routinely bi- or multi-lingual. In such a context it would be much easier than it would be now for the language of a marginalized or unsuccessful social group simply to die off. Celtic languages were certainly present in Britain during the Iron Age. Around 320 BC the Greek writer Pytheas referred to Britain as the 'Pretanic Islands', and Orkney as the 'Orcas'. These are both clearly Celtic names, as are the numerous tribal names recorded by Ptolemy at the time of the Roman incursions. The problem is that we do not know when these languages first appeared, although archaeology does give some strong pointers.

There is nothing in the archaeological record to suggest any significant infusion of new ethnic groups into Scotland (or indeed Britain or Ireland) during the thousand or so years before the Roman incursions. The wide-ranging contacts already mentioned in the context of the Bronze Age, however, required a significant degree of communication between speakers whose first languages were mutually unintelligible, as ores were obtained, traded on, and as products were commissioned, and gifts given. It would be most surprising if this fluid linguistic situation had not produced a multiplicity of creoles; new mixed languages, perhaps including the ancestors of Celtic languages. This situation is closely paralleled in the spread of other, more recent major language families, such as Swahili and Malay. In this scenario, ancestral Celtic languages evolved over a wide geographical area more or less coincident with that where they later appear in the earliest historical records. The 'coming of the Celts' was a lengthy process, not an explosive event.

People and Work

The size of Scotland's prehistoric population remains a vexed question. For the earliest hunter-gatherers, and the first few generations of farmers, the population base was small and thinly spread. However, given the marginal areas known to have been farmed during the Bronze Age, and the implications that this has for the density of lowland settlement, there is little reason to believe that average population levels by around 2000 BC were any lower than for equivalent rural areas in the medieval period. There would doubtless have been gross fluctuations due to short-term environmental downturns, crop failure and disease, but all the available evidence points to a well-populated and often intensively managed countryside.

One of Scotland's largest hill forts is on Eildon Hill North, near Melrose. The scale of the defences is impressive enough, enclosing around 16 hectares, but the main importance of the site lies in the extraordinary density of house platforms they enclose. An estimated 500 stances for circular houses, scooped from the rocky hillside, apparently date from the later Bronze Age, around 1000 BC. Once built, these platforms became the natural house stances for later generations, so it is unlikely that they represent numerous successive construction episodes (why build a new platform if an existing one is already free?). Thus the existence of around 500 suggests that very large numbers of people were resident on the hill, even if their visits were seasonal, for festivals or fairs, rather than permanent. Although we do not know exactly how individual households were constituted (they may, for example, have been defined by status or sex), each of these houses could easily have held an extended family of perhaps ten or more people, implying that gatherings of many thousands of people were not unknown on some of Scotland's largest prehistoric centres.

Such agglomerations of population were not to be seen again until well into the medieval period when the first urban settlements began to develop in Scotland. Proto-urban centres did develop in certain areas of mainland Europe, during the later part of the Iron Age (especially in the first century BC), notably the 'oppida' of central and southern France, but these large enclosed settlements, with well-defined industrial and commercial quarters, did not emerge in Scotland.

Although major centres like Eildon Hill have long been known, lowland settlement in Scotland's arable heartlands was barely recognized until the last twenty or so years. However, aerial photography has now identified thousands of enclosed and unenclosed settlements in areas such as East Lothian, Angus and Perthshire, most of which date to the centuries from around 1000 BC to AD 500. In one area of particularly dense Iron Age settlement around modern Haddington, an area of some 10 kilometres by 10 kilometres which was previously known to contain six high-status Iron Age centres is now known to contain more than sixty. These are all heavily enclosed settlements surrounded by substantial banks and ditches (although they were not defensively sited). Presumably lower-status settlements also existed but have simply not been detected. This was, therefore, an exceptionally well-peopled countryside and, given the prominence of these enclosed farms and their siting on knolls and high ground, it would certainly have seemed far more populous than the equivalent landscapes today. From a vantage point on Traprain Law, a major hill fort on the East Lothian coastal plain, one could have watched the smoke rising from hundreds of prosperous farms, not just in the immediate locality but across the Forth in Fife, far to the west across central Scotland, and south into the Lammermuirs.

Indeed, there is little to suggest that any parts of Scotland occupied in the medieval period were depopulated or empty for any significant length of time after the advent of farming. In the Western Isles the distribution of Iron Age roundhouses dating to the second half of the first millennium BC suggests population levels similar to those of the medieval period (perhaps fluctuating around 1,000 to 2,000 souls in North Uist and 500 to 1,000 in Barra, based on very rough calculations); yet even this seems to reflect a contraction of settlement to the coastal belt following the exhaustion of inland soils and the spread of blanket peat during the Bronze Age. Neolithic and Bronze Age populations in the north-west Highlands and Islands were thus at times potentially rather larger than in any period before the development of commercial fisheries and the kelp industry in the eighteenth century.

From the first introduction of farming, the vast majority of people in Scotland spent their whole lives in the business of agriculture. Wild animals declined in importance as a food source as populations quickly grew beyond the levels that could be supported by hunting. Indeed, by the end of the prehistoric period, Pictish symbol stones depict the hunting of mammals, such as deer, as an aristocratic leisure pursuit. Certain farming populations, as in Iron Age Lewis, continued to exploit red deer as a food source for several millennia (perhaps until as late as around AD 800), but these herds seem to have been managed as a resource more in tune with conventional stock-farming practice than traditional hunting. Fishing and fowling too remained important in many areas right through the prehistoric period, as would the gathering of plants and shellfish to supplement the diet, especially in times of shortage. Farming, however, was the bedrock of the economy.

There are few places where we can observe the population dynamics of these farming populations. A snapshot is provided by the people buried within the Neolithic chambered tomb at Isbister in Orkney, which was probably built a couple of centuries before 3000 BC. Communal tombs of this type were constructed by hundreds of small farming communities in Scotland, but the deposits within the tomb at Isbister were unusually well preserved. Several hundred people were represented among the bone debris, from a population which appears to have been fairly egalitarian in structure, with status based primarily on matters of age and sex rather than wealth or pedigree. Although the Bronze and Iron Age descendants of these people lived in very different societies, the physical nature of the Isbister dead is probably not too dissimilar to that of the farming majority in later times. They are probably fairly typical of Scotland's early farming communities.

The Isbister population had a generally low life expectancy, with high levels of child mortality. Even those who reached puberty could not be optimistic about living much beyond thirty, and only a small minority lived beyond fifty. Men survived on average longer than women, presumably as a result of the rigours of childbirth. Although the bones can rarely tell us what these people died of (in the absence of signs of deliberately inflicted injuries, for example), they can still provide a great deal of information. Assuming that these bones really do represent a cross-section of the community, the Isbister population had a structure not unlike many more recent pre-industrial societies: a generally young community, with few very old people (although recent advances in ageing skeletal remains suggest that such studies may have significantly underestimated the age of mature individuals). Such a structure has important implications. Old age may have been sufficiently rare to give these individuals a special status. The composition of households would have been extremely variable, given the unpredictable pattern of deaths among all age groups. This pattern is not reflective of distinctively prehistoric misery, however, but would have been familiar to rural communities in Scotland well into the present millennium. In other respects, too, members of the Isbister community were similar to their medieval descendants. They were of similar height, averaging 170 centimetres for men and 163 centimetres for women, and many suffered from degenerative disease of the spine as a result of heavy labour in the fields. Many of the women also had slight cranial deformations caused by the use of a 'brow-band' to carry heavy loads.

The agricultural economy underpinned all other elements of society, and it was the ability to co-opt and re-direct surplus production that enabled social élites to come to prominence at various periods throughout prehistory. The production and movement of prestige goods, including bronze jewellery and weaponry in the Bronze and Iron Ages, and even finely polished stone axes in the Neolithic period, presupposes the existence of an agricultural surplus which could be directed to support craft-workers in learning and practising their skills. Certain objects of metalwork, for example, the fine weaponry of the pre-Roman Iron Age, clearly denote the presence of full-time specialists, and the same may be true of the makers of bronze swords a thousand years earlier. The existence of monuments like chambered tombs as early as the fourth millennium BC also demonstrates that surplus labour could be diverted from agricultural work to engage in impressive but economically pointless projects. Clearly the cultural priorities which determined how and by whom surplus labour was expended varied greatly over the millennia.

It is impossible to generalize on the relative wealth or poverty of Scotland in prehistory, such are the vast changes in economic emphasis that occurred over eight millennia. The ability to generate an agricultural surplus shows that the prehistoric peoples of Scotland did more than scratch a living from the soil. In most periods they were closely comparable, in their levels of production and social complexity, with communities throughout northern and western Europe, with perhaps a higher density of population than was usual. The monuments of the Orcadian Neolithic, settlements like Skara Brae and monumental tombs like Maes Howe, are among the most accomplished and impressive prehistoric constructions anywhere in Europe.

In terms of the material wealth manifested at the top of the social pyramid, however, communities in Scotland were to fade rather in the first millennium BC, when an increase in contacts with the Mediterranean saw the appearance of enormously rich leaders across much of continental Europe. The lack of readily exploitable copper and tin sources meant that Scotland lacked the apparent wealth of Bronze Age centres like Ireland, and in the succeeding Iron Age communities in Scotland seem to have been rather inward-looking, with relatively few external contacts. Nevertheless, by the time of the Roman invasion the indigenous tribes were able to raise a substantial fighting force, an indicator of some prosperity.

Society, Wealth and Power

Such was the magnitude of the social changes that affected prehistoric Scotland between the first colonization and the arrival of the Romans that it is impossible to generalize about prehistoric social structure. Highly complex societies appeared and flourished, at various times and places, whose structure and values would have been quite alien to one other. A few snapshots must suffice to give a flavour of this diversity.

The relative egalitarianism of the first farming communities is reflected in the hundreds of chambered tombs scattered throughout the north and west of Scotland. The communities who built them, as at Isbister, show little sign of a rigid social hierarchy, at least in death. Their leaders probably derived their status from a combination of factors such as age, sex, and force of personality, but these individuals were not spared the rigours of menial labour, and their authority would not have extended far beyond the immediate kin group. The bones from the tombs do not demonstrate the special treatment of any individuals, either in life or in death. The intermingled remains suggest in fact that the community of ancestors was more important than the individual dead.

Studies in Orkney, most notably on Rousay where these tombs are unusually well preserved, suggest that each small farming community built its own communal tomb, partly as a burial monument and focus for religious life, but partly also as a territorial marker, helping to legitimize the group's tenure of the land. Neighbouring communities were in close contact, related by a web of kinship and social obligation, and individuals must have moved between them through marriage (if only to maintain a viable breeding population). While some groups would have been more successful than others, nowhere is there any overt sign of a higher level of authority.

This pattern of relative social equality may not have lasted long, particularly in fertile areas where population growth gave rise to conflicts over access to land and resources. Even by about 3000 BC the appearance of large communal monuments such as stone circles and henges suggests that new patterns of social authority were emerging to coordinate large-scale group endeavours. The great Orcadian chambered tomb of Maes Howe is a case in point. It was far larger and more elaborate, and absorbed much more labour in its construction than earlier tombs like Isbister. Yet it was built to contain only a few individuals rather than a whole community, and seems to reflect a significant realignment in the social relations within Orcadian society. It represents one of the first overt indicators of the emergence of a socially dominant class in Orkney, able to mobilize and direct the surplus labour of the farming population. By the time bronze objects appear in the archaeological record, it is clear that we are dealing with societies in which certain individuals or lineages had accumulated substantial levels of power over others.

As at Cairnpapple in West Lothian, substantial burial monuments, requiring the labour of large groups of people, were built to hold the remains of a single individual:

the dissolution of the individual at death into the faceless mass of ancestors had long since been abandoned. The social élite of the Bronze Age seems to have derived much of its power, in Scotland as elsewhere in Europe, through control of bronze production and trade. Command of route-ways could be as significant as control of the actual resources themselves. But this power had to be underpinned by at least the threat of physical force. As bronze technology developed, much effort was put into the production of ever more accomplished weaponry. The dirks and daggers of the earlier part of the Bronze Age gave way to highly effective slashing swords before 1000 BC, possibly designed for mounted combat. By the turn of the first millennium BC the finds from graves and hoards present a vivid picture of a heavily armed and status-conscious aristocracy, who displayed their prestige through state-of-the-art military hardware and access to a range of exotic material goods.

It is impossible to say quite how powerful individual rulers were at this period, and how large were the tribal groups or territories they controlled. These were clearly far more hierarchically ordered societies than had been the case in the Neolithic. Yet they did not represent a step on a social evolutionary ladder; with the collapse of the bronze industry in the first half of the first millennium BC, the economic basis of the Bronze Age élites seems to have crumbled and fragmented. Overt signs of individual wealth and long-distance contacts all but disappear from the archaeological record.

The succeeding Iron Age, however, was far from being a time of social chaos, even if the political groups of the period were probably rather smaller in scale than their forerunners, with far fewer signs of inter-regional contacts. For much of the Iron Age, status seems to have been derived rather more directly from the land and from agricultural wealth than from far-flung contacts and access to prestige goods. The quintessential status markers of the period are massive hill forts, monuments which emphasized linkage to the land and communal endeavour rather than explicitly glorifying the individual. Indeed burials of any kind, far less elaborate individual graves, all but disappear from the archaeological record at this time.

One quite extraordinary facet of the Iron Age in many parts of Scotland is the dominance in the landscape of substantial houses. The most familiar are the broch towers of the north and west. The best-preserved example, Mousa in Shetland, stands around 13 metres high, an extraordinary hollow-walled stone tower with an intra-mural staircase leading to the wall-head. Broch towers were originally capped with conical timber and thatch roofs, and held multiple internal floors. They were in essence monumental farmhouses, capable of housing large numbers of people – most probably extended families. Though some of the later examples formed the centrepieces of nucleated villages, many were scattered and isolated in the landscape. Their sheer numbers, in areas such as the Hebrides and Shetland, show that these were not the homes of tribal chiefs or petty kings, but were closer to the standard settlement form for land-holding families.

The stunted remnants of abandoned broch towers proved difficult for later farmers to shift, and they abound in the landscapes of the north and west even today. However, during the Iron Age these impressive structures were simply the northernmost manifestation of a much wider tradition of roundhouse-building. Timber roundhouses in the south and east of the country usually survive only below ground level. Yet originally these could have been even larger than many broch towers in terms of their original diameter, and thus floor area. Roundhouses up to about 16 metres in diameter contained an extraordinary amount of room (equivalent to the ground floors of two modern semi-detached houses), and would almost certainly have had upper timber floors like those of the brochs. With roofs rising to around 10 metres above ground level, these were as dominant in the arable lowlands as brochs were in the far north and west. Experimental reconstruction has also demonstrated the stability and durability of such buildings. With proper care and maintenance these timber roundhouses would probably have stood for many generations, and they mark a significant investment of labour and resources.

Where the evidence survives, notably in the well-preserved 'wheelhouses' of the Hebrides (so called because their interiors were divided by radial stone partitions which give a ground-plan rather like a spoked wheel), there is some evidence that Iron Age roundhouses served as a focus for small-scale domestic ritual as well as for the normal range of domestic functions. Burials of human and animal body parts in pits below the floors and within the walls of these structures suggest that key events in the life of the household were marked by religious ceremonies focused on the house. The wheelhouse at Cnip in Lewis, for example, had a complete pottery vessel and the head of a great auk (a now extinct seabird) built into its wall during its construction in the last couple of centuries BC.

The sheer profusion of monumental roundhouses – thousands rather than hundreds – during the Iron Age has profound implications for our understanding of the nature of land-holding at the time. Clearly these buildings were in part statements of the wealth and prestige of individual households or their heads. These people, however, would not have been able or willing to invest enormous resources, both of labour and materials, in the construction of such powerful statements of ownership unless they also had considerable autonomy and security of tenure. This was a period when local farming communities were not only fairly prosperous, but also sufficiently autonomous to invest their surplus labour in their own homes and farms. The appearance of souterrains in the eastern part of the country, dispersed widely across the arable lowlands, further suggests that surplus food production could be retained to serve the community, rather than disappearing to support an aristocratic 'leisure' class.

Security of tenure over generations, even centuries, also suggests stability. It implies that the Iron Age was not characterized by the sort of inter-communal warfare which would have made dense landscapes of undefended farmsteads untenable. Given that conflicts over access to land and resources seem to be a feature of more or less all human societies, and given the ease with which stock and stored produce could theoretically be removed from undefended farmsteads, the apparent lack of concern over raiding and security in general implies the existence of some higher level of social organization, to prevent such destructive conflicts occurring. This does not of course mean that organized violence was absent; simply that its manifestations, perhaps ritualized individual combat or external raids against distant communities, did not routinely threaten the destruction or appropriation of property. However, evidence for such higher authorities is difficult to find, and there is little to suggest the presence of powerful individuals until well into the Roman period.

The impression of localized control over agricultural production and wealth which characterizes much (though not all) of the pre-Roman Iron Age is thrown into sharp relief by the contrasting archaeological record of the Roman and post-Roman period. While major changes in the late pre-Roman Iron Age already hint at the re-emergence of more powerful élites – for example in the appearance of elaborate metalwork and weaponry – the destructive impact of Rome's repeated military adventures on the finely tuned agricultural economies of southern and eastern Scotland should not be underestimated. The societies which emerge at the end of the Roman period are quite unlike those which went before, and rather more akin to their remote ancestors of the Bronze Age in terms of their hierarchical structure and emphasis on a military élite.

Some of the archaeological evidence for the post-Roman period is remarkably similar to that of the Iron Age. Hill forts were refurbished or built anew, but these now tended to have strictly graded layouts, with a strongly walled citadel surrounded by terraces and enclosures, suggesting a much greater emphasis on hierarchy, division and exclusion. Unlike their Iron Age antecedents, these hill forts seem to have been monuments to the power of individual war leaders and dynastic groups. Yet while these homes of the new élite remain clearly visible in the landscape and easy to trace archaeologically, the lower classes of society virtually disappear. No longer were the arable lands of south and east Scotland dotted about with the substantial timber roundhouses of prosperous farmers. What houses have been found were much more modest in scale, and their general paucity suggests that they were far more ephemeral and poorly constructed. It is hard to avoid the conclusion that major differentiation between social classes had evolved during the first few centuries of the first millennium AD, perhaps as a result of the instability and disruption fostered by warfare related directly and indirectly to the establishment of the Roman province to the south. As well as the obvious potential effects of Roman military campaigning in the north, the presence of concentrated portable wealth in the towns and settlements of the frontier zone created an incentive for institutionalized raiding and the growth in importance of a military élite. The choicest targets for raiding of this type lay generally south of Hadrian's Wall, although small civilian settlements did briefly exist alongside some of the northern forts, notably Inveresk near Musselburgh.

Class distinctions are reflected also in the increasing dominance of items of personal adornment, brooches, elaborate weaponry and armour, that begin to appear in the archaeological record, and in the reappearance of rich individual graves. The societies which emerge during these centuries are those which find reflection later in the 'heroic' ethos of *Y Gododdin*, a series of elegies celebrating a fallen war band of the sixth century AD. The consistent emphasis on the aristocratic pedigree, military prowess and splendid appearance of the Gododdin warriors provides a remarkable insight into the chief ideological preoccupations of the social élite in post-Roman Scotland.

Death and Religion

Tombs and their contents are often used by archaeologists to infer aspects of social structure, but they also had profound cultural significance in their own right and offer rare insights into the mental worlds of prehistoric peoples. A large proportion of the material evidence for prehistory relates directly or indirectly to religion. Burial monuments and places of worship dominate the archaeological record for the Neolithic, for example, while graves and grave goods constitute much of the material remains of the Bronze Age. Before the adoption of Christianity in the post-Roman period, however, the detail of religious belief is entirely lost to us, even if certain broad trends and outlines are apparent.

The fundamentally alien character of prehistoric religious beliefs to the modern western mind can be quite jarring. It is easy to look at descriptions of the buried population from the Isbister chambered tomb, to read of their mixed farming economy, and to conjure up a vision of a rural lifestyle familiar from recent ethnography, yet the nature of burial in chambered tombs demonstrates an attitude to death and the ancestors entirely unlike any society from recent European history. Chambered tombs were not simple family burial vaults. The remains were often deliberately mixed up and rearranged into groups, for example of skulls or long bones, as if to subsume the identity of the individual within the community of ancestors. The over-representation of larger bones, such as skulls and long bones, suggests that bodies were often exposed before burial to allow the flesh to disintegrate; an act which might be seen as a means of enabling the spirit to escape from the body.

When the bones were gathered up for final disposal, fingers, toes and other small bones were either missed, or had already disappeared through animal scavenging or other forms of dispersal. Even when finally placed within the tomb, resting in peace was apparently not an option. The tombs were visited, perhaps at particular times of year, such as the summer or winter solstices, or during important occasions in the life of the community. That body parts were variously removed and reordered suggests that they were used in rituals which took place outside the tomb. Each stage in the drawn-out funeral process would have had significance for the community, and, as in some societies known through ethnographic study, certain stages may have had to await propitious conditions or specific times of year.

For later periods, it is fashionable to stress the symbiosis which early Christianity established with the emerging states of the post-Roman period. The early church was certainly closely involved in secular affairs and helped legitimize kings and states in return for patronage, land and resources. To what extent such a role is peculiar to Christianity is debatable. The centrality of religious monuments in, say, the later Neolithic suggests that religion and political power were at least as closely entwined then as during the early Christian period. Similarly the suppression of the Druids in southern Britain by the Roman Empire seems to have been intended to counter the direct political threat they posed to the new regime. It might be wiser, then, to assume that a close interplay of matters sacred and profane was commonplace throughout prehistory and continued to be so into the early Christian centuries.

Organized religion as a dominant force within prehistoric society is perhaps most obvious in the later Neolithic from around 3000 to 2000 BC. This period saw the construction of hundreds of large communal religious centres across the British Isles, most commonly stone circles or the large embanked and ditched circular enclosures known as henges. Many stone circles in Scotland are relatively small. However, there are a number of ritual complexes which were conceived and built on an altogether more massive scale. Some of the best preserved of this type survive in Orkney, notably the enormous stone circles and enclosures at the Ring of Brodgar and Stenness, and equally famously in Lewis at Calanais, where a scatter of satellite stone circles are dotted around a huge cruciform stone setting. Much less well known, but originally just as important, are major complexes of timber circles and ditched enclosures in the arable lowlands of Scotland. Major centres are known, for example, at Balfarg in Fife and Dunragit near Dumfries.

These large monuments seem to have had more than simply local significance. Pottery from Scottish henges includes styles which are replicated from Orkney to Wessex (notably the remarkably widespread 'grooved ware'). The same repertoire of design features crops up repeatedly, even though no two major henge complexes are ever quite identical. Interestingly, the Scottish examples, particularly those in the far north, seem to be among the earliest of all henges. This was clearly not a case where cultural ideas and values drifted northwards from southern Britain. Like medieval cathedrals, individual henges and stone circles evolved over many generations. They embodied an elaborate set of beliefs which doubtless changed markedly over time. Trying to understand these beliefs in detail is like trying to reconstruct Christian liturgy using only the physical remains of the ruined Border abbeys.

Clearly, however, a common pool of quite specific religious ideas underlay this extraordinary cultural phenomenon. The repeated occurrence of basic astronomical alignments within such monuments provides a strong indication that religious beliefs associated with the sun and moon played a crucial part in their development and spread. By aligning standing stones and timbers on the moon, sun and stars, the people who designed these monuments could link their own authority to the cycles of the natural world. The sun or moon rising over a particular setting during ritual performances could make the heavens seem tamed: a tremendously reassuring sight for communities whose survival depended on the weather and the predictability of the seasons.

It has been suggested that the second millennium BC saw a shift in the nature of the gods that were most venerated. The great communal monuments of the Neolithic period seem to be focused skywards, their design incorporating observations of the heavens. By contrast, the most prevalent religious practice of the later Bronze Age seems to have been based around the deposition of precious objects, including fine metalwork, into bogs, pools and rivers. This basic pattern is replicated throughout the British Isles and can be taken to represent a move away from the worship of sky gods, whose moods and actions were encoded in the sun, moon and stars, to gods of the earth or underworld. The latter are more akin to the sorts of deities who emerge in the early written sources as the pagan Celtic pantheon. They were also gods whose activities reflected the 'heroic' ideologies of the Bronze Age aristocracy. If one thinks about the shifts, ructions and complexities which have affected the development of Christianity over the past 2,000 years, it becomes immediately apparent how simplistic our understanding of prehistoric religious development must be.

Conclusion

By the time of the Roman invasion, over 80 per cent of Scottish history had already passed. At least two complex and contrasting societies, the later Neolithic with its great henge monuments, and the later Bronze Age with its sword-brandishing aristocracies, had long since flowered and faded. A third period of economic expansion and social change, the later Iron Age, was already underway. And the distinctive landscapes of Scotland, treeless moorland pasture, bleak peatlands and fertile lowland arable, were all in place, as elements of a densely peopled and intensively managed north European region. The environmental parameters for Scotland's future economic development had been set.

Scotland had generally followed a path familiar from other parts of Britain and Europe, although the nature and direction of contacts was far from uniform. Certain aspects of Scotland's prehistory are distinctively British: the great roundhouses which so characterize the Scottish Iron Age are found throughout Britain, but are quite distinct from the contemporary rectangular houses found on the continent. Their layout and design, and the frequent incorporation of ritual deposits, suggest that they embody cosmological and religious ideas in a period where overtly religious monuments and burials are virtually absent. Whatever religious ideas underlay this phenomenon they were apparently specific to Britain and may have lasted several centuries longer in Scotland than they did further south.

Scotland's is an entirely rural prehistory – unlike, say, that of France and Germany, where proto-urban centres emerged during the first millennium BC. The closest Scotland came to urbanization was probably in the agglomerations of people who built houses within the ramparts of hilltop enclosures like Eildon Hill North in the later Bronze Age, but these were probably not permanent centres of population. In other respects, prehistoric communities in Scotland fit into a wider picture of European developments. They share the phenomena of megalithic tombs, beaker pottery, 'Celtic' art, and numerous other wide-ranging prehistoric cultural traits, with much of continental Europe. By the end of the Roman period Scotland seems to have been dominated by militaristic societies similar to others which harried the collapsing Roman provinces along the 'barbarian fringe' of northern Europe. The military aristocracies which emerged in the post-Roman period were just one of many possible socio-political forms signposted by the previous five millennia of Scotland's history. Yet such élite groups were to dominate the early centuries of Scotland's written history, their pedigrees, alliances, disputes and military adventures forming the core of the literature of the early historic period. Never again did societies emerge in Scotland that were comparable with the alternative social structures apparent in prehistory.

By definition the prehistoric past was pre-literate, and it is this absence of written documents that renders it so utterly distant from us and severs its links with history as conventionally understood. Yet as the available fragments suffice to show, the prehistoric past contains a multiplicity of histories. It was never static or timeless, but its complexities can for now be discussed only in outline. Perhaps more than any part of Scotland's documented history, however, the recovery of basic data relating to the prehistoric past continues to increase. Provisional as our accounts must be for now, the future holds out considerable hope for our understanding of Scotland's most remote past.

Bibliographical Essay

Most of the available information on Scotland's prehistory is contained in academic journals, notably the *Proceedings of the Society of Antiquaries of Scotland*. Most books and monographs tend to be either works of synthesis, covering a single period (notably the recent Historic Scotland/Batsford series which form the best modern introductory texts), or a particular region, or else highly specialist excavation reports. There is little middle ground, with few books covering specific themes, such as economy, society or religion, for which recourse has generally to be made to specialist journals. The following survey of the literature steers clear of the heavyweight excavation-based monographs, although most of the works cited here give full reference to such material and provide a good way into the literature.

There are a number of good general introductions to Scottish prehistory, of which the most recent is *Scotland's Hidden History* by Ian Armit (London, 1998). This provides an overview from the first human colonization in the Mesolithic to AD 1000, focusing on 100 key sites. *Scotland: Archaeology and Early History* by Graham and Anna Ritchie (Edinburgh, 1981) acts more as an introductory textbook and, although slightly outdated, forms an excellent starting-point for delving deeper into the archaeological literature. More up-to-date and concentrating on economic and environmental archaeology is *Scotland: Environment and Archaeology*, edited by Kevin Edwards and Ian Ralston (London, 1997).

The regions of Scotland are variably served by the general literature. For many parts of the country there are weighty inventories of monuments published over many decades by the Royal Commission on the Ancient and Historical Monuments of Scotland. Among the most recent are *East Dumfriesshire* (HMSO, 1997), *South-east Perth* (HMSO, 1994) and *North-east Perth* (HMSO, 1990). These most recent volumes are extremely comprehensive and have a significance far beyond the narrow regions they cover. The usefulness of the older volumes generally relates directly to the date of publication, which goes back to the early part of the twentieth century.

In general, synthetic works are best for the north and west of the country, where the survival of monuments in the field is such that they have attracted most study. *The Archaeology of Skye and the Western Isles* by Ian Armit (Edinburgh, 1996), *The Prehistory of Orkney* by Colin Renfrew (Edinburgh, 1985), *Prehistoric Orkney* by Anna Ritchie (London, 1994), *The Archaeology of Argyll* by Graham Ritchie (Edinburgh, 1997), and *Ancient Shetland* by Val Turner (London, 1998) are all useful syntheses, each covering the whole of prehistory.

For the earliest colonization of Scotland there is little beyond the very detailed and site-specific literature of the specialist journals, although *Scotland's First Settlers* by Caroline Wickham-Jones (London, 1994) is a good introduction. More academic in tone is *The Early Prehistory of Scotland*, edited by Tony Pollard and Alex Morrison (Edinburgh, 1996), which contains a series of papers summarizing recent research.

The most recent popular synthesis for the Neolithic and Bronze Ages is Patrick Ashmore's *Neolithic and Bronze Age Scotland* (London, 1996), while the rather wider-ranging *Symbols of Power at the Time of Stonehenge* by David Clarke, Trevor Cowie and Andrew Foxon (Edinburgh, 1985) remains an important and useful work. *Vessels for the Ancestors*, edited by Alison Sheridan and Niall Sharples (Edinburgh, 1992) contains a range of papers exemplifying various current academic approaches to the Neolithic of Scotland and beyond.

Chambered tombs of the north and west are unusually well covered, mainly thanks to the work of Audrey Henshall, who has published *The Chambered Cairns of Orkney* (Edinburgh, 1989), *The Chambered Cairns of Caithness* (Edinburgh, 1991) with J. L. Davidson, and *The Chambered Cairns of Sutherland* with Graham Ritchie (Edinburgh, 1995). Her thoroughly comprehensive *The Chambered Tombs of Scotland* (2 vols., Edinburgh, 1963 and 1972) still serves as the key source for other areas. *Tomb of the Eagles* by John Hedges (London, 1994) uses the data from the spectacular site of Isbister to explore a range of social and population issues which complement the rather drier approach of Henshall's works.

Less has been written, at least in book form, on other Neolithic monuments, although Patrick Ashmore's *Calanais: The Standing Stones* (Stornoway, 1995) provides a brief popular summary of a major stone circle, while *Balfarg: the Prehistoric Ceremonial Centre* by Gordon Barclay (Glenrothes, 1993) highlights a lowland monument of comparable scale and importance in a similar fashion.

There is little in book form dealing with the important developments of the Middle and later Bronze Ages in Scotland, although *The Lairg Project: The Evolution of an Archaeological Landscape in Northern Scotland* by Rod MacCullagh and Richard Tipping (Edinburgh, 1998) provides a thorough and informative report on the most important field archaeological project of recent years on Bronze Age upland settlement in Scotland.

A synthesis of the Iron Age is provided in Ian Armit's *Celtic Scotland* (London, 1997). *Beyond the Brochs*, edited by the same author (Edinburgh, 1990), comprises a series of more strictly academic contributions dealing with the Iron Age in Atlantic Scotland. A shorter and more popular account of broch studies is available in *Dun Charlabaigh and the Hebridean Iron Age* by Ian Armit and Noel Fojut (Stornoway, 1998). Iron Age monuments other than brochs are generally ill-served by monograph publication, although Ian Morrison's *Landscape with Lake Dwellings* (Edinburgh, 1985) provides a readable introduction to the study of crannogs. A wider geographical perspective on Iron Age developments in Britain is provided in two books by Barry Cunliffe, the brief survey *Iron Age Britain* (London, 1995), and the much more comprehensive *Iron Age Communities in Britain* (London, 1991), although the Scottish material in the latter is not as well covered as that relating to southern England.

For the Roman period the most accessible introductory text is undoubtedly *Roman Scotland* by David Breeze (London, 1996), while the same author's *The Northern Frontiers of Roman Britain* (London, 1982) forms a rather more detailed analysis. Bill Hanson in *Agricola and the Conquest of the North* (London, 1991) focuses on the initial Roman incursions, while Gordon Maxwell's *A Battle Lost: Romans and Caledonians at Mons Graupius* (Edinburgh, 1990) gives a short but compelling summary of the issues surrounding the first Roman invasion and Scotland's first documented battle. *Rome's North-West Frontier: the Antonine Wall* by Gordon Maxwell and Bill Hanson (Edinburgh, 1983) provides a detailed account of Scotland's principal Roman monument.

2

The Formation of the Scottish Kingdom

THOMAS OWEN CLANCY
BARBARA E. CRAWFORD

Scotland: the Northern Mosaic

What makes a country? Is it language or landscape, politics, peoples or territory? In all these respects, Scotland during its earliest history is not a fixed and labelled destination, but a constantly shifting theatre of change. Even as late as the fourteenth century, Scotland as we know it was still evolving, first into a kingdom and then a nation, defining its borders and amalgamating its startling range of peoples and languages. It is the ability to track these developments as they happen which, more than anything else, separates the early medieval period from prehistory. For the first time there are written records, written within Scotland itself as well as by outside commentators. These records are not exhaustive, and in order fully to understand the early medieval period, scholars turn to art historical and, of course, archaeological evidence, as well as the study of place-names, a prime source for following the development of the multiple languages of Scotland in its earliest historical period. What the evidence of all these sources shows is that despite continuities both from the Roman era and also forward into the medieval and modern periods, early medieval Scotland was its own particular place, a complex puzzle of cultures and political units, very different from the nation which the term 'Scotland' brings to mind.

Land and Nation

If there is an unchanging aspect to Scotland's past, it must appear at first sight to be the landscape, the geography of a country whose history and perhaps psyche is shaped so markedly by wind and weather, and whose political divisions seem inscribed by the firths which separate north from south, by the mountains which separate east coast from west. In the early medieval period such boundaries were important, and sometimes formed barriers or frontiers which are now less easy to recognize. A warrior of the sixth century is described as hailing from 'beyond Bannawg', the mass of high hills including the Campsie Fells and the Kilsyth Hills, a boundary now obliterated by the M80 motorway. An eighth-century Pictish king is described as reigning 'this side of the Mounth', suggesting the division between Moray and the rest of eastern Scotland which was also prominent in the twelfth century. If the political divisions formed by upland regions might be mutable, the social reality of them was not. They made passage in winter difficult, effective control unfeasible, and swift communication improbable. In the summer, though, the uplands which fringed the more hospitable and agriculturally fruitful lands of Angus and the Mearns, Fife or Lothian, were in constant use as grazing land. A succession of place-names in every language used in Scotland during this period testifies to continuity of agricultural use against a changing record of the linguistic and political affiliations of the people farming the land. And the routes through the mountains, whether by boat and foot along the Great Glen, or through the passes along Loch Rannoch or Loch Tay or down Loch Lomond, remained constantly crucial mediators of communication and conflict.

The sea too, though influencing Scotland's political make-up, played different roles in the past than are now apparent. On one hand, the Firth of Clyde, and the Firth of Forth together with its sodden Carse, formed a frontier between peoples for much of the early Middle Ages. On the other, the North Channel (Gaelic *Sruth na Maoile*), was a link which made the sea-kingdom of the Gael in the west prosperous and well connected with the outside world. The record of trade which may be found in the remains of pottery and glass at prestige sites such as Dunadd and Whithorn shows the easy changeability of the tide of commerce. Throughout the sixth and seventh centuries, the Irish Sea was abuzz with material and intellectual exchange, from Gaul to Britain and Ireland and around the points of this open salt-water loch. By the eighth and ninth centuries the tide had changed, and the east coast, with rapidly developing trading centres in southern England, now wielded artistic and social influence. And the prominence of the sea reminds us that we must allow for an inversion of our normal way of thinking about Scotland: from 800 AD, the engine of influence on Scotland's future lay in Orkney and Shetland, and in the North Sea-based kingdoms of sailors for whom the Hebrides were the *Suðreyar*, the Southern Isles.

As a territorial unit, Scotland was late in forming. The idea of a kingdom or country defined by territory is inseparable from the growth of a unified kingship, capable of defining borders rather than merely exerting overlordship. As such, Scotland as a nation or a legal entity was a work in progress which only began in earnest in the ninth century. Before this period, and for some time after, Scotland should be thought of as a complex of interlocking lordships, some small, some great, based on military might and command of a system of contractual loyalties which allowed for the extraction of wealth from the land. Stronger, more centralized kingships emerged from time to time, but these were scarcely respecters of our modern notion of Scotland's boundaries. Northumbrian English kings who ruled over York also ruled over Lothian and the eastern Borders in the seventh century, as well as Galloway in the eighth and ninth. Norwegian kings laid claim to the Northern Isles, and by 1100 also to the Hebrides. Sixth- and seventh-century Gaelic kings of Dál Riata in Argyll held lordship over Irish territory in Antrim. Viking kings ruled over Dublin, Man and Galloway in the tenth and eleventh centuries. Only as a centralized kingship, under one dynasty based in the central and eastern lowlands, emerged in the tenth and eleventh centuries can one begin to talk of Scotland as kingdom and territory. Even then, centuries lay between this dynasty and its assertion of rule over such neighbours as Galloway, the Western Isles, Caithness, or the last piece of the modern map, Orkney and Shetland in the years 1468–9. And some pieces of territory were acquired by Scotland during the Middle Ages and then lost, such as Cumberland, Berwick-upon-Tweed, and the Isle of Man.

Nevertheless, this book is the history of a modern territory, and our attention must necessarily be on the interaction of peoples and polities within the rough bounds of the modern nation. Here, too, we must brace ourselves for complexity and change, as Scotland's early medieval past boasts perhaps the most diverse collection of peoples and languages to be contained within any emerging medieval nation-state. The multilingual and multicultural nature of Scotland's past is still writ large in place-names, which testify not only to the strata of individual linguistic groups who settled and named the landscape, but sometimes also to their interaction with each other. Kincardine (comprised of Gaelic and Pictish elements), Gilmerton (Gaelic and English), Corstorphine (Gaelic and Norse), Edinburgh (British and English) and Innerleithen (Gaelic and British) exemplify this mixing in the environs of Lothian alone.

The Earliest Historical Peoples

At no time in Scotland's history can we ignore the interaction between peoples, questions of colonization and conquest, and the presence of incomers and natives. There is no 'original Scot' who will sit comfortably on the page without a mess of caveats. At the dawn of documentary history, the island of Britain was inhabited by Celtic-speakers from south to north. In *c.*320 BC, the Greek geographer Pytheas voyaged, reputedly, to the British Isles, and among the names he recorded was that of the cape of *Orcas*, Duncansby Head, facing the Orkneys (named later as the *Orcades*). This makes the name of the Orkneys one of the oldest recorded still in use in Britain. *Orcas* is a Greek rendering of a Celtic word – the term **orkos* or 'pig' is at its root – and so we know that Celtic-speakers existed in northern Scotland as early as the fourth century BC. And yet, we know from place-names that there are dozens of names of rivers and islands (the Naver and the Spey; Rum and Islay) which belong to unknown, long lost languages perhaps unrelated to Celtic. How had Celtic 'arrived' in Britain, and how was it that probably by the fourth century BC, and certainly by the first century AD, Celtic languages were universal throughout Britain? We do not know, but it seems naive, in the face of the brutality of human history, to imagine that it was entirely by peaceful osmosis, or through the simple exchange of one language for another. Though we do not know when or how Celtic-speakers gained the upper hand in Scotland, it is the first clearly visible example of ethnic change and conquest.

The information later writers traced to Pytheas's voyage also included the name of Britain and its surrounding isles, as the *Pritanic* islands. Once again we are dealing with a Greek version of a native name, this time for the inhabitants of the island, the **Pritani*. Here we have another name with a long subsequent history, for it lies behind the modern Welsh for Britain, *Prydain*, and behind 'Britain' itself. As Scotland emerges into history during the conquest of Britain by Rome, it is as *Britones*, a Roman mangling of **Pritani*, that the natives, north to south, are consistently identified. When the Roman historian Tacitus described the inhabitants of Scotland whom his father-in-law, the general Agricola, encountered during his campaigns of 79–84 AD, he called them Britons and thought of them as related to their southern neighbours, though he noted that they were taller and possessed of reddish hair. The names given to landscape, tribes and individuals in these first-century sources, and also in the slightly later cosmography of Ptolemy, demonstrate the linguistic affinity between north and south. All spoke a Celtic language which we could most easily call British and all possessed a fairly consistent package of words for settlements and landscape, though in many features of material culture and no doubt of detailed social make-up there were some variations across the country.

Some of these differences were ancient and determined by geography as much as by cultural preference (upland Scotland is dominated by hill forts in the Iron Age, as are the uplands of southern England, while the lowlands display a variety of enclosed or unenclosed settlements); others seem to be of recent vintage, a result of some centuries of exposure of the southern parts of Britain first to Roman trade and abortive conquest, and then later to the neighbouring Roman colony of Gaul. For instance, during the late first century BC and the following century, coinage came steadily into use throughout much of south-eastern Britain, and while coins are found fitfully at this period in the north, here they were clearly not part of any emerging coinage-based economy.

The process by which southern Britain began to assimilate the characteristics of Rome and Romanized Gaul (at least at the level of the wealthy and influential) was greatly accelerated as a result of its successful conquest, sometimes gradual and sometimes violent, by Rome during the middle decades of the first century AD. Although there was much resistance initially, many of the powerful members of the British aristocracy – perhaps often those who had been disenfranchised by earlier native regimes – rapidly adopted Roman names, architecture and fashion. The northern parts of Britain, however, proved harder to conquer, and ultimately mostly lay outside the control of the Roman governors. The limits of their attempted conquest are constantly being pushed further and further north in Scotland by archaeology, but the limits of effective control remain in the lasting monuments of the fitfully manned Antonine Wall, stretching from Clyde to Forth, and in the more permanent boundary marker of Hadrian's Wall, from Solway to Tyne.

Although there is now clear evidence of a more lasting and complex relationship between Roman and native north of Hadrian's Wall – not least in the decidedly non-Roman origin of most of the army garrisons in the north, many of whom came from other Roman frontier societies like Germany and Spain – there remains a great difference between this superficially conquered, often merely bought-off region, and the imperial infrastructure of cities, roads, towns and villas south of Carlisle. This difference created in Scotland a two-tier world of enemies, who in documentary sources slowly crystallize into alliances of tribes. In the second century, and into the third, we hear of two 'large tribes', the Maeatae, living nearer to Hadrian's Wall, and the Caledones beyond them. The names of both these folk are preserved in the landscape, the Maeatae in Dumyat and Myot Hill in the environs of Stirling and Falkirk, the Caledones in Dunkeld and Schiehallion in northern Perthshire, but these merely localize them, and give us no sense of the extent of these peoples. Most likely they were amalgamations and alliances of smaller groupings, as neither name is known in the more detailed geography of Ptolemy earlier in the second century. Both groups seemed to have had treaties with Rome, but equally, in the years around 200, both groups revolted against their Roman neighbours, provoking a renewed set of campaigns in Scotland.

This tendency towards larger conglomerations is magnified from 297 onwards, when the non-Romanized natives north of the wall begin to be called *Picti*, 'Picts', by Roman observers. It is difficult to be sure whether this change in nomenclature reflects a change in politics or in perception. It may suggest that centuries of separation from their Romanized British neighbours had made the peoples of the north essentially identifiable, either to themselves or to the outside world, as a different nation. They were no longer simply groups of Britons external to the Roman province, as they had seemed in the previous century. It may otherwise suggest that the potential for conquest and the rise of effective war-leaders had provoked further political cohesion among the northern peoples. In either case, the emergence of the Picts must be seen primarily as that of a new polity, though this may well have been accompanied by linguistic and other divergences from the Romanized Britons. What this means is that speculation on the 'origins' of the Picts, both medieval and modern, is misplaced. The Picts did not 'come from' anywhere: history, time and the varied weight of Roman influence upon different regions created them from solidly British roots.

The Picts were undoubtedly one of the main factors in the gradual disintegration of Roman control over the course of the fourth and fifth centuries. Whether on their own or in alliance with the *Scoti* (the Gaels of Ireland also resident in Argyll) and the unidentified *Attecotti*, the Picts made persistent assaults across the Wall during these centuries. It is in the context of fragmenting internal control, both on the local level of the effective government of Britain, but especially on the grander level of the control of the Empire, that we see new arrivals in Britain in the fourth and fifth centuries. More Gaels settled in the west, in scattered colonies along the western seaboard, and Saxons and other Germanic settlers in the east, arriving both as raiders and as mercenary defenders of the eastern and southern shores. As Roman government and military defence was withdrawn and effective concerted government of Britain gradually collapsed, some of the local polities which re-emerged as kingdoms were in the control, not of natives, but of these invasive entrepreneurs, both Saxon and Gael.

Conversely, however, in the north the collapse of Roman rule, and the incursion into Britain of peoples distinct in culture and language, may well have served to blur once more distinctions between Briton and Pict. By the sixth century, a double vision is perceptible among the British concerning the Picts. To the Britons of the south, the Picts were known as *Prydyn*, a name which comes from *Priteni*, a people term very close to that which lies behind *Prydain*, the British name for Britain. This suggests, as has been seen, that these were once one people, the divergent names perhaps reflecting merely dialectal difference. But the fact that in the sixth century British poets could refer to the Picts simply as *Prydyn* suggests they were none the less identifiably cohesive, and yet different from the Britons. On the other hand, the same poetry suggests that warriors from among the Picts might be found accompanying British war bands. Thus, though separate linguistically and politically, the two sets of peoples do not seem to have been greatly divided. The real rise of a new, historical Pictish identity resulted most probably from their continued trend towards consolidated leadership, contrasted with the fragmentation of Britons into smaller sub-kingdoms which gradually lost dominion and territory to more effective political powers.

The Britons: the Men of the North

The poetry preserved from sixth- and seventh-century northern British kingdoms is set against this backdrop of loss, struggle and defeat, but is more acutely important in providing something of an insight into the culture, ideology and personnel of an otherwise poorly documented period and place. The poems, composed by Taliesin, Aneirin and their contemporaries in an early form of Welsh (which we shall call 'British' here, though 'Cumbric' is often used), illumine the violent and fractious world of cattle raids, hostage-taking, casual battles and bloody aftermaths which made the constant backdrop to early medieval Scottish society.

These poems give us some sense of the political geography of the time, for which we have little other evidence. Although we can have no absolute confidence in our reconstructions of this period, by the sixth century we can point to the existence in the north of a series of British kingdoms and lordships of varying size. Some, such as that of the Gododdin, centring on Edinburgh, seem to inherit the tribal or administrative mantles of the Roman and indeed pre-Roman world: *Gododdin* is linguistically the British descendant of the tribal name recorded by Ptolemy for the people of Lothian, the *Votadini*. Other kingdoms seem to be based on territory or location: the kingdom of *Al Clud*, 'The Rock of the Clyde', depended on Dumbarton Rock; the territory of *Aeron*, based on the river Ayr; the kingdom of *Manaw*, the name of which is preserved in Clackmannan and Slamannan. Still others are based on landscape terms, and are recorded in the poetry, though we know them best as kingdoms or regions taken over at a slightly later date by the Angles and given anglicized names: Bernicia (*Berneich*) in modern Northumberland, perhaps 'the land of the mountain pass(es)'; Deira (*Deur*), corresponding to parts of Yorkshire; Elmet (*Elfed*), the area around Leeds. Elmet and Deira were both forest names originally.

From the poetry we can also build up a valuable and instructive portrait of one ruler in this new post-Roman world: Urien, king of Rheged in the last decades of the sixth century. A series of some nine praise poems, composed by Urien's court poet Taliesin in honour of the king, and also of one of his sons, survive in one late Welsh manuscript. Although we have little historical documentation concerning Urien, in combination with these poems a clearer picture emerges.

A war leader, possibly ousting the traditional rulers of his kingdom, he ruled over territories in and around the Eden valley in modern Cumbria. One poem depicts him rescuing his kingdom, Rheged, from ignominious decline through a series of successful battles. These battles were fought against many neighbours and those in other British kingdoms, and also against the Angles settled in the east. Individual poems put flesh on this bare list. In one, the poet envisages his patron setting off with his war band to raid Manaw, the kingdom which encompassed the area around Falkirk and Stirling. He returns with the spoils:

> Herds of cattle surround him.
> Battle-keen conqueror,
> Well-armed, weapons gleaming,
> Like death his spear
> Mows down his foes.

In another, the poet depicts a pivotal battle at a place called Argoed Llwyfain. Here, Urien and his son Owain, 'bane of the east', face down English enemies, rulers of the recently established kingdom of Bernicia. They refuse to negotiate, or to hand over hostages, and charge the English. We know from a later poem, an elegy for Owain, that the Bernician ruler was killed in the conflict: 'When Owain cut down Fflamddwyn,/No more to it than sleeping.'

Urien emerges not just as a successful king over a small province, but also as a northern overlord, extending his sway and tribute far to the north-west and south-east of his Cumbrian base. He is called 'the defender of Aeron' (Ayrshire), but also 'ruler of Catraeth (Swaledale) beyond the plains'. Mustering his army entails levying hosts from different districts within his realm. And it is as emerging overlord of the north that a later historical source depicts Urien at his death. Besieging the English rulers of Bernicia who were holed up in Lindisfarne, Urien is accompanied by three other powerful northern kings. One of these, Morgant, has Urien assassinated through jealousy and fear of his pre-eminence.

This is the world of a military aristocracy which controls their liegemen by distributing the spoils of battle. Taliesin emphasizes time and again the rewards he expected for his poetry: precious metal jewellery, clothes, horses and land. The world of the warrior élite is nowhere better delineated than in the great series of elegies by Taliesin's near contemporary Aneirin, called *Y Gododdin*, a corporate poem lamenting the defeat of warriors of the kingdom of the Gododdin in Lothian, and those who joined them in setting out from Edinburgh to face a battle at Catterick against the Bernicians. They lost cataclysmically, but Aneirin evokes both the animal ferocity of these men in battle, and the ethos which lay behind their struggle. They had been given food and drink, feasted and hosted by the ruler of the Gododdin; now the warriors would pay for their mead:

> Men went to Catraeth, in high spirits their war band.
> Pale mead their portion, it was poison.
> Three hundred under orders to fight.
> And after celebration, silence.
> Though they go to churches for shriving,
> True is the tale, death confronted them.

Other aspects of this British society emerge from this poetry. It was fundamentally, although perhaps casually, Christian. Warriors gave alms to the church before setting off to battle. They performed penance. They inhabited a world defined as *bedydd*, 'the baptized', which can be set against others, who are 'pagans'. This aristocracy also had a different, less violent side to its culture: shy flirtations between young men and women, a love of fine poetry, beautiful cloth and ornament, a devotion to hunting. One stray poem which became accidentally included in the text of *Y Gododdin* is a lullaby sung by a woman to her son. She sings to him of the speckled pine-marten coat she made him, and of his father's prowess at hunting with his dogs, Giff and Gaff, his cudgel in his hand. It seems elegiac in tone, as if the boy's father will never return home, but still it gives us a rare domestic vignette among sources dominated by male military violence.

These sources provide a bright witness in an age when such sources are scarce. Equally important, perhaps, many of the aspects which define the British warrior kingdoms were shared with their Pictish, Gaelic and English neighbours. Old English poetry manifests the same strong emphasis on the mead hall, on the men of the war band as retainers of the ruler, and on the distribution of spoils to the brave. It shares the animalistic language of bravery: the soldier as boar, bear, lion in battle. Early Gaelic law texts show us this system of small-scale kingship combined with tributary overlordship in theory, as Taliesin shows it in poetry. And the emblems of the dominant mounted warrior, the images of broken spear and ingathered jewellery, bedeck the sculpture of the contemporary Pictish nobility. These were the sort of men in control throughout the northern half of Britain in the early Middle Ages.

The Picts

At a certain level, then, the ruling élite throughout northern Britain, of whatever ethnic background, shared common aims and ethical constraints. On other levels, however, there were marked differences among Picts, Angles, Gaels and Britons. The Picts were linguistically and culturally closely related to the Britons, but seem to have had an intermittent political cohesion which distinguished them from their southern neighbours. Religiously, many parts of Pictish territory remained pagan long after the people of the British regions were describing themselves as 'the baptized'. Other factors have been adduced to symbolize the separateness of the Picts, but not all of these would now be accepted. For instance, the Pictish language, often portrayed as a mix of Celtic and non-Indo-European elements, has recently been championed as demonstrably Celtic, and closely related to British. Similarly, the idea that kingship among the Picts was determined by an allegedly non-Indo-European custom of matrilinear succession has been shown to be at best an exaggeration of the truth. Instead, the Picts shared with their neighbours the custom of allowing succession to go through the female line in cases of dispute, but perhaps used the custom somewhat more frequently or openly.

What undoubtedly was distinctive was the series of symbols employed by the Pictish nobility to decorate the monuments which stud the Pictish landscape. In their earliest phase these monuments were frequently undressed boulders or reused Neolithic standing stones, inscribed with pairs of symbols, sometimes accompanied by one of a collection of auxiliary symbols. These pairs of symbols include abstract designs or schematic depictions of broken spears, jewellery, cauldrons and the like, as well as animal symbols. Examples, in the arcane modern jargon used to describe the symbols, would be the 'double-disc-and-Z-rod, plus serpent; with mirror' of Aberlemno, or the 'crescent-and-V-rod plus "tuning fork"' of Abernethy. We have no key to their meaning, and if the Picts remain to many people doggedly 'mysterious', despite growing historical confidence concerning them, it is as a result of these mute yet eloquent inscriptions. For it is as inscriptions, whatever their meaning, that these symbols should be read. They emerge contemporaneously with the post-Roman Latin memorial inscriptions which pepper the British landscape as far as the Forth, and are found in approximately similar situations.

None the less, the main interpretable message of the symbols for the modern witness is a distinctive and unifying culture among the Picts, a shared emblematic language and practice. Symbol stones are found from Skye to Fife, with significant concentrations in the Northern Isles and Caithness, the Moray Firth area, Aberdeenshire and the lands on either side of the Firth of Tay. They seem most prominent in good agricultural regions, and testify perhaps to the centres and concerns of the emerging Pictish land-holders and nobility. These suggestions are reinforced by the subsequent use of the symbols on monuments which also employ Christian imagery, and more obviously manifest the concerns of the aristocracy through scenes of hunting, hawking, horse-riding and battle.

The Angles: Germanic Settlers of the South-East

There are, of course, details of social organization which seem similar yet perceptibly different among Britons and Picts, but the broad range of culture and language tends to point towards close affinity. This is clearly not the case with the two more intrusive groups in early medieval Scotland, the Angles and the Gaels. Each of these groups spoke a language quite distinct from the Brittonic Celtic of Picts and Britons. Although Gaelic was a related Celtic language, it was more second cousin than half-sister. The Angles spoke a Germanic language, the ancestor of modern lowland Scots and English, and were thus perhaps more definitively 'other' to Picts or Britons than were the Gaels. The Angles were also pagan, at a time when at least the British nobility seem to have espoused Christianity, and in any case the nature of their pagan religion was somewhat different from that which lay in the past of the Christianized Britons. As recent immigrants, the Angles also brought with them from their homelands in northern and eastern parts of Europe a package of social customs, architectural and land-management norms, legal practices and literary memories which marked them as radically different from their neighbours.

Of the Angles' earliest settlements along the east coast of modern Northumberland and Yorkshire we know little, though the paucity of archaeological records from the fifth and sixth centuries, as compared with the thickly clustered graves and settlements further south, suggest both that these settlements were later, and perhaps on the whole thinner than those of southern England. This may also be suggested by the greater continuity of British language and custom in the northern English kingdoms. The best demonstration of this is that the names of the two main kingdoms established by northern English warlords during the course of the sixth century were merely those of the previous British regions or kingdoms: Bernicia and Deira.

Although we know of earlier English settlements in great numbers in the region of York in the kingdom of Deira, it was Bernicia which would in time gain the upper hand politically. In the later sixth century and based at Bamburgh, the kings of Bernicia were besieged by British kings at Lindisfarne in the 580s. The dramatic expansion of Bernicia is likely to have resulted from a combination of fragmentation and fratricide among the British kingdoms, and the brilliance of a series of Bernician kings, beginning with Æthelfrith who ruled from *c.* 592 to 616. Æthelfrith first united the two northern kingdoms under his authority, creating the prototype of the combined kingdom of Northumbria. He also extended his dominion over British regions, though it is not clear which these were. He was followed both in dual control of Deira and Bernicia, and in aggressive expansionism, by his successor and enemy, Edwin of Deira.

The Gaels: Colonizers of the West

It is a mark of how dominant the two intrusive peoples had become in the north that the real mark of Æthelfrith's power was his defeat, in 603, of a war band of Gaels from Argyll who had pushed deep into Bernician territory. It is perhaps further a mark of their importance that it was to the Gaels that his two younger sons ultimately fled in exile after his death at the hands of Edwin – his eldest stayed in exile among the Picts. We do not know for how long Gaels had been settled in northern Britain. Elsewhere, it seems likely that their presence in Wales and Cornwall in the fourth and fifth centuries was the result of entrepreneurial and colonizing efforts during the declining centuries of Roman power in Britain. Argyll may be a different case – there are longstanding indications of close cultural relations between the north of Ireland and Argyll, and little sign of anything like a 'migration'. Nevertheless, by the sixth century new political dimensions to the Gaelic settlement there are evident, with an aggressive and expansionist dynasty comparable with that in Northumbria.

Gaelic Argyll belonged to a linguistically and culturally unified region which extended right down to the south of Ireland. Although also Celtic in language, and hence sharing linguistic, legal and cultural affinities with Britons and Picts, there is much about Gaelic society in the early Middle Ages which is quite distinct. Strongly kin-based in law and in political organization, its practices seem largely to have been applicable throughout the Gaelic-speaking area. Kingships remained small-scale in Ireland, and perhaps in Argyll, during the sixth and seventh centuries, though it is clear that the dominance as overlords of a number of Irish dynasties had transformed the political map. The Uí

Néill in the northern half, and the Eóganachta in the southern, had established strong dynasties that controlled power by alternating rule among a restricted number of lineal branches.

At least by the eighth century, and probably much earlier, the ruling nobility of Argyll comprised three or four main related kindreds, who alternated succession to the over-kingship of the whole region, called Dál Riata. In effect there were two competing lines, the Cenél nGabráin of Kintyre, who dominated the sixth and seventh centuries, and the Cenél Loairn of Lorn, who rose to prominence towards the end of the seventh. The Cenél noengusso of Islay were a sidelined but no doubt prosperous kindred, while the Cenél Comgaill of Cowal only gradually emerged as a separate entity.

The Gaels of Argyll may be seen as closely comparable to their Irish relatives in their system of clientship and tiered rankings of overlordship. Although the terrain of Argyll gave rise to new modes of organization (lords assessed their clients by the number of seven-bench boats they could man), expectations of render and obligation seem closely matched in each region. Later examples in the Scottish law of inheritance deriving from common early Gaelic law is best explained by its first use in early Argyll. Gaelic Argyll also shared its religion with Ireland: by the sixth century it was Christian, and churchmen there were exporting the Christian faith to pagan regions among the Picts, and soon would be involved in converting the pagan Angles.

By around 600, then, Scotland had emerged as a land occupied by 'four nations and five languages', in the words of the Northumbrian monk Bede, written around 731 (the passage refers to Britain as a whole). The Britons still held kingdoms in the south and west, but were soon to lose their eastern kingdoms to the Angles, whose expansionist kings would conquer much of southern Scotland. In the north, the Picts were becoming the consolidated and prosperous people who would dominate the later seventh and eighth centuries. And in Argyll, Gaels had begun to edge eastwards as settlers, missionaries and warlords. In the period from 584 to 711 each of these four peoples recorded significant victories in the lynchpin kingdom of Manaw, often gaining temporary overlordship of the region. There was nothing inevitable about the course of Scottish history in this crucial period of the shaping of the country.

Life in the Northern Mosaic

It is the very diversity of cultures, as well as of potential mixing and cross-influence, which makes any generalization about life in early medieval Scotland impossible. This is compounded by the sources, which are scarce and incomplete. We have looked briefly at the poetry of the northern Britons, which bears witness to the lives of the warrior aristocracy. There is little available to supplement the poetry in our attempt to understand the northern Britons: they are without doubt the most elusive of the northern peoples.

Little survives in the way of archaeological evidence – no grave goods in their long-cist cemeteries; little by way of certainly dated domestic architecture; forts which yield only limited information beyond the general sense that this period, from the sixth century through to the ninth, is dominated by craggy fortresses like Edinburgh's Castle Rock and Dumbarton Rock on the Clyde. Buiston crannog, near Kilmaurs in Ayrshire, is more eloquent. This artificial island on a now drained loch was certainly the site of a lordly hall for a British nobleman or ruler, and was occupied in the sixth and seventh centuries. A sizeable dwelling, the roundhouse here revealed in excavations offers evidence of a relatively high-status lifestyle, with gold rings, imported pottery and glass vessels sharing space with weaponry and evidence of metalworking.

Others of the four nations have more eloquent testimony, but again it remains patchy. The Picts have left us no literature of their own (though doubtless they had some), no manuscripts, no laws. Their sculpture, however, demonstrates many aspects of con-
-temporary life, from the dress of rulers and warriors and the use of brooches as marks of status (women depicted on Pictish sculpture often wear very large brooches), to their very clear depictions of the animals both of their everyday life and of their nightmares. On sculptured stones at Meigle in easternmost Perthshire, men are stalked by long-nebbed man-headed griffins, chased by two-tongued apes, devoured by bears, bulls and serpents. Hunting was a clear preoccupation, and sculpture depicts this on many social levels: on stones in Angus, nobles and their hounds bring down stags at Kirriemuir; a hooded, bearded man stalks a menagerie of creatures with a crossbow at St Vigeans; a scrawny lad brings home a brace of ducks dangling from his hands at Eassie.

Other sources, too, shed light on the lives of the Picts. Archaeology has been particularly revealing in recent decades, with forts such as Dundurn in Perthshire, settlements such as Buckquoy (Orkney), and dwellings like Easter Kinnear (Fife) all contributing to filling in the Pictish landscape. At a site like Gurness on Orkney, we can see a Pictish village taking shape in the shadow of a prehistoric broch; excavations at Buckquoy suggest the methods of rearing livestock. At the lordly site of Brough of Birsay nearby, the great numbers of cattle bones suggest a rich diet based on the importation of meat. Easter Kinnear is a relatively humble farmstead site whose rectangular buildings, contrasting with the round architecture of Orkney, suggest that there was great variation in the type of houses occupied by Picts. Easter Kinnear also shows, in its very close proximity to another excavated farmstead, the fairly dense cultivation of the land in the sixth and seventh centuries. Place-name studies have in recent years also enhanced our understanding of the Pictish landscape as one of a settled, farming society.

Historians have practised their own archaeology on the social institutions of the Picts. They have turned to some of the unique features of Alba, the core kingdom of the later Scottish nation which comes into being around 900. Many of these features seem to be based on underlying Pictish inheritances. For instance, the division of estates into portions implies settled and aggregate forms of land exploitation, and the use of the Pictish term *pett*, a 'portion of an estate', by later Gaelic landowners demonstrates the earlier roots of this system. The 'shire', as the main unit of such land-holding and lordship, maintained territorial continuity into the twelfth century, and historians have inferred from this its basis in much earlier periods. The evolution of the role of the *mormaer* ('great steward') has been thought to be a Pictish contribution to a more layered system of governance, with superior noblemen subject to the king replacing smaller independent kingships. The word *mormaer* is ultimately of Pictish origin. He is the 'earl' of the later medieval period, who first comes to our attention in the tenth century.

It is, however, the incomers, the Gaels and the Angles, who have left perhaps the clearest records of their societies. For a rich and varied panorama of the life of the Gaels, we may turn to the enormous corpus of Irish law composed largely in the seventh, eighth and ninth centuries, partly on a traditional framework, and subsequently elaborated by glosses and adjustments. Early Irish law is largely descriptive rather than prescriptive, and so the texts on the laws of status detail, sometimes to the point of straining credulity, the different types of houses and possessions one would expect a man of a certain rank and occupation to hold. For example, the text called *Críth Gablach*, which dates to around 700, profiles the *ócaire* or 'young lord':

What is his property? He has seven means of support: seven cows with their bull; seven pigs with a brood sow; seven sheep; a horse both for work and for riding. Twenty-one *cumal* worth of land . . . He has a quarter share in a plough: an ox, a ploughshare, a goad, a halter, so that he has the ability to become a partner. A share in a kiln, in a mill, in a barn; a cooking-pot.

The size of his house: it is larger than a *tech nincís*, for the size of the latter is seventeen feet. It is of wickerwork to the lintel. From there to the roof-beam, feathers between the two courses of wattles. Two doorways in it: a door for one of them, a hurdle for the other, the hurdle without wattles, without bulges. A bare fence of boards around it. An oaken plank between every two beds.

These laws can illuminate rural life: we have texts on the best points to look out for when purchasing a horse, on bee-keeping, on the diseases of cats and dogs, on the maintenance of roads, and on the features which add value to land. In Professor Fergus Kelly's translation:

A securely constructed bank or wall adds the value of four cows to a *cumal* area of land. Four cows for a full mill-weir; two cows for a half mill-weir. A cow for a well which does not dry up; and two cows for an iron mine; four cows for a copper mine. Two cows for an estuary which always has fish. A cow for a fixed road to a wood or onto a mountain or as far as the sea.

From these texts we are gaining a clearer insight into the complex world of Irish status, of compensation for crime, of the making and enforcing of contracts, of the multiple levels of marriage and the legitimate reasons for divorce, and manifold other aspects of human relationships and the management of land and livestock.

It is difficult to know to what extent such laws were applicable in Gaelic Scotland. On the one hand, we know that Gaelic terminology for clientship obligations such as *cáin* (tribute), *coinnmed* (hospitality or billeting) and *slogad* (military hosting) survived to be used in the charters of the twelfth and thirteenth century in eastern Scotland. On the other hand, a document like the *Senchus Fer nAlban*, a political survey of Argyll deriving from a core text of the seventh century, shows the variations to which Irish law could be subject in a different geographical situation. The sizes of families' possessions in the *Senchus* are reckoned by the number of boats of seven benches a landowner could provide; the land's capacity is reckoned in 'houses', a feature which has some counterparts in later charters from Islay and other parts of the west. In one region, Lennox, Professor Archie Duncan has pointed to the survival of the 'house' as the unit of assessment for render (often in cheeses), as well as the use of the Gaelic term for the plough (*arachor*) for divisions of land, an instance of localized regional variation in custom.

None the less, a law such as the *Lex Innocentium*, the 'Law of Innocents', also known as the Law of Adomnán, established in 697 by the ninth abbot of Iona and guaranteed by kings of both Gaelic Argyll and of Pictland as well as those of Ireland, was broadly applicable to Scotland as well as Ireland. Its text reveals some of the dangers a woman could expect to be exposed to during her life. We are told that an angel commanded Adomnán to establish a law 'that women may not be killed by a man in any way, neither by slaughter nor by any other death, nor by poison nor in water, nor in fire, nor by any beast, nor in a pit, nor by dogs, but shall die in their own lawful death'. The subsequent details of fines and punishments meted out for injury to women are of interest. The law envisages partial culpability for industrial accidents and dangerous workmanship or manufacture ('ditch and pit and bridge and hearth and doorstep and pools and drying kilns, and every other harm besides'), and for the dangers of the countryside ('perishing in a quagmire, wounding by tame beasts, and by pigs and by cattle'). There are provisions for injuries resulting from raiding parties, as well as from slanderous allegations; but there are also intriguing notes on what is to be done when a secretly buried corpse is revealed, or when members of a person's kin aid and abet a crime, or try to cover it up and condone it.

Gaelic territory has also produced some revealing archaeology, especially at royal sites like the fortress of Dunadd in Argyll, and also at monastic sites like Iona, where excavations have shown the monastery to have been engaged in metalworking and leatherworking, and have contributed to our knowledge of the diet of the monks. Iona too has provided us with an eloquent historical document, the *Life of St Columba*, written by Adomnán around 700. Designed to celebrate the holiness of Iona's founder saint, it reveals, out of the corner of its eye, important details of daily life: the seal grounds owned by the monks for culling for meat and skins; the timbers felled from the north Argyll mainland for constructing the large monastic buildings; milk pails inhabited by demons, stake-traps set for game, the harvesting of reed-plots, the dangers of the seaways, of childbirth, of drought, plague and ambush.

Perhaps our fullest picture comes from the Angles of Northumbria. A Germanic people, their connections to their continental homelands are revealed in their preference for certain types of jewellery (bow-shaped brooches as against the Gaelic and Pictish preference for the hand pin and the penannular brooch), and imagery and techniques which are paralleled in finds from Germany and Francia. One of the principal types of dwelling, the *Grubenhäuser* or sunken-floored house, may be found alongside other types of rectangular timber buildings in Northumbria, and have parallels on the continent. Although the north is not as rich in burials stocked with grave goods as the south of England, some graves from Northumbria do confirm that the Angles practised the pagan custom of burying a man with his weapons and finery.

Yet in Northumbria these distinctive features must be balanced against evidence of adoption of aspects of life from the native Britons of the north. Most of the important royal or noble sites we know of in Bernicia, for instance, seem to be developed from earlier British foundations: Dunbar, Bamburgh and Yeavering all go back to British roots in name and archaeology. It has been suggested that the use of rectangular timber buildings alongside the Germanic sunken-floor houses is an adaptation of a native British housing type. Much of the political geography of Northumbria, a conquest kingdom as it was, is founded on that which they gradually took over in the seventh century. Indeed, our best evidence for burials among the Angles of Bernicia comes from long-cist cemeteries in Lothian: if these are Angles, they had adopted both the religion and the burial customs of the people they conquered.

The picture of the political and social life of Northumbria can also be filled out from documentary sources, and to some extent from comparison with their southern English neighbours. Seventh- and eighth-century Northumbria produced a rich harvest of literature, both in Latin and to a lesser extent in Old English. Some of these sources, such as saints' lives and histories, can shed important light on Northumbrian society, and indeed on that of their neighbours. Chief of these sources is undoubtedly the *Ecclesiastical History of the English People*, written by Bede in 731. From his work we can assemble a reasonably detailed, if not necessarily perfect, sense of Northumbrian political geography, complete with different types of royal residence and fort, and rankings of sub-kings who ruled over different parts of the expanding Northumbrian hegemony. Descriptions of royal councils fill out this picture of government. Bede is, of course, first and foremost a churchman, writing church history. His utterly convincing narrative, even where we might doubt its secure basis in fact, puts flesh on the conversion of the English to Christianity. There is nothing more striking than his description of the conversion of King Edwin at Goodmanham in Yorkshire, advised by his pagan priest Coifi, who dramatically becomes the first to turn his back on the old ways:

So he formally renounced his empty superstitions and asked the king to give him arms and a stallion – for hitherto it had not been lawful for the chief priest to carry arms or ride anything but a mare – and, thus equipped, he set out to destroy the idols. Girded with a sword and with a spear in his hand, he mounted the king's stallion and rode up to the idols. When the crowd saw him, they thought he had gone mad; but without hesitation, as soon as he had reached the temple, he cast into it the spear he carried and thus profaned it.

The Coming of Christianity

It was Bede who characterized Britain as inhabited by 'four nations and five languages'. Bede's fifth language, alongside the native tongues of British, Pictish, Gaelic and English, was Latin. As he saw it, the four nations were unified by the language of the church. In a very real sense, the presence of Christianity among all four peoples shaped and defined their competing claims to overlordship, and gave an extra dimension to conquests, both military and cultural. If the history of Scotland up to 600 is dominated by political fragmentation and cultural intrusion the process of conversion to Christianity would be an overarching factor in the events of subsequent centuries.

That process of conversion begins, inevitably, in Roman Britain. Scholars are still debating the extent to which Christianity had taken hold by the time of the collapse of Roman rule, but there can be no doubt that it was a significant element within late Roman Britain. Bishops from Britain participated in the earliest of the ecumenical councils, like the first at Nicaea in 325, and British churchmen were still actively involved in the affairs of the European church even in the midst of the turmoil of the fifth century. Indeed it is quite likely that the turmoil gave a consolidating edge to the church and effected an equation between Britishness and Christianity, much as fifth- and sixth-century rulers seemed to have espoused lingering images of *romanitas* in their titles and inscriptions.

All this pertains to southern Britain; the north is much more obscure. It is impossible to say much about the early period of Christianity north of the Wall, though there is some evidence of late Roman Christianity in its vicinity. In the past, some confidence in the shape of the Christianization of the northern Britons was possible due to a belief in a fourth-century date for St Ninian, founder of the church at Whithorn, as given in a twelfth-century life of the saint. This is no longer credible, in light of the excavations at Whithorn which show 500 AD as a clear horizon for the development of a church there. Instead we must consider a number of pieces of evidence which show that, whatever the circumstances of the conversion, there was a solid Christian church present in the northern British kingdoms by the sixth century.

The evidence consists of inscriptions, cemeteries, place-names and poetry. Of these, the inscriptions are quite the most concrete and eloquent. A thin scattering of monuments from Kirkmadrine in the Rhinns of Galloway to Kirkliston (near Edinburgh airport) bear post-Roman Latin inscriptions of dates ranging from the fifth to the seventh century. These are clearly Christian inscriptions, employing Chi-Rho symbols, invoking God, and naming priests, deacons and bishops. The most remarkable thing about these inscriptions is that they demonstrate the adoption by the northern Britons, so long outside Roman control, of Latin writing and Roman styles of monument in the post-Roman world. It can be no accident that their adoption accompanied Christianity in each case. Like their southern neighbours – perhaps even more radically – Christianity and *romanitas* seem to be part of the attempt to define 'Britishness' in a world of fragmentation and conquest.

As mentioned earlier, this can also be seen in the sixth-century poetry, which perceives its British, civilized world as *bedydd*, 'the baptized', and perceives its enemies as *gynt*, 'gentiles'. In the poetry we are confronted with an aristocracy which goes to church, gives alms to priests, confesses sins before battle, and is hopeful of heaven after death. Some traces of their churches may be found at least in place-names. A series of names which appear as variants of Eccles (from British **eglés*, 'church') may be found in southern Scotland: Eaglesham, Eccles, Eaglesfield, Ecclefechan. This appears to be the main term for small churches in the post-Roman British church, and the Eccles-names continue into Cumbria and far south in Britain, with impressive clusters in Yorkshire and the north Midlands. Added to all these pieces of evidence is that of the long-cist cemeteries which begin to be used for burial probably during the sixth century in the north, notably in the area of the Lothians. These cemeteries, usually oriented and lacking in grave goods, are evidently Christian ones, and would appear to mark changes of belief as well as of burial practice. There is occasional correlation between these different items of evidence: the Catstane at Kirkliston is surrounded by a long-cist cemetery; Eaglesfield in Annandale coincides with probable early Christian burials.

We can therefore say with some confidence that Christianity was the religion at least of the nobility among the northern British kingdoms. Equally clear, however, is that this was not the monastic church so often associated with the insular early Middle Ages. The most sensible interpretation of the data so far discussed is that the church was organized around the small regions and lordships controlled by the aristocracy of the period, and that the sort of personnel recorded on the inscribed stones (priests, bishops, deacons – these are also mentioned in other sixth-century British writings in Latin) provided the infrastructure of the church. During the course of the sixth century, however, a movement towards a more radical and ascetic vision of the Christian life now sprang up throughout Britain. This movement had begun some centuries before in the deserts of Egypt and Syria, and had taken firm root in Italy and Gaul. Congregating around charismatic masters, some sources relating to the sixth century give an impression of whole generations opting out of society. Although it is possible that persistent plagues during the course of the sixth century, especially the virulent outbreak of the 540s, contributed to this enthusiasm for the untrammelled spiritual athleticism of the monastery, the sources allow only guesswork about the progress of this sea-change in the religious culture of Britain.

Some whiff of the spirit of the age may be received from two sources. One is a seventh-century or later *Life of St Samson of Dol*. In Samson's early career in south Wales he progresses through a training course of monasteries, from the large, lucrative and lax, through the more rigid and demanding. Ultimately he branches out on his own to found a small house with two companions, whom he leaves periodically to adopt the lifestyle of a hermit. The other source is the virulent attack on the spiritual complacency of his compatriots by the polemicist historian Gildas. Gildas's pen-portrait of his *bête noire*, Maelgwn, king of the northern Welsh kingdom of Gwynedd, describes the ruthless politician toying with the alternative life of the monk, studying the monastic rule, and even briefly joining a monastery.

These activities were taking place in Wales and the south-west, but may be typical of the course of Christianity in all the British kingdoms. Further north there is some evidence to suggest similar developments. First is the appearance in Whithorn, in the early years of the sixth century, of archaeological evidence suggesting a monastic settlement with, significantly, siting and trading links broadly similar to those in south Wales. Second is the possibility, perhaps even probability, that a churchman who wrote to Gildas for advice on monastic discipline, a scholar and bishop by the name of Uinniau (appearing variously as Finnian, Winnin and other permutations), was based in south-west Scotland and had links with early Whithorn. Uinniau was the author of one of our earliest documents on monasticism in Britain and Ireland, the *Penitential of Vinnian*, which gives some insight into the interface between monastic and lay Christians. Uinniau was also one of a number of early British churchmen active in Ireland. As probable founder at least of the monastery of Moville on the Co. Down coast, he provides a strong link between the earliest British monasticism and the influential monastic founders who grew up in Ireland in the middle of the sixth century.

Christianity had probably been planted in Ireland partly through the slave trade (see below) and mercantile relations, as well as through the contact and influence that resulted from Ireland living cheek-by-jowl with Roman Britain for four centuries. All this was in advance of the rather more famous episcopal missions of the fifth century. We know little about the episcopate of Palladius, sent by Pope Celestine in 431, though what little we know tends to localize him in southern Ireland, and place his mission in the context of the combat of heresy in Britain. Patrick, a Briton from a clerical family, gives us more detail, but not enough to locate his Irish activities, or indeed the site of his home, firmly in time and space. However, both these instances confirm the existence in the fifth century of a Christian community in Ireland, and Patrick's writings suggest that he was successful in the conversion of sizeable numbers of the nobility, and in the establishment of churches and perhaps even of some monastic centres as well.

Despite this, it seems likely that it is in the sixth century we should place the real burgeoning of Irish Christianity, coincident with the rise of monasticism in Britain; there is much traditional and some more concrete evidence that British monastic founders and thinkers were active in Ireland during the middle years of the sixth century. Irish churchmen of later years looked back to Britain as the homeland of their Christian culture, and had strong cults of British saints like David, Gildas and Samson, all of whom were believed to have visited Ireland during their careers. One of the most significant of these British churchmen was Uinniau of Moville, mentioned above. He had a reputation as a great trainer of monks, and prominent among his students was Columba, a member of the powerful northern dynasty of the Uí Néill, who trained with Uinniau as a deacon. In following this chain of teaching, from the seminal monastic thinker Gildas, to Uinniau, to Columba, one has a sense of the rapidity and closeness of the transmission of ideas in Britain and Ireland in the sixth century.

The espousal of Christianity by the main political families in Ireland, both south and north, marks something of a watershed in its development. This seems to have been achieved by mid-century, and the early training of Columba in the church signifies the beginning of a more intimate relationship between the church and secular powers. This marks out the monastic experiment which Columba engaged in, beginning in 563. The debate trundles on over whether Columba left Ireland for religious reasons, or for political expediency as a result of some risky involvement, or indeed a combination of the two, but it should not be allowed to obscure the significance of the monastic system established by Columba and his relatives and followers in Scotland. Partly favoured by the local rulers of Gaelic Argyll, but no doubt also patronized by his own kin, Columba created a monastic archipelago which separated out the different levels of discipline into distinct monastic communities. Iona was the centre, a fairly sizeable community by the end of Columba's term, engaging in a wide range of activities, from manual labour to book production and theology.

Iona seems to have been a strictly monastic community, with little trace in these early years of a lay population on the island. Lay people seeking regimes of penance were sent to the other large monastery of Mag Luinge on Tiree. There also, monks and penitents engaged in extensive agriculture, and Mag Luinge may have provided the bulk of the food for the other monasteries. A third island, the unidentified Hinba (either Oronsay-Colonsay or Jura), housed two centres, one a smaller subsidiary of Iona, and the other a collection of cells for anchorites who had attained the necessary level of perfection in the religious life.

Columba was clearly a man of enormous drive. Also established during his lifetime was a monastery in the midlands of Ireland itself, Durrow. Later, and perhaps even at the time, it may have been the most accessible to the lay population. Iona was involved in providing for the needs of the local Christian population, though not on the island itself: baptizing, healing the sick, counselling fraught married couples, giving penance and the hope of forgiveness. We know of at least one small monastic church on the shores of Loch Awe connected with Columba's Iona, and there must have been others.

Alongside Columba's, there were several other significant monasteries in Gaelic Argyll (Lismore, Kingarth, Artchain on Tiree), and the heavy presence of small churches, many probably of early date, give the impression of Argyll as a Christian region even in the sixth century. This impression is bolstered by the close relationship between Columba and the local magnates, the rulers of the Cenél nGabráin. Adomnán's *Life of St Columba* depicts the saint involved in the ordination of the kings of this dynasty, and most especially in that of the powerful king Áedán mac Gabráin, even praying for Áedán's success in battle. This of course needs to be set against some strong criticism by Columba of other, renegade, members of the kindred; none the less the rapprochement between church and secular authority was here very close indeed.

Less clear is the nature of the involvement of any of these Argyll monasteries in the evangelizing of the Picts. Although there are signs of earlier exposure to Christianity in southern Pictland, clear efforts at evangelization of the northern parts seem to begin with Columba, and perhaps Columba stands at the head of a movement carried out in reality in the decades following his death. There is little evidence for his own active missionary efforts; his journeys into Pictland seem geared towards getting protection for his monks working in Pictish territory, and produced only small crops of conversions. In spite of this, the evidence of the seventh century shows that the Christianized Picts looked largely to the abbots of Iona as their Christian mentors and ecclesiastical authority, thus suggesting that Iona lay firmly behind the poorly understood conversion of the region.

This discussion encompasses merely the signposts of conversion: Christian artefacts, names, officials, narratives. Inescapable is the sense that at no time do we really encounter the reasons, motives and processes behind conversion. Still less do we have any clear notion of what individuals were converting from, in Ireland or much of northern Britain. This makes for an unsatisfying and often fragmented narrative, yet perhaps an honest one. Between a pre-Christian and a Christian society lie a host of individual and social compromises and adjustments. Even in societies which provide much fuller documentation, this makes the picture of the evolving church a fuzzy one: how much more is this true of Scotland, where the evidence is so thin and scattered?

Seventh-Century Interactions: Warfare and Overlordship

It is impossible to understand the development of Scotland during the seventh century without first having set the scene with the four overlapping peoples of the Picts and Britons, Gaels and Angles, and also outlining the growing influence of the church on society and politics. The seventh century is strongly characterized by the mixing of these peoples across a range of activities, and the bonds forged among them by marriage or conversion, as well as attempted political dominance, explain much about aspects of Scottish society, art and language in the succeeding centuries.

The most obvious way in which these four peoples related to each other is in the various attempts by the dominant kings of each of them to become overlord of all during the course of the seventh and eighth centuries. Although this frequently took the form of the subjection to tribute of regions belonging to the neighbours of dominant kings, some of the texts of the period give these acts of aggression an ethnic tone. Such overlordship was impermanent and personal, extracted at the sword's edge through victories in open and often seemingly random battles, rather than protracted sieges or planned warfare. An early example of aggressive expansionism is that of Aedán mac Gabráin, king of the Cenél nGabráin and ruler over Gaelic Argyll from 574 until *c.* 608, an uncommonly long reign. Over the course of his career, we find Aedán campaigning not just to secure his own kingship, as he did in a battle early in his career when he defeated his rivals, but also to cow or subject his neighbours. Some of these expeditions may have been simply punitive or pre-emptive. His expedition to the Orkneys around 580 may be counted as such: Orkney was at this stage clearly Pictish, and such an expedition is likely to have been more to impress than to conquer. His battle in the central kingdom of Manaw in about 582 is another matter. Here sources record a great victory, and there is good reason to suspect that Manaw was subjected to Gaelic rule as a result. However, two battles late in his life suggest an expansionist king at the utmost stretch of his power. In *c.* 598 he was defeated in the far east of Pictish territory, and in *c.* 603 his army was crushed by the Northumbrian king Æthelfrith. It is significant that this defeat occurred in Northumbrian territory: Aedán's ambitions clearly involved complete dominance of the north.

Aedán's successors were unable to maintain this position. His warfare had been largely successful, but had cost him the lives of many of his sons. Although at least one of his sons is recorded as king of the Picts, this was a temporary situation. His grandson Domnall Brecc proved a singularly ineffectual king. The tributary lordship of the Argyll Gaels over Irish Dál Riata in Antrim, which had been forged in a royal conference the previous century, was lost in battle around 639. Domnall also lost battles, apparently within or near the borders of his Scottish domain, around this time. And in 642, in a battle in which he lost his life, the tributary dominance of the Gaels over Manaw was severed. The victor was one Owein, son of Beli, ruler of the British stronghold of Dumbarton, and his triumph was celebrated in verses:

> I saw stalwart men, they came at dawn.
> And crows pecked at the head of Domnall Brecc.

It may be that Owein's resistance to Gaelic imperium was provoked by the loosening of yet another overlordship, that of the kings of Northumbria. After the death of Æthelfrith, his rival and successor Edwin had ruled the twin kingdom and had expanded its borders greatly, in particular making conquest of some of the northern and western British kingdoms. He was in due course killed by Cadwallon, the British king of northern Wales, in alliance with the pagan ruler of the English midlands, Penda. When Cadwallon was himself defeated and the sons of Æthelfrith restored in Bernicia, Northumbria gained new heights of dominance. Oswald, Cadwallon's slayer, was a Christian and a charismatic leader, and is reported as having had Gaels, Britons and Picts subject to him, as well as English. Other evidence combines to suggest that he managed to effect some sort of loose lordship over the remnants of the northern British kingdoms, and over southern Pictish territory and Gaelic Argyll. When Oswald was slain in 642, his personal hold over these disparate kingdoms was released, and it is in this context that the jockeying for power which led to Domnall Brecc's death should be seen.

Oswald's successor and brother, Oswiu, did not effectively regain power throughout Northumbria until more than a decade later. He did, however, retain a hold in Bernicia and probably in Lothian and Manaw. Forced to flee by the now powerful Penda in 655, Oswiu took refuge in his fort at Iudeu, the once-British stronghold on Castle Rock in Stirling. There he was forced to pay massive compensation to Penda and his allies, many of whom were British kings. However, snatching victory from the jaws of defeat, Oswiu killed Penda in battle as he retreated south. During the course of the 650s and 660s, Oswiu expanded the power of Northumbria far to the south, and renewed its lordship over British, Gaelic and Pictish territories in the north. This in turn was continued by Oswiu's son, Ecgfrith, under whose rule the subjection of neighbouring peoples began to attain greater structural permanence and governmental force: British kingdoms were forfeited and the lands of the British church distributed to new Northumbrian dioceses; a new bishopric over southern Pictish territory was established at Abercorn on the Forth. When in turn Ecgfrith was defeated in battle, his death was depicted as the gaining of freedom for neighbouring subject peoples. Bede writes:

From this time the hopes and strength of the English kingdom began to 'ebb and fall away'. For the Picts recovered their own land which the English had formerly held, while the Gaels who lived in Britain and some part of the British nation recovered their independence.

The victor in this battle, fought at Dunnichen Moss near Forfar in 685, was the Pictish king, Bridei, son of Beli, and his triumph was the beginning of more than a century of Pictish dominance in the north. It is significant that he was the brother of Owein, son of Beli, whose victory in 642 spelt the downfall of Gaelic power. It suggests that both the once British kingdom of Dumbarton and the main Pictish territories were in the control of the same (Pictish) family. And although the parameters of Pictish territory changed over the following century, and though Gaelic settlement seems to have moved steadily eastward in circumstances still little understood, and though Northumbrian kings successfully trained their expansionist pretensions on the new western front of Galloway and Ayrshire, yet it was Pictish kings who had the upper hand in battle and conquest during the course of the eighth century.

Seventh-Century Interactions: Marriage, Exile and Alliance

Underpinning this bold pattern of violent conflict and forcible subjection among the rulers of the peoples of Scotland is a more subtle background which reveals these rulers to be joined by strong threads of alliance through marriage and exile. The names of the sons and grandsons of Aedán mac Gabráin suggest that marriage into the noble families of his neighbours accompanied his military conquests (we should remember here that multiple marriages were permissible under Gaelic law). His sons Rigullán and Artúr have British names; Conaing, the name of another son, is borrowed from the English word for 'king'; while his son Gartnait's name was Pictish. The victors of the two most important Scottish battles of the seventh century, Owein and Bridei, were both the sons of Beli, who had ruled in the British kingdom of Dumbarton. Yet the genealogy of these two kings suggests that the power of each derived from membership of a strong Pictish family, and that each initially ruled over a separate sub-kingdom: Owein, and later his descendants, over Dumbarton, and Bridei over Fortriu (centred on Strathearn). In addition, we know that Ecgfrith, king of Northumbria, who was Bridei's enemy at the battle of Dunnichen in 685, was also his cousin: it has been proposed that their mothers were sisters. As in Europe during the *ancien régime*, antagonists on the battlefield were frequently members of a complex, widely ramified, family tree.

The best illustration of this is the case of the three sons of Æthelfrith, ruler of Bernicia and of Northumbria, who were exiled after his death in 616. We are told that they went to live, with their retainers and other noblemen, among the Picts and Gaels. The eldest, Eanfrith, who succeeded to the kingship of Bernicia for one short year, had been in exile among the Picts, where he fathered a son, presumably with a woman of Pictish royal stock. This son in time gained the kingship of the Picts. Talorcan, son of Eanfrith, ruled from 653 to 658, and may have signally aided his uncle Oswiu (who was perhaps not much older than himself) in his struggle to regain control of Northumbria.

Oswald, on the other hand, was exiled among Gaels, probably in Gaelic Argyll. Here he became a fluent Gaelic speaker – he later acted as interpreter for his Gaelic bishop – and converted, with his retainers, to Christianity. Eanfrith amongst the Picts had been converted, we are told, but apostasized on regaining the kingship. Oswald's faith was deeper: he may well have attributed his success in battle against Cadwallon to the aid of St Columba. His first act after gaining the victory was to send to Iona for churchmen to renew the flagging Christianity of his kingdom. After a false start, Iona sent Aedán, who became first bishop of Lindisfarne and abbot of the monastery there; he opened the gates to three decades of strong and steady Gaelic influence on the church in Northumbria.

Oswiu, meanwhile, had also been exiled among the Gaels, but at least part of his exile was spent in Ireland. It is there, we must presume, that he fathered a son with a woman called Fín, daughter or granddaughter of a king of the Uí Néill, the oddly named Colmán Rímid ('Colmán the Calculator'). After the death of Oswiu's immediate heir, Ecgfrith, this distant son was the choice of the men of Northumbria to succeed to the kingship. He was called Aldfrith, but had a Gaelic name, Flann Fína, and had gained a reputation during his life in Ireland for wisdom and learning. When his half-brother died in battle and noblemen were sent to fetch Aldfrith, we are told that he was studying on Iona. His reign saw close relations between himself and his erstwhile teacher, Adomnán, abbot of Iona.

Oswiu had been a man of multiple marriages. At some point in his life – perhaps during the early years of Oswald's reign – he married a British royal heir, Rhiainfellt, granddaughter of one of the prominent British rulers of the north. His two children by this marriage must later have been considered less important, though they were used to cement important marriage alliances with Oswiu's English neighbours, and for a time his son Ealhfrith was caretaker king of Deira. But it was his son Ecgfrith who was groomed for kingship. He was son of Oswiu's most official and prestigious union, with Eanflæd, a daughter of the former family rival, Edwin, king of Northumbria. That union had several important repercussions.

The most obvious is that Eanflæd, raised in exile in Kent, had grown up in a different Christian milieu, in which there were a number of variant practices. The Gaels, like the British, had retained a conservative method for calculating the date of Easter, although in the course of the late sixth and early seventh century the rest of the Christian church, at least in the west, had gradually adopted a new system. That new system was being actively espoused by the popes in Rome. During the first half of the seventh century, conformity to this new system had become something of an ecclesiastical touchstone: southern Ireland largely agreed to conform in the 630s, but many of the northern churches, including Iona, refused to do so, probably because it conflicted with the teachings of the founders of their traditions, and also smacked of disloyalty.

The great disadvantage of these competing systems of calculating Easter was that it sometimes led to the various traditions celebrating Easter on different days. For a married couple like Eanflæd and Oswiu this must have been a great trial, as it entailed for each of them different dates for the ending of Lent. None the less, they had lived with the situation for some fifteen years before a council was called to resolve the conflict of practice. It is hard to avoid the conclusion that the timing, if not the object, of the council held at Whitby in 664 was largely politically motivated – an attempt to restore authority by Oswiu within his uneasy kingdom. After much debate, Oswiu made his decision for the Rome-backed system of Easter calculation, and almost instantly began a rapprochement with Rome which would launch a golden age of Northumbrian art and scholarship.

Seventh-Century Interactions: the Church

The history of the seventh-century church in northern Britain has often been sketched out in the light of the Synod of Whitby in 664. This is portrayed as the meeting of two great opposing camps, the Roman (allegedly southern English, imperialist, doctrinaire) and the Celtic (allegedly Scottish and Irish, victimized, ecumenical), with the Celtic side losing. Such caricatures do no justice to the reality of the age, and simplify the complex intermesh of cultures and traditions which comprised the Northumbrian Christianity whose fate was being decided. Profiles of some of the members of the debate reveal that complexity: Oswiu himself was an English king who had been raised in Ireland, and spoke Gaelic. Bede gives a startling picture of Oswiu as evangelist, arguing theology with his neighbouring kings, and for much of his reign accompanied by the former Iona monk Fínán, bishop of Lindisfarne. Of the two main churchmen who disputed the issue in front of the king, Colmán, Fínán's successor in Lindisfarne, was indeed a passionate supporter of the traditions of Iona, and Wilfrid, arguing the Roman side, does appear rather arrogant to the modern reader: even the kings and fellow bishops with whom he consorted later in life routinely fell out with him. Still, we know that other supporters of the Roman Easter were there: Agilbert, the able Frankish bishop for whom Wilfrid spoke; and Rónán, a southern Irish churchman who had vociferously promoted conformity with the Catholic Easter throughout the English kingdoms. Rónán is portrayed by Bede as even more fierce-tempered and provocative than Wilfrid.

There were also many English monks on the conservative side of the debate. When Colmán lost, he left Lindisfarne, taking some of Áedán's relics with him, as well as some thirty loyal English monks. The fate of these monks gives us some insight into the cross-cultural nature of the church in these decades. They followed Colmán to Iona and then to Inishbofin, an island off the west coast of Ireland; unhappy there, they were settled by Colmán in their own monastery on the mainland, at Mayo. This English monastery continued to prosper, and was still English, with a reputation for great faith and learning, in the 790s. We may also note the presence of Cedd at the Synod of Whitby, an English monk and bishop of Essex, trained under Áedán at Lindisfarne and interpreter for all present. Finally, in trying to distinguish nationality from persuasion on the issues of the day, mention should be made of Colmán's successor after he left Lindisfarne: Tuda was an English monk trained in southern Ireland. He thus had a training that was at once Gaelic and sympathetic to the ethos of the previous Iona incumbents of Lindisfarne, but orthodox in practice.

Eighth-Century Interactions: the Conforming of Iona and Pictland

It is important to keep these complexities in mind, for the seventh- and eighth-century Northumbrian church which came to dominate the Christian culture of much of southern Scotland (Coldingham, Melrose, Hoddam, and Whithorn at its height, were all Northumbrian monasteries) was a product of this mixed background, even if by the end of the seventh century its strongest influences were those wafting over from the continent. One final figure makes sense of the permeable world of this church. Ecgberht was a monk trained largely in southern Ireland in the mid-seventh century. Stricken by a plague there as a youth, he promised God his life as an exile and ascetic if he survived. Desperate to begin a mission to the still unconverted continental German peoples, he was thwarted in this desire by a dream conveyed to him by a monk of Melrose: he was commanded to preach among the monasteries of St Columba instead, and bring them round to the Catholic observance of Easter. Ecgberht nevertheless acted as teacher to many of the early English missionaries to the continent. He lived out his remaining life in Ireland and Scotland, among the Gaels and Picts, and was extremely influential in the eventual conversion of Iona, in the year 716, to orthodoxy on the Easter question. It was a time of division in that monastery, of a slow hammering-out of compromise and change. The final reform may well have been provoked by events to the east where the Pictish king Nechtan, after assiduous study of the issues, decided to convert the practice of his kingdom to the Catholic Easter, and sent to a Northumbrian monastery for help and advice, and architects to build a new, continentally inspired church dedicated to St Peter. In the course of this, in an event we still do not really understand, the monks of Iona were 'expelled' from his kingdom.

Pictland had long been beholden to Iona in religious matters. Much of Pictish territory had probably been converted to Christianity by churchmen from Iona, and there are indications that at the end of the seventh century this relationship had strengthened. Both Bede and Adomnán wrote as if the Pictish church looked to St Columba as its overall patron. Adomnán, abbot of Iona from 679 to 704, was a campaigner for conversion to the Catholic Easter, though he seems to have valued the unity of his community above compliance on the issue. He was a skilled diplomat, and in 697 he succeeded in establishing the Law of Innocents, mentioned above. This protected non-combatants – women, children and clerics – from violence, and instituted severe punishments for any violence, physical or verbal, against women. The law was signed by forty churchmen on both sides of the Easter controversy (Ecgberht may have been one), and some fifty kings throughout Ireland and Scotland. The Pictish king, Bridei, son of Derile, was signatory to it, as were two churchmen active in Pictland: Curetán, bishop of Rosemarkie, and Cóeti, bishop of Iona and founder of churches in Atholl.

Yet in the years before 717, Bridei's brother and successor Nechtan seems to have turned his back on this influence, and embraced both the Roman Easter and the continental exoticism of the Northumbrian church. This, like the Synod of Whitby, has often been portrayed as the act of a king nervous of Gaelic influence on his church, seeking to rid himself of such 'Celtic' inconveniences. Nechtan was, however, half Gael himself, his father being of the kindred of Cowal in Argyll. Moreover, it seems likely that both Bridei and Nechtan had been actively involved with Adomnán and his successors in forging a church in southern Pictland. Once more, the complex eddies of influence in these years reassert themselves: it seems quite likely that the main impetus for change in Pictland was from reform-minded abbots of Iona.

Nechtan's actions certainly initiated a closer relationship between Pictland and Northumbria, two regions which had since the mid-seventh century been intertwined on occasion through close marriage alliances. The most striking aspect of the new relationship between the Picts and northern English is the artwork which blossomed through the combining of strong elements of each tradition. The vivid vine-scrolls, alive with birds and beasts, which creep up the sides of monuments in English churches like Hoddom, Abercorn and Aberlady may be found framing the Pictish symbols and hunting-parties, set on a background of Irish-inspired designs, which can be seen on sculpture such as the Hilton of Cadboll stone from Easter Ross. In the seventh century, animals which once were emblems of the Pictish nobility took their place in Gospels illuminated – or at least used – by English monks. The art of the eighth century makes this point well: the high crosses of Iona, echoing in shape, though not in ornament, the free-standing crosses of Northumbrian south-west Scotland; the Hunterston brooch, blending English and Gaelic elements; Pictish figurative sculpture, with its classicizing tendencies; and the artistic kaleidoscope of the Book of Kells, hinting at two centuries of creative cross-influence among the peoples of Scotland.

Northern Overlords: Pictish Rule in the Eighth and Ninth Centuries

Bede's description of Nechtan's enforcement of the Catholic Easter throughout his kingdom is striking, if for no other reason than its picture of the Pictish church as an efficient body, responsive to the king's command. What emerges from this event is how the Pictish kingdom, more than any other, had forged something close to a state from the conflict and change of the previous centuries. The eighth-century evidence reinforces this view. The British kingdoms of southern Scotland had gone, one by one, under the spreading cloak of Northumbrian domination, though the population of southern Scotland remained largely British-speaking. Only the kingdom based on Dumbarton seemed to remain significant; in the south-west, Northumbrian kings were eating away at Galloway, at Carrick and Kyle. Despite this progress of overlordship, Northumbria remained a fractious and enfeebled kingdom for much of the century, on too many occasions outflanked and outmanoeuvred by rival English and Pictish kings. In Gaelic Argyll, despite evidence that Gaels were on the move, settling north and east into Pictish territory, Dál Riata too was torn by inter-dynastic warfare.

The Pictish kingdom rises above this scenario. Although the years from 724 to 731 were dominated by a fourfold contest for the Pictish kingship, this was a brief interregnum between the strong kingships of Bridei and Nechtan, the sons of Derile (697–724), and that of Unust, son of Uurgust (Óengus, son of Fergus) who reigned from c.729 to 761, and was succeeded by his brother, Bridei, for a further two years. Still later his son, Talorcan, came to power (780–82). After another brief interregnum, Constantin, son of Uurgust, perhaps a member of the same dynasty, took the kingship, reigning from 789 to 820. His brother Unust succeeded him, followed by each of their sons in turn: first Drest, son of Constantin, then Uuen, son of Unust. Constantin's nuclear dynasty reigned unbroken for half a century. Only a battle in 839, a sort of Dark Age Flodden which saw the death of many of the most prominent reigning nobility, signalled the end of this dynasty.

But it is not merely dynastic continuity which makes Pictish kingship over the course of the eighth and early ninth century outstanding. These kings were outward-looking, expansionist both in terms of territory and connections. Nechtan's overtures to Northumbria, his importation of architects and perhaps artists, is one side of this issue. Unust, son of Uurgust, was expansionist in other ways. He sacked Dál Riata and cowed its rulers on many occasions. He formed alliances with the kings of Mercia, in the English midlands, allowing him to dominate Northumbria. In 756, he formed an alliance with Eadberht, king of Northumbria, to achieve the submission of Dumbarton. Having gained it, he seems to have turned coat and, in alliance with the Dumbarton British, attacked Eadberht's army, with massive slaughter. This event was probably on the mind of Bede's continuator when he spat out Unust's obituary: 'Oengus, king of the Picts, died. From the beginning of his reign right to the end he perpetrated bloody crimes, like a tyrannical slaughterer.'

Constantin too extended his power beyond the bounds of Pictland, setting up his son in 811 as king in Dál Riata, where he ruled until 835. These twenty-four years of joint rule, combined with Unust's earlier overlordship, suggests a scenario for the mixing of Gael and Pict in a political arena which would bear strange fruit in the 840s.

The names of Unust and Constantin, son of Uurgust, are found inscribed in the *Liber Vitae* of the community of St Cuthbert in Northumbria; Unust appears alongside the Emperor Charlemagne, king of the Franks. It is in the reflected glow of the emperor that these Pictish kings should be seen. Sculpture from what was probably a palace at Forteviot bespeaks wealth and power. The prominent masterpiece of Unust's reign, the St Andrews sarcophagus, is a heady mix of continental inspiration and native ornamentation: in both it is designed to articulate the power of the king. The imagery of David displayed so relentlessly on Pictish monuments of the eighth century suggests that they saw themselves, much as Charlemagne did, as linked to that biblical *imperator* in practice and authority. The kings of the eighth century seem also to have taken their religious aura seriously: Nechtan, Unust, Constantin and his brother Unust, all were linked in one way or another with the establishment of churches, the movement of relics, and the endowment of new foundations.

The most potent emblem of this late Pictish kingship is the Dupplin cross. Set on a hill not far from the palace of Forteviot, it is inscribed with the name of Constantin, son of Uurgust. The king appears, dominant and moustachioed, mounted above panels of serried spearmen. David wrestles the lion and plays the harp, twin images of masculine guardianship and cultural largesse. The cross is embossed and displays a craze of vines and foliage. Constantin was aptly named: the motto under which the first emperor Constantine fought at the battle of the Milvian Bridge in 312, *In hoc signo vincet*, seems singularly appropriate for this emblem of kingship and religious government.

Yet within a century of Constantin's death in 820, under another Constantin, his kingdom had been renamed and refashioned, its dominant language had become Gaelic, and its sights were set on new and ambitious objectives. In many ways it looked similar: the power, prosperity and machinery of the Pictish kingdom laid the foundations for the Scottish one that would take its place. Yet culturally it had lost out. To understand the great sea-change of the ninth century, we must first record the arrival of a new player in the fourfold game of politics in Scotland. These were the victors of the battle of 839, who had been harrying the coasts of Scotland for fifty years: the Scandinavians.

Scotland in the Viking Age

This period in the history of Scotland (between 800 and 1100) prepared the way for the birth of the Scottish nation, or rather, saw its conception and gestation. We can now begin to trace the development of the medieval kingdom's shape and form: to see the different cells or component parts come together and develop, foetus-like, recognizable features of the fully-fledged creation. The head, the heart, the limbs all come into place, and, if we use the medieval analogy of the body for the state politic, the growth of the Christian church is regarded as the soul. However, much of this process is hidden from view, primarily because we still lack full written sources.

The component parts of the medieval kingdom – Gaelic Argyll, Pictland, the northern British kingdoms, and English Bernicia – and the complex relationships between their ruling dynasties have been discussed and their very different cultural and political characteristics defined, as far as the sparse historical sources allow. A short chronicle of events in the joint kingdom of the Picts and Gaels now begins to provide a brief political narrative (the 'Chronicle of the Kings' or 'The Scottish Chronicle' – see page 64); however, documents are few and inscriptions remain difficult to interpret, often neither legible or intelligible. Place-names, on the other hand, increasingly help to provide some understanding of linguistic situations. There is little archaeological evidence to come to our aid, for pagan graves do not exist and excavated settlement sites of this period are very elusive in the Pictish heartland; battle sites are usually unidentifiable. The impressive hill forts and defended tribal centres of the post-Roman period were abandoned, and the lowland centres of power which replaced them have not left much evidence of their significance, having been overlaid and quite altered through continuity of habitation in the following centuries. Strangely enough it is the Vikings who have left dramatic accounts of their settlements around the northern and western coasts and of their way of life: the sagas, although written down much later, provide us with some valuable glimpses of the peoples against whom they fought and with whom they intermarried. These mobile incomers also left unmistakable material remains which provide rich evidence of their way of life. Pagan graves dating from the ninth and tenth centuries and distinctive longhouses have been found throughout the Northern and Western Isles.

It is through knowledge acquired from the neighbours of the Picts and Gaels, as much as from indigenous sources, that we can understand the growth and formation of the northern kingdom in this period. Comparisons with better-documented societies will help to put Scotland's early history into its north European context. The power of Christianity in shaping northern society is, for instance, better appreciated in the context of the church's assertion of its authority in other kingdoms, its relationship with kings, and its impact on daily events in other parts of Europe. We can only appreciate the remarkable life of Queen Margaret written by her confessor, Turgot (discussed at the end of this chapter), if we understand the writer's background and clerical training, his expectations of an anointed woman's role in creating a more devout society, and his own ambition to bring the church in Scotland into line with that of mainstream Europe. But the world of Turgot and the world of the Vikings are utterly different and one of the challenges presented by this period is to bring together the diverse elements making up the amniotic fluid with which Scotland was surrounded, in an attempt to understand their effects on the infant Scottish kingdom which was about to be born.

The North European Background in AD 800: the Viking Impact

One of the main puzzles of this period is how the Gaels came to dominate the kingdom of the Picts. What population movements and political endeavours did the Gaels use to take over the reins of power in the central Pictish province of Fortriu? The fate of the Picts and their strongly developed culture was linked to this process, and the eventual growth of the new territorialized political unit called Alba. None of these happenings is explained by any contemporary chronicler, and later theories have to be treated warily. We shall never fully understand the processes by which they happened. We can only proceed by hypothesizing, and new and plausible hypotheses are shaping our understanding of this remarkable political and cultural phenomenon. One such hypothesis stresses the importance of the Vikings in these developments.

From the late eighth century to the mid-tenth century boatloads of mobile warriors poured westwards out of Norway and Denmark across the North Sea and left an indelible mark on the countries raided and settled by them. The Vikings' impact on Anglo-Saxon England, on Francia and on Ireland is taken very seriously by historians today, and they are regarded as a formative element in the social, economic and political development of all three geographical areas. It is less easy to be so positive about their impact on north Britain, where they have been regarded as a negative force of mere nuisance value. William Ferguson, author of *The Identity of the Scottish Nation* (1998), has reiterated that 'the main contribution of the Norse was destructive'.

From a geographical perspective it is of course undeniable that the whole of north Britain, including Argyll, the Hebrides and the eastern seaboard, was exceedingly vulnerable to ship-borne invaders from north and east. Maritime links across the North Sea may have been established before the Viking Age proper, which is considered by historians to start with the raids on Lindisfarne (793) and Iona (794). The impetus which instigated the arrival of these raids is disputed. Scandinavian over-population may have been the stimulus, but whatever the compulsion, the intentions of the Norwegian seafarers were honed by a desire for land. The mute evidence of the graves of Vikings found on the islands and in the sand dunes of the northern and western coasts of north Britain shows that they came in family groups ready for settlement, and not only as boatloads of warriors. The thousands of place-names in the Northern Isles and the Hebrides are permanent linguistic testimony to this last major population movement into north Britain.

In fact the linguistic testimony of Scandinavian settlement is seen in more southerly locations also, but the scattered evidence in Fife and Ayrshire, Dumfriesshire and Galloway is not so simple to pin down in time or origin. Scandinavian-speakers in these areas were more probably of Anglo-Danish extraction moving north from the Danish-settled areas in northern England (the 'Danelaw') some generations later. The Danish raiders-turned-settlers (who established the Danish kingdom of York in the second half of the ninth century) created a political and trading network linked up with the Viking kingdom of Dublin. This presented another predatory, mobile and very unstable power bloc with whom the various native kings in Scotland had to negotiate and fight, and come to terms in the course of the tenth century. On different geographical fronts the Scandinavian arrivals from north and west, as well as south and east, added an important new linguistic and ethnic component to the now Gaelic-ruled kingdom in the old Pictish heartland.

Looking at those other parts of northern Europe which experienced similar disturbances from raiding and settling by Norse and Danish invaders, we get a clear picture of motive and method. The popular image of sea pirates looting and destroying peaceful monastic communities is a cherished one which some historians and archaeologists have tried hard to overturn. Unremitting violence against Christian centres is confirmed by the case of the one well-documented monastic community in Scotland, Iona, which is recorded by the literate Irish annalists as having suffered repeated raids (in 795, 802, 806 and 825) but never being completely abandoned as a Christian powerhouse of prayer. Indeed, it became a spiritual centre for the Norse settlers themselves once they had adopted the religion of the societies they were attacking. This 'conversion' (we do not know how such a change of belief was brought about in the Hebrides, perhaps through a process of syncretism) occurred in all the localities where Vikings met stable, long-established Christian societies. It was part of the integration process which Christian rulers all over Europe encouraged, as in England where the Danish Guthrum agreed to be baptized at King Alfred's insistence (878), and in Francia when Rollo of Normandy accepted Christianity in return for control over the lower Seine valley granted by Louis the Fat (911).

Such adaptability was probably quite calculated, the newly-converted realizing the advantages of being acceptable to God and the local king. The Vikings are not notable for their amenability in general. In fact they were exceedingly successful in their exploitation of native societies in the process of acquiring wealth 'coldly and ruthlessly'. Politically they dominated the societies they raided by exaction of tribute, by appointment of puppet rulers who collected the tribute for them, and by the taking of hostages. Domination must inevitably have meant the subjection of those already in authority and playing off one faction against another. In England and Ireland they can be seen playing these games to perfection, thanks to the survival of documentary sources such as the Anglo-Saxon Chronicle. But such activity was not necessarily destructive. Some constructive motivating purpose probably underlay the remarkable mobility and the co-ordination of activity which can be glimpsed in the documentary record, and which mark out the Vikings' singular contribution to the history of the period.

The Response to Viking Raids: Political Change

Our starting-point is an entry in the *Annals of Ulster* for the year 839 which tells briefly of the battle fought in central Scotland (and already referred to) by the 'gentiles' against the 'men of Fortriu', of whom a large number were killed, including the king, Uuen, son of Unust, and his brother Bran. From this we see clearly that the Scandinavians had penetrated into the interior far from their coastal and insular bases; such a devastating defeat of the native leaders on their home ground must have had some critical effects on the ability of the Picts to maintain the integrity of their defences against the invaders. It is this situation which would suggest that the Vikings had a role to play in the contemporaneous movement of Gaels into Pictish territory: they could have been taking advantage of the power vacuum which such a disastrous encounter must have created. The list of Pictish kings suggests that there were two lines of succession for a period thereafter, and the strong expansionist Pictish dynasty that we know existed in the late eighth and early ninth centuries must have been fighting for its life in the unstable circumstances which had developed.

Thus it is possible to say that the Vikings had as momentous effects on the development of the Scottish situation as they clearly had in Anglo-Saxon England. The native Pictish dynasty was supplanted by its Gaelic rivals from Argyll who, if not pushed out of their Dál Riatan homeland by the incoming Vikings, decided to move east in sufficient numbers to fill the political and cultural vacuum which probably existed in Pictland. How much violence or assimilation accompanied this extraordinary political change is the subject of much debate. What is clear from recent work is the later Scottish massaging of the record to enhance the significance of Cinaed mac Ailpín (popularly Kenneth MacAlpine) as the founder of a new dynastic succession, and to emphasize the righteousness of the Scottish cause. What is not so clear (but rather likely) is the active role of a reforming Gaelic-speaking church in the ensuing demise of Pictish culture and language.

The new Gaelic rulers of Pictland (Cinaed mac Ailpín's successors) now had to defend their acquired position of authority during the next phase of Viking raiding. In 866 a mixed band of the 'Foreigners of Ireland and Scotland' led by named Vikings, Olaf and Audgisl, raided in Fortriu and took hostages throughout Pictland (as pledges for tribute, according to the later Irish commentator, An Dubhaltach Mac Fhir Bhisigh). Olaf, the Viking ruler of Dublin, stayed some months in central Pictland in charge of operations, which suggests that the combined kingdom of the Gaels and Picts was going the way of many other west European kingdoms in the face of Viking policies: like Northumbria, overrun by Danes who took the city of York in 866. This phase was taken a dramatic stage further in 870, when Olaf and Ivar, 'two kings of the Northmen', besieged the fort on Dumbarton Rock for four months, destroying and plundering it.

The capture of the citadel of the Britons of Strathclyde was a remarkable achievement and indicates that Viking domination of the central lowlands in the late ninth century was a real possibility. The control of such an important waterway as the Clyde, leading into the heartland of central Scotland had undoubted logistical significance for the economic and political strategies which the Vikings were pursuing at this date, one of which was the operation of a slave market based in Dublin, fed with English, British and Pictish – and Irish – captives. This desperate situation made clear leadership and military organization absolutely necessary.

It was forthcoming from the new ruler of Pictland, Constantín mac Cinaeda (Constantine I), who fought a battle with Danes at Dollar in 875, was driven north into the security of highland Atholl, and finally met his death 'slain by the Norwegians' at the battle of 'Inverdufatha' (perhaps Inverdovat at the mouth of the Firth of Tay) in 877. The Danish ships most probably came from eastern England, and Halfdan (brother to Olaf and Ivar) is recorded as having led expeditions against the Picts from a base on the river Tyne, being accredited some centuries later with the martyrdom of St Adrian (Ethernan) on the Isle of May. This was the period of the heaviest attack, and the east coast location of these events indicates a hard-fought struggle to maintain freedom from Danish raiders along the eastern waterways.

This is also the time of the expansion of the Norse earls of Orkney into the northern mainland of Scotland, evidence for which derives entirely from the Icelandic saga of the earls, for there is no reference to the earldom in the sparse documentary record of the Scottish kingdom. When all the disparate sources of evidence are taken into consideration it would appear that the Scandinavians were here to stay, and set to take a dominant position in the southern kingdom as they were doing in the Northern and Western Isles.

Purpose and Effects of Viking Raids

What was the strategy and purpose of the Scandinavian activity? In north Britain, as elsewhere in the Viking sphere, the aim was to seize strategic points for raiding or directing trading endeavours (such as the Isle of May or Dumbarton Rock); to exploit the rich lowlands of central and eastern Scotland by demanding tribute and putting in place puppet rulers to extract it for them; and to settle and dominate native societies if they had sufficient manpower. However, all the surviving evidence suggests that the Vikings did *not* succeed in dominating the Scottish lowlands permanently, or in stamping their own cultural identity on the political structures which were in the process of adapting to this Scandinavian element in their midst. There is no archaeological evidence of permanent Norse settlement in central Scotland, as there is in the Northern and Western Isles, in the form of pagan graves and excavated settlements of Scandinavian type. The lack of pagan burials (only one possible grave known in eastern and one in south-western Scotland), the scatter of Scandinavian place-names, and the strange burial monuments known as 'hogback' tombstones (discussed below) tell another story – of mixed beliefs and conversion to Christianity, and of integration of small groups of incomers into mainstream native societies.

The continued existence of a Christian kingdom in the central and eastern lowlands is one of the most remarkable survival stories in the whole history of ninth-century Europe, although mostly unrecorded and therefore unappreciated. We do not know what submissions, or agreements, or alliances, what adjustments, or what coming to terms there may have been. Despite the disruption, the underlying strengths of the Pictish kingdom were a firm basis upon which the new Gaelic masters could successfully defend their kingdom against continued raids. The historical record tells us that after plundering Dunkeld and then suffering a defeat by Constantín mac Aeda (Constantine II, son of Aed) in Strathearn in 904, the Northmen were contained – and moved elsewhere to carry on their raiding.

It is possible to draw the conclusion that the impact of the raiders from north, west and east had some very significant effects on the political structures of the emerging nation. First and foremost is the development of a Gaelic-speaking royal dynasty in place of – although based on – the old Pictish one. The simplistic interpretation that Cinaed mac Ailpín moved east from Dál Riata, took over the Pictish kingdom, and destroyed the culture and identity of those people is one that no longer bears credence, and is now seen as part of the propaganda about origins propounded by later chroniclers. None the less, the disruption caused by Viking raiders, whose impact is visible in the Scandinavian place-names throughout the Hebrides and more sparsely on the western seaboard, meant the displacement of the Gaelic political structures, which henceforth were cut off from Irish homeland and tribal connections.

It is clear that Pictish language and culture suffered a catastrophic decline and was replaced by Gaelic. One of the most telling and visible sources of evidence for this comes again from place-names: in eastern Scotland place-names are predominantly derived from Gaelic, although with a scatter of Anglian names in Fife and Angus and with a few — very few — Pictish elements assimilated into the total toponymy. The strongest indicator of the previous Pictish territorial or social structures is the distribution of place-names which begin with the element *pit* or *pett* — such as Pitlochry or Pittoddrie. Yet the specific (descriptive) element of these names is almost always derived from Gaelic, telling us of the adoption of some land-holding pattern already in place, but taken over and stamped with their own cultural definition by the new Gaelic-speaking aristocracy.

The Kingdom of Alba

The arrival of Gaelic-speakers is coincident with further striking developments. There is evidence of what historians call a 'dynastic kingship', which by the tenth century was monopolized by the descendants of Cinaed mac Ailpín. The short dynastic 'Chronicle of the Kings' ('The Scottish Chronicle') is a contemporary or near-contemporary account of the combined kingdom of Dál Riata and the Picts and 'a self-conscious history of that kingship' which looks emphatically to Cinaed as the founding father. However baffling the king-lists are as evidence of inheritance customs, they do tell us that male descendants of Cinaed dominated the inheritance of the kingdom, and that there was no sharing of power. Strong rule was essential for the preservation of integrity and effective resistance to the invader. This concentration of political authority allowed the growth of territorial lordship, and earlier provincial divisions were brought firmly under the overlordship of one dynasty.

Most remarkable of all is the appearance of a new term, Alba, for this kingdom. About the year 900 Pictish terminology was dropped and in its place a new vocabulary was adopted, based on the word Alba, an old Gaelic term for Britain, but taken now to apply to the area between the Forth and the Spey, and east of Druim Alban (the 'ridge of Britain'). This is the former territory of southern Pictland, while the northern and western parts of the larger Pictish imperium had fallen under the control of the Norse. Did a learned counsellor at the heart of events devise the use of this old term for a new political unit? It is understood to be a very significant change of terminology, indicating a conscious development of a new territorial concept: a manifestation of a new Scottish dynastic pretension, and a strong indication of the demise of the Pictish element. This new northern kingdom of Alba can be seen as emerging out of the maelstrom of Viking turbulence, just as contemporary political structures did in Anglo-Saxon England and the Frankish empire.

Three features of this new kingdom should be emphasized. First, there is the increasing centralization of the regime, with formerly independent sub-kings being cast, from early in the tenth century, as *mormaers*. However, the names for the *mormaers'* provinces, Moray, Strathearn, Mar, Buchan, Angus and the Mearns, suggest that there was a new and perhaps more centrally administered structure in place of the old Pictish provincial divisions. Again it is the period of Viking raids and disruption, necessitating efficient military organization, which is likely to have been the main reason for this development. The concomitant of this was, of course, the need for strong leadership, the streamlining of inheritance of authority and the reins of power under the control of one kindred, within increasingly tight bounds. Second, there is the Gaelic nature of the political, social and cultural characteristics of the new, united kingdom, resulting in the rapid demise of the distinctive Pictish cultural forms (notably the cessation of Pictish symbols on sculptured stones), with the Pictish language being the first to become extinct in the British Isles in the historical period. Third, there is the use of the church as an instrument of kingship (although there is little doubt that this was also a feature of Pictish kingship). The movement of Columba's relics to Dunkeld by Cinaed mac Ailpín, and the freeing of churches from various secular obligations by kings such as Giric mac Dúngaile and Cinaed mac Maíle Choluim (Kenneth II), reveal a pattern of synergetic relationships between cult and dynasty, based on the mutual support services provided by kingship and ecclesiastical hierarchy. This process is well known and attested to in all other Christian kingdoms of eastern and western Europe in this period. Learned clerics provided administrative support, conducted inauguration ceremonies (as we have seen they had done in Dál Riata much earlier) and 'advocated an ideology which . . . supported the aspirations of kings'.

What did all this mean to the bulk of the population? Alba was a *political* term devised for the construction of a state identity. To the Anglo-Saxon chronicler of this period the northern king was a 'king of Scots', and a sense of national identity was probably beginning to develop at this time in the kingdom of Alba. This newly united and powerful kingdom, which at its widest covered the fertile east from Lothian to the Moray Firth, and along the fringes of the highlands of Druimalban, gives some impression of being a strong Gaelic cultural unit. As in Anglo-Saxon England, which was 'united' under the kingship of the house of Wessex at the same time, political unity was probably less real than might appear. The remarkable tribal diversity had disappeared, but regional identity remained strong north of the Mounth. The church was probably a powerful force for Gaelic culture, and one of the few recorded ecclesiastical events shows King Constantín (II) mac Aeda and Bishop Cellach committing themselves to maintain church laws and customs 'as the Scots did' (*pariter cum Scottis*) in 906. The flourishing *céli Dé* (Culdee) monastic order, which had been brought in from Ireland, became closely associated with the kings, and was richly endowed by them.

Alba was not, however, the only success story amidst the violence of the age. Despite the sacking of Dumbarton in 870, by the early tenth century a new kingdom south of the Clyde had been forged, based not on Dumbarton but on the royal centre at Govan, further up the river Clyde. This kingdom of Strathclyde (or properly Cumbria), for all it seems at times to have been a client kingdom to its northern neighbour of Alba, was aggressively expansionist. By the first quarter of the tenth century it held the corridor from Govan to Penrith, two markedly similar power centres. This was a period of linguistic resurgence, with the coining of new British/Cumbric place-names, and the exportation of the cults of saints Constantín and Kentigern/Mungo into Dumfriesshire and northern Cumberland. Characteristic of this new kingdom is an art style with eclectic influences, seen most dramatically in the monumental sculpture at Govan, with the massive 'hogbacks' (large stone grave covers with curved roof ridges) pointing to links with the Scandinavianized world of Northumbria.

It was not yet the end of the Viking age. Throughout the tenth century the kings of Alba were sucked into the unstable situation prevailing in northern England, where the Danish kingdom of York maintained an independent existence until 954. Constantín (II) mac Aeda had a close relationship with its kings, sometimes friendly and sometimes hostile, and involving marriage alliances which put him into the camp of the pagan as far as the kings of Wessex were concerned. This king of Alba may have been a very skilful manipulator of circumstances, and he certainly exercised much energy and resources in striving to benefit from the opportunities offered in Northumbria. His prime strategic considerations were southward-looking, with the ultimate aim of expanding his frontier beyond the Forth into Lothian and Strathclyde.

The Tenth Century: Expansion Southwards

We may wonder today why the northern part of the Anglian-speaking territory of Northumbria, nominally controlled by warlords based at the coastal fortress of Bamburgh near Holy Island, should have been so attractive; and why the kings of Alba expended so much energy and commitment to bring it within their kingdom (as Cinaed mac Ailpín had already done in the ninth century). Here was a land of opportunity with a power vacuum which any Dark Age warlord would want to fill. A tenth-century king of Alba would seize the opportunity to lead his army south to acquire fame and booty, as well as to extract wealth from a grain-growing, settled population. There was also the possibility of controlling lucrative trade routes within the economic sphere of the Danish dynasty which ruled both York and Dublin. This was the period when these two cities were burgeoning trading and manufacturing centres. The political links between them were based on economic contacts, which meant the maintenance of trade routes. One of these routes passed through the central lowlands of Scotland: access from west to east across the mires and bogs around the headwaters of the rivers Carron and Kelvin, or Loch Lomond and the Forth, was probably one reason for the battles fought in the ninth century.

Accommodation was reached with the kings of Alba in the tenth century on freedom for warrior-traders to move around the routes and waterways of the Clyde, Forth and Tay, although the historical accounts are more concerned to record the violent activities of Vikings such as Ragnall, grandson of Ivar, who was in control of York from *c.* 911. The underlying economic enterprise stimulated by Viking commercial activity has been most dramatically brought to light by the excavations of recent decades in York and Dublin, with evidence of crowded urban communities engaged in trade and manufacture in the tenth century. Tanneries, manufacture of combs and other objects of bone, together with metal workshops, all provide evidence of the more durable objects made and traded from York. But there would be much more besides which has not survived in the archaeological record, such as furs and pelts brought in from Scandinavia and, in the case of Dublin, slaves. Luxury goods would have been traded around the coasts of east and west Scotland and up the Firths of Forth and Clyde, although no archaeological evidence of such trade exists. Nor are any trading centres known except for Whithorn, where excavation has revealed a small-scale manufacturing community with Irish Sea trading connections. Doubtless it was the merchant traders known as 'Hiberno-Norse' and 'Anglo-Dane', active in the waterways of southern Scotland, who were responsible for the deposition of the silver hoards dating from this period and found scattered around coasts and rivers.

Some of the mobile and historically unrecorded individuals were probably prepared to settle under the protection of different native rulers. The hogback tombstones are thought to be evidence of these communities, for they are cultural identifiers which were a distinct feature of the burial customs of colonial settlers who retained them, even when the settlers became part of the host society. The oldest and most prestigious burial places usually possess one or more (including Govan, Abercorn, Inchcolm and St Andrews). Often they are hacked, despoiled and re-used by later generations, rarely surviving as well as the huge examples in the impressive collection at Govan on the river Clyde. The general distribution of these distinctive colonial monuments shows that those who commissioned them were not confined by any political frontiers. The men they commemorate must have been mobile in life, and many of the Scottish examples are near or on the main waterways or land routes across the central lowlands. They are best identified as the tombs of warrior-merchants, or maybe mercenaries, who had been given, or bought, land on which to settle. These men may have owed allegiance to their own Norse-speaking leader, or the Gaelic king of Alba, or the British king of Cumbria – or more than one of these. They adopted the Christian faith, for their monuments (some of them with Christian symbols) are all found in long-established Christian burial grounds.

The wealth which enabled the hogback tombstones to be commissioned was also an attractive feature of the Anglo-Danish world of Northumbria (where the hogback monuments originated): and it was this world over which Constantín was striving to establish some control when he fought Ragnall and the 'grandsons of Ivar' on the river Tyne in 918. However, he then came to terms with those kings of York and Dublin, who probably realized how important it was to have good working relationships with the kings of Alba (and of Strathclyde) if they were to succeed in ruling both Dublin and York jointly. To do this, they had to have unhindered access via the waterways and land routes across the central lowlands and north Pennines. Constantín entered into alliances, and – significantly – Norse names appear in the following generations of royal princes; Constantín's daughter was eventually married to a later king of York and Dublin, Olaf Guthfrithsson, who was still pagan. These relationships were regarded as idolatrous by the kings of Wessex.

One important result of Constantín's involvement in the affairs of Anglo-Danish Northumbria was the close encounters with King Alfred's son and grandson which followed: the beginning of a long and usually uneasy relationship between the Scottish and English royal dynasties. On two occasions meetings are recorded as having taken place between the kings, along with the rulers of Bamburgh, Cumbria and York, at which Constantín 'submitted', first, to Edward the Elder in 920; and, second, to Athelstan in 927. We should, however, be very wary of accepting the Anglo-Saxon version of the tenor of such occasions. These would have been meetings at frontier locations when the relationships of all the parties were equal. The English kings would have had to accept the claims of the Scots and Danes, and their position in northern England, although insisting that they 'cease from idolatry', which probably meant that social and matrimonial links with the pagan Hiberno-Norse were to be severed.

Brunanburh and After

The situation was too volatile to be permanent, and a few years later Athelstan succeeded in repulsing the heathen ruler of York and gaining control of Northumbria, from where he launched an invasion of Constantín's kingdom. It is unlikely to be a coincidence that this took place in the same year that the pagan Olaf Guthfrithsson succeeded to the kingship of Dublin, although it is impossible to say that the invasion happened as a direct result of Olaf's accession. One commentator said that Athelstan's invasion was due to Constantín and Owein, king of Cumbria, breaking the pledges that they had formerly made, in which case it could have been justified as a reprisal (with the church's backing) for action against a dangerous pagan alliance. If Athelstan had hoped to bring Constantín to battle on his home ground he failed, although he raided as far as Dunottar on the east coast (between Arbroath and Aberdeen), while his fleet may have sailed further north. This show of strength did not frighten his opponents into inactivity and three years later (in 937) a response was orchestrated by Olaf Guthfrithsson, Constantín and Owein of Cumbria, with the support of many Viking warlords from the Hebrides, York and the English Danelaw. The conjunction of such disparate component forces tells us of the threat which Athelstan's previous raid was understood to present to the northern rulers. The combined response to that military threat is unprecedented evidence for the ability of these rulers to coordinate large, mobile forces and put an ambitious military strategy into operation.

Constantín's participation must have been central to the success of the combined force and his role was clearly a critical one; in references in contemporary and later poems on the ensuing battle, one refers to 'the aged Constantine, the hoary warrior'. His heroic defeat at the battle of Brunanburh, and the heroic nature of the event, was dramatic enough to inspire such poetry – an unusual inclusion in the Anglo-Saxon Chronicle. 'A great battle, lamentable and terrible' is how it was described in the *Annals of Ulster*, but nowhere was it described comprehensively enough to know exactly where it took place. The invasion force certainly penetrated deep into the kingdom of England, probably south of Northumbria, and this brings sharply into focus the dramatic developments which had taken place in Constantín's reign. A king of Alba, who at the beginning of the century was just beginning to cross the Forth in the hope of expanding his southern frontier, was thirty years later part of a coalition of Scottish, British and Hiberno-Norse armies pushing deep into Saxon territory. This development may not have been in the best interests of the kings of Alba but was an inevitable result of being caught up in the ambitious ploys of the mobile Scandinavian warlords who were still swirling around the northern kingdom, dominating the Irish Sea and the routes between Dublin and York.

However, both Constantín and Olaf Guthfrithsson survived the carnage at Brunanburh, although Constantín's son Cellach did not. Constantín's defeat must have meant a significant loss of prestige for the old king, and would have rendered him incapable of maintaining any effective influence south of the Forth. Athelstan's successors continued to pursue the same goal by pressing north with the intention of making Northumbria fully part of their kingdom, which they eventually succeeded in doing. This was not achieved without difficulty and the next Viking warrior to appear as the power-seeker in northern England was Eirik 'Blood-axe', son of the king of Norway, repulsed by his brother, who made a bid for control of all the Scandinavian settlements in Britain and Ireland. He launched an expedition from the Orkneys accompanied by the earls Arnkell and Erlend, and drew in Vikings and warlords from the Hebrides. He did not succeed in dominating Dublin and probably received no welcome in Alba. It was not possible for an outside adventurer, however well supplied with longships, to make much permanent impact on the volatile political situation in north England. Although Eirik ruled York for two brief periods he met a violent end in 954 at Stainmore, on the Yorkshire–Westmorland border, where the two Orkney earls fell with him. The Old Norse poem *Eíriksmál* composed in his honour describes the heroes' welcome in Valhalla for Eirik and the five kings who are said to have died with him. Although we have no evidence of Eirik having much involvement with the Scottish dynasty, his brief career, and the Wessex take-over of the pagan Norse kingdom of York which followed his death, marks the end of an era in British and Irish history. The links between Dublin and York were broken, which meant that the descendants of Constantín were no longer drawn into ambitious plans such as those which the kings of York had attempted to pursue.

It is unlikely in the aftermath of Brunanburh that any gains made by Constantín in extending his power over the lands south of the Forth were maintained, although his successors were certainly in control of Edinburgh and (after 973) Lothian. This remarkable king's main achievement was to maintain the integrity of the kingdom of Alba in a situation in which it might also have fallen tributary to the kings of York and Dublin. It has been claimed by the historian Professor Alfred Smyth that he 'provided a stabilizing influence which went far to prevent the complete Scandinavian conquest of Britain'. This was probably achieved by negotiation and compromise with the pagans in a way of which King Alfred might not have approved. Nevertheless, the results for his kingdom, and for the survival of Christianity, were of a permanent nature, and the length of his reign is in itself a notable fact which must have done much to make the Scottish dynasty a stable and unshakeable feature of the north British political scene. Just as remarkable is the evidence that Constantín retired from kingship to enter a life of religion as a member of the *céli Dé* community at Cennrígmonaid/Kinrimund (St Andrews), perhaps in the aftermath of his defeat in battle against Athelstan.

Power Centres and Saintly Patrons

This provides the first indication of the importance of St Andrews as a royal centre, although the existence of the prestigious carved panel from a sarcophagus dated to *c.* 750 (and now in the St Andrews Cathedral Museum) confirms the status of Cennrígmonaid (Kinrimund) as a burial-place, surely for a Pictish ruler, a century or more earlier. It is one of the few power-centres of this period in a coastal location, and as such open to sea-borne influences, especially from the south. Our knowledge of the structure and affiliations of the Pictish church remains imperfect, but we have seen how influences had been absorbed from both the Columban church in the west and from the Northumbrian church to the south. The Gaels moved into Pictland with their own strong and distinctive culture, of which their Columban spiritual affiliations were a significant part. Some of Columba's own relics were carried east, and one of the few contemporary pieces of information about Cinaed mac Ailpín says that he bestowed these on the church of

Dunkeld. There was clearly an intention to make Dunkeld a new Iona in the heart of the new Gaelic–Pictish kingdom, and a spiritual and dynastic power-house for the incoming Gaels. In the following century the two sources of spiritual influence in Alba, from the west and from the south, may not have co-existed easily. However, the ebb and flow of Ionan and Northumbrian cults, ritual, and ecclesiastical personnel are not easy to follow.

During the period of Viking incursions any monastic and dynastic centre was likely to be a target for raids, inhibiting the development of royal power centres which were vulnerable to attack from the sea. This may account for the use of Forteviot in Strathearn as a royal residence (and burial-place of Cinaed mac Ailpín) in the ninth century. By the mid-tenth century, Cennrígmonaid was a centre of royal patronage, in Constantín II's case because of his expansionist policies south of the Forth. We cannot be sure exactly when the cult of St Andrew developed: later foundation legends suggest that some relics were brought to Cennrígmonaid in the eighth century. It is likely that kings like Constantín – whose attention was focused southwards – would have been familiar with the Northumbrian ecclesiastical centres such as York, with its minster dedicated to Peter, and Hexham, with its abbey church dedicated to Andrew. These manifestations of powerful Roman saints must have made the Scottish kings aware of the value of having an apostle's protection in a power centre of their own.

Yet Columba apparently retained a role as protector of Constantín's army, and his staff Cathbuaid (meaning 'battle triumph' in Gaelic) was carried south with the Scots in 918, helping to bring them victory against Ragnall. We should also recognize the significance of the name Malcolm (Mael Coluim means 'servant of Columba') occurring in the Scottish dynasty in the tenth and eleventh centuries. Above all there is the tradition that Iona continued to be used as a burial-place by kings of Alba throughout this period. If this can be believed, it tells us a great deal about the emotional links with the west and the continued regard for Iona as spiritual home of the Gaels. Thus the tenth-century kings derived their spiritual strength from the Hebridean world, but by virtue of their base in the eastern coastal zone came into close contact with Northumbrian influences. The resulting mixture of Gaelic and Anglo-Danish foreshadows the future eclectic nature of Scottish culture.

Constantín's reign is also significant for the first mention of Scone, the place which later (and maybe earlier, although there is no written record) was so important as a royal inauguration site of the kings of Scots. Early in his reign (906), Constantín and Bishop Cellach had a meeting at Scone when they both swore an oath to protect (*devoverunt custodire*) the church laws, customs and rights on the Hill of Faith/Belief (*montem credulitatem*). Here is dramatic documentary corroboration of the significance of an assembly site at Scone, used for the promulgation of joint church–state regulations. The commitment so seriously promulgated must have affected church rights, and is further evidence of the Gaelicizing process that was permeating the political and ecclesiastical structures of the kingdom. From this important chronicle entry we learn incidentally that bishops were influential, dynastic centres existed, and the kings of Alba acted at the behest of the church to alter or strengthen church rights and privileges – and no doubt wealth.

It was just at this time that the new designation of 'Alba' came into use, and it may be significant that this occurred in the aftermath of the cessation of raiding in the central lowlands. Constantín's struggles with the kings of Dublin and York, and then the Anglo-Saxon kings, took place in Northumbria, so that the main theatre of war was now removed from the heartland of the Scottish kingdom. Such a situation would seem to provide suitable circumstances for the development of political structures, and the strengthening of royal control over the component parts of Alba.

Respite from External Threat. Internal Conflict and Consolidation

However, the sources do not provide clear evidence that this was happening and inheritance struggles dominate the second half of the tenth century. The apparently unregulated system of succession stemmed from Irish patterns of inheritance, where there was no recognition of primogeniture, and different 'segments' of a ruling dynasty had rights to claim the throne. Of course, the longer a dynasty continued to rule the greater the number of 'segments' which could establish themselves with valid claims to power. Even a long-lived (and still-living) king such as Constantín (II) mac Aeda was not immediately succeeded by either of his sons, but by a second cousin, Mael Coluim (Malcolm) mac Domnaill. The claim of his 'segment', descendants of the eldest grandson of Cinaed mac Ailpín, were strong and undeniable. After his death in 954, power passed back to Constantín's son Idulb/Indulf (who was later said to have been killed by Norse raiders at Cullen in Banffshire) and then again to Mael Coluim's son Dub, to Indulf's son in turn and then back to Dub's brother, Cinaed mac Maíle Choluim (Kenneth II). There were therefore two alternating lines during the second half of the tenth century, one holding full authority as king of Alba, although they would both have had their own lands – and probably some of the former provinces – to keep them happy in the periods when not in power.

According to the fourteenth-century chronicler John of Fordun, Cinaed II (971–95) attempted to create a more directly regulated succession system, and gained the agreement of the nobles to establish a direct line to his collateral descendants, even if an heir were under age. We can imagine that his ecclesiastical advisers would have been behind such a move, although the role of the church in these events is never mentioned. Any such agreement did not prevent Cinaed from meeting a violent death, however, 'killed by trickery and craft, at Fettercairn: falling by the deceit of Finella, Cuncar's daughter', as recorded in the one king-list. The event was later elaborated by Fordun into an amazing account of a mechanical trap which loosened cross-bolts when the king touched it, with fatal consequences. After Cinaed's death in 995, power passed to Aed's line again under Constantín III for two years and Cinaed III of Dub's line for eight years, before Mael Coluim (II) mac Cinaeda (Kenneth II's son) succeeded by violent means in forcing the descent of kingship to his grandson. The system by which power passed to and fro was not conducive to peaceful reigns, but did allow the strongest candidate to emerge, strength coming presumably from the military following that each aspiring king could attract – as in most other north European societies of the time.

Another aspect of Celtic inheritance customs was the arrangement called 'tanistry' (Gaelic *tánaise*, or 'second, next'), whereby the heir-in-waiting from another 'segment' was acknowledged, and could be given a portion of the kingdom to govern meanwhile. It has been suggested that the kingdom of Strathclyde may have provided a power-base for such heirs-designate, although the evidence for this seems to lie more in historians' desire to identify such a system than in hard fact (only one early eleventh-century reference indicates that such an arrangement existed). Without doubt the fall of the capital of Dumbarton to the Vikings in 870 had struck a severe blow to the old British kingdom, and in the fraught period of Scandinavian invasion it may have come under the control of Cinaed mac Ailpín's descendants. But the native dynasty reasserted itself in the later tenth century and Strathclyde continued to possess something of an independent existence until the death of Owein the Bald in 1018. The south-west may, unusually, have benefited from the disturbed times of Danish rule at York, for it would have been in the interest of the kings of Alba to ensure the cooperation of the Cumbrians while they themselves were campaigning in Northumbria, thus keeping their western flank secure and protected from the Hebridean and Irish Sea Vikings. The Anglo-Saxon kings also had an interest in having some control over the land of the Cumbrians, and Edmund was able to ravage the area in 945 when he is said to have 'commended' Cumbria to Mael Coluim I. Frontier lands could suffer terribly from competing claims of neighbouring ambitious kings, each striving to assert authority over intervening territory. It would be a remarkable thing if the south-west managed to retain any provincial integrity between such competing overlords, but it has been argued that Cumbria did do so, and the remarkable collection of hogback tombs at Govan provides mute evidence of the power and wealth of one group based on the Clyde at this date.

Northern Dynasties

Moving to the northern periphery of the kingdom of Alba, we can more easily recognize the provincial integrity of the eastern firthlands of Ross and Moray. This territory had a remarkable geographical and cultural identity, the history of which is unrecorded and was deliberately forgotten by medieval kings of Scots. The ruling dynasty later derived its descent from the Cenél Loairn branch of the Gaels of Dál Riata who had apparently moved up the Great Glen into the fertile lands of the northern Picts and developed a powerful province quite independently of the southern kingdom. Kings of Alba usually came near to the northern frontier beyond the Mounth at their peril, a fact which probably helps to explain their absorption with Northumbria, an easier area into which to expand and gain personal advancement.

The ruler of the province of Moray, who is called 'earl' in the *Orkneyinga Saga*, was sometimes called 'king' (Gaelic *rí*) in the Irish annals, although he was a *mormaer* (great steward) to the kings of Alba. All these titles meant something rather different, but they were given from the viewpoint of Moray's neighbours, and it is unknown how the ruling members of the Moray dynasty defined their own status. None of this makes much difference to the reality of power which these war leaders must have exercised over a wealthy province, with a long and rich heritage extending back into the Pictish period. That reality is dramatically visualized in the highly impressive Sueno's stone, a carved monument outside Forres, which represents armed conflict on one face and Christian circumstances on the other. It is not known when or why or by whom this stone memorial was erected, probably in the tenth century, but it appears to commemorate a victorious encounter in the history of the dynasty of Moray.

At some point (perhaps through marriage with a daughter of Cinaed II), the ruling family of Moray was linked to the southern dynasty, a link which gave it thereafter some claim to power in the kingdom of Alba on the death of Mael Coluim (II) mac Cinaeda in 1034. This probably helps to explain Macbeth's appearance on the political scene, suggesting that he was more than just a violent usurper of power.

Before we introduce the most famous Scottish king of the period, we have to move even further north and consider what was happening in the Viking coastal fringe of north Britain. Internal faction attracted Scandinavian adventurers like wasps to a honeypot, and it was fortunate for the kingdom of Alba that the period of dynastic instability of the second half of the tenth century occurred mostly during a period of calm in the Viking world. However, circumstances in the Scandinavian areas of northern and western Scotland were themselves changing, and the political development in the earldom of Orkney introduced a new and powerful – and very mobile – warlord into the story. The earls of Orkney were to become an important element in the looming contest between the kings of Alba and the rulers of Moray.

As early as the late ninth century, according to the saga of the earls, the family of Rognvald of Møre in Norway had established control over the islands of Orkney and Shetland and raided the north Scottish mainland as far south as Moray. This brought them into conflict with the rulers of Moray, and there is no reason to doubt the saga's account of battles which took place throughout this area, although the accuracy of the details always has to be questioned (as the sagas were written by Icelanders several centuries later). Remarkably, the names of some of the ninth- and tenth-century rulers of Moray are remembered in Icelandic tradition, and we know from Scottish sources that these names occurred among the Moray dynasty at a later date (dynastic names were always likely to re-occur). Earl Sigurd I of Orkney is said to have died after a battle with Earl Mael Brigte of Moray, which would have taken place along the frontier territory in Ross, as Sigurd was buried on the banks of the Oykell: and indeed his burial mound may have been at the place later known as Cyderhall ('Sigurdshowe') in Sutherland. Leaders called 'Magbiotr' (Macbethad) and 'Melsnati' (Mael Snechta) are named as having been killed in the north in the later tenth century fighting with succeeding earls of Orkney, which shows that Norse settlement of the north mainland was not easily won. However, with the dominance of Sigurd (II) Hlodversson (died 1014), and his son Thorfinn 'the Mighty' (died c.1065), the earldom reached its furthest expansion, Caithness and Sutherland were brought firmly within the earls' control, and Norse settlement extended into Ross under their protection. Expansion also took place down the west coast, where these two earls appear to have exercised some authority over the mixed Gaelic–Norse society in the Hebrides, perhaps as far south as the Isle of Man.

An important dynastic marriage between Earl Sigurd II of Orkney and a daughter of a 'Malcolm, king of Scots' (most likely Mael Coluim II of the kingdom of Alba) is recorded in the *Orkneyinga Saga*. This tells us that the northern earls were considered to be valuable allies in the early eleventh century. The main reason for this must be linked with the threat the province of Moray presented to both. It made good sense – as always – for the rulers on each side of a powerful dynasty to ally and divide their common enemy's military strength between two frontiers. This was particularly important for Mael Coluim II when he was faced with the growing threat of the Danish conqueror Cnut on his southern frontier, and needed to ensure that he was not troubled by ambitious rivals in Moray.

These intermarriages between the families of the rulers of Alba, of Moray and of Orkney, brought powerful claimants to the political scene of Scotland in the first half of the eleventh century. First, though, having mentioned the Danish conqueror Cnut, we must turn again to the Scandinavian warriors who were once more arriving on the south-eastern shores of England.

The Second Viking Age

The northern kings escaped the worst of the impact of the so-called Second Viking Age. Swein Forkbeard of Denmark, followed by his son Cnut, and Olaf Triggvason of Norway led repeated raids against the England of Æthelred the Unready, starting in the 980s and continuing until the conquest of the kingdom by Swein and Cnut in 1013–16. The Scottish chronicler John of Fordun credits Mael Coluim II with success against Scandinavian raiders, fighting a heavy battle in Banffshire against a large band of Norwegians – perhaps from Orkney. The anonymous (but near contemporary) commentator writing 'The Prophecy of Berchán' calls Mael Coluim 'enemy of Britons, scourge of Norse, voyager of Islay and Arran'. These attacks around Scotland were not, however, part of the focused and deliberate campaigns which were led against England for the purpose of extorting Danegeld, a tax or 'protection money' which was paid in huge amounts of silver coin. Perhaps Scotland's lack of coinage made her a less attractive target, although the increasing evidence of silver hoards from this period indicates that there was plenty of material wealth in circulation in the form of foreign coin and 'hack-silver' (cut-up items to be weighed for bullion). These probably originated from trading ventures and mercenary activities on the part of Scandinavian settlers and visitors.

It may even be the case that Swein took refuge in the north, for a German cleric, Adam of Bremen, writing about Swein in the eleventh century, said that he spent fourteen years in exile with a 'king of the Scots' during a period of difficulty after his father, Harald Bluetooth, died in 986. It is tempting to identify him with the 'Swein, son of Harald' who raided the Isle of Man in about 995. King Æthelred considered the situation unsatisfactory enough to lead an expedition to the north-west and plunder Cumbria in the year 1000, although the English sources give no reason for this campaign. Fordun provides some confused information about Mael Coluim (probably in fact a king of Cumbria), who during Cinaed III's reign had refused to render the tribute necessary for payment of Danegeld. He is said to have 'supported the Danes against his oath of allegiance' to Æthelred: this might suggest that a king of Cumbria had indeed given refuge to Swein, a situation which could satisfactorily explain how Swein came to be raiding the Isle of Man c. 995.

The effects of the final Danish conquest of England and the imperial ambitions of Swein's son Cnut 'the Great' changed the situation once more because of the Northumbrian power bloc, granted by Cnut to his most powerful Scandinavian earls. Mael Coluim II had taken advantage of the uncertainty in the years after Cnut's final assertion of power in 1016 to lead a very successful raid into Northumbria when he won a battle at Carham (in 1018) against Eadulf Cudel of the native dynasty of Bamburgh, which gave him control as far as the Tweed, and established the southern frontier of the medieval kingdom. The powerful Norwegian 'jarl' Erik of Lade was given Northumbria by Cnut in the same year, which he ruled as an independent province. Mael Coluim would have to defend his gains against this newly-established Scandinavian warlord on his southern frontier.

It has been suggested that Cnut was very concerned to ensure that his wide-ranging North Sea political ambitions should not be upset by Scottish non-cooperation. But he had enough to do with establishing his authority on both sides of the North Sea before tackling the Scots, and it may not have been until the late 1020s that he turned his attention to the northern kingdom. The statement in the Anglo-Saxon Chronicle about Cnut's campaign in the north is dated to 1031. There is evidence from a French chronicler, Rodulph Glaber, that warfare between Mael Coluim and Cnut was more long-lasting than a single campaign. Glaber knew that Mael Coluim was a great warrior as well as a 'truly Christian king', and he suggests that the strife between the two kings was brought to an end on the advice of Duke Richard of Normandy (whose sister Emma, widow of King Æthelred, Cnut had married in 1018).

Although there is no mention in this French source of any submission to Cnut by Mael Coluim, we can be certain that it did occur, for one of the English chronicle texts provides the remarkable information that *three* northern kings acknowledged Cnut's authority when he entered Scotland: Mael Coluim, 'Maelbeathe' (presumed to be Macbeth, ruler of Moray at that time), and 'Jemarc' (presumed to be Echmarcach, king of the Rhinns of Galloway and perhaps of the Isles, and later of Dublin). This unique piece of evidence tells us that Cnut considered all three to be important elements in his global imperial schemes. Fordun suggests that the main focus of Cnut's attention was Cumbria and does not mention any submission by Mael Coluim. But the significant phrase in the skaldic poem in praise of Cnut (*Knuts drapa*), 'the heads of famous foreign lords . . . journey from Fife in the midst of the north', stressing that there was a 'peace-buying', is supporting evidence for the English chronicle's report of the three rulers' submission.

English, Norman and Scandinavian sources, therefore, tell us of the threat to Mael Coluim's independence from the greatest ruler in the northern hemisphere. Some close alliance between Normandy and the Isles is also hinted at in the Norman source, and reveals continuing links among the Viking colonial settlements. Whether we can rely on the interesting information that peaceful relations between Mael Coluim and Cnut resulted in the latter acting as sponsor at the baptism of a son of the Scottish king is uncertain. Certainly no such son survived to adulthood. It is likely that the satisfactory resolution of the situation with the Scottish king would allow Cnut to go on pilgrimage to Rome, which he did sometime in the late 1020s or early 1030s.

The comment (in one text of the Anglo-Saxon Chronicle) that Mael Coluim's submission did not last long may merely reflect expectation of Scottish faithlessness. This king had more important things to worry about at home, such as ensuring the continuation of his own line to his grandson, Donnchad (Duncan); Mael Coluim (Malcolm II) had no sons, only a daughter. It would be surprising if rival segments would ever have accepted such an abnormal progression of inheritance of power through a daughter. Clearly they did not, for in 1033 Mael Coluim was induced to have either his second or third cousin slain (a grandson, or great-grandson of his own father, Cinaed III). Whatever the relationship, this deed provided Gruoch, granddaughter of Cinaed, and at that time married to Macbeth (her second husband), with a justifiable desire for revenge against Mael Coluim. The response from other dynastic rivals was swift and Mael Coluim himself was killed the following year as the result of an ambush at Glamis.

Macbeth, Mormaer *of Moray and King of Alba*

This violent end did not, however, prevent Mael Coluim's plans for the inheritance of his kingdom from succeeding and his grandson Donnchad did indeed rule for six years, but probably only with the strong backing of his father Crínán, (lay) abbot of Dunkeld. The disastrous end of Donnchad's reign, with defeat at Durham and death in the north at the hands of Macbeth all in one year (1040), suggests some inability to judge the strength of the powers facing him on both his kingdom's southern and northern frontiers. Macbeth's attack on his overlord probably had many motivating factors: as ruler of Moray he was considered their subordinate by the kings of Alba, and no doubt deeply resented this demotion. We do not know if this was his position when, along with Mael Coluim II, he joined the submission to Cnut; but he is referred to as Donnchad's *dux* (by Marianus Scotus), which might be regarded as the Latin equivalent of *mormaer*. The variety of terms used to describe the ruler of Moray (noted earlier) tell us that their exact status was disputed; no doubt this was the cause of intense feelings of aggression against the southern dynasty, which constantly attempted to dominate. This rivalry would be the major factor lying behind Donnchad's violent end: Macbeth is said in most of the sources to have been responsible for Donnchad's death near Elgin where, according to Fordun, the king was taken to die. An assassination is implied, engineered by Macbeth who evidently disputed his authority to enter Moray. In addition there was the deep-seated desire for revenge, revolving around the murder in 1033 of Gruoch's nephew (or even son). It would probably not be far from the truth to allow Macbeth's wife (Gruoch) close involvement in Donnchad's demise, and thus give Shakespeare's dramatic creation some credibility.

Macbethad mac Findlaích of Moray (Macbeth, in modern usage) himself had strong claims to the kingship of Alba for four reasons. First, he is suspected of being a grandson of Cinaed II (although proof of his mother's blood-line is wanting); second, he was married to a daughter of Boite, whose close relative had been murdered, and he was therefore bound to continue her family's feud against Mael Coluim II's line; third, he was a vigorous military leader and hereditary ruler of a powerful province who probably regarded the possessor of power in Alba as having no valid claim to inheritance through the female line, and who was in any case discredited as a warrior; fourth, he killed Donnchad in some encounter on the frontier of his territory, and was left without rival except for Donnchad's two young sons, who soon fled into exile. There have been many less justifiable seizures of power in the history of medieval Europe than Macbeth's.

Power Struggles in the North

So little is understood of the violent and dramatic events in the history of this period that we have to cherish all sources, however difficult it may be to ascertain their validity and meaning. One such source, written a century and a half later in the quite different literary and cultural milieu of Iceland, gives us a dramatized but credible narrative of the events in northern Scotland at this very time. This is the history of the earls of Orkney (*Orkneyinga Saga*) mentioned earlier, which includes important skaldic verses written by Arnorr *jarlaskáld*, the court poet of Thorfinn 'the Mighty', who ruled Orkney and Caithness from the mid-1020s to *c.* 1065. This earl was the grandson of Mael Coluim II from Earl Sigurd's marriage – suggested above to be a political alliance designed to keep the rulers of Moray in check. Indeed, Thorfinn's early career was directed towards maintaining control of his northern Scottish territories in the face of aggressive campaigns launched from the province of Moray.

The main protagonist in this struggle for power in the firthlands of Ross and in the waterways around the Orkneys was 'King Karl', son of Hundi, a name which links him with the enemy of Earl Sigurd II at the battle of Duncansby in *Njal's Saga*, who was also called Hundi. These Scottish warriors can only have been rulers of Moray: no king of Alba possessed the power to penetrate so far north, or had the fleets necessary for fighting naval encounters around the Orkney islands. Donnchad mac Crínáin was unable to cross the frontier into Moray without losing his life. The use of the term 'king of Scots' by the saga's author is entirely understandable if we identify Karl Hundason with Macbeth, a ruler of Moray who took power from the murdered Donnchad and became king of the southern Scottish kingdom.

For the period of Thorfinn and Macbeth's rise to power, probably in the 1030s, there has survived a brilliant account in Icelandic of the battles fought between these young warriors (and possible cousins). The first encounter was off the east coast of the Orkneys:

> Made clear then to King Karl
> the close of his iron-fate,
> east of Deerness, defied
> and defeated by warrior-kin.

> Confronting the foe, Thorfinn's
> fleet of five ships
> steered, steadfast in anger
> against Karl's sea-goers.

Finally at Torfness (probably Tarbat Ness in Easter Ross) Thorfinn won another victory against Karl which 'ended with Karl on the run' and 'some people say he was killed there'. The writer of the saga was not at all sure what had happened to King Karl after Torfness, most probably because he disappeared south as ruler of Alba.

The aftermath of such a defeat would have allowed Thorfinn the freedom to raid widely and enrich himself and his followers. In addition, the vacuum left in Moray by Macbeth's assumption of power in southern Scotland in 1040 may have given Thorfinn a commanding position in the north. The saga refers to his conquests as far south as Fife, and also to rebellion against his rule, which was met with harsh reprisals and the taking of many captives:

> Shattered were the Scots'
> settlements that fear-day.
> Thatch smoked, fire
> flared over fields.
> The true prince took
> payment for treachery,
> thrice in one short
> summer he struck them.

It is likely that Thorfinn and King Macbeth/Karl Hundason eventually reached a settlement because of the changed circumstances in which Moray and Alba were ruled together for fourteen years. As far as Macbeth was concerned, the new situation required peaceable relations with the Norse world of Orkney and Caithness to enable him to rule his acquired kingdom without the distraction of northern warfare. Evidence of events during his fourteen-year reign is exiguous in the extreme (even for this period of Scottish history), a circumstance which might be taken to indicate that there were peaceful conditions and, therefore, not much to record.

The best-known fact concerns Macbeth's pilgrimage to Rome in 1050 when he bestowed gold generously on the poor, perhaps on an ecclesiastical foundation for Scottish pilgrims. Such a pious and peaceful religious journey was accomplished by several lords of northern lands at this time, some of them probably in emulation of Cnut the Great's pilgrimage of c. 1030. It entailed absence from their kingdom for months and could only be achieved if conditions were indeed peaceful at home, which suggests that Thorfinn was now an ally. Significantly, some rival Irish kings are known to have gone on pilgrimage together in this period as a sign of penitence for past enmity and pledge for future friendship. Is it pure coincidence that Earl Thorfinn also went on pilgrimage to Rome at about the same time as Macbeth? The two did not travel out together, for Thorfinn went via Norway, Denmark and Germany, nor can his 'famous journey' be pinned down to a particular year. Nevertheless the possibility remains that the two visited the pope together. The main motivation for both rulers was probably the need for remission from the sin of murdering a rival in their accession to power. Both would have been obliged to make compensation in the form of generous benefactions to the church in their territories, as we know they both did. It is tempting to speculate that, as warring cousins, they also committed themselves to bettering their relations in future under the seal of papal forgiveness. There is no evidence that Macbeth needed to take special care over the security of his northern frontiers during the time he was ruling in the south, which could suggest the development of amicable relations with Earl Thorfinn.

Evidence that Macbeth made generous provision for the church in his kingdom comes from the record of a grant to the *céli Dé* foundation of St Serf on an island in Loch Leven, which included certain lands in Fife. This charter also associates his wife, Gruoch, called daughter of Boite and *Regina Scotorum* (queen of Scots), with the grant, an unusual event in any part of northern Europe in this period of history. What can we deduce from such a remarkable piece of evidence? Were the lands part of Gruoch's patrimonial inheritance? Did she also need to gain remission of her sins for partnership in her husband's violent accession to power? The document does not tell us, but it bears out Macbeth's standing as a benefactor of the church, as later expressed by Wyntoun in his verse Chronicle:

> And all tyme oysyed he to wyrk
> Profitably for Haly Kirke.

Whatever crimes he had committed on his path to becoming the first king of Scots to rule both Alba and Moray, Macbeth compensated with generosity and the promotion of good relations with the church; actions for which he would have received ecclesiastical support in return.

Mael Coluim III mac Donnchaid 'Cenn mór' (Malcolm Canmore): Exile and Restoration

Macbeth's rule of fourteen years (1040–54) was remembered as a time of peace and plenty, but his line did not displace the southern dynasty permanently. Donnchad's eldest son was Mael Coluim 'Cenn mór' ('Big Head'), who is usually known as Malcolm III or Malcolm Canmore (the anglicized form of his name will be used here). He was restored with the support of the Anglo-Saxon king and Earl Siward of Northumbria. Once more the Scandinavian element had a role to play in the internal development of the Scottish kingdom.

The earldom of Northumbria had been ruled since 1016 by the Norwegian Erik of Lade and from 1033 by the Dane Siward Bjornsson, two of Cnut's most formidable military lieutenants. The Scottish kings perceived the necessity of developing alliances with these Scandinavian warlords in Northumbria even though they constantly tried to expand southwards into northern England. It is likely that Donnchad himself had been married to a member of the ruling Northumbrian family, so it was natural that Malcolm should flee south in the years following his father's death and Macbeth's assumption of power. His brother Domnall went to the Isles, probably the Hebrides. The two princes, heirs-in-waiting, were thus in exile for fourteen years, one under the tutelage of the Danish earl (with access through him to the Anglo-Saxon court), while the other was brought up in the Gaelic–Norse world of the Western Isles.

This was a situation which was not uncommon in northern Europe at this date. Edward the Confessor was brought up at the court of his mother's family in Normandy for twenty-six years, and he is said by Fordun to have received Malcolm favourably at the Anglo-Saxon court 'for he too like Malcolm had recently lived in exile'. Exile in England strengthened the ties of the Scottish dynasty with its powerful southern neighbour. Symbolic of these close links was the grant of estates in Northamptonshire (probably by Siward) to provide income, and a residence *en route* to London, for Malcolm. The future relationship of medieval kings of Scots with England is clearly foreshadowed in this significant period of exile.

Provision of refuge for Malcolm in Northumbria meant the Anglo-Danish regime in England was given a very valuable pawn to hold in the game of influence and overlordship of the Scottish kingdom. Malcolm was eventually restored to his father's inheritance with military backing, and trained household troops known as *huscarls* were provided by both Earl Siward and King Edward for the famous campaign into Scotland in 1054. Yet we know that Macbeth also hired foreign troops, Norman knights who had been expelled from England in the turbulent events of 1052 when Edward's Norman followers were ousted by Earl Godwin. These two forces met north of Dundee where a famous and decisive battle took place, traditionally located near a hill called Dunsinane. The encounter between *huscarls* and knights foreshadows the battle of Hastings twelve years later, but on this occasion the Norman knights did not prevail. Macbeth fled north to his patrimonial lands and Malcolm is said by most commentators to have been restored to power over the southern parts by Siward. However, by the fourteenth century Fordun complained that everything was ascribed to Siward, and Malcolm deprived of all glory 'when in actual fact Malcolm alone with his own men and standard-bearer was responsible for the whole victory'. It can hardly be doubted that Siward would make the most of his pawn and require some reward for his outlay:

control over Cumbria may have been part of the bargain, for evidence suggests he had some authority in lands north of the Solway.

Practicalities and theoretical overlordship did not always match: but Siward was dead the next year, and Malcolm won glory on his own account two years after that by hunting down his enemies and dispatching first Macbeth, and then Gruoch's son by her first marriage, Lulach, in military encounters in the north-east. Few returning claimants from exile have ousted those in possession of power and established themselves more decisively. Malcolm's kingship was a military and political reality, and the way was clear for the re-establishment of the dynasty descended from Cinaed mac Ailpín without rival.

This was more than just a re-establishment. It was a re-formulation. The new king had spent his formative years in exile at the courts of Siward and Edward; he must have returned to Scotland speaking a heavily Scandinavianized form of northern English, in addition to his paternal Gaelic tongue. Undoubtedly Malcolm also returned home with a following drawn from the Anglo-Danish community of Northumbria among whom he had grown up and with whom he must have forged bonds of loyalty and military companionship; the obvious parallel is Edward's return to England from Normandy in 1042 with some powerful French knights and churchmen who became very unpopular with some sections of the Anglo-Scandinavian ruling elite. Such followers expected to be rewarded with land and rights. Moreover Siward's expedition north of the border had resulted in a great slaughter of 'all that were best there in the land', according to the Anglo-Saxon Chronicle. Thus a new raft of nobility would have been installed in Malcolm's kingdom, alongside those surviving members of the old Celtic families who had remained loyal to the exiled prince during Macbeth's rule (first among them being MacDuff, according to Fordun's story). This situation, of Malcolm's triumphant return to his rightful inheritance, would seem to provide the right circumstances for the importing and implanting of Northumbrian agricultural, legal and social terminology later found throughout southern and eastern Scotland.

The social framework of Macbeth's kingdom with its predominant Gaelic culture would have become inevitably more 'anglicized' through this dramatic change of political fortune. The arrival of Northumbrian warriors from an Anglo-Danish society, who would have been given estates in the fertile lowlands of Lothian, Fife, Angus and Perthshire, must have started a reversal of the previous spread of Gaelic language and culture south of the Forth, and implanted a Northumbrian element in the political heartland of the Scottish kingdom. This was a significant step in the formation of the Scots language and in determining the cultural mix of the Scottish kingdom.

Scotland and 1066

As a hardened warrior who had been schooled in the tough Anglo-Scandinavian world of northern England, this Scottish king had a different outlook on life from the previous holder of power, whose experiences had been formed in the Gaelic north. Malcolm III resided mostly in Dunfermline, facing south across the 'Scottish sea' (Firth of Forth), and his knowledge and understanding of the political, social and cultural scene in Northumbria repeatedly drew him southwards. If the number of his campaigns is anything to build on, then his priorities were directed towards confirming his authority and power south of the established border and to acquiring the debatable lands between Tweed and Tyne. Five times he led armies south, eventually losing his life in a treacherous attack near Alnwick.

Throughout Malcolm's reign the situation in Northumbria was, of course, one of permanent change and continuous disturbance due to the events leading to the Norman conquest of England, and then the aftermath of King William's consolidation of his authority in the north. Malcolm seems to have attempted to make capital out of this situation by trying to ensure that he acquired as much as was attainable in another power vacuum in northern England. His interest in Northumbria and his intentions were made abundantly clear by 1061, when he ravaged the area in the absence of Tostig Godwinsson, who had been given the earldom by King Edward on the death of Siward in 1055.

It might have been thought that a marriage with Northumbrian interests would have been suitable for the young king installed with Northumbrian support – and with possible family links in the area already. But there is no evidence of any such liaison – although this means little, as there is in any case no Scottish evidence for his first marriage. Knowledge of this first marriage to Ingebjorg, widow of Earl Thorfinn, is only contained in the *Orkneyinga Saga*. There it is said that after Thorfinn's death towards the end of King Harald of Norway's reign (presumably 1064–5), Ingebjorg, the earl's widow, married Malcolm, king of Scots, 'known as Long-Neck. Their son was Duncan, king of Scots.' No other source reveals who was the mother of Malcolm's eldest son Duncan, and probably also the mother of his second son Donald.

The saga's validity has been questioned because of Ingebjorg's presumed age, and historians have suggested that the woman concerned might rather have been a daughter of Earl Thorfinn. But the saga is quite specific about the marriage – and never mentions that Thorfinn ever had a daughter. There must have been compelling reasons for the young king to negotiate a marriage alliance with the not-so-young widow of the earl of Orkney, and those reasons can be linked with the ambitions of the Norwegian king, Harald Sigurdsson, to win power in England on the death of King Edward with no direct heir. The marriage would have taken place at the time when the question of the inheritance of the Anglo-Saxon throne was the main political issue throughout the British Isles.

There were three powerful claimants with ambitions to gain Edward's throne by force, all from widely differing backgrounds. Harald Godwinsson, the most powerful noble in England, moved fast to get acknowledgement from the *Witan* (Council) as soon as Edward was dead in January 1066. William, Duke of Normandy, had a kinship relationship with Edward and a desire for vengeance against Harald, whom he regarded as a faithless vassal. Harald Sigurdsson of Norway's claim was inherited from the Danish dynasty's period of rule in England in the earlier part of the eleventh century. Of these three aspiring claimants, the king of Norway's northern base and direction of approach required the cooperation of the Scottish king. The likelihood that he might indeed be the victorious candidate made him the obvious horse for Malcolm to back. In these circumstances a marital alliance tying Malcolm to Orkney and Norway would be judicious: Ingebjorg's family were among the most powerful in Norwegian society. She was a cousin of King Harald's first wife Thora, and it is probably significant that the saga's author stresses this fact when he tells of the aftermath of the battle of Stamford Bridge. We do not know of the negotiations and promises that must inevitably have been part of the creation of such an alliance but we can guess that Malcolm's ambitions on his southern frontier would have formed part of any bargain. Tostig Godwinsson as earl of Northumbria was also deeply involved. A dangerous and ambitious power-broker, his role in the events of 1066 as the Norwegian king's ally – and in opposition to his own brother – was one of the many personal twists of fate brought about by the events of that year.

The Scottish king was therefore once again party to Scandinavian ambitions in northern England. But Malcolm did not join the Norwegian expedition, apparently keeping himself free of personal involvement in this last Norwegian military bid for power. He left it to his allies Tostig and King Harald of Norway, and his stepsons Paul and Erlend, earls of Orkney. Tostig and Harald failed to return from their bid for the throne of England, having met their death on the battlefield of Stamford Bridge, but their intervention was decisive in the eventual outcome of the three-way contest. Harald Godwinsson's diversion to the north to deal with the Norwegian invasion allowed the Norman claimant to land at Pevensey and to become established in a favourable situation at Hastings, ready for the tired Anglo-Saxon *huscarls* to return and be defeated.

So the outcome was probably the one least expected by the king of Scots, who then acquired the dangerous and unwelcome role of protector of those opposed to the new Norman regime. Moreover, Malcolm very definitely cast in his lot with the surviving members of the Anglo-Saxon dynasty by taking for his second wife Margaret, sister of Edgar the Ætheling, who was the figurehead of the English resistance. Edgar and his sisters and mother fled as fugitives to the Scottish court in the aftermath of the Norman conquest and successful military occupation of the north of England by William the

Conqueror. This second marriage of Malcolm, to the granddaughter of Edmund Ironside, must have seemed a dangerous alliance to William, who did not lose much time in bringing his formidable military machine to bear on his northern neighbour. He decided in 1072 to settle the issue of overlordship and penetrated to the heart of Malcolm's kingdom by land and with a naval force as far as Abernethy, on the south side of the Firth of Tay. As in 1031 this was apparently a peaceful meeting between the two kings, when the terms of their relationship and of the extent of their territorial possessions would have been discussed, as well no doubt as Malcolm's relationship with the English exiles. Malcolm submitted and gave hostages, probably among them Duncan, his young son and heir by Ingebjorg. These dramatic events were driven by the rapidly changing circumstances in England, and the potential, and very real, threat from Scandinavia and Northumbria to the security of William's new kingdom. All this made Scotland a pawn worth securing on the chessboard of northern history in the eleventh century.

Malcolm and Margaret, Agents of Change

The written accounts resulting from involvement with the new Norman regime and from marriage with a member of the Anglo-Saxon royal house help us to gain some valuable knowledge of the situation in late eleventh-century Scotland. Inevitably this reflects the interest of the southern chroniclers and, as far as they were concerned, it was Malcolm's continued raiding into Northumbria and the Norman response which were worth recording. The year 1079 saw him daring to cross the frontier again, which prompted a retaliatory invasion of Scotland as far as Falkirk by the Conqueror's eldest son, Robert. The absence of King William II (Rufus) in Normandy in 1091 gave Malcolm another opportunity to lead a raid south and acquire more booty. That provoked William and Duke Robert into campaigning into Lothian, when Malcolm submitted and swore fealty, receiving confirmation of his English lands and an annual payment of 12 marks as a retaining fee. He was now firmly a feudal vassal of the Norman king: he was tied by an oath of homage and the reciprocal grant of land into the sort of relationship which underlay the Norman kings' successful governmental methods. This did not mean that there was any attempt to deprive Malcolm of his royal status, and the raids into Northumbria seem to have been recognized as a permitted expression of unrest by a subordinate king, rather than a dangerous attempt to undermine the superior authority of his overlord, the king of England. Malcolm's son Duncan, still a hostage at the Norman court, did not suffer any mortal consequences as a result of his father's actions.

We are now looking forward into the Middle Ages and the Scottish kingdom is about to be born. The king of Scots was ruling a territorial entity with established boundaries which were scarcely to change for the next two centuries, and with a personal relationship of 'feudal' character ensuring its recognition according to contemporary norms. His wife remains a familiar figure as a saint and holy patron of the Scottish royal house. He sired a string of sons from two marriages, and he and Margaret had two exceedingly marketable daughters, one of whom became queen of England, and the mother of the Empress Matilda, Henry I's chosen heiress to his kingdom. The other was married to Eustace, Count of Boulogne, and thus the mother of another Matilda who married King Stephen of England. The regular sparring with the Norman kings and the frequent cross-border raids furnished Malcolm and his followers with booty to enrich their coffers and aid their conspicuous consumption, familiar features of the medieval kingdom. The Viking age was over. The turbulent Scandinavian component no longer caused disruption, and the buffer provided by Northumbrian warlords with Norse and Danish networks behind them had vanished. The medieval kingdoms were in place and 'Scotland' and 'England' recognizable territorial dominions, although 'Scotland' remained a remarkable amalgam of a variety of different linguistic groupings.

Court and Culture

How distinctively Scottish would Malcolm's court have appeared to the visiting Norman knights and churchmen of the new regime established at the White Tower in London? To what extent did the central institutions conform to a medieval norm?

The mixed culture of life in the royal circle at Malcolm's court is evident from the remarkable *Vita* of his second wife, Margaret, written by Turgot, her confessor, prior of Durham and eventually bishop of St Andrews. This account was written after Margaret's death as a model of queenship for Margaret and Malcolm's daughter, Matilda (Edith), queen of England, and purposefully records Margaret's religious zeal and ascetic lifestyle, probably with an eye to her future sanctification. It is a product of ecclesiastical learning and Latin culture by an Anglo-Norman churchman about the life of a princess of Hungarian and Anglo-Saxon ancestry. What it reveals regarding the life of the Scottish court is inevitably heavily impregnated with the outsider's view and reflects the superior attitudes of the Roman church. None the less, this is the first full narrative account, virtually contemporary with the events it records, which has survived from Scotland, and it gives us remarkable glimpses of the daily events and relationship of a native king and his foreign queen.

Margaret's influence on the life of the court was clearly significant, as has always been recognized, but not always appreciated. The choice of names for her sons, five of them Anglo-Saxon and commemorating her nearest relatives and forebears, is a clear indication of her fervent desire to perpetuate her own culture and dynastic origins. In the circumstances of the Norman domination of England and threat to Scotland, and the dramatic demise of the Anglo-Saxon royal dynasty, this can be seen as politically significant, and suggests that she saw herself as the surviving representative of an ancient lineage which she was determined should not be forgotten. This Anglo-Saxon queen put a firm stamp on cultural, social and religious matters in her new kingdom: maybe also economic ones – her biographer comments that she encouraged foreign merchants to bring in new and exotic goods (of which we have almost no other contemporary evidence, historical or archaeological).

Margaret's most lasting contribution was essentially that of 'modernizer' of the Scottish church, in that she brought north the latest in reformed orders, learning and personnel, from the Anglo-Norman world of which, from the time of her marriage, England formed a part. The evidence shows that she was very much in touch with Norman standards of reformed cult and worship, requesting Archbishop Lanfranc to send a complement of Benedictine monks from Canterbury for the church dedicated to the Holy Trinity which she and Malcolm founded (as a daughter house of Christ Church, Canterbury) at their dynastic centre of Dunfermline. This royal and ecclesiastical powerhouse, furnished by her with a dazzling array of secular and ecclesiastical treasure (according to Turgot), puts the royal patroness into the European league of noble and royal women who made their mark on the religious and cultural scene of their countries, such as Matilda of Tuscany or Adela of Blois. Margaret can be esteemed as one of the earliest of such remarkable women in a world emerging from the 'Dark Age' of early medieval European history.

Turgot tells us that she was involved in many other activities which suggest that she was deeply concerned to direct the religious life of Scotland along lines which would be acceptable to reformist criteria. Her attendance at church councils where she criticized traditional archaic aspects of liturgical practice in the Celtic church is relayed perhaps more for the unusual nature of a queen's participation than for the momentous changes that resulted. An extraordinarily eclectic range of institutions received her patronage: she visited hermits with whom she enjoyed conversing; she and Malcolm continued to be benefactors of the Loch Leven *céli Dé* community of St Serf (as Macbeth and Gruoch had been in the previous reign); an interest in Iona and particularly in St Andrews shows that she patronized the ancient centres of the Scottish church; she encouraged pilgrimage by establishing hospices and the 'Queen's Ferry' for the free passage of pilgrims across the Firth of Forth; her foundation of the Holy Trinity church at Dunfermline was according to the latest reformed Anglo-Norman precepts. All this demonstrates a deep and concerned involvement in the established religious and cultural life of her adopted country as well as a desire to reform certain aspects of it, although she can only have had a minor impact on the way the church's establishment went about its daily business, and the episcopate can hardly have been touched by her desired reforms. There may have been attempts by Malcolm and Margaret to bring the bishop of St Andrews under the authority of the archbishop of York, but those writing about it are probably expressing a wishful thought rather than actuality. Nevertheless Margaret's legacy must have been an enduring one, particularly in respect of the outer world's regard for her religious status; her personal contribution to Scotland's standing and reputation is quite inestimable. She brought enormous prestige to the Scottish dynasty and propelled it to the forefront of European royalty. To be revered as a saintly queen, and to be the mother of three kings of Scotland and of a queen of England is a personal achievement hardly equalled by any other medieval woman.

Tensions and Troubles Herald a New Age

However, Margaret's contribution was not appreciated by some sections of society within her kingdom, and the enduring nature of her legacy was very uncertain in the years of civil disturbance which erupted in 1093. Both Malcolm and Margaret died within a short time of each other: the king and his eldest son were caught in an ambush near Alnwick, and on hearing the news Margaret expired (through grief, it was thought at the time, although Turgot makes it clear that she had been ill). Reaction was immediate and, the Anglo-Saxon Chronicle tells us, 'the Scots chose as king Domnall, Malcolm's brother, and drove out all the English who were with King Malcolm before'. This must have included all the surviving princes except Duncan, the eldest son of Malcolm, who was still resident at William II's court, and who was immediately sent north with a military force as the representative of Anglo-Norman interests. It is hard not to invest these rivals to the Scottish throne with ethnic and cultural characteristics which symbolize the divergent forces at work in late-eleventh-century Scotland. But the line-up is not absolutely clear, for Duncan II was the offspring of Malcolm and the Norwegian Ingebjorg, although thoroughly assimilated into the Anglo-Norman world. The alliance between his uncle Domnall Bán ('the White', anglicized as Donald Bane), considered to represent the traditional Celtic order, and Duncan's half-brother Edmund, who was Margaret's son and thus represented the English influences at the Scottish court, was a very mixed combination indeed.

In truth these power-seekers were reacting as effectively as they could to the political vacuum created by the sudden departure of the dominant duo, and the alliances and murderous combinations were forged according to the immediate circumstances and opportunities which were under offer, not according to the set political agenda of those involved. It had probably always been thus, but whereas in the ninth and tenth centuries the Scandinavian element had been the most actively fermenting component in the north British melting-pot, it was the Anglo-Norman spice which added a rich and powerful element to the Scottish stew of the late eleventh century. As the representative of Anglo-Norman interests Duncan would be familiar with castles, knights, towns and silver coinage – the apparatus of Norman control and the means by which the conquerors of England maintained their power. The south-east was very soon going to enter this new world, opened up by Malcolm and Margaret. It would be surprising if some of these social and cultural features were not already beginning to make an appearance in Scotland as part of the turbulent events by which first Duncan and then his half-brother Edgar seized power with the military support of William Rufus.

The old order probably changed little in the north and west. In the last decade of the eleventh century another mobile Scandinavian – although now one who was king of all Norway – once more sought power and wealth in the islands and in Ireland. According to the *Orkneyinga Saga*, Magnus Barelegs (*Barfotr*) took over the whole of the Hebrides and was allowed to keep all the islands which he could sail around, while the Scandinavian settlements on the north and west seaboard were yielded to King Malcolm (or one of Malcolm's successors). Magnus was killed during a second expedition in 1103 in a skirmish in Ulster, which aptly symbolizes the end of Norse aspirations to control Celtic dominions in the old way. Scandinavian incursions had ceased in the rest of Scotland, and 'Scotland' is indeed the appropriate term to use of the kingdom about to be born. The medieval Scottish identity was fast taking shape, and even though the geographical limits had not been reached in every direction the territorial extent was recognized and attainable. The kingdom was defined, the unified kingship was in place and a single dynasty was able to exercise authority over the limbs, that astonishing cultural mix of languages and peoples who looked to it for protection and government. The unifying process would continue, and although the masking of the cultural diversity seems regrettable today, it was the fate of most minorities facing the realities of medieval power politics. The combined partnership of church and state created a medieval norm which emerging kingdoms had to adopt if they wished to be active participants in the new world order.

Bibliographical Essay

Strikingly, there is only one recent full history focused on this period, A. P. Smyth's *Warlords and Holy Men: Scotland AD 80–1000* (London, 1984; reprinted Edinburgh, 1989); despite the subtitle he has a stimulating discussion of the eleventh century. A. A. M. Duncan's still important work, *Scotland: The Making of the Kingdom* (Edinburgh, 1975), covers the period in some detail, and takes in the centuries after 1100 as well. The first volumes of the recently completed translation of Walter Bower's *Scotichronicon*, edited by D. E. R. Watt (Aberdeen, 1987–98), make this late medieval account accessible as a source for the early history of Scotland. A. O. Anderson's *Early Sources of Scottish History, AD 500 to 1286* (Edinburgh, 1922; revised edition by Paul Watkins, Stamford, 1990) remains the most valuable collection of sources in translation. The poetry of the period, which is sometimes an important historical source, has been published recently in translation: T. O. Clancy (ed.), *The Triumph Tree: Scotland's Earliest Poetry, AD 550–1350* (Edinburgh, 1998).

There are a number of picture-dominated introductions to the visible remains of the early Middle Ages. *Invaders of Scotland*, by A. Ritchie and D. Breeze (Edinburgh, 1991), provides a short archaeological overview, along with the much fuller study by L. and J. Laing, *The Picts and the Scots* (Stroud; first published 1993, but reissued in 1994 with some important corrections). For Scotland north of the Forth, the best overview is Sally M. Foster, *Picts, Gaels and Scots* (London, 1996; revised edition 1998). A political narrative of the period is offered by Benjamin T. Hudson, *Kings of Celtic Scotland* (Westport, Conn., 1994). The best introductions to the landscape and rural economy of early medieval Scotland remain those of G. W. S. Barrow, and can be found in the first chapter of his *Kingship and Unity: Scotland 1000–1306* (London, 1981), and in several important essays in his *Kingdom of the Scots* (London, 1973) and *Scotland and its Neighbours in the Middle Ages* (London, 1992). A good overview of the evidence for exchange on the western sea routes is Ewan Campbell, 'Trade in the Dark Age West: a peripheral activity?', in B. E. Crawford (ed.), *Scotland in Dark-Age Britain* (Aberdeen, 1996); that collection contains several other important essays on the period. The study of place-names continues to be vital to an understanding of language, history and society in early medieval Scotland. The best introduction is W. F. H. Nicolaisen, *Scottish Place-Names* (1976; 2nd edn., London, 1979), while for close discussion of many terms, the standard reference work is still W. J. Watson, *The History of the Celtic Place-Names of Scotland* (Edinburgh, 1926; reprinted 1993). He covers the early evidence for Celtic speech in northern Britain. An account of the earliest documented terms may be found in A. L. F. Rivet and C. Smith, *The Place-Names of Roman Britain* (London, 1979).

The nature of the Picts and their language was tackled many years ago in *The Problem of the Picts*, edited by F. T. Wainwright (Edinburgh, 1955), and some essays in that volume remain the starting-point for various contentious issues, particularly Kenneth H. Jackson's 'The Pictish Language'. This has been severely criticized recently on methodological grounds by Katherine S. Forsyth, *Language in Pictland* (Utrecht, 1997), where she comes to quite different conclusions. Forsyth's statement is now the prevailing view among many scholars of the period. Several good accounts of the Picts have been published recently, mostly by archaeologists: Anna Ritchie, *Picts* (HMSO: Edinburgh, 1989) and her Groam House Lecture, *Perceptions of the Picts: From Eumenius to John Buchan* (Rosemarkie, 1994); Sally M. Foster, *Picts, Gaels and Scots* (mentioned above), and the somewhat problematic *Surviving in Symbols: A Visit to the Pictish Nation* by Martin Carver (Edinburgh, 1999). None of these entirely supersedes the historical and artistic discussions in Isabel Henderson, *The Picts* (London, 1967), although aspects of that work are now dated. The matriliny question has been most thoroughly addressed by Alex Woolf, 'Pictish Matriliny Reconsidered', *Innes Review* 49 (1998), with a more straightforward discussion by Alasdair Ross, 'Pictish Matriliny', *Northern Studies* 34 (1999).

Leslie Alcock has been the chief essayist on northern British material culture, in *Arthur's Britain: History and Archaeology AD 367–634* (Harmondsworth, 1971), *Economy, Society and Warfare among the Britons and the Saxons* (Cardiff, 1987), and his Groam House Lecture, *The Neighbours of the Picts: Angles, Britons and Scots at War and at Home* (Rosemarkie, 1993). Buiston Crannog has now been examined in detail by Anne Crone, *The History of a Scottish Lowland Crannog: Excavations at Buiston, Ayrshire, 1989–90* (Edinburgh, 2000). The poetry remains an important and contentious source for this group: see T. Clancy, *The Triumph Tree*, mentioned above, and most recently J. T. Koch's controversial *The Gododdin of Aneirin: Text and Context from Dark-Age North Britain* (Cardiff, 1997). Alan Macquarrie's chapter, 'The Kings of Strathclyde, c. 400–1018', in A. Grant and K. J. Stringer (eds.), *Medieval Scotland: Crown, Lordship and Community* (Edinburgh, 1993), is a useful listing of the rarely documented kings. A recent good introduction to the Britons and the Anglian settlement in Northumbria can be found in C. Lowe, *Angels, Fools and Tyrants: The Britons and the Anglo-Saxons in Southern Scotland* (Edinburgh, 1999). Fuller studies of Northumbria can be found in D. P. Kirby, *The Earliest English Kings* (London, 1991); P. Hunter Blair, *Northumbria in the Days of Bede* (London, 1976); and more problematically in N. J. Higham, *The Kingdom of Northumbria, AD 350–1100* (Stroud, 1993). Northumbrian Galloway received its first detailed overview in Daphne Brooke, *Wild Men and Holy Places: St Ninian, Whithorn and the Medieval Realm of Galloway* (Edinburgh, 1994).

The Gaels have received recent and revisionist attention from Ewan Campbell in his excellent introductory study in 'The Making of Scotland' series, *Saints and Sea-Kings: the First Kingdom of the Scots* (Edinburgh, 1999). He takes issue with a number of points in what is still the most thorough treatment of the documentary evidence, John Bannerman's *Studies in the History of Dalriada* (Edinburgh, 1974). Foster, *Picts, Gaels and Scots*, mentioned above, is also an important recent account. Gaelic law, as represented chiefly by Irish texts, can be best explored through Fergus Kelly, *A Guide to Early Irish Law* (Dublin, 1988), while his *Early Irish Farming* (Dublin, 1998) is a masterly compendium of what we know through law texts and other sources about rural life in early medieval Ireland. T. M. Charles-Edwards's *Early Christian Ireland* (Cambridge, 2000) now provides a masterly survey with much direct commentary on Scotland. For western Scotland, the seven volumes of the Royal Commission for the Ancient and Historical Monuments of Scotland's inventory of Argyll are a superb guide to the remains and their historical contexts, while G. Ritchie (ed.), *The Archaeology of Argyll* (Edinburgh, 1997) provides an overview by various authors.

Most of the important sources for early Christianity in Scotland are available now in translation and in good editions. Bede, *Ecclesiastical History of the English People*, is in edition and translation by B. Colgrave and R. A. B. Mynors (Oxford, 1969), and in Penguin and Oxford Classics translations. Adomnán, *Life of St Columba* is also in full edition and translation by A. O. and M. O. Anderson (Edinburgh, 1961; revised by M. O. Anderson, Oxford, 1991), and in a stimulating and copiously annotated Penguin Classic, translated by Richard Sharpe (Harmondsworth, 1955). The early poetry relating to Iona and the early Columban monasteries is in translation in Clancy, *The Triumph Tree*, cited above, and with original text and extensive commentary in T. O. Clancy and G. Márkus, *Iona: The Earliest Poetry of a Celtic Monastery* (Edinburgh, 1995).

Iona and its early medieval legacy remain the most comprehensively studied aspect of the early medieval Scottish church. Máire Herbert's magisterial monograph, *Iona, Kells and Derry: The History and Hagiography of the Monastic Familia of Columba* (Oxford, 1988; reprinted Dublin, 1996) is now the essential historical introduction, but Anna Ritchie provides a more Scotland-focused overview in *Iona* (London, 1997). The archaeological and art historical material is best encountered in the Royal Commission's *Argyll*, vol. 4: *Iona* (Edinburgh, 1982). The 1997 centenary of Columba's death produced a wave of research, some of which may be read in the essays collected in Cormac Bourke (ed.), *Studies in the Cult of Saint Columba* (Dublin, 1997), and Dauvit Broun and T. O. Clancy (eds.), *Spes Scotorum – Hope of Scots: St Columba, Iona and Scotland* (Edinburgh, 1999). Whithorn's long-term excavations have come to published fruition in Peter Hill's important report, *St Ninian and Whithorn: The Archaeology of a Monastic Town* (Stroud, 1997), and though it sheds much light on the early periods of that site, the problems of St Ninian remain unsolved.

Alan Macquarrie's *The Saints of Scotland: Essays in Scottish Church History AD 450–1093* (Edinburgh, 1997) has intelligent discussion and wide coverage, but the post-700 period is still woefully lacking in published historical synthesis. Three important essays begin to point in the right direction: A. Macquarrie, 'Early Christian Religious Houses in Scotland: Foundation and Function', in J. Blair and R. Sharpe (eds.), *Pastoral Care before the Parish* (Leicester, 1992); Benjamin T. Hudson, 'Kings and Church in Early Scotland', *Scottish Historical Review* 73 (1994), 145–70; and Kenneth Veitch, 'The Columban Church in Northern Britain, 664–717: a reassessment', *Proceedings of the Society of Antiquaries of Scotland* 127 (1997), 627–47, though the latter two have factual and methodological flaws. Also of importance are several investigations into the church and early place-names by Simon Taylor, for which see his 'Place-names and the Early Church in Scotland', *Records of the Scottish Church History Society* 28 (1998), and the references there cited.

For the late eighth- and early ninth-century Pictish kings and their world, the most illuminating source is Sally M. Foster (ed.), *The St Andrews Sarcophagus: A Pictish Masterpiece and its International Connections* (Dublin, 1998), with an important essay on the kings by Dauvit Broun. Broun is also the prime essayist on the creation of the kingdom of Alba. An important paper, though not the most recent, is 'The Origin of Scottish Identity in its European Context', in B. Crawford (ed.), *Scotland in Dark-Age Europe* (St Andrews, 1994); a more recent view is in Broun and Clancy, *Spes Scotorum*, cited above. Máire Herbert provides important thoughts on this topic in Simon Taylor (ed.), *Kings, Clerics and Chronicles in Scotland, 500–1297* (Dublin, 2000), which includes other relevant essays. The main text for the period is by M. O. Anderson, *Kings and Kingship in Early Scotland* (revised edition, Edinburgh, 1980), and is translated by Ben Hudson as 'The Scottish Chronicle' in *Scottish Historical Review* 78 (1998), 129–61. For the kingdom of Cumbria in the same period, see the papers in A. Ritchie (ed.), *Govan and its Early Medieval Sculpture* (Stroud, 1994), and the recent work by Stephen T. Driscoll, 'Church Archaeology in Glasgow and the Kingdom of Strathclyde', *Innes Review* 49 (1998), 95–114. There are important reassessments in progress from T. O. Clancy and A. Woolf.

For Scotland in the Viking age there is a strong contrast between central Scotland and the Highlands (whose history is poorly recorded and where written sources are very thin on the ground), and the Northern and Western Isles, where archaeology provides another dimension, and the later Icelandic sagas also draw a vivid literary image of the life and deeds of the warrior earls and kings. Thus we have in the *Orkneyinga Saga* an account of the dynasty of earls in Orkney from the late ninth to the twelfth century which 'every Scottish historian regards with envy'. It is easily available in a good modern translation by H. Palsson and P. Edwards (Harmondsworth, 1978, and reprinted many times since), although there are also older versions with different introductions and notation. Older historical studies, such as J. Storer Clouston, *A*

History of Orkney (Kirkwall, 1932), used saga information as the basis for a historical narrative, but modern commentators are much less confident, and B. E. Crawford, *Scandinavian Scotland* (Leicester, 1987) and W. P. L. Thomson, *The History of Orkney* (Edinburgh, 1987) take a more critical approach. Crawford's book was the first multi-disciplinary study of the Vikings in Scotland, using archaeology and place-names in an assessment of the total impact of the Vikings on Scotland up to the mid-eleventh century. The volume of place-name studies, *Scandinavian Settlement in Northern Britain*, edited by B. E. Crawford (Leicester, 1995), brings together new work on this important resource, since W. F. H. Nicolaisen's pioneering article of 1969 ('Norse Settlement in the Northern and Western Isles'), which is reproduced in his *Scottish Place-Names* (1976).

Viking archaeology has been the foundation of one of the most popular historical developments of the twentieth century, and the Vikings in Scotland have been central to many general studies. Those which focus primarily on north Britain are Anna Ritchie's *Viking Scotland* in the 'Historic Scotland' series published by Batsford (London, 1993), the recent *Vikings in Scotland* by James Graham-Campbell and Colleen Batey (Edinburgh, 1998), and Olwyn Owen's *The Sea Road: A Viking Voyage Through Scotland* (Historic Scotland's new introductory series, 'The Making of Scotland', Edinburgh, 1999). More detailed studies of the Vikings in the Hebrides can be found in I. Armit, *The Archaeology of Skye and the Western Isles* (Edinburgh, 1997), and M. Brown, 'The Norse in Argyll', in G. Ritchie (ed.), *The Archaeology of Argyll* (Edinburgh, 1997).

Turning to historical developments in central Scotland from 800 to 1100, we are still reliant on the general histories already mentioned, and sometimes have to resort to the century-old volumes by W. F. Skene, *Celtic Scotland: An History of Ancient Alba* (3 vols., Edinburgh, 1886–90), and A. H. Dunbar's *Scottish Kings: A Revised Chronology of Scottish History, 1005–1625* (Edinburgh, 1899) for older views of the period. Benjamin Hudson's *Kings of Celtic Scotland* (1994), already mentioned, his pioneering study of *The Prophecy of Berchan: Irish and Scottish High-Kings of the Early Middle Ages* (London, 1996), and his translation of 'The Scottish Chronicle' mentioned above are helping to make this period more accessible. Histories of medieval Scotland usually open with a preliminary chapter on the eleventh century, such as B. Webster, *Medieval Scotland: The Making of an Identity* (Basingstoke, 1997), which has a particularly valuable discussion of different aspects of Scottish identity; and J. Roberts, *Lost Kingdoms: Celtic Scotland and the Middle Ages* (Edinburgh, 1997), which must be used carefully. More reliable are Broun's publications on the growth of the Scoto-Pictish kingdom and the genesis of Alba, some of which have already been referred to. In addition there are: 'The Origin of Scottish Identity', in C. Bjorn, A. Grant, and K. Stringer (eds.), *Nations, Nationalism and Patriotism in the European Past* (Copenhagen, 1994), 35–55; and 'Dunkeld and the Origin of Scottish Identity', *Innes Review* 48 (1997), 112–24 (reprinted in *Spes Scotorum*, mentioned above). Sally Foster's last chapter in *Picts, Gaels and Scots* (above) gives a useful overview, and she looks at the power centres of Alba in A. I. MacInnes (ed.), *Scottish Power Centres from Early Middle Ages to the Twentieth Century* (Glasgow, 1998). In the same volume S. Driscoll has a theoretical and stimulating chapter entitled 'Formalising the Mechanisms of State Power: Early Scottish Lordship from the Ninth to the Thirteenth Centuries'. This follows up his earlier 'The Archaeology of State Formation in Scotland', in W. S. Hanson and E. A. Slater (eds.), *Scottish Archaeology: New Perceptions* (Aberdeen, 1991), which focused on the significance of the early thanages, as had

G. W. S. Barrow, in *The Kingdom of the Scots* (London, 1973), in a chapter called 'Pre-feudal Shires and Thanes'; see also A. Grant, 'Thanes and Thanages, from the Eleventh to the Fourteenth Centuries', in Grant and Stringer, *Medieval Scotland: Crown, Lordship and Community* (above).

The most important eleventh-century royal personalities (from the number of works devoted to them) are Macbeth and St Margaret. Not all the studies are entirely historical: P. Berresford Ellis's *Macbeth: High King of Scotland, 1040–57 AD* (London, 1980) being less than historical. G. W. S. Barrow's study, 'Macbeth and the Other Mormaers of Moray', in L. Maclean (ed.), *The Hub of the Highlands: The Book of Inverness and District* (Edinburgh, 1975); N. Chadwick, 'The Story of Macbeth', *Scottish Gaelic Studies* 6 (1949); E. J. Cowan, 'The Historical Macbeth', in D. Sellar (ed.), *Moray: Province and People* (Edinburgh, 1993), are all valuable. Margaret has received either unsympathetic treatment at the hands of older historians, or laudatory assessments by generalists like Lucy Menzies in her *St Margaret, Queen of Scotland* (London, 1925). However, recent studies by L. Huneycutt, 'The Idea of the Perfect Princess: the *Life of St Margaret*', *Anglo-Norman Studies* 12 (1989); V. Wall, 'Queen Margaret of Scotland. Burying the Past, Enshrining the Future', in C. Duggan (ed.), *Queens and Queenship in Medieval Europe* (Woodbridge, 1997); and D. Baker, '"A Nursery of Saints": St Margaret of Scotland Reconsidered', in D. Baker (ed.), *Medieval Women* (Oxford, 1978), all present her and Turgot's *Life* in a more considered light. Benjamin Hudson helps to put the early eleventh-century Danish imperial impact on the Celtic world into clearer focus in two useful articles: 'Knútr and Viking Dublin', *Scandinavian Studies* 66 (1994), 319–35, and 'Cnut and the Scottish Kings', *English Historical Review* 107 (1992), 351–8.

Little of significance has been written about the eleventh-century kingdom otherwise, except on the dispute over the reliability of the early documentary sources, printed in A. C. Lawrie's *Early Scottish Charters prior to AD 1153* (Glasgow, 1905). A. A. M. Duncan first discussed them in *Scottish Historical Review* 37 (1958), and after an attack on their authenticity by J. Donnelly in the same journal in 1989, came back recently with a major examination and defence of their authenticity: 'Yes, The Earliest Scottish Charters', *Scottish Historical Review* 78 (1999). A new study of *St Cuthbert and the Normans* (Woodbridge, 1998) by W. Aird has a most useful analysis of Malcolm III's raids into Northumbria.

3

Medieval Scotland, 1100–1560

DAVID DITCHBURN
ALASTAIR J. MACDONALD

In the summer of 1328 the townspeople of Berwick were busily engaged in preparation for a wedding. It was to be a sumptuous and lively occasion: a churchyard wall was demolished by boisterous revellers and a poor woman from Musselburgh was knocked over as the groom's party returned from the festivities. The father of the groom, King Robert I of Scotland, had spent over £2,400 to furnish the guests with sufficient food, adequate (perhaps excessive) amounts of drink and new outfits. Whether the couple appreciated the efforts made on their behalf is less certain. David Bruce, the groom and Robert's heir, was four years old and Joan Plantagenet, the bride, and sister of King Edward III of England, was only seven. Moreover, political and family tensions somewhat spoiled the event. The wedding was intended to mark a conclusion to thirty-three years of intermittent warfare both among Scots and between Scots and English. It was a war from which the father of the groom had emerged victorious and it was as a token of Plantagenet defeat that Joan's mother, Isabella, had promised to return the Stone of Destiny to King Robert. With other sacred relics of Scottish kingship, it had been plundered by the bride's grandfather, Edward I, at the outset of his bloody but futile attempts to conquer Scotland from 1296. Unfortunately, Isabella's plans were thwarted when a London mob clamoured against the removal of Westminster's war trophies. Joan came without the stone. Moreover, although Isabella was accompanied by her lover, Roger Mortimer, she was without her son, Edward III. Edward refused to attend a wedding which, in English eyes, symbolized a shameful peace with Scotland. In a fit of pique the groom's father decided to absent himself too. It was put about that the one-time usurper and thug, but now respected and statesmanlike king, lay ill at Cardross on the Clyde. Within weeks, however, the old warrior had set sail for Ireland to accompany his young nephew, William de Burgh, to his earldom of Ulster.

The Medieval Economy

1. Population and Plague

At first sight the celebrations of 12 July 1328 were an extraordinary event. Few weddings were as politically symbolic as this one was intended to be; few festivities were as lavish; few couples married at such a tender age; and few women and men married in a town, for medieval Scotland was an overwhelmingly rural society. Berwick, indeed, was extraordinary even among towns. If comparing it, as one chronicler did, with the Egyptian city of Alexandria was ridiculous, it was still the largest and most prosperous Scottish town of the twelfth and thirteenth centuries. Berwick's size did not match that of Amiens or Arezzo, let alone Alexandria, and its population probably numbered a few thousands; but this was large when compared with Dunfermline, in size a far more typical Scottish town, which could boast few more than a thousand inhabitants by 1500. Admittedly, estimating the population of Scottish towns is largely guesswork. No statistics of the kind used by modern demographers survive to calculate the size of Berwick's, or indeed of Scotland's, population in the Middle Ages. There is, however, a consensus that in Europe as a whole population levels generally rose from about 1100 and that they fell substantially after *c.* 1300. In Scotland evidence of population growth in the earlier period (and, indeed, back into prehistory) is chiefly adduced from the expansion of cultivated land. Put simply, more farmed land was required to feed more mouths. As a consequence, agricultural settlement advanced up hillsides – in the Lammermuirs to altitudes never since achieved – while wastelands were ploughed and wooded areas were cleared. That was the intention behind Alexander II's grant, and many like it, of the otherwise unremarkable lands of Corncrain 'in the wasteland of our forest of Banff' to an obscure Roxburghshire knight in 1242: the recipient was to convert wasteland into farmland. Simultaneously there was an increase in the physical size of towns. Some new towns, such as the Newburghs in Aberdeenshire and Fife, were established on green-field sites and other towns expanded. Many of modern Scotland's best-known urban thoroughfares were established around this time to house a presumably growing population in towns. Aberdeen's Upperkirkgate, for instance, was laid out in the mid-twelfth century, as was Perth's High Street and probably also Dundee's Nethergate.

It seems likely that population levels reached a peak in Scotland, as elsewhere in Europe, towards the end of the thirteenth century. At that point there were perhaps a million inhabitants of the medieval kingdom. All but a few thousand of them were located in the countryside, rather than in the towns, and they were much more equally dispersed between Highland and Lowland regions than they are nowadays. From the end of the thirteenth century, population levels probably remained at best stable for about fifty years. Natural growth was negated by war casualties (during the fighting of 1296 to 1328, and in the renewed Anglo-Scottish and civil warfare of 1333 to 1346), and by what are likely to have been serious famines in the 1310s. Worse was to follow. In October 1347 a Genoese ship docked at faraway Messina in Sicily. Within weeks most of Sicily had been infected by plague and thousands were dead. The Black Death, as it became known from the sixteenth century, soon fanned out along Sicilian trade routes to most of western Europe. Carried in the bloodstream of black rats, and transmitted by the flea *Xenopsylla cheopsis*, bubonic plague reached Scotland by 1349. It is difficult nowadays to imagine the impact of this deadly, but to medieval people completely incomprehensible, disease. The late twentieth-century AIDS virus provides the closest modern parallel, though plague infected substantially more people throughout Europe than AIDS has yet done. The prospect of death loomed large for those who contracted plague. Bubonic plague killed between at least a half and two-thirds of those it infected, while the fatal impact of the pneumonic and septicaemic strains of plague was almost total. Plague also killed more quickly than AIDS. Those who contracted bubonic plague were usually dead within about five days. The pneumonic strain, which is passed from human to human by spitting, sneezing or coughing and the subsequent inhalation of infected dust particles, killed within about three days. Victims of the probably rare septicaemic variety, caused by intense infestation of the bloodstream by plague bacilli, were dead within hours.

The Black Death killed more people in Scotland than any other single occurrence in the country's recorded history probably before or certainly since. Yet precise quantification of its impact remains elusive. In Europe as a whole, despite the sometimes wildly excessive guesses made by chroniclers, it is now estimated that between a quarter and a third of the population died, though in some places mortality was higher, and in some lower. The late fourteenth-century Scottish chronicler John of Fordun guessed that 'nearly a third of mankind were thereby made to pay the debt of nature'. If Fordun too was exaggerating, the Scottish death toll in 1349–50 was perhaps closer to the lower European limit. Since bubonic plague generally thrives in warmer climes than those of Scotland, this seems feasible. Nevertheless, it would still mean that a pre-plague population of about a million had fallen to about 750,000 in the space of just a few months. A further outbreak of plague is recorded in 1362 and more were to follow, many of them in the winter months and probably therefore of the more deadly pneumonic variety. These later outbreaks were often localized, but at least one incidence of plague is recorded somewhere in Scotland in almost every decade between the 1370s and 1550s. Although these later outbreaks did not kill as many people as the first, their cumulative effect was to postpone the recovery in population levels.

In this, plague was aided and abetted by other deadly diseases. Tuberculosis and leprosy were ancient diseases. The latter was suggested by several foreign chroniclers as the cause of Robert I's death in 1329, though the word 'leprosy' was used by contemporaries to describe many different ailments. Dysentery was common enough to be advanced as an alternative explanation for the probable murder of David, Duke of Rothesay, heir to the Scottish crown, in 1402; and it is perhaps to be equated with the fatal outbreak of 'wame ill' recorded in 1439. 'Quhew', perhaps to be identified as whooping cough, is recorded in 1420; and 'grandgore' (almost certainly syphilis) arrived in Aberdeen in 1497, just two years after it was first recorded in Italy.

The effects of plague and other ailments on population levels were exacerbated by those of emigration. It is a fallacy to assume that the Scottish diaspora was a modern phenomenon first associated with either pioneers in colonial America or the victims of eighteenth-century Highland clearance. Thousands of Scots departed their homelands in the Middle Ages too, large numbers of them permanently. Many sought service as mercenaries, especially in Ireland from the thirteenth century, in France from the fifteenth century and in Scandinavia from the sixteenth century. From the later fifteenth century hundreds more headed both to England and to Poland, Prussia and Scandinavia, where the word 'Scot' was to become synonymous with pedlar. As with the victims of disease, it is impossible to be precise about the number of emigrants, but between 1419 and 1424 over 15,000 Scots were engaged in French military service alone – or about 2 per cent of the post-plague population. Although some women can be traced among the emigrants, more generally the greatest opportunities abroad were for men. The impact on domestic population levels of such a large exodus of men, when they might have been expected to be fathering children at home, was probably significant. It certainly did nothing to counteract demographic loss through disease; and it seems unlikely that Scottish population levels recovered their late thirteenth-century heights until well into the sixteenth century.

As population declined, the overall demand for food and goods obviously fell too, though probably not in direct correlation with population loss. Put crudely, the living inherited from the dead. As a result, the disposable income of many people is likely to have increased temporarily in the aftermath of a virulent outbreak of plague. Moreover, so great was population loss that it had a profound impact on both wages and prices. The specifics of this are masked by a rampant inflation which caused the abbot of Dunfermline to lament in 1409 that 'all things are dearer than they were in times past'. This, at least in part, was the consequence of a currency depreciation and the devaluation of the pound Scots; but although many prices were inflated, not all of them rose in real terms. Those of livestock and oats, for instance, remained comparatively depressed for much of the later Middle Ages, and the real price of rented land too appears to have fallen sharply soon after the first outbreak of plague. Moreover, although in Scotland the post-plague labour shortage is unlikely to have been as severe as it was, for instance, in Castile, wages probably rose as wage-earners discovered they could demand more for their labour. It was only with the 'price revolution' in the sixteenth century, when wages had probably stopped rising, that inflation began to work markedly against the interests of the poorest, landless sections of society. In the meantime, many husbandmen (the more prosperous among the peasantry) had been able to acquire larger parcels of land.

For landowners, on the other hand, the economic trends of the post-plague era were less favourable. Previously, with population levels high, peasant competition for land had been intense and labour was both plentiful and cheap. In these circumstances landlords had been able to drive hard deals with their social inferiors, and since leases were generally renewed annually, landlords had been able to strike these deals frequently. As the population declined, however, and labour became scarce, it was now landlords who competed with one another to find tenants and labourers. Initially, at least, they were forced to do this on an annual basis, by offering labourers higher and higher wages and tenants lower and lower rents – and sometimes longer leases too. The slump in many agricultural prices further diminished the income of landlords as their outlay in wages rose. This prompted many landlords to rent out what remained of their demesnes (those estates which they had had cultivated for their own needs) in order to avoid paying labour costs. But since rents were falling, this offered no real solution to landlords' problems, especially since a growing number of rents were paid in cash rather than in kind or labour services, which to some extent were inflation-proofed. By the later fifteenth and sixteenth centuries many landlords had resorted to feuing their lands, granting lifelong tenancies in return for substantial one-off payments. Between 1464 and 1514 the abbey of Coupar Angus had already leased most of its lands on a five-year basis; by 1539–60 life tenancies had become the norm on the monastery's estates.

Still, even before the intensification of feuing, all was not economic gloom for landlords. They could make ends meet at least partially through the acquisition of more land. Opportunities for such advancement came with the forfeiture of many aristocrats who had fought on the losing side in the early fourteenth-century wars discussed later in this chapter, just before the advent of plague. In this the Stewarts and Douglases were notable winners, both families acquiring extensive estates in the south-west, the Borders and elsewhere. But even a lesser man, such as the Berwickshire knight Adam Gordon, could find his political loyalty rewarded with the grant of extensive Aberdeenshire estates, in Strathbogie. Another means of shoring up incomes was to obtain supplementary revenues from the church. That Alexander Bur, bishop of Moray from 1362 to 1397, encountered difficulty in the payment of taxes which he owed to the papacy was partly because much of his traditional ecclesiastical revenue had been siphoned off by greedy, but probably in their own eyes needy, local barons. Crown revenues were an equally attractive honey-pot for aristocratic appropriation. Between 1412 and 1422 the Earl of Mar received the enormous sum of £4,238 from the crown, most of it in the form of pensions and annuities granted for no specific purpose – this, we may note, at a time when a highly skilled carpenter or mason earned perhaps £10 a

1. (*left*) This richly decorated silver-gilt brooch with amber settings, found at Hunterston in Ayrshire, is an outstanding example of sophisticated Early Christian craftsmanship *c.* AD 700. On the back, a later owner of the brooch, at some time in the tenth century, reinforced his pride of ownership by scratching 'Melbrigda owns this brooch' in runic graffiti.

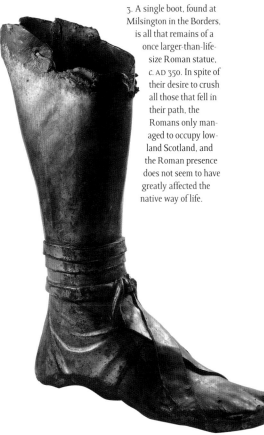

3. A single boot, found at Milsington in the Borders, is all that remains of a once larger-than-life-size Roman statue, *c.* AD 350. In spite of their desire to crush all those that fell in their path, the Romans only managed to occupy lowland Scotland, and the Roman presence does not seem to have greatly affected the native way of life.

2. (*left*) Examples of regalia made for clan chieftains, dating from the third millennium BC to the seventh century AD. Designed to impress the bearer's opponents and underlings with fine craftsmanship and conspicuous use of precious metals, the manufacture of such objects was carefully controlled by those in power.

Power, Authority and Status

4. Belt pistol, 1645, used in Scotland in a period that witnessed a number of atrocities sanctioned by the State, the most notorious being the massacre at Glencoe in 1692.

Sacred Symbols and Messages

1. (*left*) This enigmatic female figure carved from oak with quartzite pebbles for eyes was found buried in a peat bog at Ballachulish in Inverness-shire. Dating from between 730 and 520 BC, it is thought to show a goddess. The incised right hand of the figure holds a phallic object that suggests she may have played a part in a Bronze Age fertility rite. Her state of preservation when first found implies she was deliberately buried during the ritual.

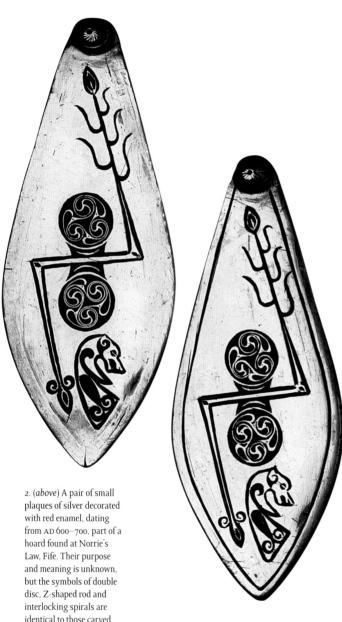

2. (*above*) A pair of small plaques of silver decorated with red enamel, dating from AD 600–700, part of a hoard found at Norrie's Law, Fife. Their purpose and meaning is unknown, but the symbols of double disc, Z-shaped rod and interlocking spirals are identical to those carved into stones and monuments by Pictish peoples.

3. (*left*) An illumination from 'The Forman Armorial', a late sixteenth century manuscript of heraldic drawings, portraying Mary, Queen of Scots and the Dauphin François of France, who married in 1558. Mary bears the arms of Scotland on her skirt and holds a thistle in her hand.

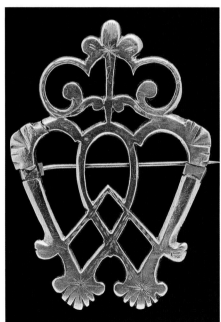

4. A typical 'Luckenbooth' brooch, a centuries-old love token still sold in Scotland today. The brooches take their name from the locked booths of the medieval jewellers who made them on Edinburgh's Royal Mile. The symbol of interlocking hearts was also used as an amulet to fasten the christening shawl of a first baby.

5. Oak figure, *c.* 1500, depicting St Andrew, the patron saint of Scotland, whose cross forms the saltire of the national flag. By the ninth century the cult of St Andrew had joined that of the missionary St Columba as an influential force in Scotland. The belief was that the relics of the apostle had been brought by St Rule to the place now known as St Andrews in Fife.

The ballade of ane right noble victorius & mychty lord Barnard steWart lord of Aubigny erle of Beaumont roger and bonaffre consaloure and chamlane ordinare to the maist hee maist excellēt & maist cryftyn prince Loys king of france knyght of his ordoure Capitane of the kepyng of his body Cōquereur of Naplis and vmquhile cōstable general of the fame Compilit be Maiftir Willyam dumbar at the faid lordis cũyng to Edinburghe in Scotland fend in ane ryght excellēt emballat fra the faid maist cryftin king to our maist Souuerane lord and victorius prince James the ferde kyng of Scottis.

+ Walterus + chepman +

1. (*left*) A page from one of the earliest known Scottish printed books, from the press of Andrew Myllar and Walter Chepman, who received a royal patent from James IV in 1507. Though most books of the period are in Latin, the poem that appears on this page, above Chepman's initials, is that of a Scottish poet, William Dunbar, and is written in the native vernacular.

Scotland's Voice

2. (*right*) The Lamont harp, or *clarsach, c.* 1500, used to accompany the songs and tales of Scotland's bards, whose continuance of the Celtic oral tradition kept the histories of Gaelic ancestors, chieftains and clans alive in the Highlands and Islands. Enthusiasm for Gaelic culture spread nationally as the Renaissance took hold.

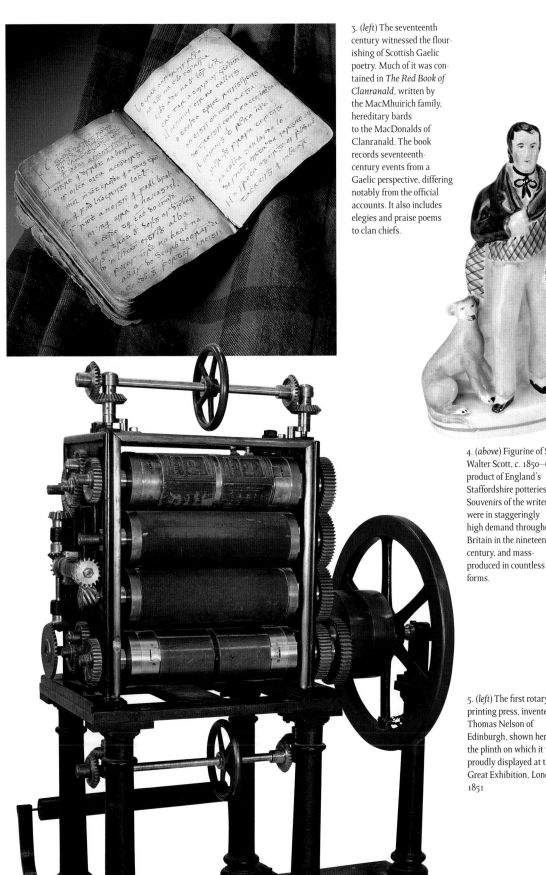

3. (*left*) The seventeenth century witnessed the flourishing of Scottish Gaelic poetry. Much of it was contained in *The Red Book of Clanranald*, written by the MacMhuirich family, hereditary bards to the MacDonalds of Clanranald. The book records seventeenth-century events from a Gaelic perspective, differing notably from the official accounts. It also includes elegies and praise poems to clan chiefs.

4. (*above*) Figurine of Sir Walter Scott, *c.* 1850–60, product of England's Staffordshire potteries. Souvenirs of the writer were in staggeringly high demand throughout Britain in the nineteenth century, and mass-produced in countless forms.

5. (*left*) The first rotary printing press, invented by Thomas Nelson of Edinburgh, shown here on the plinth on which it was proudly displayed at the Great Exhibition, London, 1851

Spinning and Weaving

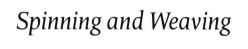

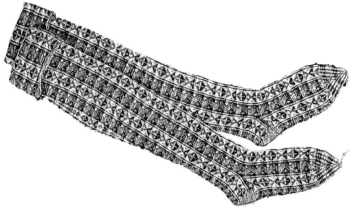

2. Edwardian mahogany spinning wheel inlaid with ivory, similar to a model shown at the Glasgow Exhibition in 1911. For many centuries, the tasks of spinning and weaving came second only to food production in importance for most Scots. By the end of the eighteenth century, women using the two-handed spinning-wheels could make 8 pence a day, more than they could in agricultural work

1.(*above, left and below*) Just two examples of distinctive Scottish textiles which remain popular throughout the world: paisley, an imitation Indian print which took its name from the town where it was originally produced; and Fair Isle hand-knitting from Shetland, the manufacture of which survived commercially long after machine-knitting had become commonplace.

3. Medieval tools used for preparing flax, the raw material for linen. Scotland's long-established linen industry reached its height in the late eighteenth century.

4. (*right*) Grave goods from a ninth-century AD boat burial, Scar, Orkney, deemed essential equipment for a Viking woman in the after-life. Among them are a whalebone plaque possibly used for smoothing linen, a spindle-whorl, shears, and a small spear, all used in weaving textiles.

5. (*below*) Flat-irons, standard household equipment of the nineteenth century. By this time, cotton was the dominant product of Scotland's textile industry, and the laundry maid or housewife had to wage a daily war against creasing. They were used in pairs: one would be heating on the fire or stove while the other was in use.

Tartan

1. (*below*) A late eighteenth century figure of a kilted Highlander with his powder horn, used to advertise tobacco. With the expansion of Glasgow's tobacco trade, the figure became fixed in the imaginations of non-Scots as the archetypal image of the Highlander.

2. Flamboyant uniform of the Royal Company of Archers, dating from 1713. Tartan clothing was fashionable at the time as an expression of anti-Union and pro-Jacobite sentiment, and many of the Company were known Jacobites. In 1747 the wearing of Highland dress was even temporarily outlawed by Parliament. But after George IV's state visit to Scotland in 1822, the once-inflammatory plaid ironically became a fashion cult among the British royal family.

3. A portrait of Baron Sirdar Iqbal Singh, the current Laird of Lesmahagow, by the artists Amrit and Rabindra Kaur Singh, 2000. The painting celebrates his commissioning of the first officially registered tartan for Scotland's prominent Asian community – the Singh tartan. The Scottish Tartan Society's register of at least 2,500 known tartan designs increases by 35 to 40 each year.

year. Moreover, when economic trends were at their worst for aristocrats in the later fourteenth and early fifteenth centuries, Mar and many others received further rewards from French kings and Burgundian dukes in return for military service or vaguer promises of political loyalty. The aristocracy found means of riding the economic storm.

2. *Feast and Famine*

Broadly speaking, although overall demand for food and goods fell as population levels dropped in the later medieval period, *per capita* expenditure remained rather more buoyant – even, as we have seen, among the aristocracy. So, on what did people spend their money? Many husbandmen and townsmen invested much of their surplus capital in land and, like the aristocracy, probably in better housing too. In all households, however, the most essential item of routine expenditure was food. The demand for particular types of food was a complicated business, determined at least in theory as much by religious considerations as it was by matters of taste. To see how this affected specific consumption habits, let us return to the royal wedding celebrations of 12 July 1328. It was a Tuesday, and in preparing the matrimonial menu King Robert had purchased copious supplies of wine, along with almonds, rice, sugar, an array of exotic spices (including cinnamon, cumin, galingale, ginger, mace, nutmeg, pepper, saffron and spikenard), vinegar, verjuice, olive oil, honey and white peas. All of this came from the Netherlands. More came from Scottish producers: malt, barley and oats (which were probably used by the cooks to prepare ale and bread), along with the carcasses of 171 cattle and 473 sheep; and there was fish too: foreign eels, along with porpoise and sturgeon.

This provides us with an indication of what the crown expected of a good medieval party. Yet, had the festivities been held on a Wednesday, a Friday, or a Saturday, or in Lent, the menu should have been different. On these days all but the most disadvantaged were expected to abstain from the consumption of meat and dairy produce. The rationale was simple. When God discovered that Adam had been tempted by the pleasures of Eve's flesh, he had retorted 'cursed is the ground for thy sake'. Accordingly everything that walked on land – both man and beast – was deemed inherently sinful. This was an intensely religious society. When the religious calendar dictated that sin ought to figure prominently in human thoughts – on Wednesdays (since Judas Iscariot had accepted his thirty pieces of silver to betray Christ on a Wednesday), Fridays (in memory of Christ's crucifixion) and Saturdays (in commemoration of the Virgin Mary) – meat, dairy produce and, for that matter, sex, were supposedly abandoned. Fish remained acceptable, for by living in water fish had both escaped God's wrath and succeeded in associating themselves with Christianity's most potent symbol of purification, water.

The devout genuinely attempted to conform to this dietary regime and those of elevated social status who could not, or would not, do so sought personal permission from the pope to disregard the conventions. In 1379, and in anticipation of her death, the Countess of Douglas petitioned Christ's vicar in Rome to be allowed meat on days when it was restricted, while in 1381 the bishop of St Andrews 'on account of his advanced age' received papal permission to eat eggs and milk in Lent and to commute his normal Wednesday abstinence to some other act of piety. Religion, however, was not the only determinant of diet. At least for the aristocratic members of society, taste also mattered. The medieval Scottish aristocracy was established from the fusion of indigenous stock with immigrants originally of French descent who had settled in Scotland from early in the twelfth century. In the wake of their arrival, native tastes were gradually melded with a palate formulated in northern France and born of French agricultural circumstances – a palate introduced not just into Scotland but across much of northern Europe too. Aristocratic cuisine was thus an international cuisine. Indeed, the menu served up at Berwick in 1328 would not have seemed strange had it been served up anywhere from the Baltic to the Bay of Biscay. Moreover, what was fitting fare for aristocrats became a fashionable diet to which other social groups might also aspire.

These broad outlines of dietary requirements determined what actually appeared on people's plates. 'Fish days' constituted roughly half the year and on these days there were few taboos regarding the type of fish which was deemed suitable for consumption. At the monastery of Whithorn, for instance, archaeological evidence points to the consumption of cod, conger eels, flatfish (probably plaice), herring, ling, ray, salmon, shark and wrasse. On meat-eating days preferences were equally liberal: beef and veal, mutton and lamb, pork, poultry and rabbit were all commonly consumed in Scotland, as they were elsewhere in the wider world of French cultural dominance. Game (both venison and birds such as partridge, pheasant and swan) were even more highly prized, though less frequently devoured. The slaughter of deer, unlike that of sheep or cattle, was an aristocratic leisure pursuit, often accompanied by lavish ceremony, and this, coupled with the enclosure of deer in forest land which was subject to special regulation, ensured that game was symbolically and physically detached from the rest of society – though no doubt some was poached. On the other hand, taboos against the consumption of horsemeat, cat or dog flesh were as widespread among all sections of medieval society as they are nowadays. In 1310, according to one chronicler, severe dearth led many to feed 'on the flesh of horses and other unclean animals'. When such creatures were consumed, it was in desperation.

Fish and meat were ideally accompanied by a combination of grain and grape-based products. For aristocrats generally, bread was best eaten white and wheaten, and it was in somewhat defensive tones that the scholar John Major admitted in 1521 that he would rather eat oaten bread than that of wheat or barley. Major was probably somewhat unusual among those of his social standing. The wealthier members of society tended to leave oatmeal for their horses, while bread made from rye was more fitting for charitable distribution than it was for aristocratic dining-tables. At a lower social level oat-based products (bread, cakes and gruel) were the normal fare. If not served with water, they were usually accompanied by ale, made from either malten oats or barley. While ale was also consumed by the aristocracy, the wealthier sections of society could afford to vary their drinking preferences. Wine was popular throughout the period. Although probably drunk daily only by the wealthy, it might be consumed by anyone in the taverns, which were apparently open for business even in rural areas by the early thirteenth century. It seems unlikely that these establishments relied only upon the occasional custom of the solitary local knight. From the fifteenth century muscadet and sweet wines, such as osay and malmsey, began to make inroads into the wine market, though without challenging the predominance of traditional reds and whites, mainly from Gascony and the Rhineland. Beer, too, with its aromatic flavour of hops, found increasing popularity from much the same period, though whisky is first recorded in royal accounts only towards the end of the fifteenth century. Even then it seems to have been consumed rarely at court, though it was perhaps already a favoured lower-class drink, as it remained until the nineteenth century. There was certainly no place for it amid the alcoholic Christmas festivities mounted by the urban élite of Dunfermline in 1503, who spent 61 per cent of their budget on beer, 29 per cent on wine, 6 per cent on ale and the minimal remainder on bread and coal. On this occasion the amount spent on beer is striking; but in early sixteenth-century Ayr and elsewhere wine remained the favoured drink for entertaining anyone of note who visited the town, be they great earls and archbishops or the 'Egyptians' (gypsies) who danced before the town's bailies (magistrates) in 1540–41.

Fish, meat, grain and, for some at least, wine and beer were the staples of diet. The environment was better suited to supply some of these religiously and culturally determined preferences than others. In most years fish and meat were readily available. The wealthy possessed their own fish stocks – the monks of Dunfermline abbey maintained a fishpond in their gardens and in 1504 James IV had the moat at Stirling castle stocked with pike – but 'even the common people', noted the future Pope Pius II after a visit to Scotland in 1435, 'eat flesh and fish to repletion'. His comments were indicative of a healthy fishing industry; and of an agriculture which was based largely on animal husbandry and in which (though the balance between the two varied) sheep and cattle predominated. That was probably the case throughout the period, and in almost all regions. If anything, the proportion of livestock farming increased from the later fourteenth century after the catastrophic population losses caused by plague. Animals required less human attention than crops and in the wake of depopulation much arable land reverted to pasture – for instance on the high peaks surrounding the Bowmont valley in the Cheviots. In the south especially there was a further inducement towards pastoral farming, in the shape of warfare. That the Gallovidian peasantry moved cattle and sheep into Inglewood forest in 1307 is a reminder that animals could be moved more swiftly than crops out of the path of hostile, hungry armies. This combination of demographic and political factors not only encouraged animal husbandry, as opposed to arable cultivation, it also ensured that later medieval cattle prices were comparatively low. There was often a glut of fresh beef after Martinmas (11 November), when many animals were slaughtered in order to avoid providing them with winter fodder. Yet preserved, salted beef was not markedly more expensive than fresh meat and so for much of the year beef was even within the budget of some poorer households. Fish too was dried, smoked or salted for consumption out of season. The significance of salt in such culinary preparation is self-evident, for while spices were merely an adornment to taste, salt was an essential preservative.

The importance of animals in medieval agriculture had other dietary spin-offs. Dairy products – milk, eggs, cheese and butter – were comparatively abundant too, though they do not seem to have been regarded as essential components of diet. Fruit and vegetables also provided an addition to the staples. Indeed, berries were so plentiful, according to Don Pedro de Ayala, the Spanish ambassador to Scotland in 1498, that Scots did not know what to do with them; the frequent deposit of their seeds in cesspits suggests otherwise. Evidence of apple, pear and plum orchards is more limited. Some were located in monastic gardens, but secular landlords too planted orchards. That established by James IV at Stirling between 1501 and 1504 was furnished with 1,500 plum trees bought from Culross abbey; and he acquired other fruit trees from the monasteries of Coupar Angus and Lindores, and from the carse of Gowrie. The extent of this plantation notwithstanding, it remains doubtful whether fruit constituted an essential component of aristocratic diet; indeed, it was still something of a luxury in eighteenth-century Edinburgh. Although onion and cabbage were planted in the royal garden in Stirling, and peas and beans elsewhere, the same was probably true of vegetables in the Middle Ages.

If, in its supply of meat, fish and dairy produce, Scotland was normally well provisioned, it was less well equipped to furnish at least aristocratic society with its other esteemed articles. Scotland lay well to the north of viticulture limits, so wine was imported. So was beer, since hops were not widely grown, and so too were considerable quantities of malt (the key ingredient of ale), even though malt was also produced throughout Scotland. Although oats and the hardy variety of barley known as bere thrived in the dreich Scottish environment, climate and soil quality were less favourable for the cultivation of wheat. This was especially the case in the north and the west, and is reflected both in the paucity of wheat remains found by archaeologists at the monastery of Whithorn and in the comparatively high price which wheat fetched in Galloway. Further east, from Orkney to Berwickshire, wheat cultivation was more common, especially perhaps in the north-east, where later medieval wheat prices were generally lower than those elsewhere. In the east, wheat yields were generally as good as those expected in France: a fourfold return on each seed sown was apparently the norm. This was higher than the anticipated yield for oats (which was normally 3:1), though largely because wheat was grown on better land than oats. It would be misleading, however, to assume that even in the east most land was well suited to wheat cultivation. Though yields were as good as those abroad, later medieval Scottish prices were generally higher than those in countries such as Poland. This suggests that supply did not match demand, and it is not difficult to guess why. The onset of climatic deterioration after about 1300 made wheat cultivation even more difficult. The demographic factors and military conflict which encouraged a transfer from arable to pastoral farming were correspondingly detrimental to the interests of the wheat-eating population. Wheat continued to be grown, but by 1457 the paucity of its cultivation had led parliament (in other words, the wheat-eating aristocracy) to decree that each man with eight oxen (in other words, the non-wheat-eating peasantry) should plough one firlot of wheat, probably equating to 19,776.82 cm^3. It would seem that the aristocracy was attempting to skew arable cultivation as much as was environmentally possible in order to satisfy its desire for wheat.

For all sections of society the undistinguished status of fruit and vegetables might have made for a deficiency in vitamin C. A similar disregard for dairy products can make for deficiencies in vitamins A and D. On the other hand, skeletal remains from around the country provide only limited indication of diseases such as scurvy (caused by a lack of vitamin C) or rickets (caused by a lack of vitamin D), though there may be some bias in favour of the better-off among those bodies which have been excavated. Even if not greatly esteemed, it would seem that fruit, vegetables and dairy produce were generally consumed in adequate quantities, though additional supplies of vitamin D may have come from fatty fish or offal. The most common possibly nutritional ailment evident in excavated bodies is iron deficiency, which may reflect prolonged breast-feeding or the high fish content of diet. More positively, both rich and poor obtained protein and calories from a diet rich in fish and meat, while grain products (especially oats) provided fibre. All in all, by the standards of other medieval countries (though not by those of today) this was a comparatively healthy diet. Indeed, the greater significance of offal and oat-based products in the diet of the poor arguably provided them with a more balanced diet than that of an aristocracy encumbered with wheaten preferences. Yet such dietary advantage as the poorer sections of society may have enjoyed was dependent on an adequate supply of food; there was no such guarantee.

The food chain was liable to disruption by adverse weather conditions, by disease of crops and animals, and through man-made hazards such as warfare and fire. In recent climatological studies it has been argued that from about 1100 until the early fourteenth century northern Europe enjoyed a period of comparatively mild weather conditions. The Scottish evidence, limited though it is, would appear to confirm this. Walter Bower, writing in the mid-fifteenth century — a late and not necessarily reliable source —

recorded crop failures only in 1196, 1205, 1209, the early 1260s (which conforms broadly with similar conditions then prevalent in Ireland), 1272 (perhaps a mistake for 1271, when poor harvests are recorded in both England and Ireland), and in 1293 (which is again in accordance with the fuller Irish evidence).

From the fourteenth century, however, climatologists suggest that average temperatures declined. The change was not dramatic: average summer temperatures dropped by perhaps only 1°C. But in marginal farming areas this, and slightly greater rainfall, resulted in a crucial shortening of the growing season and a greater chance of crop failure – from perhaps one year in twenty in the thirteenth century to one year in five by the fifteenth century. Again, the patchy and not necessarily reliable Scottish evidence tends to support the evidence of less propitious climatic conditions from the fourteenth century. Individual years of localized harvest mishap (such as those recorded in Lothian in 1358 and in the Borders in 1435) were augmented by more general shortages in, for instance, 1337, 1438, the early 1450s, and 1550). In addition there were (probably) two cumulative harvest failures in the early fourteenth century. The first of these was between 1308 and 1310. Bower ascribed this to the effects of war, which is possible, but the fuller evidence for Ireland suggests that there, at least, there was a climatically induced famine in 1310 and that it came on the back of poor harvests in 1308 and 1309. In Ireland this was the first cumulative disaster since the 1220s, but it was soon followed by another between 1315 and 1318 which affected not only Ireland, but the whole of north-western Europe. This, moreover, was one of the most extreme famines ever known in Europe, before or since. While there is little scientific or documentary evidence to illustrate the impact of this famine on Scotland, it would be unwise to conclude that Scotland escaped what neighbouring countries undoubtedly endured. It is perhaps telling that raids for 'goods and chattels' were mounted on Anglesey and Ireland in 1315 and that English officials at Berwick reported 'many dying from hunger' in 1315, and again in 1316. In the latter year the town's English garrison mounted a foray in search of food: in their quest for sustenance they foraged as far as Melrose, some 40 kilometres away.

Climatic mishaps, which could affect both crops and animals, were compounded by the impact of disease among livestock. Again, the evidence for this is patchy. Bower recorded, but left unexplained, the death of many animals in 1272. Cattle, deer and above all sheep had also perished in 1268 and great numbers of poultry were to succumb to an unidentified disease in 1344. At the turn of the thirteenth and fourteenth centuries there is more specific evidence of sheep scab ('pluk'), which prompted governmental instructions for the cull of infected animals and restrictions on their movements, though localized outbreaks recurred, on Deeside for instance in 1328. Given the significance of livestock farming, the impact of such loss was cruel. In 1272, according to Bower, 'the poor died of their poverty'. Moreover, the natural catastrophes of the later thirteenth and early fourteenth centuries were made worse by the effects of warfare, even in the north. According to John of Fordun, the civil and Anglo-Scottish warfare of 1337 left much of Gowrie, Angus and the Mearns 'reduced to a hopeless wilderness and to utter want'.

It was much more difficult for medieval society to overcome short-term catastrophes in the food cycle than it is for modern western societies, especially when short-term climatic fluctuation, disease and warfare were compounded to make for a prolonged shortfall in production, as they did especially between the 1290s and 1310s. A proportion of the meagre crop yields was required for sowing the following season, so crop loss had implications not just for one year's dining-tables, but also for those of the following year. One locality's shortfalls were not readily compensated for by another's surpluses because of the rudimentary transport infrastructure. Shortages pushed prices up, and this too affected the poor disproportionately.

Thus, despite the theoretically healthy diet of the Scottish population, even short-term disruptions in the food chain made for periodic malnutrition. This was probably one important factor in explaining why the average adult height was apparently lower than nowadays: in excavations of monastic burial-grounds in Aberdeen, Linlithgow and Whithorn the average height of medieval men was found to be about 169 centimetres. That compares with 173 centimetres nowadays. Female height was about 156 centimetres at Linlithgow and Whithorn, and 158 at Aberdeen, where greater consumption of fish perhaps led to a more protein-rich diet. Even in Aberdeen, however, female stature was still slightly short of the modern norm of 160 centimetres. And it must be borne in mind that skeletons buried on urban or monastic land are unlikely to be truly representative of those which belonged to the great majority of the population, the rural poor.

3. Craft and Commerce

Women and men did not, of course, live by bread alone. They required clothes and they desired other artefacts and possessions to enliven and facilitate their lifestyles. As with food, we may presume that the crown set the domestic benchmark of fashionable clothing and manufactures and, since its budget was the largest of any single household, it was more able than most to indulge its modish fads. Certainly, a good proportion of the sums forked out by Robert I for the wedding festivities of 1328 went on clothing. Knights received new uniforms made from both striped and coloured cloth purchased in Flanders, while cheaper continental cuts were obtained to dress the squires and crown officers, along with surcoats and caps, some made from budge (a dressed lambskin), and others from squirrel fur. What these actually looked like remains unknown, but artistic representations of Scottish clothing generally portray few striking differences from wider norms evident in north-western Europe. Likewise, foreign visitors had little to say about the Scottish dress they encountered, save for commenting on the striking headdress of women. There may have been some grounds for these observations, for in

1458 parliament demanded that burgess wives conform to the headdress worn in Flanders and other countries.

More unusual attire was probably to be found in the Highlands. One Picard chronicler noted that some of those on their way to the First Crusade of 1096 – probably Highlanders – bore 'bare legs and shaggy cloaks [and] a purse hanging from their shoulders', while in the twelfth century a Cambrai monk recalled how many Scots wore no drawers, but covered themselves with garments which were left open underneath and at the sides. In this they were not entirely unique: the lack of underclothing worn by Cistercian monks (in their case as a mark of asceticism) was to provide a perennial source of humour to others. Social as well as regional distinctions were marked by clothing. This was true especially when men were decked out for war, since the richest were better armed and accompanied by a horse, which socially and physically elevated them above the common foot soldier. But with more money in their pockets in the later Middle Ages, the more affluent townspeople, and perhaps the upper echelons of the peasantry, could afford to buy better clothes. This was a matter of some concern to the aristocracy, which, through parliamentary edicts of the fifteenth century, sought to preserve the distinctiveness of its rank by curtailing what others might wear. In 1471, for instance, it was ordained that only minstrels, heralds, knights and the wealthy might wear gowns and cloaks made of that ultimate in luxury cloths, silk – though how, and how frequently, such sumptuary measures were policed remains uncertain.

Silk was to clothing as wheat and wine were to food consumption, and it too was imported from abroad. More commonly, clothing was made of locally available products. Linen, for instance, was made from flax. Although this industry is poorly documented and archaeologically almost invisible, some of its tools, such as the flax-breaking mallet discovered at Perth, have survived, along with evidence of exported linen. The latter demonstrates that it was clearly an important industry. More clothing was made from animal products such as wool and hides. Before wool emerged as woollen cloth and animal skins as leather, they both went through several specialized stages of production. Clipped wool had to be combed or carded before being spun, a process which was increasingly undertaken on the thirteenth-century invention of the spinning-wheel. After spinning it was woven (by 'websters') and then fulled with 'fullers' earth' (by 'waulkers'). The waulker then pounded the cloth, often with bare feet or in one of the fulling mills which are recorded from the second half of the thirteenth century. This thickened the cloth before it was passed on for finishing. Once shorn of bobbles, it might then be sent to a dyer, whence it progressed further to tailors, bonnet-makers, glovers or merchants. Similar specialization is evident in the process by which the remnants of cattle and other animals were processed into items of leather clothing such as jackets, leggings, belts and footwear. Fleshers and tanners turned carcasses into leather which was passed on to cordwainers and other leather-workers for finishing and then transformation into shoes and other goods.

Tanning was a particularly unpleasant task which involved steeping unprocessed animal hides in a chemical solution usually made of tannin, a product of oak bark. The lengthy process produced an offensive aroma and noxious effluent, which explains why tanneries in Aberdeen, Inverness, Linlithgow and elsewhere were located close to a supply of water and on the outskirts of the built environment. Tanning was a necessary process in leather production, but in remote rural areas some of the other tasks associated with both wool and leather production, especially finishing, dying and retailing, might not have been undertaken at all. Other activities would have been staged either within the family or perhaps collectively by village communities – and probably on a part-time basis. In towns, where the more concentrated urban market was swelled by rural visitors, the volume of production was greater. This made full-time craftwork feasible. It also permitted greater occupational specialization, particularly in the textile industry, and the more highly skilled textile workers proved adept at protecting their status and income by excluding others from such work. Dyers, for instance, made use of local dyestuffs, such as weld, heather or even onion; but the brightest blues, reds and yellows were derived from imported mordants such as woad, madder and saffron. These were expensive materials, so dyers required capital; and by the early thirteenth century Perth's dyers had protected their investment effectively by prohibiting the inhabitants of the town's extensive hinterland from dyeing cloth. Yet, even with such restrictions, the dyers' position was not secure: for the wedding festivities of 1328 the crown had bestowed its patronage not on Perth's dyers, but on those of Flanders and the merchants who fetched their cloth from abroad.

Other industrial workers faced similar overseas competition. This was less of a problem for those who made perishable goods or for those who worked with locally acquired plant and animal remains, such as bakers, brewers or fleshers. Indeed, an industrial use was found for virtually every bit of a carcass. Meat and skins aside, bones were turned into knife handles, combs, dice and even ice skates; and tallow into soap and candles – the most common source of artificial lighting for housing. Construction workers were somewhat more reliant on foreign imports, especially towards the end of the period. Stone was locally quarried for the construction of castles, churches and other public buildings, though houses made of stone were only for the privileged few. Most houses were timber constructions, usually made from wooden posts intertwined with wattle, and daubed with clay, mud or turf to provide insulation and structural solidity. They were simple affairs, with a natural lifespan of perhaps at best twenty-five years, and were easily reconstructed with minimal skill. According to the fourteenth-century Netherlandish chronicler Jean Froissart, the Scots made light of their destruction, saying that 'with six or eight stakes they would soon have new houses'. When, due to weathering, warfare or fire (a perennial urban hazard), reconstruction proved necessary, the biggest problem may well have been the acquisition of timber.

Demand for wood was high, and not just for building houses or ships. Carpenters needed timber to make furniture, coopers needed it to make barrels, wheelwrights needed it to make that most vital of ancient inventions, the wheel, and it was also used as fuel. Particularly in the vicinity of large consumers, local supplies were quickly exhausted. As early as the thirteenth century the monks of Lindores in Fife sought timber supplies from as far away as Glen Errocht in Perthshire. This gives some credence to Robert Lindsay of Pitscottie's sixteenth-century remark that, once James IV had felled all the trees required for constructing the 'Michael', 'the greattest scheip that ever saillit in Ingland or France', all the woods of Fife were denuded, save for those around the royal hunting lodge at Falkland. Timber shortages had become so marked by 1555 that parliament passed legislation to curtail the felling of woodland.

Long before this, local shortages had prompted other conservation measures. When in 1236 Alexander II granted the lands of Alloway to the townspeople of Ayr it was on condition that they used its timber stocks only for building and not for burning. Due to the shortage of timber, peat was more normally favoured for fuel, especially in the domestic household, though it often had to be transported some distance. Aberdeen, for instance, obtained its supplies from the forest of Stocket, on the outskirts of the town. Coal, too, replaced timber for heating purposes, not least in the households of the poor. Although its use was more geographically restricted than that of peat, it was mined with comparative ease where it cropped near the surface, and the monks of Dunfermline, among others in the vicinity of the Forth, had supervised its extraction since at least 1291. Widespread use of other substances for fuel did not, however, solve the timber shortage and as a result timber was increasingly imported. Small quantities of Baltic origin were delivered in the fourteenth and fifteenth centuries and, following the development of saw-milling techniques in Scandinavia, centuries of dormant commercial interaction with Norway were reactivated towards the end of the fifteenth century as more substantial quantities of timber began to be shipped westwards, especially for use in large-scale construction projects such as shipbuilding.

For all its scarcity in particular locations, local timber supplies never disappeared completely. Metals, and metal works, were rather more scarce, even though metallic objects were of fundamental importance to all sections of society. Nails, knives, tools and ploughshares were almost indispensable for peasant farmers; urban craftsmen required ferrous tools to ply their trades; armour, weaponry and precious artefacts were distinctive symbols of the aristocracy, as (more discreetly) were horseshoes and lead roofing; and the minting of coinage was the monarchical right *par excellence*. Yet the extent to which all these objects were manufactured in Scotland of Scottish produce is questionable. Much of the original Scottish coinage derived from the Cumbrian silver mines possessed by the crown from 1136 until 1157, though thereafter a substantial proportion was minted from melted-down foreign coins. Even then, foreign coins circulated freely in Scotland and there is little evidence that local silver or gold was mined in any quantity. Despite the crown's attempts to lure foreign gold prospectors to Leadhills in the sixteenth century, disappointing results ensured that the first European gold rush came not in Leadhills but in Latin America after the Spanish conquest. Among other minerals, salt, lead and iron were the most commonly used. Quantities of all three were imported; but Scottish salt was also produced, the bulk of it from coal-fired iron pans in the Forth basin. Lead and iron, by contrast, were extracted in industries often conducted in remote rural areas. It was presumably locally mined lead which was transported from Crawford Muir to Rutherglen in the mid-1260s, and there were reports of its extraction on Islay and Lismore too by the 1540s. Likewise, the remnants of an ancient iron industry, based on the working of poor-quality bog-ore, are scattered across areas such as Rannoch Moor; although of an unidentified date, these works have been speculatively labelled as medieval.

However shadowy, these enterprises are a reminder that although much industrial activity was conducted in or near towns, medieval and early modern industry was not a peculiarly urban phenomenon. Indeed, it would be wrong to draw a sharp economic distinction between town and country. The two were interdependent. The urban crafts-men depended on the supply of raw materials from rural areas, while the rural inhabitant could only purchase some of the more skilfully produced manufactures in urban markets. As late as the sixteenth century, even the larger towns retained a strong rural complexion. The countryside was readily accessible from the built environment which, in the case of Aberdeen, Dunfermline and most other towns, could be traversed on foot within ten minutes. Besides, the familiar hallmarks of rural life did not cease at town gates. When in 1551 a mad cow charged into Thomas Galloway's Dundee brewhouse, the unusual sight was not the cow, but its state of mind. Animals routinely cluttered the backlands of urban properties, and their secretion and excretion contributed to the probably foul odour and undoubted filth of even then the biggest town of all, Edinburgh.

What made towns different from the countryside was not the absence of agricultural activity from the former, nor the absence of industrial activity from the latter, nor even the occupational structure of towns – since not all urban trades were formally regulated or privileged. More significant was the distinctive legal entity of 'the burgh' and, for some burghs, their independent political persona, once those which belonged to the crown acquired the right to parliamentary representation in the fourteenth century. Even then, legal autonomy and political rights should not be exaggerated and it is rather to the urban market-place that we should look for the key distinction between both town and country and town and burgh. While all burghs held markets, it would be difficult to accept that all burghs were genuine towns. Indeed, many burghs – especially the dozens of baronial burghs which were established in the later fifteenth and sixteenth centuries – could scarcely be distinguished physically, economically or socially from surrounding rural farm 'touns' or townships.

Only the larger burghs were truly towns, distinctive because of the commercial concentration which conditioned their socio-economic environment and the substantial number of their inhabitants whose livelihoods depended on craftsmanship or commerce. Most were located on crown lands, though some, such as Dunfermline, belonged to churchmen. Genuine towns boasted not only weekly markets, but also trading monopolies over geographically extensive and jealously guarded precincts. They traded in a more diverse array of goods than those available in most burghs. They hosted annual fairs which lasted for several days at a time and which attracted merchants and merchandise from further afield. Their inhabitants traded abroad. Towns were, in short, a form of commercial organization and it is this which explains their predominantly southern and eastern location: their vista was not only on their rural hinterlands, but also on foreign markets which mostly lay across the North Sea.

This is not to argue that regions which boasted no towns were commercially moribund. There were no towns, or burghs, in the great swathe of Highland territory skirted by Dumbarton, Perth, Kintore, Inverness and Dingwall. Yet Highlanders clearly traded and did so not only among themselves or in the distant Lowland towns but also abroad: their poetry reveals a familiarity with imports such as wine and silk while their ships docked in Bristol and Ireland during the thirteenth century. Argyll merchants were said in the same century to have visited Ireland 'frequently' in the past and some appear to have been members of the Dublin guild merchant in the thirteenth century. The forms of Highland commerce were less regulated and less routine than they were elsewhere, but trade was still taking place.

The commercial sophistication of such contact is more doubtful. Thirteenth-century Christendom witnessed a 'commercial revolution': new developments in ship design and business partnership accompanied the more widespread use of credit arrangements and the introduction of bills of exchange (effectively paper money). But in Scotland much about commerce remained simple, especially in the north and west, and trading contacts were fundamentally aimed at alleviating the mismatch of domestic supply and demand. It was this, and also in the east coast towns profit, which encouraged merchants to seek out foreign markets where excess fish, wool, leather and animal skins might be offloaded. By way of return they sought out wine, wheat, a range of manufactured goods (especially ferrous objects, particular types of cloth and clothing, furniture and artistic goods) and, increasingly from the fifteenth century, timber. Sale and purchase were most conveniently and profitably undertaken in one, preferably close-to-hand, location since this served to minimize transport costs.

No single foreign location fitted this commercial template precisely. Those which came closest in the twelfth and thirteenth centuries were Flanders and Artois. Flanders was then the most densely urbanized region of northern Europe and its expanding urban population required fish, along with other foodstuffs, to feed itself. By the thirteenth century *aberdaan* was synonymous with cod in Flanders, and Scottish herring and salmon probably also found their way to continental Europe. A sizeable proportion of the burgeoning Flemish and Artesian population was engaged in a local textile industry whose manufactures were exported as far away as the Mediterranean. This made for hungry looms, as well as mouths, and it was an appetite which both aristocratic and peasant wool producers in Scotland were quick to satisfy, with perhaps as much as half of later medieval wool exports derived from peasant producers. Hides, meanwhile, were required in the Low Countries for much the same purpose as in Scotland.

In exchange for these goods, merchants were able to purchase not just the internationally renowned Netherlandish cloths. Everything from the wine consumed at the 1328 wedding festivities to the wheelbarrows used in the construction of Aberdeen University in 1495 could be purchased at Bruges and its satellite ports. Bruges was the greatest commercial emporium north of the Alps, an urban superstore where goods of local origin were sold alongside those from other parts of Christendom. In the twelfth and thirteenth centuries there was little need to trade elsewhere – except, that is, for wheat. By medieval standards, a highly urbanized region such as Flanders was unlikely to produce surplus grain, so the demand for wheat and to some extent wine was satisfied mainly from the east coast ports of both Ireland and England in exchange for the traditional Scottish exports, most of which were probably resold in Flanders.

Flanders was to remain an important trading partner throughout the Middle Ages. Indeed, so important was Flanders that from the early fourteenth century until 1477 most Scottish exports were legally directed to a 'staple', usually located at Bruges. There was good sense behind this single-minded focus of commerce on Flanders: elsewhere there was minimal demand for Scottish produce, and in return for promising Flanders the Scottish wool clip, the Scottish merchant community received commercial privileges from the Flemish authorities. Nevertheless, traditional trading patterns were increasingly recast from the mid-fourteenth century. Political realignments played their part in this. Localized strife within Flanders, together with regional conflict between Flemings and their French overlords, and the international warfare associated with the Hundred Years War (1337–1453), all periodically disrupted Flemish and Artesian cloth production and with it the demand for Scottish wool.

In the longer term, however, the economic consequences of depopulation and the development of major centres of cloth production in the more northerly Netherlandish provinces and in England were to have an even more profound effect. On the one hand, demand for Scottish wool fell as the European population dwindled; and on the other, growing competition prompted the traditional centres of the Netherlandish textile industry, such as Ypres, together with their imitators, such as Leiden, to re-orientate production towards the output of quality woollens. These were made only from the best wools, which largely emanated from southern England and Wales, and Scottish wools were increasingly sidelined. Some were still used in the famed Flemish draperies for the manufacture of coarser cloths, which were chiefly for sale to the poor; others were used in less prestigious manufacturing centres such as Audenarde and Dixmuide – where they faced competition not just from indigenous and poorer English wools, but from the early fifteenth century increasingly from those of Spain.

4. Boom and Bust?

The effects of these structural changes in the Netherlandish economy are evident from the volume of Scottish wool exports. Exports reached a peak in the early 1370s but were running at only about a quarter of those levels by the early fifteenth century. Despite some subsequent improvement, they never again reached the levels of the 1370s. Moreover, the fall in wool exports, coupled with a less substantial drop in hide exports from the 1390s, was compounded by other factors. Anecdotal evidence suggests that there was a significant decline in domestic craft production but no fall in the insatiable demand for imports. In an oft quoted passage, Froissart reported that 'there was neither iron to shoe horses, nor leather to make harness, saddles or bridles: all these things came ready made from Flanders; and should these fail there was none to be had in the country'. Since exports were falling, good housekeeping would suggest they could not be afforded. This too is the implication of the severe shortage of bullion which was evident during the fifteenth century. That parliament repeatedly attempted to limit the export of hard cash suggests that money continued to flow out of the kingdom, partly to pay papal taxation, but also to pay for imports.

Insufficient data survives to estimate the effect of this drain on the money supply, but the amount of coinage in circulation probably declined in the fourteenth century, and further still in the fifteenth century, rising again only from about the 1540s, once supplies of American silver and gold began to reach Europe. Other adverse monetary developments are more readily quantified. The art of making more money from less metal was well understood by the crown's 'moneyers'. The metal content of silver coins was steadily reduced from their thirteenth-century optimum and the metal content of gold coins (introduced in the fourteenth century) followed suit. Furthermore, 'billon' coins, made from debased silver, began to circulate from the reign of Robert III (1390–1406), while the need for coins of small denomination to facilitate basic, everyday commercial transactions was met later in the fifteenth century by the introduction of a new copper coinage. Pejoratively termed 'black' money, this was itself subject to periodic debasement, especially in the early 1480s. There was, however, a price to pay for manipulation of the coinage. Currency depreciation and debasement led to a fall in exchange rates. Whereas in 1428 £2 Scots was equivalent to £1 Flemish, by the 1490s it took at least £3 Scots to purchase £1 Flemish.

These commercial and monetary problems were accompanied by other gloomy developments. Emigration, for instance, might be interpreted as a consequence of economic hardship. Signs of urban decline are evident too. With exports in decline, it was reported that no ship had visited Banff for some years before 1389; the thriving thirteenth-century town of Roxburgh was completely abandoned in the fifteenth century; and by 1537 it was reported that Inverkeithing was 'deceyit and fallin in povertie'. Less obvious to contemporaries, but of fundamental importance, was the limited scale of technological and scientific development. This, together with the reliance on limited supplies of organic fuels, drastically impeded both agricultural and industrial productivity. Medieval society fostered a sharp environmental awareness which was exemplified not just in the measures to conserve timber stocks, but also in a sensitive appreciation of the industrial and medicinal purposes to which plants and animals could be put; but it did not comprehend how difficult economic circumstances could be ameliorated through increased efficiency. Commerce or death, rather than industrialization, remained the answer to shortages.

All this may suggest that later medieval Scotland was living beyond its means. If so, it makes for a stark contrast with the twelfth and thirteenth centuries when wool, as the historian Alexander Grant has observed, had emerged as the equivalent of oil in the twentieth century. Just as oil brought a measure of prosperity to parts of twentieth-century Scotland, so wool brought a degree of prosperity to twelfth- and thirteenth-century Scotland. Prosperity was not, of course, uniform, as many a peasant in search of land might have testified – had he or she been literate. Neither was wool the only factor behind the fat years of the twelfth and thirteenth centuries. David I's occupation of Cumbria, or more particularly its silver mines, was to provide much of the initial wherewithal for developing a hard-cash economy. Nevertheless, the buoyant Netherlandish demand for wool was to spawn a further and dramatic rise in the money supply. Foreigners paid for wool with cash and the amount of money in circulation in Scotland accordingly rose from (at a conservative estimate) £50,000 in the mid-thirteenth century to about £180,000 or more by the end of the century.

The contrast between a prosperous high Middle Ages and an impoverished end to the period, two extremes which swivel around the grim reapers of fourteenth-century war and plague, is not, however, entirely convincing. Some of the apparent signs of later medieval depression are deceptive. For a start, currency depreciation afflicted all of Latin Christendom to varying degrees. As gold and silver passed to the Middle East in return for silk and spices, precious metals became scarce throughout the continent and the silver and gold content of coins fell almost everywhere. Indeed so scarce had silver, in particular, become by the mid-fifteenth century that many mints in north-western Europe, including that of the French crown at Tournai, struck virtually no coinage at all between 1440 and 1465. This was a fate avoided by the Scottish mint which continued production, albeit at more modest levels, throughout the great fifteenth-century silver dearth. Viewed comparatively too, the falling Scottish exchange rate was not markedly out of line with developments elsewhere. Against the Florentine florin, a coin which unusually retained most of its weight and purity, the French *livre tournois* lost about 74 per cent of its value between *c.* 1300 and *c.* 1500, while the

Milanese (and probably Scottish) currencies lost about 81 per cent and the Castilian *maravedi* an astonishing 98 per cent. That silver was still reaching the Scottish mint when the silver dearth was at its most acute and that devaluation was not as great as in some countries suggests a less gloomy economic climate than the tales of monetary woe emanating from parliament would imply.

What, then, of the other signs of depression? While some towns clearly declined in economic significance, this was paralleled by the seemingly inexorable commercial advance of Edinburgh: by the 1470s more than half of Scotland's overseas trade passed through its port of Leith; and by the 1530s more than two-thirds did. Of course, Edinburgh was grabbing a larger share of a diminishing cake, but in an era of dwindling population some decline in export levels was to be expected. A reduction in exports was not by itself reflective of economic depression. Indeed, whether industry remained quite as depressed, and imports remained quite as buoyant, as the anecdotal evidence suggests is doubtful. Froissart's jibe that there was no leather in the country is frankly ludicrous. While his allusion to the import of wheelbarrows — an assertion repeated in the anonymous fifteenth-century poem *The Libelle of Englyshe Polycye* — might be interpreted as symbolic of a shortfall in both timber supplies and craft skills, we should remember that wheelbarrows are useful implements in which to pack other goods. They may have been purchased for that reason, or for their own intrinsic value, or simply because Flanders did a nice line in wheelbarrows that year: but it is ridiculous to assume that there were neither the materials nor the craftsmen to make a single wheelbarrow in Scotland. Indeed, the falling exchange rate served to inhibit imports; and by making them more expensive it ought to have stimulated domestic craft production. If Scots continued to purchase harness, saddles, bridles and wheelbarrows abroad that was a matter of choice, based upon an assessment of the price, quality or fashion of each item. Presumably, however, it was a choice that could be afforded.

In assuming that a great trade deficit was built up in the later Middle Ages, much too great a significance can be read into the demise of the wool and leather trades. Wool and leather were not Scotland's only exports. A Baltic market developed in the fifteenth century for poor-quality woollen cloth whose sale was proscribed in the Low Countries presumably because it might otherwise have undercut Netherlandish manufactures. Small quantities of coal, salt, wool, lambskins and leather were also dispatched thither. More significantly, there was still a market for fish, and also for linen cloth, in much of western Europe. Fish, it is true, is hardly the most glamorous item of trade; but some indication of its value is to be found from the goods unloaded by the 'Clement' of Kirkcaldy when it docked at Hull on 20 February 1541. Its cargo included salmon, herring, other unspecified types of fish and fish-oil (valued at £41 6s. 8d.), linen (£1 6s. 8d.) and 'wild' leather (8s.), making a total cargo value of £43 1s. 4d. When the 'Clement' left port on 8 March, its hold was laden with saffron and mace; woollens, worsteds, velvet, linen and satin, along with six carpets and twenty-three coverlets;

soap, pitch and tar; and pewter ware, numerous pots and shovels, ten kettles, three dripping-pans and that almost indispensable Scottish culinary accoutrement, the frying-pan (five of them). Together their value was assessed at £25 15s. 8d. Even once the English customs duties had been paid, this left £13 16s. 5d. (in English money, which suffered far less than other currencies from devaluation) as profit and to cover other costs. The voyage made by the 'Clement' is significant precisely because, by later fifteenth- and early sixteenth-century standards, and perhaps by earlier standards too, it was unremarkable. Numerous Scottish ships were arriving in eastern England, unloading similarly unglamorous goods and then re-loading with spices, cloth and manufactured goods, and doing so at an ostensible profit. There are two further important points to note about this incident. First, many of the goods which the 'Clement' picked up in Hull were manufactured and many (such as the spices and perhaps some of the manufactured goods) were not of English origin. While Robert I had purchased his pots and pans for the 1328 wedding in Flanders, from the later fifteenth century the role of commercial entrepot traditionally performed by the Netherlands was, for Scottish merchants, increasingly being assumed by England. More importantly, while the reduced volume of wool and hide exports continued to be sent to the Scottish staple in the Netherlands (located from 1508 at Veere in Zeeland) and to France, the 'Clement's' cargo of rather different Scottish exports was far from worthless. Their sale went some considerable way to compensating for the fall in wool and hide exports.

So we must be careful in presuming that exports fell in the later medieval period and that a trade deficit ensued. Besides, there are other indications that this was not quite the 'poor little country' which the Scots themselves portrayed, more with an eye to winning papal pity than prizes for economic analysis, in the Declaration of Arbroath of 1320. As we have already seen, general economic trends worked to the advantage of at least some sections of later medieval society. Moreover, inflation from the fourteenth century was not simply a consequence of currency depreciation and bullion shortage. A recent authoritative study of prices, by the historians Elizabeth Gemmill and Nicholas Mayhew, has suggested that part of the price hike which afflicted many, though not all, commodities was demand-based and suggestive of economic growth. The physical evidence of that growth is perhaps best seen today in the architectural achievements of the fourteenth, fifteenth and sixteenth centuries, in royal palaces such as Falkland, Linlithgow and Holyrood; in cathedrals such as those at Aberdeen, Dunkeld and Elgin; in the baronial tower houses which sprang up across southern Scotland; and in the bridges which sprouted over rivers such as the Garnock and Dee.

Among other indicators of economic fortunes, there remains the conundrum of emigration. This, however, was not necessarily a reflection of a depressed economy. Foreign military service offered a career unavailable at home since no standing army developed in Scotland. Many soldiers were probably recruited with the expectation of lucrative remuneration. Some did indeed prosper; and although many lived out the rest of their lives abroad, others were medieval *Gastarbeiter* who sent money home on a regular basis, thereby compensating, partially at least, for the drain of money from Scotland. Meanwhile, the apparent growth of non-military emigration from the later fifteenth century roughly coincided with the intensification of feuing; and there was perhaps a link between the two. Not everyone could afford the substantial initial payments which landlords often demanded before conceding more secure tenancies. Some lost their lands, which may explain an apparent increase in the number of beggars from the fifteenth century and the acceleration in the pace of emigration. Times were difficult for many and they demanded adjustments in the face of the prevailing post-plague economic trends; but neither were times as bleak as is often portrayed, even for many of those whom the emigrants left at home.

Medieval Society: the Construction and Collapse of a Catholic Community

For rich and poor alike, medieval Scotland was a Christian society. There were no Muslims and few, if any, Jews to complicate the country's otherwise overwhelmingly Christian complexion. As for witches, there were probably few of these in medieval Scotland – despite an anonymous chronicle report that many were publicly burnt in 1479. Although other vestiges of paganism remained, for instance in folk-tales and names such as MacEachern (meaning son of a horse-lord), they did so, even in 1100, with a thickly applied Christian gloss which effectively and increasingly obliterated the heathen past from contemporary human memory. Medieval Scotland was Christian and all that was left in doubt was which brand of Christianity it was to adopt. There were several possibilities. In the eleventh century the chief battleground lay between, on the one hand, a Celtic model of worship and, on the other, a Roman and continental model. By 1100 the die had already been cast in favour of the latter and it is Margaret, the Anglo-Saxon wife of King Malcolm III, who is normally credited by historians with having cast it. Margaret is known to posterity chiefly due to the labours of her monkish hagiographer, Turgot. His eulogies of the queen suggest a woman forthright in speech and interfering in disposition. She fulminated against the lax observance of Sunday prayer and the reluctance to take communion at Easter, as well as against Celtic peculiarities in the calculation of Lent and the tantalizingly unspecified 'barbarous rites' by which, at least in some districts, mass was celebrated. The impact of these intemperate tirades was somewhat blunted by their expression in an Anglo-Saxon language which few understood. Turgot credits Margaret's husband with their translation for a wider audience. But we may doubt whether her reforms could have been achieved without the wholehearted support of a sympathetic body of clerics and an equally committed husband; or whether the Celtic eccentricities which she so despised were as swiftly and uncontroversially eradicated as Turgot implied. Margaret was not, however, a genuine radical. The invitation which she extended to three Benedictine monks of Canterbury to establish a cell at Dunfermline was more than matched by her patronage of the existing Celtic monasteries at Iona and Loch Leven; and her lambastes completely ignored clerical celibacy and lay control of the church, the burning issues of the day elsewhere in Christendom. None the less it is beyond doubt that, in time, the limited initiatives with which Margaret has been credited were implemented.

More followed. During the twelfth and thirteenth centuries most of the familiar institutions of Roman Catholicism were extended or newly introduced into Scotland. Episcopal dioceses were demarcated and subdivided into parishes, and although the latter were markedly more numerous in the south and east than in the north and west – there were only twenty-three in the diocese of Caithness by *c.* 1300 – each parish supposedly had its own stone-built church. Meanwhile, continental models of monasticism were established; and tithes and papal taxes were levied, the former to pay for the upkeep of the church and its staff, the latter to pay for crusades and the expanding papal bureaucracy. Perhaps most significantly, the newly-established ecclesiastical courts adopted a new form of law – canon law – whose provisions extended into almost every facet of human interaction. This, moreover, was not a law simply for clergymen: secular society too was expected to abide by its stipulations.

These developments were common to much of Christendom and they were to ensure that Scotland became an integral component of a wider Christian community bounded by Scandinavia, the Mediterranean, Ireland and Hungary. This was the Latin west and throughout this area the bishop of Rome (that is, the pope) was recognized as the spiritual leader. Papal leadership was no fanciful conception. From 1096 sponsorship of crusades against the Muslims of the Mediterranean world, and, latterly, against the pagans of the Baltic, provided substance to papal pretensions of leadership by tapping a popular and widespread religious impulse. Despite their geographical remoteness from the main theatres of crusade, Scots were enthusiastic about these holy wars. Even in 1096 many had 'abandoned their fleas', according to the chronicler William of Malmesbury, to join in Christendom's common enterprise of 'recovering' the Holy Land from Islamic control. In later years many others were to follow their example.

Papal leadership was not confined to external affairs. Through its espousal of moral reform and its desire to rid the church of secular control in the later eleventh century, the papacy had come to adopt a much keener interest in the internal affairs of Christendom too. Initially the issue of priestly celibacy lay at the heart of this interest, for if clerics married their offspring might seek to inherit, and thereby alienate, ecclesiastical land – much as David, son of Peter, parson of Stobo, inherited his father's lands in the later twelfth century. That hundreds of Scottish clerical offspring petitioned successive popes for dispensation from the defects of illegitimacy suggests that clerical concubinage was to remain problematic throughout the medieval centuries. It was clearly with difficulty that strictures emanating from the papal court were converted into obedience in the corners of Christendom.

Yet this was not for want of effort, since the papacy had devised a great chain of clerical command stretching from the humble priest to the papal court itself. Each priest was accountable to his local bishop. Bishops were expected to train priests before their ordination and to satisfy themselves as to the ongoing spiritual rectitude of their subordinates. Hence they familiarized priests with the dictates of popes and general councils of the church through their own episcopal statutes, warning priests, for instance, of 'that filthy contagion of lustful naughtiness whereby the good name of the church is shamefully discredited', and threatening errant priests with dismissal if they did not dissociate themselves from their concubines. Such orders required policing if they were to prove effective. It was to this end that, at least in theory, churches were also subjected to annual inspections. In 1242, for instance, David Bernham, bishop of St Andrews, instructed that every church in Lothian should be visited each year by the archdeacon or dean (the other promoted clergy within a diocese) and that 'all deficiencies in churches and churchyards, books and ornaments' be brought to his personal attention. Not all bishops, however, were as assiduous as Bernham appears to have been in his duties, and in 1549 it was frankly admitted that deans had often been bribed to ignore the existence of concubines.

In the localities, then, good conduct depended on the diligent supervision of the senior clergy. For their part bishops were made accountable to archbishops: those of the Isles and of Orkney to the Norwegian archbishop of Trondheim and those of Galloway (until 1355) to the archbishop of York. The archbishop of York had also claimed jurisdiction over the other Scottish bishops. While, with royal support, they had evaded his claims, English lobbying at the papal court successfully blocked the appointment of a Scottish archbishop. Instead, from 1189 until 1472, the remaining Scottish bishoprics were categorized as a 'special daughter' of the papacy and made directly answerable to the pope. But it was clearly impractical for a distant and busy pontiff to summon the Scottish bishops for an annual investigation of moral deficiencies in Scotland.

It was to this end that in 1225, following a proposal made by the bishops themselves, a provincial council of the Scottish church was established, chaired in rotation by an episcopal 'conservator' and composed of not just the episcopate but other clergymen too. This was an unusual, but not entirely satisfactory, substitute for archiepiscopal oversight, since the decisions of the council seem to have been neither binding on its members nor subject to papal scrutiny. These problems were not entirely overcome when St Andrews was elevated from a bishopric to an archbishopric in 1472. Petty episcopal jealousies sent several other bishops scurrying to Rome to seek dispensations from the new archbishop's jurisdiction and in 1492 Glasgow too was elevated to an archbishopric. More importantly, the belated introduction of archiepiscopal oversight did little *per se* to raise the moral calibre of either the episcopate or the lesser clergy.

While bad apples had always existed in the episcopal barrel – for instance Glasgow's Robert Wishart (1271–1316) was a notable pluralist, nepotist and most probably a fornicator – the challenge of Protestantism in the sixteenth century more than ever required exemplary spiritual and moral leadership. The episcopal response was ultimately too patchy to be effective.

It would, however, be misleading to assume that frequently bickering bishops enjoyed unfettered episcopal authority, even on their own diocesan patches. The papacy's efforts to establish a clear structure of line management had been accompanied by the steady erosion of episcopal independence. During the thirteenth century, for instance, the important role which bishops had often played in the recognition of new saints was superseded by the papal monopoly of canonization: hence the eleventh-century Queen Margaret was canonized by Pope Innocent IV in 1249. Meanwhile, certain religious establishments (such as the Benedictine monastery of Iona) were granted independence from episcopal oversight and instead were made directly answerable to the pope. Appeals were encouraged on matters of canon law from the episcopal courts to those at the papacy, and from the fourteenth century the papacy (then normally resident at Avignon) also began to appoint clerics to a substantial number of ecclesiastical offices. It is symptomatic of these trends that, whereas not a single papal letter to Scotland survives from before 1100, a trickle of twelfth-century correspondence was to become a deluge in the later medieval period, most of it in response to clerics seeking preferment to ecclesiastical office.

This enormous accretion in papal power, little diminished by the papal schism of 1378–1417, caused remarkably little opposition. Papal justice remained popular. Petitions from ordinary Scots – pleading for dispensations from canon law provisions regarding illegitimacy or marriage, requesting spiritual privileges or confirmation of lands feued by the church and even seeking absolutions for murder – continued to flow to the papal courts until the Reformation and after. Even the crown, which relied upon literate and trustworthy clerics to run secular government, was muted in its criticism of papal authority. In part this was because popes rarely made appointments to the higher ecclesiastical offices which were unacceptable to the crown, even though it was only in 1489 – much later than for some other countries – that the pope formally ceded the right to appoint the more important clerics to the crown. This, however, was an important and symbolic concession, for, while the papacy continued to respond to popular appeals for its jurisdiction, by the sixteenth century it had abandoned even the pretence of offering firm spiritual leadership. It was with impotent dismay that the papacy was left to watch the Protestant fracture of Catholic Christendom during the Reformation and its late manifestation in Scotland, the Protestant revolution of 1560.

The Bonds of Medieval Society: Belief and Birth

1. Devotion and Dissent

Much has been written about ecclesiastical institutions and structures, but such studies reveal little about the impact of religion on ordinary lives. To examine how religion shaped everyday life we can return to the wedding celebrations of 1328. We do not know for certain where in Berwick David Bruce and Joan Plantagenet were married. In all probability it was in the churchyard of the town's parish church. Marriage was normally celebrated outside rather than inside a church, and it was the walls of this churchyard which were reduced to rubble by the boisterous guests. The parish church of the Holy Trinity was a location to which this particular couple rarely returned, but in this they were probably highly unusual. Few among the medieval population were as itinerant as David and Joan, and most couples are likely to have revisited the site of their marriage often. Such visits were not occasioned by sentimental nostalgia. Sunday mass was an important religious occasion at which most, if not all, members of the local community would gather. The weekly service was supplemented by other moments of ecclesiastical contact and spiritual contemplation which marked important stages in both secular life and the Christian calendar. Baptism, as far as is known, was universal for medieval Scots; communion, following the decree of the Fourth Lateran Council in 1215, was celebrated annually in parish churches at Easter; holidays were holy days, accompanied by special religious celebrations; and at the end of the life cycle the dying craved for priestly absolution of their sins before death and Christian burial.

In this the Scottish experience of medieval religion was similar to that of other countries. Indeed, had the ordinary Berwick parishioner been set down in a church in Bern or Braga, much would probably have seemed familiar. The clergy who conducted services were trained similarly across Christendom and the church services over which they presided were conducted in the same – and to most people unintelligible – Latin language, according to a similar ritual. The same Father, Son and Holy Ghost were worshipped across Christendom, along with a cohort of internationally revered saints. And the same important feast days, especially those associated with the Virgin Mary (such as her Nativity on 8 September) and Christ (Easter, Christmas and from the mid-thirteenth century Corpus Christi), were observed in Scotland as elsewhere. Despite the largely successful attempts of sixteenth-century Protestant iconoclasts to extinguish the evidence, Scottish churches were also decorated in much the same way as their foreign counterparts. Wall paintings, stained glass and statues depicted aspects of biblical stories and saintly lives, and many churches possessed sacred relics of venerated saints. Glasgow cathedral, for instance, boasted fragments of the Virgin's girdle and hair, along with droplets of her milk, while in 1455 Edinburgh's parish church obtained an arm bone of its patron, St Giles, which was proudly displayed on 'Relic Sunday'.

As well as the components of a broadly universal religious message, the church provided ample scope for individual, familial and local piety. For the wealthy, the most conspicuous display of piety was through patronage of a religious foundation. At its most generous this prompted twelfth-century kings in particular, but others too, such as Walter Comyn, Earl of Buchan, to found monasteries – in Buchan's case the Cistercian house of Deer, which was established in 1219. The lavish patronage required to establish monasteries was less readily available in the harsher economic climate of the later Middle Ages, but smaller donations of land and money to the church continued apace, directed above all towards the urban friaries (developed from the thirteenth century) and the colleges of secular clergy (founded mainly from the fourteenth century). Charity was not, however, the only means by which to express piety. Individuals and families with an interest in crusading, itself an act of piety, often displayed devotion to St George, whose banners accompanied the crusading armies in Prussia. The Christian name George became popular among such families and some, such as the Earl of Crawford in 1406, patronized altars in the saint's honour. For many others St Roche, a victim of plague, proved increasingly popular in the aftermath of the Black Death. In some cases particular saintly attachments were proudly displayed on seals. The Caldecote family seals depict scallop shells, the internationally recognized symbol of St James and his shrine at Compostela. Compostela, Rome and the Holy Land were the three most important centres of pilgrimage, and the adoption of the scallop device by the Caldecotes and others suggests that an ancestor had undertaken the arduous devotional voyage to Spain.

These individual or familial saintly attachments were in turn supplemented by more widespread local affiliations. Berwick, for example, was St Cuthbert territory; and although the seventh-century monk was virtually unknown in Switzerland or Portugal, his was a popular cult in the Anglo-Scottish borders. The Berwickshire parish church of Channelkirk (where he was said to have been born) was one of three dozen dedicated to Cuthbert in Scotland and his feast day (20 March) was probably a day of celebration in all of them, as it certainly was in Holyrood abbey. Many Scots also visited the chief shrines for Cuthbert's relics, at Farne and at Durham. Among them was the future King Alexander I, who was the only layman to witness the translation of Cuthbert's relics at Durham in 1104. Several Scottish aristocrats followed in Alexander's footsteps, as did an array of anonymous other Scots, at least some of whom were shackled in iron fetters as they humbly performed penance for their sins before the saint. Cuthbert's status in southern Scotland was replicated by countless other saints in other localities, many of them with their own local relics and shrines. All were important in the creation of a strong local identity, as well as being foci of devotional practices.

National expressions of piety, on the other hand, developed more slowly. Even though the relic casket of St Columba accompanied the Scottish army into battle at Bannockburn in 1314, St Columba was never a truly popular national saint until the Disruption of 1843 spawned a sentimental rediscovery of ancient Celtic Christianity. St Ninian had perhaps greater claims to national affection in the Middle Ages. Certainly it was to him that many of the altars maintained by emigrant Scots were dedicated – for instance in the Netherlandish towns of Bergen-op-Zoom and Bruges, and in the Danish towns of Copenhagen and Elsinore. Nevertheless, it was St Andrew who emerged as the patron of the medieval nation, his distinctive cross displayed on the official seal of government which was adopted in 1286. As brother of St Peter, the pope's patron, Andrew was also used adeptly in diplomatic propaganda, such as the so-called Declaration of Arbroath of 1320, which was designed to win papal support. But Andrew's cult was also popular in Italy – there was a major shrine dedicated to him at Amalfi – and in the Netherlands too, as is still evident in Amsterdam's distinctive coat-of-arms. Andrew was not therefore peculiarly Scottish.

Indeed, it was only towards the end of the fifteenth century that a deliberate attempt was made to focus Scottish veneration in a specifically national direction. Leading clergymen placed the relics of hitherto largely forgotten Scottish saints on public display, and campaigns were mounted for the canonization of other ancient holy men with Scottish associations. This policy met with royal approval and, for contemporaries at least, its most vivid expression was perhaps less in the intellectual endeavours of Bishop William Elphinstone of Aberdeen (1431–1514), who compiled a new martyrology of Scottish saints, but rather in the regular peregrinations made by James IV to the shrine of the rediscovered St Duthac at Tain. None the less, even Duthac's popularity remained marginal in comparison with that of the great international saints such as Mary or Andrew; and Elphinstone's attempts to promote the celebration of Scottish saints in the church calendar failed to stem the import of foreign liturgies whose references to Scottish saints were minimal. The extent to which crown and mitre might influence popular religious sentiment was evidently limited.

Expressions of piety and the assemblage of spiritual images and objects which adorned many churches reveal something about ordinary people's understanding of Christianity. Up to a point, at least, iconography constituted an alternative bible for an overwhelmingly illiterate society. It also supplemented aural means of communicating religious knowledge, for instance during confession (which the Fourth Lateran Council had decreed should be undertaken at least annually) and in sermons (though their delivery was not regular). Religious processions and plays provided a further mechanism of instruction and by the fifteenth century these were regularly staged in towns, notably on Corpus Christi ('the body of Christ') day. It was the widespread public impulse to venerate the Host – the communion bread which became the flesh of Christ – which had first served to popularize the Corpus Christi celebrations, the Host acquiring the status of a relic of Christ himself as well as symbolically representing the unity of the church in Christ's body; but the eucharistic focus of the original processions was soon supplemented by other playlets with a biblical motif. Unfortunately, little Scottish evidence survives to illuminate the explicit content of these forms of instruction, though one prop employed in Dundee's Corpus Christi play appears to have been a wooden sculpted serpent designed to recount the tale of Adam and Eve.

If Scotland followed the example of other countries, we may assume that there was a reasonable familiarity not only with biblical stories (such as that set in the Garden of Eden), but also with the statement of belief known as the Creed, some saints' lives and such concepts as the Ten Commandments, the Seven Deadly Sins and their counterpart, the Seven Christian Virtues. Together these provided a rough-and-ready exemplar for the conduct of life. Beyond that, a belief in God's omnipotence is also evident. This in part explains the importance of prayer, as it was the means by which God might be approached. Prayer, and contact with relics, was also a means for communicating with the saints, who might in turn intercede with God to effect miracles. Indeed, the vibrancy of a saint's popularity depended on his or her ability to effect miracles. Cuthbert's miraculous prowess, for instance, was attested in popular tales. A twelfth-century collection of his miracles was in part compiled from stories circulating in Galloway, while in the fifteenth century Walter Bower credited Cuthbert's favour for a victory supposedly achieved by William Wallace in 1298, and Cuthbert's wrath for the defeat suffered by David II at Neville's Cross in 1346.

The medieval religious mentality was, however, concerned as much with the afterlife as with life itself. In 1215 the Fourth Lateran Council had proclaimed that 'not only virgins and the continent but also married persons might find favour with God by right faith and good actions and deserve to attain eternal blessedness'. Heaven was now open to secular society. However, for those who died having repented of their sins but without having performed penance, celestial ascent was complicated by a detour via purgatory. Purgatory did not become an article of faith until the fifteenth century. Belief in the existence of this hell-like antechamber to heaven had, however, grown from the thirteenth century and it was in purgatory that post-mortal penance could be undertaken. Still, there were means by which remission could be obtained on the time to be spent suffering its paradoxically timeless pain. Prayer was one such device, and the benefactors of religious institutions expected prayers to be said for their souls in return for donations. In addition, remissions could be stockpiled prior to death through the acquisition of indulgences. The church granted indulgences to those, such as pilgrims or crusaders, who had undertaken what were deemed to be good works. The length of these concessions varied. In 1249 pilgrims who visited St Margaret's shrine at Dunfermline on her feast-day received indulgences of forty days – an inducement sufficiently great for an English army to abandon its siege of nearby Loch Leven and hasten to Dunfermline in 1334. Meanwhile, a full, or plenary, indulgence was granted to those who made the pilgrimage to Rome in the jubilee years declared by popes periodically from 1300. By the sixteenth century plenary indulgences were available in return for alms-giving too.

The grant of any indulgence was dependent upon confession and the indulgence was therefore a useful means by which to reinstate sinners within the community of the church; but Protestant reformers were incensed at what they interpreted as a sale on sin.

The sixteenth century was to witness the disintegration of medieval Christendom in the midst of confessional wars between Catholics and Protestants. Protestantism was not, however, the first challenge to Catholic orthodoxy. In 1222 Bishop Adam of Caithness was murdered at Halkirk by what his horrified episcopal colleagues deemed 'satellites of the devil'. In less emotive phraseology they were probably disgruntled parishioners, affronted by the bishop's zealous, and apparently unaccustomed, collection of a tenth (in Scots 'teind'; in English 'tithe') of their income to pay for the upkeep of the church and its institutions. This event is a reminder that, however orthodox medieval Scotland might have seemed, dissent was not unknown. By comparison with many other countries, documented dissent in Scotland is none the less remarkably limited. Heresies such as Catharism and Waldensianism, which bedevilled Catholic uniformity in France, Italy and Germany (strictly the Holy Roman Empire), had little discernible impact in Scotland, though Lollardy, which had taken its cue from the fourteenth-century Oxford academic, John Wycliff, made somewhat greater headway. It was a Lollard, John Resby, who became the first recorded heretic to be burned for his beliefs in Scotland; but that was as late as 1408. Although others were to be accused of Lollardy – notably a group of thirty Ayrshire men and women who were brought before an ecclesiastical court in 1494 and tried in the presence of King James IV – Resby's fate remained highly unusual. The Ayrshire Lollards were acquitted and even in the prelude to Scotland's 'velvet reformation' of 1560, when Catholicism was supplanted by Protestantism as the country's official religion, religious persecution remained unusual. While in many countries thousands died for their beliefs during the religious struggles of the sixteenth century, Scotland's Protestant martyrs – those judicially killed for their beliefs – were to be numbered in no more than double digits.

Two very different explanations may account for the comparative scarcity of religious executions in Scotland: either the Catholic church was complacent in its defence of orthodoxy; or heresy had little appeal for anyone other than a committed, but tiny, minority of religious zealots. On this historians remain divided – not least with regard to the popularity of Protestantism before 1560 – but in considering the issue it is important to exclude the notion of inevitability from our calculations. It does not follow that because there was a Reformation in 1560, medieval religion 'must have been' in a state of decay. There were certainly abuses – such as James IV's scandalous and nepotistic appointment of his illegitimate, eleven-year-old son Alexander as archbishop of St Andrews in 1504; and unsuitable appointments increased once the crown had formally wrested control of ecclesiastical appointments from the papacy. Partly as a consequence of such appointments, there was also a lack of effective Catholic leadership, both from Rome and from several episcopal palaces up and down the country – despite the best efforts of some leading clergymen, such as Archbishop Hamilton of Glasgow, to provide a focus for revitalizing the old religion. Yet it is extremely doubtful whether the calibre of sixteenth-century churchmen was any worse than it had previously been, or whether the sixteenth-century church was any more worldly, wealthy or corrupt than it had been in the thirteenth century. Moreover, public displays of conventional piety were as evident on the very eve of the Reformation, and after, as they had been previously. And the yearning which many Protestants expressed for a more austere and pure religion had its parallels in the Cistercian expansion of the twelfth century and the mendicant ideal of the thirteenth. Protestants and Catholics might argue over which brand of Christianity was best; but the Christian culture had been so well embedded since the twelfth century that no one denied that some form of religion was essential to the fabric of society. Faith was not a matter of choice. It was a way of life.

2. Family and Fertility

The overarching importance of religion to the mentality and culture of medieval society was reflected in secular allegiances too. Let us turn again to the wedding festivities of 1328. To modern eyes perhaps the most striking aspect of this particular marriage was the age of the central participants. David Bruce was four years old, Joan Plantagenet was seven, and they had never previously met. Even for the Middle Ages the couple were unusually young. Canon law stipulated that men should normally be at least fourteen years old when they married and women at least twelve. This, by modern standards, very liberal notion was based on the presumed age of puberty and the first assumed stirrings of concupiscence, though by medieval standards it was also a safeguard against the sin of adolescent fornication. Yet while consent to marriage from both groom and bride was an imperative, age stipulation was more of a guideline. Many couples were much older when they married, but there was a vague area of discretion in canon law which also permitted younger couples to marry, providing they consented (either explicitly in words or implicitly by the act of consummation) to the union once authoritatively able. This loophole in canon law was often taken advantage of in the sort of circumstances which arose in 1328 – when it was deemed politic to give speedy effect to other agreements associated with a marriage, in this case an Anglo-Scottish peace treaty. This, quite clearly, was an arranged marriage and making the arrangements had involved protracted negotiations between the families of the bride and groom as to what resources each partner was to bring into the marriage. In that sense it was not unusual, for even marriages which resulted from courtship rather than parental design were frequently preceded by similar familial negotiations.

Among the élite at least, the outcome of premarital deliberations was normally enshrined in a formal marriage contract. This was what, in this particular instance, the 1328 treaty essentially constituted. By such agreements it was normal for the wife to be accompanied by a fitting dowry (in Scots 'tocher'), though in the Bruce–Plantagenet marriage of 1328 King Robert appears to have waived the conventional expectations of a father-in-law. Joan's dowry was, in effect, English recognition of Scottish independence. More conventionally the dowry came in the form of property, money, animals or chattels. Since there are indications that by the sixteenth century – by the thirteenth century, if Scotland followed the pattern of other countries – the size of dowries was subject to gradual inflation, a posse of marriageable daughters was an expensive business for a father. As a consequence, elsewhere in Christendom, but perhaps in Scotland too, many couples preferred cohabitation to marriage. Cohabitation avoided the customary necessity of providing a marital dowry, though from the fifteenth century canon lawyers came to regard longstanding cohabitation as *de facto* marriage. Although concubinage among the laity was prohibited by the church in 1514, following the deliberations of the Fifth Lateran Council, we may presume that little changed in reality and that some couples continued simply to live together. Meanwhile, dowry inflation was not matched by a corresponding rise in the value of the dower (in Scots 'terce'), which a husband traditionally provided for his wife and which was regarded as a wife's security in widowhood. In the Bruce–Plantagenet marriage, the dower was suitably large for Joan's status, amounting to the annual rent of £2,000 worth of land. Amid these political calculations and financial negotiations, personal feelings counted for little. Although consent to marriage was essential, emotional attachments were not, even after marriage, and they may never have followed for David and Joan. She, at least, spent the last three years of her life in England, while the king cavorted at home with his mistress, Margaret Drummond.

While the object of medieval marriage was not always the fulfilment of personal relationships, it did serve other important purposes. Some marriages were contracted to underpin an existing alliance between families. Some, like the Bruce–Plantagenet wedding, were intended to symbolize reconciliation between warring families. Others had significant socio-economic results and may have been arranged with these factors in mind. It was normal to marry within the same social status, but since wives often bestowed their status and wealth on their husbands, the wealthy heiress was also an attractive proposition for lesser men. The hand of Marjorie, heiress of the last Celtic earl of Buchan, enabled William Comyn in 1212 to become the first descendant of an Anglo-French immigrant to obtain the prestigious title of earl. By marrying Isabel, Countess of Mar, in 1404, the illegitimate adventurer Alexander Stewart acquired status and wealth which, as a bastard, he would otherwise probably not have attained. Much the same went on in urban society. In 1503, for instance, it was by marriage to Katherine Pratt, the heiress of an Aberdeen guild member, that George Bisset obtained entry to the socially exclusive guild – as 136 other men were also to do by marriage between

1399 and 1510. And although the marital arrangements of peasant society remain more obscure, it seems likely that, albeit with fewer rewards, similar trends were at work. The number of heiresses in any given section of society should not be exaggerated; and equivalent mechanisms for the social advancement of women are markedly more difficult to trace. Nevertheless, in this otherwise rigidly stratified society a good marriage was a scarce means of social advancement.

Neither the political match nor the socio-economic one was in conflict with the religious vision of marriage. For theologians, marriage was a means by which Christian affection was spread between families and it was for that reason, coupled with the horror of incest, that the church proscribed marriages between members of the same family. This required a definition of what constituted a family. In 1215 the Fourth Lateran Council liberalized the existing definition by prohibiting marriages between men and women who were related within four degrees – that is, couples whose relationship was that of third cousins or nearer. Previously it had been within seven degrees. These prohibitions applied to blood relations and also to relations created by affinity – that is, the relatives of someone who had married a blood relation. Further, though less draconian, restrictions were placed on marriage to the relatives of godparents. Yet although the 1215 regulations marked a liberalization of earlier proscriptions, they still presented a major problem for society. Few people nowadays could name all of their third cousins. Perhaps in the less mobile society of the Middle Ages this was less problematic, but even so, in the small village community, or in aristocratic society, it remained difficult for people to find a partner who was of their own social rank and to whom they were not related. Salvation was, however, at hand: in return for a fee the rich at least could seek papal dispensation for a marriage within many of the prohibited degrees.

The important role of parents in marital negotiations reflects the social importance of the family. The family was the most basic social unit of all and at its most basic it provided both an individual and a collective identity in the bestowal of a name. Christian names often ran through generations: there were eight Robert Bruces before the last of them became King Robert I. It was also in the Middle Ages that the use of patrilineal surnames became common, though they were still not uniformly adopted in Highland regions even in the eighteenth century. Elsewhere, as names passed from generation to generation, those derived from an ancestor's Christian name, or place of origin, or occupation, might become increasingly devoid of their original meaning. Thus Christopher of Cologne, one of the merchants who delivered supplies for the wedding festivities of 1328, had little to do with the German city of Cologne. Though his ancestors may have come from Cologne, he himself was born in Flanders; he became an established merchant of *ante-bellum* Berwick, and was imprisoned during the wars of independence for his Scottish sympathies. 'Of Cologne' had become his surname. Women, meanwhile, carried their surnames into marriage and did not adopt the surname of their spouse.

Their names, as well as their terces, indicated that while they might join a family through marriage, they were not fully part of it.

A surname provided a family with a distinct identity. Family members also possessed an identity of place. At the aristocratic level of society, generations of families might live in the same castle, barring political misfortune. In these circles family solidarity and distinctiveness were further enhanced by symbolic devices, such as coats-of-arms, and from the fifteenth century by genealogies, as many families invented august origins for themselves. The Lennox family of Drummond, for instance, claimed to have originally come from Hungary in the entourage of St Margaret, while the Campbells of Argyll put it about that they were actually descended from a French family called 'de campo bello'. Of course, these were fantasies. Yet behind such nonsense was not just a fashion, but an indication that lineage mattered. As we have already seen, aristocrats took to emphasizing and differentiating their status by the clothing they wore and which they permitted others to wear. It seems that a distinctive lineage mattered increasingly in the post-plague era, when aristocrats were financially hard-pressed and nervous of their social position. Demonstrations of familial antiquity mattered less to the poorer sections of society. Yet even in these circles there are glimpses of the significance of the family to individual identity. When the records of Coldingham Priory tell us of an impecunious mid-thirteenth-century Berwickshire landlord 'selling' Stephen, the son of his former serf, and his offspring to a monk, it is a potent reminder that social status at all levels of society was inherited from parents.

Within the family the eldest male was the dominant figure. His pre-eminence was of pre-medieval origin, but it was subsequently reflected in and justified by much Christian literature of that period. Women everywhere struggled to overcome the negative role model provided by Eve, seducer of Adam in the Garden of Eden and betrayer of man. If they did, they fell short of their other male-inflicted role model, the Virgin Mary. She at least was a positive image – the most powerful of the saints, a worker of miracles, and someone to whom men as well as women prayed. Unfortunately, she was also, alone of all her sex, such a benign force that few if any women could replicate her worthiness. Women's entrapment in their biblical shortcomings made it fitting for St Paul to decree, in his enormously influential letter to the Ephesians, 'Let wives be subject to their husbands because a husband is head of the wife, just as Christ is head of the church.' Such pronouncements were endorsed by evidence of an allegedly medical nature, which prompted the influential thirteenth-century theologian St Thomas Aquinas to opine that a woman's lack of mental and physical strength made her unfit to play a central role in human affairs. The principal exception, of course, was in motherhood.

The authority of the husband was both reflected and enshrined in common law. Upon marriage the husband acquired a measure of legal authority over his wife and all her possessions. She could not make a will without her husband's consent and he was permitted to speak for her in court proceedings. He was also entitled to chide her 'by words and blows', whereas she was restricted to the use of a sharp tongue. This is not to argue that wives had no rights: the husband could not, for instance, unilaterally dispose of her property and possessions, and he owed her, much as she owed him, the marital debt of sexual relations. Indeed, impotence and non-consummation were two of the very few admissible grounds for the annulment of a marriage. Nevertheless, although in theory husband and wife were regarded as equals in marriage, Christian tradition and secular law regarded the husband as head of the family, which in practice meant that wives were of secondary status. This was mirrored by the limited opportunities for independent employment which were open to wives. We rarely, for instance, hear of queens involved directly in politics until their husbands were dead; we rarely hear of merchants' wives conducting trade unless their husbands were away; and the bonnet-makers of Dundee were not unique in 1496 when they restricted female member-ship of their guild to the widows of male brethren.

Of course, that is not to argue that women did not work. It is difficult to believe that queens suddenly found an aptitude for politics once their husbands were buried; that merchants' wives suddenly developed an acumen for business in the absence of their husbands; or that Dundonian widows suddenly discovered a talent for bonnet-making. The actual working environment, especially in agrarian communities, was probably a good deal more cooperative than the male terminology normally used in official documentation and reflected in Christian commentaries on marital relationships would suggest. Still, the opportunities for widows in all of these occupations derived from the occupations of their dead husbands rather than from their own independently chosen skills and aptitudes. Wives followed husbands to work and only in towns can women be easily identified pursuing independent careers. Even there they tended to work in occupations where little formal training was required and which were frequently similar to the mundane chores they performed in the domestic household. Domestic service, retailing, prostitution, baking and brewing were notably female professions: there were more than 150 female brewers in Aberdeen in 1509 and more than 230 of them in Edinburgh in 1530. If brewing was female work, this was partly because it was a part-time occupation and largely undertaken at home with utensils – pots, vats, ladles, straining cloths – which were readily to hand in the domestic kitchen.

Of course, female employment was subject to pregnant pauses. Some aristocratic women spent a considerable part of their married life in a state of pregnancy: Mary of Guelders was with child for six years of her eleven-year marriage to James II. This was probably not the experience of most ordinary women. Although even the peasant women of Montaillou in France hired a wet-nurse when necessary, poorer women were more likely than queens to breast-feed their children. Lactation reduced female fertility. As we have already seen from the skeletal evidence, breast-feeding was probably a more prolonged process than nowadays – medieval medical treatises normally recommended a period of two years, and other continental evidence confirms that children were not normally weaned until the age of about eighteen months.

Once older, children were reminded in the Book of Deuteronomy to 'Honour thy father and mother, as the Lord God hath commanded thee'. If they did not, St Margaret was perhaps not untypical in devoting some severity to chastising her children. She knew, her biographer Turgot tells us, the maxim that 'he who spares the rod hates his son', and she sanctioned whippings of her offspring when they erred in infantile naughtiness. As children grew older they expected a greater say in their own lives. The test of generational wills was perhaps at its most acute when marriage loomed. Janet Stewart was not alone in alleging before an ecclesiastical court in 1522 that her parents had compelled her by force and fear of death into marrying a man for whom she had no affection: she was rather more unusual in publicly challenging the parental will by bringing her case to court and obtaining an annulment on the grounds that she had not consented to the marriage. Yet even this example bespeaks a keen parental interest in the future welfare of a child. There were, of course, pragmatic grounds for such concern. Especially in poorer households, children were a useful source of cheap labour and although this was less important in the aristocratic milieu, where young children might be farmed out to wet-nurses and older ones to tutors, children were of vital significance in a society where lineage mattered. Marriage too was a matter of familial honour. For these reasons alone it remains difficult to accept the view advanced by some sociologists that because death rates were so high among medieval children, parents formed an emotional detachment from them. Indeed, there is some evidence to the contrary, such as the clear distress which overcame James I when he dispatched his eleven-year-old daughter Margaret overseas for her marriage to Louis, dauphin of France. Orphans, meanwhile, were often objects of pity and charitable bequest.

The Bonds of Medieval Society: Class and Hierarchy

Relations between, as well as within, families were organized along broadly hierarchical lines. Such stratification was reflected in the religiously infused belief in a 'Great Chain of Being' which ascended from hell to heaven. Every organism had its divinely appointed place in this order and such cosmic understanding could be applied to earthly society to legitimize class differences. While such theorizing was no doubt more familiar to academics than it was to peasants, so far as is known the concept of a hierarchical society provoked remarkably little criticism in medieval Scotland. Another God-given social demarcation existed between those whose function it was to work (the peasantry), those who fought (the aristocrats) and those who prayed (the clergy). Townspeople, and women, fitted uneasily into this conception. For rural society, however, the term 'feudalism' has tended to dominate historical discourse about social hierarchy in the Middle Ages, even though it is a term loaded with difficulties and a word not invented until after that period. The image that 'feudalism' may still conjure up – of a pyramidal society, with the king at the top, barons in a secondary layer and a mass of labouring peasantry, tied to the land, at the bottom – is not particularly useful. Even historians who deal with the heartland and birthplace of what has been termed 'feudalism', north-western France, have found that the feudal pyramid crumbles: the term is not found to be easily definable and coherent.

In relation to Scotland it could be argued that the utility of the term 'feudalism' is even more limited. Scotland was not an area in which feudal institutions developed from within the indigenous society; instead feudalism in Scotland was imported by foreigners, from Normandy, Flanders, Brittany and England, who were encouraged to settle by successive kings in the twelfth and thirteenth centuries. In Scotland too, feudalism has to be seen gradually establishing itself alongside older, pre-existing patterns in which tenure of land and social organization was structured by ties of kinship. Recent research has demonstrated that feudalism cannot be said to have replaced these older institutions. Fife was one of the earliest Scottish provinces to be granted by crown charter to its native lord as a feudal fief (by David I in c. 1136.). Thereafter, Fife was ruled by the same comital family of ancient lineage, but now holding its lands as tenants of the crown and in return for military service, while the title of earl passed through the generations by primogeniture – a new system of inheritance whereby the eldest male heir usually succeeded to the bulk of the family properties.

Yet the neat transition to feudal tenure suggested by much of the extant documentation is misleadingly simple. In Fife, the feudal earls co-existed and shared power with a collateral line which represented older, Celtic, kin-based structures of lordship. The leader of kin-based society in Fife was not necessarily the earl but the holder of the title 'MacDuff' – a patronymic meaning 'Son of Dub' or 'Son of the Black One', likely to have descended from the Dub who was king of Scots from 962 to 966. It was MacDuff, when the earl was a minor, who was to be found leading the men of Fife at the battle of Falkirk in 1298; and the feudal military obligations many of them doubtless performed may well have been little more than a terminological change from the more ancient responsibility of all men to serve for perhaps forty days in the common army of the kingdom. The ancient and local legal traditions known as the Law of Clan MacDuff also retained real force, even in sixteenth-century Fife. The term 'feudalism', in short, is inadequate to describe the complex and varied patterns of landholding and social obligation that resulted from the Scottish amalgam of native influences and foreign innovations.

Having said this, we cannot ignore the salient fact that Scottish kings encouraged and invited what can loosely be termed Anglo-French incomers into Scotland. These new arrivals not only brought with them, as we have seen, new culinary influences.

They also introduced novel institutions of landholding which were adopted by the native aristocracy. Scottish kings, too, found it desirable to articulate their rights of lordship over their subjects in concrete legal terms which were inscribed in charters by sophisticated clerks. We must bear in mind the changes that occurred, but instead of concentrating on the narrow legalities of feudalism it might be more useful to examine in practice the lifestyles of the two broad groupings that dominated rural secular society. These were the aristocracy, who owned the land, and the peasantry, who lived on and from it.

1. The Peasantry

The more difficult group to understand is undoubtedly the peasantry. Common people were largely voiceless in medieval societies; empowering them with speech several centuries later is not easy. Yet what we term the peasantry constituted numerically the vast majority of all medieval societies. Scotland was no exception to this. Statistics are hard to come by but one recent estimate is that the aristocracy amounted to only around 1 per cent of later medieval Scotland's population – and the urban population was scarcely larger. The peasantry did not write, and they were rarely of enough individual prominence to attract the attention of those who did write, the chroniclers and the government officials. What can be gleaned of their lifestyles, attitudes and place in society as a whole? For one thing, we can perceive a great diversity of experience among the 'peasantry', for this term, like so many others, is only a convenient label. It groups together an array of people whose standing in society and wealth varied enormously. The peasant class was labelled with many different names: leaseholders, tacksmen, husbandmen, cottars, labourers, hurd-men, neyfs, serfs – and many others. The very diversity of the terms used to describe 'the peasantry' begins to hint at the complex layers of social structure and material standing evident in rural society.

One means of differentiating the diverse groups which constituted the bulk of the population is to utilize the categories 'free' and 'unfree'. In this sense, those at the bottom of the social tree were outright slaves. Scotland in 1100 most certainly tolerated slavery; documentary evidence attests to this. It seems, also, that early invasions of England, at least for many of the Scots involved, were expeditions whose purpose was the acquisition of slaves. The northern English chronicler Symeon of Durham suggested that the Scottish invasion of 1070 was so geared to this aim that in its aftermath every hamlet and hut in Scotland had its English slaves. We must beware of propagandist exaggeration, but English chroniclers could still maintain that the invasion of David I in 1138 was at heart a slave-hunting exercise for many in the Scottish host. In common with the broader pattern in western Christendom, however, slavery was a dying institution by the twelfth century.

Yet the end of slavery did not mean that peasants were thereafter uniformly free. The great majority of them remained subject to the constraints of serfdom. The term 'serf' in itself encompasses an array of different patterns of social and legal obligation and great variations in wealth. At one level the serf lowest in legal status was literally 'unfree' in that he was tied to an estate and obliged to perform labour services for the landowner. This serf could be bought and sold with the land. The ownership of men, as well as of land, was a subject for aristocratic dispute into the fourteenth century. But serfdom in this sense – being legally tied to the land – was in decline by the late thirteenth century, and it seems to have disappeared completely in the fourteenth century. Economic factors perhaps best explain this process. If the Scottish pattern fits with the wider European model, then the thirteenth century was, as we have seen, a time of economic expansion and population growth. A buoyant population and plentiful labour seems to have rendered it unnecessary for aristocratic landholders to tie Scottish peasants to the land. And it seems that landlords during the wars of independence, perhaps as a result of economic dislocation, were increasingly happy to exchange labour services owed by their peasants for rents in hard cash. Servile labour was certainly the glue with which peasants were most readily stuck to the land, and in Scotland it was loosened early. Relevant, too, was the fact that Scotland did not generally feature terrain well suited to arable cultivation of the lord's demesne. These factors together help to explain the decline of serfdom in Scotland and its apparent disappearance in the fourteenth century while it was still an entrenched, if not quite flourishing, institution in some other areas of the Latin west.

Was the decline of serfdom a sign that the social condition of the Scottish peasantry was more than usually healthy relative to European norms? Not necessarily, for most peasants were certainly not 'free' in the modern sense. Peasants in fourteenth-century Scotland may not have been tied to the land, and frequently may not have been obliged to undertake servile labour – ploughing, harvesting and so on – on the lord's demesne; but they were still legally bound to grind their corn in their lord's mill, to endure their lord's justice and to shoulder other obligations, such as 'merchet' (a payment for the lord's authorization of a daughter's marriage) and 'heriot' (an inheritance payment on the succession of an heir). This should not surprise us. There was at the heart of medieval society an exploitative relationship between landholders and peasantry. Arguably, the key element in the introduction of feudalism, at least at the local level, was a firmer definition of just how landlords could extract the profits created by the surplus of their tenants' labours. This might entail serfdom in the classical form – the tying of tenants to land and their physical exploitation to farm the lord's estates. As we have seen, even after the death of serfdom there remained other ways in which landlords could appropriate the surplus produced by peasant labour. And in any case, legal status may have been far less significant to a peasant than his modes of access to wealth and the share of surplus which he could enjoy.

Examining the physical manner in which land was exploited by the peasantry provides a further insight into the social organization of the medieval countryside. The dominant economic and social unit in rural society was the farm toun. The forms which touns could take, the ways in which they were exploited and the forms of peasant tenure within them varied enormously. They were not of standard size. Nor were they farmed in an identical fashion. Two significant features of land usage in touns were, however, widespread throughout Scotland. One was runrig farming, the system whereby the territory of a toun was shared by more than one tenant and then divided into strips of land for individual cultivation. Another important feature was the division of touns into infield and outfield, in which the former was exploited intensively and the latter only on a rotational basis; beyond this were outlying common pastures, where sheep and cattle were grazed. Those who rented touns were the wealthiest and most visible sector of the peasantry in the historical record – husbandmen.

Estate rentals for Coldingham Priory and Kelso Abbey (dating from *c.* 1300) and for the secular landlord Sir James Douglas of Dalkeith (dating from 1376–7) provide some help in seeking to understand this section of the peasantry. It is clear, for instance, that husbandmen often rented their lands on a communal basis with as many as ten husbandmen sharing the rent of some of Douglas's touns. After the Black Death, prosperous husbandmen were able to acquire lands in several touns. In the Dumfriesshire barony of Buittle, for instance, Gilbert Gilbertson rented land in four touns as well as the local mill. Under normal conditions husbandmen were probably able to feed themselves and their families quite comfortably and they could hope to benefit from the sale of surplus production. Another key characteristic of rural society was the usual mechanism by which peasants held their lands – an annually renegotiated (and probably verbal) agreement of rental. This certainly rendered the livelihoods of the sitting tenants perennially insecure and gave landlords the opportunity to strike a better deal for themselves, especially in the period before *c.* 1300 when the population was reasonably buoyant and land consequently scarce. From the fourteenth century, however, and especially after the Black Death, this form of tenure may have suited the peasantry better: annual renegotiations of leases in a period of labour shortage was surely in the interest of tenants. The growing population in the sixteenth century altered the balance once more in favour of the landowner.

Estate records give some detail regarding the position of husbandmen, but less on those at the next level down in peasant society, such as cottars. It is clear, though, that cottars (presumably greater in number than the more prosperous husbandmen) rented small amounts of land from husbandmen. They were also used as a labour force by husbandmen. Even below the level of cottar the historian Professor Archibald Duncan has posited 'the existence of a rural proletariat which figures in no charter'. Their number probably included those who were severely disabled, infirm or terminally sick (such as lepers), who usually at best made do with occasional distributions of aristocratic charity and the relief provided in hospitals, of which there were about sixty by 1300 and a growing number in the fifteenth and sixteenth centuries. Meanwhile, the able-bodied proletariat constituted an essentially landless, mobile labour force: it was hired by husbandmen and by cottars, and also by landlords, since demesne cultivation required paid labour over and above the obligatory services owed by peasant tenants. The role of husbandmen and even cottars in utilizing paid labour warns us, then, against picturing a simple social structure whereby peasants toiled and aristocrats exploited. In the stratified society of the countryside wealthier peasants also exploited their inferiors in the attempt to take what surplus they could from their lands. These labourers also serve as a warning against applying too strictly a dichotomy between 'free' and 'unfree' in rural society. Landless wage labourers were certainly free – but their social position and wealth was well below that of the peasant tenants whose tenures bore the distinct, albeit fading, marks of bondage to their superiors.

The glimpse of landless workers raises wider questions about the lower orders and their status in society. By reference to the labouring classes of much of Christendom, the decline of serfdom would appear to suggest that the social condition of Scottish peasants was relatively healthy. This could be taken further. Scotland would appear to have been free of the violent social confrontations so apparent in other areas of the Latin west. In France, for instance, the peasants' revolt of 1358 witnessed class struggle of great brutality; there is no hint of anything similar in Scotland. In 1385 French knights who visited Scotland were much put out by the upstart nature of the Scottish peasantry. When French esquires were dispatched to seize supplies in the Lothian countryside, they were resisted with violence by the locals. At the very least there is a suggestion here that different expectations existed in French and Scottish society regarding the acceptable conduct of the peasantry towards their social betters and of the aristocracy towards their inferiors. Similarly, rural inhabitants objected to the damage done to their lands by the crowds attending the coronation of Robert III in 1390. Their gesture of discontent seems to have expressed long-established and accepted methods for drawing the attention of the powerful to the concerns of ordinary people. And our source suggests that the appeal of the peasantry met with a receptive royal response.

All of this may not quite add up to a vision of Utopia for Scottish peasants, but it would seem to suggest that their lot was relatively comfortable, at least in social terms. Can we explain this? Attempts have certainly been made. One approach is to stress that Scottish society was never fully 'feudalized': the kindred-based ethos of pre-existing social patterns in Celtic Scotland blunted the hard edge and binding legalities of feudalism found elsewhere in Christendom. Also, Scottish lordship was strongly regional in nature. Substantial landholders often enjoyed heritable jurisdictions in their domains – rights transmitted by inheritance, which meant that most aspects of justice were the responsibility of the local lord rather than the central government. Local justice may, as a result, have been much more understanding of regional concerns than the more distant state was. Local communities clearly also policed themselves. Mechanisms existed for dispute settlement which entailed local arbitration, and customary fines were paid to wronged parties for the killing of a relation – the amount of compensation depending on factors such as the status of the victim. This was the crime resolution of the community; it was an expression of authority calculated to paper over the cracks in local social patterns, aimed less at punishment than at re-establishing social harmony. And customary mechanisms of arbitration and compensation were also the means by which blood feuds – characteristic of medieval societies in which ties of kin were central to social organization – were resolved. Public ceremonies of contrition helped to appease the honour of injured parties, while the strength of regional lordship meant that this form of conflict resolution could be enforced effectively. A third explanation for the apparently tractable nature of the lower orders has also been offered: burgeoning national identity was fostered by the wars with England from 1296. It has been argued that this consciousness, shared across all levels of society, militated against the expression of class conflict.

Consensus has not been reached on these points. One of the reasons for this, again, is that the evidence relating to the peasantry is patchy and ambivalent. For instance, in 1305 an enigmatic appeal was sent to Edward I, the English king, then in reasonably secure control of much of Scotland, requesting that Scottish peasants should enjoy the same, more secure tenure as that which prevailed in England. On one reading, this petition might attest to the self-confidence of the Scottish peasantry: they had a voice, and they expected it to be listened to at the highest governmental level. Another approach would be to focus on the nature of the complaint itself, with its indication of discontent at the insecure manner in which land was leased.

Despite tenurial insecurity, some peasants were, as we have seen, wealthy; and there was also a substantial element of rural society which, in the wrong economic conditions, would have been desperately poor. The latter is evident in government legislation of the later Middle Ages dealing with landless men and with beggars. One process which may have added to the largely hidden experience of peasant misery was the development and extension of feuing, the holding of lands by tenants in feu-ferm, during the later Middle Ages. In this form of landholding the tenant was given tenure for life, or even heritably in perpetuity. Conversion from short-term leases to the security of feu-ferm came, though, at a price. A substantial initial cash grant had to be paid to the landlord, and the annual payment was often significantly higher than the old rent had been. Conversion to feu-ferm was available only to those who already possessed capital. For old sitting tenants without the necessary hard cash the result was eviction, followed by movement to a farm elsewhere in Scotland or a future in the ranks of the landless poor – or, possibly, recourse to emigration. The introduction of feu-ferm was no doubt an important economic development for landholders; but its greatest impact may have been at the level of the peasantry. For those with some cash and an entrepreneurial spirit there were significant opportunities for advancement. For many, however, the reality was disenfranchisement and expulsion. This is hardly a comfortable image of the position of the peasantry at the end of the Middle Ages. Early sixteenth-century literary works bear this out: the court poet of James V, Sir David Lindsay, depicts in his poetry an embattled and aggrieved peasant class.

Even the absence of peasants' revolts in Scotland is not particularly telling evidence of social harmony. Uprisings elsewhere in Christendom tended to occur in regions of relative wealth, and in areas where there were significant urban accumulations. Scotland possessed neither the rich arable territory, nor the sizeable towns. Perhaps this, rather than a broad social harmony, more readily explains the apparent lack of class struggle. Certainly, the limited written sources for Scotland seem to suggest no greater aristocratic tolerance of social inferiors than is found elsewhere. Walter Bower was happy to compare peasants to dogs. He also strongly condemned the English Peasants' Revolt of 1381. This was an expression of powerful social prejudice on the part of Abbot Bower. His chronicle is remorselessly anti-English, yet when peasants dared to threaten the fabric of English society, Bower's class allegiances emerged triumphant. In short, a vision of elements of the Scottish peasantry as a desperate and disempowered class could be portrayed quite as easily as the image of a relatively comfortable social grouping, with an articulated and respected place in society.

Modern research on the nature of later medieval politics would seem to support the grimmer assessment. The later Middle Ages were marked, according to much recent political history, by brutal struggle in the localities between power-hungry magnate factions. At the cutting edge of these conflicts were local communities, terrorized into submission by regional warlords. This image does not fit, at all, with the other picture, of a fairly secure Scottish peasantry, generally at one with the ruling classes. We have, then, conflicting images of the social position and material well-being of the peasantry. There may be some truth in both images, but there is clearly no current consensus on the standing of medieval peasants within medieval Scottish society.

2. The Aristocracy

There is no such debate concerning the social position of the aristocracy. This group inhabited the same realm as the peasantry, but when dealing with this class we seem to find ourselves in a quite different world of markedly broader horizons. Here again, though, we must be sensitive to the use of such a blanket term as 'aristocracy' to describe a complex and varied social grouping. One suitable definition of the aristocracy would be that class which consisted of freeholders, those who held land securely, and usually acquired charters to prove the point. If we use this definition, the aristocracy was numerically minute in relation to what we have termed 'the peasantry'. Yet in terms of importance, of prominence in national affairs, in governance, in political power, it was dominant. This dominance was, however, by no means evenly distributed among 'the aristocracy'. At the lower level are what we might call lairds or gentry, small landholders; at the top, the politically dominant higher nobility, the magnates of the realm — a group with considerably more land, whose number has been estimated to have hovered at around fifty in the later Middle Ages.

The higher nobility was clearly a very exclusive club. The great magnates typically possessed wide territorial and jurisdictional authority and a voice that would be heard in the running of government. As with so much else, however, the magnate class of Celtic Scotland was transformed in complex ways by the influx of foreign influences introduced into Scotland during the twelfth and thirteenth centuries. The new arrivals were hardly numerous, consisting of aristocrats and their adherents, although their influence ultimately extended throughout lowland Scotland. Many of the Anglo-French incomers established magnate dynasties founded on extensive royal patronage. But the Celtic aristocracy was not displaced. Rather, it adopted and assimilated many of the aspects of the new lordship and the culture that went with it. The magnate class of thirteenth-century Scotland was a Celtic and Anglo-French hybrid. The descendant of Anglo-French incomers, Robert I was clearly at home in the Gaelic milieu of western Scotland and Ireland. Native earls, meanwhile, adopted primogeniture and the charter — the written document which specified the legalities of the new type of lord–vassal relationship. As this hybrid aristocratic society developed, the new languages of Latin, French and (latterly) English, which the immigrants brought with them, steadily advanced, even north of the Forth.

One result of the Anglo-French influx was that the aristocracy could now be easily identified as belonging to a European élite. Their concerns, their interests, their position in society: these the higher nobility of Scotland shared with other aristocracies and their peers elsewhere in Christendom. This is readily illustrated. Some Scots who participated in the First Crusade were, as we have seen, remarkable to continental observers for their uncouth mannerisms and appearance. In later centuries Scots were much more readily assimilated into the aristocratic brotherhood of international chivalry. So we find that Scottish noble houses are well represented in the *Armorial de Gelre*, a late fourteenth-century *Who's Who* of the European aristocracy. Scottish nobles also adorn the pages of Jean Froissart's *Chronicles*, a work devoted to the martial deeds of the same international class. The multifaceted connections of the house of Douglas with the states and magnate families of later medieval Christendom amply demonstrate that in practice, too, the magnates of Scotland interacted as equals with their continental peers. James, the future ninth Earl of Douglas, was a celebrated enough figure amongst the continental aristocracy to inspire the leading exponent of Burgundian chivalric endeavour, Jacques de Lalaing, to travel to Scotland in 1448 and engage him in personal feats of arms.

One way to analyse the status, lifestyles and concerns of the later medieval Scottish nobility is to examine the activities of an individual whose career would appear to encompass many of the themes important to the class as a whole. One such character is George Dunbar, tenth Earl of March, who was active in the late fourteenth and early fifteenth centuries. In common with many Scottish magnates of the time, the Earl of March enjoyed jurisdiction and wide powers in distinct regional locations. His earldom encompassed much of south-east Scotland and included extensive lands in Berwickshire and East Lothian. He was also lord of Annandale, in the western Borders. March was not notably active at the Scottish court – but his status enabled him to suppose that he should be consulted on, and involved in, the major matters of policy which confronted central government. More normally, though, the earl's concerns were regional. He was interested in the management of his extensive estates; and he was interested in making money from them in a period when, perhaps, circumstances were not always favourable for aristocratic finances. This economic concern is markedly pointed by March's mercantile contacts, which extended from his own port of Dunbar, across the border to Newcastle and to London, and reached as far as the Baltic.

Another sphere of interest of the Earl of March that reflected a wider aristocratic concern was his enthusiastic involvement in warfare. By far the most successful Scottish warrior of his time during a period of intense Anglo-Scottish conflict, March was involved in all the major campaigns and battles of the period. This activity identifies him also with the strongly Scottish attitude (amongst the aristocracy certainly, and surely at lower levels of society as well) of entrenched anti-English feeling. Yet the Earl of March defected from the Scottish allegiance in 1400 and chose to fight in the service of the English king against his countrymen in the early fifteenth century. A different, overlapping aristocratic loyalty proved, for him, more powerful than his sense of national belonging. It was a slight to the earl's family pride that drove March into the arms of the English. His daughter Elizabeth had been betrothed to the heir to the Scottish throne, the Duke of Rothesay, and their relationship had, it seems, been consummated. But Rothesay rejected the earl's daughter and married instead the daughter of the Earl of Douglas. No doubt political manoeuvrings played a part in this development, but the root cause of the March defection was slighted family pride.

The Earl of March was finally to return to Scottish allegiance and die, probably in the early 1420s, aged over eighty. Perhaps the most powerful elements in his world view were pride and status. But we also see in him the other characteristics of the magnate class. Strong regional powers and interests did not undermine an internationalism of outlook, sensibility and class loyalty. This helps to explain why a powerful sense of national identity did not rule out March's transferral of allegiance in 1400. The imperative of familial advancement; a relish of warfare; conventional piety, very local in the direction of its patronage; an eye on the profit motive. These concerns were not just those of the Earl of March. They were the common currency of the magnate class of Scotland and, indeed, the aristocracies of Christendom as a whole. Yet in some senses the magnate class was on the brink of great change as the earl's career drew to a close. March exercised extensive regional powers, as great magnates in Scotland always had.

Increasingly, during the fifteenth century, the crown was reluctant to concede such authority. Great regional power blocs were broken up and redistributed. Most notably the successively assertive kings, James I and James II, destroyed the two greatest of Scottish magnate houses, those of the Albany Stewarts and the Douglases. In its traditional sense, at any rate, the era of the great magnate was coming to an end. Regional power became less extensive; an ethos of crown service became more than previously the key to advancement. In tandem with these profound developments went changes in the nature of lordship. From the fifteenth century, written records exist of formal expressions of the relationship between lords and men, known as bonds of manrent. A personal element to lordship was not new, but as the regional authority of local magnates became less secure, these undertakings were a means of bolstering noble power. Loyal service was offered to the lord; the man received maintenance, the promise of powerful support. For all that the truly great magnate had been removed from the scene by the mid-fifteenth century, it was still the great noble, albeit through different mechanisms, who dominated secular society as the Middle Ages drew to a close.

Yet as the Middle Ages came to an end greater prominence beckoned for the lesser nobility, that class of the aristocracy which came to be termed lairds. This group had always been important as the mainstay of local administration in the vast regional tracts dominated by the great lords, and they had always been vital as the primary military supporters of the magnates. As freeholders, this class had wealth enough to avail itself of suitable military apparel. The house of Douglas, for instance, in the fourteenth and fifteenth centuries took some trouble to cultivate links with the lairds of 'the Forest' in the central Borders, and to harness to their own ends the military abilities of family kindreds like the Kerrs, Scotts, Pringles and Turnbulls. Families such as these were not only crucial adjuncts to magnate influence; they could also act without the overt leadership of the great men of the realm – it was famously the 'middling folk' who supported William Wallace (himself a lesser noble) in his rising of 1297. One thing that Wallace's leadership suggests is that at this early stage the distinction between the great aristocrats and those who possessed a merely regional prominence was somewhat blurred. Wallace, though patently not of the first rank of nobles, was not out of place leading the Scottish host in war. Nor did his status prevent him from acting as guardian of the realm.

Only from the 1440s does a legal distinction emerge between the majority of freeholders and the minority who formed the ranks of the higher nobility. This was the development of lords of parliament, which gave the higher nobility the right to be summoned personally to parliament. This distanced them from the lairds. Yet this ostentatious mark of status should perhaps be seen as a sop to magnate insecurity rather than as a backward step for the lesser nobles. By the mid-fifteenth century the truly great magnate territorial power bases were being dismantled by assertive royalty. One ally of the crown in this process was the increasingly assertive class of lairds, particularly in the destruction of Black Douglas power in the 1450s. The opportunities of royal service, furthermore, offered promise for the laird on the make, and a king such as James III, at odds with much of the magnate class, sought to use the gentry as a powerful counterbalance. The rural representatives of the 'middling sort' could not be ignored by the sixteenth century. By 1560 the lairds were decisively on the march, the foot-soldiers of the Reformation in Scotland.

3. The Clergy

As far as the countryside is concerned, there remains one social group to consider – the clergy. Clerics were involved in battle on behalf of secular souls, and their function in this intensely religious society was not deemed an easy one even when compared with the rigours of fighting and working. Yet the position of these professional Christians, of whom there were perhaps four thousand, was ambiguous. On the one hand, they formed a distinct social group, differentiated from others by their admittance to holy orders, their appearance (they were tonsured and generally clean-shaven) and by their exclusive accountability to ecclesiastical courts. Many ministered directly to the laity as priests – these are known collectively as the secular clergy. Others lived in cloistered premises, undertaking God's work in accordance with a rule (hence their designation as regular clergy) which entailed varying degrees of prayer, manual work and study. Among the latter were monks, canons-regular and friars. Besides the sparse remnants of the Irish monastic tradition (for instance at Iona), the Benedictines had been the first to arrive, settling initially under the patronage of St Margaret at Dunfermline and eventually taking over the Iona community in 1203. They were followed (notably at Paisley) by others who followed the stricter exemplar of Benedictine life pioneered at the French abbey of Cluny; and then by the still more fashionable Cistercians and Tironensians (who in the main settled in what were originally isolated locations in the south and east of the country) and the Valliscaulians (whose three Scottish houses were located in the north). The austere Carthusians, taking their name from the abbey of La Grande Chartreuse near Grenoble, were late to arrive, establishing their Scottish house at Perth only in 1429.

While there was little practical difference between the ethos of monks and canons-regular (the latter too came in several variants: Augustinian, Trinitarian and Premonstratensian), the mendicant orders of friars were the church's response to growing urbanization. They also came in different guises (Dominican, Franciscan, Carmelite, Augustinian and others) and became an established feature of the urban landscape from the thirteenth century. The location of their houses, indeed, provides a rough-and-ready distinction between genuine towns and the great mass of smaller burghs. Aberdeen and Edinburgh each had three friaries on the eve of the Reformation; but of ninety-seven burghs of barony established between 1450 and 1560, only one (Kingussie) had a friary

(Carmelite). Opportunities for religious women were markedly more limited. Only fifteen nunneries were established in Scotland, and four of them were suppressed before the Reformation, compared with over a hundred establishments founded for men.

There was something else which broadly distinguished the clergy from other sections of society: their education. Admittedly, this should not be exaggerated. Gaelic society was capable of producing medical treatises which were informed by the standard Arabic and Greek texts on the subject and, at least towards the end of the period, secular schools became increasingly common in the urban environment. By contrast, many humble priests probably stumbled through mass in a Latin learned by rote; in the later fourteenth century only some 20 per cent had experience of a university. Nevertheless, throughout the period many of the higher clergy were formally educated. A significant proportion of them attended university: between 1350 and 1425, for instance, at least 80 per cent of bishops were university graduates. Medieval universities were male and essentially religious establishments – and for most of the medieval period those who wished to matriculate at them were forced to travel abroad. Oxford and Cambridge were popular with Scottish students until the thirteenth century, as were Paris, Orleans and Bologna throughout the medieval period and, latterly, the new universities of Cologne and Leuven, founded respectively in 1388 and 1425. Many Scots continued to receive a foreign education even after the foundation of three Scottish universities at St Andrews (1411–12), Glasgow (1450–51) and Aberdeen (1495).

Yet, although distinctive in function and to some extent education, clerical society was never entirely detached from more worldly concerns. In some ways education bound at least the higher clergymen more closely to the élite of secular society since the latter relied predominantly upon literate clerics for their administrative services. The great offices of state were frequently held by clerics. Regulations on clerical celibacy, even though not always observed, meant that the church always had to recruit in the secular world. New recruits tended to bring secular attitudes with them. While it was possible for a man of urban origins, such as David Bernham, bishop of St Andrews (1239–53), to attain high ecclesiastical office, those at the pinnacle of clerical society usually came from privileged and landed families. It was with an eye to the wealth and influence which accompanied high ecclesiastical office that the church was deemed a suitable career for many younger sons of baronial background. Few of such origin would have been satisfied with the meagre incomes set aside for humble priests and some shamelessly exploited ecclesiastical resources for familial ends. In 1426 the abbot of Benedictine Iona complained that his noble predecessor had kept noblewomen as concubines, fathered offspring by them, and then siphoned off the monastery's wealth to provide his bastards with lucrative dowries. God, it seemed, worked in sometimes mysterious ways.

4. The Townspeople

Scotland was an overwhelmingly rural society, and the peasantry, aristocracy and clergy shared mainly rural concerns. Their lives were structured and ordered around the necessities of agricultural production. The inhabitants of towns, as we have seen, did not fully stand apart from the countryside economically, but were distinctive because of the concentration of commercial activities which took place within the urban milieu. Similarly, in terms of social organization the towns, like the countryside, featured strong hierarchical structures, though their nature was dictated by the overriding imperative either to manufacture goods or to buy and sell them.

The ruling urban élite were the burgesses, initially those who held property directly of the burgh's overlord, and later those who were accepted as such by the town authorities. These were the wealthy of the town – the more prosperous among the craftsmen, but especially the merchants. These men formed an exclusive club. Of the thousand or so inhabitants of early sixteenth-century Dunfermline, only about 140 were burgesses. It was this urban plutocracy alone which had a political voice. Moreover, its spheres of interest, occupations and political pretensions were protected by social confraternities, institutionalized as guilds. These were essentially exclusive clubs for the richest merchants and craftsmen of the towns. Admission to the Dunfermline guild, if not inherited, normally required a payment of forty shillings, plus a donation of spices and wine. This was beyond the reach of all but the fairly prosperous; and in Dunfermline only about a third of the burgess population joined the guild. Guild members had a powerful part in electing, from amongst the burgess community, the administrative officials who ran towns and who expressed the external voice of the urban communities. Furthermore, in the later medieval period there are signs that the merchant burgesses sought increasingly to keep power in their own hands and out of the sphere of the craftsmen. There was no question, needless to say, of the labouring poor having a direct voice in towns or the opportunity to wield authority. We might expect this narrow concentration of urban power to have caused social discontent but, as in rural society, manifestations of this are hard to discern. Just as there were no peasant revolts in rural Scotland, there were no popular uprisings in urban Scotland of the sort evident in many continental towns. Resistance to merchant plutocracies is, at most, a muted rumble, though rumbles there certainly were. They were especially common in the later fifteenth and early sixteenth centuries, as craftsmen agitated (ultimately successfully) for some greater representation on town councils and for the right to establish their own guilds.

Protection of social and economic status was not, however, the sole concern of the urban élite. What we also find among burgesses is an aspiration to reach beyond the rickety fences which constituted most urban perimeters as rich townsmen strove for advancement into the ranks of the rural aristocracy. This ambition, of course, required land – and merchants were well placed to gather the necessary capital for investment in property. Acceptance into the ranks of the nobility could certainly be achieved by at least the later fourteenth century. Sir John Forrester of Corstorphine, for instance, was a burgess of Edinburgh and bailie of the town as well as a rural landowner who led a military retinue in the Scottish débâcle at the battle of Humbleton in 1402. Meanwhile, the converse was also evident: in the later fifteenth and sixteenth centuries the landed aristocracy increasingly began to purchase residential accommodation in towns. Increasingly, too, the social stratification of urban inhabitants was complicated by the emergence of professionals, in the main lawyers, whose number mushroomed especially in Edinburgh following the creation of the College of Justice, the central court for civil matters, in 1532. Yet for all the growing social complexity of the urban milieu, the defining characteristic of social life in the later Middle Ages depended not so much on whether the primary locale was rural or urban, or even on wealth. Instead, as in the countryside, it depended on position and status relative to others.

The Bonds of Medieval Society: Leisure and Recreation

How close can we get to understanding the cultural concerns and interests of the peoples who constituted the hierarchical society of medieval Scotland? The most difficult group to reach, again, is the peasantry. Our impression of peasant life might in general be one of struggle, but we can see none the less that peasants did not spend their whole existence trying to eke a meagre living from the land. The 'rustic demonstration' of 1390 already referred to shows us that the peasants had a voice that could, on occasion at least, reach the ear of the very highest in medieval society. The demonstration also hints at elements of peasant popular culture. Clearly, the harvest celebration was an annual event in the lives of peasants. The safe collection of the harvest inspired a procession, featuring both men and women, accompanied by music and the veneration of the landscape's fertility by the construction of a 'corn dolly' – apparently termed a 'rapegyrne', at least by the peasantry of the Perth area in the late fourteenth century. Our evidence from the 1390 incident tells us little more than this of peasant popular culture – but we can surely assume that harvest festivities also featured a certain amount of feasting, dancing and drinking. We can be particularly confident about the latter if estimates that one-third of grain production was turned into ale are accurate.

The peasantry certainly had time to spend on leisure activities: Holy Days were times of rest, the rhythms of agricultural production did not require constant work, and people may not in any case have had a sufficient calorific intake to undertake physical labour every day. One means to help us sample the flavour of daily life is governmental and ecclesiastical legislation which attempted to control certain activities. In the diocese of Aberdeen it was decreed during the thirteenth century that wrestling and other sports should not be allowed in churches and churchyards, an indication not only of rural pastimes but also of the centrality of the parish church as a social focal point. We know also that Scottish peasants of the fifteenth century played both football and golf. In 1424 James I legislated against football and in 1458 James II extended the prohibition to golf. This was surely directed at the lower orders in society: the aim was to focus recreational activity on to the more militarily useful pastime of archery, and it was from the peasant classes that archers came. Such legislation clearly failed to stop ordinary people playing golf and football, and the Scottish government felt the need to repeat these statutes in 1491. Archaeological evidence provides a further insight into lifestyles. Urban finds tell us that people in towns possessed ice-skates, that they played dice, and that they owned chess pieces. Townspeople were also enthusiastic about plays. We have already encountered religious playlets. Although these probably dominated the genre, Robin Hood plays were popular in some towns too. To Walter Bower in the 1440s it was the 'foolish populace' who celebrated the English outlaw. Perhaps there was national animosity in the chronicler's attitude towards a recognizably English folk-hero, as well as social snobbery. In any case, at a relatively lowly social level it appears that Robin Hood's status as an honourable outlaw was more important than his national origins. On the other hand, plays such as Sir David Lindsay's famous *Ane Satyre of the Thrie Estatis*, produced in the sixteenth century, were tailored to a relatively sophisticated audience. Poetry too was produced in the towns, none finer than that penned by the Dunfermline schoolmaster Robert Henryson, though whether it was intended for an urban audience as well as for aristocratic and court-based consumers remains unclear.

Scottish aristocrats, for their part, shared cultural tastes with the nobility of Latin Christendom, to which they emphatically felt they belonged. The late fourteenth-century magnate Sir James Douglas of Dalkeith left a will which illustrates this. The goods he bequeathed included both equipment for jousts and holy relics, the latter a typical expression of conventional aristocratic piety. Douglas also possessed books relating to the governance of Scotland, grammar, logic and romance. He was clearly a borrower of books as well as a purchaser and was keen to ensure those borrowed were returned to their owners at least after his death. Although Douglas may have had a greater than normal enthusiasm for reading, there had been a tradition of Scottish writing aimed at a lay audience since the late fourteenth century, when John Barbour produced his epic poem *The Bruce* in the vernacular. One romance translated into Scots in the fifteenth century was *The Buik of Alexander*; dealing with the more recent (but still imaginatively rendered) Scottish past was *The Wallace*, produced by 'Blind Harry' in the 1470s. Literary entertainment was not, however, the sole preserve of English-speaking regions: the sixteenth-century Gaelic compilation *The Book of the Dean of Lismore* includes poems, several of which were written by aristocratic women. There are, indeed, hints of a well-educated circle of women in the *Gaidhealtachd*, the Gaelic-speaking area whose literary accomplishments attracted the attention of Gaelic-speaking Ireland too.

This does not, of course, exhaust the range of aristocratic interests of which we have evidence. War, as indicated by much of their preferred reading matter and enthusiasm for the tournament, was not just a way of noble life, but a hobby as well. In this sense involvement in the crusade can be instructive. Many nobles may have been genuine soldiers for Christ, but in the later Middle Ages their journeys to the Baltic to assist the Teutonic Knights have a considerable air of recreational jaunts. Feasting, chivalric interaction and demonstrations of status and prestige were key constituents of the northern crusades in which the knightly classes of Christendom were so keen to be involved. Another preoccupation the nobility shared with its European counterparts was building. Stone castles, introduced from the later twelfth century, were not merely functional; they were also decorative and symbolic. The original thirteenth-century castle of Bothwell in Lanarkshire, and others like it, were modelled on French exemplars, such as Coucy-le-Château; and when in the early fifteenth century Archibald, Earl of Douglas, updated the fortifications at Bothwell he again incorporated contemporary French architectural design characteristics in the process. In the changing architectural styles of castles and their decorative features we see reflected once again the concern of Scottish nobles to announce their status, and to adapt to changing fashions evident in the wider world of Christendom.

These are some of the activities enjoyed by the peasantry, the townspeople and the aristocracy. These neat divisions in society can, of course, dissolve when we examine cultural pursuits more closely. Golf and football were clearly diversions for the ordinary people, but James IV seems also to have engaged in both activities, and games of cards too. Chess pieces have been found in towns, but games were certainly a pursuit of the aristocracy and their households also. Excavations have uncovered gaming pieces made of wood and shale at the castles of Threave in Galloway and at Finlaggan on Islay. The famous chess pieces discovered in Lewis in the nineteenth century are reckoned to have been made in the twelfth century, their fine design leaving little doubt that they belonged to a local aristocrat. Communal town entertainment, as with markets and fairs, surely attracted outsiders from the countryside. It is hardly conceivable that ordinary rural folk would not have sought to involve themselves in the pageantry of the Robin Hood plays and Corpus Christi processions, even if only as spectators. And towns were attractive to the nobility as well, partly for their commercial services, but increasingly also as loci for second homes. Alexander Stewart, Earl of Mar, was perhaps unusual for his class in disporting himself in Aberdeen taverns in the early fifteenth century, but by – and even occasionally before – the sixteenth century the spread of aristocratic townhouses indicates a much changed pattern of residential inclination among rural landowners. Clergymen, meanwhile, were as keen as aristocrats to employ masons skilled in the most fashionable continental designs: the Frenchman John Morow, for example, plied his craft on ecclesiastical buildings at Melrose, Paisley, St Andrews and Lincluden in Dumfriesshire. And by the fifteenth century aristocrats, clergymen and even townsmen were active in continental art markets: in the 1430s, for instance, William Knox from Edinburgh purchased a gilded panel by the Mechelen artist Jan van Battel in Antwerp.

The cross-social nature of cultural and recreational behaviour can be illustrated further by reference to two other activities: ballads and prostitution. The ballad form has been seen as one means towards understanding the outlook and attitudes of ordinary people. It is, after all, an oral form – ballad singers would perform their works and a wide audience would be able to understand the material. Things are, however, a little more complex than this. Ballads of early composition seem essentially to belong to an aristocratic milieu, and their celebration of martial values and heroic narrative patterns fits well with 'chivalric' literary forms. In *The Battle of Otterburn* the noble protagonists, Sir Henry Percy and James, Earl of Douglas, arrange a date for the coming battle with mutual courtesy and respect while quaffing a shared pipe of wine. Ordinary people were certainly involved in ballad composition and transmission and would understand them; but this does not mean that they reflect the attitudes of most ordinary people. While the cultural form was the same (a ballad), the way different social groups related to it was not. Ballads composed in the sixteenth century seem to give more of an insight into 'ordinary' society – in *Kinmont Willie* the hero is clearly of quite a different class from Percy and Douglas and an exponent of the cattle raid. Still, we must remain keenly aware of the regionality of ballads and we must not suppose that the insights they reveal necessarily apply to ordinary medieval Scots more generally, or that aristocrats were by this time uninterested in the form. Careful reading is required, but both aristocratic and 'popular' concerns can be detected in ballads.

Our evidence, when we turn to prostitution, is more sketchy. There are some hints of it, such as James IV's occasional payments for the services of 'Janet bair ars', and more concrete evidence in the edict of the Edinburgh town council in 1556 which sought to prevent prostitutes from dressing as 'honest men's wives'. Elsewhere, where good evidence exists, prostitution, or at least payment for sexual gratification, can be traced in all localities and among every class of the Latin west. In the French village of Montaillou, for which we possess excellent records, early fourteenth-century peasants commonly took themselves to the town to visit prostitutes; and in fifteenth-century Castile the clergy of Seville cathedral owned a brothel. Indeed, the historian James Brundage has remarked that the fifteenth century 'seems to have been the heyday of publicly operated prostitution'. Here we may be in the realm of universal human behaviour and we must assume that it is the scanty nature of the Scottish evidence rather than the unique moral character of Scots which clouds a perhaps common pastime for men and potentially significant employment opportunity for women.

Women's sexual desires are even more difficult to pinpoint. A rare glimpse is delivered in an explicit satire written by a fifteenth-century Countess of Argyll about her chaplain's penis, an indication that private spiritual occasions lent themselves to other encounters too – and it was no doubt with this in mind that thirteenth-century church statutes decreed that priests should hear the confessions of women 'not out of sight of men'. Sexual encounters outside marriage suggest a final and important point in dealing with social lives. Specifically Scottish patterns of human behaviour and social organization are to be expected, but we must also take account of the evidence provided by other societies in Christendom. In terms of social patterns, we are dealing in the Middle Ages firstly with humans; secondly, with citizens of Christendom as a whole; and only thirdly, with people who happen to be Scots.

The Bons of Medieval Society: National and Regional Identities

There is something of an obsession in Scottish historiography with searching after the nature of national identity, and much of this search has been focused on the medieval period. This is perhaps understandable, given modern Scotland's unusual status as a nation and yet not a nation (in the sense of not having full political independence). In some senses, though, it is rather easy to identify evidence demonstrating that 'Scotland' meant something; that 'Scots' were perceived to be a people with their own characteristics. If we look abroad, even before achieving their particular notoriety from 1296 as the perennial scourge and haters of the English, Scots were regarded as an individual people with their own traits. In French literature from the eleventh to the thirteenth centuries, Scots are characterized variously as gluttons with poor table manners, as wandering rogues, and as hardy fighters. The country itself is depicted as being backward and poor. The thirteenth-century French king Louis IX (according to his biographer Joinville) famously referred to Scotland as a distant and outlandish place. Outsiders affixed stereotypes to 'Scottishness' – the concept meant something to them. A sense of 'national' attitudes was undoubtedly sharpened by Anglo-Scottish war. As early as 1297 (one year after the start of war) jurors in Yorkshire felt able to equate 'Scottishness' with wickedness. As for the Scots, signs of anti-English feeling are equally easy to trace. Inhabitants of Berwick were able to insult the besieging English in 1296, making reference to their alleged tails. This, from inhabitants of the area most exposed to, and most familiar with, English people and English influences, surely does not mean that they believed their adversaries actually had tails. It shows instead that even at the outset of the wars, they had a sense of the difference between themselves, as Scots, and their English opponents.

War alone did not create the perception that other people were somehow different and alien. War between Scotland and England produced an immediate and emotive response. This was clearly not the result of careful consideration of conflict and a resultant rational attachment of blame, any more than it is in the modern world. The immediate response to war suggests, rather, that pre-existing loyalties − what we term national ones − suddenly began to express themselves more clearly. Attached to these loyalties, once war became prevalent, was the edge of bitterness and hatred that would be a striking characteristic of Scottish and English attitudes to each other throughout the Middle Ages.

Identifying a sense of Scottish national identity is not, in truth, difficult, even before 1296. There was, for instance, a distinct Scottish church which was able early to defend its institutional separateness from the jurisdiction of the English church. Most obviously there was a king of Scots, whose title was not entirely meaningless. Scots were, prior to 1296, subject to the authority of a royal line which distributed patronage (confirmed by seals and charters), issued brieves, founded burghs, appointed sheriffs and justiciars. All of this was justified because the ruler was *rex Scotorum*, king of Scots. Yet the inhabitants of the kingdom had other, perhaps far more powerful, ways of expressing their identity. Their lives were conditioned by the regions in which they lived and the social strata to which they belonged. They spoke various languages and existed in a diversity of cultures. Their Christian belief gave them a place in the international community of the faithful; and they had a perhaps overriding loyalty to kin and family. The problem, then, is not pinpointing 'national identity' in the pre-war period − it comes rather in trying to assess the power of the impulse as a factor motivating Scots and dictating their behaviour in the Middle Ages, especially, as ever, when we attempt to understand the lower orders in society.

The magnifying glass has most often, of course, been applied to the period of the wars of independence: how strong a factor was 'national identity' in moulding Scottish behaviour? Perhaps a concrete example might help to demonstrate how problematic this issue is. In 1298 Sir William Douglas, known as 'le Hardi', died in English captivity, having engaged in the rising involving William Wallace in the previous year. Douglas had not taken his captivity lightly: prior to his death his warden described him as 'very savage and very angry'. The son of this figure, Sir James Douglas, was to become the great military leader for Robert I; the stalwart upholder of the cause of Scottish independence; the indomitable anti-English warrior. Do we see here the carrying forward of an idealistic family tradition of patriotic valour? In part, maybe, but there are plenty of other potential explanations for the behaviour of both father and son. Certainly, Sir William Douglas was fierce and aggressive long before confrontation with the English became important. His son may have pursued his military activities for a number of reasons: family tradition, as much as national sentiment, may have moved him; he had the direct impulse of the recovery of his family lands to drive him on (they had been forfeited by the English and given to the Clifford family); his relationship with Robert I clearly developed as one of great loyalty and trust − Douglas met his death attempting to carry the king's heart on crusade. Finally, it would be hard to ignore the central rationale for Douglas's behaviour posited by his late-fourteenth-century biographer,

John Barbour. Douglas, in common with many of his aristocratic caste, was a lover of war, a proponent of chivalry. A sheer love of the struggle drove him on. If it is difficult to account for the behaviour of one of Scotland's great patriots of the national struggle for independence, we perhaps begin to see how nebulous and difficult a concept that of 'national identity' is in the Middle Ages. National identity may have helped shape the actions of the Douglases; but the family achieved substantial and tangible rewards for its actions. Sir James Douglas's descendants, building on these rewards, eventually established themselves as the mightiest noble house in Scotland. Thus there was a tangle of possible motivations in shaping the behaviour of Sir James Douglas, and the actions of others in the period.

It is correct to place medieval national identity among a clutch of competing or complementary identities and loyalties. These could be familial, regional, linguistic, ethnic or international. Indeed, it is well known that Scotland developed from a hugely diverse melting-pot of peoples with different languages, ethnicities and regional bases. These divergent loyalties can in no way be said to have been subsumed by any striking national loyalty before the wars of 1296 – although national identification does appear to have been increasing in strength. After 1296 war certainly forged a sharper sense of national self-identification, as opposed to these other loyalties, but not to the extent that they were totally eclipsed. This process of sharpening identity, moreover, was not even equally spread throughout the kingdom. Indeed, in the western Highlands and Islands the process may well have been one of reversal. Here, a regional loyalty seems to have gathered in strength from the time of the wars. Scottish royal authority, advancing in the thirteenth century under Alexander II and Alexander III, went into retreat. The pull of loyalty towards the local lord in these areas outweighed that of the crown, or the less concrete 'nation'. The chronicler John of Fordun famously articulated a cultural and social distinction between Lowlanders and Highlanders in the later fourteenth century. The Highlanders, as the chronicler pointed out, spoke a different language; but they also dressed differently and behaved with greater savagery than the peace-loving Lowlanders of the kingdom. Even so, the Highlanders were faithful subjects of the Scottish crown, if properly governed. Fordun's text is not unremittingly hostile to the Gaelic world (the people are also clever and attractive) in the way that later Lowland diatribes against Highland barbarity tend to be. Fordun does, though, suggest a deep divergence between Highlanders and Lowlanders, even if the distinctness of the two groups of peoples was not so neat as he suggested. Alexander Stewart, Earl of Buchan and 'Wolf of Badenoch', pursued a late-fourteenth-century career as a Highland magnate and leader of the trademark Gaelic warrior groups known in the Lowlands as 'caterans'. Yet Buchan was a son of the first Stewart king, Robert II, and thus a member of a family very much in the mainstream of Scottish political life, rather than on the Gaelic margins.

Nevertheless, an increasing sense developed during the later Middle Ages of the separateness of the Gaelic world from the rest of the kingdom. The most self-confident expression of this trend was the Lordship of the Isles. The MacDonald lords of the Isles wielded great regional powers in the western Highlands and Islands in the later Middle Ages. Linguistically and culturally, this sphere remained Gaelic. In social organization the main secular link was the kin-based tie of Gaelic lordship. The lordship was also politically powerful. Monarchy failed to make its authority felt effectively there, while successive lords toyed with English alliances aimed against the Scottish crown. In terms of identity the people of the lordship looked westward, to Celtic Ireland. A pan-Gaelic cultural identity has been noted, and we need to accept that this runs strongly against the perceived power of national identity in medieval Scotland. Even the regime of Robert I, which utilized so effectively propaganda invoking a sense of Scottish national struggle, was able to take the seemingly contradictory step of appealing for Irish support with the claim that the Scots and the Irish both belonged to one nation.

Even more complex patterns of loyalty are perhaps to be found in the Northern Isles. For most of the medieval period these belonged to the Norwegian crown. It was only in 1468 and 1469 respectively that the Scottish crown acquired control of the islands. By then there was probably little confusion of national loyalties in Orkney: the earls of Orkney had normally been Scottish since the thirteenth century, and judicial business was being conducted in the Scots language from the 1430s. By the fifteenth century Orkney had been substantially 'Scotticized' although regional loyalties were not, of course, smothered in the process. In Shetland the situation was different. Ruled directly from Norway, Scottish influence had been minimal there before 1469. Even after that date we can hardly expect a Scottish identity immediately to have replaced pre-existing affiliations in a region whose ethnic profile, language and culture was Norse. Indeed, the Norse language was still used in seventeenth-century Shetland. For its part, the Scottish crown remained ambivalent about its relationship with the Northern Isles and in 1524 it even offered to mortgage the islands in return for a substantial amount of hard cash from the Danish king Frederick I.

If we turn to the Borders we find another area with some ancient distinctive identities, and we are forced again to recognize the complexity of concepts of identity when scrutinized against the backdrop of regional diversity. Before the wars of independence there was a strong regional identity, expressed, for instance, in the cult of St Cuthbert. There was also a powerful international ethos. This was notably evident in the chronicle compiled at Melrose Abbey, one of a clutch of rich monasteries in the area. The chronicle, composed in the thirteenth century, devoted most of its pages to the great international events of the day (crusades, clashes between popes and secular monarchs, heresy) and markedly few to the seemingly unfamiliar terrain north of Melrose. Nevertheless, except for the Gaelic region of Galloway, the Borders were well integrated into the mainstream of the Scottish kingdom. Two of the largest of the realm's towns, Roxburgh and Berwick, lay in the region. Indeed, the area was part of the heartland of the realm, in which successive kings spent much of their time. There is no indication that the English-speaking inhabitants of the Borders felt themselves to be, politically, anything other than subjects of the Scottish crown. From 1296, however, war – at first intense, then intermittent – impacted heavily on the region. Closest in proximity to England, substantial areas of the Borders came under English occupation for lengthy periods of time. The dislocation of war impacted on economic life, providing a stimulus to pastoral farming and discouraging arable cultivation, and eventually cutting cross-border land-holdings, previously quite common, as aristocrats were forced to make a mutually exclusive choice between adherence to either Scottish or English kings. It affected religious life too. Cross-border cults – such as those of St Cuthbert and, in the west, of St Mungo – declined, as did international monastic contacts. War also encouraged the development of administrative institutions to cope with the defensive needs of the region and the policing of the frontier. Local lifestyles were adapted to the prevalence of war. What effect all this had on the identities, regional and national, of the local inhabitants is difficult to quantify (although on this issue many sweeping generalizations have been made).

During the fourteenth century there does not appear to have been a noticeably less 'patriotic' attitude among Borderers than is evident throughout Scotland. Indeed, border attitudes seem often to have been expressive of greater than usual belligerence towards the English. From the early fifteenth century, though, Anglo-Scottish warfare became far less a predominantly national concern and much more frequently a matter of local clashes. In tandem with this change there undoubtedly developed a stronger sense of the region's people being somehow set apart from the wider realm. By the late fifteenth century the exercise of governmental authority in the Borders was beginning to be perceived as problematic. In the sixteenth century the culture of cross-border cattle raiding, enshrined in local ballad tradition, further distanced the inhabitants of the region from the rest of lowland Scotland. It would be difficult to say to what extent the region's inhabitants felt themselves to be Borderers as opposed to Scots, though in 1583 the Englishman Thomas Musgrave had no doubts. 'They are,' he wrote, 'a people that will be Scottish when they will and English at their pleasure.' Such verdicts often came from those appointed to police the region, but they are evidence none the less of conflicting identities in the Borders that had not obviously been present 200 years before. In dealing with identities, as with much else, we must be aware not only of regional gradations; we must, too, cast a sensitive eye on changes wrought by altering circumstances and the passage of time.

The Domestic Exercise of Power

1. Kingship

The problematic nature of national allegiances is further demonstrated by the Anglo-Scottish peace treaty which accompanied the wedding between David Bruce and Joan Plantagenet in 1328. Some of those who attended the wedding came from families which, before the wars, had held lands on both sides of the border. Many landholders naturally desired a return to the *status quo* when peace was restored between the two kingdoms. The treaty itself contained a (now lost) clause which provided for re-inheritance. But cross-border land-holding remained a vexed issue until the renewed Anglo-Scottish warfare from the 1330s ultimately cemented individual landholders to either a Scottish or an English allegiance. Exceptions, such as the continuing connection of Dundrennan Abbey with its Co. Meath estate at Burtonstown in English-controlled Ireland, underline the tenacity of territorial connections which might run counter to national imperatives. Nevertheless, in other ways the 1328 treaty represented the crystallization of themes of national allegiance. The independent status of the Scottish kingdom, as defined by its boundaries in 1286, was recognized by the English, who further promised not to aid anyone who waged war on the king of Scots in Man and the Western Isles, an indication that the crown remained nervous of loyalties in the west. Admissions of Scottish subjection to the English crown, wrought by the invaders during the preceding wars, were to be returned, as were two powerful symbols of Scottish kingship – the Black Rood of St Margaret (an indication of the holy status of Scottish monarchy) and the Stone of Destiny (expressive of the ancient lineage claimed by kings of Scots). Robert I was seeking to re-establish the kingship of his MacMalcolm predecessors.

The MacMalcolm dynasty, ruling in Scotland from the start of our period until 1286, has usually been viewed by historians as an incredible success story. Before the reign of Malcolm III (1058–93) kingship was subject to transfer within different branches of the same kin group. After his son Edgar (1097–1107) became king, by contrast, there was a continuous line of descent following the rules of primogeniture until the reign of Alexander III (1249–86). During this period the territorial authority of the Scottish monarchy was enlarged and its status was bolstered. Most notably, the monarchy had assumed leadership of westward expansion. The Norwegian crown's efforts to retain possession of the Western Isles finally foundered in the stalemate of battle at Largs in 1263 and the death of the Norwegian king Hakon IV shortly afterwards. Three years later, by the treaty of Perth, the Norwegians agreed to transfer the Isles and Man to Scottish overlordship. It is tempting, perhaps, to view this process as somehow unstoppable and pre-ordained. It is only in retrospect, though, that the MacMalcolm dynasty looks so secure and naturally expansive. It experienced consistent difficulties in extending royal authority into the peripheral areas of the kingdom to the north, south-west and west. From these areas also there emerged rival claimants to the throne. Most persistently, the MacHeth and MacWilliam kindreds from their northern bases offered repeated challenges to the ruling dynasty. The seriousness of the threat can perhaps be gauged by the brutality of its eventual end. As late as 1230 the last, female, child of the rival MacWilliam dynasty had her skull crushed against Forfar mercat cross.

If this suggests a certain lingering Dark Age savagery during the reign of Alexander II (1214–49), it also illustrates the real dangers felt to be posed by potential rival lines to the MacMalcolms, even when the latter had been established in an unbroken line for well over a century. There were certainly weaknesses at the heart of MacMalcolm kingship. The Scottish realm was, for instance, by no means an easily unified entity: it was of large extent and difficult terrain in much of its area; and the peoples of the kingdom were a very diverse assembly, emerging from the early medieval groupings of Picts, Scots, Britons, Angles and Norwegians, and entailing also twelfth- and thirteenth-century Anglo-French incomers. Another weakness was that for long there was no convincing element of sanctity attaching to the royal dynasty. Its kings were not crowned and anointed; they lacked powerful and persuasive symbols that they had been appointed by God to rule. One element of this missing sanctity was eventually provided by the figure of Queen Margaret, Malcolm III's wife. A process of lobbying at the papal court in the 1240s finally achieved her canonization, and in June 1250 her relics were ceremonially transferred to a new shrine in Dunfermline Abbey. The interest that Alexander II had shown in sanctifying his ancestor suggests royal awareness that a hallowed pedigree was a source of symbolic strength. It is no coincidence, either, that the campaign on behalf of St Margaret was contemporary with Scottish attempts to secure the rights of coronation and unction at royal inaugurations. English pressure did much to foil this initiative as both the Scottish and English royal lines understood the power of religious symbolism. In the event it was not until the coronation of David II (1329–71) that the Scottish kingship was graced with these important elements and their aura of holy legitimacy. To some extent, then, the grace of God was only rather unconvincingly seen to reside in the person of the Scottish ruler.

More impressive, possibly, was the MacMalcolm line's claim to represent an ancient ruling dynasty. Scottish inauguration ceremonies prominently featured the recitation by a Gaelic bard of the royal lineage, a lineage that stretched back into the Dark Age past. This, rather than the late acquisition of a royal saint, underpinned the dynasty's special status. The MacMalcolm kings were heirs to a centuries-long legacy. A powerful claim to legitimacy was founded in the ancient credentials as native rulers in Scotland which individual monarchs could present. An added back-up to this position was provided by the Scone inauguration stone; the placing of kings there provided visual and symbolic support to the lengthy heritage claimed by Scottish kings. Equally vital to the strength of the dynasty was its establishment of primogeniture – descent normally from father to son – as a rule of succession. Despite numerous challenges, this system remained in place from the time of the sons of Malcolm III. In this sense the Scottish monarchy shared the strengths enjoyed by the Capetian monarchy in France, where primogeniture was established early and biological chance enabled direct male succession to the crown between 987 and 1328. It was not only in the strength of primogeniture (and the lucky chance of a continuous chain of male heirs) that the MacMalcolm line bears comparison with the Capetians. The Scottish house may indeed have borrowed directly the Capetian practice of designating the heir to the throne during the lifetime of the reigning monarch. In the middle of the twelfth century, David I (1124–53) took steps to ensure that his eldest son, Henry, was accepted as heir to throne; and when Henry died in 1152 his eldest son, Malcolm, was paraded around the kingdom as the new heir. Although a minor, Malcolm IV (1153–65) duly succeeded to the throne on David's death. Alexander II was similarly designated as heir during the reign of William I (1165–1214).

The need for such designations could be interpreted as a sign of immediate royal weakness. They indicate that the ruling house was aware of the existence of potential royal alternatives and was fearful that these rivals might attract support. In his 1152 procession the young designated heir, Malcolm, was accompanied by a substantial armed force. A blunt message about military might was being conveyed to the Scottish provinces, as well as a clear statement on the issue of the succession. In the end Malcolm IV did have to face considerable domestic opposition during his reign, emanating from the peripheries of the kingdom where royal authority was at best insecure and where native magnates were resentful of the continuing advance of Anglo-French influences. Nevertheless, the purpose of designation was ultimately served and the establishment of primogeniture was most certainly a factor strengthening the position of the ruling dynasty. The dynasty was thereby able to avoid one of the problems besetting, for instance, the German monarchy. Although this imperial realm was ruled successively by the Hohenstaufen, Luxemburg and Habsburg dynasties, strong guidelines on succession by blood failed to develop in the empire. Instead, the imperial monarchy developed into an elective institution. Often, the crown was kept within one ruling line, but it did not become hereditary. This was a weakness of the dynasties which ruled in Germany and a source of strength for their subjects. Monarchies in which the succession was elective invited challenge. By contrast, the MacMalcolms were ultimately able to establish that succession should pass from father to son as of right.

Hereditary succession, of course, depended upon the existence of a son. When Alexander III tumbled off his horse (presumably by accident) in 1286, there was no royal son to inherit. Nevertheless, the Scottish kingship retained its previous strengths despite passing to the usurping Bruce dynasty in 1306 and then to the Stewart dynasty in 1371, both of which were merely elevated from the ranks of the aristocracy. Surely important in this retention of strength was another factor: Scottish kingship came to be linked with resistance to England. This was explicitly laid forth in the famous remonstrance of the Scottish barons to the pope: the Declaration of Arbroath of 1320. Forty-eight nobles – equivalent to virtually all of the higher nobility – associated themselves with the eloquent Latin prose of the Declaration and insisted that early fourteenth-century Scots fought for the freedom of their kingdom and that they supported their king (Robert I) only because of his prowess in leading the national struggle. The sentiments the Declaration lays forth cannot, however, be taken as representative of baronial attitudes since in all probability the supposed authors were neither present when the Declaration was drafted, nor involved in dictating its contents. Instead, the Declaration was a piece of highly effective royal propaganda, formulated in the royal chancery, in which royal clerks sought to justify their patron's usurpation of the kingship by suggesting that Robert, unlike his predecessor John, was capable of resisting the southern foe.

Nevertheless, the fourteenth century did see a great sharpening of concepts of national identity. The status of the monarchy, its appeal to the inhabitants of the realm, was certainly tied up with its insistence on independence. The authority of Robert II (1371–90), who was immediately faced with an obscure but threatening Douglas rising on his succession in 1371, was quite deliberately bolstered by the playing of the patriotic card. Robert II immediately renewed the Franco-Scottish alliance, and took an altogether tougher diplomatic stance towards England than had been pursued by David II. Military attacks on England were promoted and encouraged by Robert's regime, at first cautiously, but eventually openly. John Barbour's poem *The Bruce*, giving a version of Scottish resistance to England earlier in the century, was sponsored by the new king. Developing national sentiment became a prop of kingship, although for monarchs seeking friendlier relations with England this could prove to be a disadvantage. Both David II, after his return from lengthy captivity in England in 1357, and James III (1460–88) encountered opposition partly, at least, because of their pliant approach to relations with England.

Finally, there was another strength of Scottish monarchy which is perhaps easily overlooked: royalty possessed sheer power greater than the various forces which may have sought to destroy or supplant it. The big battalions underpinned royal authority. This best explains why successive kings of the twelfth century found it so pressing to introduce Anglo-French personnel, with their new and effective military techniques – the heavily armoured mounted knight and the latest methods of castle construction. The process was potentially, and at times actually, divisive, but the reward was coercive power. Kings of the MacMalcolm dynasty were able to outface all the internal military challenges they encountered. Their resources were greater than even the mightiest of their subjects, and even powerful subjects had persuasive reasons for cooperating with the royal line. When, in 1187, the severed head of William I's northern rival, Donald MacWilliam, was presented to the king, it was the outcome of a successful campaign by Roland of Galloway. A former rebel from a highly troublesome province had found it expedient to act decisively in the royal interest. The royal house was more powerful than its subjects, and it remained so with the Bruce and Stewart lines of later centuries. Striking examples of this are the destruction of the Albany Stewarts, a family of the blood royal, eliminated with dismissive ease by James I (1406–37) in 1425; and the fall of the extremely powerful Douglas family, whose leader was murdered by James II (1437–60) in 1452. On neither occasion was there an effective and sustained response from the crown's victims and their friends. More strikingly still, perhaps, Alexander, lord of the Isles, was deserted by two of his allied clans in 1429 when the opposing force revealed the royal standard. This, moreover, occurred in Lochaber, in the heartland of the Gaelic world.

One of the latent advantages enjoyed by many of the Stewart monarchs was, paradoxically, the repeated and often lengthy occurrence of royal minorities in the fourteenth, fifteenth and sixteenth centuries. Such gaps in the continuity of adult kingship created conditions in which magnate factions could seize and manipulate the levers of power in a hugely decisive manner. The iron hand of strong, even ruthless, kings like James II and James V was, for much of the aristocracy, preferable to the factional turbulence of their minorities. This is not to argue that, during their adult reigns, kings had it all their own way: James I was assassinated and James III was killed after a battle against rebellious forces at Sauchieburn in 1488. On neither occasion, however, was the Stewart dynasty supplanted. A 'body count' approach to political interaction may be misleading in some senses, but in terms of depositions and violent deaths it is worth stressing that the crown in later medieval Scotland bears healthy comparison with other medieval monarchies. France, admittedly, struggled through its later medieval civil wars without any violent removal of the (from 1328) new Valois line of kings. Perhaps Castile is a more typical example. There, ruling dynasties were removed by force on two occasions, both after lengthy civil wars. None the less, except in unusual circumstances, respect for the representatives of ruling lines was the norm in the medieval west and Scotland fits quite comfortably with the European pattern.

Little consensus, though, has been reached on the general nature of crown–magnate relations in the later Middle Ages, and whether they were of a particularly conflictual nature or not. What seems clear is that personal interaction between the figure of the king and the politically powerful elements in society was vital in dictating the course of crown–magnate relationships. For a king who had the knack of dealing capably with his magnates on a personal level the crown was not structurally weak. James IV (1488– 1513) is a case in point. He aggressively pursued royal rights, particularly in terms of finance; yet he met with little domestic opposition or apparent unpopularity. James IV had the gift of appealing to those classes which possessed a political voice. Powerful testimony to this effect comes in the form of the impressive and broad-based army with which James invaded England in 1513, coming as it did after a century in which Scots had been highly reluctant to cross the border in a full-scale invasion. Personality remained the key to the successful practice of medieval kingship, in Scotland just as elsewhere.

2. Government

The development of the monarchy and its continued status and authority is a consistent theme throughout our period. Yet while the institution of monarchy ultimately relied on the chance of personal ability to function adequately, kingship also relied on governmental structures which developed and became steadily more sophisticated. One central aspect of kingship was the existence of the court, peopled by the king's counsellors and immediate retainers, men who exercised considerable influence or who were, at any rate, closely linked with the exercise of royal power. The composition of the king's household varied in personnel, but on the basis of charter evidence it mainly consisted of men of Anglo-French stock in the twelfth and thirteenth centuries, with 'native' appearances more irregular. Highlanders, with the exception of the Campbell earls of Argyll, remained rare even in the later period.

As well as being cosmopolitan, the twelfth-century court was also a highly itinerant institution. A peripatetic royal establishment was quite sensible in these times: given the rudimentary transport infrastructure it was easier for the limited personnel of the court to travel to the source of its supplies than it was to deliver bulky produce to a central location from disparate royal estates. So the produce of royal land went directly towards maintaining the court; and many royal rights were rendered in kind and consumed as the household moved around the kingdom. Just as the personnel attending the court tended increasingly to be 'foreigners', so the geographical location in which the king was to be found was, from the time of David I, mostly inclined to a heartland which was non-Gaelic. Favourite locations of the MacMalcolm kings varied from reign to reign, but the undoubted general inclination was towards the southern and eastern Lowlands. This was the area that was most subject to influences from the Anglo-French settlers.

Both of these factors – the ethnic make-up of the court and the locations in which kings spent the majority of their time – were significant. While native magnates were not excluded specifically from the court – they were notably present on high-profile governmental occasions and did not have their traditional powers challenged in the localities – government was still conditioned by the attitudes and outlook of the king; and from the time of David I the king's retainers, closest companions and advisers inhabited a largely Anglo-French cultural world. An early thirteenth-century English chronicler was able to state, although perhaps not with total accuracy, that the kings of Scotland actually regarded themselves as Frenchmen and had reduced the Scots to servitude. Later, as Anglo-French incomers and native aristocrats intermingled, this sense of division was much less pronounced. The Bruce family, although of Anglo-French origin, was clearly at home in the Gaelic cultural world of the west, and so was the Stewart dynasty which was to rule after it. As time went by, the necessity for the royal household to be itinerant also declined. Growing fiscal sophistication meant that dues to the crown were far less likely to be paid in kind. Individual monarchs were more able to gravitate towards particularly favoured royal residences. Edinburgh increasingly became the location where government business was transacted, but different monarchs favoured different subsidiary centres: for James I it was Perth; for James II it was Stirling; and James V (1513–42) was frequently to be found at Falkland and St Andrews. The king's household, rather than an established capital, remained the decision-making heart of the realm.

In medieval Scotland, then, the court was the main institution of government. Judging by their households it seems also that kings from the time of David I existed predominantly in an Anglo-French cultural milieu. We know little detail of the culture of the early Scottish court, but we would probably not be too far off in imagining that it adhered to the norms evident in other courts of the Latin west. Regarding literary taste, there is good evidence that the French-speaking court circle of twelfth- and thirteenth-century Scotland appreciated the romantic verse forms then prevalent in France. *The Romance of Fergus*, largely set in Scotland and displaying an accurate knowledge of the kingdom's topography, may even have been composed by a member of William I's court circle. There is also evidence of other normal patterns of behaviour and interests at the Scottish court: conventional piety, enthusiasm for hunting, enjoyment of martial display. Over and above these interests we can tell much more about the cultural leanings of the royal household from the fifteenth century onwards due to more plentiful sources of evidence. The Stewart monarchs seem to have been keen patrons of literature: James I is reckoned to have personally executed a skilled poetical work, *The Kingis Quair*, during his lengthy captivity in England from 1406 to 1424. The later Stewarts seem generally to have had wide cultural interests, influenced by contemporary continental developments. In their building works these kings incorporated the latest architectural fashions, and up-to-date innovations are evident in the coinage minted by James III. Artists and poets, along with musicians from the Gaelic-speaking world and from continental Europe, were certainly patronized by the Stewarts, even if perhaps the most famous of them, the poet William Dunbar, believed he deserved greater remuneration than he received from James IV. There was, indeed, something akin to a renaissance spirit of experimentalism and lively inquiry at James IV's court. James paid volunteers to submit to tooth extractions conducted by the royal hand. James's orthodontic dabbling may not have advanced scientific understanding very far; but other developments in his reign, such as the establishment of the first Scottish printing press in 1507 and the first Scottish medical faculty at Aberdeen, may well have been intended to do so. One of the attractions of the court, at least in this later period, was the conscious attempt to portray an image of a confident, European, outward-looking monarchy.

In spite of its cultural allure, the court continued to serve primarily as a governing institution. Of the king's household officers, two probably deserve particular attention – the chancellor and the chamberlain. The chancery (known as the chapel) was a major element of medieval governance: it was the state's writing office, responsible for the promulgation of the royal will in the form of brieves, charters and diplomatic correspondence. Although its chief officer, the chancellor, was normally to be found with the king, the chapel was usually based in Edinburgh Castle. The chamberlain, responsible for fiscal matters until many of his powers were given to the new office of treasurer in the early fifteenth century, similarly stayed with the royal household and, in a sense, he remained someone who carted a bag of the king's coins around. We can still see this in the reigns of James III and James V, who were both in physical possession of chests of coinage at the time of their deaths. Neither a permanent treasury, nor an exchequer department, developed to oversee the kingdom's finances. Audits of the crown's income and expenditure were instead conducted by the appointment of auditors on an annual basis. In these key aspects of government we do not see, in Scotland, the development of a full-time civil service. The court, in short, continued to dictate the expressions of central government, which was essentially the king's will, and tended to do so on the hoof. The household, and household institutions, grew in sophistication without becoming hugely elaborate as a method of governance.

Yet ancillary institutions did emerge. Parliament was the first, though its importance should not be exaggerated. It is quite misleading to assume that an oft-quoted passage from the Declaration of Arbroath (which appears to suggest that kings could be legitimately removed if they failed to live up to wider baronial expectations) bore any resemblance to constitutional reality. The Declaration was not a constitutional treatise. Nevertheless, for important royal decision-making there had always been recourse to a wider body than the royal council, a gathering of prominent clerics and aristocrats of the realm whose approval was sought or to whom, at least, the opportunity of airing opinions was given. These occasional gatherings were not styled 'parliament' until the 1290s, but there was clearly an established tradition of such meetings before then and they became relatively frequent thereafter. The king and his council normally set the agenda and made decisions in what was always a unicameral body, composed of prelates, nobles and, from the fourteenth century, townspeople; but there was a strongly entrenched tradition that suggested that these three estates, as they became known, should be consulted. This expectation accorded with wider European patterns: throughout the Latin west, monarchies, influenced by ecclesiastical models of con sultation such as councils and synods, involved assemblies of various types in the business of government. The process fitted well with medieval political theories. It was a commonplace that kings should keep good council; and there was a concept, growing in power, that 'that which affects everyone should be universally approved' – never literally everyone, but rather the male élite who, it was supposed, might represent the views of the entire community of the realm.

Parliament's role was not, however, merely to advise the sovereign. It also passed legislation and its statutes modified and added to the customary Scottish common law set out in the fourteenth-century compilations *Regiam Majestatem* and *Quoniam Attachiamenta*. Its legislative competence included taxation. This is probably why the urban élite, with its ready access to cash, first won the right to attend parliament, though in the event, while *ad hoc* levies were occasionally approved (notably to pay the ransoms demanded for David II and James I), no regular system of national taxation, other than customs levied on exports, was ever introduced in the medieval period. Since parliament made law, it made sense that it should also decide the law. Thus parliament emerged as the highest court in the kingdom, with its sub-committees by the fifteenth century hearing appeals and complaints from secular courts held in the localities. It was increasingly assisted in this by the king's council, acting separately and in a part-time judicial capacity. As the pressure of judicial business came to overwhelm these bodies (not necessarily a sign of rampant lawlessness, but rather of popular faith in royal justice), the Lords of Council and Session emerged as a specific central court of justice, usually sitting in Edinburgh and hearing matters pertaining to civil law, from about 1490; this in turn proved the precursor of the College of Justice, established in 1532, novel only in the sense that it was staffed by fifteen effectively professional and (theoretically) paid judges. There was no similar body dealing with criminal law until the seventeenth century.

However, the medieval kingdom of Scotland, like that of France and Germany, was not a notably centralized state. Galloway can exemplify this. Crown authority intruded into the area in a slow and hesitant manner; and it relied more on local, native forces to maintain order than central institutions. When the rule of William I was undermined by his capture while invading England in 1174, the slow outward progress of the central authority was subverted. Native turmoil and violence broke out, directed against the expressions of royal authority, but also featuring internal power struggles, complete with the threat of English intervention. Accommodation was finally reached with Roland of Galloway, who triumphed in the province's power struggle. He retained wide authority within Galloway, and was able to act as a crown enforcer in, for instance, defeating the MacWilliam uprising in 1187. Yet direct royal intervention in Galloway remained limited and regional loyalties remained strong. During the wars with England from 1296 the region's ties of loyalty to the Scottish crown were evidently still weak. To win over the Gallovidians Edward I deemed it useful to return the bastard son of the last native lord of Galloway with promises of support for Gallovidian autonomy.

Galloway stands as a prominent example of a commonplace of medieval Scottish governance. The crown frequently exercised only indirect influence, by relying on native lords in its quest to 'control' the provinces. Indirect control, but of a kind much more reliable in royal terms, could also be exercised by introducing Anglo-French landholders into troublesome or remote regions. 'Feudalism', as we have seen, accompanied these foreign incomers but their importance was great also in terms of the expression of royal power in the localities. Their bonds of allegiance, at least initially, were stronger to their royal patrons than to the natives of areas, such as Moray, in which they were settled, though the far north and west, in particular, were never controlled by such means.

More direct efforts to extend the crown's authority were also undertaken through the intrusion of royal officials into the localities. Sheriffs, introduced by David I, were borrowed from English practice. Their initial purpose was to supervise royal rights in given localities and at first this was achieved in areas where the king had firmest control. Shrieval authority was normally bolstered by royal castles and royal burghs, which were often located at the *caputs*, or administrative centres, of sheriffdoms and frequently featured foreign immigration. The network of sheriffdoms, from its eastern and southern central core, was steadily extended into more troublesome and remote locales. The whole kingdom, finally, featured this expression of royal authority at the local level.

As well as representing the royal will and (until the fifteenth century) collecting royal dues, sheriffs also administered royal justice and entertained appeals from baronial courts. In this they were periodically assisted by visiting royal justiciars. The justiciars were usually prominent regional magnates and their office was a significant element in crown patronage. They held twice-yearly courts in each of the sheriffdoms of their regions. In addition to hearing appeals from lower courts they had an exclusive right to entertain cases, called pleas of the crown, relating to murder, rape, arson and theft, except in regalities granted autonomy from their (and shrieval) oversight. There were three justiciars by the thirteenth century (another introduction of David I), whose jurisdictions were split along geographical lines: one north of the Forth, one in Lothian and one in Galloway. By the later medieval period the separate Gallovidian justiciar had disappeared and there remained only the north–south split.

The itinerant nature of the justiciarship was an important factor in explaining why a centralized and professional judicial system was so slow to emerge. Another factor was the vitality of regional legal traditions and practices which co-existed with royal justice. In Galloway, for instance, local forms of justice appear to have flourished until the end of the fifteenth century. In this region leaders of kindred groupings had authority over 'sergeants' who had wide-ranging police functions. These included rights to administer summary justice to those caught red-handed in robbery. Sergeants were empowered to arrest and accuse criminals, upon whom the burden of proving innocence fell. In parliament Archibald, lord of Galloway (and later fourth Earl of Douglas) was asserting the autonomy of the region's legal traditions as late as 1384. The durability of such traditions militated against the full expression of the crown's justice in the localities.

As a consequence, especially in the Western and Northern Isles, royal justice for long remained in competition with older Celtic or Norse forms of seigneurial justice.

Provision of justice was, however, one of the key expectations of kings in the Middle Ages. In this regard, although evidence is frequently negative (in that there are few recorded complaints) or inferred, Scottish monarchs seem to have performed their role adequately. In the sphere of justice, as in much else, medieval kingship remained highly personal, and rulers, such as Malcolm IV, who left the kingdom to campaign on the continent, and James III, who threatened to undertake continental adventures, were kings who bred domestic dissatisfaction. An absent king was a king who could not deliver justice. These, though, were exceptions. The nature of the crown and its ruling dynasty, as we have seen, together with its techniques and institutions of governance, all made for an expansive and dynamic kingdom in the twelfth and thirteenth centuries. Scottish government never became highly centralized, nor did it develop a complex bureaucratic machinery. It should not, though, be assumed that lack of sophistication amounted to a failure of government. Crucially, Scotland did not – or could not – develop a system of payment for military service, either in terms of payment of mercenaries or as an inducement for Scotsmen to serve in the royal armies. In other realms, such as France in the fourteenth and fifteenth centuries, the need to organize armies on a paid basis was a vital engine of developing governmental sophistication. Scotland lacked this, but whether it was a well-governed kingdom or not by medieval standards is a question that cannot be answered by reference to its level of bureaucracy. Effective governance in any given locality depended much on the abilities and propensities of regional magnates. And the effectiveness of central government was above all a question of the character of the ruling monarch.

The International Exercise of Political Power

1. Scotland in Britain, c. 1100–1403

Along with the provision of justice, the other main expectation of a medieval king was that he should defend the realm. For Scottish kings there were two potential external threats, one to the west and north, the other to the south. Despite the attack mounted by Eystein, king of Norway, on Aberdeen in 1151, the Norwegian threat was a diminishing one. The Western Isles, as we have seen, became a domestic rather than international problem after they were wrested from Norse control in 1266. Similarly, Orkney and Shetland were acquired in 1468–9, mortgaged to the Scots by Christian IV, king of Denmark-Norway, since Christian was otherwise unable to find a dowry for his daughter on her marriage to James III. There was one component of these former Norse domains which did not remain Scottish: the Isle of Man. Although ceded to the

Scots in 1266 it was occupied by Edward I in 1290, back in Scottish possession by 1322, but repossessed by Edward III in 1333. We should not assume that the Manx population was unhappy with its ultimate fate. Scottish rule had provoked an uprising, savagely repressed, in 1275. Nevertheless, the island's history demonstrates clearly that the principal threat to the Scottish realm lay to the south.

In 1328 that threat appeared to have been neutralized. The marriage between David Bruce and Joan Plantagenet was intended to be the harbinger of peace between the two previously warring entities of England and Scotland. It was accompanied by admissions of war guilt and of Scottish independence from the former, and promises of £20,000 in return for peace from the latter. This was a substantial sum: in the later 1320s the crown's annual revenue from its lands and export duties, together its most important sources of income, amounted to only around £4,000. The agreement of 1328 did not in fact mark a great turning-point in Anglo-Scottish relations, although the outbreak of war between the two realms in 1296 is usually thought to have been just such a moment. This idea relies to a large extent on the contrast with supposedly peaceful Anglo-Scottish interaction before 1296.

We should not, though, imagine that peace and harmony were the sole constituents of Anglo-Scottish relations in the previous two centuries. In 1251 another Anglo-Scottish royal marriage was celebrated between Alexander III and Margaret, daughter of Henry III, at York. Even during this early attempt to cement good relations between the two kingdoms, care was taken that the Scottish party should be housed in quarters separate from English guests to prevent violent disputes from breaking out. This was also the century that saw Alexander II invade England as far as Dover while intervening in the English baronial rebellion against King John in 1215. Alexander's real design was to recapture the northern counties of England, previously held by David I, and this was an ambition not formally renounced until the Treaty of York was agreed in 1237. Even then, this concession did not foster harmony in Anglo-Scottish relations. As early as 1244 the military resources of both realms were mobilized, because the English king Henry III perceived that the Scots were flexing their muscles on the border and feared that they were inclining towards a French alliance. During the minority of Alexander III, Henry III had less defensive reasons for adopting a threatening posture towards his northern neighbour. In 1251, when Alexander married Margaret, Henry's daughter, the English king attempted to obtain from his new son-in-law an oath of homage for the kingdom of Scotland. Foiled in this, Henry still sought thereafter to exercise a degree of control over the Scottish minority governments. He was willing also to back up his influence with personal visitations to the border line agreed in 1237 and by concrete military preparations.

Still, the middle of the thirteenth century onwards did see increasingly amicable Anglo-Scottish relations. Familial ties between the royal houses no doubt played a part in this. Certainly, there are hints of friendship beyond the conventional confines of diplomatic niceties in some of the extant correspondence between Edward I (king of England from 1272) and Alexander III. Much stress has been placed on the various cross-border ties which had arisen between the realms and which were a factor militating for peace. Significantly, too, both Edward I and Alexander III could channel the expansive energies of their subjects and satisfy state-building imperatives by expanding into Wales and the Western Isles respectively. Most telling of all as evidence of amicable relations before the wars is that the Scots turned so readily to Edward I as their aid and potential arbiter when dynastic disaster struck the MacMalcolm dynasty on Alexander's death in 1286, and again on the demise of his granddaughter, Margaret, in 1290. Yet even in the temperate international climate associated with Alexander and Edward, there was room for raising the issue of homage by the English king in 1278. In this, its most peaceable phase, the relationship between Scotland and England could not but contain submerged tensions that were capable of informing ordinary interaction with a distinctly flinty edge.

If we cast our gaze further back, before 1237, conflict is more liberally sprinkled among the periods of peace. The defining characteristic of Scottish foreign relations was interaction with England, and it would seem at first glance that the Scottish kingdom was always going to be the less powerful of the two realms that came to dominate the British mainland. There is some substance to this viewpoint. From a modern perspective the match of the twelfth-century realms of England and Scotland would seem to be no real contest. In population, in wealth, in the strength of government institutions and in military clout the English kingdom would appear to be dominant. After 1066, also, the English crown was part of a wider empire, stretching under Henry II from the Cheviots to the Pyrenees, an empire that often drew the English crown's energies away from the British Isles itself, but which underlined nevertheless a huge divergence in the status and power of the two realms. When military conflict had occurred, shows of English military force had drawn forth Scottish submissions, often ill-defined, but quite explicit in the Treaty of Falaise, 'agreed' between Henry II and William I in 1174. The treaty followed William's capture while campaigning to regain the northern counties, though it was subsequently quitclaimed by Henry's son, Richard I, in 1189. Scottish military activity, on the other hand, seems to have been successful only at times when there were other major distractions for the English crown.

This surface assessment of the relative strengths of the two realms, however, may be misleading. A forceful case has been made for the Scots under David I coming very close to holding permanently Northumberland, Cumberland and Westmorland, the northern counties of England which were conquered during the mid-twelfth-century turmoil of the English civil war between Stephen and Matilda. The 1140s may, then, have held out the prospect of a lasting 'Scoto-Northumbrian' realm. It is true, certainly, that much as we perceive in hindsight the greater strength of the English state in relation to Scotland, there is no indication that the contemporary players had so clear a vision of their own strengths or those of other states. Moreover, David I was a capable king, and the state over which he ruled was expansive and strong. Mere chance, most notably the early death of David's son and heir, leaving the minor Malcolm IV to become king in 1153, undermined the likelihood of the northern counties being more effectively cemented to Scotland. Most tellingly of all, English royal authority had never been securely exercised in the north. It was not inevitable that the region's future lay with the English crown. In the early twelfth century the English king Henry I felt it expedient to double his personal bodyguard when venturing north of the Humber.

All this is persuasive enough, especially in the particular circumstances of David I's reign, but should not be taken too far. Contemporaries may not have fully appreciated the fact, but an undisturbed England could always avail itself of greater force than was available to the Scots. Once David I was dead a strong and active English king, Henry II, established both his control in northern England and his superior status in relation to his Scottish counterpart, Malcolm IV, with telling rapidity. It is useful, none the less, to accept that England was bordered on the north by a state powerful in its own terms. The Scottish kingdom was by no means a pushover. The idea that two 'superpowers' emerged in medieval Britain is a suggestive concept. Both kingdoms were strong. Were they too big for the same island? The long catalogue of later medieval Anglo-Scottish conflict would suggest that this was the case, that there was a structural appropriateness in a battle to the death between the two kingdoms.

The Anglo-Scottish struggle that began in 1296 had its roots in dynastic accident. Alexander III's son and heir died in 1284; the king himself was found dead near Kinghorn in 1286 after a nocturnal attempt to visit his second, recently married, queen, Yolande. A further heir remained: Alexander's granddaughter Margaret, an infant in the Norwegian court. The Scottish political leadership accepted her as heir, and arranged her betrothal to Edward, the son of Edward I. This solution to the dynastic crisis, outlined in the Treaty of Birgham (1290), envisaged a joint Anglo-Scottish monarchy, in which the integrity of specifically Scottish political and ecclesiastical structures would be maintained. A peaceful solution, however, was not to be. Margaret, the 'Maid of Norway', died – of seasickness according to one account – on her way to Scotland.

Human tragedy, when the players were royal, led to crisis in the polity. Scotland was without a ruler, or an agreed heir to the throne, and there was a real prospect of civil war. Once again, the Scots turned to England in their travails, this time to the jurisdiction of Edward I in the quest for an agreed ruler. In the Great Cause of 1291–2, the rights of thirteen claimants who sought the Scottish crown were investigated. Edward I's deliberations were thorough, and his choice of John Balliol was reasonable on accepted legal grounds. But Edward simultaneously took advantage of Scotland's leaderless state to gain recognition of his suzerainty over the kingdom. The claimants agreed to this, though John was among the more reluctant to do so. Edward had no intention, meanwhile, of stopping at mere paper recognition of his status. John's kingship

(1292–6) was bedevilled by Edward's insistence on a real exercise of overlordship. He encouraged appeals to his courts, thereby diminishing John's status as the fount of Scottish justice; and in 1294 Edward demanded that John and his barons perform military service against the French king. This was not a mere gesture of political submission, but an unwelcome imposition on the higher nobility of Scotland. It was politically untenable for John to undertake, and to impose on others, service abroad at the behest of another monarch; and economic madness, since the French king controlled Flanders, the chief source, from wool sales, of Scotland's foreign revenue. The only road was defiance, and the chosen method was to make common cause, in 1295, with Edward's enemy, Philip IV of France.

The Edwardian backlash to this defiance entailed the rapid conquest of Scotland in 1296. Berwick was stormed and sacked, the Scottish host was put to flight at the battle of Dunbar, and John was deposed in Kincardineshire. Edward, after a neat and painless progression through Scotland, returned across the border bearing with him the regalia of Scottish monarchy, the Black Rood of St Margaret and the Scone inauguration stone. This was symbolically expressive of Edward's intentions for Scotland. He had no wish to establish another potentially troublesome client king on the throne. Instead, Edward appointed English administrators and commenced ruling Scotland directly. Scotland was soon no longer a kingdom, but a 'land' subject to the English crown. These were momentous events – only the start, of course, of the long and bitter Anglo-Scottish wars. Initially, though, these were Edward's wars, the product of his ambition; and his behaviour has prompted his vilification by successive generations of Scottish historians. Edward's actions throughout the Scottish crisis had been opportunistic, manipulative and ruthless. Yet placing moral judgement on Edward I is essentially unhelpful. He exploited the possibilities of the situation with determination; increase of power was, after all, the currency of kingship. Edward's conduct towards the Scots was of the same stamp as the recent expansionist policies towards the Western Isles under Alexander II and Alexander III. We are better placed if we judge Edward's treatment of Scotland on the basis of the soundness of his approach, the effectiveness of his strategy. And here, in the longer view, we can only assess Edward's Scottish policy as badly miscalculated. For despite a seemingly unstoppable march to initial success, the longer legacy of intervention was that Scotland became a drain on English resources and manpower throughout the medieval period. Firstly in 1297 and 1298 William Wallace provided a focus for resistance to Edward I. Defeated at Falkirk in 1298, he provides modern Scots still with a largely mythical folk-hero, and late twentieth-century screenwriters with an easily adapted heroic model. Resistance continued after Wallace gave up the guardianship of the kingdom, but it was a problematic struggle fought in the name of an evidently uninterested King John, enjoying a quiet retirement on his estates in Picardy until his almost unnoticed death in 1313.

Scottish resistance was finally, it seemed, broken by Edward I in 1304 and new ordinances were laid out for the governance of the 'land' in 1305. How effective these might have been is unknown: in 1306 Robert Bruce, who had inherited the family claim to the Scottish throne rejected in favour of King John, made his bid for power. Robert I (1306–29) gave to resistance an active royal focus, but he also sparked open and intense civil war in Scotland. The factions which had supported the Balliol kingship were by no means unanimously enthusiastic about a Bruce usurpation; the powerful Comyns and their allies were trenchant rivals of Bruce, who, just before seizing the throne, had murdered John Comyn, lord of Badenoch, the leader of the family. Scotland's external and internal wars were infused with great bitterness. In these wars of terror, Robert I ultimately triumphed. His domestic enemies were eliminated, English strongpoints in Scotland were gradually reduced. For a full victory, though, Robert needed not only to gain physical control in Scotland; he also needed to achieve international recognition of his position as rightful monarch of an independent realm. A diplomatic offensive was launched to this end, whose most famous expression was the so-called Declaration of Arbroath, which contains much fine rhetoric on the Scots' struggle for independence. The real key lay in persuading England to recognize Scottish independence. And it was really only military force which could elicit this concession. Specifically, Robert I oversaw the launch of repeated raids of savage destructiveness in northern England. Ireland was another zone of English vulnerability and Scottish operations there, again of devastating, if ultimately futile, effect were carried out between 1315 and 1318. These years were also, of course, marked by crop failure, cattle disease and famine across north-western Europe. Scottish chroniclers' later chivalric gloss on Robert I and his captains should not obscure the grim brutality of the business which they undertook and of the times in which they operated.

These themes have much more to say about the successful assertion of independence than the surprising victory achieved in the set-piece battle at Bannockburn, near Stirling, in 1314. Bannockburn did nothing to solve the international impasse between Scotland and England, and was of far more moment in the domestic politics of both realms: the victory did much to vindicate the rule of Robert I; and it undermined the position of Edward II (king of England since 1307) in his own realm. Certainly, one of the main reasons for the success of Robert I was the inadequacy of Edward II as a ruler compared with his father. Domestic turmoil racked Edward II's reign, and it was this circumstance that enabled the Scottish king, finally, to force recognition of his own kingly status and the independence of his realm by the Treaty of Edinburgh-Northampton in 1328. With hindsight, at any rate, the 1328 treaty recognizing Scottish independence was a freak occurrence. The outcome of Anglo-Scottish wars thereafter was repeatedly stalemate. Only exceptional circumstances allowed Robert I to prise a suitable diplomatic settlement from the insecure, usurping English regime of the time (Edward II had been deposed by his wife and her lover in 1327). Such circumstances were never to be repeated. Neither, given the mood of resistance inculcated among many Scots over thirty years, was the prospect of English conquest liable to be achieved. This much was made evident in the renewed wars of conquest launched by Edward III when his personal rule had been established on the English throne. The peace treaty of 1328, and the royal marriage which cemented it, did not end the Anglo-Scottish wars. It only marked a hiatus in what was a century marked by war.

From 1332 the Bruce dynasty and the integrity of the Scottish realm were again gravely threatened. Edward III's approach was new, although his vision for Scotland was similar. He still sought English dominance, but by establishing Edward Balliol, son of John, as king of a truncated Scottish realm, while controlling and administering the southern counties of Scotland himself. The Balliol dynasty still enjoyed considerable support in Scotland and English backing for the Balliol 'Edward I' in 1332 was replaced in 1333 by direct military intervention, attended by striking initial success. So potent was the danger to the Bruce regime that Robert I's successor, the young David II, was dispatched to France for safety. When exactly we should regard this renewed threat as having significantly diminished is difficult to establish. Edward Balliol did not die until 1363. From 1337, however, English attentions were focused more on continental war than attempts to subdue the Scots. On the ground, Bruce fortunes were restored; by 1341 it was felt that Scotland was secure enough to accommodate the return of David II from his French refuge.

This was another period of intense Anglo-Scottish warfare and in this context it is important to recognize that the treaty of 1328 had not in any sense marked the end of the wars of independence. Similarly, the re-establishment of the Bruce dynasty in the late 1330s and early 1340s had no finality either. Scotland's independence was more strongly established, but, crucially, it was still felt to be threatened. There was sufficient reason for this. While leading an invasion of northern England in 1346 David was captured following the battle of Neville's Cross. Yet another English occupation of southern Scotland followed. Lands under English control were only gradually regained by the Scots in the latter part of the century. English kings, meanwhile, invaded Scotland in person in 1385 and in 1400. Their claims of overlordship relative to Scotland were never shelved. Scotland was faced on the south by an overtly hostile state, and one which, it was increasingly clear, was of far greater strength.

Hindsight tells us that the English threat to Scotland diminished rapidly after 1337 and that any long-term conquest of an intransigent Scotland was an unlikely eventuality. Nevertheless, the politically influential classes in Scotland did not have the benefit of hindsight. A central consideration faced by these political decision-makers was of a real, constant threat from a powerful neighbour. In the course of the fourteenth century this threat gradually became more latent than direct, and more occasional – but it was still the dominant factor in dictating Scotland's foreign policy. So, when we encounter the seeming anomaly of large-scale and regular Scottish attacks on England in the late fourteenth century, after the wars of independence were seemingly over, there is a ready explanation. The Scots felt that the English threat was merely in abeyance, not over, and they sought to re-create the conditions in which Robert I had been able to wrest acknowledgement of Scottish independence. Militarily the Scots were successful against a troubled English polity in the 1370s and 1380s. The final failure of Scottish military coercion only came in 1402 when a large invading army was catastrophically defeated at Humbleton Hill. Only after this signal defeat did the Scottish political leadership come to accept that they could not gain their core diplomatic objective through warfare. The English government, meanwhile, had altered its focus of military ambition towards France. Warfare between Scotland and England from the early fifteenth century onwards was dictated far more by local than national considerations, or was at least aimed towards precise territorial targets. In a real sense the wars of independence ended in the early fifteenth century: there was no longer a realistic prospect of the English conquest of Scotland; and the Scots had failed to force explicit recognition of this fact from their more powerful neighbours.

2. Scotland in Europe, c. 1337–1560

Conflict with England in the traumatic fourteenth century had numerous important consequences in Scotland. In terms of the political shape of the kingdom, the domestic exercise of power and the national psyche the wars wrought fundamental changes. They also changed completely Scotland's standing on the international stage, both as perceived by outsiders and by the Scots themselves. Most fundamentally, in terms of diplomacy, the wars greatly, though temporarily, raised Scotland's international profile. As entrenched enemies of the English crown, the Scots were valuable allies to those in whose interest it was to oppose England. The French crown did indeed find itself regularly in conflict with England in the later Middle Ages, so much so that the intermittent wars between France and England from 1337 until 1453 have been given the blanket title the 'Hundred Years War'. This Anglo-French conflict was a fight to the death in much the same way as the Anglo-Scottish wars were. In this context the Scots constituted important allies for the French. Geographical alignments made the Scots and the French natural allies in any conflicts with England. The two kingdoms had found it convenient to club together on occasions in the past, but with the establishment of entrenched Anglo-Scottish enmity from the late thirteenth century, the Franco-Scottish alliance – the 'Auld Alliance' – became an established feature of the diplomatic scenery of later medieval Europe. Scotland's value to France, even before the Hundred Years War is taken to have begun, was based on the military threat the Scots could pose to England. To uphold this useful check on the English the French materially supported the Scottish resistance in the early fourteenth century. Once the Anglo-French cold war became real war from 1337 the French had even more cause to bolster their allies. Their main utility to the Scots was now diplomatic: the French made sure that the Scots were included in any continental truces, ensuring that the Scots did not have to face their greatest fear – isolation against English military might. The alliance, then, was essentially defensive, intended to cope with the palpably more powerful English state. Sometimes the alliance operated in a more ambitious fashion. In 1385, at a particularly low ebb in English fortunes, the French and Scots concocted plans for combined military operations which, it was hoped, would lead to the invasion of England and its defeat. These grandiose plans failed. The French expeditionary force which did arrive in Scotland in 1385 returned home amidst evident acrimony between the allies, caused by personal animosities, clashes over strategy and the fact that the promised French invasion of southern England did not materialize.

International usefulness depended on the military threat which the Scots could pose to the English. After its defeat at Humbleton Hill in 1402, when the potency of aggressive Scottish military action against England was heavily undermined, Scotland's international prominence began to decline. If the Scots were unable to launch large-scale, concerted and damaging attacks against northern England, then their value to the French crown was much reduced. Thus the nature of the aid the Scots could offer the French crown changed from the early fifteenth century. Large mercenary forces were dispatched from Scotland to assist in the resistance against the real threat of conquest in France which the English, initially under Henry V, posed from 1415. Tellingly, this was not primarily a Scottish governmental initiative, but private enterprise. Coincidental with the decline in importance of Scotland internationally was the emergence of the Duke of Burgundy as a prominent player in the Anglo-French dialectic of the fifteenth century. By the 1420s the duke's territories included not just Burgundy, but also most of the Low Countries. This posed a further political dilemma for the Scots for, whereas in previous centuries their vital Flemish wool markets had been theoretically under French authority, they were now under Burgundian control. Moreover, the emergent Burgundian state (and from 1477 its Habsburg successor) was often at odds with France, notably from 1419 to 1435 and again in the early sixteenth century. The dilemma was self-evident: did Scots follow their commercial interests and acquiesce in Burgundian/Habsburg anglophilia, or did they retain their sentimental attachment to French anglophobia? For much of the fifteenth century they prevaricated, but in this new alignment of states a Scotland which, it was now evident, could not potently threaten England's northern border was of little relevance. Paradoxically, the relative decline in Scotland's status coincided with the rule of successive kings of the Stewart line who were anxious to stamp the presence of their realm, and so confirm their position as important players, amongst the international community in the fifteenth century. The Stewart rulers saw themselves as natural members of the élite club of important European monarchies. James IV exemplifies this trend. There was more than just rhetoric in his attempts to be the arbiter of disputes among his fellow sovereigns and in his expressed wish to lead a Christian army to the gates of Constantinople. The construction at huge expense of a royal navy with great warships scarcely functional for his limited purposes tells of the same impulse. In an antiquated gesture of close affiliation to France, James led the assembled Scottish host to its slaughter at Flodden in 1513 largely, one suspects, because there was a wide European conflict going on at the time in which he really felt he ought to be involved.

One legacy of James IV's reign was to prompt more Scots to question whether their long-term future internationally should be as a regime aligned in traditional fashion towards France, or whether closer relations with England were desirable. Even after the spectacular cull of the Scottish nobility at Flodden, however, the Scottish minority administration was still willing to work in concert with a French expeditionary force in attacking England in 1523. That on this occasion the Scots were exceedingly reluctant to enter English soil is perhaps a portent of changing attitudes. Even more tellingly, from 1524 the factions competing for political power during the minority of James V can be identified as either pro-English or pro-French. As James entered on his personal rule in 1528 a complicating, and intensifying, element of the question of Scotland's international allegiance was the Reformation, the religious breach within Christendom that began in the early sixteenth century. International politics in this era was highly charged. Scotland's importance internationally was again enhanced: would Scotland act as a northern bulwark of the old faith alongside France or would she turn towards England, which broke with Rome in 1533–4, to form an island fortress of the new religious belief? This was an important question and, during the personal rule of James V, all the major European powers had an interest in seeking alliance with the Scottish king. There is little sign that he was tempted by the option of England. Both of James's marriages were to Frenchwomen – Francis I's daughter Madelaine, and Mary of Guise-Lorraine. It was as a Catholic that James died following another offensive against England, which failed at the battle of Solway Moss in 1542.

Thereafter Scotland once again became far more of a pawn than an active player on the international stage, for James was succeeded by a female infant – Scotland's first queen regnant. Strenuous efforts were made by the English king Henry VIII, and the minority regime which followed his death, to gain the young Queen Mary's marriage to Henry's son, Edward VI. A marriage agreement to this effect, the Treaty of Greenwich, was agreed with the Scots in 1543, but was repudiated by them later in the same year. Military force was the next option, but despite another crushing victory for English arms at the battle of Pinkie in 1547, the brutal campaigns aimed at forcing on the Scots an English match for Mary – the so-called 'Rough Wooing' of 1544–7 – only had the effect of ushering the Scots into the welcoming arms of the French alliance. Mary's marriage to the heir to the French throne, Francis, was agreed in 1548 and contracted in 1558. Forces from France helped the Scots to rid themselves of English garrisons stationed in their country; and Mary's politically able French mother, Mary of Guise, assumed control of Scottish government on her daughter's behalf in 1554. Scotland's strongpoints were now occupied by professional forces from France, while French officials wielded great influence in the governance of the country. With the prospect of a Franco-Scottish union of crowns within a generation, it was as a Catholic French satellite that Scotland's future loomed.

The final and decisive event which influenced the future direction of Scotland's international leanings came with the Scottish Reformation of 1559–60. Even in the mid-1550s it was far from inevitable that Scotland would adopt a Protestant creed. Although by then the new religion was well established elsewhere in northern Europe, Scottish religious affiliations were less redolent of those in Scandinavia or the northern Netherlands and rather more akin to those evident in Ireland and Italy. There, despite vocal criticism of the Catholic church (espoused by orthodox Catholics as well as a small but enthusiastic group of Protestants), there were no Reformations; and, but for political developments, historians might still be asking why there was no Reformation in Scotland, as other historians continue to ponder with regard to Ireland and Italy. Religion alone did not make a Reformation. Protestantism was, however, given an enormous boost in Scotland, especially among the governing classes, by the suffocating political embrace of Catholic France. The threat to Scotland's independence seemed to come most potently from France, not England, after 1548 and especially from 1558; and absorption by France was not a future that appealed to Scots of the mid-sixteenth century. Neither did it appeal to Elizabeth I of England. With English aid the French occupying forces in Scotland were expelled. From 1560 Scotland's international future lay in closer relations with Protestant England.

Conclusions: Myth, Reality and the Medieval Legacy

Coming to terms with the English remains one of the medieval past's most enduring legacies. In 1995 past and present merged in the phenomenally successful Hollywood production of 'Braveheart' to produce what the *Irish Times* described as 'a crass exercise in anglophobia'. The more discerning among the film's audience were no doubt aware that 'Braveheart' contained gross historical distortions and inaccuracies. Yet such flaws were forgiven by most, and the film's stirring patriotism was loudly applauded by many. Rather than attacking the film's central ethos, popular criticism was generally confined to more muted derision of actor Mel Gibson's inauthentic accent and inappropriately diminutive stature for playing the reputedly gigantic Ayrshire hero, William Wallace. 'Braveheart' was a reasonable representation of what many modern Scots, and others, understand of Scotland's medieval past. Even if we know neither the tone of Wallace's accent nor the physical dimensions of his body (since it was cut into pieces), there is no doubt that anglophobia has medieval roots. The prerequisites for this sentiment, Scotland and England, are both medieval relics since it was in this era that both kingdoms came to take their present geographical forms.

Anglophobia, as typified by 'Braveheart', remains one enduring psychological scar of the Middle Ages. Innate conservatism, vividly and sometimes shockingly portrayed in the fatalistic drug culture of the 1996 film 'Trainspotting', is perhaps another. Overt social unrest, radical religious impulses and newfangled initiatives in government, periodically evident in France, Italy, Spain and the Netherlands throughout the Middle Ages, were rare in Scotland after the arrival of the twelfth- and thirteenth-century Anglo-French immigrants. The comparative lack of dissent and deviation arguably inhibited innovation, intellectual curiosity and enterprise. Anglophobia and conservatism aside, many more tangible aspects of modern Scottish life have similarly medieval origins. The genesis of the present legal and educational systems, together with the topographic rationale of town and country, the location of government institutions in Edinburgh, and the boundaries of local authorities also lie in the Middle Ages, the latter almost unaltered until the Local Government (Scotland) Act of 1973. It is thanks to the Middle Ages too that fish still adorns Friday menus in many canteens across the country and it was in the Middle Ages that many popular recreational pursuits, such as football and golf, first took shape.

It is a cliché, perhaps, to suggest that a study of the medieval past (and before) is essential to understanding the nature of modern Scotland and the mindset of modern Scots. Nevertheless, there is some merit to the argument: such study helps to disentangle powerful myths from, albeit often barely discernible, realities. Yet separating myth and reality is all the more difficult since myths are not merely a modern creation: they often informed medieval attitudes and propaganda too. The twelfth-century Muslim historian who compiled the *Book of Roger* for the Norman king of Sicily, Roger II, utilized the accounts of others in describing Scotland. Yet it is telling that, while England was described as a land of teeming population, healthy towns and productive agriculture, Scotland was 'uninhabited and has neither town nor village'. In their propaganda later medieval Scots sometimes found it useful to endorse such inaccuracies and depict themselves as inhabiting a small and impoverished realm 'beyond which there is no dwelling place at all'.

The reality was somewhat different. Between 1100 and 1560 Scotland developed into an integral component of Christendom. Politically, this transformation is reflected in the crown's marital policy. In the eleventh century Malcolm III was an attractive match for an Anglo-Saxon refugee with no assets and dim prospects. By 1548 Mary I was deemed a suitable partner for the heir to Henry II, king of France, and arguably the most powerful of European monarchs. The contrast is a concise indication of Scotland's growing international stature. Whether as an individual force to be wooed or as a puppet to be manipulated, Scotland became widely recognized as the political counterpart to England in the Latin west. This reflected the steady, if unspectacular, advance of the crown's domestic authority. To be sure, this was neither a perfected nor an irreversible process. Nevertheless, Mary's medieval predecessors had bludgeoned domestic rivals into early graves; and for the most part they satisfied their remaining subjects' limited expectations that kings provide justice against injustice and that they defend their realm against external aggression. In return, the crown was generally rewarded with loyalty.

These developments provided a common point of reference with other medieval kingdoms. So too did the structures of society and economy. Society was bonded and underpinned by a universal religious faith, though this it would finally lose with the advent of the Reformation, to be replaced by the internationalism of Protestantism and Catholicism. On the other hand, Christian values, familial and class bonds, together with international, national and regional identities, proved more enduring – and to different degrees they continued to shape social relationships, in Scotland as elsewhere, in later centuries. However, even during the Catholic centuries their comparative potency, among individuals, in regions and across time, varied. National allegiances, for instance, were generally sharper in 1560 than they had been in 1100, while regional affiliations, though still vibrant, had been weakened, not least by the collapse of cohesive regional lordships and the spread of greater linguistic uniformity. There had been modifications too in class relationships. Slaves, serfs and the legally 'unfree' disappeared from the medieval landscape, to be replaced by beggars, migrants and the new, economically 'unfree'; genuine freedom, as John Barbour suggested, remained 'a noble thing'. Nevertheless, middling sorts had begun to emerge in the fertile land between the social extremities, in the shape of the wealthier husbandmen and merchants, and also members of the nascent professions, especially lawyers, who were to play an important role in the reception of the Reformation in towns like Edinburgh. While Scotland remained an overwhelmingly agrarian country, the cashless self-sufficiency and unwritten legal systems of 1100 were being increasingly overtaken by commercialization and formal litigation. Many certainly prospered in the process.

This is not to argue that medieval Scotland was a resounding tale of success. Simple notions of benevolent 'progress' through the centuries should be rejected. It could, for instance, be argued that the position of women declined as the early modern era dawned. Male iconoclasts vilified that previously positive example of womanhood, the Virgin Mary; and the benign image of the Virgin was replaced by the nightmare spectre of the witch. The Reformation also ushered in sterner attitudes towards prostitution. Female employment opportunities perhaps declined more generally as population grew in the sixteenth century. John Knox, meanwhile, ranted against the 'monstrous regiment' of female rulers. It could indeed be argued that the later fourteenth and fifteenth centuries witnessed the high-water mark of female status, at least in some senses, until the twentieth century. In part, of course, this was a consequence of the Black Death and the ensuing labour shortage which had probably opened up employment opportunities for women.

Beneficial as some of its side-effects may have been, the Black Death was the single most calamitous event to have struck Scotland in recorded history, and although population levels began to increase towards the end of the period, this owed little to developments in health care or medical science. Scotland remained a harsh and brutal society for the disabled and the sick, for the poor and even for a male aristocracy of a still belligerent temperament. Despite growing secular literacy and the production of accomplished poetry from the later fifteenth century, medieval Scotland was never Christendom's cultural beacon. Its foremost intellectual, John Duns Scotus, had made his reputation abroad during the thirteenth century; and print, together with Protestantism and exploration, the hallmarks of the early modern civilization, were belated arrivals in Scotland.

It is perhaps worth remembering that while similar political, social and economic developments to those found in Scotland occurred all over medieval Europe, they rarely coincided. Italy and Germany lost the political coherence to be found in Scotland, while the Netherlands and Ireland never quite found it. Fifteenth-century Czech society found a bond in the Hussite heresy at the effective price of expulsion from Christendom; on the other hand, in the Iberian kingdoms social tensions were exacerbated by the presence of large non-Christian minorities and only partly resolved towards the end of the medieval period by forcible conversions and draconian expulsions. Meanwhile in Poland, while political coherence and religious uniformity developed, different economic trends ensured that the country's wealth became even more concentrated than in Scotland, as servile status was introduced for the great mass of the peasantry. Yet in combining so many of the elements only to be found in a great medieval power such as France, Scotland was unusual. It also succeeded in this despite (if the evidence of Wales and Ireland is considered) its initially unpromising start as a partly Celtic society. A remarkable native dynasty transformed and enlarged its authority in ways not quite seen elsewhere in the Latin west. The fierce test of the English wars moulded the character of this state and did much to define the attitudes of Scots in the wider world of Christendom. Scotland was perhaps a third-rate power, but it *survived* in the shark-infested waters of international interaction. And from kings to commoners Scots can be seen ceaselessly striving to engage as equals in the bloody games played by medieval nations.

Bibliographical Essay

This volume attempts to chart the history of a nation. The national framework is a common and legitimate approach to interpreting the past, but not without its disadvantages. It implies that it was through national eyes that women and men of the past viewed their world. In the Middle Ages many did not, or at least did not do so exclusively. Local affinities, to parish, market and landlord, dominated daily life. At the same time, an intrusive and international religious faith pervaded almost every facet of human existence and made for a genuinely cosmopolitan streak to the medieval mind. Among the upper levels of society this was augmented by an international chivalric culture. It follows that arguably the best introductions to medieval Scotland are to be found either in local or in international surveys. Unfortunately, few of the former exist, though E. P. D. Torrie, *Medieval Dundee: A Town and its People* (Dundee, 1990) and J. Bannerman, 'Macduff of Fife', in A. Grant and K. J. Stringer (eds.), *Medieval Scotland: Crown, Lordship and Community* (Edinburgh, 1993) provide excellent examples of what is possible. Approaching Scotland from the European perspective is in practice equally problematic, since most general histories concentrate on the Anglo-French axis and have little to say about Scotland. Three lucid and recommended exceptions are Robert Bartlett, *The Making of Europe: Conquest, Colonization and Cultural Change, 950–1350* (London, 1993); R. Frame, *The Political Development of the British Isles, 1100–1400* (Oxford, 1990); and R. R. Davies, *Domination and Conquest: The Experience of Ireland, Scotland and Wales, 1100–1300* (Cambridge, 1990). These may be usefully complemented by A. Mackay and D. Ditchburn (eds.), *Atlas of Medieval History* (London, 1997), which includes maps and accompanying texts on Scottish themes by Alexander Grant.

For all its inadequacies it is, however, within a national context that most historians have attempted to reconstruct medieval Scotland. The simplest introduction remains that by W. C. Dickinson, *Scotland from Earliest Times to 1603*, revised and edited by A. A. M. Duncan (Oxford, 1977), ideally supplemented by P. G. B. McNeill and H. L. MacQueen (eds.), *Atlas of Scottish History to 1707* (Edinburgh, 1996). Rather more challenging are the concept-driven volumes of *The New History of Scotland*: G. W. S. Barrow, *Kingship and Unity: Scotland, 1000–1306* (London, 1981); Alexander Grant's excellent *Independence and Nationhood: Scotland, 1306–1469* (London, 1984); and Jenny Wormald, *Court, Kirk and Community: Scotland 1469–1625* (London, 1981). Less user-friendly are the relevant volumes of *The Edinburgh History of Scotland*: A. A. M. Duncan, *Scotland: The Making of the Kingdom* (Edinburgh, 1975), a book brimming with ideas, but one which requires careful reading and re-reading; Ranald Nicholson, *Scotland: The Later Middle Ages* (Edinburgh, 1974); and Gordon Donaldson, *Scotland: James V to James VII* (Edinburgh, 1965).

Coverage of specific themes is patchy. The most authoritative works on the economy are Elizabeth Gemmill and Nicholas Mayhew, *Changing Values in Medieval Scotland: A Study of Prices, Money, Weights and Measures* (Cambridge, 1995); and A. J. S. Gibson and T. C. Smout, *Prices, Food and Wages in Scotland, 1550–1780* (Cambridge, 1995). Both include material of a highly technical nature, while also offering wider insights into the economy. Overseas trade and the urban economy have received attention in article form, in volumes such as M. Lynch, M. Spearman and G. Stell (eds.), *The Scottish Medieval Town* (Edinburgh, 1988). By comparison, and with the exception of R. A. Dodgshon, *Land and Society in Early Scotland* (Oxford, 1981), the rural economy is adequately covered only from the sixteenth century, for which see Margaret Sanderson, *Scottish Rural Society in the Sixteenth Century* (Edinburgh, 1992) and R. A. Dodgshon, *From Chiefs to Landlords: Social and Economic Change in the Western Highlands and Islands, c. 1493–1820* (Edinburgh, 1998). Ian Whyte offers the most up-to-date synthesis in *Scotland before the Industrial Revolution: An Economic and Social History, c. 1050–c. 1750* (London, 1995).

The boundary between economy and society is historiographically blurred and many of the works cited above have much to say about both. Women and peasants remain disgracefully neglected, though Elizabeth Ewan and Maureen M. Meikle (eds.), *Women in Scotland, c. 1100–c. 1750* (East Linton, 1999) offers a starting-point on the former. There is no adequate monograph on the peasantry, though J. J. McGavin, 'Robert III's "Rough Music": Charivari and Diplomacy in a Medieval Scottish Court', *Scottish Historical Review* 74 (1995) is important. Predominantly about aristocratic men, G. W. S. Barrow, *The Anglo-Norman Era in Scottish History* (Oxford, 1977) offers a detailed analysis of 'feudalism'; a contrary interpretation is advanced by Susan Reynolds in *Fiefs and Vassals: The Medieval Evidence Reinterpreted* (Oxford, 1994) and, for a later period, by Jenny Wormald in *Lords and Men in Scotland: Bonds of Manrent, 1442–1603* (Edinburgh, 1985). National identity is discussed most recently in D. Broun, R. J. Findlay and M. Lynch (eds.), *Image and Identity: The Making and Remaking of Scotland through the Ages* (Edinburgh, 1998). The renaissance in urban social history is largely the achievement of E. P. D. Torrie (now Dennison) and her essay in S. Foster, A. Macinnes and R. MacInnes (eds.), *Scottish Power Centres from the Early Middle Ages to the Twentieth Century* (Glasgow, 1998) provides a good starting-point. In the same volume Richard Oram discusses monasteries, though medieval religion more generally is best approached either from the European perspective, adopted by R. N. Swanson, *Religion and Devotion in Europe c. 1215–c. 1515* (Cambridge, 1995), or from the rich archaeological evidence assembled in works such as P. Hill (ed.), *Whithorn and St Ninian: The Excavation of a Monastic Town, 1984–91* (Stroud, 1997), and J. H. Lewis and G. Ewart, *Jedburgh Abbey: The Archaeology and Architecture of a Border Abbey* (Edinburgh, 1995). Specifically Scottish and historical studies of the Reformation abound. I. B. Cowan, *The Scottish Reformation: Church and Society in Sixteenth-Century Scotland* (London, 1982) is perhaps the most readable.

Domestic politics has traditionally been approached from the monarchical angle. David I remains neglected, though G. W. S. Barrow's pamphlet, *David I of Scotland (1124–1153): The Balance of New and Old* (Reading, 1985) is a starting-point. The same author's introductions to the first two volumes of *Regesta Regum Scottorum* (Edinburgh, 1960 and 1971) are indispensable for the following two reigns; William I is also the subject of a less specialized synthesis by D. D. R. Owen, *William the Lion: Kingship and Culture, 1143–1214* (East Linton, 1997). A study of Alexander II is in preparation (edited by Richard Oram) and a similar volume already exists for his son: Norman H. Reid (ed.), *Scotland in the Reign of Alexander III, 1249–1286* (Edinburgh, 1990). Later kings have been better served by modern biographers, and none more so than Robert I in G. W. S. Barrow, *Robert Bruce and the Community of the Realm of Scotland* (3rd edn., Edinburgh, 1988). While David II has yet to find his Barrow, the Stewart dynasty has been tackled with verve by Stephen Boardman, *The Early Stewart Kings: Robert II and Robert III,*

1371–1406 (East Linton, 1996); Michael Brown, *James I* (Edinburgh, 1994); Christine McGladdery, *James II* (Edinburgh, 1990); Norman Macdougall, *James III: A Political Study* (Edinburgh, 1992) and *James IV* (Edinburgh, 1989); and J. Cameron, *James V: The Personal Rule, 1528–1542* (East Linton, 1998). All focus on crown–magnate relations, a subject also addressed in K. J. Stringer, *Earl David of Huntingdon, 1152–1219: A Study in Anglo-Scottish History* (Edinburgh, 1985); Alan Young, *Robert Bruce's Rivals: the Comyns 1212–1314* (East Linton, 1997); Michael Brown, *The Black Douglases* (East Linton, 1998); and K. J. Stringer (ed.), *Essays on the Nobility of Medieval Scotland* (Edinburgh, 1985), which includes Jenny Wormald's controversial but seminal article, 'Taming the Magnates'.

Domestic political studies also comment on Anglo-Scottish relations. In addition, Keith Stringer, *The Reign of King Stephen* (London, 1993) is highly illuminating on David I's intervention in the English civil war, as is the under-appreciated chapter by Judith Green, 'Anglo-Scottish Relations, 1066–1174', in Michael Jones and Malcolm Vale (eds.), *England and her Neighbours, 1066–1453* (London, 1989). Amid much dross published on the wars of independence, Fiona Watson, *Under the Hammer: Edward I and Scotland 1286–1307* (East Linton, 1998); Colm McNamee, *The Wars of the Bruces: Scotland, England and Ireland, 1306–1328* (East Linton, 1997); and R. Nicholson, *Edward III and the Scots* (London, 1965) provide the most authoritative recent accounts. Later fourteenth-century Anglo-Scottish relations are tackled in *Border Bloodshed: Scotland and England at War, 1369–1403* (East Linton, 2000) by A. J. Macdonald. Relations with other countries have received less attention, though *Scotland and Scandinavia, 800–1800* (Edinburgh, 1990), *The Scottish Soldier Abroad* (Edinburgh, 1992), and *Scotland and the Low Countries, 1124–1994* (East Linton. 1996), all edited by Grant G. Simpson, and *Scotland and Europe, 1200–1850* (Edinburgh, 1986) and *Scotland and the Sea* (Edinburgh, 1992), both edited by T. C. Smout, provide a basis for delving at particular points.

All the works cited above are the product of two fundamental processes. Historians require evidence, and only when that has been assembled and digested is it possible to offer (hopefully accurate) narrative and (sometimes even stimulating) interpretation. The most recent source guides remain B. Webster, *Scotland from the Eleventh Century to 1603* (London, 1975) and G. Donaldson, *The Sources of Scottish History* (Edinburgh, 1978), though both have been overtaken by the publication of additional source materials. The most significant landmark among such work is D. E. R. Watt's nine-volume edition and translation of the fifteenth-century *Scotichronicon* by Walter Bower (Aberdeen, 1987–98). Bower's chronicle offers more than just a narrative of events from the creation of the world to the fifteenth century. Emotionally laced with religious moralism, social snobbery and ardent patriotism, *Scotichronicon* provides a true flavour of the clerical mentality; and arguably a better insight into the Scottish Middle Ages than any other published work, except, perhaps, the Bible.

4
Reformation to Union, 1560–1707

KEITH M. BROWN

In August 1560, some 130 of the leading representatives of the Scottish political nation gathered in Edinburgh for the sitting of a parliament. It was a tense assembly that met at the end of what had been a bitter civil and religious war involving significant military intervention by France and England, rivals for influence in Scotland. The last remnants of the once dominant French army had already embarked for home, their departure watched by English soldiers whose bombardment had brought to an end France's recent political hegemony in Scotland. For once, the English, who also returned home at the end of hostilities, had been welcomed by many Scots, resentful of the growing French presence and the taxes required to sustain their large professional army. Others were relieved that the Protestant Queen Elizabeth had tipped the military balance against the forces defending the Roman Catholic church.

Now, under the terms of the Treaty of Edinburgh, signed on 6 July, the French and English left the Scots to settle their own affairs. Hence the parliament summoned by authority of the absentee Queen Mary and her husband, Francis II, king of France and king of Scots. Instructions from Paris were to avoid any discussion of religion, but that is exactly what the noblemen who had led the revolt against France and Rome wanted to talk about. The Protestant lords packed the parliament with their supporters, frightening off most of the Catholic bishops and leaving the Catholic laity without any leadership. Organized and with a clear sense of purpose, the Protestants petitioned parliament to redress those abuses which 'by the malice of Satan and negligence of men' had crept into the church. Parliament's response was to declare unequivocally for a new beginning, displaying a radical degree of self-confidence in a different kind of future that few modern legislatures would dare emulate, severing Scotland's centuries-old relationship with Rome and its pope, 'that Man of Sinne'. The latter's authority was overturned, the mass, that central ritual of the church, was outlawed, and a new, almost brash, Calvinist Confession of Faith was adopted. Even without royal ratification, parliament had taken a momentous decision, one that would prove to be irretrievable, and one that would define the nation and its identity throughout most of the next five centuries.

One hundred and forty-six years later, in the autumn and winter of 1706–7, parliament again met in Edinburgh to take a decision on Scotland's future. Once again there was an absentee queen, Anne, an Englishwoman and the last of the Stewarts to rule the kingdom. Once again Scotland was being squeezed between the might of England and France, between securing Protestantism and the largely imagined threat of Catholicism, and between those who advocated revolutionary political ideals of resistance against tyrannical rulers and those who defended the rights of monarchs against their subjects. As in 1560, parliament met amidst enormous political tension, conscious that it was faced with a choice that would have great consequences for the nation. Yet the assembled company of men who sat in the Parliament House, built facing St Giles cathedral in the 1630s, was not so very different from that in 1560. Although the parliament of 1707 was a bigger body than at the Reformation, it was still dominated by the landed nobility, with many of the same families prominent in 1560 again centre stage in 1707. The overwhelming majority of the population remained outside the political process, although in 1707 the mob did make its voice heard in the streets of Edinburgh as it howled abuse at those who supported closer union with England. This time the debate within parliament was more open, but in the end there was overwhelming backing for union. On 28 April 1707, the Scottish parliament was dissolved, a historic moment that Chancellor Seafield recognized as 'the end o' an auld sang'.

As in 1560, Scotland's political leaders in 1707 took a leap of faith, turning their backs on old traditions, envisaging a better future unshackled by the legacy of the past. Yet while the road towards Protestantism, a limitation on royal power, and friendship with England was first marked out in 1560, the journey that followed was never a smooth one: there was nothing inevitable about what occurred in 1707. Nevertheless, these themes linking the two parliaments, surely the most significant in Scottish history, shaped the intervening age and continue to resonate down to the present. Anyone looking for the birth of modern Scottish identity will find it in the period of the Reformation and the Union with England.

The Reformation, 1560–1603

1. Long-Term Perspectives

The Protestant Reformation, which had its origins in Germany in 1517, was the single most important event in European history between the Renaissance and the period of Enlightenment, industrialization and revolution that unfurled in the later eighteenth century. In Scotland, where it occurred relatively late, Reformation unleashed ideas and energies that established the agendas in religion, politics and social change throughout the entire sixteenth and seventeenth centuries, only beginning to wind down in the mid-eighteenth century. It continues to shape lives today, often in ways that people fail to recognize, for example in Scots law, or in educational traditions. However, the main themes that flowed from the Reformation are religious beliefs, political ideas, union with England, heightened literacy and greater social control. The one important development of this period that was distinct from Reformation was population growth, although it did dovetail with social control in that the propertied ranks increasingly shared with the clergy a desire to regulate the behaviour and movement of these large numbers of people. However, population growth was more an indication of the recovery of late medieval society after the impact of the fourteenth-century plagues than an indication of any new capacity by early modern Scotland to sustain a population greater than ever before. That hurdle was only overcome in the later eighteenth century. Furthermore, while there might have been more people around than there had been for 150 years, their experiences of material life were not very different. The real changes of this period were principally religious, political and ideological, and their impact was primarily on the élites of society.

Of course, not everyone in Scotland became a Protestant overnight in 1560. Nor did all those who converted to Protestantism understand what they were doing. On the other hand, within a very short time most of the country was exposed to a different kind of religion, and the differences were both visible and audible. We should not underestimate how shocking this might have been for a society conscious of the need to placate a God who would condemn to eternal hell those who got it wrong. By the end of the seventeenth century, a Protestant ministry was established, the new belief system was widely adopted and the religious revolution had gone through a second phase of heightened activity in the 1640s. This last contained the seeds of Protestantism's own inescapable tendency to fragment, and the Episcopal–Presbyterian and Remonstrant–Resolutioner divisions (discussed below) were merely a foretaste of the secessions of the eighteenth century. Nevertheless, these were conflicts within a Calvinist community of believers, and there was little deviation from that consensus.

Embedded in the Protestant Reformation of 1559–60 was a revolution against the crown as represented by Mary of Guise, legitimate governor of the kingdom and representative of the absentee Francis II and Mary. For Protestants, worried about how this action could be justified, and in order to answer their critics, arguments were brought into the public sphere by John Knox, who advocated a limitation of royal authority as a means of resisting tyranny. Kings who abused their authority should, he argued, suffer 'according to Godis law, nocht as a King, but as an offender'. A second revolution against Mary in 1567 required that an even more sophisticated ideology of resistance be refined by George Buchanan, the most profound intellectual sixteenth-century Scotland produced. Thereafter, a blend of Knoxian and Buchananite thought haunted the Stewart monarchy until the 1689 revolution when a reigning king, James VII, was forfeited by parliament for his usurpation of absolute authority in the state.

In the intervening years, ideas about resistance to kings were spread down through the social hierarchy, repeatedly clashing with forms of royal absolutism, both in public debate and in rebellion. James VI was subjected to such revolutionary politics in action at the Ruthven Raid in 1582, when he was kidnapped by a faction of Protestant nobles, and it was deployed by successive Presbyterian critics like Andrew Melville and David Calderwood, who chipped away at the crown's claims to supremacy over the church. In the 1640s, Charles I was destroyed by these ideas, which were further developed by the Covenanters (see below) who took up arms against the king, gradually giving up the excuse that he was blinded by bad counsel to attack the very foundations of monarchical authority. The young Charles II was left in no doubt in 1650–51 that while the Covenanters disapproved of his father's execution, he would never be permitted to exercise the kind of power to which James VI laid claim. The nobility's reactionary conservatism after 1660 appeared to signal a return to a form of absolute monarchy, but the genie could not be put back in the bottle. The Covenanters' resistance ideas, along with their religious beliefs, were too deeply shared in Scottish society. The very radical, almost republican tendencies of the Cameronians in the 1680s might have been out on a limb, but the ease with which James VII was deposed in 1689 indicates that Buchananite notions were just below the surface even of élite society.

The road from Knox, Buchanan and Melville through the Covenanters to the revolution Whigs was a bumpy one, and there was nothing inevitable about the failure of royal absolutism. However, the enforced abdication of Mary, the defeat of Charles I and the forfeiture of James VII each made the monarchy's recovery less likely. By 1706, it was relatively easy to offer the throne to a distant German prince. Never again would kings wield the power to which Stewart monarchs aspired, never again would subjects be so in awe of their kings, and while forms of religious persecution continued, never again would the crown use legitimately authorized violence to enforce religious conformity. This continuing debate was conducted in religious and secular language, but the debt to the Reformation was immense and – especially at a popular level – it was religion that fuelled each succeeding conflict.

Union with England was no more inevitable than the defeat of royal autocracy. Yet here too the Reformation set a course that made it more likely and more desirable. Reformation in 1560 brought Scotland into line with Protestant England in the face of the threat, real and imagined by turns, from counter-Reformation Europe. Fears about Philip II's Spain in the later sixteenth century, the Holy Roman Emperor during the Thirty Years War, or Louis XIV in the later seventeenth and early eighteenth centuries created a strong sense of common bonding against foreign oppressors. English policy towards Scotland after 1560 was largely benevolent, an Anglo-Scottish League was formed in 1586, and by the time of the Union of the Crowns in 1603 there had been no hostility between the two kingdoms since the 1550s. There is no doubt that this regal Union was at times unsatisfactory, and a separation of the ways was possible in 1649 (when the English advocated it) or in the early 1700s (when a faction of the Scottish parliament appeared to desire it), but the combination of a common religion and monarchy was a powerful one, to which can be added a more or less common language and a convergence of trading interests. England pursued no ambitions in Scotland, the conquest of the 1650s being reluctantly undertaken after the Scots had provoked war, and most of the time the English were not very interested in Scotland, far less so than they were in Ireland. That in 1705, amidst a massive continental war, the English Whigs decided the Scots should be forced to choose between a Hanoverian monarchy with England, or a Stewart monarchy in enmity with England, was understandable. Fortunately, Scotland's politicians took the sensible course, agreeing to a parliamentary and economic Union. That decision massively shaped Scotland's future, positioning it close to the heart of an Anglo-centric imperial trading system. The claim by Tories, Jacobites and modern-day nationalists that this was unfair, unconstitutional, or mistaken need not be taken seriously.

The Reformation stimulated significant change in the social and cultural sphere, including the drive to promote education and literacy. This does not mean that there were no schools before 1560, but the rapid expansion thereafter, especially in the Lowlands, was a direct product of the Protestant church's publicly stated commitment to establishing a school in every parish. What slowed that policy down was the greed of landlords unwilling to fund education adequately, the kirk's own meagre funds having in the first instance, to be ploughed into church buildings and ministerial salaries. Of course, the growth of the printing business facilitated the spread of literacy, but Scotland's printing industry was in no significant way unique. Its presence does not explain rates of literacy by the mid-seventeenth century which were comparable with the best in Europe. Even if these literacy rates have been exaggerated as part of the national myth, the evidence from signing and of the creation of schools points to a society with a high commitment to elementary education in a wide segment of the population. The effect was to create a people deeply influenced by the Bible, but also able to assimilate much of the pamphlet material about religious topics and related political ones. It is not unlikely, therefore, that many Covenanters were directly exposed to the writings of Knox, Buchanan and Samuel Rutherford.

Greater literacy also provided a wider pool of educated people, particularly important in a small population, who were able eventually to contribute their intellectual energies to solving society's problems. The flow of ideas from the Reformation through to a thoughtful, self-examining and socially critical religion fused with relatively widespread literacy to create the reservoir from which the Enlightenment, secure in a British Whig state, flowered in the eighteenth century.

The period from 1560 to 1707 saw a greater degree of social control being exercised by the propertied ranks in alliance with the church. In part this was a product of the population rise that placed more pressure on land and food, stirring unease among landowners as large bodies of poor moved around the country seeking employment and nourishment. However, social control was also an aim of the Protestant church, concerned to regulate social behaviour according to its evangelical mission. Thus sexual activity was much more carefully divided into what was acceptable and what was undesirable, being regulated with previously unimagined levels of moral policing. The church's very real desire to alleviate the lot of the impoverished, disabled, sick and widowed was handicapped by inadequate resources, hence its co-operation with civil magistrates in distinguishing between deserving and undeserving poor, and in controlling domestic migration. Witchcraft emerged as a perceived threat to political hierarchy, religious beliefs and community values, triggering periods of intense persecution. More than ever, crime was against God's laws, an affront to the king's authority, and was seen as a threat to property and privilege. This in turn led to greater efforts to regulate a wide range of behaviour and a harsher criminal code with more emphasis on punishment than compensation. Crown, kirk and community all saw a need for more regulation that, at a parish level, the highly devolved Protestant church was best placed to administer.

At the end of this burst of energy generated by the Reformation, what were the consequences for Scotland and for its people? Politically, the independent Scottish state was compromised by the 1603 Union of the Crowns, disappearing altogether in the 1707 Union of the Parliaments. This was no bad thing in the context of the time since international security was better provided within the orbit of English influence than outside it. The threat from arbitrary kings receded never to re-emerge, and the aristocratic oligarchy that replaced it provided much better government than was to be found in most neighbouring states. The regulation of people at the parish level, by noble courts of barony and regality, and by the kirk, was the best that a society at this stage in development could expect, upholding the values of the whole community within a recognized hierarchy. The commitment to education was a real one, affirmed by parliament again in the important 1696 Education Act, even if the vision continued to be impaired by funding difficulties. The religion of the individual was still largely determined by family tradition, local loyalties and clerical leadership, but much more so than before 1560, people were able to reflect on a variety of religious routes to follow. However, in the provision of material goods, and in greater freedom from the fear of famine, disease and unemployment this period made few advances, although one should be careful about attributing to early modern people any expectation that life should improve. The imagination and energy required to make advances in these fields of human experience would have to come from a different source than the Reformation.

2. A Religious Revolution

The pre-Reformation Roman Catholic church in Scotland was certainly not wholly corrupt, nor had it entirely lost the trust and confidence of all the Scottish people. Pockets of real spirituality existed in the monasteries, there were priests who laboured hard in their parishes, the laity still observed many of the rituals of the church calendar, good works were evident in the hospices and in alms-giving, and educational provision was far from non-existent. On the other hand, a robust, vibrant, self-confident church would not have been swept away so easily in 1560. Abandoned by its bishops, undefended by an often ill-educated clergy with low morale, and earning little respect from a literate laity that was angered by abuses within the church and enthused by the fresh ideas emanating from Protestant Europe, Scottish Catholicism collapsed almost immediately as the protection of French military force was removed.

Protestantism benefited from that association in popular perception of an unwanted French presence in the country with the defence of the church. The Protestant Lords of the Congregation became national leaders of the patriotic cause in the course of 1559–60, but the religious battle was not only decided by rival French and English armies promoting their faiths. Among those whose beliefs mattered – nobility, clergy, lawyers, merchants, the tenantry and craftsmen – Roman Catholicism had a precarious and often superficial hold, leaving it vulnerable and fragile. Protestantism might only have convinced a relatively small minority of its spiritual and moral superiority, but that minority had the commitment and the organization to succeed. Given their opportunity by the collapse of the Guise regency, the departure of the French army and the summoning of a parliament, the Protestant leaders acted decisively, sweeping out the old religion and introducing the new.

What the Reformation parliament of July 1560 did was to alter the official religion of the country. However, it was 1567 before the crown gave its formal assent to the religious transformation of Scotland, so that the new Protestant Church of Scotland remained politically insecure. It is important to appreciate that from the 1560s Protestantism in Europe was on the defensive as the papacy and its secular allies rolled back the frontiers of the new faith, while at the same time Roman Catholicism expanded rapidly in the New World. There were certainly no grounds for thinking in 1560 that

Scottish Protestantism was safe, especially as the country was ruled by the Catholic Queen Mary. The latter's return from France to Scotland in 1561, following the death of her husband, made that insecurity all the more apparent. The willingness of a great magnate like the fourth Earl of Huntly to put himself forward now as a Catholic champion, the presence of a majority Catholic population in Edinburgh, and the benign interest of other Catholic powers, all point to what Mary might have achieved had religion been her first priority. Instead, the queen focused on her claims to the throne of England, a country that had reverted to Protestantism at the accession of Elizabeth I in 1558, and on cultivating a broad domestic support, including that of the Protestant church to which she gave financial aid. The inept handling of her marriages allowed her most severe critics their opportunity in 1567 to replace Mary with her infant son, James VI, who could be moulded into a Protestant ruler. Any lingering belief that Scottish Catholicism might still stage a political revival was killed off in the subsequent civil war of 1567–73.

What survived was a form of seigneurial Catholicism, living under the protection of powerful Catholic families. While rebellions were mounted in the later 1580s and early 1590s by Catholic nobles in league with Spain, these had little realistic expectation of achieving anything more than limited toleration, and were entirely dependent for their success on foreign intervention. The Catholic religion hung on in increasingly isolated pockets, encouraged from time to time by the newly-founded Roman Catholic Jesuit order which made episodic appearances in Scotland from the 1580s. However, it was only in 1622 that the Sacred College of Propaganda at Rome began to develop a more coordinated approach to mission. In the summer of 1625, 198 people were converted on the island of Eigg by Cornelius Ward, a Franciscan and the first Catholic priest to set foot there since before the Reformation. Yet in spite of these minor successes, the Catholic community remained weak and scattered. Apart from the few Roman Catholic noble families dispersed throughout the north-east, like the Gordons of Huntly, and some west Highland clans, the Scots were a Calvinist people. While physical persecution was modest by contemporary standards, social and financial pressures were placed on Catholics, and hostility to them was commonplace – hence the observation by an English traveller in 1617 that in Scotland, 'To be opposite to the Pope is to be presently with God.'

Nevertheless, while Protestantism was politically secure by the 1570s, it was by no means universally understood, and the degree of popular identity with it remained shallow for a generation. The problem facing the new church's leaders in 1560 was that most of Scotland's population was at best apathetic towards their agenda, and the massive financial resources of the pre-reformed church had fallen into the hands of secular landlords. With the latter unwilling to relinquish control of the ecclesiastical estates, the likelihood of addressing the former problem was greatly diminished. In *The First Book of Discipline*, hastily drafted by the Protestant clergy in the winter of

1560–61 in preparation for Mary's return to the country, the church proposed a scheme by which the wealth of the old benefice system would be invested in a programme of sustaining a well-educated ministry, and building and maintaining kirks, hospitals, hospices and schools. It was a visionary programme, but while the nobility gave lip-service to it, they were unwilling to surrender the lands that had progressively fallen into their hands since the early sixteenth century. Instead, the crown brokered a series of deals by which it acquired a share of the income from these former ecclesiastical estates along with the new church, but in which the greater part, including all the former abbatial lands, remained with the nobility. Mary agreed to the first of these arrangements in 1563, and others followed over the succeeding years as the church campaigned relentlessly for the restoration of the lost patrimony. Unfortunately the Protestant kirk never had the wealth of its Catholic predecessor, thus putting most of its social and educational aspirations on hold.

Even in its most fundamental ambition of providing a qualified parish ministry throughout the country, the church had to be patient. In the first place, while many former priests and monks did convert, there was an inadequate number of ministers. The 'New Foundation' at the University of St Andrews in 1579 created a Protestant intellectual powerhouse that addressed the staffing issue, especially after the appointment of Andrew Melville as its principal in 1580. But the filling of parishes was patchy, and many localities remained without an effective Protestant ministry for decades. North Ayrshire had a full complement of clergy by the end of the 1560s – hardly surprising for a locality at the forefront of the Reformation. Similar success stories could be found in Fife, Angus and the Mearns, Lanarkshire and Peebles, while a Highland region like Argyll benefited from the patronage of its Protestant earls. In other localities the Protestant Reformation made a slower impact. Catholic nobles did what they could to hamper the new church, and parts of East Lothian, Dumfriesshire and Aberdeenshire laboured under the obstructive activities of the Lords Home and Maxwell, and the Earls of Huntly. Elsewhere, geographic remoteness and a shortage of qualified ministers conspired to keep churches vacant. In the south-west there was no Protestant minister in any of Eskdale's five parishes before 1600, and a Protestant minister did not set foot on the Hebrides before 1609.

Not surprisingly, therefore, Catholics could be found in all walks of life, even among the highest ranks of the nobility, or in the greatest crown offices, while from the 1580s a new generation of counter-Reformation Catholics provided a more intellectually self-assured core of recusancy. Persecution of Catholics who persisted in attending mass was allowed by law, John Knox and his colleagues having persuaded parliament that any form of worship 'inventit by the braine of man' was 'Idolatorie'. Yet, by the standards of the day, Scottish Protestants were reluctant to create martyrs. The greatest pressure was applied to noblemen and their families, making it more and more difficult for them to exercise authority, or retain their local pre-eminence while remaining practising Catholics. The real challenge to the Protestant church lay not so much in an educated and articulate Catholic critique as in the persistence of old customs and practices among the mass of the populace. Thus on 30 December 1574 the people of Aberdeen were charged with 'plaing, dancing and singing filthy carols on Yule Day'. Preventing people from singing Christmas carols, observing holy days, masking, or discouraging beliefs in the efficacy of sacred wells, prayers for the dead, or the intercessory powers of the saints, proved more frustrating to parish ministers than the activities of Jesuit missionaries. Even in 1624, the Privy Council had to order local magistrates to prevent the 1 May barefoot pilgrimage to Christie's Well in Menteith. Persuading people that most of the former church's ritual was irrelevant, and asking them to accept instead a more cerebral and less visual religion that centred on preaching, was difficult. Perhaps it was unsurprising that in 1616 Perth kirk session decided that its session officer should carry a red staff to church services on a Sunday 'therwith to wauken sleepers and to remove greeting [crying] bairns furth of the kirk'.

A church created out of persecution and revolution was always likely to contain within it the potential to subvert the political order, but mostly its courts were deployed to reinforce existing hierarchies. In 1598, Glasgow presbytery initiated action against a youth who had failed to lift his hat to his father in passing, thus upholding paternal authority. These church courts were staffed by clergy and laity, and were constructed from the base of parish kirk sessions through provincial synods and up to the General Assembly of the Church of Scotland. During the 1570s, presbyteries were developed as an intermediate church court between the kirk sessions and the synods. However, it was kirk sessions that dealt largely with issues of immediate concern to individual parishes, principally sexual misdemeanours like fornication and adultery, drunkenness and non-observance of the Sabbath, and they were responsible for charitable relief and education. Between 1573 and 1600, St Andrews kirk session dealt with 1,716 offences against the church's discipline – one a week – with 57 per cent of these being sexual crimes, chiefly fornication, and 29 per cent being for disorderly conduct, including breaches of the Sabbath. A fornicator could expect to be fined two pounds, more than twice the average weekly wage, as well as having to endure a public rebuke and ritual humiliation. Similar campaigns were waged in every parish up and down the country. Here in the kirk session the minister and his lay elders, commonly respectable men chosen from within the community, provided a form of self-regulation and social control, investigating paternity, disciplining those who offended against communal values, deploying fines to help widows or the disabled, and taking responsibility for the Christian instruction of the parish. Presbyteries and synods generally dealt with more difficult cases, for example those involving errant ministers, or nobles, certain types of crime like Roman Catholic recusancy and witchcraft, recidivists, and supervisory activities like the visitation of parish churches and the licensing of new ministers. The

General Assembly sought to reflect the mind of the whole church and to act as a final court of appeal.

Running through all these levels of church life was a very strong sense of independence from the crown, partly a product of the circumstances of the 1560s when a Catholic queen made it impossible to recognize any formal role for the monarch, but also because the Calvinist theology of the kirk was hostile to the idea of crown authority over it. That idea of a church distinct from the crown was not new at the Reformation, but it was reaffirmed in the light of the late medieval experience when kings had acquired too much say over church affairs. Throughout the 1560s and 1570s, crown and church clashed largely over the practical issue of resources, with the former finding that bishops continued to be the best means of getting access to ecclesiastical finances, especially if inappropriate and venal kinsmen of powerful lords could be appointed to these offices. Disgust at this corruption hardened the General Assembly's opposition to bishops, and in July 1580 it declared them to have no scriptural authority and to be a corruption in the kirk.

However, the church's political independence was unacceptable to the crown, even to a sound Protestant lord like James Douglas, fourth Earl of Morton and regent from 1572 to 1578. It was even more distasteful to the men who gathered around the king after Morton's fall in 1580. The church's attacks on Catholics at court, like the French Duke of Lennox, its backing for the political *coup* against the king's advisers in the Ruthven Raid of 1582, and its ongoing criticism of any attempt by the crown to exercise influence over religious affairs, hardened the young James VI's resolve to re-establish royal control over the kirk. In 1584, under the menacing gaze of Chancellor Arran, parliament passed the so-called 'Black Acts', creating an Erastian royal supremacy over the church and establishing government by bishops, this being the most amenable means by which James could exercise control. Meanwhile Patrick Adamson, archbishop of St Andrews, gave some intellectual credibility to the doctrinal argument in favour of bishops. The king's political weakness was such that over the next few years the Presbyterian element in the church fought back, and in 1592 parliament recognized their preferred system of government.

However, there was no real agreement between the king and men like Andrew Melville, who were determined on a separation of church and crown on terms James VI could never accept. At a conference in the autumn of 1596, Melville grabbed hold of the king, calling him 'God's silly [simple] vassal', and warned that 'there is two Kings and two Kingdoms in Scotland. There is Jesus Christ the King, and his Kingdom the kirk, whose subject King James the Sixth is, and of whose Kingdom not a King, nor a Lord, nor a Head, but a member.' A few months later, with James's political grip growing more assured, the pendulum swung away from the Presbyterians following an anti-Catholic riot in Edinburgh. James exploited the nobles' fears over the politically subversive potential prevalent in Presbyterianism, and a compromise was reached. The king retained his royal supremacy over the church with royal appointees acting as ecclesiastical managers, while at the same time the General Assembly remained relatively independent and the lower church courts continued to operate. It was a good deal less than the king wanted, there being no secret about his preference for bishops, but in the circumstances it was the best he could expect. Meanwhile, the more radical Presbyterians had been isolated by their own intransigence, their constant refrain that the church was in danger from within being ignored by the great majority of parish clergy and their congregations who wished to be left in peace to worship their God.

3. A Crisis of Authority

The revolution of 1559–60 did more than eject French troops and Roman Catholic doctrine from Scotland. It also overturned the power of the crown, asserting the rights of subjects to resist the legitimate authority of the king, or in this case Queen Mary, who was represented in the person of the regent Guise. Of course, this was not the first time a Scottish monarch had faced rebellion, but the last successful occasion had been in 1488 when James III was replaced by his son in a very conservative *coup*. Scotland lacked a coherent ideology of resistance until the Reformation, when John Knox articulated the duty of godly subjects – meaning the Protestant nobility – to overthrow an evil ruler. It was an idea that Protestant leaders found more useful than persuasive, and Knox was soon frustrated by their unwillingness to carry his arguments forward once the Reformation dust had settled. The death of Francis II in December 1560, and the decision of the widowed Queen Mary to return to Scotland the following summer, brought Knox face-to-face with a monarch who had no intention of relinquishing any of her inherited power. Most of the nobility immediately rallied behind Mary, hoping to distance themselves from the events that ended the Guise regency. Stewart monarchy would continue as though nothing had happened.

Mary's initial success was stunning. She rallied her nobility, crushed a rebellion in 1562 in the north-east by the fourth Earl of Huntly, the most powerful Catholic in the country, steered a moderate course with the Protestant church, established a glittering court, made popular and effective progresses around her kingdom, and pursued clever diplomacy designed to persuade Elizabeth I to recognize her cousin as her heir. Until 1565, when Mary married Henry Stewart, Lord Darnley, another cousin and a rival claimant to the English throne, the queen could do no wrong. Even when that marriage lost her the support of her principal adviser, James Stewart, first Earl of Moray, who tried to reunite the coalition of 1559–60 against his half-sister, Mary emerged triumphant. The Chaseabout Raid of 1565, when the royal army pursued Moray and other rebels around the central Lowlands and into exile, was clear evidence that crown authority remained resilient, even when wielded by a young woman.

Within two years Mary had abdicated and was a prisoner in Loch Leven castle in

Fife. Her downfall was dramatic and largely her own fault, but it was also brought about by a shift in the foundations of the monarchy that had taken place in 1560. The collapse of the queen's marriage to Darnley, a man of few talents and many vices, was not merely occasioned by two people who did not get on. Mary refused to allow her husband to be king in anything but name. Darnley in turn participated in the bloody and terrifying Rizzio conspiracy against his wife in 1566 when her Italian secretary was murdered in the palace of Holyrood. The birth of their son, James, on 19 June 1566 weakened the queen by providing an alternative focus of loyalty, but in the short term it rendered Darnley superfluous. Discarding a husband was not easy, divorce having too many complications that would compromise the legitimacy of Prince James. Darnley's death was the best option available to Mary. In conniving in the murder of her husband in February 1567, Mary had widespread support: it was only her subsequent dependence on his killer, James Hepburn, fourth Earl of Bothwell, that created scandal in Scotland and throughout the royal courts of Europe. Rumours of the queen's sexual misconduct appeared to be confirmed by marriage to Bothwell in May 1567, providing her more outspoken enemies with a popular cause to rally around. If the queen could not be shown to be tyrannical simply because she was a practising Roman Catholic, she could be accused of murder and quite possibly adultery. Even among her closest supporters there was disgust at the Bothwell marriage. At the very least, Mary had shown appalling political misjudgement, and a broad coalition emerged demanding that she end the relationship with her new husband, something to which the now pregnant Queen could not agree since it would affect the status of her unborn child. Faced with almost certain defeat at Carberry on 15 June 1567, Mary surrendered to her opponents, led by more radical Protestant lords like the Earl of Morton, who never had any intention of allowing her to govern again. She was escorted back to Edinburgh, where the mob demanded that her captors 'burn the whore', but was then taken to her island prison.

The enforced abdication of Mary was really an opportunistic strike by the Protestant nobility to conclude what they had begun in 1559–60. Having possession of the infant James VI gave them all the political legitimacy they required; Mary's signature to her abdication was merely a recognition of a *fait accompli*. Moray was proclaimed regent, James was crowned king, the Protestant church received the statutory recognition that had been withheld by Mary, and parliament gave its backing to the new religion. However, this more extreme course worried political conservatives who had aimed only at the removal of Bothwell. Mary's escape, defeat at the battle of Langside on 13 May 1568, and her flight into English captivity strengthened the hand of the shaky regency government which still had to fight a civil war to establish James VI's authority. That war, which claimed the lives of three regents including Moray, ended in 1573 when English military assistance again proved crucial. Scotland's move into a Protestant and pro-English posture was complete.

The double blow to royal authority of the successful revolts of 1560 and 1567 was immense. This was especially so because of the context of two long minorities dating from James V's death in 1542 to when James VI took up governing by himself in about 1585. Even more importantly, not only did John Knox provide Protestants with good cause to overthrow the ungodly tyrant, but George Buchanan evolved a sophisticated, secular argument for resisting tyranny, grounding his ideas in the manipulation of Scottish history: he invented a form of ancient constitutionalism that advocated popular sovereignty. Thus kings were entrusted with power by the people (meaning the political community), who have the right to withdraw their allegiance when that contract between ruler and ruled was demonstrably broken. However, as tutor to James VI, Buchanan was more successful in teaching Latin than in indoctrinating the young king with his political ideas. James had Buchanan's books burned and outlawed at the first available opportunity. Nevertheless, Buchanan's ideas, along with those of Knox, were now rooted in the political landscape, and would have huge influence among the generations of nobles, ministers and relatively ordinary people who found in them an inspiration to stand against their kings.

James VI's minority was not unlike that of his predecessors, only worse. In addition to baronial factionalism and feuding, there was deep religious division, and the crown's political decline from the heady days of the king's grandfather was exacerbated by a chronic shortage of money. Yet James VI was not ill-served by those who governed in his name. The regent Morton endeavoured to make the peace settlement negotiated in 1573 endure, he worked hard at restoring law and order, especially on the Anglo-Scottish borders, he tried to uphold royal authority over the church, and he pursued a policy of friendship with England. In all this, Morton created enemies who engineered the premature ending of James's minority in 1578 when the king was only twelve years of age, and resentment against the former regent was pressed home two years later when he was arrested and executed for his part in Darnley's murder. Without a regent, Scottish government slipped further into the politics of feud and faction as a succession of *coups* and rebellions punctuated the years that followed, lasting well into the king's adult reign. It was 1595 before James VI, aged twenty-nine, could claim to have mastered his kingdom. Compared with most of his Stewart predecessors, it was a very poor beginning to his personal rule.

Why was James VI so inept? To some extent his personality was at fault; he lacked the clear-sighted ruthlessness of James V, being more inclined to negotiate solutions to problems. While this might have been an advantage in diplomacy and in ecclesiastical policy, it proved a disadvantage in dealing with noble factionalism. He also faced greater difficulties, most obviously the fact that the new Protestant kirk presented the king with more complex issues of crown–church relations than earlier governments had faced. The other problems confronting the young king were the English succession, noble power, lack of money and the debate over authority.

In foreign policy, James VI had to walk a careful line between cultivating Elizabeth

I in order to win her support for his right to succeed to the English throne, while avoiding becoming a tame English client. The latter fate had befallen the regent Morton who pursued policies designed to persuade Queen Elizabeth to enter an alliance. Elizabeth, however, exploited Morton's dependence on England and the fact that Mary remained her prisoner. She was also reluctant to formalize a relationship with what was still in the eyes of many European states a rebel government. Morton's requests for financial aid went unheeded, leading to his fall in 1578. His execution in 1581 took place in defiance of English military threats, exposing Elizabeth's unwillingness to repeat the interventions of 1560 and 1573. Although the Scottish governments of the early 1580s flirted with pro-French policies, the real intention of Chancellor Arran was to press Elizabeth I to take James VI seriously, a lesson the young king learned and was to repeat time and time again. Elizabeth withheld any formal recognition that James was her heir, but the Anglo-Scottish League of 1586, signed amidst English fears of Spanish invasion, Mary's execution with Scottish connivance a year later, and the payment of a pension to James, brought the two countries into a relatively close alliance. James's marriage to Anne of Denmark in 1589, strengthening ties with another Protestant state with which Scotland had strong commercial links, was sufficiently neutral to win Elizabeth's approval. Although James flirted with Spain in the hope of pressuring Elizabeth into making further concessions, and while the latter attempted to use the pension to influence Scottish domestic policies, neither had much success. Especially after the final defeat of the Catholic earls in 1594, Anglo-Scottish relations were good, and none of the minor diplomatic spats that followed could rock the alliance. James VI continued to worry about the English succession, working hard to persuade the rest of Europe of his case. It was more difficult to influence the debate in England since Elizabeth had forbidden any discussion of the subject, and it was only from 1600 when James was able to open up a secret correspondence with Sir Robert Cecil, the English Secretary of State, that he sensed the prize was within his grasp.

Relations with England were far from being James's only concern and his foreign policy was influenced by his reliance on the nobility at home. The enduring power of nobilities in early modern Europe is widely recognized. That power was locally based, grounded in extensive land ownership, hereditary jurisdictional authority, and lordship over other men, all of which gave the greater nobles regional influence and leverage at the centre of the kingdom. Kings needed to employ these lords to do their business in the localities because they had no alternative, while their own government and court was strengthened by having such powerful figures involved there. The king never considered excluding the great magnates from the centre, and more often than not James VI had difficulty persuading enough nobles to sit on his Privy Council, attend parliament and come to court. But the king also faced the problem of presiding over a world in which royal authority was flouted in the localities as nobles conducted their own blood feuds, or private wars, many of which spilled over into national politics. The paralysis of the king's authority continued throughout the 1580s, reaching a climax in the spate of feuding and rebellions of the early 1590s. Two rebellions in the south-west and three in the north-east, all combining elements of blood feud and Catholic conspiracy, were only the more blatant examples of the crown's weakness. Royal authority was eventually restored in 1594–5, but not before the warden of the West March was slain, defeated in the battle of Dryfe Sands by rebels on 6 December 1593, and the king's Lieutenant was forced to flee the field at the battle of Glenlivet on 3 October 1594. Much of the Borders was ungovernable, and large swathes of the Highlands were no-go areas for royal officials. James VI's effective rule extended over less than half his people. Even in a shire like Ayrshire, close to the heartland of the kingdom, the murder of the fifth Earl of Eglinton in 1585 set off a round of killings between the Cunningham and Montgomery families that the king could do little to quell. The near impotence of the king was epitomized in the career of the fifth Earl of Bothwell, who was first charged with witchcraft and treason in 1590, but who succeeded in defying James for five years, conducting a series of raids against royal palaces until he was forced into exile in 1595.

What changed the political environment was James's recognition that his best hope for stability was publicly to pursue a pro-English foreign policy, to seriously confront his Catholic rebels, and to allow the Presbyterians to retain the initiative in the church. The recognition by the sixth Earl of Huntly in the autumn of 1594 that he could not force the king to side with Spain, or even grant limited Catholic toleration, ended any hopes of a counter-Reformation. The subsequent exile of the Catholic lords along with Bothwell allowed the king the opportunity to make himself the head of the biggest faction in the country. Yet it is too easy to imagine that James VI achieved much of permanence before 1603. Had he been assassinated in the Gowrie conspiracy of 1600 (when the Ruthven family unsuccessfully attempted to kidnap him at Perth), he would have been succeeded by a six-year-old boy during whose minority Scotland would quickly have reverted to the political chaos from which it had so recently emerged.

Nevertheless, between 1595 and 1603 James VI was able to make progress in imposing a greater degree of law and order on the country, even addressing the deeper roots of noble violence. The king admitted that there was nothing much he could do about most of the sources of noble power, like hereditary jurisdictions. However, in concert with the church, and with the cooperation of many of those nobles on whom he relied, it was possible to persuade the nobility to exercise their power more responsibly. Thus the blood feud was brought inside the framework of the law in 1598, duelling was outlawed, restrictions were placed on the carrying and use of firearms and on the employment of retainers, or armed followers. Yet even in the 1600s nobles were being slain on the streets of Edinburgh, and Ayrshire experienced a large-scale private battle between rival factions of the Kennedy kindred on 11 December 1601.

However, the tide was turning as the nobility embraced a less martial identity. Against a background of ever-improving Anglo-Scottish relations, some progress was made in the Borders and even the notorious West March, where another warden was slain in 1600, saw a decline in lawlessness. A Highland policy proved more difficult to implement, and attempts to colonize Lewis by the Gentlemen Adventurers of Fife in 1597 proved wholly abortive. The crown had little choice other than to go on relying on magnates, like the seventh Earl of Argyll, to maintain a form of order. Certainly, the explosiveness of the region was unchanged. A few weeks before James succeeded to his English throne, a Macgregor raid on Glenfruin resulted in the bloody slaughter of the Colquhoun clan and a number of the citizens of Dumbarton who were unlucky enough to be in the wrong place at the wrong time.

The financial weakness of the Stewart monarchy in the later part of the sixteenth century also made James VI's task of ruling difficult. The great cash windfalls from which James IV and James V benefited were generated by feuing, but the mid-century inflation drastically reduced the value of these fixed rents. Meanwhile, customs revenue remained stagnant, the opportunity to acquire significant new land from the church was squandered at the Reformation, and there was little possibility of squeezing additional money out of feudal dues without risking the wrath of the nobility. For Mary, the problem was less drastic than for her son since she had the additional French income she received as dowager queen of France. Mary, therefore, could afford an expensive Renaissance court that in the early 1560s appeared to promise a return to the heady days of her father and grandfather.

James VI had no such resource on which to call, and during the twenty years that followed Mary's abdication, the real value of the royal income declined even further. King James built no palaces or navy, his court was modest with little cultural impact, even Prince Henry's baptism in 1594 being heavily dependent on borrowing, taxation, and the English pension. By the 1590s, crown income stood at around £250,000 per annum with the extraordinary income from the English pension contributing an average of £30,000 per annum and taxation another £25,000 per annum, a fifth of the total and almost as much as the income from customs. The crown's precarious financial position was not helped by a king whose generosity to favourites fell far short of prudent. All early modern governments were desperately short of money, but James VI was poorer than most, and less responsible. Even when in 1596 the Octavians, a group of financially conservative officials, offered him a route to a balanced budget, James undermined them, giving in to the pressure from courtiers and nobles for pensions.

Until the execution of his mother by Elizabeth I in 1587, James VI's authority in Scotland remained in some doubt, and the king was placed in the awkward position of ruling by right of the revolutionary politics he had grown to despise. The kirk's continuing demand to be allowed to govern itself was also a threat to the high claims for royal authority made at parliament in 1584 when the royal supremacy over the church was recognized. With the establishment of a degree of political stability after 1595, and with the king's regaining of the initiative in the church in the following year,

James VI took up his pen to defend his own views on royal authority. In a theoretical advocacy of the idea that kings ruled by divine right, *The Trew Law of Free Monarchies* (1598), published anonymously but with the authorship widely known, James challenged the idea that kings were elected by their people, were subject to the law, or that even tyrants could be removed. For James VI, monarchy was a form of government that 'approacheth nearest to perfection', and for a people subject to a tyrant, there was no alternative but patience and prayer. It was an eloquent rejoinder to Knox, Buchanan and Andrew Melville. However, James VI was no mere intellectual writing about kingship in the abstract, and in his *Basilikon Doron* (1599), a handbook of practical advice on kingcraft which he wrote for his son, the king offered a pragmatic insight into ruling Scotland. James's political writings might have claimed that 'Kings are called little Gods', but he also recognized that in the world of politics a successful ruler would have to be flexible and realistic. Nevertheless, James's political aspirations were clear, being diametrically opposed to those of his old tutor and of the men who carried through Reformation in 1560 and who made him king in 1567. This argument between divine right monarchy and contractual monarchy would be repeated again and again in the conflicts that followed over the course of the seventeenth century.

When in March 1603, James VI received the news that Elizabeth Tudor was dead and that he had been proclaimed king of England and Ireland, he immediately set about leaving Scotland to go and make good his claim. The kingdom of Scotland he left behind was in good order, even if James had taken unusually long to get to grips with it. However, he had done little to change it, having succeeded merely in restoring royal authority to something approaching that of his grandfather, James V. There had been no fundamental shift in the balance of power between crown and nobility, or centre and locality; the institutions of government continued to be as rudimentary as ever, its financial base precarious, its theoretical underpinning more controversial than ever before. It remained to be seen what impact the removal of the king to London would have on this already highly decentralized kingdom and its people.

The Economic Context

1. Population

The nation ruled by James VI and his Stewart successors expanded from a population base of some 700,000 people c. 1500 to perhaps one million by c. 1700, though most of the growth probably took place between c. 1540 and c. 1640. The increase was evenly spread throughout the still sparsely populated countryside, both Lowland and Highland, but its most dramatic effects were seen in the growing share made up by towns.

However, population growth continued to be affected by the twin evils of disease and food shortage. The sustained outbreaks of bubonic plague that occurred in 1568–9, 1574, 1584–8 and 1597–1609 were concentrated mostly in the fertile south-east of the country. The death toll was probably highest among the lower ranks in society, and towns suffered especially badly because of overcrowded and poorly built dwellings. In the small town of Perth, 1,427 people died between September 1584 and August 1585. For the nobility, plague was largely an inconvenience, as in 1606 when parliament had to be switched to Perth to avoid the risk of contamination in Edinburgh. Dr Gilbert Skene, who wrote a tract on the plague in the mid-sixteenth century, was in despair over the contempt shown by the rich for the fate of the countless poor struck down by plague, being regarded as no more than 'beasts degenerate fra mankind' by their social superiors. When plague struck Crail in 1602, the infected families were driven out of the town and took to wandering the countryside looking for food, increasing the chances of the disease spreading, until the sheriff took it upon himself to provide relief. Skene knew there was a link between dirt, stagnant water, spoiled food and disease, and that it was spread by contagion, although shooting stars also figured in his analysis, but neither the preventative actions of the magistrates or the skills of the medical profession could do much to stem these dreadful culls on the mass of the population. For the next three decades there were no significant outbreaks, but in 1644 plague returned, killing an estimated 9,000 people in Edinburgh alone. Three years later, Aberdeen made every effort to keep it out, sealing off the town, but unfortunately an infected Brechin woman gained entrance. Over the weeks that followed 1,760 people died in a population of around 8,000. In Brechin, from where the carrier had come, a third of the people died, a devastating local visitation that is concealed in the figure of 2 or 3 per cent mortality from plague for the entire country. Thereafter plague receded, and Scotland escaped the recurrences that affected other European states in the later seventeenth century, possibly because of strict quarantine procedures.

The repeated dearths or food shortages of the later sixteenth century, especially in 1562–3, 1571–3, 1585–7 and 1594–8, had a greater effect on prices than on population, although there is little doubt that people did die of starvation. The impact of these local harvest failures was accentuated by poor overland transport and marketing, the efforts of government to hold back exports during such episodes being an indication of the fact that food was available elsewhere in the kingdom. Food prices were set locally at sheriff courts by 'fiars', a jury of landlords, farmers and merchants, and there was considerable fluctuation from one year to another and from one region to another. However, food shortages rarely affected the entire kingdom. A notable exception came in 1623 when famine was catastrophic on a national scale, killing thousands and devastating entire communities like Kelso, where one in five people died of starvation or associated diseases. Fortunately, famine on this scale did not recur until the 1690s when repeated bad harvests in the Highlands from 1693 spread to the Lowlands three years later, creating crippling food shortages and untold human misery that was not relieved until the better harvest of 1700. Food prices soared and the parish system of localized poor relief proved wholly inadequate. Aberdeen was unable even to feed its own poor with the meagre handouts usually on offer, let alone the beggars who flooded into the town. Nationally the population fell by 13 per cent due to deaths from starvation and disease related to malnutrition, a fall in the birth-rate caused by inadequate diet, and as a consequence of unusually high levels of emigration.

Not only were there many more people, they also moved around more than ever before, most commonly in search of work or alms. Vagrancy represented a form of subsistence migration, creating fear among the propertied ranks in times of high unemployment, or food shortages, and resulting in strict measures to regulate movement. Kirk sessions were required to issue certificates to those with legitimate reasons for being on the move, and magistrates could resort to quite savage punishments like scourging and branding for those who persisted in flouting the law. Nevertheless, by the latter half of the seventeenth century, changes in farm management were encouraging a migration from upland parishes of the eastern Borders into Edinburgh and its satellite towns. Most people involved in this opportunity migration were young and single, a high proportion were female, and most were looking for employment, often finding it as apprentices, servants and labourers, for whom there was a steady demand. Already by *c.* 1700, Lowland towns were sucking in excess Highland labour: for example, one in twenty people living in Greenock had been born in the Highlands.

A great many people left Scotland altogether in search of better opportunities elsewhere, continuing a long-established pattern which would influence the country's population profile and economic performance for centuries to come. Government played little direct part in this, although some colonial schemes were developed. James VI's plans to colonize the Western Isles with stout and godly Lowlanders came to nothing, there being a negligible flow of population in that direction. However, royal policies in Ireland from the 1610s created a demand for settlers, especially in Ulster, and some 30,000 to 50,000 people crossed the Irish Sea over the next three decades. The flow of people continued later in the century with as many as 50,000 going there in the 1690s alone. Poland drew thousands of merchants, pedlars and soldiers who often settled in the country, creating an exile community of between 30,000 and 40,000 people by the early decades of the seventeenth century. The loss of population to England has never been calculated, but there was certainly a growing Scottish community in London, and Scots were also to be found scattered in English colonies in North America and the West Indies. For the whole of the seventeenth century, population depletion owing to emigration might have been as high as 250,000 people, helping to keep the total population relatively static and acting as a drain on manpower. On the other hand, it did lessen the impact of Malthusian disasters when they struck.

One particularly well-documented form of emigration was created by the demand for soldiers on the continent. As many as one in five young men may have gone into foreign military service in the first four decades of the seventeenth century, and the Privy Council authorized 47,110 men to enlist as mercenaries between 1625 and 1642. In every army engaged in the Thirty Years War there were Scottish soldiers: the Munro kindred alone had 3 generals, 8 colonels, 5 lieutenant-colonels and 30 captains engaged in the armies of the Swedish king, Gustav Adolph. Few of the ordinary soldiers ever returned home, most dying miserably of sickness and starvation rather than on the battlefields of Breitenfeld and Lützen. In 1612, Colonel George Sinclair took 900 men to Norway to fight for the Swedes, only for them all to be killed in an ambush shortly after their arrival. Even the successful officers might not return; Patrick Gordon was buried in Moscow in 1699, having carved out a remarkable career in the service of Peter the Great. By reducing the pool of men of marriageable age, this type of emigration may also have raised the age at first marriage for women, thus reducing overall fertility and compounding the check on demographic expansion.

2. Agriculture

For the great majority of the population, farming was their livelihood. After the high incidence of dearth in the later sixteenth century, Scottish farming responded to the improving conditions of the early seventeenth century with sufficient robustness to ensure that normally there was an adequate food supply. Indeed, in most years a grain surplus was exported to the more profitable markets of the Netherlands, Germany and the Baltic. To cope with the demands of a growing population, and in the absence of new methods that might increase crop yields, more land was cultivated than at any time since the beginning of the fourteenth century, leading to a growth and spread of farm touns or settlements. Scottish landlords, like those throughout Western Europe, turned their backs on the demesne farming that was so attractive to their counterparts east of the Elbe, but their dominance over the tenantry did allow them to take the initiative in improvements. Clearly this was not on the scale of the eighteenth century, but early seventeenth-century landlords were experimenting with the enclosure of formerly common land, consolidating holdings, reclaiming marginal land and adopting liming, and there was great enthusiasm for tree-planting and cattle-breeding.

The estate economy in much of the Lowlands also became overwhelmingly a cash economy, except in big grain-growing districts like Angus or Buchan, and even Highland landlords were demanding at least part of their rents in fixed silver sums. Just as the sixteenth century saw significant changes in some rural communities as kindly tenants were displaced by feuers able and willing to pay higher rents to landlords, so in the seventeenth century the pressure for leases from land-hungry tenants ensured a ready supply of cooperative tenants prepared to carry out improvements and to pay more for their leases. This is most evident in the spread of single-tenancy farms, between 50 and 70 per cent in eastern Aberdeenshire being single-occupancy farms by the later seventeenth century. Here individual opportunism and ambition were replacing what may have been the less productive joint-occupancy farms of earlier in the century, reducing former tenants to the level of labourers.

Easy and relatively cheap credit, which fell from an official maximum rate of 10 per cent set in the later sixteenth century to 8 per cent in 1633 and to 6 per cent at the end of the century, led to heavy investment in castles or country houses and their surrounding parks. However, improvements were not without risk. The entrepreneurial Andrew Fraser of Philorth who developed Fraserburgh at the turn of the century went bust and was forced into heavy selling of land. Unfortunately, the heavy debts incurred during the mid-seventeenth-century convulsions took decades to repay, and after 1660 risk capital was difficult to find. Obviously, some landlords recovered quickly and some even profited from the misfortunes of others, but the assurance of the early seventeenth century was lacking. Military quartering and the fining of landlords and tenants for their Covenanting sympathies also depressed economic progress in some localities.

Parliament passed legislation to encourage improvement, for example the 1661 General Enclosure Act strengthening the rights of landlords in order to facilitate enclosures, or the 1695 Division of Runrig Act which permitted landlords to consolidate land into larger fields. But a sympathetic legislative climate could not make landlords put money into improvements, and estate surveys in the 1690s discovered few enclosed farms larger than 250 to 300 acres. The first call on any disposable cash still tended to be rebuilding, or renovating, the family seat, while the entail legislation of 1685, restricting the freedom of heirs to dispose of their land on the market, acted as a depressant on improvements, making it very difficult to sell land. Compared with the best farming in Holland, or in the south of England, Scottish landlords were lagging behind in terms of organization and technology, but comparisons with much of France, Spain or Scandinavia were more favourable.

On the whole, therefore, farming methods changed little and only very slowly over this period. The inefficient, if socially desired, runrig system, in which sub-tenants farmed strips of land scattered throughout a farm toun, still dominated the landscape. Land continued to be divided into infield and outfield, a form of farm management usually associated with low crop yields. The intensely farmed infield comprised continuously cultivated and heavily manured land on which cereals were grown, while outfield land was more marginal, its usage switching between coarse oat production and pastoral farming. The proportion of land allocated to each category varied greatly from one locality to another, and in some Lowland areas well over half the farm might be infield. Farming technology remained stuck where it had been for centuries. For example, the thirteen-foot-long wooden plough commonly in use required teams of between six and twelve oxen to pull it and was very difficult to turn. There was little innovation in the type of cereals and root crops grown, nor were there any improvements in sheep and cattle breeds until the last quarter of the century, when cattle-breeding became more sophisticated in response to the demands of the English market.

3. Trade

Poor overland communications undoubtedly hampered domestic trade, although this factor can be exaggerated. Already in the early seventeenth century Dumfries had a nine-arched bridge of squared stone, wide enough for two carriages to drive abreast of one another. Where there were no bridges there were ferries, as at Aberdeen where there were two over the river Dee. Government too began to take some initiative in encouraging improvements. In 1635, the Privy Council instigated an investigation of the depth of the river Forth by the civic authorities of Burntisland, Kirkcaldy and Dysart. Parliament created the legislative framework for sheriffs to impress local labour into repairing roads and bridges in 1669. In effect there was no national road system, and while there was a legislative framework for the maintenance of roads by local magistrates, there was no sustained effort by government at enforcement.

The creation of hundreds of fairs and markets, the improvement of harbour facilities and the building of bridges indicate an awareness among landlords (particularly grain-growers) and burgh magistrates of the need to facilitate the marketing of their produce. Before 1660, there were only fifty non-burgh markets in the country, a number that had risen dramatically to 186 by 1707 as landlords sought to improve their marketing opportunities. By the later seventeenth century a little under a fifth of the country remained more than 25 kilometres from either a licensed market or fair. Meanwhile, an open border with England facilitated overland communication southwards. Cattle farmers were making their first inroads into the English and Irish markets, and even in the early part of the seventeenth century, border landlords like the Earls of Buccleuch were expanding their sheep flocks in Teviotdale in response to the domestic and foreign demand for wool. While the take-up of new farming technologies, products and management was slow, landlords were important innovators and opinion leaders. The scale of cattle, wool and grain production, as well as the opencast coal mining on estates, was all geared to the market (export wherever possible) through a developing system of fairs, markets, drove roads, harbours and merchant partners.

In the first half of the seventeenth century, Scotland's international trade was still centred on the North Sea, with links to Scandinavia, the Baltic, Flanders and northern France. This is evident in the customs revenue, which in 1621–3 saw 32 per cent of imports arriving from the Netherlands, 22 per cent from the Baltic and northern Germany, 22 per cent from England, 18 per cent from France, and the remaining 6 per cent from elsewhere. The principal destinations for ships leaving Leith, Scotland's busiest port at this time, were Veere, London, Amsterdam and Königsberg (Kaliningrad in modern Lithuania). Naturally this was subject to fluctuations created by diplomacy and war, for example in the 1620s Franco-Scottish trade collapsed because of Charles I's war with France. Fortunately the total volume of trade, as measured by customs duties, grew as Scottish exports were soaked up by the Netherlands and England. New markets also opened up from the 1660s in Spain, North America and the West Indies, where the Scots had had a foothold in Barbados as early as the 1620s.

However, the biggest shift in trade patterns over the course of the seventeenth century was the growing importance of the English market to Scotland. The heavy losses in manpower, shipping and coin during the warfare of the 1640s, and the English military occupation of the 1650s, took another two decades to recoup, while confidence was sapped for a generation, discouraging economic risk. Against this background, the country's dependence on trade with England grew more prominent. The latter might have happened anyway in the context of a regal union in which the English economy was about to accelerate at a rate the Scots could not hope to emulate, but from the 1650s Scotland could only watch from the sidelines as the English vied with the Dutch for commercial primacy. From the 1660s, the opportunities for trading beyond Europe were restricted by protective English legislation (collectively known as Navigation Acts) that prevented Scottish ships from carrying goods to and from English colonial ports. The Scots petitioned against what they perceived to be unfair English practice, yet were not slow to follow suit, prohibiting the import of Irish cattle, beef and grain in 1667. In such a cut-and-thrust mercantilist environment it was impossible to stand aloof.

At the same time, Scotland was subjected to the inconveniences of England's wars with the United Provinces in 1652–4, 1665–7 and 1672–4, which sabotaged the growing Dutch trade. Further wars with France in 1689–97, the War of the League of Augsburg, and from 1702–13 the War of the Spanish Succession, brought the Scots close to desperation as another important market for fish, wool and linen was sealed off by a combination of high French tariffs and privateering. Against a growing balance of trade deficit, the country relied more and more on the cattle and linen trade with England. Unfortunately, this trade was far more important to the Scots than the English who repeatedly showed no interest in commercial union, and this dependence was underlined when the English parliament threatened to cut it off with the Alien Act in 1704–5 in order to force the Scots to negotiate the Hanoverian succession.

Yet it would be a mistake to imagine that the Scots simply accepted this drift into a form of economic dependence on England. Some indication of entrepreneurial energy was apparent in the low-profile, illegal trade between Glasgow and the American colonies, and there were signs that the initiative in international trade might be switching to the west. Glasgow's investment in a new dock at Broomielaw in 1663, and the purchase of land five years later on which Port Glasgow was built, indicate a vision of a more commercially expansive role for the city. As early as 1680, an anxious Scottish government began to coax merchants out of their conservative attitudes, looking for ways to overcome the balance of trade disaster facing the country. The beginnings of a trade and colonial policy emerged in that decade, but progress was stalled by a shortage of capital, confidence and shipping. In 1692, Leith officially had only 29 ships with a total of 1,700 tons and Glasgow had 23 ships totalling 1,200 tons.

The crown also proved unhelpful, being mindful of the monopoly interests of English trade, especially the powerful East India Company. In June 1695 William II finally conceded a charter to the Company of Scotland with a remit to open up Scottish trade in America, Africa and the Far East. A month later, the formation of the Bank of Scotland highlighted the new awareness of the opportunities available for risk capital that had been created by parliament over the last few years. Already by 1695 there were forty-seven joint stock companies operating in the country, all established within the previous five years. The result of the Company of Scotland's grand ambitions, however, was the tragi-comic opera that is known as the Darien Scheme, a fiasco of stunning proportions in which vast sums of money, thousands of lives, and national prestige were lost in a futile effort to plant a colony in the Spanish territory of Panama between 1698 and 1700. The idea had been sold to the Privy Council in July 1695 by William Paterson, a financial entrepreneur addicted to big risks, who described it as 'one of the most beneficial and best grounded pieces of Trade at this day in Christendom'. Hyperbolic advertising and wishful thinking led to a rush of Scottish investors, large and small, who ploughed their money into an enterprise doomed to failure amidst the economic and political struggles of greater empires.

Scotland's underlying problems lay not only in its political and diplomatic vulnerability in a more competitive international context, but in the imbalance of its trade. This was recognized at the time, and in 1681 a memorial prepared for the Privy Council recommended addressing this problem and stimulating both navigation and shipping 'which is the life and substance of all well ordered commonwealthes'. On the whole, Scottish imports were manufactured and more exotic goods along with some locally unavailable raw materials. For example, very large quantities of timber were imported from Norway, and by the later seventeenth century 360,000 deals, or sawn fir planks, were imported each year. Iron arrived from Sweden, mostly for Glasgow; from the Netherlands came fine textiles, fancy goods, a dyestuff called madder, and dried fruits all the way from the growing Dutch colonial enterprise in the East Indies; leather and hops for beer-making were imported from England; wine, brandy and manufactures from France, most of the wine arriving in Edinburgh's developing consumer market from Bordeaux; cooking-pots and brassware was purchased in the markets of north-western Germany. As yet the rum and tobacco trade from the New World was relatively small, although Glasgow had staked its claim to exploit this market. Nevertheless, measured in numbers of ships, the principal arrival points for imports were around the Forth estuary, where 69 per cent of ships docked in 1680–86. This enormous business in luxury imports, from rare foodstuffs to expensive fabrics, jewellery, weaponry and furniture, all point to the growing wealth of the nation (or parts thereof) and to the aggressive trading activities of its merchants. At the same time, it highlights just how much the Scots relied on imports, and how much they had to earn in exports to pay for it all.

Unfortunately, the country was almost entirely reliant on the export of a narrow range of raw materials and a handful of manufactures to earn the currency to purchase these expensive imports. Thus in 1611–14, of the £736,986 worth of goods that left the country, just over half was agricultural with another fifth fish, and under a quarter was manufactured goods, mostly woollen cloth. However, Scotland's portfolio of exports changed over the course of the century. Hides, one of the staples of Scottish exports for centuries, fell dramatically in terms of volume and value. Some 200,000 skins were exported yearly to the Baltic states alone in the early seventeenth century; by 1660 this had fallen to 93,000 per annum. Fish continued to be successful until the 1680s, when the market collapsed.

In the early decades of the century, coal and salt proved to be vigorous new industries, but salt stagnated from the 1650s, the fall in demand in Norway being one factor in its decline. Coal had a more sustained economic impact. In the 1610s and 1620s the landlords of the Forth valley became increasingly alert to the value of their coal deposits, entering into partnerships with merchants, lobbying government for helpful economic policies, and pushing into the Dutch and English markets. Among the wonders of the age was the development of Sir George Bruce of Carnock's mine at Culross which involved tunnelling under the Forth estuary, a project in which 'many poor people are there set to work, which otherwise through the want of employment would perish'. Sadly, the mine was destroyed by a storm in 1625. Nevertheless, coal exports doubled from the 16,000 tons per annum early in the century to twice that volume by the 1680s, when they too suffered decline because of international instability. By the 1700s both the salt and coal lobbies were advocating conservative and protectionist economic policies designed to sustain their frail businesses in the face of the threat of a free market with England.

Grain exports continued to expand, again fuelled by better production and marketing strategies adopted by landlords and their merchant partners, until the 1690s when production was devastated by poor harvests. The only real growth sectors of the economy that were export driven in the later seventeenth century were linen and cattle, for which there was enormous demand in England. The former compensated for the continued decline of wool exports and sustained a cottage-based estate industry chiefly benefiting landlords. The highly profitable cattle trade earned much valued sterling for big landowners, especially on the borders and in Highland estates connected by drove roads to market centres like Crieff and Falkirk from where their beasts were moved on to Carlisle and ultimately London.

Efforts to create new industries in the early decades of the seventeenth century through crown-granted monopolies, for example in tanning and glass-making, were never sufficiently successful for those industries to become exporters, but they are testament to an entrepreneurial spirit. Some twenty such businesses were active by the 1650s, but there was little increase on this until the 1690s, when the number shot up to almost fifty. Most of these enterprises were based around Edinburgh and Glasgow, close to concentrations of landed and merchant capital that was invested in the form of joint stock ventures, and with access to a pool of skilled craftsmen attracted to the growing cities. In the case of Edinburgh, there were five businesses in the city itself with another twelve at Leith, three at Bonnington, two at Cannonmills and Dalry, and one each at Newhaven, Restalrig, Musselburgh, Morrison's Haven, Braid and Colinton; thirty in all. Manufacturing, therefore, did establish itself in a number of limited fields like wool, glass, paper, cloth and metal, chiefly for domestic consumption, although linen had established the basis for future successes in the textile market. On the whole, Scottish trade remained stuck in a rut, and while the possibility of free trade with England did excite some when it was discussed, the overwhelming concern of the conservative merchant interest was to protect the domestic market, to shore up the weak linen manufacturers, and to guarantee buyers for Scottish coal and salt.

4. Towns

The vital connection between the surplus-producing landlords and tenants on the one hand and European markets on the other was provided by towns. Royal burghs continued to have an exclusive right to engage in foreign trade, and within the burghs it was the merchant burgesses who dominated both that trade and the politics of the town. Such a monopolistic structure to international trade probably was advantageous in the first half of the seventeenth century, allowing a concentration of capital in Edinburgh without being unduly stultifying. Edinburgh clearly dominated Scotland's international trade. In 1563, 25 per cent of the total tax assessment for all Scotland's burghs was paid by Edinburgh, Dundee was well behind at 12 per cent, Aberdeen paid 9 per cent, Perth 7 per cent and St Andrews 3 per cent of the total. By 1635, Edinburgh was paying 30 per cent of the total burgh tax assessment. Dundee remained the capital city's nearest rival, but its share had fallen to only 9 per cent, followed by Aberdeen, Perth and then Glasgow which had overtaken a declining St Andrews. By 1670, Edinburgh's share had risen to 33 per cent, and by 1705 it was 35 per cent. Meanwhile the relative wealth of Dundee fell as the burgh slipped to fourth place, Aberdeen remained third, although its percentage share of the total tax burden fell and the town was a good deal poorer in 1700 than in the prosperous 1630s. Glasgow's precocious rise in prosperity and population was reflected by its move into second place by 1670 with 12 per cent of the tax assessment, rising to 20 per cent in 1705. By the first decade of the eighteenth century, Edinburgh and Glasgow were paying 55 per cent of the total burgh tax assessment, reflecting the huge shift that had taken place in the shape of the country's urban economy from a predominantly eastward base to a new east–west axis.

Closer examination of the burghs also reveals that the early seventeenth-century prosperity of Fife towns like Anstruther and Crail, demonstrated in the latter's expansive town planning, had dissipated as Edinburgh tightened its regional grip. Similarly in the west, Glasgow's success was bought at the expense of Ayr and, to a lesser extent, Dumfries. The latter's prosperity in the early decades of the century, when one traveller described it as 'a pleasant, flourishing town', was followed by ruin, and then a slow and partial recovery based on control of the tolls over the river Nith, and the siting there after 1660 of the headquarters of the king's customs for the Solway Firth. However, it was not simply a case of the bigger towns overwhelming their neighbours. While the early seventeenth-century trade with Zeeland in the Low Countries was predominantly carried on by the large burghs of Edinburgh, Dundee and Aberdeen, their trade gradually shifted away from Veere to the more dynamic cities of Amsterdam and Rotterdam, leaving smaller towns like Dysart and Kirkcaldy to pick up the Zeeland trade, their business being carried out in small colliers. The 1672 Act Anent Trade of Burghs, reducing the royal burghs' monopoly over foreign trade, also provided opportunities for some baronial burghs to carve out for themselves niches in the market that their bigger competitors had overlooked, or were unable to exploit.

Towns had to be alert to more than competitive disadvantage. In December 1584, Robert Henderson, a baxter's boy, was burned alive in Edinburgh as punishment for setting fire to his father's house and that adjoining, thus endangering the entire town. Such severity underlines, among other things, the threat posed by the insubstantial nature of the largely wooden town buildings of this period. Three-quarters of Dunfermline burned down in 1623, Kelso suffered a similar conflagration in 1645, and Glasgow had serious fires in 1652 and 1677. Nevertheless, between the mid-sixteenth century and the early eighteenth century the growth in the size of the urban population, and its share of the total population of Scotland, was significant. In *c.* 1550, only 1.5 per cent, some 13,000 people, lived in towns with populations greater than 10,000. This compares with 3.5 per cent of the population of England and Wales living in similarly sized towns. By *c.* 1600, the Scottish urban population had grown to 30,000 people, some 3 per cent of the population. For the first half of the seventeenth century the urban share grew only very slowly as war and plague took a heavy toll, and by 1650 this figure was just 3.5 per cent. However, the seventeenth century saw a more dramatic surge of people moving into large towns, and by *c.* 1700 the urban population stood at 53,000, a little over 5 per cent of the total Scottish population, although this remained well below the 13 per cent urban population found in England and Wales.

Edinburgh, which was by far the largest Scottish town, grew in size from around 12,000 people in 1560 to perhaps 30,000 in 1640, and by the 1690s this had risen further to between 40,000 and 47,000 inhabitants. Increasingly the city was becoming a centre of professional services and luxury provisions with lawyers, doctors and ministers catching up fast on merchants in numbers and wealth, while a whole new range of craft and retail services like stationers, tobacconists, wigmakers, confectioners, silk weavers and perfumers appeared over the course of the century. These specialists clustered in towns because demand for their services lay there, but their presence also attracted more nobles and gentry to the city, there being 332 recorded in the poll tax returns of the 1690s compared with only 372 merchants. However, the largest occupational group in the 1690s was domestic servants, there being 3,276 female and 1,082 male servants compared with 311 tailors, the largest craft, and 732 apprentices in all trades. Something between 4 and 5 per cent of the country's population lived in the capital city, a figure that was still modest when compared with London which accounted for 10 per cent of England's population, but which was much more typical of continental Europe. Glasgow, with a population already somewhere between 10,000 and 12,000 in the 1630s, also experienced a burst of growth in the seventeenth century that confirmed its place as Scotland's second city. By the 1690s, around one in eight people was living in a town of more than 2,000 inhabitants, a proportion close to Ireland or Denmark, though somewhat less than England. Although Scotland remained an overwhelmingly rural country, the pattern of urban expansion had been set.

Accompanying this increase in the urban population, there was a growth in the number of burghs. Only twenty-one new royal burghs were created between 1560 and 1707, nineteen of these before 1650, but 231 burghs of barony were founded in the same period. There was a high concentration of these new foundations on the east coast, a third of the new royal burghs being on the Forth river and its estuary, reflecting the eastward orientation of Scottish international trade. There were success stories. Peterhead was created as a burgh of barony in 1587, being just beyond the reach of Aberdeen, and thus able to develop its servicing of the local hinterland. Its hopes were pinned on fishing, but while twenty-seven boats were registered by the early seventeenth century, these were at least as busy in carrying grain. When the medical qualities of St Peter's Well were highlighted in 1636 by Andrew More, a native of the town and Professor of Physic at King's College, Peterhead also became a relatively popular spa town. By the 1680s the town was a major centre for white fishing in the region.

However, the number of medium-sized towns remained low – by the 1630s only ten towns had populations greater than 4,000 people – and many burghs were no more than sprawling villages, few of the new burghs growing above 500 inhabitants. Even a very old and well-established town like Dunfermline had only 220 houses and 287 families in 1624, representing a population of some 1,200 people. As engines of local economic activity, the new towns had a limited impact, rarely managing to compete with older burghs, and 140 of the 231 new burghs of barony proved to be non-viable. The baronial burgh of Rattray in Aberdeenshire was created in 1563, but it failed to develop. Falling into the hands of outside control, its harbour had silted up by the 1650s, and the 1696 poll tax schedule showed at most three feuers living in a village which was owned by the minister of nearby Crimond.

The Conditions of People

1. The Landed Nobility

For the Scottish people, the period from Reformation to Union was one of both enduring social continuities and shocking political changes. The mid-seventeenth-century Covenanting revolution led to the overthrow of the Episcopalian church, the execution of a king, and the temporary removal from local and national government of most of the higher nobility. The reverberations of the 1640s were still being felt for the remainder of the century, but Scotland remained a society of distinct and hierarchic orders. A century earlier, the medieval concept of the three estates still dominated the thinking of political theorists about how society was organized. After the Reformation, the first estate, the clergy, ceased to have a distinct political identity and was in the process of becoming a profession, and it was only in parliament that the episcopate preserved the idea of a clerical estate. The third estate was made up of the representatives of the burghs. The second estate grew confused as the nobles came to be equated with the titled peerage, while the barons effectively constituted what had the appearance of a fourth estate inside parliament, even if on the outside, in society at large, they were part of the nobility. What this demonstrates is the inadequacy of using parliament's increasingly archaic notions of how society should be to describe how society was in reality.

By 1560, the nobility formed a large body of landlords divided into a peerage (52 in 1560, 59 in 1603, 102 in 1637, 137 in 1714) and an untitled baronage, all tenants-in-chief to the crown with their own coats-of-arms and hereditary courts. The nobility was ranked by title and creation, and there were huge disparities of wealth, office and control over men, but the hundreds of heads of houses formed an open-ended and large body, closer to the European model than the exclusive English example in which only peers were accounted noble. Over the course of the seventeenth century there appeared the first indications of a governing élite of aristocrats emerging from this amorphous landed nobility, a process of differentiation that accelerated in the following century.

Noble power was based primarily on their very considerable dominance of land, a dominance that increased in the later sixteenth century at the expense of the church and the crown. Huge tracts of former ecclesiastical lands were acquired by secular landlords. Thus the estates of Newbattle abbey came into the hands of a branch of the Ker kindred, establishing the house of Lothian among the top ranks of the nobility. Other ecclesiastical land was feued to secular tenants, ranging from small 'bonnet lairds' at the bottom of the propertied community to the higher nobility. Even the 'teinds', or tithes of the income of certain land, formerly payable to the church, became the preserve of secular landlords. One effect of this windfall was to disperse landholdings so that while most noble houses retained a territorial core of estates around their principal residence, landed possessions were scattered. By the early seventeenth century, the dukes of Lennox held property in fourteen shires, and the marquises of Hamilton owned land in thirteen shires. Some forty-eight noble houses had a landed portfolio extending to more than four shires, while 106 noble houses owned property in two or more shires.

In spite of high levels of 'wadsetting', or mortgaging by landlords, Charles I's efforts to reverse the noble land grab accompanying the Reformation, or the financial misfortunes that characterized the mid-century political turmoil, the nobility retained their supremacy over landed society. In Aberdeenshire in 1667, 1.25 million acres were owned by 799 'heritors' (landowners), but a mere twenty-one peerage houses owned 28 per cent of the land, with the baronial families possessing another 36 per cent. Noble dominance is underlined by the fact that of the leading twenty-five landed families in the shire, twenty had a significant presence there dating from the fourteenth century, six being of the Forbes kindred and four were Gordons. Furthermore, noble dominance of the land market increased as many small bonnet lairds whose families had acquired a stake in land during the sixteenth century were squeezed out in the second half of the seventeenth century when big estates proved more profitable. Thus in Aberdeenshire there was a fall in the number of heritors by 25 per cent, benefiting the large feudal landlords.

For those nobles who gained access to court and political office there were also rich rewards not available to outsiders. In the course of the seventeenth century, great magnate families like the houses of Hamilton and Argyll were brought back from the edge of destruction by royal patronage, while the Murrays of Atholl, and the Dalrymples of Stair, experienced a meteoric rise in fortune as a consequence of the king's largesse. At every level it was the nobility who swarmed over offices in the state, and only the 1649 Act of Classes, which excluded from public office large numbers of the higher nobility who had taken part in the Engagement (see page 249), threatened that near monopoly. At court, in the Edinburgh administration, in the central law courts, in military offices, and above all in local justice, the nobles were pre-eminent, whether they were magnates protecting their enormous interests by way of political office, or small barons using a legal career to raise their fortunes, or as a means of entry to royal office and a much sought-after hereditary title.

While noble authority had been unquestioned before 1637, after 1660 the determined conservatism of the nobility reflected a nervousness about preserving their wealth and privileges. Their control over other men was also less secure. Lordship of the kind familiar throughout late-medieval Scotland continued to be practised by the generation of nobles who came to adulthood under James VI, but from the early seventeenth century it was reshaped by new challenges. In the Lowlands, the vicious blood feuds that forced lords into strategies designed to protect their followers and strengthen their own military potency were pacified. Consequently, military retaining grew less useful, and bonding ceased to be deployed to strengthen lordship. Already relations with tenants were predominantly commercialized, landlords preferring cash rentals to other forms of service. The clientage networks that linked lesser nobles with the magnates ceased to carry the obligations of lord–man relationships, being renegotiated as alignments in which magnate patrons mediated royal offices and rewards to their local clients in return for political support. The mid-century civil war made the change complete, accelerating all the above developments, and adding the ingredient of a peasantry that now made up its own mind about political and religious affairs. Nobles continued to act as patrons with enormous economic, judicial and political power in rural communities, but they were ceasing to be lords. Only in the Highlands did clan chiefs continue to exercise quasi-military authority through their tacksmen and tenurial arrangements. They inspired personal loyalty from their men by a commitment to the shared paternalistic values of their communities, and by the extraction of surplus which was used to feast and feud.

2. The Middling Sorts

Below the nobility was a differentiated body of professional and quasi-professional occupational groups, wealthier burgesses, and lesser landowners (heritors). While some corporate identity was provided by bodies like the Convention of Royal Burghs, the General Assembly, or the Faculty of Advocates (1532) and Society of Writers to the Signet (1594), there was no common identity linking these 'middling sorts'. Of the professions, the twelve hundred or so ministers are most easily identified. Already by the early seventeenth century, a generation of married clergy were forming a hereditary identity as fathers passed their parishes on to their sons. Between 1616 and 1638, 17 per cent of the 1,232 ministers were sons of the manse, a figure that had increased to 27 per cent by 1648. It was also a profession that was entirely university educated, and it was growing in wealth as stipends were pushed up, especially under James VI and Charles I, to their highest value in relation to the rest of society at any time in history. The average stipend was £391 in 1617, £544 in 1631–7, £576 in 1641–8, and stood at £674 in 1649–50. These were men of significant social standing, important and articulate community figures who could and did act as an alternative focus of leadership to the nobility.

Lawyers were also increasing in number and in wealth, while their professional standing was enhanced by developments like the centralization of the Court of Justiciary in Edinburgh in 1672 and the creation of the Advocates' Library in 1682. The size of the Faculty of Advocates also grew from fifty-four members in 1587 to 200 by 1714. By the

1690s, there were practising in Edinburgh 36 advocates, 5 commissaries, 38 notaries, 15 procurators, 49 writers to the Signet, and 179 writers. Yet the corporate identity of the profession was stretched by the enormous disparity between country notaries, or solicitors, on the one hand, and on the other hand rich Edinburgh judges who might have a noble lineage, a country estate and a high political profile. Like the ministers, legal families were often dynastic, and a great many kinship connections can be traced among the 210 judges who sat on the Court of Session between 1532 and 1688. It was the success of one generation after another that took the Hopes into the top flights of the peerage by the end of the seventeenth century. Lawyers often participated in politics, being professionally useful to kings, as was the case with Thomas Hamilton, first Earl of Haddington, who served James VI, or George Mackenzie of Rosehaugh, who held office under Charles II and James VII. But their political role might also be subversive, the careers of Archibald Johnston of Wariston and James Dalrymple of Stair both demonstrating how a keen legal mind might dismantle the high claims of the crown.

On the whole, however, lawyers were a socially conservative body of men, closely tied to the landed nobility by birth and marriage, and by the fact that their most lucrative business came from servicing that sector of society. In the period up to 1688, half of all advocates were the sons of landed families with the trend moving towards an ever greater connection with landlords. In the period 1645–60, fifty-seven of the ninety-five new admissions to the Faculty of Advocates were from a landed background; by the period 1690–1705 the landed element among new admissions had grown to 116 out of 126, with an increasing number of these being eldest sons. By contrast, sons of burgesses among the ranks of advocates declined markedly from one in three before 1560 to one in six between 1600 and 1660, following which there were scarcely any sons of burgesses. There were a great many more sons of the manse after 1600 than formerly. Even in 1560, lawyers were among the wealthiest members of the community in Edinburgh, and the relative wealth of judges and advocates increased over the course of the seventeenth century. Yet this rising prosperity and the overlap with another profession like the clergy did not lead to anything like a separate social consciousness critical of the nobility. At the top of the legal profession, judges were likely to be noble, or to become noble, while elsewhere in the ranks of lawyers their most important social bonds were likely to be hierarchic rather than horizontal.

By the later seventeenth century other small professions were emerging. Among the most prominent were physicians who, along with surgeons and apothecaries, were in the top bracket of wealthy householders in Aberdeen in 1696. The establishment of the Royal College of Physicians in Edinburgh in 1681 was a significant step forward in the profession's development, which was becoming more scientific in approach, slowly abandoning earlier interests in astrology. Soldiering was increasingly adopted as a profession, and while military leadership remained very close to being a noble monopoly, it did offer a route to rapid social advancement. Men like Charles Middleton, first Earl of Middleton, who fought for the Covenants and for Charles II, or David Colyear, first Earl of Portmore, who served William II, were both catapulted from obscurity to titles, wealth and high office through their military skills and usefulness to the crown. All these groups had a distinct professional identity, but what was entirely lacking was any sense of identity with one another, and there is no evidence that Edinburgh's lawyers, physicians, schoolteachers, ministers, musicians and fencing masters experienced any sense of belonging to similar stations in society.

Nor did these professionals necessarily have much in common with those urban dwellers, chiefly merchants, whose wealth separated them from their own communities. At a legal level, burgh society was divided into those who held burgess status and the rest of the indwellers of the town. Yet within the former, it was clear by the end of the sixteenth century that population growth and greater wealth had accentuated the process of social differentiation. Already, 10 per cent of Edinburgh's population owned 56 per cent of the city's wealth, while in Aberdeen by 1608 a similar proportion owned 38 per cent of the town's wealth. Over the course of the seventeenth century, that wealthy sector increased its financial dominance in the community, even if it was not composed of the same families. Those richer merchants involved in international trade were forming an urban élite, and it was from the ranks of these men that burgh councils were drawn, creating small, wealthy oligarchies far removed from the mass of burgesses in their towns.

Most merchants were not international traders, being mere stallholders who carried on a local trade. Entry to merchant guilds varied from one town to another, for example the entry fee and the required level of wealth to qualify for entry was lower in Glasgow than in Edinburgh. It was also possible for craftsmen to enter the merchant guilds by way of marriage. Craft guilds continued to act as welfare institutions for their members, while ensuring that highly conservative and protectionist production and pricing arrangements preserved their monopolies. Here too hierarchy was extremely important. When in November 1567 Charles Sandeman, a cook, was made a member of the guild of Edinburgh, he had to give an undertaking never to be seen in public carrying dishes of food to his clients. Instead, he promised to employ a servant for such tasks, restricting himself to serving within his tavern. During the later seventeenth century, the increasing differentiation of craftsmen, and the shift in relative fortunes of crafts in response to domestic demand and international trade, which, for example, depressed the standing of skinners while enhancing that of tailors, began to fracture the traditional structure of burgh society. Distinctions between those with burgess status and the 'unfree' became less important than occupation and wealth, and by the later seventeenth century many of the town's professionals might not hold burgess status.

One physical manifestation of this social differentiation in towns was the greater segregation of living space. Thus in Edinburgh there was a growing concentration of rich householders in the north-west of the city, between the Castle and Parliament

House, with expensive new tenements like Gladstone's Land being erected. From the 1670s, the Lawnmarket also began to develop as a desirable residential area. By contrast, the south-east and the area to the south of the Grassmarket was taking on the appearance of slum dwellings for the very poor, particularly those newly arrived in the city. Not all urban communities had the same social profile, however. The 1691 hearth tax reveals that Linlithgow had a high percentage of wealthy inhabitants, much greater than Dumfries, but both towns had developed an upmarket residential area, in the south-east of Linlithgow, and in the Lochmaben district of Dumfries.

Nevertheless it proved difficult for merchant families to consolidate their wealth from one generation to another, largely because of the precarious nature of their business in which great riches could be made, or more easily lost, in a short time. Relatively few of the leading merchant families of Edinburgh at the Reformation were still at the top of their community by 1637. Furthermore, this group suffered particularly badly over the next two decades, and the richest merchant in the kingdom, Sir William Dick, was bankrupted as a consequence of his support for the Covenanters, dying a pauper in an English prison in 1655. Unlike similarly ruined nobles, he did not have the landed reserves, or social connections, to recover. If the burgh commissioners did take a more aggressive role in the parliaments of the 1640s, they spent most of the remainder of the century keeping their heads down, attending to their own affairs. Yet the conservatism of the merchant community concealed changes taking place within burgh society as the very concept of royal burghs with trading privileges, and of a select community holding burgess status, was subverted by the market. That conservatism, though, ensured their acceptance of a hierarchic social order, preventing the evolution of a self-conscious identity with professionals, or with those lesser landlords and wealthier tenants who occupied a middling place in rural society.

Indeed, the same divisions and solidarities can be identified outside the small towns of seventeenth-century Scotland. In rural society, the evidence for the equivalent of England's 'mere gentry' and yeoman farmers is slight. However, there were occupiers of the land who were above the level of landless labourers or cottars, and yet who were not noble. In the Highlands the *fine* existed in this space between chiefs and their tenants, but these clan gentry were so obviously part of a lordship hierarchy that it makes little sense to associate them with any middling order. In the Lowlands the picture is more complex. There the feuing of the previous century had created many more owner-occupiers on the land, especially in shires like Fife and Ayrshire, and it was these bonnet lairds who formed the backbone of the Covenanting movement both in the 1640s and again in the Restoration era. While the sixteenth century saw an increase in small-scale proprietors and feuers, their numbers decreased in the later seventeenth century as low grain prices and the strict entail all conspired to favour the economies of scale available on the bigger estates. These families struggled hard to survive in circumstances that proved too adverse for many, and the connection has been made between their socio-economic condition and their attraction to political dissent and evangelical religion. In the following century, similarly placed men in the north-east of the kingdom were likely to be Episcopalian dissidents and Jacobites. Undoubtedly, many of these farmers and their families were no longer prepared to be the mute followers of great lords, nor were they willing to give unquestioned obedience to the king. However, their solidarity was primarily a reflection of shared religious ideas rather than a product of economic circumstances.

Although land in Scotland was owned by relatively few people, most had access to some share of it in the form of sub-tenancies of one sort or another. In the countryside there was a regional and even a local variety of tenancies and sub-tenancies, each carrying a different status. Increasingly leases were written: 80 per cent of those on the Crawford estate in Lanarkshire in 1638, but only 33 per cent of the leases on the Strathbran estate in Perthshire in 1701. Some tenants were even relatively wealthy. Generally, paternal landlords operated a system of preferential treatment for sitting tenants and their families who had a surprising degree of security of tenure in spite of often having short leases. The absence of subdivision among heirs did work against younger sons, although it had a more positive impact on the landed economy generally, preventing the continuous subdivision of land into uneconomic farms. All but a few tenants, however, struggled to make a living, consuming perhaps a third of the farm's produce, while similar proportions were set aside for seed corn and rent. Periodic rent arrears were common, landlords usually allowing 'rests' on the basis that tenants could not pay what they did not have, and from time to time these were written off altogether.

Social mobility took place within the tenantry as families increased, or decreased, their holdings, and the feuing movement of the sixteenth century followed by sharp inflation did cause significant redistribution among the tenantry in many localities. This varied greatly from one estate to another, with 70 per cent of feus on the abbatial lands of Scone, Paisley and Coldingham being granted to existing tenants, while less than 40 per cent of sitting tenants acquired feus on the estates of the abbeys of Kelso, Arbroath and Crossraguel. Undoubtedly, there were losers among those families dispossessed, although the eviction of kindly tenants was never easy. Others seized the opportunity to acquire heritable possession of their lease, becoming in due course the bonnet lairds who were especially numerous in shires like Fife, Stirling and Ayrshire. However, analysis of estates like that of Panmure in Angus in the seventeenth century suggests there was relatively little movement into the ranks of the propertied, or down into that of the landless poor. On the whole, the tenantry continued to enjoy a period of prosperity in the early part of the seventeenth century, even with the successive rent increases negotiated by landlords who were determined to overcome their own financial difficulties. Especially in the western Lowlands, where cash rentals were more common on the predominantly pastoral farms, landlords squeezed their tenants harder, reducing margins and causing greater indebtedness and ruin.

Social mobility might traverse all ranks of society. A few individuals had remarkable stories to tell, like George Davidson, born illegitimate in the late sixteenth century in the parish of Tarves in Aberdeenshire. Illiterate and with no social connections, he managed to get started as a packman, or pedlar, and by 1626 had been admitted a burgess of Aberdeen. Five years later he was contributing towards the fund for the restoration of Fittie kirk, and in 1643 he bought 16,224 merks' worth of land in Belhelvie parish. The new laird of Pettens continued to add to his estate, paid for a stone boundary wall around Fittie church, built two bridges in the parish, and when he died in 1663 was memorialized with a substantial and ornate tombstone. George Davidson's experience was unusual, but by no means unique.

3. *The Labouring Sorts*

The bulk of society was made up of a range of differentiated common people, many of whom lived close to the margins of subsistence. In rural communities these might be cottars who farmed strips of land on which they grew a little food for their own family's consumption, had some grazing rights, and who worked as labourers for the landlord, or for his tenants. Within this society the numbers of servants and hired labour varied greatly depending on farm sizes. Thus the larger farms of the south-east required much greater numbers of servants and labourers than Aberdeenshire with its predominantly small, family-run farms. Rural communities also contained a range of craftsmen and tradesmen, somewhere between 3 and 5 per cent of the male working population, who might provide services as weavers, tailors, leather-workers, smiths and wrights, but also farm a smallholding. Their wealth and status fluctuated between that of the tenantry and labourers. However, in some localities the size of this workforce might be much higher. In Aberdeenshire in 1696 as many as 25 per cent of the male working population of some parishes around the town of Aberdeen were employed in craft and manufacturing activities, while in Buchan a fifth were weavers. Concentrations of workers were also found at coal mines and salt works, their freedom having been restricted by an Act of 1606 imposing a form of serfdom on them. The legislation, which was added to over the succeeding decades, was intended to protect the rights of owners from competitors who might poach their labour force, providing relatively secure employment and reasonable wages in return for being unable to leave their employer's service. In towns perhaps half the population was made up of servants and workers providing a ready pool of hired labour and often participating in a 'black economy'.

In the regulated economy, the chief concern of employers was to keep wages from rising beyond agreed limits, hence the 1621 Act of Parliament designed to punish 'the fraude and malice off servandis'. Of course, it was 'unscrupulous' landlords and masters who undermined such legislation, offering higher rates of pay in a labour market with a skills shortage. Wage levels, therefore, were regulated by magistrates in town and country, punishing masters and employees who breached agreed maximum wage limits. This did not always disadvantage workers. In Dundee in 1659, six master masons were permitted to combine to protect their jobs from 'insufficient men' who threatened their livelihood. In return for official support, they agreed to work a twelve-hour day, from six o'clock in the morning to six o'clock in the evening with a half-hour rest in the morning and an hour at midday, at a rate of 16s. 8d. without drink, or 13s. 4d. if drink was supplied by the employer. As in this example, it was not uncommon for payment to be partly in kind, food, drink, clothing and housing all being offered along with money. Over the first fifty years of the seventeenth century, wages for skilled craftsmen continued to rise quite sharply as they caught up with the inflation of the mid-sixteenth century that had so badly eroded the purchasing power of workers. However, from the 1660s stability set in, and the real value of wages never climbed back to pre-inflation levels.

The picture was much the same for unskilled labourers, who earned around half that of their skilled counterparts. Urban wages were slightly higher, although this was offset by rural labourers having access to some plot of land on which they grew their own food. Of course, the 17s. a day that could be earned by a mason in mid-century, or the 6s. a day earned by a rural labourer in winter, was never guaranteed. From a pool of sixty-five labourers on the Yester estates in East Lothian in 1687–96, five men worked less than twenty days in a year, only three worked more than 280 days, with the largest number, thirty-two, working between 220 and 279 days. Female workers were paid less than their male counterparts – two-thirds less for the same job in Aberdeenshire in the 1690s.

As well as skill and sex, the impact of geography, economic and political conditions, and the cycle of family life, all affected the remuneration of wage-dependent workers. Predictably, poverty was most pronounced when a married couple had to support children too young to work, and in old age. As for the other necessities of life, there is little evidence to suggest a significant increase in material goods at the lowest levels of society; clothing was made of coarse linen fabrics, shoes (if any) remained the most basic form of leather wear, and only crude tools, utensils and pottery were affordable. Rural housing was unchanged from medieval times, essentially consisting of one-chamber constructions of wood and peat, roughly six metres by four metres, containing people and animals. These dim, smoky, damp dwellings encouraged ill-health and hastened death.

When the naturalist John Ray visited Dumfries in 1662, he could not help observing that the countryside around 'abounds with poor people and beggars'. These unemployed, wandering poor were subject to the harsh Poor Law legislation of the later sixteenth century, with its emphasis on helping the sick and aged, not the able-bodied poor, who were regarded as a menace. These latter were subjected to strict controls on their movements, to whipping and branding. Parliament continued to reflect the concerns of landlords and merchants who feared a loss of social control, hence from the 1570s the increasingly harsh penal code for the treatment of the unemployed or gypsies. This trend continued into the following century with the 1663 amendment to the Poor Law allowing manufacturers to press able-bodied vagrants into service, and the 1672 legislation that gave permission to local authorities to create workhouses. In 1698, in a time of national famine and job scarcity, Andrew Fletcher of Saltoun estimated that 100,000 vagrants were wandering the land, offering a threat to the propertied orders. Women were more likely to be numbered among the poor than men, although they were less likely to be vagrant because many were elderly or had children to care for. In the East Lothian parish of Dirleton in the 1670s three-quarters of the poor were female.

It was the church that championed the cause of the weak and powerless in society. At a national level this was more pronounced during periods of Presbyterian church government, when there was a General Assembly to provide a platform for ministers concerned at poverty-related issues. In May 1574, for example, the General Assembly condemned Robert Gourlay, an Edinburgh merchant who exported grain at a time of shortage. In spite of the protection he enjoyed from government, Gourlay submitted to the church and did penance for his sinful behaviour. Local churches also made some effort to bridge the gap between government policy and the needs of their communities, using fines levied on the parish for playing games on Sunday, drinking offences, or defamation, to fund the Poor Box. Clackmannan kirk session provided 4s. for a poor, blind woman on 15 September 1639, and new cups and a basin for a poor widow on 30 November 1680; in April 1687 it was able to report that there were only five poor people living in the parish. Kirk sessions prioritized the needs of local people who had fallen on hard times, a large proportion of whom were women, but in some circumstances extended quite generous relief to vagrants passing through the parish in search of work. Even those who had offended against communal values could be given some help. In 1680, Dirleton kirk session gave £1 13s. to a pregnant woman known to be a notorious fornicator when she was unable to get help from her home parish which had banished her three years previously. The Dirleton session provided maintenance 'lest the child should perish', even if it had little sympathy for the behaviour of its mother.

In the towns, the custom by which the poor were sustained by burgh councils keeping down food prices was difficult to maintain in the first half of the seventeenth century, but thereafter proved more effective. Landlords also played their part with various degrees of enthusiasm, for example 'resting' rents in years of bad harvest or distributing alms at the gates of their houses. On the whole, such social obligations were more closely observed in the Highlands by clan chiefs. On Barra, the McNeil chief was responsible for finding wives and husbands for widowers and widows, replacing the cattle of tenants lost in bad weather, and maintaining old people in his home. Elsewhere, poor relief varied enormously from parish to parish depending on how the local heritors interpreted the legislation, but in general landlords were resistant to taxation. Even in the midst of the famine of 1623, East Lothian heritors protested against Privy Council recommendations for a local levy on the grounds that it was 'odious and smellis of ane taxatioun'. In the famine of the 1690s only one in five of those parishes whose records survive voted a local assessment to provide poor relief, the more generous communities being in the south of the country, for example in the Lothians. By contrast, in Aberdeenshire only one parish voted in favour of assessment.

For the poor, the weather was everything, determining whether they would eat or starve. Terrible frost and snowfalls between mid-January and mid-March of 1571 caused enormous hardship, especially the violent storm of 22 February when the snow, hail and wind were so severe that 'nae man nor beast might take up their heads, nor gang, nor ride, and many beasts, and mony men and women, were perished in sundry part, and all kinds of victuals right dear, and that because nae mills might grind for frost'. There were some very severe famines, as in 1623 when in Dumfries 10 to 15 per cent of the population died, two-fifths of these being children, and again in the mid-1690s. However, there were severe food shortages in only ten years of the seventeenth century.

While food was not significantly more or less scarce than in previous centuries, the rise in population had consolidated a shift from meat to cereal consumption, with fish as a welcome addition where available. In 1605, Sir Thomas Craig of Riccarton suggested that Scotland 'lacks none of the necessities of life', and pointed to the oatmeal diet of servants that ensured they were 'hardy and long-lived'. He was not far wrong, as the farinaceous diet of ordinary people, who rarely ate meat or dairy produce, was highly nutritious. The orphans at Hutcheson's Hospital in Glasgow in 1649 consumed some 2,800 calories per day, largely made up of oatmeal, herring, cabbage, a little beef and four pints of ale. Some four-fifths of calorie intake was acquired from oatmeal and ale, even if deficiencies in calcium led to problems for growing children and lactating mothers, and the shortage of vitamins A and C created eye and skin disorders. All told, this was in some ways a healthier diet than that enjoyed by the nineteenth-century working classes.

Most people were born into households that were essentially nuclear, rarely containing more than two generations of parents and their children. Marriage was not a sacrament, being essentially a civil contract entered into by mutual consent, and the law recognized 'irregular' (though binding) marriage by habit or repute. However, the church success-fully sought to control marriage through the proclamation of banns and the pronounce-ment of a blessing, and in seeking to limit expenditure on wedding festivities. There was little it could do to stifle the celebrations of the rich, and even among the less well-off people were usually prepared to pay what amounted to a fine for exceeding what the kirk deemed to be 'seemly enjoyment' of a wedding day. The church did find an ally in parliament over the issue of regular marriage, landlords being worried about the impact of irregular marriage on lines of succession. As early as 1562, Aberdeen kirk session began to crack down on 'handfasting', a marriage contracted without the church's blessing. Especially outside the propertied ranks of society, individuals usually chose their spouses, marrying relatively late, in their mid-twenties, and they were likely to experience a succession of partners due to early death, creating fluid families in which step-relationships were common. The kirk imposed a strict view of incest, extending it to sexual relations between a man and woman with no blood relationship. Thus 'a man may not marry any of his wife's kindred nearer in blood than he may of his own, nor the woman any of her husband's kindred nearer in blood than her own'. However, divorce was easier after the Reformation, even if community pressure made it unusual.

Sexual intercourse was a pleasure mostly confined to marriage. The kirk was keen to wipe out the sins of fornication and adultery, increasingly frowning on any form of physical contact between the sexes, and putting much energy into uncovering every form of what it called 'filthiness'. Its agenda was largely in tune with the wider community which knew well the disadvantages to all but absent fathers of unwanted bastards. In fact, the kirk session proved to be highly effective in persuading men to admit to paternity, some two-thirds agreeing to face up to their responsibilities, except in Ayrshire where the figure was closer to a half. Consequently, illegitimacy rates were relatively low at some 5 per cent of all births, with Fife and the Lothians being the lowest, and they continued to fall throughout the century to nearer 3 per cent by about 1720. Even intercourse between betrothed couples was relatively uncommon, only 3 per cent of legitimate first births being conceived outside marriage: a low figure in a society with no effective contraception, and much lower than in contemporary England.

Couples who anticipated their marriage might be subjected to public humiliation by the kirk session. More serious punishments might be inflicted on sexual 'deviants'. Capital punishment by the state was imposed on those who persisted in incestuous or, very rarely, in adulterous relationships, corporal punishment and banishment being commonly employed, and for the relatively unusual crimes of sodomy, bestiality and the murder of new-born infants, this last being recognized as a distinct crime by parliament in 1690. Child abandonment was uncommon, largely because it was difficult to dispose of an unwanted child without the community knowing about it. Ayr experienced only four cases between 1661 and 1690. If necessary, the parish would take care of foundlings, but its resources were sparse, and at Perth in 1700 the authorities decided that a five-year-old child was old enough to beg for its own living.

Early death was commonplace in this society, and the ritual of dying was a public one. This does not imply that attitudes to it were casual. Indeed, the church taught that all life was a process of dying, that death itself was a moment for which all that went before was a preparation. At that point, and only at that point, did the poor claim equality with their social betters, who nevertheless sought to make social distinctions in their magnificent funeral processions and grand funerary architecture, like the monument to the first Earl of Dunbar in Dunbar parish church. Old age and death for most people who attained adulthood occurred in the early to mid-fifties, but many died much younger, especially of disease. Leprosy lost its hold on the popular imagination in the early seventeenth century, the last leper being admitted to the Aberdeen Lazar House in 1604, but plague was still the most feared killer of the period.

Early modern society had few resources to deal with the trials of sickness. Even the rich received largely ineffective medical care, as when influenza swept through the royal court in 1562, or in the following year when Henry Sinclair, bishop of Ross, went to Paris for a lithotomy only to die of an infection in the wound some months later. The growing interest in medicine and science generally in the latter half of the seventeenth century did improve medical care for the higher ranks of society, but had little impact on the mass of the population since it was beyond their reach. Even the educated continued to apply quack medicine to their ailments, for example, going to London to be touched by the king for scrofula, the 'King's Evil'. The minister of Blantyre recorded in his diary in 1670 that an infected ear might be cured by grinding worms, boiling them in goose fat, and pouring the mixture in the ear. Many pre-Reformation hospitals survived, as at Dundee or Lanark, while new establishments were founded at other sites, for example at Aberdeen, where two new institutions supplemented the three existing hospitals. Further north, new hospitals were founded at Inverness and even on Orkney. Some burghs retained surgeons to care for the poor, while the charters establishing the Faculty of Physicians and Surgeons at Glasgow in 1599 and the College of Physicians at Edinburgh in 1681 both contained an obligation to treat the poor. However, all hospitals were very small, most being run along strict lines for select members of society, often guild members, and they were certainly not adequately resourced to deal with the scale of disease.

4. Crime and Punishment

Not only was this a society of orders, it was an orderly society. At first glance this is not at all apparent. Blood feuds were still a feature of Lowland society in the later sixteenth century, with over 365 having been identified. These ranged from bloodless disputes between neighbouring lairds to regional civil wars like that which raged throughout much of the north-east in the later 1580s and early 1590s claiming the lives of hundreds of individuals, including the second Earl of Moray who was butchered by the Gordons at Donibristle Castle in Fife in February 1592. At the root of these feuds lay a combination of political instability, an honour culture in which individuals and kindreds were easily slighted and demanded vengeance, military lordship that brought with it the widespread carrying of arms by nobles and their followers, and a system of justice in which compensation had to be forced from an offending party by applying escalating forms of pressure. Although the most extreme kinds of violence tended to be associated with the Highlands and Borders where government was least effective, blood feuds were found throughout the country with localities like Ayrshire and Angus being among the worst. Even the High Street of Edinburgh saw the killing of the first Lord Spynie and the first Lord Torthorwald in the early 1600s.

Feuds were occasioned by disputes over property or natural resources, jurisdictional quarrels between lords, injuries done to kinsmen or dependants, and issues of personal honour. They could be of short duration, or they might drag on for decades, and because they most commonly involved neighbouring families, their own histories associated earlier quarrels with more recent ones, creating an imagined memory of perennial feuding. However, by about 1610 a combination of changing attitudes within the honour culture, a coordinated campaign by church and state to reduce private violence, and the altered political context in which the need for a highly martial nobility declined, all conspired to undermine the hold of the blood feud. It survived for longer among Highland clans, remaining potent for the remainder of the century, but the legitimacy of feud was no longer an issue.

The Highlands were subject to other forms of lawlessness such as cattle rustling and blackmail, both of which were largely eradicated from the previously notorious border region. There crown terror in the decade after 1603 changed for ever the idea that such activities formed an integral part of the local culture. The high-profile execution of the ninth Lord Maxwell for murdering his Johnstone rival in 1608 sent out a powerful signal that no one living on the former West March could fail to observe. All gentlemen continued to carry swords, and duelling was a feature of noble life, claiming the lives of a number of prominent individuals like the fourth Duke of Hamilton who was slain in Hyde Park in 1712. However, the Scots never became as dangerously obsessed with the notions of punctilio that caused such bloodletting among some continental élites. Increasingly the martial qualities of the nobility were placed at the service of the crown, illegitimate violence was condemned, and there was no question of defending the right to private violence after the early years of the century. Of course, some nobles continued to engage in violent and high-handed behaviour, and to escape the rigours of the law for all sorts of crimes. In 1685, one of the sons of the ninth Earl of Morton got away with killing a footman in a quarrel over a dog, and in 1704 another son was cleared of a rape charge.

The complex and overlapping system of royal, ecclesiastical and private courts provided justice that was intensely local. Every locality had, in addition to its access to the higher courts, a barony court with its own officers and a kirk session with its elders chosen from the community. At a local level there was often close cooperation between secular and ecclesiastical courts. In November 1664, the barony court at Stitchill in Berwickshire incorporated the acts of the kirk session into its own statutes 'for advancing the glory of God, the cherisheing and nourisheing of piety and vertew'. The new office of commissioner of the peace was introduced in 1609, when 404 officers were appointed. They had little immediate impact, but the commissioners proved more useful after the Restoration. By 1663, there were 733 commissioners of the peace throughout the kingdom, with East Lothian having expanded its numbers from 17 to 38, Argyll from 10 to 29. Disputes were commonly resolved by arbitration, or taken immediately to court; those who committed crimes were quickly identified, usually they were caught, and punishment was immediate and effective. Only civil cases between the propertied orders in the Court of Session tended to be long and expensive. The Court of Justiciary continued to be the highest criminal court and sat in Edinburgh. In 1628 the long hereditary possession of the Justice Generalship by the earls of Argyll was surrendered – although they retained authority over Argyll and the Isles – and in 1672 the court was thoroughly reformed, with new circuit judges being appointed to take royal justice more effectively into the localities.

Standards of proof and methods of determining fact and responsibility were very different from twentieth-century practice. Those subjected to the criminal courts, especially for serious crimes carrying the death penalty, were at the mercy of the courts, which seem on the surface to have had little interest in mitigating circumstances or motive. However, the courts did try to uncover the truth and a high proportion of prosecutions were dismissed. On 4 December 1675, Melrose regality court, a private, heritable jurisdiction, found that James Turner was unable to prove a case of theft against a former female servant, and he was fined £10. Confession was also important, the reconciliation of the accused with God, the community and either their victims or their families being a necessary preparation to the execution of justice. Nobles were also expected to make full confessions in treason cases, often trading these for less degrading forms of execution. Such was the fear of eternal damnation that it was not uncommon for the accused to break down before ministers of the church, saving their souls at the cost of their earthly lives. Torture was not routinely employed in criminal cases, except for witchcraft, and lawyers like Sir George Mackenzie of Rosehaugh were sceptical of its use. The boot and thumbscrews were used more widely by Restoration governments determined to extract confessions in political cases, but after 1689 this practice was forbidden without proper authorization. The idea that a corpse would bleed if touched by its killer was widely believed and was employed to confirm the guilt of a beggar who slew another of his kind in a quarrel over the coins scattered at the Duke of Lauderdale's funeral at Haddington in April 1683. The man was subsequently hanged.

Punishments were meted out rapidly and, to modern eyes, sometimes barbarously. They might involve various forms of execution, including beheading, hanging, burning, pressing, drowning with gradations of mutilations often preceding death, for traitors, witches, homosexuals, murderers, thieves, fire-raisers, forgers, rapists, and persistent adulterers. Even animals were not entirely spared punishment. When in 1675 a man was found guilty at Inveraray sheriff court of committing bestiality with a mare, he was strangled at the stake and burned, the horse also being put to death for its role in the crime. Most penalties involved fines, imprisonment being rare, other than for debtors. Jails or 'tolbooths', like the new one erected at Clackmannan in 1592 at a cost of £284, were chiefly used to hold prisoners awaiting trial. Transportation to Ireland was experimentally used to deal with border criminals in the early 1600s, but with little success. The use of more distant penal colonies was introduced by the Restoration government to get rid of (among others) political prisoners and prostitutes, 258 individuals being shipped off to Barbados in November 1679 only to be shipwrecked in the Forth with the loss of all but thirty lives.

Court records indicate a low level of criminal activity, mostly petty pilfering and bickering between neighbours. However, the crown was not only concerned about crime, social control being a significant factor in the shaping of the criminal law and in the activities of magistrates. This has already been alluded to in the management of vagrancy, and is apparent in legislation like the 1661 Act imposing the death penalty on sane children over the age of sixteen who cursed their father or mother. Disorder, in the sense of representing a threat to hierarchy, was rare, although it did occur with the connivance of people of rank. In the spring of 1615, the Queen's chamberlain and his officers were attacked and beaten in Burntisland by a crowd of women of the 'bangster [unruly] Amazon kind' intent on preventing them enforcing a court order. Clearly there had been collusion by the town magistrates and minister who was deprived of his post and sent to another parish. However, when on 3 May 1682 there was a riot in Edinburgh against the impressment of some apprentices for military service in Flanders, the local community was able to frustrate the crown. The mob smashed the windows of government officials, soldiers fired on the crowd, killing a score of people, and arrests were made, but in the subsequent trials the assize refused to allow any convictions.

Witchcraft represented a quite different threat to the spiritual order of the community with belief in the demonic powers of those individuals who had bonded themselves to Satan spreading down from the intellectual élite in the later sixteenth century to the rest of society. Among magistrates there was a good deal of ambivalence about witchcraft. Even James VI, who initiated the first witch hunt in 1590 and forced assizes to return guilty verdicts, was within a few years much less convinced of the threat witches posed, a change of mind that is already evident in his 1597 book, *Daemonologie*. After the terrible killings of the 1590s, prosecutions remained constant if undramatic in number, but rose again from the 1620s, peaking in 1643–9 with a final outbreak in 1661–2, before setting in to a steady decline as the élites grew more sceptical. Something of the scale of these outbreaks can be seen from the 350 commissions issued to arrest suspects in 1649. The majority of the unfortunate victims were women from the lower ranks in society. In Renfrewshire in 1697, a child levelled accusations against twenty individuals, seven of whom were put to death in spite of the fact that magistrates were much less willing to investigate or convict than they had been fifty years earlier. The acquittal rate among witches tried before the High Court of Justiciary in the late seventeenth century was over 50 per cent, a figure which excludes cautions, banishments and corporal punishment. However, even when the courts did clear the accused, the local community might not be satisfied. At Pittenweem in 1705 a woman was stoned to death after being released by the Justiciary Court at Edinburgh.

Culture: Between Renaissance and Enlightenment

1. Education

Towards the close of the sixteenth century, Scotland was in the midst of a late flowering of the northern Renaissance. By comparison with the artistic achievements of contemporary England and Holland this was unimpressive, but Scottish cultural developments were comparable with those of states of similar size, such as Denmark or Portugal. In the area of education the country's achievements were a good deal better. The church's commitment to a parish-based educational system available to everyone was an ideal beyond its means, but the aspiration was a worthy one, and parliament did give it progressive statutory backing with Acts in 1616, 1633 and 1646. Many localities lacked church buildings as well as schools in 1600, but the steady advance of both into remote communities was already paying dividends by mid-century. By the 1630s, all the more remote shires had a scattering of schools: 6 in Ross and Cromarty, 3 in Orkney, 3 in Caithness and 5 in Argyll, while on the former border shires there were 27 in Berwick, 6 in Selkirk, 11 in Peebles, 21 in Roxburgh, 8 in Dumfries, 6 in Wigton and 7 in Kirkcudbright. In Fife there had been 3 schools before the Reformation; there were 13 by 1590, and by 1633 this had risen to 43.

Many schools were very basic buildings offering only rudimentary education, but some were the beneficiaries of substantial bequests, like Aberdeen Grammar School which in 1633 received an endowment of land from Patrick Dow, the late principal of Marischal College. Grammar schools in the larger burghs were generally able to offer a more advanced curriculum, preparing scholars for entrance to university and providing the sons of merchants with the literary and arithmetic skills needed to conduct their business. Scotland was well on the road to being among the most literate societies in Europe, being on a par with most of north-western Europe in teaching its population to read and write. Nevertheless, the system's shortcomings were not ignored by parliament and the 1696 Education Act attempted to address these. It required heritors in every parish to provide a school building and a stipend for schoolmasters, but while the presbyteries were given leave to petition commissioners of supply to find funds, the weakness of the legislation continued to lie in the absence of any mechanism that would compel landlords to pay up.

The result of this commitment to schooling was impressive. For the period 1640 to 1699 comparisons with the ability of people to sign their own names in the north of England are generally favourable. Illiteracy was virtually unknown among the male ranks of the nobility and the professions, while 65 per cent of noblewomen were literate. Something like three-quarters of male craftsmen and tenant farmers could write their names, a proportion that was rising over the course of the century. There were some variations within trades, for example wrights and maltmen had a very high literacy rate, at over 90 per cent; some three out of four baxters, brewers, chapmen, innkeepers and tailors were literate; but for weavers, smiths, carters, shoemakers and butchers the illiteracy rate was 50 per cent. Illiteracy among labourers was high, only one in five being literate, and millers and sailors were almost universally illiterate. In every case, the few women in these trades were much less likely to be able to sign. Nevertheless, it was at this level in society, especially in urban communities where these trades were concentrated, that Scotland's schooling provision had its greatest impact in comparison with England.

By the end of the late-medieval era, Scotland had three universities: St Andrews, Glasgow and King's College, Aberdeen. Two more were added in the later sixteenth century. The provision of a college at Edinburgh from 1583 proved to be the basis of a new university, and in 1593 Marischal College, Aberdeen, was founded by the scholarly and very wealthy George Keith, fifth Earl Marischal. None of these institutions was a centre of European excellence before the eighteenth century, but neither were they backwaters. They were staffed by scholars most of whom had studied on the continent, many having European reputations. They included men like Andrew Melville, Samuel Rutherford, and David Gregory who worked on geometry and optics at Edinburgh before moving to Oxford in 1692, where he was closely associated with Isaac Newton. Even those whose significance has since declined should not be overlooked, scholars like George Sinclair who attempted to demonstrate the existence of witchcraft by scientific method in his *Satan's Invisible World Discovered* (1685). Until the 1660s, the university syllabus was dominated by Aristotelian metaphysics; after this, new scientific and philosophical ideas rapidly gained ground, introducing students to a Copernican universe, Cartesian thinking, and Robert Boyle's chemistry. Primarily training colleges for the Protestant clergy, the universities also educated the expanding number of lay lawyers, and provided nobles with the necessary skills to participate in the society of gentlemen where Latin, rhetoric, philosophy and ancient history offered access to a common European culture. Many of these nobles, along with the brightest clergy and most ambitious lawyers, continued studying throughout Europe, especially in France and Holland. Over fifty Scots had matriculated from Leiden University by the early 1700s, their academic credentials from St Andrews or Glasgow opening doors in what was a highly mobile world of learning.

2. Artistic Achievements

The intellectual and cultural products of this enthusiasm for learning were modest but energetic. Two factors acted as constraints on what was achieved. First, in contrast to the early sixteenth century, the royal court was poor after 1567 and in 1603 it removed entirely to England. Queen Mary was able to sustain a glittering court because of her French income, and the 1566 baptism of Prince James was an occasion that drew admiration from the many foreign guests who attended. In 1594, James VI managed to put on an equally impressive display for the baptism of his eldest son, Prince Henry, but he had to beg and borrow to pay for it. There was little else of note at James's court, although the impecunious king did manage to patronize a number of promising poets, the 'Castilian Band'. There were certainly no royal architectural commissions beyond the repair or improvement of existing palaces, such as at Linlithgow prior to the king's visit in 1617. After 1603 the crown no longer sponsored the visual and dramatic arts, and a literature of criticism and compliment directed towards kings was muted. Even more than between 1603 and 1637, the absence of a royal court in Restoration Scotland was telling. Consequently, when the Duke of York set up residence at Holyrood in 1679, there was a rush of enthusiasm to be associated with his court by the nobles, but also by professional bodies like the Royal College of Physicians, incorporated in 1681, and the Faculty of Advocates, whose Library was established a year later.

Second, a kirk that was much less wealthy than its medieval predecessor was unable to provide the artistic patronage that allowed the pre-Reformation church to have such an enormous influence on the course of the Renaissance in Scotland. Besides, regardless of the form of church government, Scottish Protestantism was suspicious of any form of visual art in church buildings, seeing in every painting or sculpture the potential for idolatry. The desacralization of the mass, and its replacement with a commemorative ceremony, saw the altar displaced in favour of a space in which to site the communion table, and a new emphasis on the pulpit as the focus of attention. The very real poverty of the church allowed it to make a virtue of austerity, but some finely carved pulpits were commissioned, and from the early seventeenth century a few bells were imported from Holland. Lack of money also retarded building plans, most ministers being concerned just to have a church building and manse that could be kept waterproof.

More often than not extensions to existing buildings took the form of burial aisles for local nobles (who footed the bill), for example the Kinnoul aisle, built in 1635. Nobles also invested in ornate seating for their own families, constructing lofts that emphasized the social distinctions of the community; there is a fine example at Kilbirnie barony church, and that built in 1634 for the Forbes family at Pitsligo church. In some cases nobles built entirely new churches, as at Dirleton in 1612, where the first Earl of Kellie was the patron. Burghs too demonstrated pride in their kirks. A new building was finished in East Anstruther in 1644, while Ayr built the Auld Kirk in 1666. Apart from a few exceptions like Dairsie church, where Anglican influences are clearly visible, the plainness of church architecture and interiors, along with the unwillingness even of the bishops to act as artistic patrons, produced its own form of Protestant culture, as valid in the statement it made as any other.

There is no denying the effect of this austerity in retarding the decorative and expressive arts. However, the setting of the Psalms to unaccompanied singing produced a richly textured music that brilliantly expressed the sense of awe so central to the Calvinist view of a righteous and holy God. The church also largely withdrew its patronage from drama. Initially it concerned itself with stamping out 'clerk plays', and in 1574 the General Assembly forbade any plays based on the scriptures, allowing only secular works. The later sixteenth century, therefore, saw theatre tolerated in a censored form. In June 1589, Perth kirk session allowed a company of comedians to perform on condition there would be no swearing or scurrility that would be 'a scandal to our religion'. Companies of English players also continued to tour the country, and in 1603 *Philotus* was published, a sexual comedy and satire of marriage written in Scots. However, the seventeenth century saw the development of an increasingly stern attitude towards acting that in time stopped the performance of plays altogether.

In the absence of royal or ecclesiastical patronage, the arts had to look to the nobility, and even after 1603 nobles retained this role since only a very few decamped entirely to London. Their enthusiasm for education and travel gave nobles international tastes, encouraging adaptation or imitation of what they read and saw elsewhere. Their castles became more comfortable and ornate, decorated with features that were pleasing to the eye, but often requiring to be read as complex texts. This iconic form was most apparent in the painted ceilings that were so fashionable in the later sixteenth and early seventeenth century, a particularly good example being Chancellor Dunfermline's Pinkie House at Musselburgh. This was a form of artistic patronage not confined to the very rich and powerful, as is apparent in the homes of lesser nobles at Earlshall, outside Leuchars, and at Culross. The exteriors of buildings were similarly treated to interpretative design; the rebuilt Strathbogie Castle, home of the first Marquis of Huntly, is a fine example from the early part of the century. After the Restoration there was a distinct shift in style away from Renaissance ideas, but architecture remained the principal beneficiary of noble artistic patronage, allowing Sir William Bruce to express his genius in the likes of Kinross House as well as completing royal commissions that included the redesigning of Holyrood Palace.

Portrait painting was much in vogue from the later sixteenth century. Initially Scottish nobles had to employ foreign artists like Frans Purbus, Adam de Cologne and Adrian Vanson, but the native-born George Jamesone was the most popular artist of the early seventeenth century, and while his works cannot stand comparison with those like Daniel Mytens, who painted the third Marquis of Hamilton at the London court, he was on a par with English provincial painters. Music too had its place in country houses, as it did in popular culture, with virginals and lutes imported to complement the sound of harps, pipes and fiddles. While spiritual music still featured largely in popular taste, more secular interests began to be reflected in the collections of noble enthusiasts of the early seventeenth century like Sir John Skene of Curriehill, Sir William Mure of Rowallan, and Anne Ker, Countess of Lothian, who also composed. Native composition was for the great hall, the chamber and the tavern, a rich sound of Gaelic bardic poetry, popular ballads and dances, and light entertainment. At its best, Scottish architecture, art and music embraced whatever styles were found elsewhere, blending them to suit a native environment. The effect was bold, colourful and noisy, a mixture of the erudite and the playful, of high and popular culture, of classical and baronial styles.

A similar eclecticism can be discerned in the literary productions of the period, there being nothing that might be described as a Scottish school. The outpourings of the Castilian Band of poets in the 1590s, the most prominent of whom was Alexander Montgomery, was continued by a number of figures associated with the London court after 1603, men like John Murray, Sir Robert Ker of Ancram and Sir William Alexander of Menstrie. The tradition also survived in William Drummond of Hawthornden, a courtier poet who did not reside at court, preferring to cultivate his ideas of Stoic retreat from society. In his sonnet, 'The Praise of a Solitarie Life', he concludes, 'The world is full of Honours, Troubles, Slights, / Woods harmlesse Shades have the only true Delightes'. A more worldly character was Sir John Scott of Scotstarvit, an official of Charles I's government, who was an enthusiastic collector of Scottish poetry, publishing *Delitiae Poetarum Scotorum* in Amsterdam in 1637; he also promoted Scotland's first atlas. If much of this is inaccessible today, especially Menstrie's voluminous Latin verse, it is more because of changes in fashion than because it was not thought well of at the time. The content of most of these works was uncontroversial, being the typical mixture of love poetry, advice to gentlemen and classical allusions, but along with conventional suggestions for the good government of the commonweal, there is also criticism of courtly morality and political vice. Menstrie with his visions of British imperial greatness, seeking inspiration in ancient Rome and imagining expansion in North America, comes closest to innovative ideas. The last of Scotland's Renaissance writers, Sir Thomas Urquhart of Cromarty, produced a range of works that spanned the middle decades of the century. His bizarre writings, including *Epigrams, Divine and Moral* (1641), the mathematically obscure *Trissotetràs* (1645) which set out to explore trigonometry, his fantastic *Introduction to the Universal Language* (1653), and his enigmatic and imaginative *The Jewel*, written during his imprisonment in the 1650s, besides his translations of Rabelais and a family history, are the literary equivalents of the painted ceilings. As for style, the Scots were already floating free of any one dominant linguistic form. In addition to the Scots tongue, George Buchanan and Arthur Johnston were among

Europe's foremost Latin poets. Others, like Alexander Ross, made their career in England, while bards like the MacDonald poet, Ian Lom, composed in Gaelic. In the later seventeenth century, Gaelic was still spoken in half the Scottish land mass. In 1706 much of Sutherland and Inverness-shire was composed of monoglot Gaelic communities, and there were large Gaelic-speaking populations in Aberdeenshire, Angus and on the island of Arran, suggesting that as much as a third of the population was predominantly Gaelic-speaking.

Unlike Gaelic poets who performed in an oral culture, the Lowland poets published their works in a period that saw the book market expanding rapidly. By 1600, there were a mere twenty book traders, printers and sellers in Scotland, a number that rose sharply, attaining a peak of ninety in the 1680s before economic depression cut their numbers over the next two decades. Initially confined to Edinburgh, St Andrews and Stirling, the printing business spread to Aberdeen in 1622 and Glasgow in 1638, and it was these two towns, along with Edinburgh, that dominated the trade. Book-selling spread more widely from its sixteenth-century bases in Edinburgh, Stirling, Perth, Glasgow and St Andrews, to Aberdeen in 1613, Peebles in 1630, Dundee in 1662 and to a further ten towns before the end of the century. Initially, religious works dominated the trade in books. In fact, the Protestant Reformation placed great emphasis on the availability of religious texts, especially the Bible, and in 1579 the General Assembly applauded the 'days of light' that had been made possible by the widespread circulation of accessible Bibles. Nevertheless, before the late 1620s less than twenty-five items, including books, pamphlets and news sheets, were produced each year, before religious controversy sparked an outburst of publications. This peaked in 1648 when there were forty-eight different publications; after this, printing dropped back to between twenty-five and fifty items per annum until the 1680s.

Scotland's own book-publishing output was small, the bulk of it being provided by school textbooks, government publications, and religious items like the highly controversial 1637 Prayer Book. Secular historical writing, of which the most notable in the first half of the century was the *History of the House of Douglas*, emphasized the great deeds of ancestors, leading up to present achievements, and reflecting once again the optimistic message of successful noble dynasties. For more robust writings, one had to turn to religious controversy, although the best of this genre, by David Calderwood, did not see the light of day until 1678. Censorship clearly did restrain writers, and almost all the banned literature before 1700 was concerned with religious themes. However, in 1579 two poets were executed for writing libels against the fourth Earl of Morton. George Buchanan's works were publicly burned by order of his former pupil, James VI, and the Restoration governments tried hard to restrict the circulation of publications critical of church and crown. Increasingly, seventeenth-century governments found censorship difficult to enforce, and after 1689 publishing was less regulated. While much of the religious writing of the period had a very transitory shelf-life, some books, like Henry Scougal's *Life of God in the Soul of Man* (1677), remained classics of their genre for decades.

In the last two decades of the century new secular issues grew in importance, providing a catalyst for the printing business, and in 1695 250 items were printed in the country, 15 per cent of which were about Darien. The market was provided by ministers, lawyers and nobles, who also bought books from all over Europe on every conceivable subject. Some buyers, like the regent Moray in the 1560s and the first Earl of Buccleuch in the 1620s, collected sizeable libraries, in the latter case chiefly of a historical and military nature, while Archbishop Robert Leighton's 4,000 volumes ranged across the classics, divinity, philosophy, science and medicine.

The Scots' concern to embrace new ideas and learning was already apparent in the radical nature of the Reformation, the commitment to parish schooling, the foundation of new universities, and in James VI's decision to start the New Year on 1 January 1600 (instead of 25 March, as continued to be the case in England), according to the custom 'in all the well-governed commonwealths'. What gradually emerged in the later seventeenth century was a spirit of more rational and scientific inquiry, epitomized by men like Sir Robert Moray, a politician and a founder-member of the Royal Society. Sir Robert Sibbald, too, was catholic in his interests, which covered medicine, botany and geography, and in the 1680s he was very much at the centre of the outburst of intellectual energy that included the lawyer and royalist political theorist, Sir George Mackenzie of Rosehaugh. However, the intellectual giant of the era was Sir John Dalrymple of Stair, whose massive *Institutions of the Law of Scotland*, published in 1681, shaped Scots law for centuries, placing current practice within a rational philosophical and historical system. These interests in science, medicine, political theory and law would underpin the Enlightenment of the eighteenth century. There was a steady stream of scientific inquiry from John Napier of Merchiston, the inventor of logarithms, to Sir Thomas Urquhart of Cromarty, with his bizarre mathematical calculations and scientific observations in the 1650s, to Moray and Sibbald later in the century.

What was new was the greater public awareness of what previously had been highly esoteric investigations conducted largely in private. The coffee-house culture of late seventeenth-century Edinburgh, the popularity of masonic lodges like that at Kilwinning which in 1643 had twenty-six members and was already describing itself as 'the ancient lodge of Scotland', the growth of the medical and legal professions, the expansion of the secular market for books on gardening, military science and gazetteers – all these pointed to a public demand for knowledge. And it should be remembered that the Scots continued to be open to the very best of what the rest of Britain and Europe had to offer, sharing in the discoveries of Descartes and Newton and the world they were reinterpreting. Nevertheless, religion continued to arouse enormous interest among pamphleteers, devotional writers and chroniclers of the times. Scotland was certainly not on the edge of a new secular age, and the point is emphasized in the execution in

1696 of a foolish and stubborn Edinburgh student, Thomas Aitkenhead, for holding deist ideas and arguing that 'theology was a rhapsody of feigned and ill-invented nonsense'.

Kings and Covenants, 1603–60

1. Regal Union and Absentee Government, 1603–25

In James VI, the Scots possessed a tried and able king whose early errors of judgement had made him wiser, who had reigned for thirty-seven years and ruled as youth and man for twenty of them. Though his judgement was still marred by over-confidence, he was fortunate that his northern kingdom had much to be confident about. The nation had not experienced foreign invasion since the 1540s, the civil war that had ended in 1573 was a distant memory, the Protestant Reformation was secure, the last Catholic rebellion having fizzled out in 1594, and the country was among the most peaceful in war-torn Europe. The economy was recovering from the hardships of what contemporaries perceived as runaway inflation, the slump in European trade, and a high incidence of dearths caused by bad weather. Food production could apparently sustain the new, higher levels of population. As early as the 1600s there were hints of an economic boom that would bring new wealth to landlords and merchants, stretching the gap between rich and poor.

In some respects Scotland remained a disorderly kingdom with widespread, if declining, feuding, especially in the Highlands and Borders; it was plagued by a fear of witches, burning hundreds in an orchestrated panic in the 1590s; and the governing élites worried anxiously about crime levels among the increasing numbers of the propertyless. Religious divisions among the literate and the articulate had created deep fissures in society, but persecution was surprisingly bloodless in what was a deeply intolerant age. In short, Scotland was prospering, if not rich; it was at peace, if not entirely peaceful; it was united, even if religious disputations prevented the full measure of conformity the king wished to create. Scotland had the appearance of a kingdom blessed by good fortune, and it was a matter of no great surprise to the Scots that God chose one of their Stewart royal line to unite the crowns of England and Scotland on Elizabeth I's death, creating a concentration of power never seen before in the islands of Britain and Ireland.

Uniquely, perhaps, James VI and I had no difficulty in imagining Great Britain as a mighty Protestant empire with himself at its centre, a second Constantine, Brutus and Arthur rolled into one, presiding over a restored Golden Age. The king's liking for ancient British iconography was to be a key feature of his reign after 1603, reflecting wildly optimistic expectations of his ill-assorted kingdoms. James hoped for a Great

Britain with a unified monarchy, a single parliament, a congruous church, a unified legal code, an interdependent economy, an integrated élite, and, in due course, a British people. What he got was an empty title of king of Great Britain that scarcely anyone used, a flag, a coinage, some intermarriage between courtier families, and a multi-kingdom state system that pleased no one. His efforts to persuade the two parliaments to unite were rejected by the English and the Scots (although the former were prepared to consider admitting Scots to their own parliament); legal unification never got off the ground, and the idea served only to alienate the excessively conservative English common lawyers; after an experimental period of abolition, customs tariffs were reimposed in 1611 because the king needed revenue; and although some progress was made in bringing the Scottish church more into line with the Church of England, the separate jurisdictions of the two were strictly maintained, the Church of Scotland being administered by the archbishop of St Andrews who answered directly to the king. The English were especially sceptical of the advantages the king's publicists recommended. Sir Henry Saville, Warden of Merton College, Oxford, had reason to ask, 'As for ritches, what have they to enriche us withall? What merchandize of worthe? What freedomes, what libertyes to endow us with?' The birth of a new British age proved to be stillborn, and only James's zeal kept alive even the pretence that the regal Union had resulted in anything other than one king ruling three kingdoms.

Yet there is no doubt that for Scotland the world would never be the same again. An absent king did not make for a kingless kingdom, but it certainly left a vacuum at the centre of what was already a highly decentralized state. It also raised the international stature and the potential domestic resources of the king of Scots above any of his predecessors. The king was now in London, as were his household and court, political institutions which retained enormous significance. More people were employed in the London court than in the entire administration of Scotland. Henceforth, Scottish politics would be played out both in Scotland, at parliament, in the Privy Council and its committees, in the courts of law, and in the castles and houses of the nobility. However, political developments would also unfold in the labyrinthine, faction-ridden maze of the London court. For the remainder of the century, successful Scottish politicians had to be able to move freely in both environments, creating and being a part of bonds of clientage in each. For some noble families, like the house of Lennox, this resulted in complete anglicization, others like the house of Hamilton successfully bridged the two worlds, and some slipped into provincial obscurity, denied access to the centre of political life at court.

For all this, it would be untrue to suggest that Scotland was now governed from London. James VI was too skilful a king to ignore the advice and expertise of the men he left behind in Edinburgh as officers of state, Privy Councillors and judges. Many decisions, often over matters of precise detail, were made at court by the king and a handful of Scottish councillors and advisers. Herein lay the temptation to adopt a more absolutist style of government, decreeing from a distance. Yet under James VI these London-based policies could be overturned, or moderated, by Edinburgh politicians who were granted considerable freedom to get on with the job of governing. Thus Highland policy after 1603 was gradually shifted away from the king's more extreme ideas of exterminating native clans and replacing them with Lowland colonists, to a more practical reliance on local nobles and chiefs to police their own lands. Similarly, while James did drive his ecclesiastical policy through the General Assembly and parliament against the advice and wishes of reluctant Privy Councillors, after 1621 their covert refusal to enforce it was ignored by a king sensible of the realities of political life and also running out of energy.

The regal Union had both a real and a perceived impact on the relationship between the king and the nobility. James VI had faced many palace *coups* and rebellions during his reign in Scotland, the last of these being the ill-fated Gowrie Conspiracy of 1600. In London such a threat to the king's security was unlikely, even if the Gunpowder Plot of 1605 was a reminder to an ever-nervous king that no early modern ruler was entirely safe. Only five years later Henry IV of France died at the hands of an assassin. However, combinations of nobles could no longer force themselves on the king, or easily pressure him into changes in policy. James VI's son and successor, Charles I, acted instead as though the king could enforce his will on the nobility, that the idea of divine right monarchy could be translated into a form of conducting politics by fiat. In fact there had been no decline in noble power in the localities, and as the crown had no independent military force it was vulnerable to pressure from that quarter.

James VI, with his keen awareness of the local basis of that power, fully realized this. He never set out to undermine his nobles, knowing that royal government worked best when that local dominance was harnessed to his own national interests. Thus he wrote in his book *Basilikon Doron* that the nobles must be cultivated because 'they must be your armes and executoners of your lawes'. A handful of mavericks were executed, like the ninth Lord Sanquhar, hanged in London in 1612 for having a fencing master murdered after the man had injured him; some Catholic lords suffered imprisonment or exile, like the tenth Earl of Angus, who retired to a French monastery to end his days; and some awkward characters like the vicious old fifth Earl of Caithness were forced into line by the manipulation of their debts. But there was little sympathy for these nobles from their peers who courted and respected a king who, more than any of his predecessors, showered them with honours, riches and offices.

In some respects, the governing of Scotland was made easier by the regal Union. Foreign policy lay within the sphere of the royal prerogative exercised by the king, and after 1603 that policy was determined at the London court. That James VI was determined to pursue peaceful policies, ending England's long war with Spain in 1604, made it easy to accept that foreign affairs were beyond Scottish control. It was not until the mid-1620s, when Charles I dragged the Scots into England's pointless wars with Spain and France, that the dangers of this became apparent, disrupting Scottish trade for no obvious advantage. More obviously, Scotland no longer required a foreign policy towards England. The countries had been allies since 1586, but the regal Union removed the need to regard the Borders as a special zone requiring its own form of jurisdiction. This was a development James VI had foreseen, predicting that the Anglo-Scottish marches would become the 'middle shires'. In the short term, the region's peculiarities were recognized, a joint border commission being established in 1605, and a decade of savage policing rooted out the worst elements of border gangsterism. In its first year the commission executed seventy-nine individuals, and in the following years scores – if not hundreds – of the killers, cattle rustlers, and blackmailers whose types had tyrannized the region for centuries were hanged or transported. By the early 1620s, this brutal policy had been so successful that the crown was able to scale down its operations.

The Highlands were less easily subdued, but again the regal Union made a difference, altering the relationship between Scotland and Ireland. James ended the long-running Irish rebellion in 1604, cutting off the demand for Highland mercenaries, or *buannachan*, and making it easier for Edinburgh to coordinate naval expeditions into the Western Isles in 1605 and 1609. Experiments in colonization, the prototypes for Ulster, were tried out by Lowlanders on Lewis and by the Campbells on Kintyre and Islay. The former failed miserably, the latter succeeded because the house of Argyll had the military muscle to make it succeed. And this was an environment where violence still mattered, where warlords like Coll Keitach prospered, making himself master of Colonsay after slaughtering Malcolm McPhie of Colonsay and his close followers in February 1623. However, Highland lords and chiefs were also learning how to manipulate the crown, and increasingly it was the partisan deployment of royal commissions rather than private blood feuds that settled issues. Thus Campbell resources were deployed viciously in attempting to exterminate the bandit Macgregor clan in the king's name, and the crown also relied heavily on the power of the Gordon house of Huntly and the Mackenzie house of Seafield in the north. On Orkney and Shetland, the crown was particularly aggressive, replacing Norse Udal or Odal law with Scots law in 1611, and executing the second Earl of Orkney for treason four years later.

Yet while the traditional form of magnate policing remained the key to governing the Highlands, the 1609 Statutes of Iona, which were enforced on the clans, did represent a more coherent and ideologically driven attempt to alter the nature of the region. The Privy Council, concerned about the 'grite crueltie and inhumane barbaritie' of the region, set about civilizing the Highlands and Islands by coercing the chiefs into acting as crown agents. It tried to make them responsible for the good behaviour of their men, for the planting of churches and the payment of ministers, the erosion of the martial culture of their society, and the Lowland education of the sons of the clan *fine*. The moral tone of this crusade was also indicated in Lowland concern at 'thair extraordinair drinking of strong wine and aquavite'.

Three decades after the Statutes of Iona were first agreed, the crown's policy was still a long way from being fulfilled, but the region was quieter than at any time since the collapse of the lordship of the Isles in the fifteenth century. More importantly, the growing financial pressures on Highland landlords who needed cash to pay crown fines and their Edinburgh creditors led them to pursue more commercial estate policies that eroded the basis of clan relations. Had civil war not erupted in the 1640s, the long-term effect of crown policies and economic change might have been gradually to demilitarize the region, allowing Gaelic culture to make a more acceptable accommodation with Edinburgh and London than the one ultimately imposed on it in the mid-eighteenth century.

Another obvious advantage for a Scottish king after 1603 was the immense enhancement of his wealth. The English treasury was not bottomless, and it was not long before James came to realize just how parsimonious the House of Commons could be, but the income from Scotland now formed only 2 per cent of royal finances. The Scottish revenues could be retained in the kingdom to fund the administration, and to create a reservoir of patronage for the nobility. The latter also had access to the much greater bonanzas available at the London court. No previous Stewart king had so much wealth to lubricate the machinery of politics, and not since David I distributed Scottish lands to his Anglo-Norman followers had a generation of nobles been so richly rewarded.

Nevertheless, the underlying problem of the crown's fiscal weakness had to be addressed. In 1606, the Scottish parliament agreed to a substantial taxation of 400,000 merks, a significant turnaround from the repeated refusals James had faced in the later 1590s and early 1600s. The kingdom's growing prosperity, the willingness of the nobles to vote for taxes that would fund their own pensions, the king's undoubted popularity and effective parliamentary management delivered what the crown needed. Further taxes were voted in subsequent parliaments and conventions of the estates, and the level of crown debt fell, at least until about 1617–18, when a downturn in economic conditions and European war exposed the underlying vulnerability of the king's income. By the time the 1621 parliament voted an unparalleled raft of tax increases, including £400,000 over the next four years, Scotland had become used to continuous taxation. Clearly the king could no longer finance the governing of the country out of his own ordinary income as had been expected throughout the late medieval period. Crown lands, customs dues and the profits of justice were inadequate for the needs of the seventeenth-century state, and the crown became ever more dependent on extraordinary income in the form of taxes. In 1621, not only was the rate of taxation increased, but the tax base was widened, new taxes were imposed on 'annual rents' or earned interest – a temporary measure that was not rescinded – and on salt, coal and other consumer products. Taxation now accounted for around a quarter of the crown's annual income compared with a tenth in the later sixteenth century, a measure of the success of royal officials in persuading parliament to fund the king, but also of the crown's vulnerability to political pressure. Besides, there was never enough money, and Charles I was left to inherit a financial shortfall which had no obvious solution.

In his 1598 book, *The Trew Law of Free Monarchies*, James VI argued that God vested authority over the church in kings, but it was the regal Union of 1603 that gave him the political leverage to make into reality a claim already encapsulated in statute in the 1584 Act of Supremacy. While there were large numbers of clergy and laity who rejected both Erastian ideas of a royal supremacy and a hierarchy of bishops to enforce it, the king rightly calculated that most men would follow his lead over an issue that he argued was not intrinsically spiritual, being a thing 'indifferent'. James moved slowly and softly, seizing opportunities as they arose, and there is little evidence that he was working towards a preconceived end. Nevertheless, the failure of English Puritans to get his backing at the Hampton Court Conference in 1604 was a strong signal of his preference for bishops that his Scottish critics could not fail to observe. It was here that James declared 'No bishop, no king'. When in the following year an illegally convened General Assembly met in Aberdeen after repeated postponements, the king was provided with the excuse he needed to move against the Presbyterian leadership. Always careful to operate within the limits of the law, James had Andrew Melville and his colleagues rounded up and imprisoned in England. Melville was later exiled, dying in Sedan in 1622, a largely forgotten figure. In 1606, parliament was primed, the nobility especially being won over to the royal ecclesiastical programme by the creation of new secular lordships from former ecclesiastical estates, the Lordships of Erection. The General Assembly was manipulated, able but obedient men, like John Spottiswoode, were brought to the fore and appointed to the vacant bishoprics, and apostolic authority was discreetly provided by English bishops. By the time the 1610 parliament met to give additional statutory backing to the royal supremacy, restoring most of the pre-Reformation powers to the bishops, and creating courts of high commission, the political preparation was such that it had removed any question of overt opposition.

James VI's apparent political victory over the Presbyterians in the years after 1596 concealed the fact that dissent had been driven underground. Royal confidence in the regulation of outward conformity to the monarch's chosen religion was demonstrated in the fact that the king employed a Roman Catholic Lord Chancellor, Alexander Seton, first Earl of Dunfermline. It also meant that a great many people were able to accept grudgingly the king's *fait accompli*, while privately disapproving of it. Some of these people were close to the heart of government, men such as Lord Cranstoun and Sir John Skene of Curriehill, while many crown officials and nobles were embarrassed by the religious loyalties of their wives and daughters, who attended clandestine house meetings and patronized dissenting ministers like Robert Bruce. Others were nurtured in secretive dissenting exercises, or prayer meetings, and conventicles, or open-air gatherings, by a network of ministers and lay people, especially women. Among these was Rachel Arnot, wife of a very rich Edinburgh merchant whose house became a centre of dissident activity. Her children and grandchildren were connected to prominent judges and royal servants, and her grandson was Archibald Johnston of Wariston, who became one of the most influential Covenanter leaders of the 1640s and 1650s. Elizabeth Melville, Lady Culross, was author of the highly regarded *Ane Godly Dreame* (1603); Janet Kene, the widow of Andrew Hart the printer, ran the press after his death in 1621; and Catherine Erskine, who sheltered the dissident John Livingston in the 1630s, was the daughter of Treasurer Mar and married to the eldest son of Secretary Melrose. It did not require the liturgical controversy that erupted after 1615 to create a Presbyterian underground; the continuity of personnel and ideas were there from the 1590s, beneath the surface of the king's easily bought public conformity.

There is no question that James VI ever sought to subject the Church of Scotland to Canterbury, but the king did see religion as a key to creating a more united British kingdom, and since 1603 he had come to admire the liturgy and order of the Anglican church. Attaining a degree of conformity in church government was an important step on the road to a British church; persuading people to worship according to similar rites was crucial to it. The appointment in 1615 of the energetic and ever obedient John Spottiswoode as archbishop of St Andrews allowed the king to press ahead with a revision of the liturgy. Even before the royal visit of 1617, the only one of the king's post-1603 reign, Spottiswoode ran into difficulties with the General Assembly, his own episcopal colleagues, and Privy Councillors who foresaw trouble ahead. The experience of Scottish Protestantism in the raw after such a protracted absence was a shock to the king. The exposure of many Scots to the king's Anglican chaplains and preferred forms of worship was even more worrying to austere native opinion, and at a bad-tempered General Assembly in 1618, the Five Articles of Perth were foisted on the church. The Articles made provision for private baptism and communion, confirmation by a bishop, and the observance of holy days, but the most provocative was that requiring kneeling at communion, a ceremony that to the Protestant godly reeked of Rome and was highly offensive to many who had been prepared to accept bishops. Avoidance of the Articles was widespread, especially as so many magistrates looked the other way, and conventi-cling increased markedly. The king's response was petulant, insisting on parliamentary ratification in 1621, a decision that almost cost him a raft of other important legislation, including a generous taxation. However, neither the Privy Council, nor the episcopate, was prepared to risk further public disorder by enforcement. The very existence of the Five Articles became the means by which the royal supremacy was undermined, since every person who refused to kneel for communion was also refusing to kneel before the king.

By the time of his death on 27 March 1625, James VI and I had been king of Scotland for fifty-eight years, ruling in his own right for forty-two of those years. Already, before 1603, his foreign and domestic policies had brought a greater measure of peace and stability to the country which the regal Union consolidated, allowing him further to patronize the nobility and to extend effective royal authority over peripheral regions of the kingdom. However, the deep-rooted problems of the crown's financial weakness, and of religious divisions, remained unresolved. Arguably, James had exacerbated these in the last decade of his reign, leaving his son with a legacy that would require skilled and sensitive handling. The shortcomings of the regal Union, which depended so much for its success on James VI and I's own experience of Scotland and on his personality, would now be exposed by a king who was entirely lacking in political skills or in sensitivity.

2. Charles I and Monarchical Hubris, 1625−37

In the summer of 1633, Charles I made a visit to Scotland to be crowned. While there he presided over a parliament that granted him everything he wanted, issued orders to an obedient Privy Council, commanded a church that did not question his authority, and basked in the loyal addresses of his Scottish people and the fawning obedience of his court. No Stewart king had ever appeared so powerful. Four years later, Scotland was in the throes of revolution and monarchical authority collapsed with astonishing speed. The illusion of royal power created by James VI and his son was exposed to the harsh realities of Scottish politics. As we have seen, real power was located in diverse sources, chiefly with the nobility, but also among the clergy, in burgh councils, and with clan chiefs, all of whom had been prepared to collude in the pretence of royal absolutism for as long as it served Scotland (or their own interests) well. Under Charles I, the problems already stoked up by his father were further inflamed. The result was revolution.

By 1625, many of the councillors who had served James VI so well were infirm and elderly. The Chancellor, Treasurer and Secretary were all men in their sixties, and it was unsurprising that Charles I wanted to appoint his own advisers. Unfortunately, Charles only listened to the advice of servants whose views echoed his own. A decade later, most of his father's councillors had died or retired; in their place were biddable men like the indebted and Catholic Earl of Nithsdale, career officials like Sir John Stewart of Traquair, and bishops who implemented royal directives, lacking entirely in political independence. Those nobles who tried to offer disinterested or critical counsel were ignored. Even more worrying was the treatment meted out to the second Lord Balmerino, condemned to death for treason in 1634 for having been found in possession of a petition complaining about practices that 'may seem against the constitution of a free parliament'. Yet when finally faced with crisis in the summer of 1637, many of Charles's councillors faded out of sight, barely daring to defend the king whose distant commands they had faithfully obeyed without question.

In his treatment of the nobility, Charles also provided a stark contrast with his father. The new king had his close noble friends, like James Hamilton, third Marquis of Hamilton, a man who shared his passion for fine painting, but he was determined to undermine the deep-rooted feudal power of the Scottish nobility. He signalled this intent almost immediately in 1625 with his revocation, a standard procedure by which kings repossessed lands alienated during their minority. Yet Charles was in his twenty-fifth year when he succeeded to the throne, and with only a few months of a technical minority to run he announced a plan to revoke all crown grants. Behind this scheme was a plan to refinance the church and the crown at the expense of the nobility, who were required to surrender former ecclesiastical lands prior to a re-granting, for a price, under revised conditions.

Already in 1617 the establishment of a Register of Sasines (covering land transactions and heritable bonds secured on it) indicated a greater desire on the part of crown officials, lawyers and landlords to have a better record of land ownership. But it was also intended to remodel landed society in such a way that the crown was the only feudal superior, breaking the link between the nobility and their tenants. Alongside this reform was a plan to purchase the heritable jurisdictions, putting local justice firmly in the hands of royal officials. James VI had started down this path with the creation of commissioners of the peace in 1609, deliberately modelled on English justices of the peace, and he persuaded a few sheriffs to resign their heritable offices. However, he ran into local obstruction, lacking the funds to finance a large-scale compensation package. Charles's plans backfired badly, creating panic throughout a landed community that feared massive land confiscations. The subsequent teind commission, which was established in 1627 to investigate the ownership of teinds, or tithes paid on former ecclesiastical estates, served only to alienate local communities subjected to unwanted royal inter-ference. The attempt to regain control of local jurisdictions was met with a sullen lack of cooperation, and was stymied by the absence of finance to buy out even those few nobles who offered to sell their rights. Charles's relations with the great majority of his nobles got off to a bad start with the revocation and simply got worse. No early modern king could afford to alienate so many nobles over such a fundamental issue as property rights, far less one ensconced in another kingdom.

Yet the crown did have financial problems that Charles had to address. He inherited a pensions bill of £159,000 per annum out of an annual ordinary income – that is, without taxation – of £250,000. The deficit in royal finances grew in spite of further taxes being granted in 1625, 1630 and 1633, and the pensions bill continued to soar as every effort to cut it risked the wrath of courtiers, royal officials and nobles who had become dependent on this additional income. By 1633, ordinary income stood at £238,000 per annum, while expenditure was running at £260,000 per annum, and the accumulated royal debt was £853,000. Yet more taxes levied on a public already resentful at a range of unpopular policies was politically dangerous. The burghs especially were bearing a heavy burden with no discernible benefits. The 1633 parliament doubled Edinburgh's tax, hitting hard a credit community that included half of its wealthiest 300 merchants, and lumbering the burgh with the cost of a new bishopric and a new Parliament House. By 1635–6 the city had to find £150,000 per annum to remain solvent, when before 1625 its expenditure had never exceeded a third of that sum in a year. Similarly, those nobles outside the charmed circle of courtiers, like Hamilton who earned a huge commission from acting as tax collector for the 1633 grant, grudged the incessant demands for more money. It was not so much a case of men not wanting to pay their taxes, for most had become accustomed to the idea of an annual tax, rather that they lacked confidence in a distant monarchy's understanding of how best to spend its resources.

Charles I also inherited a Scottish church that was in turmoil. Even his bishops were worried about the threat to their independence from England, as was publicly seen in Archbishop Spottiswoode's stubborn refusal to give precedence to the archbishop of Canterbury at the old king's funeral. The young monarch who replaced him did nothing to quell those fears, or heal the divisions. Less theologically literate than his father, if more pious, Charles I was determined to uphold royal authority in the church, and to push the Scots towards greater conformity with England. The new king wanted to advance his own religious preferences which were influenced greatly by William Laud, elevated to the archbishopric of Canterbury in 1633. Laud was an enthusiast for Arminian ideas, rejecting the Calvinist doctrine of predestination, and allowing the possibility of man responding by his free will to God's grace. The king also shared Laud's desire to impose order and decorum on worship, being attracted to the same theatrical devices that resulted in a ceremonial closely resembling that of Rome.

The impetus driving the Scots closer to a Church of England, itself in the process of being seized from the Calvinists by Laud and his friends, came from the court. Apart from a handful of clerics like John Maxwell, bishop of Ross, support within the Scottish church for an Arminian programme was lukewarm. In responding to the king's orders to compile a new liturgy the bishops were unenthusiastic, knowing it would never be acceptable to very many Scots, especially in the more solidly Presbyterian south of the country. Of course, at a local level the religious life of the parish was largely unaffected by these policies. On 4 January 1628, Clackmannan kirk session fined a husband and wife 13s. 4d and sentenced them to make a public repentance after they were found guilty of winnowing corn on the Sabbath. It is unlikely that this outcome would have been very different had there been no bishops in the church, and in one sense the life of the kirk carried on regardless of the arguments between the lay and clerical élites. Increasingly, however, those disputes were transmitted to the wider community.

The very close association between Charles I's religious policies and the rest of his political ambitions makes it impossible wholly to disentangle them. However, his resolution to enrich the church at the expense of lay landlords, and to enhance the role of bishops in royal and local government, awakened many nobles to the previously ignored warnings about the threat posed to their authority by a revived episcopate. The

Jeremiahs who had seen portents of tyranny in the appearance of bishops in the 1600s did not appear so hysterical by the 1630s as more and more of the episcopate appeared on the Privy Council. By 1634, eight of the fourteen bishops were Privy Councillors, Spottiswoode had been appointed Chancellor, the first cleric to hold the office since before the Reformation, and there were rumours that other powerful offices would fall to bishops who were also exercising authority in local offices. For the more Presbyterian-inclined clergy the issue of bishops was a doctrinal one, argued out over proof texts and church history, but for the middle-of-the-road laity it had become deeply political.

Like his father's visit to Scotland in 1617, that made by Charles I in 1633 proved to be a disaster in terms of public relations, especially over religious issues. The high liturgical tastes of king and courtiers were brought face-to-face with the more austere tastes of the Scots, made starkly apparent in the matter of clerical dress. While the Scots clergy had stuck with the resolution of the 1575 General Assembly that ministers and their wives must dress in clothes of 'grave colour', the king's chaplains attired themselves in more flamboyant surplices. Nevertheless, Charles pressed on zealously, a Book of Canons and a Prayer Book being produced by the Scottish bishops in close consultation with Laud. The resulting liturgical mishmash was provocative. Here was a form of worship that not only had all the hallmarks of the Church of England, a body many Scots thought had only ever been halfheartedly reformed – a view with which many English Puritans agreed – but that also appeared to be moving towards Rome. Protestantism was on the defensive everywhere in Europe owing to the military successes of the Holy Roman Emperor, Spain's renewed attacks on the Dutch and the weakened position of the French Huguenots. Furthermore, the king's French Catholic wife, Henrietta Maria, was gathering around her an increasingly influential body of Catholic courtiers. In these circumstances it was not difficult to imagine the worst. That this liturgy was to be imposed without debate, and without the sanction of the General Assembly, or of parliament, fuelled the resentment.

The debate within Protestantism about the relationship between church and crown should not be permitted to obscure the much greater agreement over other areas of religious belief. Protestant Scotland was remarkably consensual in its Calvinist theology. The Scots did not produce any significant theological thinking of their own – unsurprising perhaps amongst a clergy convinced it had a sure grasp of revealed truth – and by the seventeenth century a neo-scholastic sterility hung heavily over religious thought. At the heart of this faith was an awesome and righteous God whose more terrifying aspects served to underline mankind's utter depravity. At the same time, Christ's unconditional love, demonstrated in his bloody sacrifice on the Cross, brought forth in his undeserving people a profoundly emotional and charismatic outburst of unworthy anguish, heartfelt sorrow, uncontrollable joy and excitable worship in public and in private that is reflected in much of the literature of the period.

If most of this doctrine was little different from medieval Catholicism, Calvin's extreme emphasis on God's sovereign will and man's total lack of free choice created in predestination an intellectual and emotional problem for many Protestants that appeared to grow as the seventeenth century unfolded. If a man had been chosen by God as one of the elect, destined for eternal life, how was he to know? Without the assurance that his faith had saved him, the Scottish Protestant was doomed to a life of self-doubt, certain that everything was providential and that each man was called to fulfil a particular role in the course of his life, while knowing that he could do nothing to influence his own fate. No good works would suffice, no penitential confession would alter the course on which he was set. Instead, this sinful, worthless creature could only follow a spiritual life of religious devotions, obey God's commands, earnestly hoping that his predisposition to live in such a way was an outward sign that he was among the chosen.

Periodic evangelical revivals swept through the church, renewing the fresh start made in 1560 and energizing the faithful with a powerful sense of destiny. Thus at Stewarton in 1622, in one of the great open-air communion gatherings that was typical of evangelical Protestantism, Robert Blair preached to large crowds of people who were 'at first under great terrors and deep exercise of conscience, and thereafter attained to surest peace and strong consolation'. The signs of the times were eagerly pored over by a people convinced of God's immediate intervention in their affairs. When in 1608 an earthquake shook towns throughout Scotland, the inhabitants of Dumbarton rushed to the church in fear of God, while in Aberdeen the kirk session resolved that the event was evidence that 'God is angry against the land, and against the city in particular for the manifold sins of the people'. Apocalyptic ideas nurtured an excited expectation of Christ's imminent and triumphant return, feeding the idea of a people covenanted in a special and binding relationship with God.

3. *The Covenanting Revolution, 1637–51*

That spiritual covenant had profound practical consequences. The Covenanting revolution of the 1640s was a watershed in the history of the seventeenth century. A reigning king was defeated in what became known as the Bishops' War of 1639–40, was forced to make huge political concessions in 1641, was then defeated in two further wars between 1642 and 1648, and finally in 1649 was executed in public by order of a faction of the purged English parliament. While the Scots never approved of Charles I's death, it was they who had begun his downfall, and the Covenanters' ideas of armed resistance were widely disseminated throughout Britain. No Stewart king ever again sat comfortably on his throne knowing he was God's anointed. In other ways, too, the Covenanters turned the world upside down, establishing a form of government that sought to preserve the privileges of the nobility, but that was ultimately driven by revolutionary impetus to eject the great majority of the higher nobility from politics. English conquest in the 1650s weakened, however temporarily, the hold of the nobility over local society. Episcopalians and Presbyterians became irreconcilable enemies, while the latter also divided into warring factions, splitting the Church of Scotland so deeply that the rifts were never healed. The religious basis of political life had the effect of politicizing large numbers of ordinary people for the first time, while the clergy emerged more than ever before as leaders of local communities. The 1640s and 1650s altered Scotland in other ways. Any pretence of a regal Union of equal sovereign states disappeared when England conquered Scotland; thereafter the military and economic superiority of the former pulled further and further ahead. The kingdom's self-confidence collapsed as a consequence of English occupation, its economic and cultural energies were sapped and did not recover until the 1680s. The divergence between Highland and Lowland society became more pronounced than ever. The ways in which these changes affected later seventeenth-century Scotland are explored below, but it is important to emphasize here the searing shock that slowly impacted first on Scotland, and then on the rest of Britain as the conflict spread outwards from the Prayer Book protest in St Giles cathedral on 23 July 1637.

There was nothing spontaneous about that protest, which had behind it months of planning by nobles and clergy angered by a range of policies but focused now on the high-profile introduction of the king's provocative liturgical reforms. In August, David Dickson, minister of Irvine, presented the Privy Council with the first of what soon became a stream of supplications against the Prayer Book, and altogether sixty-nine similar protests had been made by the end of the following month, a large proportion being from Ayrshire and Fife. The purpose of the petitioning dissidents was to bring pressure on the government to back down, not to initiate revolution. For its part, the Edinburgh administration abandoned the capital and did nothing. In London, the king refused to take the petitioners seriously. By mid-November, a provisional government was in place, named the Tables after the five tables at which representative groups of nobles, barons, burgesses, ministers and an executive committee sat. In February, a National Covenant was signed by the political élite and distributed throughout the kingdom for wider subscription. This impressive document, compiled by Alexander Henderson, minister of Leuchars, and Archibald Johnston of Wariston, a gifted and evangelical young lawyer, underlined the Covenanters' hostility to any hint of Roman Catholicism. Further, it defended the 'true Religion', emphasized a commitment to government under the law, implied a profound distrust of Erastian episcopacy, and bound its signatories to the defence of God, king and commonweal on the clear understanding that the king's interests were subordinate to those of the law and the church. It declared in ringing terms, 'whatsoever shall be done to the least of us for that cause, shall be taken as done to us all in general, and to every one of us in particular'.

Only now did Charles I awaken to the possibility that what he faced in Scotland was more than a local difficulty created by a handful of unrepresentative activists. Subsequent efforts by Commissioner Hamilton to recover ground over the course of the year proved fruitless. He persuaded the king to sanction the first General Assembly since 1617, hoping to get it to agree to the legal introduction of liturgical reform, and in November 1638 it gathered in Glasgow. From the start, it was dominated by Presbyterian clergy and pro-Covenant nobles sitting as ruling elders, reviving a role they had enjoyed in the 1560s, and there was a marked preponderance of commissioners from south of the Tay–Clyde line. The six General Assemblies of 1606 to 1618 were condemned as 'unfree, unlawfull, and null', the royal supremacy, the bishops, the Courts of High Commission were swept away, and the Five Articles, the canons and the liturgy were judged to contain 'many popish errours and ceremonies, and the seeds of manifold and grave superstition and idolatrie'. Over the next two years the General Assembly and parliament dismantled James VI's carefully constructed church, breaking royal control over parliament. However, those political achievements were soundly based on military success.

Force and violence were at the heart of the Covenanting movement from the moment Jenny Geddes, an Edinburgh serving woman, allegedly initiated the riot, throwing whatever came to hand at the hapless dean of Edinburgh. It was the sheer weight of numbers, and the menacing behaviour of the armed men who flocked to Edinburgh, that persuaded the Privy Council to take flight in the summer of 1637. Similar riots elsewhere broke the nerve of Royalist councillors and magistrates. The Glasgow Assembly also met in an environment of simmering violence. The first military action took place in February 1639 when James Graham, fifth Earl of Montrose, overawed a stubbornly loyal Aberdeen, while the castles of Royalist nobles were forced to surrender. On 10 May, David Prat, a servant of the Royalist Sir George Gordon of Gight, was shot in the head by Covenanters defending a cache of arms. He was the first person to die in an escalating conflict that would in time consume thousands. Meanwhile, opponents in the kirk were removed from their charges, fifty-two ministers being dismissed in the year following the Glasgow Assembly and another twenty-six in 1640. The Covenanters, therefore, had no scruples in resorting to extra-legal actions in pursuit of justifiable ends, nor was there ever any question over fighting for principles and beliefs grounded in a heady mixture of Old Testament apocalypticism and Buchananite republicanism. To that end, the provisional government began seeking funds to buy arms on the continent at an early stage in its disagreement with the king, while shire committees of war were established to organize local recruitment and defence. Scots mercenaries were enticed home to form the core of what quickly became a remarkably professional force constructed on the model of the devastatingly successful Swedish army that had carved its way into central Europe in the early 1630s.

This determination to defend their cause was matched by the king's ruthlessness. Charles I might have been slow to react, but once he realized the seriousness of the threat to his authority, he was prepared to use the military power of England and Ireland to crush the Covenanters. Unfortunately for the king, his efforts to mobilize armies in these kingdoms, allied to effective Scottish propaganda, served only to destabilize them. Nor did he achieve anything in Scotland in the Bishops' War of 1639–40. On 28 August 1640 his ill-equipped and poorly led English army was defeated by the Scots at Newburn, and within days the Covenanters had overrun the north of England, occupying Newcastle. Charles was forced to concede all the Covenanters' demands, recognizing a Presbyterian kirk, and agreeing to the reforms carried out by parliament in the sessions of 1639 and 1640, like the Triennial Act which required parliament to sit at least once every three years. These reforms stripped the king of most of his authority, abolishing the Lords of the Articles by which the crown controlled debate and procedure within parliament, removing bishops and officers of state from it, and creating a committee system that placed power in the hands of the commissioners and their factional leaders among the higher nobility. The voting power of the barons, or lairds, was doubled, strengthening the landed vote. Parliament also took a direct role in government through the important interval committees that sat between sessions.

When Charles came to Scotland in the autumn of 1641 he found himself signing away much of his prerogative power, and while government reverted to that of the Privy Council, even its membership was now scrutinized by parliament. The clearest theoretical statement of the new relationship between king and parliament was expounded by Samuel Rutherford, whose *Lex Rex, or the Law and the Prince*, published in 1644, attacked royal absolutism in a similar vein to George Buchanan's sixty years earlier, limiting royal authority to a contractual agreement between king and people. Rutherford proved to be the Covenanters' greatest spiritual leader. Posterity best remembers his remarkable letters, first published in Rotterdam in 1664 under the title *Joshua Redivivus*, but he also wrote on church government, condemning Erastianism (the subjection of the church to the state), and freedom of conscience, and he debated the implications of predestination, attacking the Antinomian idea that man had no moral responsibility in a world determined solely by God's will.

The security of the Covenanters' gains depended on neutralizing the king's power elsewhere in Britain. Rebellion in Ireland in the autumn of 1641 led to Scottish troops being stationed there to protect the Protestant population of Ulster, and when civil war between king and parliament broke out in England in the summer of 1642 both sides were soon lobbying for Scottish support. Fear of what a victorious Charles might do to the Covenanters, and the tantalizing offer by the English to allow the Scots a hand in reshaping the Church of England 'according to the Word of God, and the example of the best Reformed Churches', proved persuasive. The Covenanters also wanted a stronger union between Scotland and England, one that would ensure the king could not keep them out of decision-making on key foreign and economic policies while also making it impossible to wage war on Scotland again, and one glued together by Presbyterianism. The final agreement, the Solemn League and Covenant of 1643–4, essentially exchanged Scottish military power in return for suggesting the Scots might have an important influence in shaping the post-war political and religious settlement.

In January 1644, the confident 20,000-strong Army of the Covenant marched into England. Although Alexander Leslie, Earl of Leven, conducted successful operations throughout the north of England, and led the Scots to playing a decisive role in the battle of Marston Moor on 2 July 1644, the Covenanters failed to deliver the expected knock-out blow. Instead they were embarrassed by the now Marquis of Montrose's campaign in the Scottish Highlands. The core of his army was an expeditionary force of Irish Catholics under the command of Alasdair MacColla, whose aim was to destroy Argyll and Clan Campbell. In a series of six stunning victories at Tippermuir, Aberdeen, Inverlochy, Auldearn, Alford and Kilsyth between September 1644 and August 1645, Montrose destroyed any notion of the Covenanters enjoying a God-given immunity to defeat. The bloody sacking of Aberdeen on 13 September 1644 (a major factor in the fall of the town's population in that decade from 9,000 to 6,000), the savage harrying of Argyll, and the dreadful slaughter of fleeing Covenanters at Kilsyth, all brought the war home with a sickening impact. Plague, food shortages, the heavy taxation required to maintain a previously unimagined level of military preparedness, and the prosecution of large numbers of witches, all contributed to a growing unease and discontent with a nervous and ever less tolerant government.

Montrose briefly threatened to bring the entire Covenanting edifice crashing down, but instead of consolidating in Scotland, he chose to go to the rescue of a king whose main field army had been torn apart by the New Model Army at the battle of Naseby on 14 June 1645. MacColla's Irish and Highland troops refused to follow Montrose, who was caught off guard by David Leslie's Covenanting army at Philiphaugh, near Selkirk, on 14 September. The apparently invincible marquis barely escaped with his life, while many of his followers were butchered in cold blood, along with their women and children. Covenanting Scotland was rescued at Philiphaugh, but the Covenanters were now the junior partners in their alliance with the English parliament. Charles hung on until May 1646 before surrendering to the Scots at Newark, believing he would get a better deal from the weaker of his enemies.

Charles I might have been defeated, but he did not believe he had been beaten, and furthermore he was still king. He arrogantly brushed aside a series of proposals for a lasting settlement placed before him by the Scots and English parliaments, and by January 1647 the Scots had had enough; they handed the stubborn king over to the English in return for the payment of the arrears due to their army, which finally returned home. However, within Scotland the nobility reacted against the revolution. Before the end of the year, moderate Covenanters, led by Hamilton, had negotiated a deal with the king that promised to restore him to his thrones on condition he imposed Presbyterianism on the Church of England for three trial years. Hamilton sold this deal, known as the Engagement, to the Scottish parliament by emphasizing the threat to the Covenants from the English sectarians. Too many nobles had become worried by the spectre of the fall of the monarchy, and by the stirrings of social change. Already within parliamentary committees, shire committees of war, and presbyteries there was evidence of lesser lairds and clerics presuming to take upon themselves the governing role formerly the preserve of the higher nobility. Yet in supporting the Engagement, the 'Engager' nobility triggered the very nemesis they had imagined. The refusal of Argyll, most of the army and the General Assembly to recognize parliament's decision prompted civil unrest, losing Hamilton valuable weeks in putting down dissent in the south-west. Hamilton's army was dismembered by Oliver Cromwell at Preston on 17–19 August 1648, and Hamilton was executed a few months later on the grounds that as an English peer (he was also Earl of Cambridge) he had committed treason.

The failure of the Engagement settled Charles I's fate. In Scotland, power was seized back by more radical Covenanters from the south-west, known among their enemies as Whigs, who marched on Edinburgh and conducted a *coup* known as the Whiggamore Raid. Cromwell's arrival in Edinburgh secured the stability of a new regime that had his approval, but was dangerously short of support among the higher nobility. A complete purge of political and civic offices followed, leaving most peers disenfranchised, a situation legitimized in the Act of Classes of 23 January 1649. Scottish government was now in the hands of a socially inferior group of lairds, merchants and parish ministers, along with a few radical nobles like Argyll. Meanwhile, in England a similar purge of Parliament removed any who remained remotely sympathetic to the king, most of these being Presbyterians. The Rump Parliament, dominated by Cromwell and fearful of the army, put Charles on trial for his life, and on 30 January 1649 a reigning Scottish king was beheaded by a faction of English sectarians.

The reaction of all Scots to the king's death, regardless of political allegiance, was, in hindsight, predictable, but at the time the leaders of the new English republic were surprised. As far as the English parliament was concerned, the Union with Scotland ended with the death of the king, since it had been based solely on a dynastic accident. However, in spite of their conflict with Charles I, the Scots remained wedded to the idea of monarchy, loyal to the Stewart family, and committed to Covenants with God that could not be overturned by the unilateral behaviour of one party and which underlined the need to maintain the regal Union. On 5 February 1649, the Covenanting government proclaimed Charles II king of Scotland, England, France and Ireland, throwing down a gauntlet that the unsteady regime in England could not ignore. Yet the young exiled king had no desire to deliver himself into the hands of those very Covenanters he blamed for destroying his father. Nor had he much faith in Montrose, who launched an ill-prepared and poorly executed expedition from Orkney, only to be defeated at Carbisdale in Sutherland on 27 April. This time Montrose did not escape and was executed in Edinburgh, being hung, beheaded and his limbs cut off to the delight of the Presbyterian crowd. Charles disowned Montrose even before his death in order to curry favour with the Scots, but still he wavered, believing the Irish were more palatable allies. Unfortunately, Cromwell invaded Ireland in August 1649, and over the next ten months subjected that kingdom to a campaign of unbridled ferocity that destroyed all vestiges of resistance. With nowhere else to go, the king landed in Scotland in June 1650, submitting to the hated Covenants and placing himself in the hands of men he despised.

The pious self-confidence of the Covenanter government had recovered from the blows delivered by Montrose in 1645–6, and had been encouraged by the defeat of the Engagers and the death of Montrose. Charles II now came to Scotland and signed the Covenants, although his scarcely disguised contempt for the Scots caused some soul-searching among the Presbyterian clergy as to the authenticity of the king's commitment and their own tolerance of his cynicism. However, it appeared that God was again blessing his chosen people in a land where the kirk's authority had never been greater, and the Presbyterian gospel was proclaimed without challenge. The business of purification continued, with 105 ministers being deposed in 1648–51. It remained only to put Charles II back on his English throne, and to reform the Church of England. These objectives persuaded Cromwell, fresh from his victory in Ireland, to make a pre-emptive strike. His campaign in the summer of 1650 foundered in the face of the clever and patient generalship of the Covenanters' commander, David Leslie. With its line of communications cut off, its supplies running short and morale low, the English faced defeat, but on 3 September Leslie was provoked into an unnecessary attack outside Dunbar by the over-confident and meddling clergy. The Scottish defeat was overwhelming, leaving Cromwell, now master of Edinburgh and the south-east of the country, to declare that 'God made them as stubble to our swords'.

Charles II was not entirely despondent. The defeat split the Covenanters into the extreme 'Remonstrants', based in the south-west, who renounced the unholy alliance with the king, and the mainstream 'Resolutioners', who decided to go on cooperating with Charles II and his supporters. Scotland was falling apart, yet few were prepared to join publicly in agreeing with the late Royalist poet, William Drummond of Hawthornden, who had argued in his tract on toleration that 'Religione can not be preached by Armes'. On 1 January 1651, Argyll crowned Charles II king of Great Britain, but the ceremony at Scone was a hollow one, its invented ritual failing to conceal the deep divisions among the factions now rallied around the king. The reality was that the kingdom was broken and exhausted. In desperation, the king led his Scottish army on yet another invasion of England, gambling on gathering Royalist support, but the English had no enthusiasm for this latest pestilence from the north. The remnant of the government in Scotland was captured at Alyth on 28 August, and Dundee was sacked on 1 September. Two days later, on the anniversary of Dunbar, Cromwell destroyed the Scottish army in the narrow streets of Worcester. Charles II escaped to continental exile, but many of the Scottish political leadership was rounded up, and before the end of the year the greater part of the country had been occupied by English troops. It is one of the enduring popular myths of Scottish history that the country has never been conquered in its entirety. That is untrue. While some spirited resistance continued in the Highlands until 1653, Scotland was by 1651 a conquered nation.

4. Conquest, 1651–60

For a people schooled to think of themselves as a new Israel, the experience of conquest was bitter, although its prophets found ready-to-hand biblical explanations in both the pride that had characterized the previous decade, and in the failure to take the 'Second Reformation' of the Covenanters far enough. Everywhere there was evidence of defeat. English soldiers were garrisoned throughout the kingdom, building new and formidable military bases on key sites at Ayr, Leith, Perth and Inverlochy. English administrators took over governing at national and local level, and the private, hereditary courts of the nobility were abolished. On the island of Arran, territory of the Hamilton family, Brodick Castle surrendered in April 1652 and a garrison was established that was to leave its alien presence on folk memory at places like Creag an Stobaidh, the stabbing rock, where an English soldier was killed. Only the church remained immune to English personnel, since Cromwell regarded the Scots as merely mistaken brethren. Nevertheless, the kirk was forced to accept the toleration of independent Protestant congregations such as Quakers and Baptists. The country was exhausted: thousands had been killed in the war, its merchant shipping had been sunk, the economy of its towns disrupted, entire localities devastated, previously wealthy merchants ruined, and the nobility exiled or weighed down by debts owing to war creditors, and now by punitive financial penalties imposed by the English. Scotland's will had also been sapped, as is evident in the absence of any resistance in the winter of 1654–5, when General George Monck mopped up the last Royalists. Too weak and divided to fight for an absent king, and encouraged by the church to endure God's divine punishment, there remained only patience and prayers for deliverance.

The nature of the English occupation eased the burden of defeat. There was never any doubt that the government rested on its military force, but it was recognized by London that the Scots could not be squeezed enough to pay for the garrison, and that in order to avoid recurrent heavy subsidies the military presence would have to be run down. Therefore, especially from 1655, Lord Broghill, the president of the ruling Council of State in Scotland, set about creating a more civilian government with a strong Scottish presence. The framework for this was Cromwell's 1651 declaration announcing his desire to include Scotland within the English Commonwealth. Discussions did take place, involving picked Scots acceptable to London, and on 12 April 1654 an Ordinance of the Protectorate government indicated a willingness 'to invite the people of that nation unto such a happy Union'. It was a union entirely on English terms, but the Scots were never treated like the Irish, who were subjected to another wave of massive land confiscations and colonization in the 1650s. Instead the model appeared to be Wales, which had been integrated into England in 1534. The Scots were offered seats in the Westminster parliament, both Argyll and Wariston being chosen, and were encouraged to participate in the administration of their own country. In the context of the seventeenth century, this was as benign a conquest as anyone could expect. Modest signs of economic recovery were also encouraging.

What ended the occupation and the republican union was not Scottish resistance, but English instability. Cromwell's death in 1658 exposed the extent to which the entire republican experiment was dependent on his forceful personality. The monarchical style of the Protectorate that had governed Britain since 1653 collapsed owing to the inadequacies of his son, Richard Cromwell, while feuding among the parliamentary generals brought England to the brink of anarchy. It was Monck who intervened from Scotland, marching his army on London where he imposed order, recalled the purged members of the English Long Parliament, and came to the conclusion that only the restoration of the king would provide stability. He left behind a small garrison in Scotland where everywhere nobles and clergy began to resume their leadership of the community, and a faction of Covenanter nobles even took over the government. Yet the initiative lay with London. The Scots waited and watched, and only when the English parliament had decided to recall the king did they act. Always loyal to the Stewart dynasty, there was never any question that the Scots would not follow in the English slipstream, restoring a monarchy the legitimacy of which had never been in doubt. As for Charles II, he was determined never again to set foot in his Scottish kingdom. Scotland would be peripheral to his interests, a provincial backwater peopled by a nation he wished to forget.

Constitutional Struggles, 1660–1707

1. Restoration, 1660–88

In 1660, no one knew what ideas Charles II would bring back with him from exile in Breda. For the most diehard Covenanters fear was uttermost. Wariston fled to Holland, only to be kidnapped three years later and brought home for execution, an utterly broken man. In the event there was no bloodbath, and only James Guthrie, the extremist Protestor minister, and an unfortunate Argyll, preceded Wariston to the gallows. Charles II, wanting the warring to end, bit back his desire for vengeance, and demanded that his Royalist supporters do likewise. But in the newly-summoned parliament of 1661, the nobles were determined to put the Covenanting genie back in the bottle. Never again must they be subjected to the humiliations and losses of the previous two decades: the nobility would place its trust in a strong king, a hierarchic but obedient church, and their own entrenched privileges. In the astonishing Act Rescissory, every piece of legislation passed by the Covenanting parliaments between 1639 and 1651 was annulled. The king's prerogatives were fully restored, and he was granted control over a small standing army that swelled to 2,946 men by 1688. Along with a generous taxation, Charles II became more powerful than his father had ever been. Finally, and to the great surprise of a king who would have been satisfied with a moderate Presbyterian church, parliament restored the bishops in 1662, placing the church firmly under the authority of the crown. As for the nobles, they resumed their control over local society, reactivating their private courts, scrambling to fill every available office, while setting about restoring their lost fortunes. In a symbolic ritual that underlined the rejection of the previous two decades, the head, limbs and body of the executed Marquis of Montrose were reassembled and buried with great pomp. The reactionary tone of the next quarter of a century was set by the 1661 parliament in Edinburgh, not by the king in London.

For the Presbyterian clergy and their loyal congregations, the ecclesiastical settlement came as a stunning shock, especially as it was mediated by one of their own kind: James Sharp, the nimble-minded minister of Crail, who returned from court as archbishop of St Andrews. Sharp took the view that it was better for men like him, with strong Covenanting pedigrees, to lead a church that the secular authorities had decided would be Episcopalian, than for others less sympathetic to fill the bishoprics. However, his action was viewed as a betrayal, and he quickly fell into the role of ecclesiastical policeman, harrying and persecuting old friends. The majority of ministers did conform, having careers to nurse and families to feed, or simply being tired of the whole business and wanting to get on with their pastoral vocation. In the north-east there was even enthusiasm for the return of the bishops. But in the south of the country, especially in the Protestor strongholds, hundreds of ministers spurned the bishops and the royal supremacy, leading their flocks off to be ministered to in field conventicles. Thus on 13 October 1662 John Livingston, minister at Ancram, preached to his congregation, telling them that while the king had civil authority over them, this was a 'limited power' not pertaining to the ecclesiastical sphere.

The old arguments had not gone away, and the crown reacted with persecution, passing legislation like the 1662 Act Anent Covenants and Conventicles, which betrayed the government's fears that recent experience had encouraged ordinary people to think they could band together against the crown. In all, 274 ministers were thrown out of their places between 1660 and 1688, the heaviest concentration of these being in Galloway, Dumfries, Ayrshire and shires around Glasgow, while one in five of all parish ministers was cited to appear before the Privy Council during that period. In the presbyteries of Ayr and Irvine, thirty of the fifty-seven ministers left their churches immediately in 1662, but their congregations continued to follow and support radical leaders like William Guthrie, Alexander Peden and John Walsh for as long as they ministered to them. Conventicling was widely spread, the most intense areas of activity being Fife and Lothian, and persecution extended to those lay people who supported their ousted ministers, some 1,901 being cited before the Privy Council between 1666 and 1685. The largest share of these came from Fife, with a quarter of the total. However, their geographic origin shifted over time so that in the early 1670s Perthshire was heavily targeted, while later in the decade the emphasis switched to Glasgow and Ayrshire. Fines and imprisonment were widely deployed, but with little effect. The Indulgences of 1669, 1672 and 1678, when the crown tried to adopt a more conciliatory policy, secured qualified submissions and therefore returned to the fold 43, 91 and 15 ministers respectively. The Restoration monarchy and church never quite recovered from this blow to their authority, swinging from policies of repression to conciliation in an effort to dragoon or persuade people to conform.

Charles II was indifferent to those religious issues that caused such anguish to the Covenanters, being interested only in outward obedience. Arguably he was content to allow some degree of dissent, tolerated by royal prerogative, as it prevented the bishops from assuming too much power. By contrast, even the celebration of public holidays such as Christmas angered many Covenanters like Walter Pringle of Greenknow, who recorded dismay and disgust in his diary on 25 December 1663, asking, 'Where will this backsliding stop?' However, the Privy Council did not interfere with the kirk's control over local discipline, and there was no attempt to meddle with the liturgy, as had occurred in the 1620s and 1630s. Unfortunately, the Edinburgh administration under the Earl of Middleton, goaded by archbishop Alexander Burnet of Glasgow, was determined to use the army to exert pressure on dissidents in the south-west. A subsequent inquiry by the government found the local military commander, Sir James Turner (puzzlingly nicknamed 'Bite-the-sheep' by locals), guilty of imposing illegal exactions on the people of the region. The outcome was predictable. Against the backdrop of the unpopular second Anglo-Dutch war of 1666—7 which caused a trade recession, there was a local uprising in the name of the Covenants. The government was at its most jittery, sensitive to the unpopularity of the levying of 500 troops for an essentially English war, but unlike 1637, no nobleman joined the ranks of several hundreds of tenant farmers and bonnet lairds who marched over the Pentland Hills towards Edinburgh in the hope of forcing concessions. They were contemptuously scattered by Sir Thomas Dalyell's dragoons at Rullion Green on 28 November. In the aftermath, executions, deportations and fines intensified the level of persecution. John Ross, a Mauchline man, had his severed head exposed at Kilmarnock and his right arm at Lanark, and Ralph Shield, an Ayr clothier, was hanged at Edinburgh. However, when eight more Ayrshire men were returned to Ayr itself for execution, the public hangman disappeared and his Irvine counterpart refused to do the job. In the end, Cornelius Anderson, one of the condemned men, saved his own life by carrying out the executions, fortifying himself with a large quantity of alcohol, and reputedly dying shortly afterwards of depression. Once again, God appeared to have deserted the Covenanters.

Those nobles Charles II charged with the government of Scotland contained a blend of Royalists and Covenanters, few of whom had a consistent record of support for either side during the wars. They included a good number of factious drunkards, crooks and thugs for whom the spoils of office meant everything. Middleton, who was the architect of the Restoration settlement in Scotland as Commissioner to parliament, was abandoned by the king in 1663 after attempting to remove from office the more politically adroit Secretary of State, John Maitland, second Earl of Lauderdale. The latter was an ex-Covenanter and an Engager who had spent almost a decade in the Tower of London. He was also by conviction a Presbyterian, although he was prepared to sacrifice those beliefs. He was by far the most skilled politician of the age, with an enormous intellect and an equally enormous appetite for high living and coarse humour. After the 1666 Pentland Rising, which left his greatest rivals, the young seventh Earl of Rothes and Archbishop Sharp, in semi-disgrace, Lauderdale ran Scotland from London. He reined in the military, placing the emphasis instead on a locally led militia, and curbed the ambitions of the bishops, having the hawkish Alexander Burnet, archbishop of Glasgow, sacked, while offering Indulgences to the deprived ministers in 1669 and again in 1672.

This policy met with limited success, but could never win over the most intractable of the Covenanters, who continued to be subjected to heavy fines, imprisonment and occasional executions. General Dalyell had learned his trade in the Russian army, and had few qualms about the effectiveness of terror on a civilian population. The arbitrary nature of much of this policing was unpopular with many Lowland landlords who found a spokesman in parliament in the person of the third Duke of Hamilton. Increasingly in Edinburgh and in London, the now Duke of Lauderdale was portrayed as despotic, and the quartering of the Highland Host for a few weeks in the south-west in 1678 appeared to confirm this image. Dalmellington had 900 men quartered on it, while Kilmarnock reported damages of £2,800, and there were numerous tales of stealing, assault, torture and rape. The crown's persistent persecution brought about an understandable backlash when on 3 May 1679 a party of the most militant Covenanters assassinated Archbishop Sharp outside St Andrews. That stunning blow against their oppressors inspired a widespread rebellion in which the crown's principal military enforcer, John Graham of Claverhouse, was defeated in an engagement with a large, armed conventicle at Drumclog on 1 June. Glasgow was soon occupied by the rebels, but again there was no support from the nobles. The rebellion lasted for seven weeks before the king's son, the illegitimate Duke of Monmouth, defeated them at Bothwell Bridge on 22 June 1679. Monmouth staged a limited purge in the weeks that followed, even offering a third Indulgence. Meanwhile, Lauderdale's failure to keep the peace made his subsequent retirement inevitable.

In Scotland, dissent did not disappear after Bothwell Bridge. The Queensferry Paper of 1680 intimated a determination on the part of radical Covenanters to overthrow 'the kingdom of darkness', meaning kings and their bishops, arguing against monarchy since this form of government was the most likely 'to degenerate into tyranny as sad and long experience has taught us'. The Sanquhar Declaration of 22 June disowned Charles II, and Richard Cameron urged his followers (known to history as the Cameronians) to fight back, initiating a nasty guerrilla war that culminated in his own death in a skirmish at Airds Moss on 22 July 1680. His military commander, David Hackston of Rathillet, was wounded and taken prisoner to Edinburgh where he was subjected to the newly-imported English method of disposing of traitors, being hanged, disembowelled while still living, beheaded and quartered. One by one the more militant Covenanting leaders were being hunted down and killed, or they were fleeing into exile.

The crushing of two rebellions in thirteen years generated a new spirit of self-confidence in the crown, a self-confidence bolstered by James, Duke of York's presence in the kingdom for most of 1679–82. The duke was an exile in Scotland while the interminable Exclusion Crisis, which came out of a desire to prevent a Roman Catholic from succeeding to the throne, raged in England. On Christmas Day 1680, the students of Edinburgh University burned an effigy of the pope, deliberately bating the Catholic duke, but on the whole the political élite rallied behind him. James's utter hatred of rebels, his contempt for Presbyterians, and his military instincts, resulted in a harsh crack-down on all forms of dissent. The 1681 Test Oath flushed out any office-holders who had doubts about a Catholic succession and the royal supremacy. The eighth Earl of Argyll and James Dalrymple of Stair, Lord President of the Court of Session, were convicted of treason and driven into exile, making them its most prominent victims. Heavy fines were imposed on dissenters, especially in the south-west, while Claver-house's dragoons were unleashed on the Covenanting underground. Twenty-nine inhabitants of Dumfries were rounded up and incarcerated in the 'Whig vault' of Dunnottar Castle near Stonehaven, and by October 1684 there were 160 men and women imprisoned in Glasgow in appalling conditions.

Not content with executions, the Privy Council introduced 'a new inventione and ingyne called the thumbekins', or thumbscrews, to complement the work of the already highly effective 'boot' that shattered a person's legs so that he or she could never walk again. At Wigton, Margaret MacLachlan and Margaret Wilson, aged sixty-five and eighteen respectively, are reputed to have been tied to stakes and drowned by the incoming tide for refusing to renounce their adherence to the ideas of the Sanquhar Declaration. The most conservative estimates suggest around 100 victims of the 'Killing Times'. These people, ordinary men and women, were martyrs for their faith and their political ideas, and were hanged, shot and drowned for refusing to acknowledge Charles Stewart before Christ Jesus. In spite of the reign of terror, protests continued to be made. In February 1682, there was a riot in Prestonpans church and the minister who had been sent to replace the deposed Covenanter cleric was hauled out of his pulpit by the outraged congregation. But this was a war the king's forces could not lose, and even before James was recalled to court in 1682, he had cowed his enemies, his own men were in place in government, and with the economy at last showing signs of growth and cultural activities rejuvenated, the House of Stewart looked unshakeable.

Yet within three years of Charles II's untimely death at the age of fifty-four on 6 February 1685, following a stroke, his brother had been driven from the throne. The fault lay entirely with James VII, a fool and a bully who deserved his fate. It was a measure of Protestant Scotland's sense of its own durability that the succession of the first Catholic monarch since Mary aroused so little protest, other than from the Cameronian remnant who declared in the Sanquhar Protestation of 28 May that the new king was a murderer and idolater. The preamble of the Excise Act, passed by a grateful parliament that year, equated the peace and prosperity of the kingdom with 'the solid, absolute authority' of the monarchy. A rebellion led by the exiled and already condemned Earl of Argyll in May–June of 1685 achieved nothing but his own execution along with seventeen heritors, a Major Campbell first having his arms cut off, and the transportation to Jamaica of another 150 followers. In the south, Monmouth's rebellion had the same result; total defeat at the bloody battle of Sedgemoor on 6 July 1685 and his own botched beheading. These military victories, and the king's strong financial position, merely encouraged James to act in an ever more arbitrary manner.

James misread support for the monarchy as personal support, believing his own absolutist propaganda, and in 1687 he deployed the royal prerogative to introduce Catholic toleration in a country where their small numbers (a mere 2 per cent of the population) was more than made up by the hatred levelled at them. The king's actions were rightly seen as an attempt to help the cause of his co-religionists rather than as deriving from any sense of genuine religious tolerance of diverse opinions. Scotland's scattered Catholic communities were largely to be found in the western Highlands (where small Franciscan and Dominican missions were active), in Upper Deeside, and in isolated noble houses. In Edinburgh there were few Catholic families (variously estimated between 100 and 500), yet it was here, in Holyrood Palace, that a Roman Catholic chapel, a Jesuit college and a printing press were established, providing the Protestant mob with a ready focus for its fury. Meanwhile, both genuine and opportunist Catholic converts, like the fraternal Earls of Perth and Melfort, were placed in key government offices. Elsewhere in James's realms, the filling of the Irish army with Catholic officers pointed to the king's more sinister intentions. In the short term, toleration appeared to benefit the Catholic community, but the royal policy backfired badly. Of more lasting benefit to Scottish Catholics was the appointment in 1694 of Thomas Nicholson as vicar-apostolic for the whole of Scotland and the fact that by 1707 there were thirty priests active in the country.

Such an emotive mixture of arbitrary government and Roman Catholicism could not fail to arouse widespread anger and fear among all Protestants. How far James could have gone in Scotland (or England) is impossible to know, but relations with parliament broke down over the toleration issue in 1686, and there were popular riots against Catholics in Edinburgh and elsewhere. However, the king pressed ahead with the 1687 Indulgence which undermined earlier successes against the Covenanters by introducing limited toleration of all religious dissidents. Ministers were permitted to hold irregular meetings outside their churches on condition these were publicly intimated. Some forty-eight clergy exploited this extraordinary concession while the bishops could only look on in exasperated disbelief. James's policies had even greater impact in England, and the birth of a male heir on 10 June 1688 signalled that his policies might outlive him. Meanwhile, the king's son-in-law, William of Orange, was deeply worried about English foreign policy, which was moving dangerously close to friendship with Louis XIV of France, who in 1685 had initiated widespread persecution of French Protestants. Assured of support in England, William invaded in November, James panicked, the Dutch army marched on London, and the Glorious Revolution handed the English throne to his daughter, Mary, and her Dutch husband.

2. Revolution and the Reign of William II, 1689–1702

As in 1660, Scotland followed the English lead, and once again the Scots were more extreme in their reaction. Support for James collapsed, but not as completely as in England, there being substantial sympathy for the king among Episcopalians, especially in the north-east and in the central Highlands. However, James's uncompromising attitude made the position of most of his Protestant supporters untenable. The Convention Parliament, packed with men like Sir Patrick Hume of Polwarth, who was still under sentence of treason, and Thomas Stewart of Coltrees, a former exile, met in the spring of 1689. The elections were manipulated by supporters of William of Orange and by Presbyterians, but popular involvement was probably greater than in any other election in the history of the Scottish parliament, with over 300 men voting in the Aberdeen burgh contest. The Convention forfeited the king, who was accused of trying to alter a legal, limited monarchy to 'an Absolute and despotic Power'. The crown was offered to William and Mary on condition they accept the Claim of Right and Articles of Grievance, the former of these documents requiring that in future 'the king at his access to the Government, is obliged to swear, to sustain the Protestant religion, and to rule the people according to the laudable laws'. The Jacobite faithful, essentially a motley collection of indebted and desperate clans fearful of the House of Argyll's restoration, and led by Viscount Dundee (Claverhouse) who remained loyal to the king, won a minor engagement at Killiecrankie on 27 July 1689. Unfortunately for the Jacobites, Dundee's death in the battle stalled the campaign. Before the engagement he allegedly addressed his troops with a stirring harangue, telling them they were fighting in 'the best of causes' for king, religion and country against 'the foulest usurpation and rebellion'. Whether this speech was ever made or not is unknown, but its refrain became part of the Jacobite myth. In reality, Dundee was defending a brutal, arbitrary tyranny and he deserved his fate. Subsequent defeats at Dunkeld on 21 August and Cromdale on 1 May 1690 bottled the Jacobites up inside their glens, allowing William to get on with the real business of defeating James at the battle of the Boyne in Ireland two months later.

Military priorities elsewhere in Britain and in Flanders made it impossible to finish off Jacobite resistance in the Highlands. Instead, the government was persuaded to accept an oath of loyalty from the clan chiefs, who sought and received James's permission to make their peace. The unnecessary tardiness of MacIan of Glencoe in making his submission allowed John Dalrymple of Stair, the Secretary of State and formerly one of James VII's ministers, to make a bloody example of his clan. Captain Robert Campbell of Glenlyon was ordered 'to put all to the sword under 70 . . . to have a speciall care that the old fox and his ones do not escape your hands'. The massacre of Glencoe on 13 February 1692 cost the lives of MacIan and thirty-seven of his clan. It proved to be the last engagement in this phase of the war for the British succession, a savage episode in successful state terror that kept the Jacobite clans cowed for a quarter of a century. It also marked the revival of Campbell power in the Highlands, provoking one MacLean poet to lament that now the Earl of Argyll can 'sink his hook into our nose'. A handful of Jacobites held out on the Bass Rock until April 1694, when they were finally starved into surrender.

While few were prepared to fight for James VII in 1689, many were uncomfortable with his removal. These people were spread across a spectrum from outright Jacobites, determined to restore James and his son to the throne, to Scottish Tories whose first loyalty was to the Episcopal church. It was the latter that was the more important constituency, particularly after the Presbyterian religious settlement of 1690 forced many Episcopalians to conclude that only James's restoration would enable them to regain the upper hand in the church. William II was a Dutch Calvinist, but he was also a reigning monarch who saw advantages in maintaining a degree of royal authority over the church, and some degree of conformity between Scotland and England. A moderate form of Episcopacy was his preferred option. However, the Episcopal church's close association with the repressive policies of the Restoration monarchy, and more recently with the Catholic James VII, left its supporters with little room to manoeuvre. Instead, the king's ministers were left to struggle with an assertive and uncontrollable parliament in which the Revolution Whigs, chiefly Presbyterians, had the upper hand. The bishops and the royal supremacy were condemned by the Convention Parliament, and thereafter it proved impossible for crown ministers to prevent the slide towards Presbyterianism. In accepting a political and religious settlement that weakened crown authority, William indicated that his priorities lay elsewhere, in the ongoing European war to prevent Louis XIV gaining ascendancy in Europe.

1. Examples of fifth- and sixth-century BC harpoon heads, carved from antler and bone, found in Macarthur Cave, Oban. Scotland's early inhabitants were highly skilled in their use of natural resources and learned how best to exploit the properties of individual substances for maximum gain.

2. Grave goods from Culduthel, near Inverness, 2300–1800 BC, including a generous supply of arrow-heads. A dead person of this period was buried with tools and treasures it was hoped would equip them for all eventualities in the after-life.

Tools for Survival

3. (*below*) Eighteenth- and nineteenth-century spoons made from cattle horn. Few possessions were more precious to a poor Highlander or Islander than their own spoon, sometimes carved with their initials. Moulding spoons from horn was an acquired skill that provided a livelihood for tinkers, who circulated their wares to those who had no access to mass-manufactured goods.

4. A pannier (*rivva kishie*) woven from rushes, dating from the eighteenth or nineteenth century and designed to carry peat, grain or other goods on ponyback. This example is from Shetland. On windswept islands where wood was scarce, plant fibres needed to be employed to construct basic containers, creels, furnishings and even parts of buildings.

Law and Order

1. The apparent potential of ordinary human beings to harness superhuman powers through the occult and supernatural was subject to both fear and fascination throughout the seventeenth century. King James VI (I of England) himself published a treatise on 'daemonologie' in 1597. As a consequence, a woman of Ladybank, Fife, was one of many suspected of witchcraft and forced to wear this horrific iron collar .

2. (*below*) Scottish temperance, teetotal and abstinence societies grew up in the first part of the nineteenth century in a powerful attempt to establish a pervasive counter-culture, using the ethos of religion to fortify the message. Here, one man pledges 'by Divine Assistance' to follow a course of self-control as from June 1878.

3. Employed at a time of great political and religious conflict, from 1565–1710, the Maiden was a characteristically swift and violent means of purging society of its undesirables.

4. (*above*) Ballot box used during the Referendum of 1997.

5. Selection of playing cards from a seventeenth-century pack showing the arms of some of the last Scottish nobles who sat in the country's own Parliament until the Union of 1707, when they voted themselves out of existence.

1. Examples of seventeenth-century jewellery worn by supporters of Scotland's Stewart dynasty. For many years after the execution of Charles I in London, such jewellery was worn to commemorate the 'Martyr King' and to foster allegiance to the Stewart cause.

Taking Sides

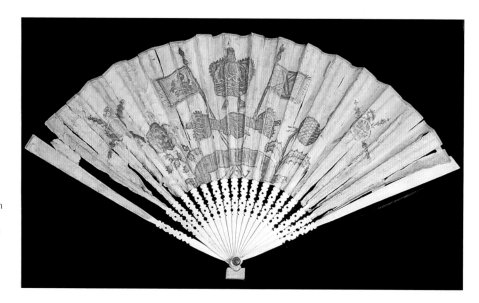

2. Ladies' fan, decorated in support of the Act of Union, 1707, with devices of both England and Scotland, flanking a cordial handshake between the two crowns.

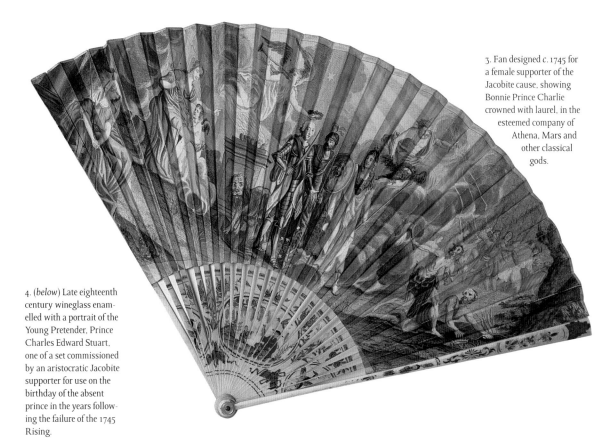

3. Fan designed *c*. 1745 for a female supporter of the Jacobite cause, showing Bonnie Prince Charlie crowned with laurel, in the esteemed company of Athena, Mars and other classical gods.

4. (*below*) Late eighteenth century wineglass enamelled with a portrait of the Young Pretender, Prince Charles Edward Stuart, one of a set commissioned by an aristocratic Jacobite supporter for use on the birthday of the absent prince in the years following the failure of the 1745 Rising.

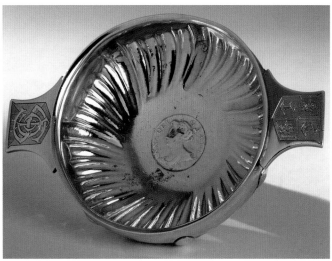

5. (*above*) The profile of Queen Anne, set within a traditional Scottish quaich wrought by Edinburgh silversmiths at the time of the Act of Union.

Leisure and Play

1. (*right*) Booklet of Border rugby fixtures from the 1930s. Although history credits the invention of rugby to Webb Ellis, at Rugby school in England, the Romans played a similar game called 'harpastum' in Scotland, and Border towns continue their ancient tradition of Border Ba' events, which involve the whole village in a game not dissimilar to rugby.

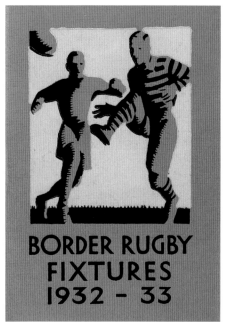

2. A slate gaming board with quartz playing pebbles, found in Jarlshof, Shetland, dating from the eleventh or twelfth century AD. One of a range of early board games of the period which have been found in Scotland almost intact.

3. Some of the famous Lewis chessmen, finely carved from walrus ivory in the twelfth century, probably first brought to the Isle of Lewis by Viking invaders. Although the Vikings ransacked the country's monasteries, they left a striking legacy of objects that were highly prized. The chessmen were likely to have been treasures of a Lewis aristocrat.

4. Avant-garde silver and purple chairs designed in 1903 by Charles Rennie Mackintosh for the Room Deluxe at the Willow Tearooms, Sauchiehall Street, Glasgow.

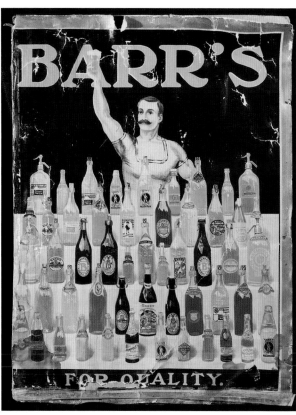

5. Irn-Bru, Scotland's 'other national drink'. 2001 saw Irn-Bru celebrate its 100th birthday. The secret recipe contains thirty-two different flavours, providing its unique and distinctive taste. (*far left*) A poster issued by the manufacturers, Barr, in 1901.

Turbulence and Unrest

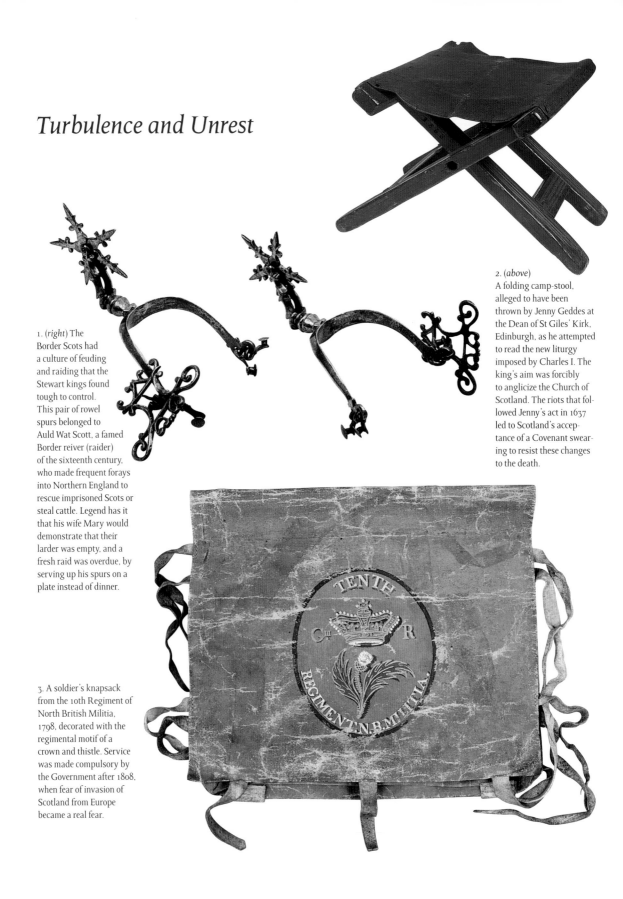

1. (*right*) The Border Scots had a culture of feuding and raiding that the Stewart kings found tough to control. This pair of rowel spurs belonged to Auld Wat Scott, a famed Border reiver (raider) of the sixteenth century, who made frequent forays into Northern England to rescue imprisoned Scots or steal cattle. Legend has it that his wife Mary would demonstrate that their larder was empty, and a fresh raid was overdue, by serving up his spurs on a plate instead of dinner.

2. (*above*) A folding camp-stool, alleged to have been thrown by Jenny Geddes at the Dean of St Giles' Kirk, Edinburgh, as he attempted to read the new liturgy imposed by Charles I. The king's aim was forcibly to anglicize the Church of Scotland. The riots that followed Jenny's act in 1637 led to Scotland's acceptance of a Covenant swearing to resist these changes to the death.

3. A soldier's knapsack from the 10th Regiment of North British Militia, 1798, decorated with the regimental motif of a crown and thistle. Service was made compulsory by the Government after 1808, when fear of invasion of Scotland from Europe became a real fear.

That the Presbyterian Church of Scotland conceded by William's ministers on 7 June 1690 should be so radical was due to the political organization and spiritual credibility of individuals who had suffered most over the previous three decades. These were the men who dominated the General Assembly that reconvened in November 1690 for the first time in thirty-nine years. Meanwhile, in the Lowland localities, especially south of the Tay, the popular mood was uncompromising. From the winter of 1688–9, Episcopalian clergy were ousted from their parishes, and in some presbyteries the purge was almost total. Subsequent efforts by the crown to put a brake on Presbyterian intolerance proved inadequate in the face of popular pressure. For the new king, the political cost of saving a clergy and a church that was so unsympathetic to William's claims to the throne could not be borne. The Presbyterians were allowed to have their way, extending parochial purges throughout the kingdom and making a clean sweep of the universities. Between 1689 and 1702, 664 ministers were driven out of their charges for refusing to recognize William and Mary. Of course, change was not immediate or dramatic everywhere. At Clackmannan, the minister, Daniel Urquhart, had faithfully preached in support of James VII, but in 1689 he simply shifted his public position, instructing his congregation to obey their new sovereigns. However, over the next few years, the session minutes were burned by David Bruce of Clackmannan, a Jacobite sympathizer who was heavily fined for refusing to take the new oath of obedience, the church funds disappeared along with the communion plate, and in 1696 Urquhart was finally deprived of his position. William's government also conceded the kirk's demands for the formal separation of church and state, a long-held Presbyterian principle, and to the abolition of lay patronage. It was a triumph of almost unimagined proportions for what had been a beaten remnant when James VII inherited the throne in 1685.

The political settlement that followed the revolution proved to be much less clear-cut. The Convention Parliament's radical agenda in the spring of 1689 stripped the crown of some of its prerogative powers, enhanced its own role in the state, and created greater protection for the rights and liberties of the subjects. The latter were to be permitted to petition freely, freedom of speech in parliament was guaranteed, the crown was forbidden the use of torture without evidence and it could no longer make subjects testify against themselves, and the fining of husbands for the non-attendance of their wives at church was forbidden. A caucus of Whig Revolution men continued to press for further reforms, their agenda being inspired by the 1641 constitution. This group, 'the Club', acted like a nascent political party, outmanoeuvring the ministry time and time again in the sessions of 1689 and 1690, confident in what James Dalrymple of Stair described as the belief that 'that king they made, they will order'. Their greatest success was in the 1689 session when Commissioner Hamilton agreed to the abolition of the hated Lords of the Articles in return for supply. Thereafter, controlling parliament was never the simple matter of stuffing this committee with crown officials and clients, and William's ministers had to work at managing parliament on the floor of the house. This was the high point of the Club's activities, and the creation of a Presbyterian Church of Scotland led to a falling away of support among the more religiously motivated commissioners. Disappointment at not being given office frustrated the leadership, especially Sir James Montgomery of Skelmorlie, an Ayrshire maverick who perversely switched his energies to Jacobite conspiracy, only to be found out and discredited.

In spite of the Club's successes, once William had accepted the crown, his supporters set to work on his behalf to prevent any further erosion of royal authority. William's choice of ministers throughout his reign was idiosyncratic, especially in the early years, being driven by a desire to avoid becoming the prisoner of a particular party. He succeeded only in creating highly unstable factions. Thus the most extreme of Whig revolutionaries, men like James Johnston, Wariston's son, found themselves serving in the same ministry as officials of the former king. William never found his Lauderdale, and one after another ministers foundered in the morass of competing politico-religious loyalties. Only in the later 1690s did William Douglas, second Duke of Queensberry, emerge as a man who might be able to straddle this beast and provide a degree of ministerial continuity.

William's principal concern was that the Scottish parliament should provide supply for the continuing War of the League of Augsburg, which had as one of its objectives the preservation of the revolution. Fighting ground on until 1697, when mutual exhaustion persuaded Louis XIV and William to declare a truce in the Treaty of Rijswijk. But even this peace was recognized at the time as nothing more than a breathing-space in the bloody business of thwarting the French king's ambitions to place his grandson on the Spanish throne. For William, all else was sacrificed to foreign policy. By comparison, the furore over the massacre of Glencoe, condemned by a parliamentary inquiry in April 1695, was a minor irritation. Similarly, the king's sabotaging of the Darien scheme occurred because it threatened to unsettle William's delicately constructed European alliances by driving a Scottish presence into the heart of Spain's South American colonial empire. William never visited Scotland; he had none of James VI's vision, none of Charles I's meddling agenda, none of James VII's crusading passions. He did not even have an heir for whom he schemed and planned. His named successor was James VII's ailing younger daughter, Anne, the last of whose many children died in 1700. The English parliament decided to look to who would succeed Anne, opting in the 1701 Act of Succession for the Protestant House of Hanover, distantly related to James VI. Already stung by the collapse of the Company of Scotland, the Scots took offence. Anti-English feeling found new roots in the soil of disappointed expectations. Scotland's Dutch king came to his own conclusion that only parliamentary union would solve the problem of his disunited kingdoms. In some respects, William II, the absent Dutchman, was the best of Scotland's seventeenth-century kings, a man too busy to interfere, sufficiently uninterested to allow the development of a church free of state control, and a parliament able to call his ministers to account. William left the Scots to govern themselves. Unfortunately, war and famine made his reign a fittingly dreadful ending to a harsh century.

3. *Parliamentary Union, 1702–7*

Queen Anne agreed with her predecessor's analysis of Anglo-Scottish relations. Following the renewal of war with France in 1702, the War of the Spanish Succession, English politicians, especially Whigs, also came to agree that the interests of English national security were best served by Union. Furthermore, the queen's ministers in London saw that the problem of persuading the uncooperative Scots to accept a Hanoverian succession might be solved by Union. In 1703, England's Tory government was unprepared to make the necessary concessions that would entice the Scots into Union, but by 1705 the Whigs were determined to settle the issue. The Scots' refusal to ratify the Hanoverian succession, while proposing no stable alternative way forward for their relations with the monarchy (or with England), only increased their vulnerability. Racked by self-doubt, and inflamed by resentment against the English, they knew increasingly that there had to be change of some sort. The Privy Council's insensitive decision to take Scotland into war with France, again without consulting parliament, exacerbated the situation. Demands that a new monarch required a new parliament grew, fuelled by English Tory ministers who believed Scottish elections would return a parliament shorn of many of the revolution men who had sat continuously since 1689.

Instead, the parliament elected in 1702 was hostile to the court and to England, forcing the usually adept Queensberry into serious concessions in the tumultuous 1703 session. Andrew Fletcher of Saltoun led the intellectual assault on the government, telling the assembly that since 1603 English ministers had undermined the country by corrupting Scottish ministers. Consequently, 'we have from that time appeared to the rest of the world more like a conquered province than a free and independent people'. Still smarting from Darien, and provoked by Saltoun, parliament asserted its control over the succession in the Act of Security (which did not receive the royal assent until 1704), over foreign policy in the Act Anent Peace and War, and over trade in the Wine Act. The crown faced the very real prospect of Scotland choosing a different monarch from England, possibly even James VIII (the Old Pretender), making a separate peace with Louis XIV, and pursuing a competitive trade strategy.

The fall of the Queensberry ministry, and its replacement with one created around the New Party led by the second Marquis of Tweeddale, was intended to pour oil on troubled waters. Tweeddale had been a critic of the corrupt Queensberry interest, and his party wanted compensation for Darien investors, but he also believed in the necessity of a Hanoverian succession. Yet he too failed to control a rowdy and militant parliament in which sat Whigs like Saltoun, hammering away at the crown's prerogatives with his proposed 'Limitations', Jacobites known to be in contact with the exiled court at

Saint-Germain outside Paris, and uncooperative members of the old Court Party who elected to be mischievous. Nor could Tweeddale settle the ugly mood of the public, which in the course of 1704 forced ministers into colluding in the judicial murder of members of the crew of the English ship, the 'Worcester', spitefully accused of piracy in a tit-for-tat struggle with the English admiralty over the last assets of the Company of Scotland. Public opinion was not helped by the publication of extreme English views, like those contained in William Atwood's *Superiority and Direct Dominion of the Imperial Crown of England over the Crown and Kingdom of Scotland*. It was the Whig government in London that finally forced the issue, passing the Alien Act that threatened Scotland with a trade embargo and the loss of those privileges of naturalization enjoyed since James VI's accession to the English throne. The Act would come into force on Christmas Day 1705 unless the Scottish parliament accepted the Hanoverian succession, or began negotiations for a parliamentary Union. It was time to choose.

The fall of the Tweeddale government, and the creation of a ministry led by the arrogant and decisive second Duke of Argyll in partnership with Queensberry, signalled the crown's determination to end the existence of the Scottish parliament. However, it was the supine behaviour of the fourth Duke of Hamilton that got around the problem of the ministry's minority position in parliament. Hamilton was the nominal leader of the Country Party, but his Jacobite connections, and the unlikely rumours that he harboured kingly ambitions of his own, made him vulnerable to political pressure. His suggestion, on 1 September 1705, to a thinly attended parliament, that the queen should nominate commissioners to treaty for Union stunned the opposition, handing the crown victory on a plate. In the words of the Jacobite George Lockhart of Carnwarth, this was the day from which was dated 'the commencement of Scotland's ruine'. The resulting negotiations in the spring of 1706 were tough and hard fought by the Scottish commissioners, but their commitment in principle to Union and Hanover made the eventual outcome inevitable. Chancellor Seafield, who led the Scottish delegation, opened negotiations by telling the English commissioners: 'We are convinced that an Union will be of great advantage to both. The Protestant religion will be more firmly secured, the designs of our enemies effectually disappointed, and the riches and trade of the whole island advanced.' This was a powerful argument that anti-Unionists repeatedly found difficult to counter. The Articles of Union, presented to a grateful queen, agreed to an incorporating Union, effectively trading Scottish political independence for access to English trade markets. Many of the articles were taken up with protecting Scottish privileges, the legal system, education, the nobility and the rights of the royal burghs, and with lessening the negative impact of free trade on vulnerable sectors of the economy. Nevertheless, the Scots would be surrendering their own parliament in order to have forty-five members in the 513-strong House of Commons and sixteen representative peers in the House of Lords.

It was little wonder that the proposals were unpopular in Scotland, but caused only a ripple of interest in England. Addresses to parliament opposing Union poured in from eighteen shires and twenty-one burghs, almost half and a third of the respective totals, concentrated in the south of the country where English commercial competition was most feared. The presbytery of Lanark protested in its address of November 1706 that Union would render Scotland subject to 'strangers to our constitution . . . who may judge it for the interest of Britain to keep us low and intirely subject to them'. On the other hand, the majority of shires and burghs did not petition parliament at all, an indication of the general uncertainty gripping the country.

The Articles of Union were presented to the Scottish parliament on 3 October 1706. The debate over the succeeding months, both outside parliament, and inside once it sat to consider them in detail in November, centred on sovereignty and trade. As early as 1695, George Ridpath had argued that there was no reason why 'Scotsmen should not defend with their pens, what their ancestors maintained so gallantly with their swords', and the opponents of the Union poured out propaganda focusing on the defence of sovereignty, a line of argument that had a broad appeal with the general public. By contrast, supporters of Union concentrated on the benefits of trade, an argument that proved more persuasive with parliament. Among the pro-Unionist writers was Daniel Defoe, the English spy and propagandist, but there were also genuine Scottish Unionists like the first Earl of Cromarty, who published *Parainesis Pacifica: or a Persuasive to the Union* in 1702, and William Seton of Pitmedden, author of the 1706 essay, *Scotland's Great Advantages by an Union with England*. Both men believed a Hanoverian succession was necessary for the future political stability of the country, and thought that Scotland's economic difficulties could be solved by free trade with England. Along with politicians like Queensberry, Argyll and Seaforth, they were also inclined to the view that Scotland's identity would not be lost simply because the legislature moved to London, there being sufficient guarantees in the Articles to prevent this occurring.

The first vote on Article one of the Act, requiring that 'the Two Kingdoms of England and Scotland shall . . . be united into one Kingdom by the name of Great Britain', resulted in a crown majority of thirty-three, a comfortable but not entirely reassuring result. The government was especially concerned about the influence of the Church of Scotland, and therefore passed a separate Act guaranteeing its Presbyterian future, at a stroke removing a good deal of popular resistance, as well as placating opposition among the Whig–Presbyterian interest in the chamber. Promises to pay off Darien investors from the Equivalent, a large lump sum of £398,085 10s. sterling, persuaded Tweeddale's New Party to unite with the court, and there is no question that Queensberry used the usual methods of bribery and coercion, including £20,000 sterling from the English treasury, to stiffen the resolve of government supporters who were awaiting the arrears of their salaries. Office-holders naturally voted with the government – for example, eighteen of the nineteen military officers in the parliament supported Union. The opposition was led by the mercurial populist Hamilton, famous for emotive speeches like that in which he asked, 'Shall we in half an hour yield what our forefathers maintained with their lives and fortunes for many ages?' His followers embraced Jacobites committed to stopping Hanover, Episcopalians aghast at the thought of an unending Presbyterian hegemony, reformers who feared that Union would strengthen the power of the crown, and those who passionately believed the Union would spell the end of Scotland. The mood of impending but inevitable tragedy was caught in the sentimental, but still moving, 'Mother Caledonia' speech of Lord Belhaven. No noble was prepared to take his opposition to the streets, where ugly mobs milled around Parliament House to cheer Hamilton and vent their anger at pro-Union members whose houses were attacked.

A nervous ministry pressed on, stiffened in their resolve by the knowledge that English regiments had been moved close to the border and to the Irish ports. Had there been a recourse to arms to save the parliament, the crown would have acted decisively to crush it. The struggle would be waged inside the parliament. Article by article, the Act of Union made its way to the end on 16 January 1707, when by 110 votes for Union and 69 against, the Act was passed with a majority of 41. The crown had safe majorities among the peers (42 for, 19 against and 16 abstentions), the shires (38 for, 30 against and 14 abstentions), and the burghs (30 for, 20 against and 16 abstentions), an unambiguous vote in favour of Hanover and Union. In some respects, this was the Scottish parliament's finest hour, settling such a bitterly divisive issue by political debate. There was no suggestion that parliament was not the constitutionally correct arena in which to settle the matter, and no one seriously questioned the political rights of its members. Popular sovereignty was never an issue. That the kingdom accepted a decision that was far from satisfactory to so many Scots underlines that it too had attained a new level of political maturity.

Retrospect

The Act of Union in 1707 marks the end of the seventeenth century and the beginning of something new. Of course no one, and no people, can leave their past behind, and the Scots carry the baggage of the Reformation and the seventeenth century with them even today. Most significantly, the decision that Scotland would be a Protestant state, that parliament and not despotic kings or the mob should be the arbiter of politics, that the Church of Scotland would be Presbyterian, and that Scotland should be a partner with England, have all shaped contemporary Scotland. Until the latter half of the twentieth century Scotland has continued to be dominated by the key decisions taken in this era. Only very recently has the Protestant, constitutional monarchy and Unionist view of the world – essentially a Whig view – been eroded, although now that erosion is very fast. No one can hope to grasp what has shaped Scottish identity over the previous 450 years without some understanding of the Reformation, the Covenanters and the Union of 1707.

Unfortunately, all too often prejudice and sentimental myths have obscured the history of the period. Of course, that prejudice and that myth-making has its roots in this period, in John Knox's own writings about the Reformation, or in Jacobite versions of the events surrounding the passing of the Act of Union. The process continued with succeeding ages: from the Enlightenment's disapproval of an earlier, less 'civilized' age, through to Sir Walter Scott's romanticism, and on into the Victorian determination to demonstrate the constitutional inadequacy of Scotland in comparison with England. Today it is not uncommon to find apparently intelligent commentators blaming the Protestant Reformation for everything from Scotland's cultural shortcomings to the sexual behaviour of the Scottish male. Curiously, the Jacobites continue to bask in positive publicity, being widely exploited for 'heritage' purposes, while the Covenanters are ignored. The Union issue continues to be controversial, but it is unusual to find those divisions based on well-informed historical knowledge of this crucially important period. Since politicians, religious leaders, writers and cultural commentators continue to appropriate Scottish history to serve their own ends, the need for contemporary Scots, and those others who wish to understand Scotland, to know about this era of its history, is as great as ever.

Disappointingly, perhaps, those early modern Scots have left little for today's generation to see, apart from some fine castles, or to hear, apart from some largely unfamiliar tunes, or even to read, other than that which is of interest to historians. Their mental and material world is not easily accessible, and to enter it is to pass into what is a very unfamiliar landscape. Little of Scotland's cultural iconography is drawn from this uncompromising era, apart from the bungling Mary, queen of Scots whose 'tragic' image continues to sell endless tourist souvenirs. Instead, Scots are embarrassed by the arbitrary actions of their kings, the burning of witches, the arcane squabbles over a religion of receding significance to them, the butchery of dreadful civil wars, the harshness of the law, and the unrelenting despair of those many thousands who starved to death in a land that is now incomparably richer. But one must resist the reaction of those eighteenth-century Whigs who looked back in disgust, shaking off the dust of this era as they embraced the economic and intellectual benefits of a British Empire in the making. They, more than any others, have shaped how we think about this century and a half, a time of dark deeds and depressing ideas, a backdrop against which to measure the Enlightened Scotland apparently brought into being by the Act of Union. They were not entirely wrong in their analysis. Yet the period has its heroic figures, and one does not have to approve of all they stood for, or did, to admire the vision of John Knox and the genius of George Buchanan, the daring and inspirational bravery of warriors like Montrose, and the stubborn patriotism of Andrew Fletcher of Saltoun. There is also much to celebrate in these decades, whether it be the insistence on giving every man an opportunity to be educated, the astounding courage of simple folk who died for their faith and their principles rather than submit to the will of a king, the evolution of a legal code that blended the best of what Europe had to offer with indigenous values, or the vision of formerly warring nations joining together in peace.

Bibliographical Essay

General

Among general histories of Scotland in this period the most accessible are J. Wormald, *Court, Kirk and Community: Scotland 1470–1625* (London, 1981), and K. M. Brown, *Kingdom or Province? Scotland and the Regal Union, 1603–1715* (Basingstoke, 1992), although the latter is predominantly concerned with political issues. Still useful are G. Donaldson, *Scotland: James V to James VII* (Edinburgh, 1971); W. Ferguson, *Scotland: 1689 to the Present* (Edinburgh, 1968); and R. Mitchison, *Lordship to Patronage: Scotland, 1603–1746* (London, 1983). The period is also well represented among the essays to be found in J. Dwyer, R. A. Mason and A. Murdoch (eds.), *New Perspectives on the Politics and Culture of Early Modern Scotland* (Edinburgh, 1980), and L. Maclean (ed.), *The Seventeenth Century in the Highlands* (Inverness, 1986). There is a mine of information to be gleaned from P. G. B. McNeill and H. L. MacQueen (eds.), *Atlas of Scottish History to 1707* (Edinburgh, 1996).

The British context to Scottish history in this period is crucial. Among the better volumes to address this issue are R. A. Mason (ed.), *Scotland and England, 1286–1815* (Edinburgh, 1987); P. Ellis and S. Barber (eds.), *Conquest and Union: Fashioning a British State, 1485–1725* (Edinburgh, 1995); A. Grant and K. J. Stringer (eds.), *Uniting the Kingdom? The Making of British History* (London, 1995); B. Bradshaw and J. Morrill (eds.), *The British Problem, c. 1534–1707* (London, 1996); G. Burgess (ed.), *The New British History: Founding a Modern British State, 1603–1715* (London, 1999); and B. Bradshaw and P. Roberts (eds.), *British Consciousness and Identity: The Making of Britain, 1533–1707* (New York, 1998). The seventeenth century is also dealt with effectively from a British perspective in B. P. Levack, *The Formation of the British State: England, Scotland and the Union 1603–1707* (Oxford, 1987); D. L. Smith, *A History of the Modern British Isles, 1603–1707: The Double Crown* (Oxford, 1998); G. S. Holmes, *British Politics in the Age of Anne* (London, 1987); and G. S. Holmes, *The Making of a Great Power: Late Stuart and Early Georgian Britain 1660–1722* (London, 1993).

Reformation

The best general history of the Reformation remains *The Scottish Reformation: Church and Society in Sixteenth Century Scotland* by I. B. Cowan (London, 1982), although it compares poorly with more recent work elsewhere in Europe. The old ecclesiological arguments between Presbyterians and Episcopalians rehearsed in G. Donaldson, *The Scottish Reformation* (Cambridge, 1960) continue to be re-run in D. G. Mullan, *Episcopacy in Scotland: The History of an Idea, 1560–1638* (Edinburgh, 1986); and A. R. MacDonald, *The Jacobean Kirk, 1567–1625*

(Aldershot, 1998) offers some refreshing insights into this tortuous issue. More specialized tastes are catered for in G. Donaldson, *Scottish Church History* (Edinburgh, 1985), and J. Kirk, *Patterns of Reform: Continuity and Change in the Reformation Kirk* (Edinburgh, 1989).

The important theme of church discipline is addressed in B. Lenman, 'The limits of godly discipline in the early modern period with particular reference to England and Scotland', in K. von Greyerz (ed.), *Religion and Society in Early Modern Europe, 1500—1800* (London, 1984), 124—45; G. Parker, 'The "Kirk by law established" and the origins of "The taming of Scotland": St Andrews 1559—1600', in L. Leneman (ed.), *Perspectives in Scottish Social History* (Aberdeen, 1988), 1—32; R. A. Houston, 'The Scots Church, Rotterdam, 1643—1795: a Dutch or a Scottish example of civic Calvinism?', in J. Roding and L. H. van Voss (eds.), *The North Sea and Culture 1550—1800* (Hilversum, 1996), 266—84; and M. F. Graham, *The Uses of Reform: 'Godly Discipline' and Popular Behaviour in Scotland and Beyond, 1560—1610* (Leiden, 1996). For local studies of the impact of religious change, see M. Lynch, *Edinburgh and the Reformation* (Edinburgh, 1981); M. H. B. Sanderson, *Ayrshire and the Reformation: People and Change 1490—1600* (East Linton, 1997); and F. D. Bardgett, *Scotland Reformed: The Reformation in Angus and the Mearns* (Edinburgh, 1989).

The political history of the later sixteenth century remains patchy. The reign of Queen Mary continues to divide opinion sharply from the sympathetic in M. Lynch (ed.), *Mary Stewart, Queen in Three Kingdoms* (Glasgow, 1988), to the highly critical in J. M. Wormald, *Mary Queen of Scots: A Study in Failure* (London, 1988). In spite of being a dry read, the best political study is G. Donaldson, *All the Queen's Men: Power and Politics in Mary Stewart's Scotland* (London, 1983). For studies of the major contemporary figures of the reign, see M. Lee, *James Stewart, Earl of Moray: A Political Study of the Reformation in Scotland* (New York, 1953), and W. Blake, *William Maitland of Lethington 1528—1573* (Lewiston, NY, 1990).

There is no good political narrative of James VI's reign in Scotland before 1603. An overarching view is offered in the provocative, if idiosyncratic, *State and Society in Early Modern Scotland* by J. Goodare (Oxford, 1999). G. R. Hewitt, *Scotland under Morton, 1572—80* (Edinburgh, 1983) is an inadequate examination of part of the minority, and M. Lee, *John Maitland of Thirlestane and the Foundation of the Stewart Despotism in Scotland* (Princeton, NJ, 1959) remains the most enjoyable political study, although it only covers a short period and is very dated. Issues of government and political power are addressed in K. M. Brown, *Bloodfeud in Scotland, 1573—1625: Violence, Justice and Politics in an Early Modern Society* (Edinburgh, 1986); J. M. Wormald, *Lords and Men in Scotland: Bonds of Manrent, 1442—1603* (Edinburgh, 1985); T. I. Rae, *The Administration of the Scottish Frontier 1513—1603* (Edinburgh, 1966); and R. H. Hannay, *The College of Justice* (Stair Society, 1990). R. A. Mason, *Kingship and Commonweal: Political Thought in Renaissance and Reformation Scotland* (East Linton, 1998) provides an insight into sixteenth-century political ideas. For regional studies during this period, P. D. Anderson, *Robert Stewart, Earl of Orkney, Lord of Shetland, 1533—1593* (Edinburgh, 1982), and P. D. Anderson, *Black Patie: The Life and Times of Patrick Stewart, Earl of Orkney and Lord of Shetland* (1992) deal with the far north, while J. M. Hill, *Fire and Sword: Sorley Boy MacDonnell and the Rise of Clan Ian Mor, 1538—1590* (London, 1993) examines the western seaboard.

Economy

By far the easiest introduction to economic and social issues is I. D. Whyte, *Scotland Before the Industrial Revolution: An Economic and Social History c. 1050–c. 1750* (London, 1995). For population, see M. Flinn (ed.), *Scottish Population History* (Cambridge, 1977), which is good on detail but its interpretations of the motors of demographic change are outdated; and R. A. Houston, *The Population History of Britain and Ireland, 1500–1750* (Cambridge, 1995). Agriculture is very well covered in M. H. B. Sanderson, *Scottish Rural Society in the 16th century* (Edinburgh, 1982); I. D. Whyte, *Agriculture and Society in Seventeenth-Century Scotland* (Edinburgh, 1979); I. D. Whyte and K. A. Whyte, *The Changing Scottish Landscape, 1500–1800* (London, 1991); M. L. Parry and T. R. Slater (eds.), *The Making of the Scottish Countryside* (London, 1981); and R. A. Dodgshon, *Land and Society in Early Scotland* (Oxford, 1981).

Studies of trade and commerce are less available, and the fact that S. G. E. Lythe, *The Economy of Scotland in its European Setting 1550–1625* (Edinburgh, 1960) and T. C. Smout, *Scottish Trade on the Eve of Union* (Edinburgh, 1963) are still the main texts is an indication of the decline of interest in economic history. However, see C. A. Whatley, *The Scottish Salt Industry 1570–1850* (Aberdeen, 1987), and R. Saville, *The Bank of Scotland 1696–1996* (Edinburgh, 1996) for more recent studies of early modern commerce. C. A. Whatley, 'Economic Causes and Consequences of the Union of 1707. A Survey', *Scottish Historical Review* 68 (1989), 150–81, is an important overview of the relationship between economic issues and politics. G. Marshall, *Presbyteries and Profits: Calvinism and the Development of Capitalism in Scotland, 1560–1707* (Oxford, 1980) makes a good attempt at exploring the Weber thesis in a Scottish context. For urban developments, see M. Lynch (ed.), *The Early Modern Town in Scotland* (London, 1987), and G. Jackson, 'Glasgow in transition, *c.* 1660 to *c.* 1740', in T. M. Devine and G. Jackson (eds.), *Glasgow*, vol. 1: *Beginnings to 1830* (Manchester, 1995), 63–105.

Society

What is known about Scottish society is in inverse proportion to the number of people in its various ranks or occupational groups. However, the only general study of the nobility is by K. M. Brown, *Noble Society in Scotland 1560–1637: Wealth, Family and Culture* (Edinburgh, 2000). There is little readily available on the later seventeenth century, but see R. K. Marshall, *The Days of Duchess Anne: Life in the Household of the Duchess of Hamilton 1656–1716* (London, 1973), and M. Lee, *The Heiress of Buccleuch: Money, Marriage and Politics in Seventeenth-Century Britain* (East Linton, 1996).

Middling and professional groups are discussed in T. C. Smout, 'The Glasgow Merchant Community in the Seventeenth Century', *Scottish Historical Review* 47 (1968), 53–70; T. M. Devine, 'The merchant class of the larger Scottish towns in the seventeenth and early eighteenth centuries', in G. Gordon and B. Dicks (eds.), *Scottish Urban History* (Aberdeen, 1983), 92–111; G. Donaldson, 'The Legal Profession in Scottish Society in the Sixteenth and Seventeenth Centuries', *Juridical Review*, New Series 21 (1976), 1–19; A. Murdoch, 'The advocates, the law and the nation in early modern Scotland', in W. Prest (ed.), *Lawyers in Early Modern Europe and America* (London, 1981), 147–63; N. T. Phillipson, 'The social structure of the faculty of advocates in Scotland 1661–1840', in H. Harding (ed.), *Law Making and Law Makers in British History* (London, 1980), 145–56; and H. Dingwall, *Physicians, Surgeons and Apothecaries:*

Edinburgh's Medical Profession, 1580–1726 (East Linton, 1996). Surprisingly, there is no study of the clergy as a profession. D. Stevenson, *The Origins of Freemasonry: Scotland's Century, 1590–1710* (Cambridge, 1990) discusses a social activity of men predominantly drawn from these middling and professional ranks.

For the mass of the population, a good starting-point is R. A. Houston and I. D. Whyte (eds.), *Scottish Society, 1500–1800* (Cambridge, 1989). A. J. S. Gibson and T. C. Smout, *Prices, Food and Wages in Scotland, 1550–1780* (Cambridge, 1995) is an excellent source book, and R. Mitchison, 'The Making of the Old Scottish Poor Law', *Past and Present* 63 (1974), 58–93, deals with what was for too many people an important issue. For sex and marriage, see R. Mitchison and L. Leneman, *Sexuality and Social Control in Scotland, 1660–1780* (Oxford, 1989), and L. Leneman, *Alienated Affections: Scottish Experiences of Divorce and Separation, 1684–1830* (Edinburgh, 1998).

The best analysis of urban society is H. Dingwall, *Late Seventeenth-Century Edinburgh: A Demographic Study* (Aldershot, 1994). While R. A. Houston, *Social Change in the Age of the Enlightenment: Edinburgh 1660–1760* (Oxford, 1994) is largely concerned with the eighteenth century, it is useful for comparative purposes. Recently, Highland society has been well documented, especially in A. I. Macinnes, *Clanship, Commerce and the House of Stuart, 1603–1788* (East Linton, 1996), which is also insightful on politics and religion, and R. A. Dodgshon, *From Chiefs to Landlords: Social and Economic Change in the Western Highlands and Islands, c. 1493–1820* (Edinburgh, 1998).

Crime is very poorly covered outside specialized works like that by S. J. Davies, 'The court and the Scottish legal system, 1600–1747: the case of Stirlingshire', in V. A. C. Gatrell, B. Lenman and G. Parker (eds.), *Crime and the Law: The Social History of Crime in Western Europe Since 1500* (London, 1980), 120–54. However, there is a good literature on witchcraft, principally C. Larner, *Enemies of God: The Witch Hunt in Scotland* (London, 1981), and B. Levack (ed.), *Witchcraft in Scotland* (New York, 1992).

Culture

Scottish education has been reasonably well served by historians of this period. J. Scotland, *The History of Scottish Education*, vol. 1 (London, 1969) remains the standard work, though very dated. A more controversial interpretation is offered in R. A. Houston, *Scottish Literacy and the Scottish Identity* (Cambridge, 1985). Houston also provides the European comparisons by which Scotland can be judged in *Literacy in Early Modern Europe: Culture and Education, 1500–1800* (London, 1989). Also useful is J. Durkan, 'Education in the Century of the Reformation', *Innes Review* 10 (1959), 67–90, and J. Durkan, 'Education: the laying of fresh foundations', in J. MacQueen (ed.), *Humanism in Renaissance Scotland* (Edinburgh, 1990), 123–60.

The Scottish Renaissance has never been adequately treated in a single volume. Its most sophisticated exponent has confined himself to the writing of essays, among which is J. Durkan, 'The Culture Background in Sixteenth-Century Scotland', *Innes Review* 10 (1959), 382–439. However, aspects of Renaissance culture are addressed in H. M. Shire, *Song, Dance and Poetry of the Court of Scotland under James VI* (London, 1969); I. B. Cowan and D. Shaw (eds.), *The Renaissance and Reformation in Scotland* (Edinburgh, 1983); R. D. S. Jack (ed.), *The History of Scottish Literature;* vol. 1: *Origins to 1660* (Aberdeen, 1988); J. MacQueen (ed.), *Humanism in*

Renaissance Scotland (Edinburgh, 1990); A. A. MacDonald, M. Lynch and I. B. Cowan (eds.), *The Renaissance in Scotland* (Leiden, 1994); D. Howard, *Scottish Architecture from the Reformation to the Restoration, 1560–1660* (Edinburgh, 1995); and S. Mapstone and J. Wood (eds.), *The Rose and the Thistle: Essays on the Culture of Late Medieval and Renaissance Scotland* (East Linton, 1998). The later seventeenth century is less well served, but see D. Allan, *Virtue, Learning and the Scottish Enlightenment* (Cambridge, 1993), and R. L. Emerson, 'Scottish cultural change 1660–1710 and the Union of 1707', in J. Robertson (ed.), *A Union for Empire: Political Thought and the British Union of 1707* (Cambridge, 1995), 121–44; H. Ouston, 'Cultural life from the Restoration to the Union', in A. Hook (ed.), *History of Scottish Literature*, vol. 2: *1600–1800* (Aberdeen, 1989), 11–32; and J. Macaulay, *The Classical Country House of Scotland, 1660–1800* (London, 1987).

For national identity, see W. Ferguson, *The Identity of the Scottish Nation* (Edinburgh, 1998); the essays by Michael Lynch and John Young in D. Broun, R. J. Findlay and M. Lynch (eds.), *Image and Identity: The Making and Remaking of Scotland through the Ages* (Edinburgh, 1998); and K. M. Brown, 'Scottish identity in the seventeenth century', in B. Bradshaw and P. Roberts (eds.), *British Consciousness and Identity* (New York, 1998), 236–58. C. Kidd, *Subverting Scotland's Past: Scotland's Whig Historians and the Creation of an Anglo-British Identity, 1689–c. 1830* (Cambridge, 1993) makes some useful observations on the seventeenth century.

Kings and Covenants

From 1603, Scottish history must take more account of the British dimension, for which see the section above. B. Galloway, *The Union of England and Scotland, 1603–1608* (Edinburgh, 1986), and R. A. Mason (ed.), *Scots and Britons: Scottish Political Thought and the Union of 1603* (Cambridge, 1994), address the ideological debate surrounding the regal Union. Also see the important essay by J. M. Wormald, 'James VI and I: Two Kings or One?', *History* 68 (1988), 187–209, which raises many issues about multiple kingship, some of which are developed in M. Lee, *Great Britain's Solomon: James VI and I in his Three Kingdoms* (Urbana, Ohio, 1990). On the impact of the Scots at court, see K. M. Brown, 'The Scottish Aristocracy, Anglicization and the Court', *Historical Journal* 36 (1993), 543–76, and N. Cuddy, 'Anglo-Scottish Union and the Court of James I, 1603–1625', *Transactions of the Royal Historical Society* 39 (1989), 107–24. The reign of James VI after 1603 is most comprehensively covered in M. Lee, *Government by Pen: Scotland under James VI and I* (Urbana, Ohio, 1980), while there are useful insights on parliament, the Highlands and Irish emigration in J. Goodare, 'The Scottish Parliament of 1621', *Historical Journal* 38 (1995), 29–52; J. Goodare, 'The Statutes of Iona in Context', *Scottish Historical Review* 77 (1998), 31–57; and M. Perceval-Maxwell, *The Scottish Migration to Ulster in the Reign of James I* (Belfast, 1973). For Charles I, two very different approaches can be found in M. Lee, *The Road to Revolution: Scotland under Charles I, 1625–37* (Urbana, Ohio, 1985), and A. I. Macinnes, *Charles I and the Making of the Covenanting Movement, 1625–1641* (Edinburgh, 1991).

Religious issues in the early seventeenth century are less well examined in comparison with the Reformation era. W. R. Foster, *The Church before the Covenants: The Church of Scotland 1596–1638* (Edinburgh, 1975) is less than satisfactory, but W. H. Makey, *The Church of the Covenant, 1637–51: Revolution and Social Change in Scotland* (Edinburgh, 1979) is an impressive study. The question of a British ecclesiastical agenda is addressed in J. Morrill, 'A British patriarchy? Ecclesiastical imperialism under the early Stuarts', in A. Fletcher and P. Roberts (eds.), *Religion, Culture and Society in Early Modern Britain* (Cambridge, 1994), 209–37. For theological beliefs, see D. G. Mullan, 'Theology in the Church of Scotland, 1618–c. 1640: a Calvinist Consensus', *Sixteenth Century Journal* 26 (1995), 595–618, and the highly sophisticated *Politics, Religion and the British Revolutions: Samuel Rutherford and the Scottish Covenanters* by J. Coffey (Cambridge, 1997). Also essential to understanding seventeenth-century religion is the fascinating L. E. Schmidt, *Holy Fairs: Scottish Communions and American Revivals in the Early Modern Period* (Princeton, NJ, 1989).

The mid-seventeenth-century revolution and wars further entangle Scotland's history with that of England and Ireland. The controversial *The Fall of the British Monarchies, 1637–1642* by C. Russell (Oxford, 1991) is a little too Anglo-centric, but brilliantly demonstrates the political entanglement of the Scots in English affairs. J. Morrill (ed.), *The Scottish National Covenant in its British Context, 1638–51* (Edinburgh, 1990) places more emphasis on the Scottish dimension without losing sight of the bigger picture. A similar intention lies behind the patchy *The Celtic Dimension of the British Civil Wars* by J. R. Young (Edinburgh, 1997). P. Donald, *An Uncounselled King: Charles I and the Scottish Troubles, 1637–1641* (Cambridge, 1990) details the high politics of the Scottish revolution, but the argument is lost amidst over-dense detail. For the standard political narrative of the Covenanting era, see D. Stevenson, *The Scottish Revolution, 1637–44: The Triumph of the Covenanters* (Newton Abbot, 1973); D. Stevenson, *Revolution and Counter Revolution in Scotland, 1644–1651* (London, 1977); and the collection of essays in D. Stevenson, *Union, Religion and Revolution in 17th-century Scotland* (Aldershot, 1997). In addition, the Irish and Highland dimension is brought out in D. Stevenson, *Scottish Covenanters and Irish Confederates* (Belfast, 1981), and the excellent D. Stevenson, *Alasdair MacColla and the Highland Problem of the Seventeenth Century* (Edinburgh, 1980). The very human tragedy of the period is also brought to life in D. Stevenson, *King or Covenant? Voices from the Civil War* (East Linton, 1996). Among the many books on Montrose, the best remains E. J. Cowan, *Montrose: For Covenant and King* (London, 1977). J. R. Young, *The Scottish Parliament, 1639–1661* (Edinburgh, 1996) deals with the important constitutional repercussions of the revolution, but is virtually unreadable. Parliamentary politics is better presented in J. Scally, 'Constitutional revolution, party and faction in the Scottish parliaments of Charles I', in C. Jones (ed.), *The Scots and Parliament* (Edinburgh, 1996), 54–73. For the 1650s, see F. Dow, *Cromwellian Scotland, 1651–1660* (Edinburgh, 1979); D. Stevenson, 'Cromwell, Scotland and Ireland', in J. Morrill (ed.), *Oliver Cromwell and the English Revolution* (Harlow, 1990), 149–80; and there is some Scottish content in R. Hutton, *The British Republic 1649–1660* (Basingstoke, 1990).

For a competent overall account of the mid-century wars, see M. Bennett, *The Civil Wars in Britain and Ireland, 1638–1651* (Oxford, 1997), and J. Kenyon and J. Ohymeyer (eds.), *The Civil Wars: A Military History of England, Scotland and Ireland, 1638–1660* (Oxford, 1998). More specific topics are addressed in M. C. Fissel, *The Bishops War: Charles I's Campaigns against Scotland* (Cambridge, 1994); I. Gentles, *The New Model Army in England, Scotland and Ireland, 1645–53* (Oxford, 1992); and J. D. Grainger, *Cromwell against the Scots: The Last Anglo-Scottish War, 1650–1652* (East Linton, 1997).

Constitutional Struggles

There is no good history of Restoration Scotland. The closest there is to a political study of the period is J. Buckroyd, *Church and State in Scotland, 1660–1681* (Edinburgh, 1980). Far better is R. Hutton, *Charles II, King of England, Scotland and Ireland* (Oxford, 1989), although Scotland only forms a part of the story. There are some insights into politics in J. Patrick, 'The Origins of Opposition to Lauderdale in the Scottish Parliament of 1673', *Scottish Historical Review* 53 (1974), 1–21, and J. Patrick, 'A union broken? Restoration politics in Scotland', in J. Wormald (ed.), *Scotland Revisited* (London, 1991), 119–28. I. B. Cowan, *The Scottish Covenanters, 1660–88* (London, 1976) is, surprisingly, the most recent book on this topic, and there is a clear need for the later Covenanters to be re-examined. However, for an unusual perspective on the topic, see V. G. Kiernan, 'A banner with a strange device: the later Covenanters', in T. Brotherstone (ed.), *Covenant, Charter and Party: Traditions of Revolt and Protest in Modern Scottish History* (Aberdeen, 1989), 25–49. J. M. Buckroyd, *The Life of James Sharp, Archbishop of St Andrews 1618–1679* (Edinburgh, 1987) provides a competent account of one of the major figures of the age. Religious issues are also dealt with in E. H. Hyman, 'A Church Militant: Scotland, 1661–1690', *Sixteenth Century Journal* 26 (1995), 49–74, and G. DesBrisay, 'Catholics, Quakers and Religious Persecution in Restoration Aberdeen', *Innes Review* 47 (1996), 136–68.

There is a useful survey of the 1689 revolution and the subsequent period to 1707 in W. Ferguson, *Scotland's Relations with England: A Survey to 1707* (Edinburgh, 1977), although the prejudices of the author are rather close to the surface. The revolution itself remains in need of a good history. Although interesting, I. B. Cowan, 'The reluctant revolutionaries: Scotland in 1688', in E. Cruickshanks (ed.), *By Force or Default? The Revolution of 1688–1689* (Edinburgh, 1989), 65–81; B. P. Lenman, 'The Scottish nobility and the revolution of 1688–1690', in R. Beddard (ed.), *The Revolutions of 1688* (Oxford, 1991), 137–62; and B. P. Lenman, 'The poverty of political theory in the Scottish revolution of 1688–90', in L. G. Schwoerer (ed.), *The Revolution of 1688–89: Changing Perspectives* (Cambridge, 1992), 244–59, all underplay the religious and ideological aspects of the conflict. P. Hopkins, *Glencoe and the End of the Highland War* (Edinburgh, 1986) provides an unrelenting narrative of the struggle in the Highlands. B. P. Lenman, *The Jacobite Risings in Britain 1689–1746* (London, 1980) is more readable, while for the undeserving hero of Scottish Jacobitism, see A. M. Scott, *Bonnie Dundee: John Grahame of Claverhouse, Viscount Dundee* (1989), and M. Linklater and C. Hesketh, *For King and Conscience: John Graham of Claverhouse, Viscount Dundee (1648–1689)* (London, 1990). The best analysis of the Convention Parliament is still J. Halliday, 'The Club and the Revolution in Scotland 1689–90', *Scottish Historical Review* 45 (1966), 143–59. William II's reign is covered, albeit dryly, in P. W. J. Riley, *King William and the Scottish Politicians* (Edinburgh, 1979).

Ecclesiastical divisions are given an airing in B. P. Lenman, 'The Scottish episcopal clergy and the ideology of jacobitism', in E. Cruickshanks (ed.), *Ideology and Conspiracy: Aspects of Jacobitism, 1689–1759* (Edinburgh, 1982), 36–48; T. Clarke, 'The Williamite Episcopalians and the Glorious Revolution in Scotland', *Records of the Scottish Church History Society* 24 (1990), 35–51; L. K. Glassey, 'William II and the Settlement of Religion in Scotland, 1688–1690', *Records of the Scottish Church History Society* 23 (1989), 317–29. The only church history remains that by A. L. Drummond and J. Bulloch, *The Scottish Church, 1688–1843* (Edinburgh, 1973).

The road to Union is well trodden, although there remain large gaps in the historiography. *The Union of Scotland and England* by P. W. J. Riley (Manchester, 1978) is the standard account, and while P. H. Scott, *Andrew Fletcher and the Treaty of Union* (Edinburgh, 1994) is not without its uses, the political message is far from subliminal. Amazingly, the only account of Darien remains *The Company of Scotland Trading to Africa and the Indies* by G. P. Insh (London, 1932), although J. Robertson (ed.), *A Union for Empire: Political Thought and the British Union of 1707* (Cambridge, 1995) places Scottish ideas about trade, empire and Union in a European and British context. C. A. Whatley, 'Salt, Coal and the Union of 1707: a revision article', *Scottish Historical Review* 66 (1987), 25–45, is useful, and the most accessible introduction to the topic is C. A. Whatley, *'Bought and Sold for English Gold?' Explaining the Union of 1707* (Glasgow, 1994).

5

From the Union of 1707
to the Franchise Reform of 1832

BRUCE P. LENMAN

The Act of Union of 1707 was strictly 'The Treaty of Union of the Two Kingdoms of Scotland and England' which was agreed in 1706 after Anglo-Scottish negotiations. It was then amended and passed by the Scots parliament and approved without change by the English one. It was a political measure, with its two most significant provisos embedded in its first and second clauses. The first provided that on 1 May 1707 'the Two Kingdoms of Scotland and England, shall . . . forever after, be United into One Kingdom by the Name of Great Britain.' The second clause provided that the succession to the throne of the new united realm, 'after Her Most Sacred Majesty' Queen Anne, should, in default of issue from Anne, go to 'the Most Excellent Princess Sophia, Electoress . . . of Hanover, and the Heirs of Her body, being Protestants'. The succession was therefore specifically subject to the rules laid down in the English Act of Succession of 1701: 'All Papists and persons marrying Papists' were excluded from succession to 'the Imperial Crown of Great Britain and the Dominions thereunto belonging'.

The rest of the Union legislation was of far less interest to Queen Anne's English ministers, who had in the end been the driving force behind the whole business. Nevertheless, it can be argued that to get what they deemed essential to the security of England and its 'Protestant Constitution' in the middle of the second great Anglo-French war which had followed the Glorious Revolution of 1688–9, those ministers, themselves a small aristocratic clique, had to come to terms with the representatives of the Scottish aristocracy. Once the Union was a fact, James Johnston, a former Secretary of State for Scotland and leading Scottish advocate of it, complained to his friend George Baillie of Jerviswood that English critics of the selfishness of the Scots nobles would not believe that 'some have done it out of love for their country'. The latter were few. By and large, Scots aristocrats shaped the details of the Union to guard the selfish interests of themselves and their allies. English ministers had had to design a package which they hoped could secure the acquiescence, if not the hearty support, of all the major Scottish social and political interests capable of blocking a Union which had come to be seen in

London as the only sure guarantee of a united Protestant succession in both England and Scotland. The Union, therefore, established a framework defined by forces other than those of immediate political expediency. It registered the power structure of early eighteenth-century Scotland by the specific concessions and provisions and guarantees which formed so much of its twenty-five clauses, and it also set the Scottish society which had generated that power-structure within a new political, and to some extent economic, framework. By doing so it laid the foundations of a Scottish *ancien régime* which lasted until Catholic emancipation in 1829, and the Great Reform Act of 1832 tolled the bells at its drawn-out funeral.

The late seventeenth-century Scots nobility had already been strongly attracted by London and the royal court. After 1707 this trend became much more marked, and the leading nobles and grander lairds tended to focus their careers and ambitions on the crown in its Westminster parliament. They went to London to live the fashionable life and solicit civil and military posts. However, the framework of a now provincial Scottish society remained firmly hierarchic and aristocratic. The collective leadership of the burghs bargained with, but did not challenge, that aristocratic framework. However vigorous they were becoming, the business class did not offer any overt challenge to the hierarchical social order until very late in this era. The 'Kirk by Law Established' spent much of the period trying to shed inherited fundamentalism and residual radicalism precisely to render itself a more acceptable partner in the patronage-bound social hierarchy. The lower orders showed little capacity or desire to challenge this *ancien régime* until the economic growth engendered within its conservative but permissive structures had begun to create new problems and a new world.

If, then, 1707 to 1832 constitutes a Scottish *ancien régime*, one of several variations on that theme in contemporary Europe, Scotland after 1707 was locked into a realm which was indeed 'confessional' and committed to a concept of monarchy which preserved the idea of 'Sacred Majesty' so dear to the hearts of the now exiled and Roman Catholic main branch of its ancient Stewart dynasty. The exiled Stewarts assumed that God disapproved of a usurping and heretical regime, and would punish Scottish and English peoples for their national apostasy. Scottish Jacobites in particular, whether Protestant or Roman Catholic (and the vast majority were Protestant Episcopalians), accepted this view in the modified form that, by violating the principle of indefeasible hereditary right, the Scottish nation had committed a great national wrong in 1688–9, and that war, famine and plague would dog its footsteps until it rectified that wrong by a second Restoration, parallel to that of 1660. Protestants who were not Jacobites had no problems over the transfer of power in 1688–9. The exiled Stewarts might think God a Roman Catholic, but Protestant Whigs, who supported the revolution, knew God was Protestant and therefore His providence would sustain the Protestant succession which alone could secure revolution principles.

Yet Scotland after 1707 was not part of a confessional state as most other European monarchies understood that concept in the eighteenth century. The United Kingdom of Great Britain could not match the monolithic orthodoxy of, say, Lutheran Sweden or Roman Catholic Spain. Even its established Protestantism was plural. The most dramatic single concession necessary to secure Scottish acquiescence in the Union had been the 'Act for Securing the Protestant Religion and Presbyterian Church Government' which, along with a similar piece of legislation 'Securing the Church of England as by Law Established', simply removed religion from the unificatory influences implicit and explicit in the Treaty of Union. Though the political system rested on a narrow base, there were potentially dynamic forces loose in Scotland after 1707 and more particularly after 1746. The Scottish Reform Act of 1832 eventually widened the franchise in Scotland vastly, much more dramatically than the English Great Reform Act, itself deemed surprisingly radical. This franchise extension in Scotland registered substantial changes in the balance of social power within Scottish society. Those shifts in power balances derived ultimately from economic developments. Massive urbanization, extensive industrial development, radical rural reorganization and spectacular levels of confessional pluralism were all in place before 1832. What is astonishing is that a social and political system which had produced the 1707 framework contrived, in modified form, to maintain even a weakened ascendancy as late as 1832.

There was no more ardent defender of the *ancien régime* towards its end than Sir Walter Scott, lawyer, poet, novelist and Scottish patriot. Yet his greatest novels were all about the tensions generated within human psyches when rapid social and economic change renders a once-honoured, still-loved set of values and loyalties obsolete. Scott underlined the deep paradoxes which abound in Scottish history between 1707 and 1832, and the extreme difficulty of establishing direct linkages between intellectual and artistic developments, which undoubtedly made this era not only a Golden Age of Scottish culture, but also of economic, social and political developments. Scott has been – rightly – seen as a founder of the Romantic Movement, but his own core values were not romantic. The eighteenth century has been described as the 'Age of the Scottish Enlightenment'. Yet some historians would trace the origins of that particular variant on the western Enlightenment far back beyond 1707, into the fertile soil of Restoration Scotland. By the last decade of the eighteenth century, when the Enlightenment in Scotland had just passed its peak, its social shallowness and intellectual limitations were becoming apparent and a powerful backlash was gathering strength. Despite this, it is clear that in a modified form Enlightenment cultural values minted in Scotland remained potent not only within Scottish society, but also in the wider United Kingdom and far beyond its limits in Europe and the Americas, in what was a constantly changing cultural complex. Its core values of order, tolerance, rationality and progressive improvement, though often challenged in an increasingly romantic, urban and divided society, remained potent, even when much of the original social order with which they first flowered had become obsolete or indefensible or both.

The keynotes of the period 1560 to 1707 had been Reformation and Union (both of crowns and parliaments). In the eighteenth and early nineteenth century they were Union in action, Enlightenment and economic change. From start to finish, Scotland in this age exhibited strong differentiation of social and gender roles. At the start it was hardly a class society, since the aristocracy and lairds were the only fully self-conscious class, the landed class. By the end of the period, middle-class self-consciousness was full-blown, and various forms of working-class consciousness were becoming political facts of life, putting the fear of death into conservatives like Walter Scott. The lifestyle of the landed classes was still the supreme goal for the socially ambitious in 1832. In 1707 the dominance of the landed classes in Scotland had been absolute. There were, particularly in the trading burghs, bourgeois entrepreneurs, but they and other members of the middling orders of society (notably lawyers) were so enmeshed and identified with the landed élite, who were by far their most important customers for commercial and professional services, as well as their political masters, that the idea of a bourgeois challenge to the existing ascendancy of nobles and lairds over a hierarchical society of orders rather than classes was unthinkable. Indeed, when the Jacobite physician Patrick Blair, the first Scot to dissect an elephant among other things, was pardoned at the last gasp before execution for his part in the 1715 rising, this was recognized. One petition on his behalf argued that when the noblemen and lairds who employed Blair joined the Jacobite army, he had to follow them, because otherwise 'there was no method the doctor could take to subsist himself and Family'.

Arguably, the prevalent neo-classical style of the fine, decorative and building arts in the eighteenth century was a visual code eminently suited to a landed ascendancy linked creatively with middle-class businessmen and intellectuals in the joint pursuit of politeness and prosperity. Neo-classicism emphasized order, restraint and elegance, and the money needed to indulge in it on any scale in architectural form. It was also a frame of mind which discountenanced extremism in politics and 'enthusiasm', the contemporary word for fanaticism, in religion. Similar social structures elsewhere in the European–Atlantic world cultivated a comparable, essentially cosmopolitan style. What is interesting is that the forces which were to destabilize this world often came to a head at the same time in widely separated, though intellectually linked, parts of that Atlantic-centred world. The underlying engine of change was the commitment of the landed élites to economic growth. In eighteenth-century Scotland and Virginia, Scots lairds and tidewater planter-gentry were at one in seeking enhanced prosperity through commercial means, in order to enable them to sustain what they hoped would be a more elegant lifestyle. It is no accident that in 1832 Walter Scott was brooding over the disintegration of his social and political worlds at much the same time as the conservative heirs of the Founding Fathers of the American republic were wincing at the final demise of their hopes for a classical republic of civic and Spartan virtue in the face of Jacksonian populist politics, evangelical religion and crass materialism. It can, therefore, be contended that the period from 1707 to 1832 in Scottish history, with all its inherent paradoxes, not to mention continuities at both ends of the era, has a distinctive character. Even the strains within Scottish society in this span of years gave that society a set of inner tensions which for long on balance contributed to its dynamism, rather than overwhelmed its essential character. However, by the 1840s change had become fundamental and this world had gone.

Demography and the Movement of People

The materials available for investigating Scotland's shifting population are not adequate to produce truly reliable figures for overall numbers before 1755. However, recent studies show that the significant overall population growth, which clearly occurred in sixteenth- and early seventeenth-century Scotland, did not continue into the late seventeenth and the first half of the eighteenth century. Regionally, one process of change associated with that earlier growth does seem to have continued: the dietary shift in the Lowlands in the earlier period from meat and animal products to a much greater reliance on oatmeal continued into the eighteenth century, spreading into the Highlands and Islands. If, as a recent calculation suggests, the population of Scotland in 1691 was some 1,235,000, the famines and epidemics of the 1690s brought the previous pattern of modest but steady overall population increase to a halt. Recovery before 1755 was extremely modest, for between 1691 and 1755, on these figures, Scotland added only some 30,000 people to its population. Behind such generalizations there lay quite sharp regional diversity. Thus the western Lowlands appear to have had a population growth of over 10 per cent between 1691 and 1755, while a county like Aberdeenshire, hard hit by the disasters of the 1690s, may have held in 1755 a population as much as 7 per cent lower than it had held in the 1690s, and that despite a doubling in the size of the city of Aberdeen in the same period. Even by the 1750s Scotland's annual population growth rate, at a mere 0.4 per cent annually, was well below England's 1 per cent.

It is only with the appearance of Dr Alexander Webster's *Account of the Number of People in Scotland* that we are on firmer numerical ground. Webster, a tall, handsome clergyman of the Church of Scotland who combined the characters of wit, *bon viveur* (not for nothing was he known as 'Dr Bonum Magnum'), evangelical saint and Enlightenment savant, was in his own body a wonderful receptacle of several of the most powerful currents in Scottish intellectual life in the mid-eighteenth century. His demographic survey used the educated manpower of the ministers of the kirk as research assistants and had, as a typical sub-plot in an age of close church–state relations, the aim of establishing the number of men capable of bearing arms potentially available in the Scotland of his day. Modern scholarly efforts to check his results suggest he was remarkably accurate. He estimated the population of Scotland in 1755 to be 1,265,380.

Roughly 53 per cent of the population lived north of the Forth. The Highlands and Islands part of that area north of the Forth held about 30 per cent of Scotland's population. Roughly another 11 per cent lived in the Southern Uplands. The bulk of the population was in the three Lowland areas: the north-east had 18 per cent of Scotland's population; the east-coast counties no less than 30 per cent; and all the west and south-west only 20 per cent. There were many more burghs on the east coast than there were on the west, and in rural areas population densities varied sharply. In the Highlands they were often under 20 per square mile, whereas in much of the Lowlands 50 to 60 per square mile was more normal.

Between 1750 and 1850 this stable population experienced, like many other European countries, unprecedented growth. By 1801 there were 1·6 million people in Scotland. By 1841 the figure was 2·6. From 1750 annual growth in numbers jumped to 1·2 per cent, which was just behind England, though outstripped by Ireland's 2·1 per cent, and by many modern developing countries. Some decades saw even faster growth. Between 1811 and 1821 the annual growth was nearly 1·6 per cent, and some regions, such as the Western Isles, saw population growth far beyond the national average. This growth from 1750 saw a break-out from a traditional pattern of high birth levels contained by devastating mortality rates, to one where, despite a somewhat downward trend in fertility, life expectancy, for reasons still debated, improved so sharply as to sustain a heavy net gain in population.

Partly this was due to the fading away of the spectre of famine, which returned only to parts of the Highlands and Islands in the late 1840s. There were real shortages in the early 1740s. The '45 rebellion in the Highlands was played out against a background of near famine, but in Scotland as a whole famine was averted. There were to be a few local areas hit by dearth in the Highlands in 1782–3, but the eighteenth century, even the 'long' one from 1707 to 1832, saw no major famine. Apart from gains due to vaccination against smallpox from the late eighteenth century, medicine, excellent by contemporary standards though Scottish medicine was, probably contributed little to the parallel fading away of epidemic diseases on the old pandemic scale. Bubonic plague just ceased to happen after the 1640s, while better quarantine procedures prevented its reintroduction. Improved incomes by 1800 may have enhanced diet and clothing hygiene. However, there was a sharp rise in adult life expectancy in the middle decades of the century whose causes cannot be linked to obvious medical or social improvements; the fall in adult mortality is doubly puzzling because it came decades before any significant fall in infant and child deaths. Thus there are still many imponderables. The fact of swift population growth, however, is central to any analysis of Scottish society between 1750 and 1832.

In the seventeenth and early eighteenth centuries, the society experiencing these changes was profoundly rural. In terms of the percentage of its total population living in towns of 10,000 inhabitants or over, Scotland came low in European ratings, being eleventh out of a 'league' of sixteen in 1600 and 1650 and still down at tenth place in 1700. Towns fell into two legal categories: royal burghs and burghs of barony. Royal burghs were self-governing, though under self-perpetuating oligarchies whose composition was defined by the 'set' or constitution of the burgh. They had a direct relationship with the crown through their representative body, the Convention of Royal Burghs. Originally, only royal burghs could conduct an import–export trade. In the early eighteenth century there were about seventy of them. They were outnumbered by some 200 burghs of barony which were dependent on a feudal superior and whose growth before 1750 is rather masked by the use of a 10,000 threshold. By 1750 they were on the verge of erasing the basic differences between themselves and the royal burghs, for in 1743 a decisive legal case between Kirkwall (a royal burgh) and Stromness (a burgh of barony) had started a fifteen-year progress to the House of Lords, where the decision finally buried the monopoly of the royal burghs. This was to be a landmark in the decline of mercantilist and monopolistic approaches to the management of economic life which had characterized at least the previous three centuries.

Even so, only a tenth of the Scottish population was urban in 1750. Thereafter, urban growth, both in absolute and relative terms, was extremely rapid. By 1800 Scotland was one of the five most urbanized societies in western Europe, and by 1850 it was second only to England and Wales. Other countries had often had a long tradition of urbanization; the Netherlands and Italy, for example. Scotland's urbanization, as it closed the gap with England and Wales, was an extraordinarily fast process. No other European nation matched the speed with which the proportion of the Scottish population in towns of over 5,000 went up between 1801 and 1831 (from a fifth to a third). There was continuing growth in the east-coast burghs. Edinburgh, with its satellite port Leith, had 82,560 inhabitants in 1801 – still bigger than Glasgow, with its 77,385 inhabitants. But by 1821 Glasgow had pulled ahead. In general, west-coast towns benefited from the enormous sustained growth in Atlantic commerce after 1750, and none more so than the port of Greenock which went from 2,000 inhabitants in 1700 to 17,500 in 1801, and 27,500 in 1831, by which time it was one of the six largest Scottish towns. Yet the growth of manufacturing industry, with its need and ability to attract migration from rural Scotland and beyond, was even more important. Of the five Scottish towns which trebled their population between 1750 and 1821 – Glasgow, Paisley, Kilmarnock, Falkirk and Greenock – only the last was primarily a port town. The others were centres of industry.

Much of the migration which swelled urban populations drew on people who had long been used to frequent, short-distance movement in the countryside. Most of those who moved into Dundee in the period 1750–1830 came from the nearby Angus countryside. Landed proprietors who set up planned villages with a view to enhancing their estates looked to local people to inhabit them. In twenty-five such villages established in the north-east between 1740 and 1850, almost all the population was drawn from less then twenty miles away. On the other hand, the presence of Gaelic chapels in Glasgow, Dundee and other cities underlined the large flows of Highland immigrants. Given the poor soil of much of the Highlands and Islands and their complete lack of minerals that could sustain industry, pressure of population on resources was becoming intolerable (as it was in many parts of western Ireland) by the late eighteenth century. The Duke of Argyll described the island of Tiree as 'over-peopled' as early as 1771. There had long been a tradition of short-term migration from the Highlands to adjacent Lowland areas for seasonal agricultural work. By the end of the eighteenth century newspapers were remarking even in Edinburgh and Lothian on the numbers of harvest workers coming down from the Highlands, driven as much by misery at home as opportunity in the Lothians. Inevitably, such migration often became permanent. As late as 1851, 5 per cent of Glasgow's population was Highland-born.

Immigration and emigration further complicated the picture. Immigration, apart from very small groups of niche-entrepreneurs like the German Jews who funded the import of flax and hemp from the Baltic to Dundee after 1800, was predominantly Irish. Seasonal labour flows from ports like Derry accelerated with the coming of steamship communication in the 1820s. More generally, the period from 1810 to 1830 saw massive migration from east Connaught, and above all from Ulster, fuelled by similar factors driving people out of the Highlands, as well as the troubles of the rural linen industry. Fully 16 per cent of Glasgow's population was Irish-born in 1841. These immigrants were often Protestant as well as Roman Catholic. They brought their feuds with them, though Protestant Ulstermen, even when Church of Ireland people originally of English stock, tended to blend into Presbyterian Scotland quite quickly, not least, as disputes in Dundee Episcopal churches showed, because they had little sympathy with what they saw as Catholicizing tendencies in the Scottish Episcopal kirk which they first attended. By the mid-nineteenth-century peak 7 per cent of the Scottish population was Irish-born, which was double the English percentage. More Scots were 'of Irish heritage', but that was a code, not for Irish, but for Roman Catholic. In fact there was little difference, apart from religion, between many of these people and those descended from Highland folk who, in the southern part of the Highlands, migrated to Glasgow in large numbers, driven by desperate poverty and often handicapped by an inadequate command of the English language. Struggling in an urban slum was still better than starving in Donegal or Lochaber. The tragedy was not that surplus population left these poor lands, but that they left still overpopulated and vulnerable societies behind them. Sometimes their urban earnings were remitted to those areas to shore up a valued, if marginal, lifestyle.

Further north in the western Highlands those who relocated were liable to choose long-range emigration rather than internal migration. Substantial migration from Skye, for example, can be shown to have developed after Norman MacLeod of MacLeod, facing imminent bankruptcy, forced massive rent increases on his tenants when he leased his estate for twenty-three years from Whitsunday in 1769. His ruthless example was promptly followed by Sir Alexander MacDonald of Sleat, the Duke of Gordon, and other landowners. By 1771 there were reports that 2,000 people were preparing to leave Sir Alexander's estates for St John's Island (now Prince Edward Island). The substantial clan gentry or 'tacksmen', who held extensive tacks or leases which they then sub-let to small farmers, were deeply disgruntled. By February 1771 ten of them were known to have signed a bond to move to Canada, and had persuaded 100 families to engage to go with them. This tacksman-led emigration to North America, from maritime Canada to the Carolinas, became a widespread phenomenon in the western Highlands and Inner Hebrides.

Famously, Flora MacDonald, who helped preserve the Jacobite Young Pretender after the battle of Culloden in 1746, sailed with her husband Allan MacDonald of Kingsburgh and her brother-in-law Coll McAllister from Campbeltown in Kintyre to Wilmington in North Carolina in August 1774. Flora had never been a Jacobite. She helped Prince Charles escape for the same reason that General Sir John Campbell of Mamore, the commander of the Hanoverian troops hunting him, was latterly clearly trying not to catch him. As patriotic non-Jacobite Scots they wanted him out of the country before his capture generated appalling embarrassment and national humiliation. Her husband and their five sons all joined the Loyalist forces fighting for King George III in the War of the American Revolution when it broke out in 1775. Highland Jacobites who had fled to America immediately after the '45 were much more likely to take the part of the rebel colonies and their Continental Congress, often serving with distinction with the Continental army, but most of the recent Highland immigrants, led by tacksmen like Allan MacDonald, were staunch Loyalists. Kingsburgh held the king's commission as a brigadier-general. He went down to defeat at the battle of Moore's Creek Bridge in North Carolina with the other Highland Loyalists from along the Cape Fear river. By 1780 Flora had returned to Skye. Allan joined her in 1784, part of the tragic Loyalist migration after the war, a migration proportionately much bigger than the *émigrés* who left France at the Revolution.

In absolute terms, this first wave of Highland migration, sadly cut across by a long, vicious war, was not very large. Nevertheless in a local context it could be dramatic, as when a whole parish of about 600 people in Knoydart, led by their priest, are said to have left for a new settlement, Glengarry in Canada, in 1785. Though firm statistics are beyond our reach, the latest research suggests that perhaps in the first period of emigration, from 1760 to 1775, about 20,000 left. In the second phase, from 1783 to 1803, the figure may have been as low as 15,000. The emigration in no way restrained the steady increase in the population of most of the Highlands, though it did at times restrain specific landlords from rackrenting from fear of losing tenants to what was in effect a rent revolt led by their one-time allies, the tacksmen.

What is clear is that in the years immediately before the American Revolution, when emigration from Great Britain to North America increased so dramatically as to be a matter of deep concern to the British government, Scotland was, with Yorkshire and London, one of the three main source areas for massive flows of emigrants. In the Scottish case they tended to be whole families on the move, though of course there were also single men and women. They came from no particular urban complex, nor did they come exclusively from the Highlands or Lowlands. Apart from a few eastern counties, all Scotland seems to have been involved. At this date the political and social establishment in Scotland, and especially in the Highlands, was passionately hostile to emigration. People were useful as tenants, labourers, servants, cannon fodder for wars, and latterly as workers in the labour-intensive kelp industry which collected and burned seaweed to make alkali. Using the landlord-dominated Highland Societies of Edinburgh and London as lobbyists, landed interests secured the passage of the Ship's Passenger Act of 1803 which, under the guise of raising standards on emigrant ships, tried to price emigration beyond the pockets of most would-be emigrants. It failed. Emigration continued, especially to America, though its social bases shifted continually; in the 1820s and 1830s it was often skilled Lowland workers, like handloom weavers, and others in trades especially threatened by mechanization, who left.

Economic Development in Town and Country

Scotland in 1707 was a country whose economy was in many ways underdeveloped and fragile. Agricultural productivity was still low in all but a few regions, those around the major towns, even if the extent of agricultural 'backwardness' may have been exaggerated. Scotland lagged behind Ireland in the size and adaptability of its commercialized market sector, and its industrial products like woollens and paper were vulnerable in quality and price to English competition. These facts go far to explain several aspects of the Union settlement, for as well as offering to lift for ever restrictions on Scottish access to English home and imperial markets, the Treaty of Union was eventually structured so as to offer protection to vulnerable aspects of the Scottish economy. Producers of malt, salt and coal all secured terms which effectively privileged them in the Scottish domestic market, while the treaty also provided for direct subsidies for woollens and for various kinds of cash transfers. Direct subsidies to woollens was one device; refunding lost capital to shareholders in the ill-fated Company of Scotland was another. Particularly for malt producers, a favourable tax regime was laid down. Not much wonder, then, that there were complaints from Ireland about excessive concessions, since her legislature had petitioned in vain for union with England in 1703.

The imperial dimension of trade concessions was probably of little importance in 1707. Scots had long traded with English colonists anyway. It was legal under Scots law. The domestic market was, however, undoubtedly very important. Probably half of Scotland's exports in 1707 went to England in the shape of black cattle and linen, over the years in roughly equal amounts by value. These were crucial underpinnings for the rent rolls of the Scots aristocracy, who in the last analysis pushed the Treaty of Union through despite much less enthusiasm among the lairds and widespread signs of popular hostility in the burghs. Going into the Union from a pre-Union depression meant that many Scots were disappointed by the failure of the Union to jump-start their economy into the sort of sustained growth which had occurred in England in the era of the so-called 'commercial revolution' of 1660–1713. However, that spurt of English growth was slowing down by 1707. It had owed much to the re-export of colonial produce, while the Scotland of 1707 tended to have surpluses in areas where normally European markets were over-supplied. For example, outside freak years like the 1690s, Scotland produced more grain than it could consume. Its own internal grain markets were active. Transportation development, such as the important Edinburgh turnpike network established from 1713, and the military roads in the Highlands, must have lain behind the substantial convergence of grain prices in regional markets that had occurred by the second quarter of the eighteenth century. Fragmentary statistics suggest that overseas trade held up and may even have slightly increased, while there may have been a modest but real increase in the volume of coastal shipping in the decade after the Union.

There must have been improvement and capital accumulation for Scotland to survive the very serious harvest failures of 1740–41, which contemporaries compared with those of the 1690s. Famine was averted primarily by the willingness of local élites to use the mechanisms of the Kirk and local government to tackle the problem of dearth by banning malting of grain for alcoholic drinks, and by being willing to 'stent' or tax in badly affected parishes for at least the minimal poor relief which helped check the classic downward spiral from malnutrition to epidemic disease. Nevertheless, improved communications and a deeper national capital base, partly due to the sustained profits derived from linen and cattle exports, certainly helped. Famine was averted. As we shall see, the poor-relief system did little to sustain the vulnerable part of the population, especially after the middle of the eighteenth century. There was a system dating from the fifteenth century, originally fairly comprehensive for those recognized as settled in a parish or town, but between 1745 and 1832 it became progressively meaner, blaming poverty and want on 'moral degradation'. It was the absolute growth of the economy which lifted Scotland from the recurrence of dearth on a national scale, even if regional episodes like that in the Highlands in the 1840s could be tragic enough.

Industrial and Commercial Expansion

The period from 1750 to 1775 saw a steady acceleration of commercial and industrial growth. The latter sector was heavily dominated by textiles. Legislation in 1727 set up a Board of Trustees for Fisheries and Manufactures which rightly identified linen as the most promising Scottish industry, and used its limited funds to encourage technological progress and high standards in linen manufacture. Its officials stamped cloth intended for sale as a guarantee of its quality, with the result that much linen produced for use within the producing household escaped their scrutiny. Nevertheless between 1728 and 1815 Board records show that the quantity of linen produced for sale in Scotland went up from over 2 million to 36 million yards and in value from £103,312 to £1,403,767. Production doubled about every twenty-five years between 1725 and 1800. The expansion was seldom continuous for more than five years; there was relative stagnation in the 1730s and 1770s and periodic acute depressions. Fluctuations were thus normal. On the whole the tendency to instability increased over time and the period 1803–5 saw wild variations in output levels for linen.

Webs of linen produced by tenants, cottars and their families helped pay rent. The landed classes also benefited from mining in areas of Scotland, nearly all in the central belt, where coal seams were to be found. As late as 1760 only half-a-dozen primitive steam engines were at work in Scottish pits. Thereafter, the rising population increased the demand for coal for heating houses, just as industrial demand escalated. All collieries near the sea were linked to a salt-producing industry which used the otherwise unsaleable small coal or 'culm' to evaporate sea-water in salt pans – vast iron pans on the shore. Not very competitive in foreign markets, Scots coal was hewn for an expanding domestic market. After 1760 investment in steam engines, an elaborate system of rail-based, horse-drawn waggon ways, and other transport developments like the Monkland Canal (opened in 1790 to take coal from Monkland to the Glasgow market), ensured a rapid expansion of production. At the same time coal prices soared, doubling in the 1790s, partly because wages in the industry were rising despite, or perhaps because of, the fact that colliers, like salt workers, were legally servile until 1800. Other workers remained reluctant to enter the industry for a couple of decades after 1800 before a horde of Highland and Irish immigrants came into the pits, and wages could be cut.

Helped by Dutch-educated Scottish medical men, who were the only academically trained chemists of their day, a Scottish chemical industry was in existence by the late eighteenth century, producing inorganic bleaching agents by 1800, to service the textile trades. In 1798 Charles Tennant established the St Rollox chemical works in Glasgow, where by 1799 he was producing fifty-two tons a year of a dry chlorine-based bleaching powder. By 1825 the figure was 9,251 tons. One by-product of this manufacture was sodium sulphate, used as an industrial alkali in the manufacture of soap and glass. With the repeal of a crushing excise tax in 1815, this inorganic alkali was to sweep aside the rival organic product produced from kelp in the Highlands. By the 1830s the St Rollox works was probably the largest chemical factory in the world.

Economic developments tend to come in clusters. The fastest-growing industry in late eighteenth- and early nineteenth-century Scotland was cotton. It clearly benefited from the bleach fields, dye works and manual spinning and weaving skills already developed for linen. The first major cotton entrepreneurs tended to be Glasgow linen manufacturers. However, cotton was also a spectacular beneficiary of power-driven machinery and mechanization. Water-powered mechanical cotton spinning mills were created all round Glasgow, taking advantage of the falls on the rivers and often creating whole new communities. Labour was not easy to obtain. David Dale, whose large mill at New Lanark commenced operations in 1786, had to make a special effort to attract Highlanders. Similar labour recruitment problems faced the Buchanans at Deanston, and other employers at Catrine, Blantyre and Ballindalloch. Water power, already long established for milling grain, lay behind the west-to-east expansion of cotton spinning, which was to spread as far as Stanley, above Perth, where huge bends in the river Tay offered unique opportunities to cut across them with 'lades' (canals) and harness a big river's energy. More generally, the application of water power to textile and other manufactures ensured that a great deal of industry developed in the countryside and remained there until the second great spasm of urbanization following the agricultural depression of the 1870s. Dura Den, a small chasm on the course of the Ceres burn in Fife, became famous after 1815 for the fossil fish which freak circumstances 350 million years before had preserved in a layer of yellow Devonian sandstone there. By the mid-nineteenth century, when the local minister who had pioneered the discovery, Dr J. Anderson, summed up his achievement in *Dura Den: A Monograph of the Yellow Sandstone and its Remarkable Remains* (Edinburgh, 1859), it had become a heavily populated industrial area with half-a-dozen water-powered linen manufacturing or timber processing sites on its short length.

Steam power was ultimately to replace water power as the principal source of energy for manufacturing processes (though water-wheels were still in use in some Scottish textile works in the 1960s), but they developed slowly from their initial role as pumping devices in mines. The sending of a few of Bolton & Watt's improved steam engines with separate condensers and centrifugal governors to Scottish textile mills in the 1780s and 1790s was an important development. When Watt's patents lapsed in 1800 there was an increase in steam-engine sales in Scotland, amounting by the 1820s to a surge. It proved relatively easy to apply steam power to spinning, but weaving was a much more delicate process and successful power looms came quite late. Meantime, handloom weavers grew in number from 45,000 around 1790 to just under 85,000 by 1840, by which time their fate was sealed by the introduction and accelerating spread of power looms. In Dundee the first skilled power-loom weavers were tentatively introduced in the late 1820s. By the 1830s, power looms were common, but handloom weaving only declined absolutely in the 1850s. Cheap labour held back the full mechanization of weaving.

The Scottish iron industry was to be the core of the heavy metallurgy and engineering-based industrial complex which in the west of Scotland, though not in the east, was to supplement the textile-centred industrial development of the period from 1750 to 1830, adding a dynamic force to the Scottish economy. Before 1800 Scottish ironworks were not particularly competitive, and but for the protection which transport costs gave their domestic market they would probably have been knocked out by cheaper English and Welsh iron. There were famous manufacturers like the Carron ironworks on the river Carron north-west of Falkirk, founded by Dr Roebuck of Sheffield in 1760. When he sold out in 1773, it received a charter of incorporation setting its capital at £150,000. However, its most famous product, the carronade (a short-barrelled, rapid-firing naval gun), was a reminder of how dependent it was on war orders. David Mushet, a foundry manager, had identified in 1801 huge reserves of black-sand ironstone in central Scotland. Combined with the coal reserves of the region, this proved crucial, but only with the invention of the 'hot blast' process by James Beaumont Neilson in 1828. This involved heating the blast of air which supplied the oxygen flow to iron furnaces. It cut costs, increased productivity, and allowed raw coal to be used rather than coke. Between 1828 and 1838 Scottish iron production soared by 500 per cent. It was a new age.

The period 1707–1832 was not dominated by such factors. Its commercial developments were only in the later decades much affected by the steam engine. Water transport remained by far the most efficient means of moving goods and in 1832 the great bulk of merchant shipping still moved under sail. Steamships were significant by the 1830s only in the shape of fast steam packets whose coal consumption was so high that they were competitive only for moving people, perishable goods or those of high value over moderate distances. Coastal shipping and harbour improvements were becoming increasingly important for manufacturing industry by the 1820s. Long-distance trade was extremely important for Scottish ports. The tobacco trade loomed very large. By 1745 Glasgow was importing 13 million pounds of tobacco annually; the Scots tobacco firms steadily increased their dominance thereafter in the expanding Piedmont region of Virginia beyond the first falls in the great rivers. By the 1770s tobacco accounted for between a third and two-fifths of Scottish imports by value. Sugar, and the increasingly popular rum, accounted for another 9 to 15 per cent. Another 30 per cent or so was composed of industrial raw materials, such as flax, wood, iron and tar products, mainly from the Baltic. Manufactured imports like woollens and metal goods came mainly from England.

The volume of tobacco imports by 1775, 46 million pounds or some 21,000 tons, alone generated a formidable volume of shipping. Most of this importation of tobacco, followed by re-export to continental Europe, was based on regulatory provisions in the Acts of Navigation, prohibiting direct trade between the Chesapeake and foreign countries. By the middle of the eighteenth century the smoking habit had become widespread among Scots males, and by 1800 it was commonplace among working women. Ground tobacco was also widely consumed as snuff by both sexes. In textile mills, where the air was polluted by fibres, it was used to clear the nasal passages.

After 1783, with most of British North America now an independent, anglophobic United States, the tobacco trade withered. However, it had in its days of greatness been one of the commercial enterprises which fuelled the precocious expansion of Scotland's banking industry. The Bank of Scotland had been set up as early as 1695. Tainted by Jacobite associations, it had to see its monopoly breached by the chartering of the Royal Bank in 1727. Both tended to be conservative in lending and suspicious of branch banking, but the British Linen Company, sponsored by the Whig man of business Lord Milton and chartered in 1746 primarily to develop the marketing side of the linen trade, was by 1747 becoming a bank with a much more positive attitude towards entrepreneurial needs than the Bank of Scotland and the Royal Bank. Even so, western businessmen and industrialists found it necessary to set up their own banks. Inevitably, there were elements of instability. The collapse of the Ayr Bank in 1772 had severe short-term consequences, not least because all banks preferred to lend on heritable land security and many substantial landowners were hard hit by this failure. Nevertheless, eighteenth-century Scotland had in many ways a more advanced and flexible banking structure than England, with an earlier and wider general use of banknotes, especially ones of small denomination, to supplement the standard commercial bill of exchange. This undoubtedly facilitated industrialization and commercial expansion.

Agricultural Developments

The complex geology of Scotland ultimately determined the range of agricultural options available to its regions, which by 1800 were all deeply affected by the shifting patterns of demand and comparative costs in distant urban and industrial markets. Scotland's agriculture was still its biggest industry and employer. The desire for national enrichment through improvement found apt expression in June 1723 when the 'Society for Improving in the Knowledge of Agriculture' was established in Edinburgh. Its driving force was its secretary, the Galloway laird Robert Maxwell of Arkland. Its membership included many nobles. Even the Lord Provost of Edinburgh, Patrick Lindesay, was to publish in 1733 a book called *The Interest of Scotland*, in which he denounced what he saw as archaic agricultural methods, such as holding land in dispersed strips (runrig) rather than consolidated fields, and the holding of grazing land in common. To be hailed as an Improver was many a landlord's ambition. Such men looked to the advanced commercial agriculture of the Netherlands or England as their model.

Yet many of the Improvers were odd men out. The Earl of Stair could afford progressive hobby farming on the back of his years in lucrative official employment. Archibald Grant of Monymusk in the north-east had been expelled from the House of Commons for fraud and theft from a major charity. Robert Cockburn of Ormiston, a great Lothian Improver, effectively went broke and had to sell his estates. The fact is that until agricultural prices rose sharply, improvement carried to any lengths did not pay realistic returns on capital invested. Attempts to improve might be viewed with scepticism by tenants or other lairds. Someone who tried to improve his land by the innovation of liming was described by the established farmers of Peterculter in Aberdeenshire as 'not wise enough' (daft). Agricultural innovation could often be only piecemeal. Landlords tried to exploit the existing system. The second Duke of Argyll tried to squeeze out the middlemen in the clan system – the tacksmen with large leases – in favour of sub-tenants who were invited to bid competitively for their farms direct from the duke. This they did, but at levels they could not afford. Argyll secured enhanced arrears rather than rents. On the other hand, there is no doubt that the expansion of the low-overhead black cattle trade to England did raise rents, which in the Highlands were often paid in cattle-drovers' bills of exchange.

Enclosing, consolidation and the enlargement of farms did gather momentum, especially in fertile Lowland areas near big urban markets like Edinburgh and Glasgow. Liming, draining and land reclamation also became common in such areas, all increasing the productivity of holdings. With the big jump in agricultural prices during the French Revolution and the Napoleonic Wars, investment could be seen to pay. Change took various forms. Orkney doubled its agricultural exports between 1770 and 1790 without reorganizing holdings but with more sophisticated techniques, like the use of systematic crop rotation and increasing commercialization. By 1832, on the other hand, William Cobbett, the agricultural journalist, could describe the big farms of Berwickshire and Lothian as outdoor factories producing corn and beef with the help of a workforce of landless labourers, and of steam power. Their efficiency helped them survive the fall in prices after the cessation of war in 1815.

In the Highlands there had been continuous, accelerating change from at least the late seventeenth century. Rentals in kind were being phased out by élites who were often driven by debt which they had incurred by conspicuous consumption as they tried to ape the lifestyle of the Lowland and English upper classes. On the MacLeod estates in Harris and Skye, rents paid wholly in kind in the 1640s were paid half in money a century later. Commercialization was becoming pervasive. By the 1720s, 30,000 or more black cattle were being driven south to the great cattle fair or tryst at Crieff. The social coherence of clans came under tremendous strain as traditional chiefs were replaced by sons with no interest in inter-clan warfare, and an obsessive interest in higher rents. Campbell of Knockbuy's rents went up 400 per cent between 1728 and 1788, largely on the back of the cattle trade.

There was forcible change in key areas such as Lochaber as a result of destructive government military action designed to compel stand-outs from the last Jacobite rising of 1745–6 to abandon the illusion that further resistance was feasible. This continued a policy of social and political integration begun by the crown in the early seventeenth century. However, most change in the eighteenth-century Highlands was generated by the indigenous élites themselves. After the '45 uprising the government pushed through legislation designed to destroy clanship by depriving the landlord-chiefs of the hereditary jurisdictions that were essential to the coherent functioning of a working clan. Legislation also attacked the outward symbols of Celtic culture such as the kilt, and the traditional culture-bearers like the bards, not to mention the Gaelic language. Yet Celtic society persisted, with its language, reasonably well until the last quarter or so of the eighteenth century. At that point huge increases in external demand for Highland products like cattle, kelp, whisky, wool, mutton, slate and timber took over from internal reorganization by local élites as the dominant force in the Highlands and Islands. Those élites, who were the gravediggers of traditional society, then started to chase windfall profits on increased prices rather than investing for managed change. Above all, they racked up rents. In Torridon in Wester Ross, rents went up 1,000 per cent between 1777 and 1805. MacDonald of Glengarry put up his rents by nearly 500 per cent between 1768 and 1802.

Highland élites, especially in the era of the Napoleonic Wars, when agricultural prices soared owing to the cutting-off of external supplies and very high levels of government expenditure generated abnormal levels of effective demand, subordinated everything to increased production and higher rents. Many tacksmen were squeezed out, though some could mobilize the capital to survive as active entrepreneurs within the new, highly commercial Highland economy. In the name of rationalization a massive assault was launched on the township or *baile* which had, down the centuries, been the basic building block of Gaeldom. Starting in the 1760s, this assault had largely succeeded by the 1830s. The successor systems were, however, by no means uniform. Indeed, the Highland economy and society had always been both varied and, whatever commentators might say, so rapidly changing as to defy the label 'archaic'.

In Argyll, Perthshire and much of the eastern Highlands, where towns like Glasgow, Perth and Inverness were adjacent and able to absorb surplus population, the trend was towards reorganization into single farms, pastoral or arable, with one tenant, though usually also with a population of servants, labourers or shepherds. In the western Highlands and Islands a very different pattern emerged, in which townships were replaced by small individual holdings or crofts which were not capable in themselves of sustaining a family, and whose grazing rights on nearby hillsides were still held in common with other crofters. Landlord pressure pushed these communities towards the seashore to clear the interior for the large-scale farming of blackface and Cheviot sheep, which were steadily moving north into the Highlands after 1760 or so. By 1802 the sheep dominated the higher land in Perthshire, Argyll and Dumbarton, and the entire west coast as far north as Skye. Only in the far north from Ross and Cromarty up to Caithness had the sheep revolution not struck home, but even there, it was clearly coming soon.

The tragedy was that as the Highlands were pulled into the position of suppliers of protein and raw materials for newly-industrialized urban complexes in Scotland and England, they were also drawn into chronic dependence and instability. Black cattle remained a viable, valuable regional export until 1815, but only because of war demand.

In more competitive markets after the war boom had collapsed, their prices plummeted. Kelp was a huge employer of the casual labour available from the crofters who had been resettled in such numbers near the sea. Though population growth in the Highlands was slowing by the 1820s, partly due to out-migration, the process of growth was not arrested until after 1830. There were plenty of hands for the collection and burning of seaweed, which was the technique for kelp production. Food supplies for these dense, marginal populations depended vitally on the high yield of potatoes grown in 'lazy beds'. These were the reverse of their name, being ridges of soil, with seaweed used as manure, laboriously scraped together. Their outlines can still be seen all over the west. In Harris in particular they run through the rocks virtually into the Atlantic, partly to minimize the endless toil of transporting seaweed manure in creels on the backs of men and women. After 1815 the renewed import of cheaper, better, Mediterranean barilla alkali led to a collapse in the kelp prices which had sustained many rent rolls. Only in Shetland, where landlord pressure on smallholders to produce economic surpluses by fishing on the rich fishing bank around the archipelago was fierce, was a population as amphibious as that in the West Highlands and Islands in the heyday of kelp, when people spent so much time on the beaches or up to their waists in the freezing water.

Paradoxically, the landlord class in the western Highlands which presided over this pattern of radical change was itself profoundly destabilized by the course of events. Many were forced into extensive sales of parts of their estates to stay solvent. Even the mighty Campbell house of Argyll, historically not much given to surrendering control of anything, was in crisis after its head became a part of the free-spending circle around the Prince Regent (after 1820, George IV). By 1819, it proved imperative to sell the possessions in Mull and Morvern which the Campbells had annexed from the Macleans of Duart in the seventeenth century. The estates of Lord Reay in western Sutherland were bought by the Anglo-Scottish wealth of the ducal Sutherlands in 1829. Lord MacDonald sold out in North Uist to preserve his Skye holdings, while his Skye neighbour MacLeod of MacLeod downsized in Skye and sold off his mainland holdings to avoid bankruptcy. The Duke of Gordon sold his lands in Badenoch and cleared out of Lochaber, where he had for so long been a thorn in the flesh of Cameron of Lochiel.

Whole territorial empires disappeared, like that of the MacDonalds of Clanranald in the western mainland and southern half of the Outer Hebrides, which was sold off between 1813 and 1838. Nor did the turnover rate among Highland estates show any sign of slowing after 1832. It was to accelerate, if anything. High living in London may explain some of the failures, but it was really the collapse of so many markets simultaneously after 1815 which was so lethal. Cattle prices halved between 1815 and 1830. Kelp halved in price between 1815 and 1820, and its decline became irreversible when techniques were developed to produce industrial alkali from salt. Untaxable illicit distilling of whisky, which enabled Highlanders to turn their meagre barley crops into valuable, easily transportable spirits, came under aggressive new regulation from a revenue-hungry British state in the 1820s. Under-capitalized Highland fishing was hit by erratic migration of herring shoals away from western sea lochs. The Highland aristocracy, and especially the ex-Jacobite families, had tried to curry favour with the British government by raising Highland regiments on an ever-increasing scale from the Seven Years War (1756–63), to the War of American Independence, to the French Revolutionary and Napoleonic Wars. This employment of surplus young males collapsed after 1815. Despite the Duke of Wellington's best endeavours to salt away as many regular regiments as possible in colonial postings to save them from a cost-cutting Westminster legislature, there was mass demobilization. Only sheep remained profitable, a fact which ushered in the second stage of clearance of population after 1820.

Clearances hitherto had been aimed at moving people out of the interior glens to crofting communities on the sea margins. Virtually no landlord wanted to lose population. However, as the profitability of the kelp and black cattle trades built up between 1760 and 1815 declined, major families such as the MacDonalds of Clanranald and the Mackenzie chiefs, the Earls of Seaforth, were bankrupted. Under such pressure landlords from 1820 began to link assisted emigration with the idea of further clearances of population to make way for even more intensive sheep ranching. In 1827, the Clanranald estate managers had planned to ship 3,000 people to Canada from South Uist and Benbecula. In practice, no rapidly bankrupting Highland estate could afford the expenditure needed to link organized emigration to evictions. Between 1820 and the 1830s, wool prices fluctuated and the earlier pattern of rapid growth in the industry stalled. Before the 1840s, when famine gave the final push towards mass emigration, the Highlands and Islands are best seen as relentlessly destabilizing at almost every level, without quite plunging over the edge into visible disaster. The old landed families of the west were, however, in final decline by 1832. The odd exception which proved the rule, like the mighty ducal house of Sutherland, owed its grandeur to external factors.

In 1785 Elizabeth, Countess of Sutherland in her own right, had married the heir to the enormous landed and industrial wealth of the Marquis of Stafford, whose resources were rooted in the English Potteries country. Raised to ducal status, and able to use English capital to expand their already huge northern lands to near county size by buying up Lord Reay's estates, the pair set out to make Sutherland one vast, modernized, profitable estate. Their man of business, James Loch, a classic product of Lowland Enlightenment values, was confident that by moving population to the coast and encouraging industry there, while simultaneously bringing big commercial sheep farmers, often Lowlanders from the north-east, into the interior parts of the million or so acres of the Sutherland estates, the local economy could be re-invigorated. Loch, a fine flower of the Edinburgh Enlightenment, had moved in circles which had included luminaries like Henry Brougham, lawyer and Whig politician, and that other legal Whig, Henry Cockburn. Loch was mildly liberal, a devotee of rational improvement and of the political economy of Adam Smith. Like most convinced liberals, he had a dictatorial streak and was so convinced he was right that evidence to the contrary made no impact. As a local minister of the Church of Scotland pointed out as early as 1818, the sad fact was that despite all the traumas he inflicted on local society, Loch failed to create a more viable economy.

The classic pattern of a dominant but economically progressive aristocracy cooperating with closely linked bankers and small businessmen to raise landed incomes by constructive change in rural areas, and development of urban markets, had imploded in marginal regions. Free-wheeling capitalist development was by the 1830s proving volatile and unpredictable, rooted as it was in a wild fluctuation of comparative advantage. Whether it was Walter Scott in the Borders, or his friend Alasdair MacDonnell of Glengarry in the Central Highlands, men with expensive aristocratic tastes and poor land were going to the wall by the 1820s. Their misfortunes were another sign that an age was coming to an end.

Whatever landlords' problems, it was the poorest who suffered most of all. Of course, Highland poverty existed before 1750. The Highland Clearances were in some ways as much a consequence as a cause of the relative deprivation of the Gaelic-speaking population. In any case, the phrase covers a vast multitude of very different landlord-initiated events which led to the displacement of tenants. Consolidation of holdings between 1780 and 1830 along the arable fringes of the Highlands involved eviction of small tenants and sub-tenants, but the dispossessed were largely absorbed as the labour force needed by the new large farms. Elsewhere in the western Highlands and Hebrides, eviction, especially after 1820, involved profound trauma; the destruction of traditional society and its culture; and widespread bitterness and physical protest. Lack of alternatives to agriculture forced many to emigrate. Gaelic society never recovered.

Only about 10 per cent of the land surface of the western Highlands and Islands was cultivable, giving farmers there many fewer options for change than their Lowland counterparts. For geological reasons, many more Lowland landlords were in a position to supplement their rent rolls from mining, especially coal, than were Highland proprietors. In the Lowlands change had proved more consistently manageable by existing landowners, partly because they moved cautiously, and acted on a large scale only when stable market opportunities and favourable price structures made it safe to do so. Even so, different regions in the Lowlands moved to quite different chronologies. Much of the Southern Uplands was as depopulated as the Central Highlands by large-scale sheep ranching, and in the eighteenth century there were significant developments in both the west and east of the region. In the west, in Galloway, there was further depopulation to make way for consolidated cattle-grazing units using drove roads to walk their product to mainly English markets, and supplementing local cattle with Irish beasts shipped or, more usually, swum over the trifling twenty miles of water between Galloway and Ulster. Resistance by threatened tenant farmers, known as Galloway Levellers because they destroyed dry-stone cattle enclosures, was put down with troops and legal severity in 1723–5. The east, in the valleys of the Tweed and its tributaries, saw towns like Melrose, Hawick and Galashiels develop a water-powered woollen industry which by the 1820s was beginning to specialize in light tweeds.

Elsewhere in the Lowlands technical problems, such as the impracticality of economic drainage of clay soils before tile drains became freely available in the 1820s, and not very dynamic price levels for arable products, kept farm reorganization and the adoption of new crop cycles (using root crops and legumes to eliminate the need for fallow) at very modest levels before the 1780s. Improvers founded societies to discuss new methods, but wiser landlords held back. It was a combination of rising population, expanding nearby and English urban markets (especially in London), and, above all, soaring wartime prices for produce, fuelled by elimination of imports and huge state expenditure, which precipitated a great wave of change to consolidated, modernized, capitalized farming in most of the Lowlands between 1793 and 1815.

The impact of progressive commercialization and rationalization of Lowland agriculture over a much longer period was nevertheless traumatic for large sections of the rural population. Many lost any significant grip on, or access to, land. In areas of mixed arable farming, tenant numbers held up quite well, but in the extensive Lowland hill-farming areas there was widespread dispossession of tenants and, to an even greater extent, of the once numerous sub-tenants. Cottars, who were given a smallholding in exchange for seasonal labour on adjacent farms, had at one point constituted from a quarter to a third of rural society. By the time of the (Old) Statistical Account, an invaluable multi-volume source for eighteenth-century population and economy compiled from ministers' returns by Sir John Sinclair in the 1790s, the minister of Kilmany in Fife could refer to 'the annihilation of the little cottagers'. With many sub-tenants, they had been turned off their land, becoming an agricultural proletariat. Nothing like the spasms of rural rebellion which occurred in contemporary France or Ireland hit Scotland, though major food riots broke out in eighteenth-century Scotland roughly every ten years. As the militia riots of 1797 showed, Scotland was not altogether a cowed society. The explanation for the acceptance of widespread dispossession, at least before 1815 in the Lowlands, seems to have been the voracious demand for labour in both urban and rural industrial activity, as well as in still labour-intensive agriculture. Living standards probably rose overall, admittedly from a low base.

Social, Legal and Religious Developments

The Roles of Women

Scottish society between 1707 and 1832 rested in the last analysis on family structures inherited from earlier centuries. Within them the procreation and rearing of future generations occurred. In a society which, like all other European Christian societies, accepted patriarchal norms as the prescriptive ones, women were supposed to find their principal fulfilment and sphere of influence in the family. In practice, work consumed the lives of most Scottish women, whether countrywomen or town-dwellers. If unmarried, the daughters of the poor people who made up the bulk of Scotland's parents would most likely be in service to another household. Married women below the level of the comfortable bourgeois household had to work to sustain family income. They were their husbands' partners, if not in a family business, then in the business of sustaining a household. They were usually junior partners, but they were not the obedient, docile spouses of a prescriptive literature often written by clerics, and always remote from reality. Countrywomen worked, often at hard physical labour, outside the no more than two rooms they called home. Domestic cleaning requirements were minimal, and cooking limited to porridge and stews at best for much of the time.

Their very patterns of courting, conception and birth-giving were determined by seasonal patterns of work, which is where they first associated with men, whether carrying peats, or assisting at the shearing, or helping to feed the ravenous gangs of harvesters. With the widespread use of the scythe replacing the traditional women's tool, the sickle, harvesting on substantial Lowland farms became dependent, literally, on a cutting edge of physically powerful males, but they had to be fuelled with food and drink as well as money. Women, with children helping, did the miscellaneous work, such as hoeing and weeding, created by the new, intensive 'improved agriculture'. They were out in the fields in all weathers. Contemporary observers remarked on the low standards of hygiene and prematurely aged faces and figures of eighteenth-century Scottish countrywomen. The availability of permanent and seasonal work for women varied from place to place. Wet-nursing around Edinburgh and boarding out of idiots in Fife and around Glasgow may be indications of a lack of alternative forms of employment. Indoors, the female domestic servants in prosperous tenant farmer households coped with the hugely labour-intensive businesses of milking, cheese- and butter-making, brewing, baking, cooking for a large household, endless laundry, sewing and child-minding.

Urban women of all but the most prosperous classes were equally hard worked. The Newhaven fishwives who carried their menfolk's catches into Edinburgh in creels on their backs to sell their fish on the streets were only the most colourfully dressed of an army of female street traders. Scottish representative peers and MPs tended to buy consumer goods on a large scale in London during their visits to the metropolis, but Edinburgh was beginning to show signs of an emergent consumer society by the early eighteenth century. When the Duke of Hamilton of that time visited Edinburgh he would bring back 'bonny things for the bairns', such as toys – often, like Edinburgh's famous claret, imported. Women manned the street stalls and the ever-growing number of small shops, as well as providing an army of domestic servants who in Edinburgh petitioned as early as 1700 for the right to establish a mutual benefit society.

Spinning, a female domestic skill, became an important industrial one as the Scottish textile trades expanded, and women moved easily from the domestic putting-out form of the spinning industry in the late eighteenth century. First, that meant into the water-powered rural spinning villages, such as David Dale's New Lanark, which spread from Dumfriesshire to Aberdeenshire in the 1780s and 1790s; and, second, into the urban steam-powered factories which sprang up in all the major cities after 1789. The Scottish economy thus made massive use of female labour in this age of transition, but women entrepreneurs, even as the old guild and urban monopolies collapsed before a new competitive free-market individualism in the 1750s, were comparatively rare. Women could and did hold individual farm tenancies on modernized landed estates, and could be aggressive to the point of violence in trying to defend their rights to profit from newly-exploitable resources. However, for many rural women, widowhood carried with it the risk of eviction. In towns, women had had the right to continue to operate their late husbands' businesses even in the heyday of incorporated monopoly groups. The King's Printer in Scotland in the early eighteenth century, a militant litigant but a poor printer, was the widow of Andrew Anderson, Agnes Anderson; she also founded the Valleyfields paper mills at Penicuik in 1709. And a woman, Christian Shaw, established the Paisley fine-thread industry after 1725.

Nevertheless, it must be recognized that most men in towns never owned their own businesses (or houses), and that the vast range of new employments which urbanization and industrialization made available to women in later eighteenth-century Scotland meant that an increasing number of women were able to support themselves and their children, and leave abusive husbands. There were plenty of the latter, but women did have a legal resort in the shape of the consistorial courts, which administered modified medieval canon law as a means of regulating the marital disputes which reached them. They were even-handed between male and female, and though the number of divorces actually granted, usually for adultery, was small, judicial separation on grounds of cruelty, usually by the husband, was more common, and by the end of the eighteenth century the judiciary was adamant that the theoretical right of a husband to inflict 'moderate correction' on his spouse was obsolete.

Amongst the lower orders, with little or no property to worry about, marriage by mutual attraction appears to have been usual. Upper-class women, those of the middling orders, and even humbler people with property, traditionally only married after a legal contract had been drawn up. Whether peer, merchant, farmer or tradesman, the bridegroom expected the bride to bring a 'tocher' or dowry into the marriage (which had to be returned if she died childless within a year), but also himself to agree to provision for the wife within marriage, and after widowhood. Often there was also a pledge of financial support for daughters, who might otherwise have been deprived of any inheritance, especially if a stepmother produced a male heir for their father. As women in the Georgian era came increasingly to think of an affective marriage based on 'falling in love', they were liable to make runaway marriages – which more often than not ended badly, leaving them without the usual legal protection of their property rights. By default, all of a woman's movable property belonged to her husband, hence the bitter hostility of propertied parents to irregular or runaway unions. By the latter part of the eighteenth century almost all parents accepted that a match required the consent of the principal parties, but no affectionate mother or father wanted their daughter to be robbed and abused by a plausible rogue who inveigled them into sudden matrimony. Even a widowed Countess of Strathmore could end up in deep trouble in 1777 when she married the Irish adventurer Andrew Bowes who, on the strength of manipulative blarney and an army commission, had already married, plundered and buried his first rich wife, a northern English heiress. Lady Strathmore was undoubtedly unwise, but she did not deserve the decade of physical and psychological abuse Bowes inflicted upon her in a barefaced attempt to seize control of her estates. She was eventually saved from the villain, whom she divorced, by an ante-nuptial settlement she had, in a rare fit of sense, unilaterally registered in 1777.

It was with the emergence of a self-conscious and ever-expanding middle class which used women as wealth-bearers and transferers, but which increasingly spurned aristocratic patterns like the negotiated marriage protected by a legal settlement, that the problem of women's property rights became acute. In 1760 there was little sense of class in a still hierarchical Scottish society which thought more in terms of 'orders' or 'estates' within the body politic. By 1830 there was plenty of class feeling, nowhere stronger than in certain sections of the urban middle class, which was concentrated in the larger Lowland towns and was disproportionately adherent to churches that had seceded from the Kirk. Initially, there was no great theological dimension to this continuing fracturing of the Presbyterian inheritance. Without exception the secessions were provoked by the implications of the restoration of lay patronage by law. However, seceding churches invariably tended to develop a populist, evangelical flavour, which appealed to rising urban business groups. Resentful of older service élites linked to the aristocracy, like Edinburgh advocates, and convinced that the self-perpetuating oligarchies which dominated the Scottish burghs were not business-friendly, the newer middle classes used dissenting religion as a form of self-assertion.

Evangelical Christianity, prosperity, and a tendency to regard multiple procreation and purely domesticated wives as status symbols, made these formidable men exponents of conservative patriarchalism. Female education in the eighteenth century had tended to be much less extensive than male, even at the parish school level, where far fewer girls than boys attended, and beyond basic literacy girls were traditionally expected to concentrate on sewing and other domestic skills. By 1766 a *Scots Magazine* reviewer complained that the newly-fashionable boarding schools for girls hardly taught traditional domestic skills, but rather inculcated social skills such as music, drawing and dancing, designed to fill more or less compulsory leisure hours. The odd remarkable woman, like the mathematician Mary Somerville who was born in Fife in 1780, managed to achieve intellectual recognition, but males had a vice-like grip on the learned professions other than teaching in the early nineteenth century, and the brave new world of the liberal bourgeoisie around 1830 was hardly a form of female liberation from the restrictive stereotype of 'the angel in the house': quite the contrary.

At lower social levels, the irony was that the very range of opportunities which offered women a new measure of independence, because of far more numerous work options, also tended to confirm their secondary status in the market economy. This was very true of the textile trades, which between 1780 and 1840 dominated industrial growth. By 1826, 90 per cent of Scots manufacturing jobs were in textiles, at a ratio of six in cotton, three in linen, and one in wool. Cheap labour crowded into textiles so abundantly that its flow retarded mechanization. By the late 1830s over 30 per cent of the poorly paid handloom weavers were Irish-born. Women were concentrated in preparatory trades and domestic spinning. The early mechanization of cotton-spinning using steam-powered spinning mules required physical strength on a scale which marginalized women spinners and enabled well-organized male spinners to control labour flows through an apprenticeship system. In Glasgow in 1837 there were only seventy female mule spinners to 1,000 male ones. When women were introduced into spinning mills it was often in an attempt to dilute expensive, strike-prone male artisans, which may be why the introduction of female spinners to the Broomward Mill in Glasgow in 1819–20 led to men burning it down. Later, in 1832, a few Glasgow women spinners were blinded by thrown acid.

The mines which, with their associated salt works, had always had a large female element in their workforce, also eventually saw dilution by cheap non-militant male Irish labour. In this case the process was complicated by the rigid bondage, akin to serfdom though not technically slavery, in which Scottish colliers and the salt workers associated with them were held in the eighteenth century. Early-seventeenth-century legislation laid down that the workers in the mines and salt works could not leave their work, to which their whole family was hereditarily attached by law, and were pursued and imprisoned if they fled. On the other hand, they could not be sold apart from their workplace; their property was their own; and though to an extent socially isolated, they had regular access to marriage and religion. They were also well paid and industrially quite militant, being given to sit-down strikes in the pits. Workers obviously would not enter an industry, however desperate for work, when they and theirs thereby entered bondage. The Emancipation Act of 1774, which began to dismantle this system, explained quite openly in its preamble that it was designed to encourage fresh entry into the industries. As it only applied to those entering after 1 July 1775, many mining families remained unemancipated until the end of the century when further legislation of 1799 finally removed all traces of a serfdom verging on slavery.

The system depended on family units working together underground. In the 1790s a Clackmannan collier, with his wife and daughter acting as bearers, could earn 12s. for a five-day week, along with a free house, yard, and perquisites worth 30s. yearly. The men with their superior power-to-weight ratio wielded the pick, but the women literally raised the coal. There was no rush of new male labour into the pits after 1800. The big expansion came much later, so employers began to think of altering the sexual division of labour by excluding women and children. Men were then the sole support of their families, which was said to have a 'steadying impact' and make them 'much more regular'. Reformers denounced as intolerable the scanty clothing and 'degrading' toil of women working underground. In fact, given the heat and effort, the clothing was sensible and the toil no different from carrying a creel of fish or peats. A third of the labour force in collieries, and more, was female in the 1830s, but by 1842 women were legally banned from working below ground. Miners could cultivate conservative patriarchy on radically reduced family incomes, which made them fear dismissal much more: that is what had been intended all along. Law was a most formidable instrument of social control and manipulation. Indeed, it is worth remembering that witches were still being prosecuted and executed during the dawn of the Enlightenment. The witchcraft statutes were not repealed until 1736 (witchcraft was thereafter deemed to be a form of fraud), but the last execution had been at Dornoch in 1727 when an old woman was strangled for allegedly turning her daughter into a pony.

Legal Developments

Scots law had a long history behind it when it and its courts were effectively guaranteed survival by the provisions of the Act of Union. Whether there was an appeal from the Scots supreme Court of Session and High Court of Justiciary in Edinburgh to the House of Lords in Westminster was a matter prudently glossed over, though subsequently that appeal was established in practice. Many ambitious young Scots crossed the border to make their careers in the English legal system, most notably William Murray, fourth son of David, fifth Viscount Stormont, a man from a family with a Jacobite background who used his Scottish connections to secure his earliest briefs at the English bar. He rose to be Lord Chief Justice of England and Earl of Mansfield. In 1771 his judgement in Somerset's case, which freed any black slave in Britain, was part of the background to the emancipation of (white) Scottish coal and salt workers from 1774.

In retrospect, the best-remembered of eighteenth-century Scots lawyers is not Mansfield but James Boswell, the son, heir and despair of Alexander Boswell (1707–1832), Lord Auchinleck, a Lord of Session. James Boswell craved social and literary success in London all his adult life. He passed for a Scots advocate in 1766, but in 1785, at the age of forty-five, he moved to London, had himself called to the English bar in 1786, and assiduously observed Mansfield's style by attending his legal sessions in Westminster Hall. He saw moving his family to London as an escape from an 'irksome' and 'narrow provinciality' in Scotland. Starting with hopes as high as they were fragile, he made nothing of it, despite trying very hard both in London and on the Northern Circuit. In the end he enlisted as henchman and toady to James Lowther, first Earl of Lonsdale, a ruthless, wealthy English magnate hell-bent on political domination in north-west England. That relationship too turned sour. Boswell learned, the hard way, that Mansfield's career was the brilliant exception, not the rule.

It was in Scotland itself, more than elsewhere in the British monarchy, that lawyers as a group rose to exceptional prominence in this era. Quite eminent figures were qualified, practising lawyers. Ludovic Grant of that Ilk, chief of a great Speyside clan, was less than enthusiastic in support of the Hanoverian government in the 1745 rebellion for various reasons, one of which was its failure to give this qualified lawyer his heart's ambition: the gown of a Lord of Session. In the controversial Appin murder trial of 1752, James Stewart of Aucharn was tried and executed for the murder of a government factor on a forfeited Jacobite estate, Colin Campbell of Glenure, the Red Fox. One of the judges, acting as Lord Justice General, was Archibald Campbell, Glenure's chief and third Duke of Argyll. Yet on the whole it was as resident managers in Scotland for an increasingly absentee, London-centred élite that Scots lawyers came to dominate Scots society. The supreme example was the able, patriotic and enlightened Andrew Fletcher, Lord Milton, Lord Justice Clerk from 1735 to 1748. Milton was local under-manager of Scotland for its dominant political boss, his fellow lawyer the first Earl of Islay, later third Duke of Argyll. Islay turned up at his own clan capital, Inveraray, for the Appin murder case, but he usually spent a disproportionate amount of his time in London. It has been shown that the absentee élite did not confine itself to using lawyers as under-managers. They were perfectly happy to use junior members of their own family, well-disposed lairds, and civil servants like the Welshman Gwynn Vaughan, who held a post in the Customs in Scotland and was a useful agent for Islay – despite his recurring tendency to run away from a country he detested. In strategic burghs like Edinburgh, the key to control over the Convention of Royal Burghs, there was always George Drummond, government nark and crooked real-estate manipulator; he was usually a reliable placeman and sycophant to Lord Islay, despite a monstrous conceit of himself that occasionally made him forget his place. His sanitized posthumous image is one of Scotland's great whited sepulchres.

Nevertheless, lawyers were very important. Their legal tradition was distinctive because Roman/Dutch, and therefore quite unlike the precedent-based common law tradition of England, Ireland and anglophone North America. Based on principle, not precedent, Scots law continued to develop the tradition of Institutes laid down by Viscount Stair and Sir George Mackenzie in the late seventeenth century. The posthumous *Institute of the Law of Scotland* (1773) by John Erskine, Professor of Scots Law in the University of Edinburgh, from 1737 to 1765, is a fine example of this continuing development. It stressed the essential rationality of law, its unavoidable social context, and the significance of the concept of public interest, which might even limit the rights of property-holders. Until the French Revolution swept over the Netherlands and broke the connection, Scots lawyers continued to complete their education with some experience of a Dutch university. It was one of the few things James Boswell and his father had in common.

The year 1747 saw a major change in the structure of Scots law in the shape of the abolition of most franchise courts or heritable jurisdictions. Before that date they had profoundly influenced the pattern of the Scots legal structure, keeping justices of the peace, for example, marginal figures compared with their centrality in the governance of the English shires. This was despite the 'Act for rendering the union of the two kingdoms more entire and complete' of 1707, which constituted the sixth chapter of the statute book of the sixth year of Queen Anne's reign (VI Anne c.6). Combined with the politically motivated decision to abolish the Scots Privy Council in 1708, this legislation in theory gave Scots justices the same powers as their English equivalents, but as late as 1730 Sir John Clerk of Penicuik could write, 'Tho' the countrey be in the hands of certain justices of the peace, as in England, yet there are some shires in this countrey where they doe not meet at all.' The reason for this can be seen in say, Lanarkshire, where there was really no business for the justices' quarter sessions. It went elsewhere: to the courts of the hereditary sheriff, the eight regalities, the two baronies, the two burghs and the numerous kirk sessions. Only after March 1748 would the suppression of franchise courts and the reduction of the power of church courts allow the justices to emerge, though never on the English scale.

The franchise courts had always excluded a very large proportion of the king's subjects from the jurisdiction of his courts. In a criminal action at local level, heritable jurisdiction would operate through a barony held by the accused's feudal superior, and from that, on appeal, through the court of the superior's lord, usually a regality. They went on being created into the early eighteenth century and, at the time of abolition in 1748, there were 160 regalities in Scotland. They varied widely in size, but the biggest ones were very large. In 1728 the Justiciary Court of Argyll and the Isles exercised authority over a huge area in the name of the Duke of Argyll, whose deputy claimed for it a jurisdiction 'as sovereign as any Court in Britain, and the proceedings of it only subject to the review of the High Court of Parliament'. It would be quite wrong to suggest that the administration of justice in heritable courts was necessarily inferior to that in royal ones, as a glance at the regality of Glasgow's records show. That regality tried many capital cases in the first half of the eighteenth century, as it dealt with the teeming population of an overcrowded, mushrooming city. A case of infanticide in 1735, for example, brought by the court's procurator fiscal before two judges (one laird, one lawyer), and a jury of fifteen, shows the quality of the procedure.

Undoubtedly all over Europe infanticide was, for largely symbolic reasons (destruction of life by a mother viscerally challenged God's providential order and male concepts of femininity, seen as part of that order), so defined as to ensure a high rate of conviction among accused women. A dead baby basically doomed the mother if she did not have witnesses to testify the death was not her fault, something a teenage servant birthing an illegitimate baby in a shed in the dark lacked. Adam Smith, lecturing on jurisprudence, said: 'The laws of most countries being made by men generally are very severe on the women who can have no remedy for this oppression.' As usual, Smith's generalization was at best half true. Early modern courts were traditionally lighter on women than men, and very reluctant to impose the harsher penalties available on female offenders, partly because they did not regard them as wholly independent agents. Infanticide was the great exception. Even when the theological imperative to fence femininity began to lose its urgency as Catholic and Protestant regimes ceased to jockey for position as the most ultra-righteous, the literati of the Scottish Enlightenment were producing a secularized version. William Alexander, MD, whose *History of Women* (1779) is an incoherent monument to obsessive scribblerism and no guide to reality, let alone female reality, as satiric contemporaries said, was at one with Smith in this, and with John Millar, who wrote on the condition of women in his *Distinction of Ranks in Society* (1771). Smith and Millar had their own oblique approach to reality, but they were far more powerful thinkers and writers than Alexander. Yet all agreed: progress for women down the ages consisted in leaving the 'primitive' world of matriarchy and women sharing the public sphere to ever greater 'refinement' and 'elevation' in modern societies where women were trained in 'graces' to make them, in the words of Lord Kames, 'objects of pure and elevated affection' – for men, of course.

There is a good deal of this built into the character of Jeanie Deans, the heroine of Walter Scott's *The Heart of Midlothian* (1818), which has been described as 'the bourgeois novel of infanticide', and is very, very loosely based on the trial of Isobell Walker for infanticide in Dumfries in 1738. Scott, as ever, wished to shore up the contemporary moral order. Jeanie Deans had to be virtue incarnate. Reality in Glasgow in 1735 was that eleven prosecution witnesses, including three surgeons who reported on the mutilated neonatal corpse, and two midwives who found abundant milk in the breasts of the woman who denied giving birth, established guilt beyond all reasonable doubt. The lawyer for the defendant then admitted guilt and pleaded, too late, exculpating circumstances; the woman, after a trial (by contemporary standards) of exemplary fairness, was condemned to death under the statute II William and Mary c.21. The same statute gave Scott his theme for the novel.

Because of its perceived – but in fact debatable – importance in sustaining the Jacobite rising of 1745, the entire system of franchise courts was undermined by the Heritable Jurisdictions (Scotland) Act of 1747 (XX George II. c.43) passed by the Westminster parliament as part of its programme of social engineering designed to eliminate the possibility of future Jacobite rebellions. The regalities were simply abolished. Loyal Whig Hanoverian regality-holders then promptly and not unreasonably demanded almost £60,000 in compensation. The jurisdiction of baron courts was restricted to a £2 fine in civil suits and a £1 fine in criminal cases. Most ceased to function because they became unprofitable. Like the regality courts, they disappeared on 25 March 1748 when the legislation took effect. Only the chivalric jurisdiction of the High Constable, largely symbolic, was retained intact. If the Middle Ages could be said to end at a given point in Scotland (which, of course, they do not), a case could be made for 25 March 1748 when Scotland was, as it has remained, under the uniform jurisdiction of the crown.

Religious Developments

Prosecuted in man's courts, many crimes were deemed also to be transgressions of God's laws. The Presbyterian Kirk remained between 1707 and 1832 the basic frame of reference in the religious sphere, as well as a vital factor in the family, social welfare and education. Its history divides in many important ways at about 1740, when the mainly theological preoccupations of the early eighteenth century gave way to ecclesiastical controversy. The party known as 'Moderates' (supporters of lay patronage) began to gain a grip on ecclesiastical power, despite the resistance of 'Popular' or evangelical opponents (defenders of at least a congregational veto on the patron's choice). The Scottish Enlightenment entered a phase which seemed to pose a subversive challenge to the Christian religion. It was a phase signalled by the publication in 1739 of David Hume's *Treatise on Human Nature*, a work which fell stone dead from the press, but proved the precursor of a cascade of disturbing and much more successful publications from Hume's fluently corrosive pen. The early eighteenth century had seen Professor John Simson of Glasgow accused first in 1716–17 of heresy on the nature of the process of redemption. He was acquitted, but rebuked for using language that laid too much emphasis on nature and reason to the disparagement of revelation and grace. By 1726 the presbytery of Glasgow was accusing Simson of Arianism: denial of the divinity of Christ. A perplexed General Assembly suspended him in 1729. He had his salary, but might not teach. There was an imputation, if not declaration, of heresy. Professor Archibald Campbell of St Andrews was accused of Rationalism in 1736 (but not pursued) after the publication of his archetypally proto-Moderate book, *The Apostles*

No Enthusiasts (fanatics). Most insidious of all before 1739 was the influence of Francis Hutcheson, Professor of Moral Philosophy in Glasgow from 1729 until his death in 1746. He developed the deist third Earl of Shaftesbury's concept of innate, intuitively known moral sense; he was accused of teaching that the measure of human merit was the happiness of others; and he minted the phrase 'the greatest happiness for the greatest numbers', which Jeremy Bentham and the English Utilitarians were to take over and modify slightly.

Theological ferment was therefore endemic in the Church of Scotland long before the age of the high Enlightenment from about 1740 to about 1790, but that was merely a sign that it was a live part of the 'Catholic' or Universal Church. There was, in fact, a whole range of theological positions in the various groups within the church, and it would be quite wrong to argue that the Moderate and Popular parties stood for distinct, polarized theologies. The Moderates as a party emerged in the General Assembly after 1750 under the leadership of William Robertson, who later became principal of Edinburgh University. Its leading members were undoubtedly heavily influenced by Christian Stoicism as propagated in the blend of Christian and classical culture that formed the core of Francis Hutcheson's teaching. However, there were important ministers like Robert Wallace, Patrick Cumming, and even Francis Hutcheson himself, who shared the theology without supporting the policies eventually identified with Moderatism. There were at least four theological positions at all times and probably in all parties, ranging from strict scholastic Calvinism, which stressed predestination; to Evangelical Calvinism, which stressed free grace; to liberal Calvinism, which was anxious to accommodate rational criticism and was reserved on strict confessional standards; to the Arianism or Pelagianism (that is, denial of the total depravity of man) of a small minority influenced by Professor Simson. Increasingly after 1750 the Popular party responded to rational Enlightened criticism by moving from speculative divinity to biblical Evangelicalism, on the solid theological ground that God did not speak to Christians by metaphysical exercises, but through revealed religion, with its straightforward demand for piety to God, charity to man, and sober and godly living.

Patronage, or the right of a lay patron (often the crown) to nominate a minister to a parish, had been reinstated in the Kirk by controversial legislation of 1712, despite Presbyterian emphasis on the right of a congregation to choose. It was only one of a range of issues that disturbed a religious community whose chief end, as modern readers may forget, was to glorify God and enjoy him for ever. However, patronage was a disruptive issue. In 1733 Ebenezer Erskine, one of the ministers in Stirling who had been prominent in a previous row over patronage in Kinross between 1726 and 1731, was suspended from his charge for refusing to withdraw a fierce objection to patronage he had made to the Synod of Perth and Stirling. Three ministers who supported him were also suspended. Attempts to appease these men by the 1734 and 1736 General Assemblies of the kirk were rebuffed when the dissenters constituted themselves a presbytery and were joined in 1737 by four more ministers, including Ebenezer's brother Ralph, minister of Dunfermline. In 1740, the Assembly deposed them. This original secession did not repudiate Establishment principles, in that it withdrew from a perceived corrupt Establishment in the hope of rejoining a pure one. Even the Erskines' sympathizers were appalled by their course of action; it established secession as a permanent feature of the ecclesiastical scene, with predictable sectarian polarization, as the secession attracted and expounded the most conservative variety of scholastic Calvinism. Successive secessions followed.

Some of the products of these further splits were theologically much more liberal, such as the Relief Kirk, which grew out of a crisis in the 1752 General Assembly, one in which the Moderate party was in firm control. Their candidate for Moderator, Patrick Cumming, won comfortably. The presbytery of Dunfermline declined to admit an unpopular presentee, and the Assembly resolved to depose one of its ministers. Fifty-two members voted to depose Thomas Gillespie, minister of Carnock, with another 102 members abstaining. The original secession of the 1730s had by 1760 spawned ninety-nine congregations in Scotland, with more in Ulster, though it was riven by faction, first in 1747 between Burgers and Anti-Burgers over the licitness of oaths taken by town councillors, and after 1795 between Auld and New Lichts over the weakening of the authority of the seventeenth-century Westminster Confession of Faith. Gillespie and his followers turned their backs on this tradition of rancour and fission when in 1761 they set up the Presbytery of Relief. They offered to hold communion with all sincere Christians of any denomination. They also queried the whole concept of a church–state link. The saintly Gillespie was less than happy about his schism, eventually urging his own congregation to return to the Church of Scotland, which they did. However, the existence of vigorous sects making a strong appeal to tenant farmers, artisans and in the towns to small businessmen, especially in the west of Scotland, meant that there was by the early nineteenth century a rapidly growing Presbyterian dissenting interest.

The early stages of this development hardly worried the Moderate party. Secession was to them an opportunity and advantage which confirmed their grip on the Kirk. They depended, crucially, on control of the General Assembly. Like the Westminster politicians with whom they were so anxious to come to terms by not challenging the fact of patronage, they grossly exaggerated the inherent powers of the particular representative body they happened to be able to control; they then used that authority to stamp on rival centres of legitimacy. Patronage was contrary to the basic tenets of Presbyterianism and of the Church of Scotland. That was not really debatable. To use the supreme court of the church to intimidate presbyteries and synods which declined to violate the law of that church, was to carry liberal pragmatism to the point of usurped dictatorial authority; but that for self-righteous liberals has often been a short road. Moderates like Principal Robertson, or his friend Hugh Blair, minister of the High Kirk of St Giles and from 1761 incumbent of a new chair of rhetoric and *belles-lettres* in the

University of Edinburgh, established and funded, modestly, by the town council, seldom doubted that they were right. These clerical Moderate literati, particularly the close-knit Edinburgh group, had a towering conceit of themselves, and seemed to work on the assumption that nobody else could show the sort of cultural awareness of which they were capable. It was not true, as was demonstrated by the row over the fact that John Hume, minister of Athelstaneford, had become involved with the theatre by writing the play 'The Tragedy of Douglas'. First performed publicly in Edinburgh on 14 December 1756, with the author and several other ministers present, it elicited censure from the presbyteries of Edinburgh and Glasgow of the play; of the playhouse itself, at a time of national distress due to a war when the poor were the prime sufferers; and of the ministers' attendance. The Reverend Alexander 'Jupiter' Carlyle, most prominent of those censured, wrote vigorously in his own cause. The (rather bad) play went on to wholly unmerited success.

A leading lay Evangelical, the advocate John MacLaurin, who was to become Lord Dreghorn when made a member of the Court of Session, wrote a reply to the defenders of 'The Tragedy of Douglas', which was written from a wide knowledge of contemporary literature and an active participation in Edinburgh literary life. MacLaurin made some telling points. He would have welcomed a great Scots tragedy. Other things being equal, ministers of the Gospel had better things to do, like succour their people's distress, than seek eminence in *belles-lettres*. If a Scottish play were to achieve success it would be better to do it on the back of merit rather than the preposterous Moderate puffing of 'Douglas'. Lastly, the Moderate literati, organized in groups like the Select Society, were becoming absurdly conceited literary dictators.

Politically, the Moderate grip on the kirk depended on the peculiar nature of the General Assembly, composed of ministers and ruling elders (ordained, but lay in outlook). As politically illiberal government rather than theological questions became the predominant issue of contention for those excluded from ruling circles in the later eighteenth and early nineteenth centuries, overt criticism of the composition of the Assembly became possible. The Popular party did in 1768 secure the appointment of a committee to correspond with the royal burghs (who controlled urban patronage), the landed interest, and presbyteries, with a view to securing parliamentary remedy for the grievances of patronage. The Moderates suppressed it the next year, but in 1769 Andrew Crosbie, a leading Popular spokesman, published *Thoughts of a Layman concerning Patronage and Presentations*. Like many opponents of the existing system, Crosbie was no advocate of 'one man, one vote' in the selection of ministers. He was a social conservative. Quite clearly most of the Popular party would have been appeased by a veto: that when the process of selection, however arranged, was complete, a candidate who in the event was still repugnant to the Christian community concerned should not be forced on it.

The reason why the Moderates saw no need to offer even token concessions to what was plainly the predominant view among church members was summed up in Crosbie's tabulation of 944 benefices in the Church of Scotland: the crown had the patronage of 334; the nobility, 309; and the landed gentry, 233. Now the nobility and lairds, especially the latter, could have Popular tendencies. However, the General Assembly always met in Edinburgh, which meant that ministers and laymen from remoter, often Popular-inclined areas, had difficulty attending, while the ruling elders in attendance always tended to be dominated by Edinburgh lawyers – some Popular, of course, but led usually by a phalanx of government supporters, including the principal law officers of the crown. An influential minority, the Moderates for a lengthy period could just about control the Assembly.

Their programme of accommodation with government was not meant to be overtly sycophantic. On the contrary, by ceasing to bang its corporate head against the brick wall of Westminster stubbornness over patronage, the Moderates hoped the Church of Scotland would eliminate any danger to the principle of Establishment, and clear the way for a constructive engagement with the state in the joint task of shaping a Christian commonwealth. If the Moderates parodied their Popular opponents in their writings as bigots and clodhoppers, they were themselves parodied by Popular pamphleteers as social butterflies with a tendency towards infidelism. As is so often the case, the literary sources were exaggerated tropes which provided little guide to the realities. Despite the worldly tone of his posthumous autobiography, the kirk records show Alexander Carlyle to have been an assiduous pastor. As a young incumbent often absent seeking literary contacts, Robertson had been a genuine pain to the fathers and brethren of the presbytery of Haddington, but he grew up to be a gravely dignified prince of his church. Moderate sermons were not always a thin gruel of humanist philosophy. Often they drew heavily on the Latin works of John Calvin. Where the Moderates could be criticized was on the unreality of their vision.

The power of the crown was given them to defeat their opponents, but the secular-minded Westminster politicians who increasingly controlled crown patronage and power never shared their vision. They were Erastians, godless Erastians in most cases, looking for an ecclesiastical manager to advise them and keep the lid on the Church of Scotland. From 1736 to the fall of Sir Robert Walpole in 1742, the Campbell brothers, Argyll and Islay, used the Reverend Patrick Cumming. Thence to the fall of Lord Tweeddale in 1746 the Reverend Robert Wallace managed matters, until Cumming made a comeback. Principal Robertson then became the dominant figure until replaced by Principal George Hill of St Andrews, who not only managed crown patronage, but also filled so many chairs in the University of St Andrews with his relatives that chapel services there were said always to start with Psalm 121: 'I will lift up mine eyes unto the hills, from whence cometh my help.'

Spiritual vitality was elsewhere. The first settled, ordained Seceder minister in Hill's own St Andrews was not a man Hill would have welcomed as a colleague. He was a former champion wrestler who had kept the inn at Gairney Bridge in Clackmannanshire when the four 'Secession Fathers' met there in 1733 to lead the first post-1712 secession. New groups were attracted, paradoxically, by what was in many ways a traditional tendency. The seventeenth-century piety of the Church of Scotland, much obscured by assiduous Victorian editing of the sources to produce appropriately sober Covenanting role-models for a puritanical bourgeoisie, was full of features which in the twentieth century would be described as charismatic. The eighteenth century saw not just survival, but also rejuvenation of this tradition, especially in the connection between mass religious revivals and the great ritual and apostolic feast of the annual communion season. Calvinist theology on the Eucharist was very 'high', to the point of being close to certain forms of Jesuit eucharistic theology. There was no doubt about the 'real presence' of Christ as the long tables of communicants were served at (in rural parishes) outdoor communion, preceded by fasting and followed by feasting. The fathers of the kirk may have failed, to their chagrin, to shift their flocks to the practice of frequent communion, but they had built in a sense of the mystical rapture of the occasion which was impressive.

Although ministers and elders, the ordained presbyters of the kirk, were all male, women had always been very important in the Presbyterian tradition, notably in late seventeenth-century conventicles. Calvin, whom Scots Presbyterians revered, had after all said he could himself see no reason why women, with a superior gift of piety to men, and the quality of intelligence, should not enjoy equal status with men in God's church. He then added he knew St Paul did not agree, and he felt he had to defer to St Paul. Nevertheless, circles of praying women had traditionally sustained and influenced leading ministers.

Nor was Scotland the only stronghold of what the embittered and sceptical Robert Burns called, in his remarkable but misleading poem of 1785, 'The Holy Fair'. Ulster, New England and the maritime provinces of Canada had by the 1740s a well-entrenched similar tradition. That was why the 'Great Awakening', which convulsed the religious lives of many from the 1740s, was a transatlantic evangelical revival, owing much to ocean-spanning figures like the English Methodist George Whitefield, who between his graduation from Oxford in 1736 and his death in Newburyport, Massachusetts, in 1770, preached some 18,000 sermons throughout Britain and America. Methodism, until it was marginalized and driven out, was a movement anxious to cleave to the Church of England, of which its founder, John Wesley, was a high church Arminian priest. The Church of Scotland was spared a similar disastrous divorce by the fact that its ministers were willing and able to participate in a vast emotional revival like the 'Cambuslang Work' of 1742, in a Clydeside parish with Covenanting traditions and stimulus from Whitefield himself. Scottish Methodism always remained small, as did the Baptist and Congregational communities, despite the fact that both denominations were able to root in the fertile soil of the ecumenical, itinerant, evangelical preaching sponsored by the brothers James and Robert Haldane of Airthrey in Stirlingshire. Between 1798 and 1810 the Haldanes sank £70,000 into their campaign, but even the Popular party in the kirk found their style unacceptable. Their habit of acknowledging only ministers of whom they approved, and the defection of one or two of whom they did approve to the Seceders, compounded their scant heed for the parochial system, not to mention their conservative support for the public administration of ecclesiastical discipline, which most Popular as well as Moderate clergy were beginning to feel was outdated.

This last point was important. Even during the Presbyterian revival of the 1690s, there were signs in the larger towns that the Kirk was having to make concessions in its enforcement of discipline. And even in the rural parishes where its power held up longer, the Kirk's ability effectively to regulate morality was waning in this period. During the eighteenth century three-quarters of north-east men accused of fornication appeared before the kirk session of their parish to acknowledge paternity; by the mid-nineteenth century less than a third did so. Changing values associated with the fragmentation of Protestantism, a revised poor law, new economic opportunities and greater geographical mobility account for this decline. Always more successful in imposing its moral and religious views on its own voluntary adherents, the kirk became less concerned with their enforcement on the whole community during the eighteenth century.

The first part of the eighteenth century had seen the failure of two alternative religious options to shake the pro-Hanoverian Presbyterian ascendancy in Scotland. Of these, the less formidable option was the small residual Roman Catholic community, or rather communities, for though individual Roman Catholics were pervasive, significant concentrations were localized in regions like the Enzie in the north-east, where there was a seminary at Scanlan on the lands of the Duke of Gordon in Glenlivet. Of the 16,500 or so Roman Catholics in Scotland in 1763, two-thirds were in the Highlands and Islands. The southern Hebrides and Arisaig had concentrations of essentially pre-Reformation Catholicism, revived by seventeenth-century Franciscan missions. The seminary had originally been on Eilean Ban in Loch Morar in Clanranald territory until the rampant Jacobitism of the host clan drew dangerous government attention after the '15 rising. There was a Roman Catholic community in Edinburgh, but virtually none in Glasgow, and elsewhere in the Lowlands there were pockets associated with noble houses. Propaganda in Rome notionally ran Scotland as a mission with two vicariates, one Highland and one Lowland. Only as late as 1827 did the influx of Irish Roman Catholics to the west of Scotland necessitate a third vicariate. For forty years Bishop John Gordon, a native of Glastirum in the Enzie and a relative of leading Jacobite families, provided exemplary, dedicated and courageous leadership before he died in 1746, but the date of his death underlines why little progress was made.

There were internal stresses, despite the tendency of both Rome and its opponents to depict Scottish Roman Catholicism as monolithic. It is quite clear from the nature of the Scanlan seminary's library in Banffshire that Jansenism (a controversial, debatably heretical tendency in seventeenth- and eighteenth-century Catholicism), with its Augustinian theology and puritanical ethos, was a major influence. In Scotland as in Ireland, Jansenism survived papal denunciation in the bull *Unigenitus*. More lethal was this minority's rampant Jacobitism, denied of course by the mission's statutes, which proclaimed strict political neutrality, but this was pure public relations for non-believers' sake. Priests were Jacobite to a man. Bishop Gordon encouraged the '15 rebellion. Bishop MacDonald blessed the '45, and ended up an exile in France, while his colleague Bishop Smith fled to England and remained there between 1747 and 1751. Government persecution was politically not unreasonable after 1746. There were other problems with Scottish Catholicism, like priestly inadequacy and apostasy. By 1776, Scots Roman Catholics were a threat to nobody, but legislative proposals of 1779 to lift many of the penal laws provoked rioting in both Glasgow and Edinburgh. This underlined the depths of popular anti-Romanism and the stresses of the American war, which had lain behind the provisions of the bill to allow Roman Catholics access to the British army.

The other failed religious alternative by 1746 was the Episcopalian option in the Church of Scotland. That is how it is best seen. The episcopate of the Church of Scotland had refused to accept the Glorious Revolution of 1688–90, leading to a purely Presbyterian ecclesiastical settlement. This was unpopular with the gentry of several regions, who remained attached to Episcopalianism and gained official toleration by an act of 1712 pushed through by English Tories. Rightly seen as Jacobites, Episcopalians were a disliked, distrusted minority. These people were not nineteenth-century sectarian Episcopalians, deeply influenced by the High Anglicanism of the Oxford Movement, and with small pockets of deep popular support supplemented by the socially ambitious carriage trade. They were Jacobite members of the Church of Scotland who wanted to keep the Episcopal order in that church in the form which had been normal in the Restoration era, when it had coexisted quite happily with most of the structures of a Presbyterian polity, from presbyteries to synods. North of the Forth, a very high proportion of the clergy were of this persuasion and, backed by stubbornly conservative lairds and nobles, they could and did hang on to their parishes. The elders of Brechin cathedral consistently refused to cooperate in 'planting' a sound Presbyterian minister, enabling the Episcopalian Jacobite John Skinner to hang on. The north-east was strongly Episcopalian, as were most of the Jacobite Highlands. Further south the situation was more mixed. There was a significant Presbyterian power in Perthshire in the shape of the first Duke of Atholl, High Commissioner to the General Assembly of the kirk in 1712–14, but branches of his family were Episcopalian and the powerful Roman Catholic nobility and gentry of south Perthshire could and did obstruct the establishment of Presbyterian ministers, even in parishes where there were no Roman Catholics outside the big house.

The failure of the '15 rebellion saw the first effective drive against Episcopal clergy.

Especially in the north-east, they had revealed themselves in their true colours in 1715. Influenced by mystical quietist traditions from France, they had depicted themselves as apolitical, and most had signed the Oath of Abjuration of the Pretender in 1712, but they openly and ardently supported the rebellion. Widespread and overdue evictions merely drove the expelled clergy into school-teaching or the households of the Jacobite lairds and nobles, where they served as tutors, chaplains, musicians and even architects, and taught their creed to the next generation. Like counter-Reformation Catholicism, it was an integrated, authoritarian world view, teaching that after the great national sin of the Revolution of 1688–9, when Scotland had spurned indefeasible hereditary right, God had visited upon her famine, plague, war and faction, which afflictions he would only lift with the restoration of the main Stewart line. It was an increasingly unconvincing argument, but it nevertheless carried the predominantly Episcopal leadership of the '45 rising through the rebellion, confirming the courage of some on the scaffold into the 1750s.

By then, the Episcopalian–Jacobite option was no longer serious either in secular politics or the church. The communion was divided between 'qualified' chapels who prayed for King George, and Jacobite hold-outs, embittered by post-1745 persecution, whose bishops finally ceased to pray for the exiled house on the death of Prince Charles in 1788. Thereafter, there came a slow but unmistakable recovery based on attracting middle- to upper-middle-class support for a dignified and moderate creed in an age of turmoil. In Edinburgh this development was symbolized by the building in 1815–18 of St John's Episcopal church, designed by William Burn, as the handsome Gothic western termination of Princes Street; it was financed by Bishop Sandford from donations and an issue of shares.

The central issues facing the Kirk at the turn of the century were, firstly, its relationship with a rapidly changing society, and, secondly, whether its relationship with the state could be so adjusted as to make of it a mutual partnership in coping with the challenges thrown out by those changes. The wars against a perceived godless French Republic and then Napoleon from 1793 to 1815 tended to make church and state cling together, but there had always been tensions in post-Union Scotland between a national church which clung to the medieval concept of the nation as an essentially homogeneous Christian community, and a social and political leadership which contained a significant non-resident element, quite often not adhering to a Presbyterian Establishment themselves, and seldom sharing fully in its ideals.

A crisis over rural poor relief in mid-century is an example of this. Traditionally, Scots poor law, set up about the same time as the Elizabethan poor law system in England, was parish-based; liberal in its use of outdoor relief to a broadly construed category of unfortunates; and ready to supplement inadequate voluntary donations for the poor by 'stenting' or assessing and taxing the better-off for varied periods. Stent was paid half by the heritors or principal landlords of the parish, and half by the other inhabitants. Increasingly, the redistributive implications of this were resented and opposed by wealthy landlords, some of the most militant of whom proved to be absentees, resident in England (especially London), and adherents of the Anglican Church. By a series of collusive actions in 1751–2 before the Court of Session, whose judges were appointed for their political loyalties as well as their legal distinction, and all of whom were, of course, themselves landlords, the traditional poor relief system was replaced by a wholly bogus 'Old Scots Poor Law'. This was remarkable for its mean-minded hostility to outdoor relief, increasing exclusion of the able-bodied unemployed, and its pathological aversion to stenting. The judgements which did the trick simply transferred control of funds wholly to the heritors, by-passing the kirk session, which was liable to include mere tenants. Since these judgements enabled the heritors to hijack in some cases significant endowments left by the charity of the past to the kirk sessions for relief of the poor, the General Assembly rightly protested the offensive Erastianism of this *coup*, for *coup* it was. The Moderates, however, made it their business to suppress this issue until it dropped out of sight.

In rural areas, as long as harvests were good, the impact of this shift of power was normally limited. Much less easy to sweep under the carpet was urban destitution. It grew as rapidly as did towns, and as industrialization became widespread so did the problem of cyclical unemployment. Then there was the fact that the medieval church had not normally provided parochial services in the burghs, where the town councils had been instrumental in the creation of great, central burgh kirks, like St Mary's in Dundee, the kirk of the Holy Rood in Stirling, St Giles in Edinburgh, and Holy Trinity in St Andrews. Even when divided up in the post-Reformation era, they were by the early nineteenth century quite inadequate, to the point where voluntary collections for the poor, the Holy Grail of the 'Old Scots Poor Law', were bound to be inadequate. It was in the towns that innovation became vigorous as the result of cooperation between church and town council. Sunday schools spread rapidly in urban Scotland in the 1780s. In 1787, the Reverend William Porteous, in the aftermath of Glasgow's first and very violent cotton-mill strike, successfully urged the city fathers to set up Sabbath schools to occupy and educate child workers on their one day of rest. In Aberdeen in 1787 the first such school was set up 'for the instruction of poor children in reading English, learning the principles of the Christian religion, and psalmody', but also in the hope that it might decrease the rate of burglary during the hours of divine service.

This was the background to the rise of Thomas Chalmers, native of Fife and graduate of St Andrews, within the Church of Scotland. A conversion to an ardently evangelical outlook came to him only in 1810, long after his 1803 settlement as minister of the rural Fife parish of Kilmany. Thence he was translated in 1815 to the prestigious Tron kirk in Glasgow. There he embarked on two main enterprises. One was to reconcile science and religion through popular lectures, such as his 'Astronomical Discourses'. The other was to re-create the self-sustaining Christian rural community in an urban context. In

1819 he persuaded Glasgow town council to create a new parish in the crowded east end of the city. By 1819 the 'Old Scots Poor Law' had reduced support for the poor to very low levels in the countryside. In the towns, the higher, more traditional, levels of support had tended to survive, and as poorhouses or workhouses were rare in Scotland, the support was outdoor, not within institutions. Depression in 1819–22 increased the fiscal burden of urban poor relief. Chalmers removed St John's parish from the statutory poor relief system, backed up ultimately by payments from the revenues raised by city rates. Instead, there was to be a purely voluntary contribution system whereby the poor were encouraged to sustain the poor through family solidarity, supplemented by a reluctant doling out of small sums by kirk elders re-programmed to give as little as possible. Supplemented by intensive evangelization and a vigorous Sunday school movement, the experiment was, like Chalmers himself in many ways, a spectacular, charismatic failure, as several sceptical ministers of the Kirk had the independence of mind to say. The experiment collapsed in the 1820s after Chalmers left the parish, but his message was so acceptable to the wealth-holders of his day that there was bitter reluctance to face the truth. Critics like the Edinburgh physician William Pulteney Alison dared to doubt whether the 'deserving' poor were a meaningful category: 'If we reserve our charity until we meet with human beings exempt from sinful propensities . . . we may reserve it for the next world.' Such an outlook made more progress as the result of the frightening cholera outbreak of 1831–2, which made it clear that abject poverty bred disease which killed rich people as well as poor ones, than from rational argument.

After 1820 the evangelical party in the General Assembly was led by the Reverend Andrew Thomson of Edinburgh, on whose death in 1831 the leadership went to Chalmers, by then Professor of Divinity in the University of Edinburgh. In the fateful year 1832, Chalmers became Moderator of the General Assembly. It was still the aim of virtually every member of that Assembly to make a success of a church–state relationship. The tremendous social problems accompanying industrialization, the rise of various kinds of Seceders, and the beginnings of mass migration from Catholic as well as Protestant Ireland, meant the Kirk had to be dynamic to avoid being threatened with the sort of moribundity which the relentless dead hand of the Whig politicians, who had usurped the powers of the royal supreme governor, had inflicted on the Church of England. Church extension beyond the limits of a parish framework only capable of a glacial pace of change, and at least some modest financial support to underline the truth of an Anglican bishop's plaintive insistence that an establishment was meant to make the state religious rather than the church political, were minimal requirements. Above all, dialogue and partnership, especially after the 1832 franchise extension, was expected. It was a naive expectation of any Westminster government. They responded to effective pressure, but the Moderates had deliberately dismantled the carefully modulated guerrilla warfare which the kirk had waged against the excesses of patronage, while stifling the Assembly's voice of protest about the iniquity of poor law 'reform', and the scandal of needless secession.

For Moderates like Principal William Robertson, the policy of accommodation with government worked. From April 1759, when he was made chaplain of Stirling Castle, he progressed from Lady Yester's chapel to the prestigious Old Greyfriars kirk in Edinburgh, to being a chaplain to the king, Principal of Edinburgh University and Moderator of the General Assembly in 1763 (the prelude to a sixteen-year ascendancy in its councils). In that same year he was appointed to the post of Historiographer Royal (vacant since the death of the genealogist George Crawfurd in 1748), with a salary of £200 per annum. Robertson took his place in that succession of influential conservative clergymen consulted by Scotland's current political manager on the use of crown ecclesiastical patronage; but by the early 1830s the failure to elicit any adequate response from government and the rise of Popular evangelical dominance in the General Assembly, at a time when the emotionally seductive, if strategically inept, option of secession was an established precedent, had created a situation fraught with the danger of a disruptive revolution of long-frustrated expectations in the Church of Scotland.

Political Life

Some would argue that politics in most early modern countries was little more than a froth floating on the surface of societies which changed very little. Historians look for the 'political moment' when the activities of government began seriously to impinge on the day-to-day life of ordinary people, and they tend to place that moment later and later. Only when it had come, goes the argument, could there be 'politicization' in any depth. Prior to that moment politics could be seen as primarily an activity of the numerically small élites at the top of essentially hierarchical societies. Even apparently draconian actions like forfeiture of estates on a large scale after the '15 and the '45 rebellions did not affect the basic position of 90 per cent of the people living on those estates. They were never, in most early modern societies, going to own land. Few did. Most were tenants, for whom the central issue was not ownership, but terms of access to land. They were never likely to be absolutely denied access to land, since an estate without tenants was a useless, profitless asset. The élite of landowners constituted the effective political nation as well as being the managers of the dominant agricultural sector. As long as they were not divided over religion or the succession to the crown, politics in the modern sense of clash of values and interests was replaced by patronage. By 1747 the Hanoverian succession and Presbyterian settlement were unchallengeable. As in contemporary Ireland with its entrenched Anglican élite, management replaced politics.

In practice, Scotland between 1707 and 1832 both illustrates and challenges this paradigm. In the early eighteenth century there was a good deal of passion in Scottish politics, going much deeper than the élite, and producing occasional violent and dramatic episodes. Yet this was not an era which saw significant change in Scottish society. Equally paradoxical are the final decades of this period. Between 1790 and 1815 French politics were tumultuous, as the Bourbon monarchy collapsed into a radical and aggressive republic which in turn mutated into a Napoleonic empire whose origin was violent and whose end was traumatic and bloody. Yet French society changed very little in the period between 1790 and 1815. In Scotland, by way of contrast, social and economic change in the late eighteenth and early nineteenth century was spectacularly profound and fast. Yet until the very end of the 1820s, the Scottish political scene demonstrated a profound immobilism. Partly, it is true, the very tumults of France were used to reinforce the *status quo* in Scottish politics, but the paradox runs far deeper than just that antithesis. It is true that throughout the period from 1707 to 1832 the distribution of loaves and fishes between members of the Scottish ruling élite remained central to that élite's perception of the function of politics, but to penetrate below the surface it is essential to address the discontinuities as well as the continuities of Scottish political history in this era.

The Era of Political Integration and Protest, 1707–36

The primary political motivation behind the incorporating Union of 1707 operated at different levels. One affected the balance between the sharply defined and bitterly competing English Whig and Tory parties in the Westminster parliament. Scottish parliamentary factions remained frozen after 1707 into the two groups which had emerged from the old Scots parliament: the Argathelians or followers of the Duke of Argyll, and the Squadrone Volante, which was led by nobles not prepared to knuckle under the Argathelian sway. A third party, the Jacobites, was technically excluded from parliamentary politics by its inability to take the oaths to post-1689 sovereigns. In practice some did, especially in the reign of Queen Anne between 1702 and 1714. She was, after all, a Stewart, and though it is clear that she never intended to allow her half-brother, the Jacobite pretender or claimant James Francis Edward Stewart, to succeed her, Jacobites could exercise their impressive capacities for wishful thinking and believe that she might arrange for James to succeed. A minority, and only a minority, of the still formidable Tory party between 1707 and 1714 was in fact crypto-Jacobite. Especially after 1715, the forty-five notoriously venal Scots MPs at Westminster became an important buttress of an often unpopular Whig ascendancy in British politics, while still retaining their old internal factional division down to at least 1746.

There is little doubt that the fully incorporating Union was profoundly unpopular in Scotland below the levels of the majority of court supporters in the old Scots parliament who pushed it through. Of course, supporters of the Act of Union denied this, but then they would. Their behaviour was a better guide to their beliefs than their words, for they did not risk an election process for the first Scots MPs at Westminster, who were selected by the discredited last Scots parliament. The Scots did have a strong, if complex, sense of identity which, from the medieval wars of independence to the Covenanting movement of the seventeenth century, had defended Scottish identity by mobilizing society at levels well below the aristocracy. Petitions, a basic form of community expression of opinion, poured into the dying Scots parliament. There was not a single one in favour of the incorporating Union. Nor was hostility to the Act of Union confined to known malcontents like Jacobites. It was cross party and faction, and well summed up by the presbytery of Lanark's petition to parliament of 14 November 1706 where a unitary kingdom with only one Parliament was denounced as 'destructive to the true interests of the nation as well as the church'. Urban mobs in Edinburgh, Glasgow, Dumfries and Stirling reinforced the point. It was all in vain.

Yet the contempt of Westminster for opinion out of doors presented a priceless opportunity to Scots Jacobites. They alone were prepared to use force, and force was the only form of discourse likely to catch the attention of the post-Union rulers of the United Kingdom of Great Britain. They were therefore in a position to capture the leadership of Scottish nationalist sentiment, a formidable addition to their core conservative, aristocratic, Episcopalian constituency. The man who seized on this truth was Simon Fraser of Lovat, crook, shyster (he employed George Crawfurd, the Historiographer Royal, to help him with his claim to the barony of Lovat and typically never paid him), and as anyone who has read his voluminous extant correspondence will agree, a truly awful human being. He was in exile in France at the time of the Union, less because of his Jacobite tendencies (which came, went, and came) than because of a well-justified charge of rape he preferred not to face. Louis XIV was desperate to escape from the huge strains generated by the War of the Spanish Succession which, thanks to the military genius of the English commander, the duke of Marlborough, and his Imperial counterpart Prince Eugene, was not going well.

Lovat sold the French crown an invasion plan, with Scotland the target. As experience already showed he was more than capable of then buying the favour of the London government by revealing to them the plans he had sold to the Jacobites and their French backers, Louis XIV very sensibly locked him up in a fortress by authority of a *lettre de cachet* (usually employed to prevent the abduction of heiresses into a runaway marriage) until the operation was completed. The plan appears to have been the only Jacobite venture in which the Old Pretender (a young man of twenty) intended to issue printed addresses only to the natives of his 'ancient kingdom' of Scotland. Landing with French troops in Fife or Lothian, James was to take advantage of the widespread disaffection with the Union to seize control of Scotland. He was then — and this was the clever bit — to rerun the Bishops' Wars of 1639 and 1640 in which the Scots Covenanters had brought Charles I to his knees, by launching an invasion to seize the source of London's domestic and industrial fuel supply – the Tyne–Tees coalfields in north-east England. The aim was not to destroy Queen Anne's regime, but to force England to the negotiating table, with a view to peace for France and independence for Scotland. Militarily, as the Commander-in-Chief North Britain later publicly admitted, Scotland was indefensible. British forces were fully committed on the continent. However, the expedition was botched. Neither the French naval nor military commander liked his assignment. Admiral Claude Forbin had been involved in the French bid to colonize Thailand in the 1680s. He made a rather better job of finding Thailand than the Firth of Forth, which he overshot so badly that by the time he beat back against the wind Admiral Byng's Royal Navy squadron could catch him and chase him off. Westminster had had better luck than it deserved.

Anglo-French war was usually good news for Jacobites, as only the French crown, among European powers, was possessed of the military muscle to underwrite a Stewart restoration, if it was prepared, which it never was, to make that restoration a first priority. Yet Anglo-French war brought into being a regular British army which proved an extremely attractive vehicle for the martial bent of the Scots ruling élite. In 1707, eighteen out of the nineteen Scottish army officers sitting in parliament had supported the Union, as had twenty-one of the twenty-seven Scottish peers serving as officers or with eldest sons in the army. The War of the Spanish Succession, like the '15 and the '45 rebellions, saw the issue of many new commissions which were opportunities for pro-Union Scots. Peerage families became military dynasties. In the period 1707–46, eight members of the Dalrymple family, for example, held commissions, notably Field Marshal John Dalrymple, second Earl of Stair. 'Red John of the Battles', John second Duke of Argyll, also eventually retired as a field marshal after forty years in the British army. A smaller number of élite Scots joined the Royal Navy, where the way to make money was to be lucky with prize captures while holding senior rank. In the army a mixture of influence and purchase would start a young man off in junior positions, which were not profitable. Once a company, and then a regiment came along, regular profit was taken for granted on basic running costs, and senior commands usually carried very significant perks and opportunities. Not only were the first, second and fifth field marshals Scots peers (the Earls of Orkney and Argyll in 1736, and Stair in 1742), but the proportion of Scots peers who became general officers much exceeded the proportion among their English and Irish equivalents. Distinguished Scots soldiers like Argyll, Stair or the third Earl of Hyndford often had second careers as diplomats, being deemed to have the ideal experience and *gravitas* for an ambassadorial post of consequence. It has to be added that they all had to have courage. An eighteenth-century battlefield was a concatenation of lethal accidents in an arena swept by whirring musket balls, squalls of lethal canister shot, and cannon balls. To have a career, an officer had to have the guts to take it, and the luck to survive.

Integration into a British élite was therefore a process which co-existed with other and sometimes opposite trends. The Scots nobility had been the key to passing the Act of Union, but they had expectations which were often bitterly disappointed by post-Union reality. English propagandists like Daniel Defoe had promised a spectacular rate of economic growth in the new common market. His motives were political and sectarian. He had no idea what would happen. The Scots peerage was further enraged when, in 1711, the House of Lords, for internal partisan reasons, ruled that the Scots Duke of Hamilton was not entitled to sit in the Lords on the strength of his newly-granted United Kingdom peerage as Duke of Brandon. The Duke of Queensberry, principal fixer for the Act of Union in the Scots parliament, had been given a United Kingdom peerage as Duke of Dover in 1708 and had sat in the Lords, but had been banned from voting for the sixteen Scots representative peers. Between 1711 and 1782 Scots peers with English peerages lost in both ways: they could neither sit nor vote for a representative. In any case, by 1710 the sixteen were infamous for nearly all being tools returned on a government list put through by patronage and intimidation. In 1713 a motion in the Lords for the repeal of the Act of Union was only narrowly defeated, and in 1715 the Duke of Atholl presented the new Hanoverian monarch, George I, with a Perthshire petition to the same effect.

The death of Queen Anne and the Whigs' virtual *coup* following the accession of George I marked the eclipse of the Tory party, whose government style had suited many conservative Episcopalian Scots. When the Whig Sir David Dalrymple of Hailes stole and piratically printed the Scots Jacobite Lockhart of Carnwath's subversive *Memoirs of the Union* in 1714, he asked rhetorically in a vituperative preface how you could 'satisfy any Revolution Protestant, why any toleration should be granted to a Scotch episcopalian'. It is interesting that the man who sparked off the greatest of Jacobite risings, John Erskine, Earl of Mar, was a disappointed office-seeker, an architect of the Union who had to talk fast to explain his U-turn on that and the House of Hanover, which he had greeted with oleaginous flattery. He left London for Fife and then for his Highland estates before he raised the Jacobite standard on the Braes of Mar in September 1715. A windbag and opportunist from Westminster like Mar would never have achieved much had he not been offering to toss a firebrand into a powder keg. Scotland was ripe for rebellion, for a complex of political, economic and social reasons. The Pretender was a peg for grievances. He came late to the rising and left from Montrose with Mar early in 1716. There were pockets of pro-Hanoverian sentiment, especially in the far north, Glasgow and the west of Scotland, but the fact that open elections returned Jacobite town councils north of Stirling underlines the widespread Lowland support for the rising. Mar, like Carnwath, was an enterprising, improving landlord with a strong interest in industrial development. What the Highlands offered was swift mobilization of armed men (not by any means always willing men) through clan structures. Given that there was a small rising in north-east England and great potential in the Roman

Catholic parts of Lancashire (where Mar's best general, Mackintosh of Borlum, ended up surrendering in Preston), it required all Mar's talent for indecision to make the rebellion go off like a damp squib. Far too late, he fought an indecisive battle at Sheriffmuir against the Duke of Argyll, who saved the Hanoverian cause by holding fast the key blocking position at Stirling.

Its failure greatly helped the Hanoverian regime, though neither disarmament or forfeiture of rebels was successfully enforced. In 1719 a farcical episode further discredited Jacobitism. As the result of an Anglo-Spanish quarrel in the Mediterranean, Cardinal Alberoni, first minister of Spain, sponsored Jacobite invasions. The invasion of England aborted. The purely diversionary Scottish one, led by Lowland exiled nobles and a few Highland chiefs, went in to defeat at Glenshiel following a prompt response by General Wightman and the Inverness garrison. When the Pretender's marriage to the neurotic Clementina Sobieska went very publicly on the rocks in the later 1720s, the public-relations damage was so massive that the principal Jacobite agent lost heart. Helped by mediation by Argyll and others, the Pretender had by 1728 returned from a brief exile in Holland to live quietly under promise, which he kept, to abstain from all plotting. General Wade, an Irishman and expert in internal security, had been brought in by the 1720s to create a strategic network of military roads in the Highlands. It was he and his troops, in association with the government's principal legal hatchet-man in Scotland, Duncan Forbes of Culloden, who put down the next serious episode of violent resistance in Scotland: the 1725 riots against a malt tax in Glasgow. When the Porteous Riot of 1736 in Edinburgh, which saw the lynching of the captain of the City Guard, Captain Porteous, was followed by the arrival of Wade and the imposition of communal punishments, such as the demolition of the Netherbow Port and a fine, it seemed that violent resistance to the London government was as dead an option as the Stewart dynasty.

The Big Sleep and the Brief Nightmare

Logically, there was nothing left to do in Scottish politics except to quarrel over the distribution of jobs. If a single person controlled the interface between aspirants and patronage, politics consisted of jockeying for a position within his distribution system. There was only one other level to Scottish politicking and that was at Westminster, where the king in his parliament was the central power in the British monarchy. The king remained the most important politician, as well as commander-in-chief and head of the executive, but he needed a minister or ministers who could obtain the consent of the two Houses to his government's measures. That minister usually lacked the local knowledge personally to handle Scottish patronage, but resisted employing another as his Scottish sub-manager (who, by definition, acquired some quasi-independent power) until the practicalities compelled him to do so. Sir Robert Walpole, who got his nose ahead of the pack in 1722, and evolved into the royal favourite of George I and, unexpectedly, of George II too, as well as becoming Prime Minister, followed this pattern. It allowed the eventual rise of Argyll's brother, the Earl of Ilay (he succeeded as duke in 1743, but is usually referred to as Ilay), as manager of Scotland for lengthy periods before he died in 1761. In the words of the Duke of Newcastle, Ilay was 'the absolute Governor of one of His Majesty's Kingdoms', but strictly on sufferance from Westminster.

The Argathelian ascendancy in Scotland was challenged by surviving Squadrone power until the resignation of the last Squadrone politician of any consequence, the Marquis of Tweeddale, from the Secretaryship of State for Scotland in January 1746 (after which his secretaryship was abolished). The '45 Jacobite rebellion had indeed been greatly facilitated by several factors, one of which was the fact that the rival Argathelian and Squadrone sympathizers within the political, military and legal structures in Scotland barely communicated, let alone cooperated. Other factors included the breakdown of the Anglo-French entente which had been central to Walpole's system. By 1744 there was Anglo-French war and the French were seriously thinking of using the exiled Stewarts, perpetuated in the Princes Charles and Henry (sole positive achievement of the Sobieski–Stewart marriage), as a political front for invasion. The Young Pretender, Prince Charles, was pencilled in to accompany a major invasion of the south of England, led by the Marshal de Saxe, in 1744, but the plan was cancelled. Aided by Franco-Scots bankers and Franco-Irish privateer entrepreneurs, as well as, covertly, the French government, which made arms, cadets and a battleship available, Prince Charles headed for Scotland in the summer of 1745. There had been a resumption of Jacobite plotting from the start of the breakdown of Anglo-Bourbon relations in 1739, but all involved, especially the Highland chiefs, rightly insisted they would only rise if French troops and funds were committed. Charles, when he reached Moidart, lied to the effect that they were, but his plan was to seize control of a virtually undefended Scotland and invade England in order to make the French re-activate their invasion plans. Given that the problems of clanship and heritable jurisdictions were unsolved; that the British government was deeply unpopular, especially in Scotland, where its ruthless use of limited patronage had left no place for principle and a large number of dissatisfied place-seekers; and that the garrison in Scotland was a small one composed disproportionately of recruits and invalids, Charles's plan proved feasible. Once he had the crucial allegiance of the Clan Cameron, he could create a force, small but capable of walking to and occupying Edinburgh. On the way he picked up Lord George Murray, the general whose talents account for most of the Jacobite military achievement. General Cope, the government commander, could raise no support in the Highlands to crush the rising at an early stage, and then saw his poor troops routed in under ten minutes at Prestonpans.

The '45 was very much a minority *coup*. No major magnate adhered to it. A high proportion of its leadership was either bankrupt, or heading that way. It had to nominate town governors, not elect them. Its core support was from the usual suspects: Episcopalians and smallish clans (the Camerons were an exception) with reason to hate Campbells. However, it seized control of a Lowland area rich enough to equip troops and fund an invasion of England which few Jacobite leaders much liked, outside the prince's immediate circle. Scottish nationalism and prudence spoke against it. Never did the Scottish leadership mean to impose on England a regime Englishmen did not want. That would have been futile, so when it became clear that widespread English support was as unreal as prior French commitment, the Scottish force staged a technically brilliant retreat, won a surprise victory over Hawley at Falkirk, and finally was destroyed by George II's younger son, the Duke of Cumberland, at Culloden, outside Inverness, in April 1746. Partly due to a successful Royal Naval blockade of French gold and supplies, the Jacobite army's days were numbered even before Culloden. There was never a chance of another rising, though a worried London government launched a further campaign against clanship, which was this time abolished; against Gaelic culture, which was hard hit; and against rebellious landlords, who really were forfeited. By 1747 Jacobitism was a busted flush, as the Old Pretender and Prince Henry, who became a cardinal, knew. When Charles finally died in 1788, his death took mainstream Scots Episcopalians off the hook of praying for the Pretender, but to everyone else it was just the demise of an Italian drunk.

Patronage, the Dundas Despotism and the Rebirth of the Politics of Principle, 1761–1832

Even before Ilay's death in 1761, Westminster politics had entered an unstable phase with the accession of a young king, George III, in 1760. King George terminated the systematic proscription of the remnants of the old Tory Party. Ex-Jacobites, like the Earl Marischal and Simon Fraser of Lovat, the younger, began to be allowed to make their peace with the House of Hanover. In 1784 the forfeited Jacobite estates were returned to their traditional owners, on the significant grounds that no families had fought harder for George III in the recent American War of Independence. The dominant landed class was no longer divided against itself on dynastic and religious issues. Episcopalian tenets were common amongst the aristocracy and gentry, but were no longer associated with any challenge to the Presbyterian settlement in the kirk. That alone removed a major source of trouble. Both the Old and Young Pretenders had been profuse with guarantees to the Church of England, but they had never been able to guarantee a Presbyterian order in Scotland, for their supporters there would never have borne it. Episcopal Jacobite ministers started to occupy parish pulpits at the start of the '15 rebellion. Since there were only 2,889 county electors in Scotland in 1820, and the burgh electorate (which was the town councils as defined by the 'set' or constitution of the burgh) only brought that number up to 4,239, of whom only a fraction were truly independent, the landed and government interest was capable of total dominance over a system which became progressively more corrupt in such matters as electoral law after 1707.

Instability in the 1760s derived from George III's inability to find a first minister to his taste who could cope with the pressures of government. His first choice was a Scot, the Earl of Bute, whose brother, James Stewart Mackenzie, ran Scottish patronage. Bute sank under a tidal wave of Scotophobia. His brother hung on until 1765, but then was sacked. Eventually, with Lord North, the king found stability, but it was undercut by failure in the American war which actually produced political debate in Scotland. The evangelicals in the kirk and most Seceders sympathized with the American Patriots, as did even a small radical wing of the nobility. Only after 1784, with the defeat of the king's arch-enemy Charles Fox and the rise of the Younger Pitt, were conditions ripe for the re-emergence of a powerful Scottish manager, in the shape of Pitt's right-hand man, Henry Dundas of Arniston. This conservative lawyer and laird had had a long run in office before he pinned his career on Pitt. Gradually, he built up a fantastic complex of patronage, as well as becoming the first Viscount Melville. Always intensely interested in an India with which he had extensive family connections, he became first president of the Board of Control set up by Pitt's 1784 India Act as a government bridle on the territorial empire of the East India Company (EIC). Walpole had used EIC patronage to sweeten Scots. Henry Dundas used the civil and military patronage of the company to gratify his fellow Scots on an unprecedented scale. He was also treasurer of the navy, and after the outbreak of war with revolutionary France he came to be the dominant figure in the British military effort against both the republican regime and the successor imperialism of Napoleon Bonaparte. When to EIC, naval and military patronage is added general government patronage appropriate to the man who was – in reality if not technically – the second most senior minister and a meticulous supervision of crown ecclesiastical patronage in Scotland after 1783, his relentlessly expanding grip on the Scottish constituencies becomes wholly comprehensible.

There were always those who did not accept his hegemony. He was not Dundas of that Ilk, and senior branches of his own family held seats in defiance of a man they regarded as an impudent upstart. Normally his power grew by mutual agreement. He offered rewards for cooperation to town councils. His deal with the Duke of Gordon's electoral interest gave him seats; the duke received an English title which exempted him from arrest for debt as a member of the Lords; and the Duchess of Gordon got a chance to go to London to sparkle and marry off daughters (very well). After Lord Melville's fall from power in 1806, his Scottish empire passed to his son Robert, in due time second Viscount Melville. It was no despotism. Rather it was an enlightened manipulation of the existing system to facilitate Scottish participation in the advantages of an incorporating union, while still upholding that distinct Scottish identity which nobody denied that the first two Viscounts Melville always showed. They even rolled back English control of Scottish life in minor ways by breaking the old rule that Commanders-in-Chief North Britain and barons of the Scottish exchequer were English.

When the second Lord Melville's power collapsed, it was due to an issue of principle: Catholic emancipation. On it he was liberal, but he declined office under Canning in 1827, and without office even a Dundas could not keep a grip on the Scottish constituencies. He compounded his troubles by junior office in the 1829 Wellington government which did pass Roman Catholic emancipation, thereby irrevocably splitting those conservative forces that had controlled the United Kingdom almost continuously since 1783. Henry Dundas died deep in debt. His son was kept poor by debts. He accepted the Whig triumph of 1832 gracefully.

His age was over. Society could no longer be contained within the old political framework. Indeed that framework had probably been preserved beyond its likely term by the great popular lurch into militant loyalism which marked the opening stages of the new French wars and totally wrecked the hopes of Whig anti-Dundas Scots peers like the Earl of Lauderdale, who was counting on war-weariness to aid his cause. There was an active movement for burgh reform, not least because a growing business class did not trust the bankrupt self-perpetuating oligarchs of the old system not to plunder new developments for revenue to service old debts. The formation of the Scottish Association of the Friends of the People in 1792 had registered the recognition by moderate burgh reformers that Westminster would ignore them until they could force a change in the Scottish parliamentary franchise. They had noticed that in 1790 only nine county or burgh constituencies in Scotland had been contested. Then the most radical elements led by men later prosecuted, like George Mealmaker and Thomas Muir, moved after 1797 into the outright subversive structures of the United Scotsmen, aiming, in close ideological cooperation with their fellow radical republican Presbyterians of the United Irishmen of Ulster, at a French-type revolution by violence. They were a dangerous, deeply unpopular minority. When he escaped from arrest to Paris, Thomas Muir, like his Irish counterpart Theobald Wolfe Tone, gave the French bombastic, unreal memos of just how ripe his native land was for revolution aided by invasion.

Such men were an asset to Pitt's government, for their cocksure arrogance solidified support for existing structures. It was only after 1815 when the wars were over that there was any real hope of change, and that by political not military means, as English agitators like William Cobbett and Major John Cartwright, who toured Scotland after 1815 relentlessly preaching parliamentary reform (by which they meant the institution as well as the franchise) as the panacea for all ills, repeatedly said. In the event, bad harvests, mass unemployment, recession fuelled by the most vicious deliberate deflation of the century, and government repression did provoke radical weavers into a political strike. A demonstration of physical force by radicals on behalf of an invisible 'provisional government' was easily crushed at Bonnymuir, near Falkirk, in 1820 by government cavalry. After the 'Radical War', forty-seven were arrested, three of whom were executed. It was the end of physical-force radicalism.

The existing regime, largely held together by fear of worse, was cracking from the early 1820s, when the Scots lawyer Henry Brougham helped George IV's disreputable Queen Caroline to defeat her even more disreputable (if more stylish) husband's bid to divorce her. Queenite agitation and mobs set in motion a sense that the weight of opinion was turning against the *status quo*, bizarre though the occasion might be. Emancipation of Roman Catholics and English Dissenters after 1829 deeply fissured the party of conservative continuity in government. In Scotland, where Catholic relief measures had led to rioting in 1778–80, Catholic emancipation was widely supported by 1829 by the educated élites, including Presbyterian clergy, though there are indications that there was still instinctive hostility to the measure among ordinary folk. Scottish reforming Whigs like the lawyer Henry Cockburn, whose posthumous *Memoirs* have so coloured our view of this period, began to sense a rising identification of patriotism with reform of Scotland's representative and municipal institutions. The case for reform was becoming overwhelming as Edinburgh, Aberdeen and Dundee all became insolvent, and John Galt's ironic novel *The Provost* (1822) was hailed as being close to the bone.

When in 1830 a Whig government achieved office and proposed reform, first of the parliamentary, then of municipal franchises, liberal aristocrats led aroused middle classes and supportive workers into a demonstration that Scotland, like England, was set for change. When it came in 1832 it was more radical than in England – the numbers of parliamentary voters went up to 65,000 from 4,500. A £10 franchise and enfranchisement of non-royal burghs revolutionized the municipal scene. The middle classes had become acknowledged partners in the formal political process. With a sixteen-fold increase in the electorate and twenty-three burgh constituencies instead of fifteen, the shift in power was irreversible.

Culture and Education in the Age of the Enlightenment

The word 'culture' is notoriously slippery and cannot be confined to the fine arts and literature. In Scotland a tiny but inordinately self-confident minority of writers saw themselves as on the cutting edge of anglophone culture, itself part of a wider, cosmopolitan, 'polite' European culture. An example of this is historical writing, which between 1750 and the outbreak of the French Revolution enjoyed an enormous vogue. Voltaire said, '*L'histoire est la partie des belles lettres qui a le plus de partisans dans tous les pays*' ('History is the category of literature with the largest number of readers in every country'). Edward Gibbon, the English historian of the decline and fall of the Roman Empire, agreed. David Hume, the Scots philosopher, who was far better known as an historian and was very proud of the success of his history books in polite circles in France, spoke of his age and his Scotland when he said, 'I believe this to be the historical age and this the historical nation.' The vast majority of Scots between 1707 and 1832 probably read little or no history. This did not mean they lacked culture (or a sense of history), merely that their version of Scottish culture was very different from that of Hume.

The plurality of cultures and the complex, variegated nature of any one major Scottish culture has to be recognized. There were a number of very different cultures in Scotland between 1707 and 1832. Radically different language, physical setting and predominant economic activities could distinguish the adherents of one major grouping from another. Equally, there were always important elements of overlap and interpenetration. Scottish cultures were always exposed to influences from the several cultures of Ireland; after 1707 to a greater and greater extent to influences from England; and also from both a wider European world and a world much wider than Europe.

In any case, 'culture' can consist of material objects as much as of products of the mind. Archaeological work takes the material definition of culture for granted, and clearly even in comparatively recent ages, with good written and visual evidence surviving from them, it is essential to re-create the world of material objects, and the techniques and rituals accompanying their usage, to convey the experience of daily life in historic communities. This level of analysis is here largely omitted, partly for reasons of space, since it would involve a survey ranging from clothing to cooking utensils and clay pipes, not to mention vernacular architecture and furniture, and partly because of the uneven coverage of these topics in the literature. Some aspects of Highland and Island material culture are well covered because, being rural, they were deemed aspects of 'folkways', a concept much cherished by romantic culture in continental Europe. The daily life of the urban poor in this period has never had the same appeal (though as it happens there is an extremely detailed chronology and typology of the clay pipes which so many of the lower orders, male and female, smoked, broke and threw away).

A broken tobacco pipe seems a trivial thing. However, it reminds us that a burgeoning variety of goods became available during this first mass 'consumer revolution'. The rapidly growing volume of tobacco imports into Britain in the early eighteenth century meant that half the adult population could have had a pipeful a day; consumption per head was probably higher then than in the nineteenth century. Tobacco became affordable before tea. Writing of the 1710s from prison in Edinburgh Castle where he spent the years from 1719 to 1743, the Jacobite brigadier William Mackintosh of Borlum deplored the increasing prevalence of tea-drinking as a part of polite hospitality. The beverage was so ubiquitous as to be found in Edinburgh's charity workhouse in the 1750s. It too had become an 'extravagance' of the poor, according to some commentators. By the second half of the eighteenth century other consumer durables were firmly within the reach of the middle as well as the upper ranks: clocks, window curtains, china and looking-glasses, to name but a few. Relieved of the need for domestic architecture to be defensive, castles and tower houses gave way to country houses, albeit sometimes in mock baronial style during the early nineteenth century. Palladian town houses and country mansions designed by William and Robert Adam, among others, housed the newly affluent classes. The élites of the late seventeenth and early eighteenth centuries had relied mainly on imported Dutch works of art. In the last third of our period their walls were graced by the paintings of Scottish artists like Henry Raeburn (1756–1823) and David Wilkie (1785–1841), who had a British or even international standing. There was food for the mind as well as the eyes. As befitted a 'hotbed of genius', Edinburgh published the second largest number of book titles of any city in Britain (after London) in the eighteenth century, and Glasgow came fourth (after Oxford). From the mid-eighteenth century Edinburgh had several regular newspapers. There was reading material for all levels of education and all pockets: the largest number of surviving chapbooks – small, cheap recreational pamphlets of at most a few dozen pages – can be dated to the years 1780–1830.

The Major Cultures

The most important cultural divide in Scotland was between that of the Gaelic of the Highlands and Islands and that of the Scots-speaking Lowlands. Geographically, the two inhabited different zones. There was arguably a third cultural zone composed of the Orkney and Shetland Islands and Caithness, where an originally Scandinavian culture, operating in physical settings much more like the Gaelic Highlands and Islands than the Lowlands, was being steadily assimilated into a wider Scottish and British context by an élite of Lowland origins. Of the three Scottish cultures, that of the Lowlands was the most powerful, and the concentration of urbanization and industrialization in the Lowlands meant that with each successive decade after 1750 Lowland preponderance became greater.

Linguistically, all three zones were fascinating, but in the Lowlands after 1707 there was a particularly important tension between the tradition of the vernacular Scots spoken in the seventeenth century, and anglicizing traditions already noticeable by 1700. Archibald Pitcairne's satire, *The Assembly* (1692), already shows class differentiation, with nobility speaking stilted English, socially aspiring lairds and bourgeoisie using an anglicized Scots, and humbler people and lairds from the notoriously conservative north-east employing primarily Scots. By 1712 the poet Allan Ramsay and his friends in Edinburgh had set up the Easy Club, one of the many which dominated the literary life of the capital. However, this one hoped its members 'by mutual improvement in conversation . . . may become more adapted for fellowship with the politer part of mankind', by which they meant the inhabitants of the London coffee-houses as reflected in Joseph Addison's *Spectator* magazine, one of whose articles they solemnly debated weekly. By 1719 there was a club for (very) young women called the Fair Intellectual Club, where female persons aged between fifteen and twenty embarked on an awesome reading schedule; harangued one another on moral virtue; denounced vice; and were chastised by 'Mrs Speaker' for the slowness with which they were adopting standard English (in truth, a very vague concept in 1719). By the middle of the century many Scots had extensive contacts with English people, and a very large and growing expatriate colony in London. There were so many Scots in London that there was a Scots presbytery, which grouped a fair number of Scottish congregations. Interestingly, it paid no serious attention to Presbyterian sectarianism as it had developed in Scotland, for Seceder congregations happily participated in the London Scots presbytery alongside those of the establishment. By the end of the century there were enduring Scots kirks like Crown Court in Covent Garden, which was rebuilt in 1777 and which, with the assistance of the Highland Society of London, built a Gaelic chapel in Cross Street, Hatton Garden, dedicated in May 1813.

Back in Scotland the desire to speak 'correct' English was becoming a passion among sections of the literati. There had been a conservative Jacobite tradition of upholding Latin as an upper-class culture and Scotland's traditional language of access to international audiences, as well as the vehicle of some of the very greatest of Scottish authors. The Jacobite physician Archibald Pitcairne wrote laudatory and satiric verse in Latin. Thomas Ruddiman, the sentimental Jacobite Keeper of the Advocates' Library in Edinburgh, wrote a Latin textbook and printed, superbly, Scots Latin classics like the works of George Buchanan, but his fervent anti-Union spirit was eclipsed by death in 1752. His successor as Keeper was David Hume. Hume produced in 1752 a collection of Scottish usages to be avoided, along with 'correct' English equivalents from the 'best authors'. Reprinted in the *Scots Magazine* in 1760, the work was criticized for its abject spirit, but even the critic reluctantly felt the exercise necessary. In 1779 Professor James Beattie, a rising literary star, produced a larger but similar work to help his country students at Aberdeen University because they had 'no opportunity of learning English from the company they kept'. From the northern cultural province's marchland, Caithness, Sir John Sinclair of Ulbster emerged as an ardent Scottish agricultural improver, but also as the author of a substantial 1782 book designed to help eradicate Scots idioms, rather than, or in addition to, words. In Orkney and Shetland, Norn, the local variation on Old Norse, had, like the ancient Galloway Gaelic of the south-west, become extinct in the seventeenth century, but had influenced the successor Scots which Sir John, who had held office in London, now wished to replace with a more appropriately British idiom.

Sir John organized the Statistical Account of Scotland, using parish clergy to write it. Its 1792 account of Mauchline (Ayrshire) says, 'The Scots dialect is the language spoken, but is gradually improving, and approaching nearer to the English.' Scots authors corrected one another for slipping into what Hume called an 'uncouth dialect'.

The Select Society, which included Hume, Adam Smith, playwright John Hume and the painter Allan Ramsay, changed its name to the Society for Promoting the Reading and Speaking of the English Language and brought in an elocution teacher in 1761 – the Irish actor, Thomas Sheridan. This was not as odd as it sounds in the sense that English, a mongrel language that combines an Anglo-Saxon base with Latin and Norman-French accretions, had evolved from the eleventh century in that part of England which was the Lordship of Ireland under a conservative Anglo-Norman nobility. Their descendants later complained in the sixteenth century that nobody spoke decent English in London now, by which they meant their Chaucerian English. Nevertheless, Sheridan was perhaps not the man to help Hume, who actually spoke Scots and French (the latter poorly, with a thick Scots accent), to blend into the eighteenth-century upper-class drawl of the London social set.

Given the social cringe behind these antics, the vernacular literary revival in eighteenth-century Scotland is all the more remarkable. It was rooted in the last flourishes of an older Scots literary tradition, and in a lyric culture which was pervasive because the upper- and lower-class musical and poetic traditions of Scotland interpenetrated one another more than was usual in the rest of Europe. It was the presence of bogus Scots airs (as well as one or two genuine ones) in a well-known English collection, Tom d'Urfey's *Pills to Purge Melancholy*, which moved Allan Ramsay to follow up his light *Scots Songs* of 1718–20 with four small volumes of *The Tea Table Miscellany* (1723–37), which became the most successful song collection in the three kingdoms. Scots was still used in lairds' houses and in the songs that were sung in them. The violin, a concert instrument, became the universal accompanist to Lowland popular dance mania. The Musical Societies of Edinburgh and Aberdeen regularly played Scots airs and had Scots songs sung in their concerts, alongside a classical repertoire of Handel, Haydn and contemporary Scottish composers like the Earl of Kellie, a Scots peer who devoted his energies to his musical vocation. It is against this sort of setting that the short life of Robert Fergusson (1750–74) must be seen.

Fergusson was the vital link between Ramsay and Burns. The latter greatly admired him, describing him as 'my elder brother in the Muse'. Fergusson was a well-educated man. He had been a student at St Andrews University, and he worked latterly as a clerk to the Commissary Office in Edinburgh, dealing with the documentation of matrimonial and testamentary cases. Classical models and older Scots literature from the medieval Gavin Douglas to the last active Jacobite who was a poet of consequence, William Hamilton of Bangour, formed the background to his verse. Much of it was in English, but the Scots poems show a power of deflative satire directed against both the Whig political ascendancy in its local Edinburgh manifestation, and the Moderate clerical élite who dominated St Andrews University and the fashionable Edinburgh kirks, not to mention a Rabelaisian vein which Burns was to mine so successfully.

If Fergusson's life was brief and difficult, that of Burns was not much longer and palpably harder, closing with premature death in 1796. Born in 1759, he was the son of a poor Ayrshire tenant farmer. By the time he began seriously to write verse, he had ruined his health with cripplingly hard physical toil on small, poor, barely viable farms. Indeed his first collection, *Poems, Chiefly in the Scottish Dialect*, produced in a small edition in Kilmarnock in 1786, seemed destined for obscurity, especially since the literary dictators of the day in Edinburgh were not, in the words of one of them, usually 'partial to the productions of the vulgar rhymers in the Scottish dialect, of whom every district has favourites'. Burns was just plain lucky. A recommendation from the blind poet Thomas Blacklock, who did not know him but was influential in Edinburgh literary circles, was the breakthrough. Burns himself was so despairing as to be on the verge of emigration to the West Indies. Blacklock had the sympathies of the Moderate literati, especially after the parishioners of Kirkcudbright had compelled him to retire on a small pension only after they had grimly resisted his nomination as their minister by the local patron. His blindness and the facility for verse composition which he unfortunately mistook for inspiration, as well as his personality, attracted the friendship of contemporaries like the Duchess of Gordon, Lord Monboddo, Adam Ferguson, Henry Mackenzie and Principal Robertson. His recommendation and Burns's merits made the Ayrshire man famous within weeks. Burns appealed to his patrons often for the wrong reasons, and never more so than when they patronized him (in every sense of the word) as a 'Heaven taught plowman'.

He was, in fact, a man with a reasonable education behind him, and an extensive knowledge of both Scots and English literature. He was an improviser of genius, as well as a poet who affirmed the centrality of spontaneous emotion, all of which made him a romantic writer. In addition he was of the Enlightenment, for he was a sceptic, an ironic wit, and a man of logic. Reason was his guide. Satire came as naturally to him as to the Augustan Englishman Alexander Pope, whom he had read. The advice he received in Edinburgh after the triumphant success of the 1786 Kilmarnock edition of his poems – to write longer works in English – was almost uniformly bad. Apart from 'Tam o' Shanter' and 'Green Grow the Rashes, O', neither of his subsequent published verse collections of 1787 and 1793 enhanced his poetic stature. What confirmed his greatness and his continuing growth in stature as a poet was his work on Scots songs. Yet to say this is rather to miss the point about them, for at their greatest they fuse completely two elements from quite different artistic modes: the words exist because the tune existed, and to read them as 'straight' poetry without the music is nonsense. Burns was a sociable man, as his enthusiastic support of such clubs as the Edinburgh Crochallan Fencibles, dedicated to drink and bawdry, shows. His talent for penning bawdy songs was considerable and not incompatible with the ability to make a song a vehicle for the most poignant expression of love's melancholy. The meeting between Burns and James Johnson in April 1787 and the poet's commitment to furnish material for Johnson's proposed collection, *The Scots Musical Museum*, which Burns virtually edited in the end, therefore ranks as one of the happiest meetings of minds.

By then Burns was employed as an exciseman based in Dumfries. His social and political relations with the ruling élite had been full of social, sexual and political tensions, slightly modified by his freemasonry, which put him in a fellowship that softened class barriers as much as a hierarchic society could bear. It was also a vehicle for Enlightenment ecumenicism and a mild radicalism. Burns, who, as he explained in a letter to the *Edinburgh Evening Courant* in November 1788, was a staunch supporter of the Glorious Revolution a century before, though with sympathy for Jacobite idealism, was an admirer of the American Revolution, which he saw as a development from 1688. The French Revolution, however, threatened the social stability of the world Burns inhabited; in deference to his patron, Mr Graham of Fintry, he had publicly to repudiate it, as well as to join a volunteer defence force.

The survival of the Scots literary tradition was remarkable, but perhaps less so than the amazing resilience of the Gaelic poetic tradition in an ever more traumatized Highland society. The immediate post-Union period was one of change in the Gaelic literary tradition, once dominated by a bardic élite using classical common Gaelic, a highly artificial literary language taught in bardic schools and looking back to Old Irish. The professional bards died out in the early part of the century with the demise of Niall MacMhuirich around 1726 and of his decidedly inferior successor Domhnall MacMhuirich, who was still active in the 1730s. Pressure to bring the literary language into line with spoken Scots Gaelic can be seen in the *Confession of Faith* translated into Gaelic by the synod of Argyll and published in 1725, which is essentially Scots Gaelic laced with common classical forms. Orthographic confusion persisted, despite the consistent system adopted in the Gaelic New Testament published in 1767. By about 1769 there were nearly 300,000 Gaelic-speakers – nearly 23 per cent of Scotland's population.

Attempts to abolish Gaelic began in James VI's reign and recurred with every Jacobite rebellion, but were essentially knee-jerk cultural chauvinism by frightened English-speakers. The idea of forcible extirpation was impractical. The Society in Scotland for Propagating Christian Knowledge (SSPCK), founded in 1709, set up schools to supplement the parochial system in the Highlands and Islands. By 1711 it had five schools, one on remote St Kilda. By 1795, it had 323. Originally it forbade Gaelic in its schools. It was a rule which from the start had to be broken, and after 1767 it was officially reversed. The pattern of survival and change, but with elements of continuity or echo from the bardic past, thus went on in a somewhat more broadly literate community.

The greatest and most innovative of the Gaelic poets, whose work came quite early in the century and left a deep mark on all subsequent poets, was Alasdair MacMhaighstir Alasdair (Alexander MacDonald), born *c*. 1690, the son of a Moidart minister of chiefly ancestry and cousin of Flora MacDonald, who helped rescue Prince Charles after Culloden. Inspired partly by James Thomson's Augustan English poems, *The Seasons*, published between 1726 and 1730, MacMhaighstir Alasdair produced a great sequence of seasonal poems, far less affected and mannered than Thomson's and far greater poetry. He is, however, best known for his violent commitment to Jacobitism and his participation in the '45, which itself led to a tremendous outflow of political poetry — exhortatory and satiric, by turn. His motivation appears not to have been blind Stewart loyalism which, like his conversion to Roman Catholicism (denounced as political rather than religious by a contemporary Gaelic poet), served as a badge for deeper passions. He was a Gaelic cultural nationalist who was also a Scottish one.

Donnchadh Bàn Mac an t'Saoir (Duncan Bàn Macintyre) came later (he was born in 1724), but he is the other of the twin peaks of the century's Gaelic verse. Employed as a forester by the Campbells of Glen Orchy, he was non-literate, though he had literate mentors and a wide acquaintance with the heritage of Gaelic verse. At one stage he lived near the manse of Killin, where the New Testament was being translated into Gaelic, and it was the son of that manse, John Stewart, who saw the first edition of his poems through the press. Donnchadh Bàn wrote praise poetry for Campbell magnates, as well as a lament for the Campbell victim of the Appin murder, but his greatest achievement is as a descriptive poet of nature, especially in such masterpieces as 'Moladh Beinn Dòbhrain' ('Praise of Ben Dorain'). He settled in Edinburgh in 1767 as a member of the City Guard — a classic precursor of the 'Hielan polis' of twentieth-century Glasgow.

Donnchadh Bàn fought unenthusiastically for Hanover at the battle of Falkirk in 1746, but he is no political poet like MacMhaighstir Alasdair, or John Roy Stewart, the professional soldier whose Gaelic verse mirrors the bitterness of the defeat he faced at Culloden and the stresses of his subsequent escape to France. Iain MacCodrum, who knew the MacMhuirichs of South Uist and was in 1763 given the anachronistic and nominal title of bard to MacDonald of Sleat, continued the process of bringing Gaelic verse into closer contact with daily life in a stream of 'village' poetry, all somehow linked to communal concerns. This trend is marked in the great poet of Sutherland, Rob Donn, whose employer was the Whig Lord Reay, but who expressed Jacobite sympathies, almost certainly as a vehicle for the Gaelic patriotism which denounced the act proscribing Highland dress of 1747 in 'Na Casagan Dubha' ('The Black Cassocks'). Highly original in his modification of the elegiac tradition, and a very important, if at times oblique, commentator on the relations between landlord, tacksman and tenant, Rob Donn was aware of the wider world of British politics. Donnchadh Bàn denounced the Scotophobic John Wilkes in verse. Rob Donn knew of the death of Prime Minister Henry Pelham in 1754, for he mentioned it in an elegy.

Dùghall Bochanan (Dugald Buchanan), his contemporary, was converted by George Whitefield, the Methodist preacher, in his second visit to Scotland in 1742, from whence sprang the sombre magnificence of the few but impressive religious poems of Buchanan. Uilleam Ros, a Skye man who lived in Wester Ross, is the last of the major eighteenth-century poets. His Jacobitism was theoretical, which is perhaps why he could write so moving a lament on the death of Prince Charles. Much of his work is distinguished by wit, humour and bawdiness, but it is for his often desolate but always tightly controlled love poetry that he is best remembered. Desolate indeed was the early nineteenth century in the Highlands. It was the century of the Gaelic diaspora. Such was the magnificence of the heritage of lyric verse from the eighteenth century that there was enough inherent quality in the tradition to enable it to survive, narrowly, in the years ahead, and even in its early years to expand into Nova Scotia where Gaelic-speaking Scots communities came into existence. The hymns of the Reverend James MacGregor, who held a charge there, were the harbinger of a flowering which included Iain MacGhill Eathain (John Maclean), who had published verse and been patronized by Maclean of Coll before leaving Scotland in 1819, and even representatives of the old bardic family of MacMhuirich.

Apart from a non-meeting of minds between Dugald Buchanan and the sceptical philosopher David Hume, the urban literati saw little and knew less of the real Gaelic culture of this era. The one important interface was with a quite exceptional product of the Gaelic world: James Macpherson. He was born on Speyside, educated at Aberdeen University (1752–5), became a teacher and then a tutor to Graham of Balgowan, through whom he met the fashionable playwright John Hume at the spa of Moffat in Dumfriesshire. Hume and Alexander Carlyle pressed him for translations of Gaelic verse, which they then showed to Hugh Blair, soon to be Professor of Rhetoric and Belles-Lettres in Edinburgh. The two sides fed on one another. Blair was looking for something 'sublime' out of a 'primitive' society. Macpherson, partly because of his extensive classical education in Aberdeen, felt that the Highlanders were like the Ancient Greeks, and like them ought to have Homeric epics. James Boswell, in a delicious fit of romantic gloom in 1764, envisaged the Scots tongue as 'being lost every day' and thought that 'in a short time [it] will become quite unintelligible', so that future Scots would have to apply themselves 'to the study of their ancient tongue as to Greek or Latin'. Macpherson similarly saw himself as living in the irreversible decay of the Gaelic tradition, and sought to prove that in its youth that tradition had the classic vigour of Ancient Greece and Rome. Over the authenticity of his publications, which began with *Fragments of Ancient Poetry* and went on to two epics, *Fingal* and *Temora*, allegedly by the bard Ossian, controversy raged from the start. After his tour of the Highlands and Islands in 1773 the London literary dictator, Dr Samuel Johnson, declared the works wholly fraudulent. Irate Irish and Welsh scholars denounced less the works than the pretentious and tendentious annotation designed to stress their classical quality.

That did not prevent a vogue for this precursor of the Romantic Movement spreading from Britain to Europe and America. The works were translated into twenty-six foreign languages. All the major English romantic poets were influenced by Ossianic enthusiasm, as were such improbable pairs as Burns and Napoleon, Goethe and the painter Angelica Kauffman, the supreme draughtsman Ingres and the musician Mendelssohn. In fact, Samuel Johnson's arrogant contempt for Gaelic culture led him greatly to oversimplify a complex phenomenon. Macpherson had, partially, real Gaelic sources, and help from Gaelic scholars. He massively amplified and modified what he had, but believed sincerely he was resurrecting ancient Celtic culture. After 1765 he went south and in London enjoyed a political career, spiced by a spell in the West Indies. Having watched his chief, Cluny, hunted for a decade after Culloden, he could indulge his mischievous neo-Jacobite spirit to make trouble for the House of Hanover, while fornicating on a Homeric scale. He died in his neo-classical mansion on Speyside, built for him by the Adam brothers, and was buried in Westminster Abbey. The misty Celtic twilight which he fashioned was endorsed by a surprising number of professors, especially in the Universities of Aberdeen and Edinburgh.

Education Systems

The need for all Christians to be instructed in the basic tenets of their faith and to be able to read the Bible lay behind the aspirations of the sixteenth-century reformers to have a functioning school in every Scots parish. There was a struggle throughout the seventeenth century to turn aspiration into reality. The Act of 1696, which laid down the basic parochial school pattern until 1872, represented part of the revolution settlement. Heritors or landowners of the parish were legally obligated to appoint a dominie or schoolmaster, to pay a minimum of 100 merks Scots salary per annum and to provide him with a house. A merk was two-thirds of a pound sterling, but since the pound Scots had stabilized at one-twelfth of the pound sterling in 1603, the salary was roughly £5 11s. sterling. Eroded by inflation, the salary was not increased, despite mid-century pressure and agitation by teachers, until 1803. A tax on land provided the money – hence the stinginess of heritors – but the actual running and supervision of the school was the responsibility of the kirk sessions, presbyteries and General Assembly. The overall result of their activities has been a source of fertile dispute among historians.

Education was neither compulsory nor free. Dominies made ends meet by acting as the minister's assistant, amanuensis and praise leader, but they were also allowed to charge fees. Sessions deliberately kept the fees for basic subjects low. Reading, writing (taught as a separate subject), arithmetic, church music and Latin were therefore cheap. Latin was the poor boy's essential entrance ticket into college, where he would take a formal degree, aided by bursaries. The better-off did not need to graduate, often contenting themselves with a selection of classes and at most a pocket of 'class tickets', testimonials from the relevant professors. Parochial school teachers charged much higher fees for 'applied' subjects like French, mensuration, book-keeping or navigation.

In addition, they could and did take boarders. It is difficult to generalize, and all sorts of modifications and adaptations were utilized, like splitting the statutory salary in two to give two schools a starting base, usually in a geographically large or divided parish. Between parochial schools, where the kirk session had the obligation to help with fees for the poorest pupils, charity schools run by bodies like the SSPCK, adventure schools run on the cheap by entrepreneurs, and other schools paid for by the parents, there was a very considerable range of educational opportunity throughout the Lowlands and at a lower, but still far from negligible, level in the Highlands and Islands. There were regional variations, of course. Orkney and Shetland were more like the Lowlands than they were like Lewis or South Uist.

The overall result in terms of basic literacy and numeracy is debatable and we can never be precise. In reaction to exaggerated hype for Scottish education, students of literacy have denied any significant Scots superiority over England or France. This is absolutely clear from the only direct and quantifiable evidence we have: ability to sign a document. By the 1790s Lowland reading literacy (always seemingly greater than the capacity to write) was clearly high, though whether it was higher than in many parts of northern Europe is questionable. Highland parishes had lower levels of achievement, usually, but some Lowland parishes were dissatisfied with their levels, while a Ross-shire parish could report that most inhabitants were capable of reading the Gaelic New Testament and Psalms, and added that many could also read the English Bible.

Scotland was comparatively well supplied with schools which could be means of social mobility for relatively humble pupils, though those who made it up from the very lowest social background were few, atypical, and usually needed patronage from benign members of the upper orders. It was the middling orders who benefited from relatively abundant, cheap educational opportunity. The burghs, especially the bigger ones, were particularly impressive in this respect. There the schooling was provided by the town council, usually in amicable cooperation with the kirk. The basic school type was the grammar school, whose curriculum was dominated by the classical languages and mathematics. In 1729 a committee of Irvine presbytery in Ayrshire visited the grammar school to check its efficiency. Increasingly, the town council not only appointed teachers but also audited them by visitation.

In the burghs there were, of course, endowed schools, such as Heriot's Hospital in Edinburgh, which had been established by pious benefactors to help the deserving poor. It was much later that they were taken over by the local middle classes (in the name of efficiency). In many burghs this period saw the development of an academy movement, which in new schools such as Perth Academy emphasized the new applied, business-oriented subjects like modern languages, book-keeping and navigation, as well as keeping up the traditional stream of classics and mathematics. Zealots like Thomas Chalmers, who were worried that the private 'adventure' schools which abounded in town and country to supplement the parochial and burghal system were often run by

Seceders, looked forward to a renewed, dynamic cooperation with the state to expand the parochial and burghal system. The Scots Whig, Henry Brougham, secured an 1818 inquiry into the public schooling in Britain. The Scottish part of the inquiry brought out just how wide a range of schooling was available, so that after 1832 the dynamism of the response to perceived need from several sources was used by the new Whig ascendancy to justify reneging on a commitment to increased public investment in education. This had the twin advantages of keeping taxes low and appeasing the dissenting, non-Church of Scotland constituencies on which Whigs often depended for main funding, votes and favourable publicity in elections.

The flexibility of the system could even overcome confessional barriers. Roman Catholics in Scotland were heavily concentrated in the western conurbation and grew in numbers from 30,000 in 1800 to 70,000 by 1827. Though the first Orange Walk was held in Glasgow in 1821 by a Protestant minority among the Irish immigrants, a Catholic Schools Society was set up in Paisley in 1816, and in Glasgow in 1817, in order to help Roman Catholic immigrants from predominantly rural backgrounds to integrate more fully into an urban setting in a new country. These societies were sponsored by Protestant businessmen like Kirkman Finlay. A joint committee, half Protestant and half Roman Catholic, appointed teachers of the latter faith who used a Protestant version of the Bible in their teaching.

Public education was largely male-dominated and orientated. Girls did attend parish schools where they were taught basic reading, writing and counting, but they were always in a minority. Figures are scarce, but in a report of 1837 it is recorded that Ballantrae parish school had 96 boys and 47 girls; about the same time the Mauchline Educational Institute had 183 boys and 50 girls. As they were excluded from universities, girls normally did not embark on Latin or mathematics above the simplest levels. Schoolmistresses were employed by burgh councils to teach them sewing instead. It was in private schools that women could have teaching and, indeed, entrepreneurial roles. In 1738 Ayr magistrates discovered that seven of the eight persons cited before them for keeping private schools were female. Small boarding schools for girls with pretensions to gentility were extremely common in and around cities like Edinburgh by the early nineteenth century. They concentrated on endowing the girls with appropriate accomplishments like a little French or Italian, and some instrumental or vocal musical skill, as well as the more 'refined' handwork such as lace-making and embroidery, all designed to enhance their marriageability. When, for example, Lady Helen Cumming Gordon found herself responsible for a niece, the natural child of a young Scots servant of the East India Company who had died aged twenty-six after fathering the girl by an Indian woman, she had to resort to boarding schools in Elgin and Edinburgh.

In 1810 the two unmarried women, Marianne Woods and Jane Pirrie, who ran the Edinburgh school, sued Lady Cumming Gordon for libel and loss of livelihood. Her ladyship had endorsed publicly allegations by the girl, Jane Cumming, that the mistresses had indulged in 'indecent practices' (that is, a lesbian relationship). The subsequent legal history was complex; the mistresses first lost, then won in the Scots courts, having the Court of Session's final verdict confirmed by the House of Lords, and finally securing a substantial settlement which was being haggled over in the courts as late as 1821 and eventually settled out of them. The case says a great deal about women's roles in education and perceptions of gender boundaries in the élite culture of the Enlightenment, where men with a classical education like Lord of Session Lord Glenlee could say in his March 1811 notes on preliminary testimony by a Miss Janet Munro: 'I have little doubt that in all ages and countries, women have enjoyed this mode of seeking pleasure.' The House of Lords showed the strength of the Prince Regent's remark that 'the Non-Conformist conscience doth make cowards of us all', stating that it regarded the central issue, lesbianism, to be publicly unmentionable.

The Scottish universities, which were the apex of the national education system, were of course exclusively masculine. All the universities, except Edinburgh, had been originally clerical corporations, products of a medieval church, and John Knox and the other fathers of the Scottish Reformation were determined to maintain the grip of the Kirk on the colleges. The latter, after all, provided the vocational training for the clergy and their secular partners, the parish dominies, some of whom were always young aspirants to the ministry awaiting a charge. Edinburgh, despite being a Renaissance 'tounis college', was not really different. It was the biggest and most prestigious of Scottish universities in the eighteenth century. Its principal was *ex officio* a member of the General Assembly of the kirk, and in the 1760s and 1770s he was usually the dominant figure in that body.

In no sense, however, were the universities subject to clerical tyranny. Edinburgh is the classic case. Its Faculty of Divinity was the senior one in terms of status and symbolism, but it produced no major works of theology. Robertson, who became principal in 1762, was an historian, while his main Moderate clerical ally, Hugh Blair, was Professor of Rhetoric. There were no confessional tests for admission as a student to Scottish universities. English Dissenters or Polish Roman Catholics were perfectly welcome if they paid the modest class fees. In theory, professors had to sign the Westminster Confession of Faith. In practice, only one professor in Edinburgh did so between 1758 and 1826. Moderate ecclesiastical historians, for instance Fraser Tytler of Edinburgh, were clear that tolerance towards all major faiths was a virtue. In lectures in 1798–1800 Tytler expressed admiration for aspects of the Koran, and saw all churches, including the Church of Scotland, as flawed products of their time.

There was a complete alliance in Edinburgh between city and university. They were interdependent. A distinguished professoriate confirmed Edinburgh's 'capital' status in the post-1707 world and attracted students. Moderate clergy drew the line at giving the infidel David Hume the chair of moral philosophy in Edinburgh, but that was not unreasonable, for they laid especial emphasis on classics and moral philosophy as giving their ordinands the broad cultural background necessary to enable them to establish a rapport with enlightened patronage-wielding landed gentlemen. In every other case, Moderates tended towards appointing the best candidate for a chair, regardless of partisan affiliation. Theirs was a regime in which divinity was offered as a fee-free option to preserve access to the ministry for the poor student with vocation. It followed that pluralism was inevitable for poorly paid professors of divinity. They had to have a parish, or other posts, or, like eminent Moderates, income from writing. Walter Scott, as late as 1816 when literary clergy were being displaced by writing lawyers as the dominant Scots literati, said that literary talent was how an enlightened clergyman attracted patronage.

Yet by then the evangelical wing of the kirk, led by the former Moderate Chalmers, was in full cry against pluralism for teachers of divinity, as well as against the abuses of patronage. A commission on the Scottish universities which sat from 1826 to 1830 (with only three clerics out of twenty-two members) endorsed the demand for more rigorous standards in divinity, as in other subjects. The commission saw the colleges as secular institutions, rather missing the point that their Moderate rulers saw them as vehicles for ensuring that clergy were in tune with the enlightened leaders of Scottish society. When in 1827 Chalmers became Professor of Divinity in Edinburgh, and made it clear he would treat the job as a full-time one, the world of the Moderates was coming to an end.

The Scottish universities they had dominated in the second half of the eighteenth and first two decades of the nineteenth century had emerged from the traumas of the Glorious Revolution and the purges which followed Jacobite rebellions, especially the '15, with two walking wounded among the colleges. These were King's College, in Old Aberdeen, and St Andrews. Both suffered from Jacobite associations, partly because of their close connections with Episcopalian and Jacobite families whose sons they educated. St Andrews had Jacobite patrons, like the Scots of Scotstarvit, who were patrons of the important chair of humanity (Latin) and even at one stage tried to give a chair of divinity to a man who was titular Jacobite Earl of Dundee. He was suspended, but held the emoluments until 1732. Sustained fiscal crisis reduced St Andrews to a mere hundred or so students. It tried hard to crawl back into favour by appointing the Duke of Cumberland as its chancellor in 1746. With the aid of one of his successors between 1765 and 1787, the ninth Earl of Kinnoull, it at least avoided total collapse, and under Principal Hill at the turn of the century it had the two successive Viscounts Melville as chancellors of what had become a Moderate bastion. In Aberdeen, King's College retreated into embittered factionalism and isolation, unable to prevent Marischal College in New Aberdeen from asserting its full university status.

Edinburgh, Glasgow and Marischal College were therefore the Scottish universities in the ascendant in the period 1746–1832, with Edinburgh working overtime, then and since, to suggest that it single-handedly sustained the 'Age of the Enlightenment' in

Scotland. It was very important, to be sure, but so were Glasgow and Marischal. Glasgow was not just the university of the west, but also of Presbyterian Ulster, from whence it drew some of its ablest students and professors, like Francis Hutcheson. Aberdeen was the university of the north-east and north, set in another big, vigorous city. There is a well-known paradigm, shaped originally for Edinburgh, which suggests that the university literati after 1750, themselves unconditional supporters of the Union and assimilation to England, provided a substitute for a lost political identity in the shape of an ultimately determinist drive to understand the forces which had brought Scotland to where she was. They made themselves an important part of the Atlantic and European 'Republic of Letters', and Scotland the Athens of Britain, while replacing the old parliament and great nobles as the articulate national voice. The universities they ran also significantly broadened their recruitment base. Universities like Glasgow could and did attract young men from tradesman or mercantile families, offering them a useful, practical education. As the flow of better-off Scots to continental universities died away around 1800, the percentage of students in Scots universities from merchant or tradesman background was rising. From being about a quarter of the student body in 1740, they went up to about half by 1830.

Their intellectual programme was important to the enlightened clerical professoriate; Moderates hoped also to carve out an area of autonomy in Kirk and university by cooperation with the state, but those who wielded the decisive influence in terms of appointments and tone were precisely the great political nobles of Scotland, semi-absentee, or almost wholly absentee though they might be in London. In the latter part of this period, with the state operating on a scale without precedent in the war decades, two great political managers, the Dundases, called the tune, though usually in cooperation with the Scots nobility. It was the first Duke of Roxburgh, the second and third Dukes of Argyll, the third Earl of Bute, James Stewart Mackenzie, the ninth Earl of Kinnoull, and the first and second Viscounts Melville who made the appointments in the intensely politicized patronage structure of Scottish academe which reinforced the changes in the direction of tolerance, a more secular society, and a more scientific outlook, which they were using their power to force more generally on Scottish society.

The three universities were beneficiaries of the fact that their own dynamism after 1750 corresponded with a lowish point in the history of most other western European university systems. The abandonment of Latin as the teaching language was not confined to Scotland in the eighteenth century, but it meant that there was a language barrier which had not existed before in, say, Dutch universities, traditionally heavily patronized by Scots. Dutch influence was still important for most of the eighteenth century in Scotland. Pupils of Herman Boerhaave (1668–1738), Professor of Chemistry at Leiden, were pervasive in the foundation and development of Edinburgh University's School of Medicine, and in the development of the Edinburgh Royal Infirmary in the 1740s as an aid to clinical teaching. The Infirmary was never significantly large in terms of the size of the city, but it did develop an admirable regimen for its longer-stay patients, based on fresh air, good food, rest and a saving sense of the limited capability of contemporary intrusive treatments. No less than 12,800 men passed through the Edinburgh Medical School between 1720 and 1790. It was big business. Glasgow medical teaching was important, but not on the same scale. Aberdeen and St Andrews could not compete.

Other subjects, however, benefited from a general expansion in the body of knowledge which made the abandonment of the regenting system, whereby a single regent guided students through the whole syllabus, inevitable. Single-topic chairs were the future, though there was a cavalier side to the way ambitious Scots academics hopped from a poorly paid chair in one subject to a better prospect in another. Sir John Pringle, a great military doctor and author of *Observations on the Diseases of the Army*, briefly held a philosophy chair. Adam Ferguson held a chair of physics (natural philosophy) before becoming Professor of Moral Philosophy in Edinburgh in 1764. Payment depended heavily on class fees, which both Boerhaave and Adam Smith, a Glasgow professor, reckoned kept Scottish academics on their toes, but could equally make a successful chemistry professor drop research and concentrate on spectacular lectures full of fireworks to pack them in by the several hundred. Other Scots professors treated their chairs, which they held for life (*ad vitam aut culpam*) and which bore no pensions, as a piece of freehold property. Some used them as a base from which to work for real money elsewhere. Others appointed sons as heirs and successors, making the chair an heirloom. Not all hereditary successions worked as well as the three medical Monros at Edinburgh. John Anderson, alias 'Jolly Jack Phosphorous', was Professor of Natural Philosophy in Glasgow University, where he had started as Professor of Oriental Languages. He left an intemperate will when he died in 1796, denouncing Glasgow professors as vain, power-mad, factious and neglectful. Anderson's plans for a rival university achieved little (due to lack of funds) before 1832, when the first of many Mechanics' Institutes in Scotland was set up in Glasgow to offer, in effect, evening classes to skilled workmen.

From no other university system did such a high proportion of the 'polite' literature of the Enlightenment emerge. With the arrival of the Romantic Movement and an increasing susceptibility to emotionally-charged bunkum, the way was clear for John Wilson, a native of Paisley who as a student at Glasgow began 'an orgiastic cultivation of sensibility', to make a good living as Professor of Moral Philosophy in Edinburgh from 1820. His appointment was a political job. His lectures were outrageous, soft-centred harangues based on material supplied by a friend. Students cheered him, regularly. Nevertheless, with all their oddities, Scottish universities were important and, by the standards of the time, mostly large. Scotland had the highest proportion of university places to population in Europe. There were only 730 students in the two Aberdeen colleges by 1824, but Glasgow by then had 1,240, and Edinburgh, 2,300. Upper-class English students were a minuscule proportion, even in Edinburgh, but there were many middling Irish, especially from the north of Ireland, and English Dissenters, bourgeois by definition, not to mention many colonial Americans in the medical schools, especially in Edinburgh. Only the rare boy of truly humble origins fed through from the parochial or burgh schools, and he needed benign patronage to afford even the modest fees and living costs.

'High' Culture, Enlightenment and Romanticism

It should already be clear that in the field of imaginative literature the Moderate literati were living at a time when very great literature was being produced in a Scots vernacular they deprecated, and in the Gaelic tongue which most of them, Adam Ferguson always excepted, could not comprehend. Their own efforts, in prose and verse in the same field, were in fact laughably inferior. Nevertheless, there is a consensus that much of the 'high' culture, literary and visual, if not musical (though a 'polite' musical culture throve in this era), is of exceptional importance and enduring value. It is seen as a 'Golden Age' of Scottish culture, particularly in the context of the Enlightenment.

This opens another major area of controversy: the nature of 'the Enlightenment'. This protean and pervasive concept is always in danger of becoming everything in general and nothing in particular. It was so different in individual national contexts that even the most brilliant attempts, such as that of the American historian Peter Gay in the 1960s, to depict it as a coherent international movement break down. Gay's Enlightenment was an informal, international movement of liberal, even radical, anti-clericals. He rightly saw the French Enlightenment as seminal, and cast the development of the whole movement in that mould. The Scots literati of the Enlightenment were also deeply influenced by French thought. French was their common foreign language. Principal Robertson, who made himself a master of Spanish sources for his *History of America*, was rather unusual, though he was followed by a lesser Hispanist, Robert Watson, Professor of Logic at St Andrews, who wrote a celebrated life of Philip II of Spain published in 1777. Yet the Scottish Enlightenment does not fit the Gay profile. It can be made to do so by the procrustean device of ignoring all Scottish intellectuals of the eighteenth century except the very atypical David Hume and Adam Smith. In reality the Reverend Doctor William Robertson was the central figure of the era of 'high Enlightenment' in Scotland. He was fully equal in stature with the two others in terms of intellectual achievement, and far more important socially and politically. The bevy of Moderate divines who were literati were the core of a Scottish Enlightenment which was choreographed by great noble patrons, and which can be described as predominantly clerical, and in political terms conservative.

The central achievement of the Scottish Enlightenment was a new capacity to recognize and interpret complex social patterns. Whereas previous Western thinkers tended to divide experience into phenomena created by God, and things which were artificial constructs of man, Scottish thinkers of the eighteenth century realized that economies, state structures, and languages were among many phenomena which did not really fit this dichotomy. They were created but not designed, yet they existed and worked, by a process almost providential. Principal Robertson, a religious man, hovers on the brink of applying this view to religions. Adam Smith, not formally religious, still needed an 'invisible hand' to make all well. Whether such insights were subversive is controversial, especially, in the case of philosophical thinkers like Adam Smith and David Hume. There are scholars, most notably the American Donald W. Livingstone, who have argued that Hume was not just conservative, the exponent of a secular and sceptical conservatism, but the originator of the only true political philosophy, conservatism. Of course, 'conservative' and 'liberal' are not metaphysical terms. They are labels whose significance varies with contemporary perceptions of the meaning of these words. Certainly it is possible to find in both Smith and Hume remarks which imply a conscious critique of aristocratic hegemony. In *The Wealth of Nations* Adam Smith hailed the Act of Union because by it 'the middling and inferior ranks of people in Scotland gained a complete deliverance from the power of an aristocracy which had always before oppressed them'. As statements go, it was a ridiculous generalization rooted in notions of Scotland's unspeakable pre-1707 barbarism, which Hume and Smith were particularly prominent in propagating, compounded by a bizarre view of the status of the aristocratic authority which undoubtedly dominated Scotland for the duration of Smith's life. Hume claimed much the same with particular reference to the Highlands in his *History of England*, where he said that Highlanders had ever since 1707 enjoyed in theory 'every privilege of British subjects', but it was only with the defeat of the '45 and the subsequent legislation 'that the common people could in fact enjoy these privileges'. The thought must have warmed the hearts of many a Gaelic-speaking tenant farmer facing eviction and emigration to Glasgow or Canada.

Hume certainly believed that there was a case for making House of Commons constituencies equal in population and having a standard, fairly high property qualification for the vote. He also argued that bishops and Scots representative peers should be excluded from the Lords as a first step to turning it into a meritocracy of life peers selected by co-option. All this was utopian, as the title of the relevant essay, 'Of the Idea of a Perfect Commonwealth' (published in 1752), shows. Since Hume was no fool, he knew there was no chance whatever of any such measures being adopted. In any case, an upper house based on mutual-admiration cronyism was an appalling concept, far worse and less defensible than hereditary succession, which at least represented established property and tended towards normal minds. Like men of the French Enlightenment, Scots ones were liable to indulge in flights of fancy, when they were sure there was no chance their ideas would be implemented. After all, they did not regard any particular point in a providentially evolving social pattern as inherently sacred.

In practice the literati were deeply committed to the established political order. That was the premise on which the whole Moderate party in the Kirk was based, though to give it its due, it meant to move on from there to a more dynamic ecclesiastical conclusion. Adam Smith ended his days, after a couple of years hobnobbing with the great and good in London, as a Commissioner of His Majesty's Customs in Scotland, a post to which he was preferred through the interest of the Duke of Buccleuch. David Hume had quite an extensive run in political office, including two years in the embassy in Paris in 1763 through 1765, and then as Under-Secretary of State for the Northern Department for eleven months between February 1767 and January 1768. When his patron, Lord Conway, retired, Hume was finished, and by 1769 he was back in Edinburgh 'done with all Ambition'.

The enlightened ones or illuminati were prepared to examine the theoretical case for reforms, but almost always came down against any specific political reform, at any particular point in time. The Moderates tended to lose their moderation in the face of the excesses of the French Revolution, denouncing Sunday schools as hotbeds of sedition, and missionary endeavour as a sign of irrational fanaticism. However, the secular-minded illuminati were not far behind in their aversion to a whole range of overdue reforms, such as the need for a reorganization of the governance of the Scottish burghs, which by the 1820s the government was opposing simply on the grounds that it would be a precedent for other reforms. The issue which underlined the immobilism of the established order in the late eighteenth century was the refusal of the Westminster government to trust Scots with a militia, despite the populist Militia Bill of 1757 which made much play of entrusting home defence in England to a freedom-loving militia rather than the regular army. Adam Ferguson was the leading figure in the Scottish Enlightenment's great age who best understood that liberty, a favourite word of English Whig discourse on which the Anglo-Scots poet James Thomson had written a celebrated poem in 1735–6, required an element of participation to be meaningful. Later in the century, the eleventh Earl of Buchan praised Thomson's 'Liberty' as a great encomium of political and civil liberty, but added, as befitted a Scots patriot with reservations about the workings of the Union, that 'Britain knows nothing of the liberty that Thomson celebrates'. Ultimately, men like Smith and Hume believed that the more rumbustious manifestations of traditional English liberties slid into anarchy, a view which was reinforced when they saw mobs in the 1760s rioting in London on behalf of the virulently Scotophobic opposition gadfly John Wilkes. Smith and Hume identified widespread participation in the political process with crude chauvinism, and what was worse, religious bigotry.

On the other hand, the classical tradition of civic humanism, to which all Whigs had to pay at least lip service, was very clear that to develop virtu (not so much 'virtue' as responsible civic spirit), the individual had in some measure at least to take responsibility for his own governance and/or defence. Governance in a managed Hanoverian Scotland was so narrowly based that the possibility of a civic-spirited militia seemed the sole remaining badge of reciprocal, interactive partnership within the Union, so the Poker Club was founded in 1762 to stir up the flames of Scots militancy on the militia issue. It lasted until 1784, achieving little but supported by most of the Moderate literati, leading Scots politicians, and (in bad faith) by Smith and Hume, who seem to have joined it mainly to make sure it never applied effective pressure. In general, the pro-Hanoverian intelligentsia believed in exercising influence on the existing power structure from within.

That accounts for the very heavily assimilationist thrust of their *belles-lettres*. In imaginative literature James Thomson was almost the *beau idéal*. He was a son of the manse whose father had died while exorcizing a ghost. Criticism by the Professor of Divinity at Edinburgh of a college exercise involving a commentary on part of Psalm 119 made him abandon divinity to seek his fortune with his pen in London. Amazingly, he succeeded, securing a sinecure through political patronage which lasted until just before his death in 1748. He was co-author of *The Masque of Alfre*, which contained the ode 'Rule, Britannia', as well as 'The Seasons' and 'Liberty'. The inevitable ambiguities of a British patriot who also stressed Scottish themes like the ancient liberties, sublime natural scenery, and the mystery and superstition of the north, prepared the way for a later romantic phase in Scottish literature, mostly produced by Scottish-domiciled writers like Burns and Scott. Would-be Scots playwrights, like the Dunbartonshire man Tobias Smollett, headed for London, where Smollett failed, but succeeded as a novelist in the 1740s. Few wrote for that provincial operation which was the Scottish stage. A successful drama was synonymous with a London première. Everyone mentions that when the great Mrs Siddons came to act in Edinburgh in 1783, enthusiasm was so great that the General Assembly of the Kirk had to adapt its schedule to allow for attendance. Fewer mention that despite her majestic milking of emotion (she always played her role in 'Douglas' carrying a huge handkerchief for the tears), her subsequent visits to Edinburgh failed because of very thin support.

Latterly only Henry Mackenzie, an Edinburgh lawyer and literatus whose life (1745–1831) spanned neatly the heyday of Hanoverian Scotland, achieved the sort of widespread acclaim through imaginative writing which so many sought. His third-rate tear-jerking novel of sensibility, *The Man of Feeling* (1771), enjoyed the sort of success for the wrong sort of reasons which an equally lamentable tear-jerker, *The Sorrows of Werther* (1774), gave to the much greater German, Goethe. Apart from Mackenzie's lucky sentimental novel, it was in the fields of history, philosophy, political economy (to be re-christened economics), and what modern scholars would slightly misleadingly call sociology, that the Scottish *illuminati* were to make their British, European and Atlantic impact. They quite deliberately bid for those markets, as Principal Robertson demonstrated after the Earl of Bute secured the principate of Edinburgh University for him in the full expectation he would develop his work on Scottish history. Robertson refused to paint himself into that corner, opting for the majestic European canvas supplied by the Emperor Charles V.

History, on a broad enough canvas, sold well. Tobias Smollett, after making his name with novels like *Roderick Random* (1748) and *Peregrine Pickle* (1751), settled in Chelsea and edited the *Critical Review*, which he tried to use to support his own heavy investment in a British identity by creating in its columns a standardized English distanced from all regional dialects and therefore universally usable. When he turned to history, he wrote three successful volumes of a *History of England* in 1757–8. David Hume watched his *Treatise of Human Nature* (1739) fall 'dead-born from the press in London'. He recovered with two volumes of *Essays Moral and Political* (1741 and 1742), and produced a simplified re-run of his *Treatise* in 1748, as *Enquiry Concerning Human Understanding*; he confirmed his reputation, made with the *Essays*, with his *History of England* in five volumes (1754–62). Obsolete as history, it is now primarily a source for Hume's 'Philosophical' Whiggism, showing him deprecating 'vulgar' Whiggism. Without endorsing Jacobitism or Toryism, Hume deliberately set out to see their point of view and undermine populist Whiggery.

Principal Robertson shared with Hume the idea of the historian as setter of the moral tone of society, albeit in his case the vision presented was rooted in Christian providentialism. Having made his name in the romantic era of Mary Queen of Scots and James VI and I, he turned his version of 'philosophical' (that is, analytical) history to the evolution of Europe in the era of Charles V. He then meant to produce a history of the Americas in two balancing parts. The *History of America*, which appeared in 1777, was primarily devoted to Spanish America, showing his unparalleled bibliographical mastery of Spanish printed (and a few manuscript) sources; as well as a strong bias towards the metropolitan authority as opposed to Amerindians or settlers and their descendants. His hidden agenda was that the Spanish empire had been too authoritarian in church and state and too protectionist, whereas the English (then British) empire had been too libertarian, but that Providence was now leading Spain towards less authoritarianism and freer trade, as it was the British empire to more decency and order. The American Revolution destroyed his architecture. The English sections, mere sketches, were published posthumously by his son. Robertson turned in the end to India, producing a slim book, *An historical disquisition concerning the knowledge which the ancients had of India . . .* (1791), which characteristically illuminated much more than Greco-Roman knowledge.

The history of the political economy, philosophy and 'sociology' of Enlightenment Scotland suffers from the fact that several of its exponents have become iconic. People find it easier to try to encapsulate an idea of an era if they can internalize a few icons, which need not be visual, but which are helped by a visual dimension. Adam Smith, with *The Wealth of Nations*, and the classical contemporary portrait medallion of him by James Tassie, is the ultimate Enlightenment icon. Unfortunately his reputation has been endlessly manipulated, often to endorse points of view he would scarcely comprehend, let alone endorse. He was a moral philosopher whose *Theory of Moral Sentiments* (1759) relied on an innate sense of sympathy (a concept Smith may have partially derived from his reading of French sentimental novels) as the root of moral instincts. By the early nineteenth century his philosophical work was forgotten and already fatuous claims were being made to the effect that *The Wealth of Nations* invented economics. The book has almost no original material in it, as far as economic theory goes. The most sophisticated concepts, such as multilateral settlement of balances of payments, had been worked out before 1700. Smith did acknowledge his debt to the French school of thinkers known as the Physiocrats, but was otherwise extremely ungenerous to his predecessors, especially to Sir James Steuart. One of the few leading intellectuals to join the '45, Steuart returned from exile in 1763 to publish in 1767 his *Inquiry into the Principles of Political Oeconomy*, which was the leading work until *The Wealth of Nations* appeared in 1776. Like most successful books, Adam Smith's work told people with influence what they wanted to hear. It was written for a society of orders, not classes, and the only order Smith thought had an interest compatible with that of society as a whole was the landed aristocracy. For businessmen he had a visceral distrust. His advocacy of freer trade and lower taxes, and his distrust of monopoly, was almost platitudinous, but embedded in a splendid, if in many places unconvincing, textbook.

David Hume is another figure who became iconic because of twentieth-century commentators' obsession with his radical scepticism about the possibility of real knowledge in the early *Treatise* of 1739. Contemporaries believed that the Reverend Dr Thomas Reid, professor in Aberdeen and then Adam Smith's replacement in the Glasgow chair of moral philosophy in 1764, had effectively answered Hume by his 'Common Sense' theory of knowledge, which was vulgarized and aggressively propagated by another Aberdeen divine, Dr James Beattie. That their 'answer' was flawed, compared with, say, modern probability theory, hardly matters. Few were likely to have their faith shaken by a Humean ontology whose logical conclusions were patently absurd. The Moderate literati of Edinburgh were friendly with Hume precisely because they saw in him no threat. Scots Common Sense philosophy reigned serenely at home and was exported to the United States of America through such channels as John Witherspoon, who left the Laigh kirk, Paisley, for the College of New Jersey (later Princeton) in 1768. He became a signatory to the Declaration of Independence and an immensely influential figure in American academe. However, to push the analysis of the influence of 'Scotch' philosophy to the point of arguing that Thomas Reid, through the mind of Thomas Jefferson, was the principal begetter of the 'self-evident' truths in the Declaration of Independence seems to press the case rather further than positive evidence can justify.

What is true is that Scots academic rhetoricians and belletrists seem to have invented the concept of English literature as an academic subject. Another sequence of scholars followed James Hutton, whose *Theory of the Earth* (1795) expounded the continuity of the earth-shaping forces through time, founded modern geology. Hutton's ideas were advertised by his friend the mathematics professor John Playfair, and then after 1830 widely circulated, if misleadingly recast, by the Forfarshire laird's son, Charles Lyell. The analysis of society, in the form of a 'scientific' history dealing with structures rather than specific events, was much more central to the intellectual life of Scotland between 1750 and 1832, producing such misunderstood texts as Adam Ferguson's *An Essay on the History of Civil Society* (1767) and John Millar's *Distinction of Ranks in Society* (1771). Much of what we take as proto-sociology in these is formed from the accepted generalizations of civic humanism – the ideology drawn from the classics and further developed in Renaissance Europe, which tried to teach men how to create and sustain a republic of virtue devoted to participative, not passive, liberty. Above all, Scottish literati saw all societies as moving inexorably through a fourfold stadial progression from hunter, to shepherd or herdsman, to agriculture, and then commerce.

Walter Scott sums up better than most the disturbing inexorability of change, so lucidly expounded by someone like Millar. Giving up the production of lively narrative verse when a better, racier rival in the shape of Lord Byron came on the scene, Scott, the amiable Border lawyer, started from 1814 with *Waverley* to mine the rich seam of the vast, predominantly middle-class, market for novels. Because of the habit of issuing them in parts (three-decker novels), authors were driven to be verbose and Scott wrote vast amounts of unworthy material after his financial collapse of 1826, heroically trying to clear debt. Nevertheless, in his half-dozen truly great Scottish novels, what is central is the tragedy of those caught with outdated loyalties in the inexorable transition between one social order and another. Romantic sensibility and Enlightenment rationality blended in Scott. In a different way, John Galt, another writer whose best work is a minority of pieces in a vast output, was anxious to write up traditional provincial Scotland, most famously in *Annals of the Parish* (1821) and *The Provost* (1822), before inexorable change eroded its national characteristics.

By the 1820s the classic balance between an accommodating aristocratic hegemony and a rapidly changing commercial society was clearly unstable. The débâcle into which Scott's attempt to sustain a generous Border laird's lifestyle led him, his publisher, and his printer symbolized this. Sir Walter, as he was after 1820, was spared the final extinction of the Dundas regime he loyally supported only by death. The neo-classical idiom which was pioneered not by the French but by the English from the 1730s was one which Scots architects could rapidly internalize and develop as an apt expression of the new stability and progress of Scotland after the 1750s. By 1830 it was becoming outdated. Famously, the young son of an Edinburgh merchant, the architect James Craig, had won the 1766 competition for a plan for the new Edinburgh to be raised on land on the far side of the drained Nor Loch, and had set a neo-classical mould which a succeeding generation of builders respected. Though the Adam brothers, the greatest Scots architectural dynasty, naturally sought commissions primarily south of the border, a good deal of their stylish neo-classicism is embodied in late work in Edinburgh, particularly Charlotte Square and Register House. The most famous member of the dynasty, Robert Adam, had set out young to catch an aristocratic Scots and English market by sending himself on the fashionable Grand Tour in the 1750s, and haunting classical sites in Italy and Dalmatia in association with the great neo-classical French draughtsman and architect Charles-Louis Clérisseau. By the 1830s the touches of 'Gothick' castellation he had allowed himself in commissions like Culzean Castle in Ayrshire were mere trivia compared with the rising wave of serious asymmetrical gothic revival. Even the classical strain in the increasingly fractured architectural scene was moving towards 'archaeological' Greek. In the same way, the images of the great portraitists, Allan Ramsay the younger and Sir Henry Raeburn, who had immortalized the male and female élites of the Enlightenment era in Scotland, were by the 1820s curiously backward-looking. The future clearly lay with different sensibilities, from the genre paintings of the young David Wilkie, to romantic history and landscape.

Conclusion

Between 1707 and 1746 the range of options available for a relevant, functional Scottish identity narrowed in the sense that Jacobitism and repeal of the Union ceased to be feasible. Most Scots had clearly reached that conclusion as early as the 1720s. Their dominant élites were uncompromisingly Unionist and assimilationist. They participated in the high Enlightenment, which was the product of aristocratic patronage and cooperative intellectuals, many of them clergymen. It was part of a Europe-wide movement away from the introspective, genocidal sectarian conflicts of the seventeenth century towards a more tolerant, prosperous, cosmopolitan and scientific-minded society. Freemasonry, which had been invented in early modern Scotland, was, of course, partly a product of Renaissance mysticism, but it also became in the eighteenth century a vehicle for specifically Enlightened values, and helped link the Scots élite to the newly-dynamic freemasonry of England, Europe and North America. Henry Dundas was a freemason, and so was Burns. Despite papal disapproval, there were plenty of Roman Catholic freemasons before 1800. Jacobite lodges used the craft to try to bridge the sectarian gulfs which were such an impediment to the Jacobite cause. Public buildings in the New Town of Edinburgh, from Register House to the new neo-classical quadrangle for the university, had their foundation stones laid with Masonic honours, as had the US Capitol in Washington.

Scotland in the early nineteenth century was not yet an industrial society. It was an agrarian one which had experienced a dramatic expansion in industry and commerce. Thus there was probably more basic significance in the development of Scottish banking — from the chartering of the Bank of Scotland in 1695 and of the Royal Bank in 1727, to what became the British Linen Bank in 1746, to the complex of urban and regional banks that developed in the later eighteenth century – than there was in fixed-capital industrial investment. As credit loosened there were crises like the collapse of the Ayr Bank in 1772, though that crisis enabled the two senior chartered banks to emerge as the dominant ones, controlling note issue and credit limits for the provincial banks. It was not radical political opposition which destabilized Hanoverian Scotland by 1832. That it could handle. It was its own inherent tendency towards accommodation, growth and change.

Scottish identities were a complex phenomenon and undoubtedly in this period a British element became very important in them. It is fashionable to stress the linkage between Britishness and Protestantism, but that stress, though partially valid, tends to underestimate two factors. One is the depth of divisions between Protestants of different kinds. The other is the extent to which the ruling élites in Hanoverian Scotland consciously, if at times discretely, repudiated the whole grievance-factory of factional and sectarian animosity which had been integral to the experience of Christendom since the Emperor Constantine established the church in 324. One consequence of the broadening of the Scottish political base in 1832–3 was to be the re-emergence of chronic sectarian rivalry as a significant aspect of Scottish life.

Obviously, Scotland shared after 1707 in the progressive globalization of European commerce, far more so than it had before the Union. The British monarchy was, by 1757, itself a global, if barely coherent, complex of interests. At one point the Scots aristocratic and mercantile élites seemed to be emerging as the Praetorian Guard of a more coherent empire, especially after the triumphal Peace of Paris of 1763, when Scots virtually monopolized governorships in the newly-conquered territories. This was all dust and ashes by 1783. The independent United States, Europe, Asia and Latin America were vastly more important for Scots business and, in the case of North America, migratory interests between 1783 and 1832, than what was left of the British Empire. Lord Selkirk went bankrupt sponsoring Highland settlement in Canada. Most Scots in the Caribbean or the Indian sub-continent were 'sojourners in the sun', desperate to get back to a lairdly lifestyle in Scotland before Scots intellectuals prominent in anti-slavery agitation succeeded and undermined the plantation system.

Henry Dundas did grasp the opportunities for imperial expansion in India, the great exception to imperial recession after the American war. Scots did take advantage of his patronage networks to get jobs in India, where a high proportion of them died after the proverbial 'two monsoons' in one of the three East India Company 'presidencies'. By the 1830s the newly-enfranchised, and aggressively assertive, Scottish merchant class was trying to use British naval and diplomatic power forcibly to open markets abroad. The Scot James Matheson, an Edinburgh graduate and a notable smuggler of opium into China, was at the forefront of demands for a 'forward policy' to force the Chinese to allow unimpeded trade, denouncing the elderly Duke of Wellington, an Irish aristocrat of the old school, as an advocate of 'submissiveness and servility' because he jibbed at war with China in 1835. It came in 1839. There were success stories of outstanding soldiers like General Sir David Baird, who made his name in India, as well as the odd wealthy ex-EIC 'nabob'. There were also failures. Henry Low, a Fife lawyer and golfer, went bankrupt in a bad recession in 1825 as a partner in a Fife bank. By 1830 he was in Australia, where the estate he ran went bankrupt. By 1833 he was in India, where he went bankrupt in Calcutta. He died in Burma in obscurity, the only triple-medal winner of the St Andrews Society of Golfers to have been declared insolvent in three continents. The life of this great man reminds us that what was distinctive about Scots by 1832 was their unique blend of experiences and identities. Between 1707 and 1832, an unstable cocktail was created in such a way that even the strongest ingredient could only contribute to an unpredictable, but always unique, final taste.

Bibliographical Essay

General

An older collection of essays which is still informative is N. T. Phillipson and Rosalind Mitchison (eds.), *Scotland in the Age of Improvement* (Edinburgh, 1970; 2nd edn., 1996). There is a broad but compact survey by Bruce P. Lenman, *Integration and Enlightenment, Scotland 1746–1832* (London, 1981; 2nd edn. Edinburgh, 1992) which tries to place political history in its wider social, economic and cultural contexts. T. M. Devine and J. R. Young (eds.), *Eighteenth-Century Scotland: New Perspectives* (Edinburgh, 1999) is a useful if incomplete guide to recent interpretations. T. M. Devine, *Exploring the Scottish Past* (East Linton, 1995) is also worth reading. The evolution of Gaelic society is conveniently and simply surveyed in Allan I. Macinnes, *Clanship, Commerce and the House of Stewart, 1603–1788* (East Linton, 1996), and also in the more challenging but highly rewarding *From Chiefs to Landlords: Social and Economic Change in the Western Highlands and Islands, c. 1493–1820* by R. A. Dodgshon (Edinburgh, 1998).

Economic and Social

T. M. Devine and Rosalind Mitchison (eds.), *People and Society in Scotland*, vol. 1: *1760–1830* (Edinburgh, 1988) is the most recent comprehensive social history. I. D. Whyte, *Scotland Before the Industrial Revolution: An Economic and Social History c. 1050–c. 1750* (London, 1995) is excellent, but stops midway through this period. T. M. Devine (ed.), *Improvement and Enlightenment* (Edinburgh, 1989) is a helpful collection of essays. C. A. Whatley, *The Industrial Revolution in Scotland* (Cambridge, 1997) is a very brief overview. On one of the central themes in early Scottish industrialization, Alastair J. Durie, *The Scottish Linen Industry in the Eighteenth Century* (Edinburgh, 1979) is good. Richard Saville, *Bank of Scotland: A History, 1695–1995* (Edinburgh, 1996) is of fundamental interest for eighteenth-century (and later) economic history. Andrew Blaikie, *Illegitimacy, Sex, and Society: Northeast Scotland, 1750–1900* (Oxford, 1993) is the most scholarly study of this interesting topic. R. A. Houston, *Social Change in the Age of Enlightenment: Edinburgh, 1660–1760* (Oxford, 1994) contains a mass of detailed research which makes the society of Scotland's capital come alive. Some other high-quality monographs dealing with social history have been produced in recent years, including Elizabeth C. Sanderson, *Women and Work in Eighteenth-Century Edinburgh* (London, 1996), and R. A. Houston, *Madness and Society in Eighteenth-Century Scotland* (Oxford, 2000). T. M. Devine and G. Jackson (eds.), *Glasgow, Beginnings to 1830* (Manchester, 1995) is good on some aspects of the history of Scotland's second city, though it is mostly about the years after 1750. R. A. Houston, *The Population History of Britain and Ireland, 1500–1750* (Cambridge, 1995) deals, among other things, with the connection between economic change and population rise. A. J. S. Gibson and T. C. Smout, *Prices, Food and Wages in Scotland 1550–1780* (Cambridge, 1995) is one of the few books which breaks new ground on population and economy in early modern Scotland. T. M. Devine, *The Transformation of Rural Scotland: Social Change and the Agrarian Economy, 1660–1815* (Edinburgh, 1994) is a good archive-based study. I. D. Whyte, *Agriculture and Society in Seventeenth-Century Scotland* (Edinburgh, 1979) is important. There is much less work on Highland economy and society, but Dodgshon's *From Chiefs to Landlords* (above) should be consulted, along with Charles W. J. Withers, *Urban Highlanders: Highland–Lowland Migration and Urban Gaelic Culture, 1700–1900* (East Linton, 1999).

Religion

This traditionally sectarian, over-written, and hagiographically inclined field has been raised to respectable academic standards of late by such works as Callum G. Brown, *Religion and Society in Scotland Since 1707* (Edinburgh, 1997); John R. Macintosh, *Church and Theology in Enlightenment Scotland: The Popular Party, 1740–1800* (East Linton, 1998); and Leigh Eric Schmidt, *Holy Fairs: Scottish Communions and American Revivals in the Early Modern Period* (Princeton, NJ, 1989). Other studies include Marilyn J. Westerkamp, *Triumph of the Laity: Scots-Irish Piety and the Great Awakening, 1625–1760* (New York, 1988), and C. Johnson, *Developments Within the Roman Catholic Church in Scotland, 1789–1829* (Atlantic Highlands, NJ, 1983). Periodicals such as the *Innes Review* and *Records of the Scottish Church History Society* continue to produce detailed studies of religious topics.

Politics

Inevitably, the absence within Scotland of the 'high politics' of policy determination after the Union of 1707 has led historians to produce 'Namierite' studies of patronage and the struggles for control of the constituencies, which produced the hard coin of eighteenth-century Westminster politics in the shape of MPs committed to one faction or another. Examples of this are Ronald M. Sunter, *Patronage and Politics in Scotland 1707–1832* (Edinburgh, 1986); John Stuart Shaw, *The Management of Scottish Society 1707–1764* (Edinburgh, 1983), but note that *The Political History of Eighteenth-Century Scotland* (Basingstoke, 1999) by the same author provides a short overview; and Alexander Murdoch, *The People Above: Politics and Administration in Mid-Eighteenth-Century Edinburgh* (Edinburgh, 1980). By contrast, Michael Fry, *The Dundas Despotism* (Edinburgh, 1992) tackles every level from constituency manipulation in Scotland to British Cabinet decision-making on domestic, foreign policy and imperial policy. On the whole, this ambitious design is successful despite a surprising shallowness on the affairs of India. For the very different politics of the Jacobite alternative, see Bruce P. Lenman, *The Jacobite Risings in Britain 1689–1746* and *The Jacobite Clans of the Great Glen 1650–1784* (2nd edn. Aberdeen, 1995). Daniel Szechi, *The Jacobites, Britain and Europe 1688–1788* (Manchester, 1994) is an excellent short and scholarly survey of Jacobitism in its full international context – this in a field which has many 'popular' studies of mixed quality.

Cultures, Education, and Enlightenment

Among modern studies of the eighteenth-century Scottish universities, Jennifer Carter and Donald Withrington (eds.), *Scottish Universities: Distinctiveness and Diversity* (Edinburgh, 1992) and Roger Emerson, *Professors, Patronage, and Politics: The Aberdeen Universities in the Eighteenth Century* (Aberdeen, 1992) are among the best correctives to the common tendency to regard Edinburgh University as the Scottish Enlightenment's sole begetter. Richard B. Sher, *Church and University in the Scottish Enlightenment: The Moderate Literati of Edinburgh* (Edinburgh, 1985) is a classic study, but the subtitle describes it better than the title proper. Sher more than made amends by co-editing Andrew Hook and Richard B. Sher, *The Glasgow Enlightenment* (East Linton, 1995). Another book worth consulting in this field is Jennifer J. Carter and Joan H. Pittock, *Aberdeen and the Enlightenment* (Aberdeen, 1987). Jane Rendall, *The Origins of the Scottish Enlightenment 1707–1776* (London, 1978), and Roy H. Campbell and Andrew Skinner (eds.), *The Origins and Nature of the Scottish Enlightenment* (Edinburgh, 1982) cover the same ground in very different ways. The former is more a source text than a study, and it is fair to say that the very best recent work on the Enlightenment is in articles and book chapters. Nicholas Phillipson's *The Scottish Whigs and the Reform of the Court of Session* (Edinburgh, 1990), shows the quality of his work on ideas, institutions and society. Anand C. Chitnis, *The Scottish Enlightenment: A Social History* (London, 1976) is useful and solid, but rather out of date. Among even older works, Gladys Bryson, *Man and Society: The Scottish Inquiry of the Eighteenth Century* (Princeton, NJ, 1945; A. M. Kelley reprint, New York, 1968) is still very well worth reading, though an excellent book consciously written as a replacement for it is Christopher J. Berry, *Social Theory of the Scottish Enlightenment* (Edinburgh, 1997). Istvan Hont and Michael Ignatieff (eds.), *Wealth and Virtue: The Shaping of Political Economy in the Scottish Enlightenment* (Cambridge, 1983) is a collection of essays focusing on the remarkable contribution of the Scottish Enlightenment to the formation of modern economics. A. Broadie, *The Scottish Enlightenment: An Anthology* (Edinburgh, 1997) provides an affordable and wide-ranging selection of important passages. The essential text on literacy is R. A. Houston, *Scottish Literacy and the Scottish Identity* (Cambridge, 1985). Houston also provides the European context in which Scotland's achievements must be judged: *Literacy in Early Modern Europe: Culture and Education, 1500–1800* (London, 1989; 2nd edn., 2002). R. D. Anderson, *Education and the Scottish People, 1750–1913* (Oxford, 1995) is useful.

On the more literary side of the Scottish Enlightenment, David Allan, *Virtue, Learning and the Scottish Enlightenment* (Edinburgh, 1993) places eighteenth-century Scottish historical writing in a much longer continuum. Colin Kidd, *Subverting Scotland's Past* (Cambridge, 1993) examines the way in which Scottish Whig historians pursued their agenda of creating a new Anglo-British identity between 1689 and c. 1830. A convenient introduction to the predominantly poetic Gaelic literary achievement is in Chapter 5 of Derick Thomson, *An Introduction to Gaelic Poetry* (London, 1974. 2nd edn. Edinburgh, 1989). Fiona Stafford, *The Sublime Savage: James Macpherson and the Poems of Ossian* (Edinburgh, 1993) probes the roots of the anglophone concept of the 'Celtic twilight'. Howard Gaskill (ed.), *Ossian Revisited* (Edinburgh, 1991) is an excellent collection. Andrew Hook (ed.), *The History of Scottish Literature*, vol. 2: *1660–1800* (Aberdeen, 1987) covers writing in all the various linguistic traditions of Scotland.

Art, Architecture and Music

Duncan Macmillan, *Painting in Scotland: The Golden Age* (Oxford, 1986) is a standard work. Sir James Lewis Caw, *Scottish Painting Past and Present, 1620–1908* (Edinburgh, 1908; reprinted Bath, 1975) is a monumental study. Andrew Gibbon Williams and Andrew Brown, *The Bigger Picture: A History of Scottish Art* (London, 1993) accompanied a BBC television series. Two important architects of the period are studied in compact modern style in Kitty Cruft and Andrew Fraser (eds.), *James Craig 1744–1795* (Edinburgh, 1995), and Margaret H. B. Sanderson, *Robert Adam and Scotland* (HMSO, Edinburgh, 1992). A. J. Youngson, *The Making of Classical Edinburgh 1750–1840* (Edinburgh, 1966) remains by far the best of its author's many books, and an enduring achievement. Thomas A. Markus (ed.), *Order and Space in Society: Architectural Form and its Context in the Scottish Enlightenment* (Edinburgh, 1982) raises some more general points. Penguin's excellent series, *The Buildings of Scotland* (Harmondsworth, 1978–), has only so far covered six regions. The much more extensive (and better illustrated, but more expensive) reports of the Royal Commission on the Ancient and Historical Monuments of Scotland are also an invaluable resource for this and other ages; it is only fair to point out that publishing of the series began in 1909. There is a charming and informative piece of musical history in David Johnson, *Music and Society in Lowland Scotland in the Eighteenth Century* (London, 1972).

6

Civil Society, Governance and Nation, 1832–1914

GRAEME MORTON
R. J. MORRIS

Between 1832 and 1914 the bargain which the Scottish élite had made at the Treaty of Union took on new meanings and posed new questions. The balance between local and central government, the Scottish nation, and Britain and Empire, provided a new context in which Scotland could grow. In 1707, the Scottish élite had sold a parliament and bought into a free trade area with a unified currency. The integrity of Scotland as a nation was embodied in clauses protecting the nation's legal, religious and educational systems and, by implication, much of local government. This was to prove a remarkably resilient structure, one with profound implications for Scottish national identity. The dominant Lowland Protestant fabric of the country's social structure survived several nasty rebellions and even more violent suppressions of these rebellions. The economy stabilized and then expanded. The Union settlement was the basis for a dynamic and thriving national character in both a Scottish and a British sense. Some features of this have gained the approval of later generations and other cultures: the freedom and world reputation of Enlightenment thinking generated by figures like Adam Ferguson; the embodiment of national pride in romantic poetry and fiction (Walter Scott); and the revival of local language in poetry and song (Robert Burns).

Other developments are regarded more equivocally. In polite society élite forms of communication converged with English, which was the dominant language of trade, industry and the state. The re-creation of the Gaelic myths of Ossian by the poet and scholar James Macpherson and of Scotland's foundation by Scottish historians at the time of Union were enthusiasms that did not last. Politics from Argyll to Dundas were re-invented as a managerial system of patronage well suited to the local/central political structures of the time. This system could deliver the occasional piece of legislation to Scotland (such as the Edinburgh Improvement and Extension Acts, which led amongst other things to the building of the North Bridge in the 1760s) and provided a squad of usually reliable government supporters to the Westminster parliament. It also left Scotland to be governed with little interference from Westminster, an outcome of either neglect or design. There was little evidence that Scotland's economy, culture or sense of national identity suffered from the lack of a parliament, but as this system was reformed in the 1832–1914 period, the modern conception of Scotland the nation was forged.

By 1914 Scotland was a nation increasingly confident in its contribution to Britain's economic development and place in the world, but it was still rooted in locality and the everyday. The village, the rural and urban parish, the town and the region retained their significance for Scottish society. The rise of the modern nation was the end product of these features. Scotland modernized its localities and its communities regrouped. It was pushed and pulled through this transition as one might have predicted of a small nation with a powerful neighbour and strong overseas trading links. Scottish history is as much about what happened on the land and territory of Scotland as it is about what happened to Scottish people. We will talk about both. And when we tie our thoughts to the flag of national identity, we again profess an awareness that the history of Scotland is far from insular. National history was and is a history of self-reflection, often formed in opposition to 'others'. England's role as the 'auld enemy', or the 'menace' of Catholic Ireland, to name but two, have done much to forge a sense of 'Scottishness', but in a period that followed a century of Union, even those are too simplistic. Scotland operated within an agreed union of incorporation during the age of nationalism in the late eighteenth and nineteenth century. Identity was a result of maturity, coalition and compromise.

Scotland had a level of governance unheard of for a nation without its own parliament. The Scots gave up their parliament by treaty, but negotiated the survival of the three institutions which were felt to be essential to its ethos. The 'spaces' left for social action and cultural development within a nation without a parliament were an important part of the story in nineteenth-century Scotland. These were the spaces of civil society, the area between household and the state where associational activity took place and where public opinion was formed. Scotland was in union with a larger neighbour, through which it shared its government, but it maintained an important layer of distinctiveness. The meanings and relationships of the Union began to change as a result of a wide-ranging series of developments. Scotland was a major player in a larger set of processes: population growth linked to patterns of emigration and rural–urban migration; urbanization, putting pressure on infrastructure, church and municipality; economic growth and changes in consumption patterns that linked world and local markets; empire becoming part of national and racial identity; and political and social individualism expressed within representative assembly and associational structures. These processes occurred against a background of legislative intervention in the national society and in the economy, but ultimately realized in the locality.

Because of the lack of a parliament, the distant nature of Westminster, and the centrality of church, law and education, civil society was constructed as the mechanism to mediate modernization. Being more formal than the family, constructed out of rules and regulations rather than blood ties or the tyranny of cousins, yet being separate from, sometimes opposed to, the state, the soul of the Scottish nation was contained therein. Being Scottish involved a series of identities in the period 1832–1914. It is commonly argued that Scots enjoy a dual national identity, where they can be British if they wish, but if not they can opt to be Scottish as well as, or in distinction to, 'Britishness'. The metaphor of concentric rings displays the Scots as having multiple identities, from the personal to those of family, region, religion, state or empire. These accounts carry the implication that the bigger identity is the more important, because it is more geographically widespread. However, this neglects the interconnection of these identities and the fact that their importance depends on the context in which they co-exist and are realized. The lesser identity may be the most acute. Events and trends make one or other national, religious or class identity raw and alive, flickering into life for a day, a few months or years, before its intensity wanes. The years from 1832 until 1914 were ones of modernization, fragmentation and dislocation, with major movements of people and capital and key changes in governance. Scottish national identity, like the history of the Scottish nation, has been neither coherent nor progressive. It ebbs, it flows, it breaks up, it muddles along. Our task in the pages that follow is to chart its path.

The Disruption of the Church of Scotland: 18 May 1843

On 18 May 1843, the day of the disruption of the Church of Scotland, many of the economic, social and cultural forces which were changing and testing Scotland become evident. At about three in the afternoon a long line of black-suited men, ministers and elders, emerged from the General Assembly, then meeting in St Andrew's Church in Edinburgh's New Town. They walked in impromptu procession through dense crowds to Tanfield Hall, a one-time oil-gas works, then a warehouse, located in the industrial suburb of Canonmills. Here preparations had been made for the first assembly of the Free Church of Scotland. The Deed of Demission was signed by 474 ministers giving up some £100,000 sterling in emoluments, as well as the shelter of manse and kirk buildings. The central issue was patronage, but it was an issue which exposed many of the fault lines of Scottish society. The ministers of the established Church of Scotland were chosen by patrons, mainly landlords and the crown, and then approved by the presbytery. Usually congregations accepted the patron's choice and a wise patron took care to see that the selection would be acceptable. This comfortable relationship was broken by the growing evangelical movement in the kirk, which worried about the inflexible parish structure and the failure of the dominant moderate section to retain the attention of the urban working classes. The Moderates, with their respect for polite learning and a stable relationship between church and state, faced increasing challenges from Evangelicals like Thomas Chalmers, with their direct and enthusiastic belief in the redemption from sin through faith in Jesus Christ and their mission, through popular preaching and missionary work, to communicate this to the working classes, whom they felt were neglected by existing structures and practices. After ten years of conflict within the kirk, the Evangelicals came to believe that freedom from the state was essential. In 1833, they gained a majority in the General Assembly of the church and passed the Veto Act which sanctioned the rejection of an unwanted minister by the parish. This was challenged by a number of patrons and ministers who forced or 'intruded' ministers on parishes that had rejected them. The Court of Session in Edinburgh upheld the rights of patrons over those of the church courts. Legal appeals to the House of Lords and debates in the Westminster parliament were unable to resolve the conflict. In 1842, the General Assembly issued its Claim of Right, a title which was significantly re-used in the early part of the campaign which brought about the current devolved Scottish parliament. The 1842 Claim asserted the spiritual independence of Scotland under the headship of Christ and the guarantees of the Union settlement. The 1843 walk-out followed.

There were many social pressures behind this event. It was a movement led by the urban middle class against overly intrusive aristocratic influence, thus marking a profound shift in the political aspirations and power of the middling ranks within Scottish society. At the same time there was a split within the middle classes between those who accepted a hierarchical view of society, mainly urban merchant élites, and those who did not, mainly those with new wealth and lower-middle-class status. They were joined by many Highland people who responded to the economic and social betrayal by the lairds, most notably represented by rack-renting and the clearances, by leaving the latter's church. The Disruption also represented a very particular nationalist feeling. The state which controlled the kirk was the Westminster state and crucial decisions which created the need for the Disruption had been taken in London. Lord Jeffrey, on hearing of the scale of the Disruption, claimed: 'There is not another country upon earth where such a deed could have been done.' It was a measured nationalism. The Reverend George Lewis of Dundee, like many who were about to leave the kirk, took care to attend the annual levée of Her Majesty's Commissioner, the Marquis of Bute, at Holyrood Palace, 'anxious to show our loyalty to Caesar when about to give to Christ the things that belong to Christ'.

While when many still believe that Scotland will only be truly free when the last minister has been strangled by the last copy of the *Sunday Post*, it is deeply unfashionable to see merit in the making of the Free Church. But in many ways the Disruption represented Scottish Protestantism at its best. There was an elemental energy in the drama of the exit from George Street, in the early open-air services and in the building of churches, schools and manses, as well as the collection of money to support ministers.

There was a self-directed discipline, a sense of freedom before God without intervention of patron or parliament which formed a powerful aspect of liberal Scotland. Although the Disruption was an aggressively male event, that sense of self-direction and escape from hierarchy lay behind the entry of many women into both secular and religious areas of public life in the second half of the century. There was a proud application of logic and reason, especially theological reason, which so impressed and terrified the English. When that most English of Englishmen, William Cobbett, visited Scotland in 1830, he paused at the border in mock terror of the Scots 'feelosofers'. Twenty years later, Hugh Miller, geologist, theologian and editor of the Free Church newspaper, the *Witness*, decided to visit England. He recorded his scorn at the poor quality of theological argument among the Methodists in a temperance coffee-house in Newcastle. It was way below that of the 'peasant controversialists so unwisely satirized by Burns. The development of the popular mind in Scotland is a result of its theology.' At the same time, the Disruption reflected cultural forces which were deeply oppressive, an effective Sabbatarianism which closed parks, libraries and sports grounds and locked away children's toys, as well as a sectarianism based not so much on hatred as on bleak incomprehension of other points of view.

The outcome of the Disruption was deeply paradoxical. The initial result was an energetic burst of investment in the religious infrastructure of Scotland. Over 730 churches had been provided by 1847, a 'sustentation' fund guaranteed ministers a minimum stipend of £122 sterling a year, which could be and was supplemented by wealthier congregations. Some 400 manses, and schools for 513 teachers and 44,000 children, as well as a college for the education of ministers (on the Mound in Edinburgh), were well on their way. It was an astonishing achievement, based on the donations and subscriptions of the congregations. Despite its lack of prominence in modern knowledge of Scottish history, in contemporary terms the Disruption was a pivotal event which incorporated and responded to many of the pressures and changes within Scottish society. Yet the outcome was very different from that envisaged by its leaders. True, all the evidence showed that in the next fifty years the proportion of the Scottish population with some sort of religious adherence rose from around 30 per cent to around 50 per cent, but in the long term it was the established church which made the gains, doubling its share to around 20 per cent, while the Free Church barely held the share of around 10 per cent evident in the 1840s. The Free Church became identified as the Highland church, and above all the middle-class church. In part this was systemic. The new churches, schools and ministers' salaries only came at the cost of donations, subscriptions and pew rents, and these only came from the middle-class merchants and shopkeepers. In turn they became the elders and managers of the new kirk. Working people felt more comfortable in the older secession churches originating in the eighteenth century, or the established church with its accumulated resources and without the insistent demands for pew rents and donations.

Ironically, given the powerful elements of social and national assertiveness it contained, the Disruption destroyed key elements which the Union settlement had sought to preserve. The parish state, the godly commonwealth of minister, dominie and kirk session which directly or indirectly provided poor relief, education and social discipline in most of Scotland, was gone. After 1843, Scotland was a pluralist religious society, a fact emphasized by the increasing numbers of immigrant Irish Catholic people during the potato famine of the middle and late 1840s. There had been legislation, local and national, from Westminster before 1843, but after 1843 the framework of Scottish poor law and education had to be provided by legislation and civil servants empowered by London, notably through the Poor Law Act of 1845 and the Education Act of 1872. After 1843, the framework was provided for Scotland and not by Scotland.

The Disruption provides one vantage point for reviewing the major changes of modernization, industrialization and urbanization which were making Scotland by transforming its civil society, governance and national identity. The structural changes involved were ones which Scotland shared with many other parts of the world, notably in Europe and North America, but such shared changes and experiences often carried with them features particular to Scotland.

Population

Between 1831 and 1911, Scotland's population increased from 2.4 to 4.8 million. This increase was one of many experiences in common with other industrializing countries. Also shared were high birth rates and high death rates. The crude birth rate was about 35 per thousand in 1861 and the crude death rate just over 22. Death rates were dominated by the huge mortality of young children, which was especially high in the growing towns. Of those born around 1871, a quarter would not live to the age of five, though even that was an improvement on the statistics for the eighteenth century. In the 1860s, the crude death rate for the four biggest towns was 20 per cent above that of other towns, and 57 per cent above the rural rates. Despite this, the high birth rate meant that Scotland was a land full of children. By the mid 1870s, the death rate began to fall and the urban/rural difference converged. In 1911, the gap between cities and rural areas was down to 17 per cent.

The change was due in part to improvements in standards of living, but also to better health and environmental management. It was also related to a reduction in the birth rate which took place from the 1880s onwards. There was little evidence of widespread use of mechanical methods of contraception, but abstinence, prolonged breast-feeding, *coitus interruptus* and perhaps an increase in abortions were part of a changing ideology of fertility which was bringing the Scots through a 'demographic transition' to lower birth rates and lower death rates. There were several distinctive Scottish elements in this experience. Despite widespread regional variations, Scottish demography was dominated by low levels of nuptiality (i.e. women married late and a high proportion did not marry at all) combined with high rates of fertility within marriage. In the early 1860s, marriages in Scotland produced a level of fertility which was 74 per cent of that which demographers consider a likely maximum. In England the level was 67 per cent. By 1911, the figures were down to 56 per cent and 47 per cent respectively, but the gap remained. Scotland also had comparatively low levels of nuptiality. In 1861, 20 per cent of Scottish women aged between 45 and 54 (and thus beyond the age when they could expect to bear children) had never been married; the figure was 12 per cent in England. By 1911, the gap had narrowed a little to 21 per cent and 16 per cent. The rate of spinsterhood was nearly twice that of England and Wales, although there was a smaller gap for men. In 1861, 13.5 per cent of Scots men aged between 45 and 54 had never married, while in England the figure was 10.5 per cent. By 1911, the figures were 16 per cent and 12 per cent respectively. In part, the lower nuptiality of Scots can be accounted for by lower wages and restricted housing availability in town and, especially, countryside, but this gap and the importance of spinsterhood for a large minority of women in Scotland were also outcomes of the most distinctive feature of Scottish demography, namely migration.

Between 1861 and 1913, some 1.46 million people born in Scotland were recorded as emigrating overseas; equivalent to 30 per cent of the 1911 population. Long-distance migration tends to be dominated by young, single males. In the 1850s, after a period of potato failure and agricultural depression, 24 per cent of men in their late teens left Scotland. The impact on sex ratios was dramatic. In 1861, there were 77 men for every 100 women in the 25–29 years age group – in which people were most likely to marry for the first time. The comparable sex ratio for England was 88. When the ladies of Scotland sang that ever popular song, 'The Flowers of the Forest', they were more likely to be thinking of young men who had gone to Canada and Australia than those slaughtered at Flodden, the ostensible subject of the ballad. There are various versions of what appears to be a lost original, but the best – and best known – is probably that by Jean Elliot (1727–1805), published anonymously *c.* 1755: 'At buchts in the morning, nae blythe lads are scorning; The lasses are lonely, and dowie, and wae . . . The Flowers of the Forest are a' wede away.' Only in Ireland and Norway did out-migration have more impact on population growth.

Migration had a widespread impact on Scottish culture and society. Folk-song collections seem always to contain a selection of jaunty and soulful migration ballads. Lowland gravestones from the nineteenth century often include the names of family members who died overseas, suggesting that in this literate and educated population, networks were maintained over very large distances. As a result of migration, the frontier of Scottish culture spread across the world, and Scots displayed an ability to sustain and develop that culture in many parts of the globe. There are to be found 39

Edinburghs, 25 Glasgows and 19 Dundees around the world, but none can top the 75 Hamiltons sited in Canada, Australia, New Zealand, Sierra Leone and the Caribbean, amongst others. It has been claimed that nine Scots or 'Scotch-Irish' were signatories of the American Declaration of Independence. Of the 29 presidents of the United States by 1921, 5 were of Scottish descent and 4 of Ulster-Scots descent.

Caledonian societies around the world continue to provide a focus for Scottish emigrants and exiles to celebrate Scottish national character in a selective historical context. They include St Andrew's societies and Burns clubs, Gaelic associations, Highland associations, Celtic associations, Bruce and Wallace associations. The oldest society in America was the Scots' Charitable Society of Boston (founded in 1657). The first St Andrew's society, the Club of Charleston, was founded in 1729. The St Andrew's Society of Montreal was founded in 1834 after parliamentary elections had 'caused revival of that national feeling which is to some extent natural to all men, and is said to exist in an eminent degree in Scotchmen'. Their St Andrew's Day dinners were chaired by leading Scots merchants, like Peter McGill, and acquired a full range of Scottish symbols, transparencies of William Wallace, John Knox, Walter Scott and Robert Burns, plus some heather, broom, whin, thistles and a 'small cask of genuine mountain dew specially sent over for the occasion'. By 1921 it was claimed for North America that there 'is no city of any size or importance in the county that does not have its St Andrew's Society, or Burns or Caledonian Club, which serves to keep alive the memories of the home-land, to instil patriotism towards the adopted country, and to aid the distressed among their kinsfolk'.

Literary connections with the homeland were particularly strong. A number of Burns Suppers were held around the world to celebrate the centenary of the birth of Robert Burns in 1859. The spirit of the author of *Waverley*, Sir Walter Scott, and his promotion of the romantic Highland condition, was developed fifty years after his death in the 'kailyard' literature. Concurrent with the revitalization of the clan societies within Scotland in the mid-1880s was a similar trend overseas. The Order of the Scottish Clans (1878) and the Daughters of Scotia (1898) were part of the late-nineteenth-century revival in clan interest in America. The Gaelic Society of New Zealand (1881) was an attempt to preserve and to celebrate the Gaelic language. The Caledonian Society of Toronto claimed in its publication of 1900 that Scotland had produced more bards than any other nation. It was a rhetoric that did little to face the reality of the economic collapse and social fragmentation of the Scottish homeland.

Within Scotland, internal migration and regional variations in fertility had important effects. The western Lowlands gained population from migration and natural increase. The three counties of Ayr, Lanark and Renfrew contained 27 per cent of Scotland's population in 1831 and 46 per cent in 1911. This area gained from the 300,000 Irish people who came to Scotland in the period. In 1851, 18 per cent of Glasgow's population were Irish-born. Others came from the Highlands, which lost population throughout the period. Such migrations provided important elements of Highland culture within the large towns. They also tied together different regions of Scottish society and economy, often perceived as separate. Wages sent home, temporary migrants returning at key points in the agricultural year, and women returning after a period as servants or textile workers in the Lowlands meant that the Highlands could never be an isolated area of 'folk' culture. This migrant link cushioned the Highland population from the pressures of economic change, especially the landlord pressures of clearance and rent increases. The Skye rebellion (discussed below) may have had as much to do with a depression in the industrial west of Scotland as with the policies of the local landlords. The overall changes in the distribution were not simply a matter of migration but also of different patterns of natural increase (the balance of births and deaths). In the fifty years between 1861 and 1911, this interaction tended to conceal the fact that many areas of Scotland experienced high rates of loss through migration. Thus in the 1860s, Berwickshire lost 16 per cent of its population through migration, higher than any of the 'crofting counties'. This was in part concealed by a rate of natural increase of 15 per cent in Berwickshire, well in excess of about 10 per cent or less in most crofting counties. Sutherland, for example, only lost 15 per cent of its population, but natural increase was a tiny (for this period) 6.8 per cent. In part these changes were one result of migration out of Scotland, but they also reflected that other flow of population from countryside to town. Scotland was an urbanizing nation.

Towns and Cities

Scottish towns were the worst and the best of places. The growth of towns and of the proportion of the population living in towns was arguably the single most important experience of the Scottish people in the nineteenth century. The influence of urbanization pervaded all aspects of life: religion, work, consumption, transport and governance. The towns provided frontiers of new experience which required and received new responses of policy and culture. The cold figures place Scotland second in the European urbanization league tables. The proportion of the population living in towns of over 5,000 rose from 31 per cent in 1831 to 59 per cent in 1911. A wide range of individual patterns was involved. In Glasgow, early experience of formidable rates of growth in the first part of the century gave way to a period of consolidation as growth transferred itself to surrounding areas. The population of the parliamentary burgh was 202,426 in 1831 and grew by 36 per cent in the following decade. Subsequent decades saw growth of between 10 and 20 per cent, except for the depression years of the 1870s. Between 1901 and 1911, the population of the old parliamentary burgh area actually fell by 4 per cent as growth moved to the outer areas.

Towns of the raw industrial frontiers of west central Scotland, like Motherwell, grew from 726 people in 1841 to 18,726 in 1891: very different from the sedate but substantial pace of Selkirk, which grew from 2,833 in 1831 to 7,298 in 1891, or St Andrews, which did not even double in size in the same period. Although by 1830 most towns had modest rates of natural increase (the high birth rate outpaced the high death rate), growth of this kind could only be sustained by massive rises in internal migration. In some cases, especially in Glasgow and the west of Scotland, people came long distances, notably from Ireland and the Highlands, but most internal migration was short-distance and within the region concerned. There are still many questions to be asked about the net contribution of migration to Scottish towns and cities. Natural increase, a surplus of births over deaths amongst the resident population, does not become visible until the 1860s, when adequate government statistics of births and deaths began to be published. In four of the next six decades which followed, the actual increase in size of Scotland's four biggest towns was less than the natural increase in population: in other words, more people left than came in. In the 1870s and the 1900s, Glasgow lost around 80 per cent of its natural increase.

Scottish towns were not simply destinations. They were locations which saw massive population flows and exchanges, inwards and outwards, and acted as social and cultural transformers on those who experienced them. The journey of William Chambers from Peebles into Edinburgh in the early years of the nineteenth century must have represented many such movements. William and his brother Robert were to become leaders in the Edinburgh printing and publishing industry. The account of this migration was part of a *Memoir* written at the end of a successful life and was as important for its mood as for the details of the journey. The memory of migration contained a sense of loss and opportunity. The brothers remembered Peebles with a sense of affection. It was a place of thatched cottages, weavers and labourers. Peebles was a knowable community, the minister, the kirk elders, the candle-maker, and Miss Ritchie who kept a disciplined and respectable inn. There was also a Covenanter: 'a tall grim and bony man'. This was a place of true kindness which did not need a poor law for mendicants (like Dafy Jock Grey of Gilmanscleugh) were always sure of help. Peebles was about simplicity and lack of pretension: 'There was much pleasant intercourse among families at a small cost. Scarcely any gave ceremonious dinners. Invitations to tea at six were common. After tea there were songs, with perhaps a round of Scottish proverbs . . .' And then there was Hogmanay, with 'a universal distribution of oat-cakes, cheese, shortbread and buns', followed by the tradesmen calling personally for the payment of their accounts. As a compliment William Chambers repeated Lord Cockburn's remark, 'quiet as the grave or Peebles', and added the tale of the local man who returned from Paris with the words, 'but still Peebles for pleesure'.

No doubt much of this reflected the reality of Peebles in the early years of the century, but the real importance of an account written in 1872 was that this was a Scotland of the mind which thousands of people carried with them as they walked or took the cart, and later the train, to the big city. It was an idealized image of Scotland which was nourished by many urban lifetimes and by a century of Scottish culture. Here was a feeling that amongst the struggles and opportunities of urban industrialism was a 'real Scotland'. This Scotland was nourished in many ways. David Wilkie's much-reproduced painting 'The Cotter's Saturday Night' (1837) had it to perfection: piety, human affection, the Bible, the fiddle on the wall and the solid, simple comfort of the room. By the 1880s James Guthrie's Berwickshire painting of the 'Hind's Daughter' (1883) portrayed a much more elemental confrontation of a sturdy-looking young lady in the vegetable patch. Novel after novel celebrated the Scotland of clachan, fermtoun, village and small burgh. John Galt's *Annals of the Parish* covered the industrializing west (1820, but editions were still being sold in Glasgow in 1895); William Alexander, *Johnny Gibb of Gushetneuk*, first published in the *Aberdeen Free Press* (1869–70); and then the so-called 'kailyard novels': 'Thrums is but two church steeples and a dozen red stone patches standing out of a snow heap', as J. M. Barrie put it in *Auld Licht Idylls* (1892). In different ways all these novels alternate between Scots and English. Scots was about the spoken word, about piety, genuineness, affection, domesticity and community; English was for the cold business of description, about the remote and the modern. This understanding of Scotland was reinforced by an especially Scottish genre of Reminiscences. Dean Ramsay's *Reminiscences of Scottish Life and Character* was first published in 1857. All the main characters were there: the weaver, the shepherd, the pillar of the kirk and the gravedigger. Even when the urban and urbane Sir Alexander Geikie, eminent geologist, produced his *Scottish Reminiscences*, they were tales of Lowland farmers and Highland ferries, as well as town life in olden times. Then there was Burns, whose poems became part of the assertion of being Scottish for all social classes.

Migration to the town did not bring the complete loss of this sense of community, even when driven by economic need and opportunity. Robert and William Chambers had come to Edinburgh because the draper's business which their father ran had failed. His father had already given up a prosperous business as a manufacturer employing up to a hundred handloom weavers. It was characteristic of many migrations that they were triggered by some personal crisis – a death, unemployment, or the failure to get a job. Technological change and the financial crisis after the French wars were only one aspect of such pressures. Again, like many migrants, the Chambers family settled in an area of the town where they found other people from their own area. In his *Memoir*, William Chambers recorded: 'According to immemorial usage, families with limited means from the southern counties of Scotland, who seek a home in the capital, sagaciously pitch on one of the second rate streets in the southern suburbs . . . sprinkled about in common stairs, they form a colony, possessing a community of south country recollections and gossip.' The attraction of the town consisted of the variety of opportunity. His father took work as the manager of salt pans at Joppa, while William was apprenticed to a bookseller and took lodgings with a woman from Peebles in the West Port area of Edinburgh.

The towns to which people like Robert and William came were in crisis. Matters were getting worse under the pressure of rapid growth. Dr James Stark, an Edinburgh physician, made a careful study of burials in Edinburgh. Although these figures were not true death rates, the direction of change was very clear. Between 1810 and 1819, the burial rate was 24.6 per 1,000 people; the figure rose to 26.2 in the 1820s. The 1830s brought the cholera epidemic of 1832 and influenza in 1837, contributing to a figure of 29.1; the 1840s saw a further increase to 30.2, partly explained by typhus, the 'famine fever' of 1847 and more Asiatic cholera in 1849. Several other factors contributed to this increase. The increasing density of population made the spread of water-borne disease much easier. Common diarrhoea as much as epidemics of measles and scarlet fever was responsible for high rates of child mortality.

The urban crisis of the 1840s and 1850s was a social as well as an environmental one. Scottish Chartism was one focus of discontent. Chartism was a major popular movement, originating in Birmingham in 1837 to campaign through mass petitions and public meetings for universal manhood suffrage. It gained extensive working-class support, as well as a wider radical representation, from the belief that legal means of manipulating constitutional power was the key to solving many social and economic problems. The leadership was divided between the moral force strategy of rational persuasion and the physical force leaders. Scottish Chartism gained a mixed reputation. There was an initial period of intense activity between 1838 and 1842, with Glasgow a centre of widespread enthusiasm for the Birmingham programme. Chartist halls, schools, churches and cooperatives spread across the industrial areas from Fife to the border textile towns. Reports of large political meetings filled the widely read *Liberator* and *Northern Star*, a Chartist press that was Scottish and British. Moral force resolutions were passed at the great meeting of 1838 which took place at Calton Hill in Edinburgh, while elsewhere these were being rescinded in favour of physical force by an active support for Fergus O'Connor, an Irish-born but English-based leader with a reputation for aggressive oratory.

The progress of Chartism in Scotland illustrates the problems of writing a specific Scottish history as distinct from simply a history of what happens to have happened in Scotland. There was little that was innovative about Scottish Chartism. Chartist churches were the most distinctive and sustained product of Chartist activity. The authority of the kirk and its associated 'parish state' was felt to be so effective in Scotland that appeals for people to turn towards independent Chartist churches were especially important for the movement's leaders. In general Scots argued out at local level the ideological positions derived from the English heartlands of Chartism. Activity was local, but within a British organization. Support was given to the Birmingham leaders. O'Connor and Julian Harney were cheered on their trips north and funds were raised for Welsh Chartists arrested after the Newport 'rising' of 1839. There was little British coherence to the movement and even less Scottish coherence. In the early 1840s references were made to William Wallace as an icon and a Central Committee for Scotland was formed, but this was dominated by Glasgow and the west of Scotland. The nature of Scottish Chartism was created by its situation as a British movement active within a Scottish culture. Chartism was inhibited in Scotland not so much by language and/or religious and ethnic division as by its place in a nation without a parliament. The target for Chartism was the Westminster parliament, and the analysis that drew Chartists together regarded parliamentary representation as the route towards the solution to a wide variety of social and economic injustices and that involved a British focus.

The debate over the 'revolutionary' or 'sleepy' nature of the Scottish working class in this period, or the physical force versus moral nature of Scottish Chartism, neglects the fact that this dichotomy represented part of the dynamic of Scottish popular and working-class experience. It was a debate which took place within Scottish Chartism, witness all the meetings with their resolutions and counter-resolutions. The external reference of the Birmingham six points (which formed the core of the movement), and of the British parliament, were problematic for Scottish Chartists, but they interacted with an environment of ideas, organization, experience and social structures accumulated over the previous fifty years and embodied in a network of trade-union and radical movements.

Authority was also challenged across many other frontiers: in food riots, in trade associations, in political meetings and in demonstrations. The radical movements of the 1790s and above all the campaign for the reform of parliament in 1830–32 had taught people in Scotland that political representation was the key to the solution of the problems of poverty and injustice, hence their ready response to the six points of the Charter. Trade unions based upon local associations of skilled males were an increasing part of the bargaining over workplace and wages. They were joined by larger organizations of colliers, spinners and handloom weavers trying to control relationships with the greater accumulations of capital in those industries. These organizations were noted for their secrecy, passwords, ritual initiation and intermittent use of violence. The trade unions were most effective at periods of increasing demand. They were most threatening to the owners of expanding industries, such as the ironmasters of Lanarkshire, or those faced with intensifying competition, like the cotton spinners of the west of Scotland.

For their part, the Scottish governing élite, especially those operating at regional and local level, like the Tory sheriff of Lanarkshire, Archibald Alison, were willing to use and extend the use of law to break this organizational power. This was demonstrated by the treatment of the strike leaders of the Glasgow Cotton Spinners' Association in 1837–8. The lodge leaders were arrested and after considerable delay received harsh sentences of transportation despite the fact that the most serious charges were not sustained. It was little wonder that the prospect of political representation attracted such people. The total and effective destruction not just of the union, but also of the credibility of union activity, opened the way for the reconstruction of the technology and labour force structures of the cotton industry.

The balance of violence and moral force was also part of the dynamics of Scottish radical and working-class politics in this period. Chartist leaders like Robert Cranston in Edinburgh were engaged in the creation of an assertive, self-respecting and disciplined radical culture. Many like Cranston were members of Temperance Associations and campaigned for working-class education through Mechanics' Institutes. They saw organization and the discipline of the mass meeting as more effective than the riot or secret lodge meeting and anonymous threats.

There was a sense of a world which was out of control. In 1857, Alexander Smith, poet, honorary secretary to Edinburgh University and one-time pattern designer in Paisley, was reflecting on Glasgow clubs and sociability, of pride in locality and easy access to the countryside and the snowdrops of Castle Milk. This was also the town which in 1848, the year of commercial depression and revolutions in Europe, 'had the bad eminence of going further in deeds of lawlessness and riot than any other city in the Empire'. The normally 'industrious Glasgow operative' cried out 'against the tyranny of class legislation . . . Hungry and tumultuous meetings were held on the Green.' As a young boy Smith had witnessed riots in Trongate and the High Street: '. . . all the civilities and amenities of life – seemed drowned in a wild sea of scoundrelism'. Gun shops were broken into, and meal carts and food shops raided, until eventually the street was cleared by soldiers.

There were many individual and group responses to this. Some gathered statistics and marshalled them into tables as they prepared to lobby for legislation and change. Others, like Thomas Chalmers, sought to reform the church and deliver knowable self-supporting communities like those of rural or small-town Scotland in a network of urban parishes. This vision of an urban Scotland ordered by a patchwork of godly commonwealths was one of the motives which drove the Evangelicals towards the Disruption of the kirk. There were those like the Chartists and radical liberals who demanded an extension of the suffrage, for they saw representative politics as the key to social order and justice. Others like Cranston, the Edinburgh Chartist, saw education and abstinence from alcohol as the key to order and self-direction. They reformed their social life around the new teetotal societies of the 1830s and 1840s. An increasing number of the middle class recognized a new frontier within the great cities dividing them from the poor and working classes. They set out to explore, to understand and sometimes to reform. They wrote like the missionaries who were beginning to report back from darkest Africa. A. de Colombel, who published his *L'Angleterre et l'Ecosse: souvenirs d'un touriste* in 1853, described the Lowlands as 'treeless' and 'melancholy'. 'Lowlanders are small, ugly and miserable! The true Scotland of European renown is to be found in the Highlands.' The German travel writer Kohl called Glasgow 'the most religious and the most drunken city in Europe or the world'. Kohl's picture of the Scottish city, full of opportunity, sometimes threatening, always out of control, was captured in 1858 by Alexander Brown, letterpress printer of Glasgow, in a patchwork of phrases:

An immense concourse of men, women and children with numbers of policemen . . . lounging in idle groups . . . oaths, recriminations and abuse . . . filthy, crowded . . . smells of whiskey . . . Irish . . . thieves and prostitutes . . . temperance hotel . . . tidy and clean . . . *Lloyds Newspaper, Family Herald* . . . numerous and respectable . . . Dixon's Govan Ironworks . . . sleepless furnaces . . . City Hall . . . Louis Kossuth . . . boys and girls whose revolutionary tendencies, from the effect of associations are shrewdly suspected.

The book's subtitle – *Social Photographs* – reflected his sense of distance, of being an observer rather than a participant, but also the need to immobilize, to capture, to take away and reflect, which was part of the new art of photography that Scots like D. O. Hill and Thomas Annan were taking up with so much enthusiasm.

Industrial Change and Economic Growth

The social consequences of rural–urban migration were a challenge of magnitude for governors and reformers alike. Sectoral shifts in industry produced geographical movements in the population. For those in search of work the town took on the symbolism of prosperity, or at least the potential for prosperity. In the period 1841–1911 there was a net increase of around 760,000 male jobs along with the creation of 285,000 female jobs. Women could find work in textile-dominated Dundee, but their wage was low and their employment marked a last-gasp attempt to compete with the dominance of Lancashire and with the export of jute from India after 1850. The imbalance between the sexes was to re-emphasize the maleness of 'work', as the prestige of new technology was allied to the harshness of the metallic and engineering trades and of coal extraction. When work was plentiful and wages were good, the hours would be long even for those with some control over their activities. The diary of a Dundee millwright, John Sturrock, recorded the pressures of his work and the tiredness he felt during a busy week in 1864. In spite of the fact that his life was governed by earning a wage, Sturrock kept up both his religious and secular instruction more than was common amongst his class.

Mon. 31. Wrought all night.

Tues. 1.11.64. Went to the library with my book and did some other small errands coming home, where I arrived a little past eight and as I was somewhat tired after last night's work I was no long in going to bed.

Wed. 2.   Wrought till eight, but cannot say I did anything before going to bed.

Thurs. 3.   Wrought till eight, then had a while writing before going to bed.

Fri. 4.   Wrought till eight and then had a while at the drawing.

Sat. 5.   Got stopped at two o'clock, then went out to my father's.

Sun. 6.   Did not get up till about nine o'clock. Went to church in the forenoon and started at five o'clock to come home. Came in by the Kellas and got an opportunity to chat a while with Anne. Came in with J. Wright and Margaret Packman. Went along to her mother and stopped a while and got home about ten o'clock. Got a newspaper at my father's today from an old sweetheart now married in New Zealand.

In the following year, Sturrock's scarce skills secured him a better than expected wage rise of 3s. to give him 19s., and he was soon to benefit from weekly rather than fortnightly pay. Regional specialism confirmed that the towns and cities were observed as the embodiment of industrial change, a theme we shall return to. Greenock was 'Old Dirty' and industrializing Coatbridge was in 1869 described as 'anything but beautiful. Dense clouds of smoke roll over it incessantly, and impart to all the buildings a peculiarly dingy aspect.' Woollen cloth, tartans, tweeds and knitwear in Galashiels, and a number of hosiery and tweed producers in Hawick, bucked the general decline in textiles. There remained a widespread reliance upon fishing and agriculture in the Highland counties. Fishing for herring made Fraserburgh grow. Prior to 1833, its market was found in the slave plantations of the West Indies, and then by exporting to Europe in the 1850s. Glasgow merchants' links to India and the Far East were part of a larger pattern. Jardine Matheson & Co. did spectacularly well through the provision of financial services to Indian traders. The port of Leith could be quiet in terms of general trade in 1838, yet still its shipbuilding yards built the 450-ton 'Seius', which took the honour as the first steamship to cross the Atlantic. There were other success stories, such as the thread-making firms of J. & P. Coats and Clarks in Paisley that merged in 1896 to become the largest manufacturing firm in Britain (and fifth largest in the world), as well as the most profitable by 1910 with a value estimated at £70 million. There was the jute industry of Dundee, which exploited the new flax that became machine-pliable when treated with whale oil and water. In 1826 Dundee had replaced Hull as the largest port in Britain for flax, and the city's jute and other rough-textile productions boomed as never before, employing upwards of 35,000 at the mid-century. Dundee's mill-owners exported their expertise to Calcutta, but in turn the Scots' own market dominance was undermined. Medium-sized towns like Kirkcaldy benefited from specialization with the production of linoleum from linseed oil and jute canvas; such specialism helped to maintain breadth in the Scottish economy. But throughout our period, the importance of regional production was masked by the extraordinary concentration of industrial development in the west-central belt. Employment in shipbuilding was a key feature of this transforming economy, increasing from 4,000 workers to 51,000 in the seven decades prior to 1911, and reaching 122,000 in 1921. Transportation and mining were the other areas of significant growth in employment.

The context was a shift in the markets for Scottish goods. The trade in tobacco to America, exploiting the fast sailing routes to the north of Ireland, and sustained by a network of highly efficient wealthy traders and financiers, had peaked in the 1770s. New markets in Asia, South America and Australia were added to the established ones of England as destinations for Scottish goods and minerals. Scotland tended to lack the latest technology which was making the impact in England in the early decades of the nineteenth century. Yet persistent low wages did make Scotland an attractive place for investment by English-based entrepreneurs. Cotton was by far the most important industry at the turn of the century: the value of its cloth stood at three times that of pig-iron in 1814. Textile production progressed slowly, through booms and slumps, but the underlying trend was one of relative decline.

In the early decades of the nineteenth century the transformation in the economy was not inevitable. The most successful foundry in Scotland was the Carron ironworks, which had grown quickly from 1759. It was dominant in what was a very weak sector until the 1830s. Its *nom de plume*, 'the English foundry', betrayed the origin of its construction and its reliance on imported technology, and in this respect it was not unique. The change came with the introduction of J. B. Neilson's hot blast technique in 1828, which used pre-heated air under pressure; this coupled with the exploitation of the then plentiful blackband ironstone, first discovered in 1801, gave the west of Scotland a technological edge. By greatly reducing the use of coal by between a half and two-thirds, the process allowed the Scottish producers to undercut the cost of iron production from England. The number of furnaces in Scotland rose from twenty-seven in 1830 to over a hundred in 1860. Scotland's share of British pig-iron production rose from 5 per cent to 25 per cent as the century's mid-point approached, reaching 29 per cent in 1852 before gently declining with the demise of easily accessible blackband ironstone. This dramatic rise in foundry work was coupled with Sir Charles Tennant's formation of the Steel Company of Scotland (founded in 1872), and the west-central belt was henceforth increasingly dominated by heavy industry both as an economic reality and as a synonym for a way of life. The Tennant empire was one of the best examples of the linkages between the railways, in this case the Caledonian Railway, and heavy industry. Pig-iron output in Scotland stood at 37,500 tons in 1830, doubled over the next five years, and then entered a new phase with production of 197,000 tons in 1840. With such a demand created by the railways in 1845, this more than doubled to 475,000 tons and reached 775,000 tons in 1852. The chemical complex at St Rollox in Glasgow was the largest in the world. The yard run by the Napiers in Govan was at the leading edge of its industry, providing the engines for all the Cunard ships in the period from 1840 to 1865.

One contemporary commentator on the Scottish coalfields, Robert Bald, looked for explanations for an already apparent growth in the demand for coal. Writing in 1832, he identified a new 'style of living of even the poor', who now used coal in the fireplace. The demand from the iron and other manufacturing trades, and the newly-introduced burning of lime in agriculture, were other causes cited by Bald. What he could not foresee was the enormous extent to which the expansion of individual producers and of large engineering complexes would stimulate the mining industry from the final quarter of the century. In 1870 coal output stood at 14,935,500 tons per annum; by 1913 it had almost trebled to 42,456,500 tons per annum.

As the century closed, Scotland was experiencing the high point in fortunes linked to empire. Models of the great ships built on the Clyde, including HMS 'Good Hope' built by the Fairfield Company, and the 'Asahi', recently completed for the Japanese navy, were popular displays at the 1901 Exhibition in Glasgow. They sat next to exhibits from two American companies, Singer's and Bissell's, which demonstrated the extent of overseas investment in Clydeside. Next were artistic displays by the home-grown engineering companies of G. & J. Weir and Colville's. But it was high noon before change. The British Linen Company had moved its office from Glasgow to London in 1888 in search of more custom. Others would follow and the rhetoric of the exhibition did nothing to hide the fact that the Clydeside yards had lost out on overseas commissions, despite remaining a major employer and a world leader in terms of output. The shipyards experienced the beginning of trends which would lead to much wider structural changes in the economy later in the twentieth century. The relative decline that had set in for so many of Scotland's heavy industries was to become an economic tragedy for the lives it touched. The first two verses of 'The Docker's Tanner', commemorating the strike for employment and a fair wage in 1890, mixes pride with sadness:

> At the docks there is a strike that the company don't like
> A tanner on the hour they'll have to pay:
> Like slaves they'd have us work far more than any Turk
> And make us sweat our lives out every day.
>
> Every morning there are flocks for employment at the docks,
> Hard-working men who scarce can get a meal;
> With wives and children dear, it would make you shed a tear
> If you only knew the hardship they feel.

That nearly half of all tonnage ordered from 1890 to 1914 was for the British navy illustrates how precarious the once proud boast, that Scotland was the workshop of the world, had become. The historical debate on economic decline has centred on the extent to which the Scottish economy was overly specialized in the Victorian period, suggesting that was the cause of the malaise which overtook it. Yet the view that Scotland was solely a nation of the west coast, of semi-skilled and skilled workers in the shipyards, steelyards, and engineering and chemical plants, was only one (albeit significant) part of the story. By 1911, the overall balance of the Scottish economy replicated the economic pattern found in the rest of Britain, mixing industrial, textile and service industries. Scotland had its own core/periphery with the Lowland regions of Strathclyde, Lothian, Central and Fife increasing their proportion of the occupied male labour force from 58 per cent to 71 per cent over the period 1851–1911. Dumfries and Galloway, the Borders, Tayside, Grampian and the Highland regions lost in relative terms, gaining employment but at a much lower rate. This regionalism, and the importance to the Scottish economy of key regional production centres, was masked by dramatic sectoral shifts. The symbolic resonance of the heavy industries was strong, but as an ideal type for the 'ordinary' Scottish people it was inevitably incomplete.

Agriculture

Scottish agriculture employed 30 per cent of the male labour force in 1851 and 13 per cent in 1911. Agriculture remained the major source of income in the countryside, especially after the decline of rural industrial employment like stocking weaving in the north-east and hand-loom weaving in the Lowlands during the 1830s and 1840s. Although regional variation was extreme, the overall change had many factors in common. It was driven by market forces closely linked to urban and industrial development; it was also linked to technological progress and to a growing scientific knowledge spread, for example, by printed media and agricultural associations. The process was dominated by powerful landowners. Indeed, land ownership in Scotland was heavily concentrated, with three-quarters of the land owned by 580 people in 1873. This was a reflection of the extensive upland estates like those of the Duke of Sutherland, but also included Lowland holdings with arable and mineral wealth, such as the Buccleuch estates. Landlord authority was augmented by a legal structure, notably through the law of hypothec, which concerned matters of debt and pledges. Crop and stock were regarded as a tacit pledge against rent and other duties and could be seized by the landlord, who thus had preference over other creditors.

Mixed farming, in one form or another, was characteristic of most parts of Scotland, with two results. First, farmers were able to respond to changes in prices and consumer incomes by switching crops like oats, turnips and barley from animal feed to feeding people or supplying the breweries; second, there was less seasonal variation in the demand for labour. In most areas of Scotland, notably in the dairy farms of the south-west, average farm size was relatively small. East Lothian and Berwickshire were among the few areas which were dominated by large capitalist farms worked by tenants and wage labour. By the 1840s, the substantial farm buildings included cart sheds, cattle courts, stackyards, turnip stores and stabling for the heavy horses upon which the farm depended. In the largest farms steam engines were added to the horse gin and, when available, water power. Farms like that of George Hope at Fenton Barns in East Lothian or nearby Sunnyside had chimneys that would have graced a small factory, while Dowlaw and Lumsdain on the Berwickshire coast took water power from artificial ponds on the nearby hill.

North-east Scotland had a wide variety of farm sizes based on an integrated system of peasant agriculture and capitalist farming that served the increasing urban demand for cattle. In the middle years of the nineteenth century, the drovers and dealers were being replaced by Aberdeen auction markets and wholesale butchers linked by rail and steamship to markets in the south, especially London. The tenants of the large capitalist farms employed, bought and sold in the cash economy. They hired labour at the feeing market, they bought store cattle from Ireland or from their own hill farmers, and purchased feedstuffs, fertilizers and consumer goods. The small peasant farmers cleared marginal land, produced their own potatoes and oats to feed the family, and relied upon family rather than wage labour. They raised cattle to sell on to the larger farms for fattening. Their unmarried sons and daughters provided much of the waged labour for such farms. As in many regions, the 1850s and 1860s were periods of sustained improvement. Fields were more systematically drained, making them easier to work with horses and improved ploughs rather than oxen. The slow spread of mechanical reapers further reduced the seasonal demand for labour. The last thirty years of the century were marked by the need to respond to the fall in grain prices in the seventies and meat prices in the eighties. The hardest hit were the profit-seeking large farms. Initially, the peasant farms survived by intensifying the exploitation of family labour, but by 1900 this was breaking up. The first generation of farmers' children to experience compulsory education was less willing to accept harsh work with the hope of getting their own farm. They increasingly took the emigration route to the cities or to Canada.

Outside the north-west, labour on Scottish farms was generally provided by farm servants hired for six or twelve months at the hiring fairs. Accommodation was provided by the farm. In the north-east, accommodation was in the bothy where the unmarried men slept and cooked in often squalid conditions. In the 1850s, ministers of the Free Church attacked this system as a source of immorality and the cause of the high illegitimacy rates of the region. The connection may have been more complex, for in nineteenth-century Banffshire there was an association between extensive illegitimacy, high levels of farm service (involving considerable geographical mobility, freedom of courtship, and transient social relations), and a shortage of rented smallholdings. The attacks made on bothies by the county medical officers of health in the 1890s are more straightforward to prove. The last years of the century saw some improvement and a return to the 'chaumer and kitchen' system which was common in many parts of Scotland (in which food was provided in the farm). In the Lothians and Borders, farmers hired married men on condition that they supplied adult female labour at harvest times: the bondager system. One aspect of the preference for married men was the need to supply cottage accommodation on the farm. In the 1850s, many of these were still single-storey, one-roomed units, but by the end of the century they were being replaced by two-storey slated houses. As a result of the six- to twelve-months-long hire, the monopoly of tied housing, concentrated land ownership and a poor law that offered nothing to the able-bodied, there was little surplus or underemployed labour in the Scottish countryside. Scotland was not a country of open villages or squatter settlements. The under-employed went into the towns or emigrated. Those who lost their place as horsemen would seek places as carters or policemen in the large towns.

On the larger farms the labour relationship was marked by several features. The labour force was organized in hierarchies. The horsemen were the élite, followed by the cattlemen and the 'orramen' – general labourers. The female servants came under the farmer's wife, while the men were managed by the 'grieve' or foreman who mediated between the farmer and the men. Hiring took place at twice-yearly 'feeing' markets at Whitsunday and Martinmas, which were also turnover dates for tenancies and sub-tenancies. Once the feeing market bargain had been struck, the men expected their autonomy to be respected and, in many areas, if a grieve was dismissed or not reappointed the whole labour force would leave: the so-called 'clean toun'. Both men and farmers depended on 'reputation' to ensure they got the best labour and the best wages possible. Ploughing matches and gossip, especially the bothy ballads of the north-east, marked out the quality both of men's work and a farm's comfort, food and horses. The secret fraternity of the horseman's word was another means by which labour enforced its areas of autonomy on the farm. The direct comparison of wages was impossible because of the importance of payment in kind for farm workers. In 1907, a Board of Trade inquiry into living standards suggested that Scottish farm workers received around 30 per cent of their income in kind: accommodation, sometimes food in the farm kitchen, a potato allowance for the married men and those living out, sometimes a milk and coal allowance. Others got allotment ground to grow their own potatoes and a place to keep a pig. Border shepherds by tradition ran sheep of their own alongside those of the farmers. The indications were that at the beginning of the century Scottish farm wages were universally below those of England. By the end of the century, wages in central and southern Scotland were among the highest in the kingdom while those in the north-west were still below average. Even that last claim needs to be qualified because the dominant form of economic relationship between labour and land was not the wage but the crofter's rent – a relationship distorted by the legislation of the Crofters Act of 1886, as we shall see shortly.

In the Highlands change was especially intense, savage and political. In some ways the best-known examples, like that of the Sutherlands, were exceptions. Between 1819 and his death in 1833, the duke and his agents engaged in a full-scale economic and social development project. Tenants were moved from inland farms to the coast to make way for large capitalist sheep farms. At Brora, £16,000 was expended on a new coal pit and £3,327 on four salt pans. Brick and tile works were established. Textile entrepreneurs were briefly tempted in to establish a flax manufactory. Most disappeared faster than inward investment on a less favoured industrial estate. The coal pit was gone by 1825. Only the model fishing village at Helmsdale had any sustained viability. Around half a million pounds was invested in a project that added little to the rent roll and a great deal to the family's unpopularity. More typical was the slow attrition of places like Morvern and Ardnamurchan in north Argyllshire where pre-existing destitution reached crisis levels with the potato failure of the late 1840s.

In the Islands and western Highlands of Scotland, as in many parts of Ireland, rising population and the spread of the potato had gone together. When a fungus blight destroyed the crop in 1846 and 1847, these parts of Scotland lost some two-thirds of their food supply. Some 150,000 people, mainly the poorest cottars and crofters, were at risk. Although on a smaller scale than the disaster in Ireland, the famine in Scotland was dangerous and destructive. The outcome was a small increase in deaths and a major increase in out-migration. This was in part a result of the greater integration and strength of Scottish civil society. Some landlords, such as the Sutherlands and Matheson in Lewis, provided exceptional degrees of help. However, in a number of cases this stopped suddenly when heavily indebted estates, for instance that of Sir James Riddell in Ardnamurchan, were placed under trustees. Government provided some help, especially in the form of steam vessels to transport grain to areas of shortage, but as in Ireland this was gravely inhibited by the ideology of men like Sir Charles Trevelyan, who believed both that relief would bring continued 'demoralization' and dependence and that the Celts were by nature indolent people who needed to be 'reformed'. In Scotland the strength of the associational culture of civil society averted major disaster. The Central Relief Board was formed early in 1847 to coordinate the activities of the Free Church Relief Committee and the Relief Committees of Glasgow and Edinburgh. Other families were rescued by the cash remittances of temporary migrants in the Lowland farms and cities. A long-term solution of sorts was found in permanent migration to the cities, and outside Scotland to Canada and Australia. Many crofters financed their own passage through savings and the sale of stock. Others were helped by landlord-financed schemes as well as by the activities of the Highland and Island Emigration Society (from 1851).

For a while, out-migration (both self-financed and assisted, temporary and permanent), together with a more cautious approach to clearance by landlords, low levels of nuptiality among those who stayed and a period of prosperity for agriculture in general, helped to stabilize the situation. This stability was broken in the 1880s. The fall in meat prices reduced landlord income and put pressure on the sheep farms. In many areas, red deer providing sport for the late-summer shooting parties were the preferred stock for hillsides which had been grazing for the sheep and cattle of small peasant farms at the start of the century. At the same time industrial depression brought a reduction in the remittances from temporary migration which had always been required to balance the crofting economy. The break came in Skye in 1882, when the crofting families of the Braes 'deforced' (obstructed) the sheriff's officer sent to enforce rent rises and eviction notices. Both sides were mindful of contemporary events in Ireland. The authorities sent a boatload of marines, then established a government inquiry, the Napier Commission. The crofters and their radical allies in the burghs established the Highland Land Law Reform Association to politicize the issues. The outcome was legislation in 1886 which increased security of tenure in the crofting counties. An increasing number of 'land raids' were initiated on Lewis, when crofting families reclaimed land which had already been cleared. These events seemed to set the Highlands and crofting counties apart in their culture, politics and legislation, but in other ways they showed how deeply the Highlands were integrated into a greater Scotland. When the Napier Commission took evidence in Morvern, an area which had suffered clearances and loss of population after the potato famine, the barrister for the crofters was financed by an association of Morvern people resident in Glasgow. The link between Highland and Lowland was much more than the Highland jaunt by a Walter-Scott-reading, train-travelling holiday population, or the appropriation of tartan as Scottish rather than just Highland dress.

Governance

Despite the absence of a parliament of its own, Scotland never lost the ability to govern itself. It was to be subject to the laws passed by a Westminster parliament dominated by MPs from England, whose keen eyes were trained more on the development of empire than on the generally loyal, but sometimes complaining, northern neighbour. Scotland, like Wales, was assumed to be too small to be a 'nation-state'. Constitutional theorists were vocal in their support for the singularity of Westminster rule within Britain. For many of these decades, Scotland's experience of Union ensured infertile ground for political nationalism. Westminster provided much of the symbolism of Britishness, but encouraged the workings of local self-administration. The result was a remarkable array of sources to enact Scotland's governance, some more independent of the British state than others, some more part of civil society than others.

The Union settlement replaced Scotland's major agency of executive government with a new Privy Council of Great Britain and it was not long before Scotland came under the control of political managers: Archibald Campbell, Duke of Argyll, Henry and then Robert Dundas. In conjunction with a range of boards or commissions based in Edinburgh, Scottish governance was enacted. This mixture of Westminster distance – and of local solutions by preference – was carried into the nineteenth century. The mechanism of Scottish governance was now more bureaucratic and more open, although far from democratic: the Board of Supervision (1845) and the Scotch Education Department (1872), based in Whitehall but with minimal staffing, were the only two purely Scottish central government departments. Yet reform of the burgh councils (from 1833) had already captured the focus of Scotland's governance. Local issues were prioritized, and the industrial and commercial élites used their representation in the council chambers to resist the growth of what was regarded as legislative interference in their affairs from Westminster.

Reform in county government was at a slower pace – not until 1889 were representative county councils established. Along with the sheriffs, the Scottish Commissioners of Supply (instituted in 1667) undertook the administration of the counties until reform. The Commissioners were a group qualified by ownership of land to the annual value of £100 in the county, who were charged with the collection and supervision of local taxation. Their meetings were also the forum of county-wide discussions, albeit dominated by the likes of Buccleuch and Roxburgh. Following changes brought in by parliament in 1857, there was an increasing role for the Commissioners, including control over the running of the county police force. They had been given the right to raise their own general levy on the county and much of the governance in welfare and issues of sanitation and hygiene were undertaken jointly with the towns. However, coherence in county government was lacking. The delay in the counties taking up police legislation was symptomatic of the fragmentation in the mechanisms of governance. The result was much duplication of work, and opportunity remained for the old county influences to structure their part of civil society. The Road Trustees were created in 1831 to instigate and maintain the turnpike roads; the Parochial Boards were established in 1845 before giving way to the Parish Councils in 1895; the School Boards, set up in 1872, were elected in each parish and burgh, and their assessments were to be collected by the Parochial Board along with the poor rate; in 1894 the Local Government Board was established in place of the Board of Supervision. Streamlining of county government had come – finally – in 1889: the legislation created the County Council and empowered it to undertake all administrative and financial affairs covered by Commissioners of Supply, the County Road Trustees and all duties covered by the Public Health Acts in the counties, except those administered by the royal burghs and the parliamentary burghs. Governance in the years immediately thereafter would develop from the introduction of any number of by-laws, sanctioned by the Secretary for Scotland, which tightened up control of local affairs.

It was the lateness, and the weakness, of this reform which provided the opportunity for the survival of aristocratic influence over the people of the county. In the Borders, the Dukes of Buccleuch and Roxburgh maintained their dominance as county office-bearers (until the reorganization of local government in 1974) and used their influence to suggest appropriate appointments for the legal office of sheriff-depute. The dukes had faced flashes of resentment over their power: the people of Hawick, for example, displayed their disapproval of Buccleuch's opposition to parliamentary reform in 1831, and of his quickness to force the council to repress popular discontent, with 'hissing and booing' for the duke and stones for his parliamentary candidate. Sir Walter Scott fared as badly, receiving a volley of stones for his public support for the Tory candidate in Selkirkshire, Lord Henry Scott. The latter – who represented Selkirkshire in parliament in 1861 – was a member of the line of Scotts of Buccleuch, and the two main branches of the Scott family dominated the representation of Roxburgh between 1830 and 1868. County government was not a world where 'a new name' would make a mark.

It was in the burghs that the impact of local government reform was probably greatest – the result of three Acts passed in 1833. The £10 property qualification for the local vote was revolutionary in comparison with the pre-reform structure, although neither here, nor with parliamentary reform (a year earlier), was the franchise universal. Added to the parliamentary electorate of householders and permanent lodgers, the local electorate included women and peers meeting the property qualification. However, restrictions on married women ensured those eligible were spinsters, widows, and elderly. Municipal elections were to be held on an annual basis and, as a counter to the self-serving reality of the pre-reform structure, one-third of the council body would step down each year, one member from each ward. Reform was aimed at administering an increasingly complex urban society. Yet, despite this new openness, the Acts adapted rather than replaced past structures. The 1833 legislation created what was called a 'dual authority structure' of police and municipal government, coexisting in the same town.

Royal burghs and burghs of barony could and did adopt a 'parallel police system', revitalizing the police legislation introduced earlier, for example in Glasgow (1800) and in Edinburgh (1805). In this dual structure, elected magistrates and commissioners of police were each given powers to raise rates. The main duties of the Police Commission went well beyond straightforward policing. Scotland's Burgh Police Acts contained much of the social legislation that was passed in this period. The police commissioners were empowered to preserve law and order in the city; to oversee its paving, drainage and cleansing; and to regulate other parts of urban infrastructure to improve sanitary standards. The police commissioners had responsibility over many issues which were covered by public health legislation in England. The right to adopt a police system was extended in 1847 to non-royal parliamentary burghs, and in 1850 to 'populous places' (over 1,200 inhabitants). These Acts and the Burgh Police (Scotland) Act – the Lindsay Act – of 1862 increased the powers of the police commissioners *vis-à-vis* the town councils, particularly in their role as regulators of building standards.

The Lindsay Act made provision for any locality of more than 700 in population to form a meeting and to vote on whether to become a police burgh, with the ensuing rights to make building and sanitary laws of their own. It was a choice indicating the ways and means by which Scotland could exert the independence of its localities from Westminster. By deepening the range of qualification to only 700, the opportunity for Scotland to govern itself, although always within the parameters set by Westminster, was immense. The Act gave county constables the authority to extend their powers of arrest into the burgh. If this was not adopted, then their powers were diminished and uniformity across Scotland abridged. Thus in 1868 the chief constable of Ayrshire highlighted Wallacetown and Newton as places of refuge, free from arrest, for certain categories of criminals from Ayr. The Burgh Police Act of 1892 and the Town Council (Scotland) Act of 1900 ended the system of dual responsibility in favour of the municipal councils. This recognition of the ultimate authority of the town council was consolidated by the Local Government (Scotland) Act of 1929, which removed much of the competing rating and administrative authorities into a more unified system of burgh and county councils and Education Authorities.

The experience of local government in Scotland was built on Westminster's absence from day-to-day events, by design as much as by neglect. In important ways Scotland was very much in charge of its own governance. The police legislation undoubtedly gave Scotland a further choice of self-regulation. It was an option for the towns if they so wished and, because it was no statutory requirement, it added to the discretionary armoury of civil society. The interaction between the bargain made at the Act of Union and the urban industrial society being created in the years following 1760 meant that such government and civil society was most active in the areas of religion, poor relief and education.

Religion, Poor Relief and Education

Scottish civil society used religion as its rallying cry and employed voluntary activity as its vehicle. The established Church of Scotland could claim the greatest number of adherents of any single religion in the 1830s, despite no longer being the people's church of the previous century. In Glasgow and Edinburgh the presbyterian dissenting congregations as a group were about equal in size with the Church of Scotland, but their numbers were not as great elsewhere. Dissent would gain impetus by the Disruption of 1843 and the union of the Secession Church and the Relief Church – creating the United Presbyterian Church – in 1847. With the creation of such large rivals rather than the more common splinter groups of the recent past, the returns produced by the 1851 religious census showed the similarity of church attendance of the three presbyterian churches. Their respective proselytizing in search of adherents made this a most lively period in Scotland's ecclesiastical history. Yet the upheaval was not to last. The established church regained its pre-eminence in most areas from the 1860s, with parts of the Highlands being the notable exceptions.

Rather than showing doubt over the centrality of formal religious worship, the fluctuating tale of Presbyterian dissent – and the growth in numbers of Catholic adherents after the Irish famine of 1848 – should be seen as evidence of the all-encompassing importance of religion to everyday life. Religiosity was a key component in social behaviour and in class formation, with so much of what we look back on as 'Victorian values' being imbued with Christian doctrine. At the same time a religious ethos dominated the provision of relief to the urban poor throughout this period. The death of David Livingstone in 1873 created an unprecedented level of interest in overseas missionary work, and it lent renewed force to long-established 'missionary' activity at home. In Edinburgh the United Presbyterian Church at Broughton Place had promoted a direct link between its home mission and its mission to Jamaica in 1835: 'The congregation was convinced not only of their duty to send the gospel to the heathen, but also to those of our fellow citizens who are no less degraded, though tenfold more inexcusable than the heathen abroad, living within the sound of the gospel of grace, and yet voluntarily despising the great salvation.' To all benevolent and charitable voluntary organizations and associations in the first half of the century, notions of a Christian mission in the world were central. This ethos of 'godliness', of righteousness and of piety was particularly strong in Scotland, a country which retained a higher level of church attendance than in England, although precise figures are unreliable. Church attendance rates did not decline as the towns and cities became larger, but rather declined when church-building failed to keep pace with this growth. Completely new communities were growing up in the mining, iron-working and textile districts of northern England, central Scotland and south Wales, often several miles from the nearest parish church. The weakness of the established churches in so many of these areas left a religious vacuum amongst this mobile population. It was soon to be filled by the remarkable attraction of non-established religions fed from the growth of industry and the intensification of class antagonisms associated with the decline of paternalism.

Evangelicalism was the motivating force behind the church extension movement – to build more churches in the soulless city – and it justified ever more intervention through voluntary organizations too. Its most active adherents believed that in all senses the industrial masses were deprived, but it was spiritual destitution rather than material poverty which had priority. Thomas Chalmers, whose early career was discussed in the previous chapter, was appointed convenor of the Church of Scotland's Committee on Church Extension in 1834. Chalmers estimated in 1837 that 40,000 individuals in Edinburgh were without church facilities. In Glasgow as many as 60,000 were without a place of worship. The struggle to bring the church to the town labourer was a great one. It involved the church's role in controlling education, as well as providing the number of seats necessary to serve the masses. The Parochial Mission for the Employment of Scripture Readers in the Old Town of Edinburgh (1854) actively intervened in the lives of the poor, inspecting living conditions, bringing coal and offering needlework to women. The élites of the city had escaped to the wide straight lines of the southern New Town from the 1760s and to the north from the 1780s, abandoning the closes, wynds and vennels of the Old Town to those with less economic resources. Here then was a response from within Edinburgh's civil society to implant religion into the minds of those it had left behind.

Chalmers experimented with his vision of a Christian commonwealth of small cooperating communities based around Christian education and Christian worship. He was determined to transplant the community ideal of the rural parish to the unpredictable and perhaps unwelcoming environment of the town. In 1819 Chalmers had begun his investigation in the Glasgow parish of St John's. Dividing his parish into twenty-five 'portions' (of about 400 inhabitants), he then recruited a number of lay officers and teachers to help him visit and minister to the needs of his people. He drew upon the support of church elders, deacons and Sunday School teachers to mix moral with practical help, and to enforce personal discipline. In all their efforts they were driven by the imperative to eradicate, wherever possible, the need to seek out poor relief from the authorities. Cases of genuine need could be met through appeals to the extended family, the neighbourhood or to philanthropic individuals.

Critics of Chalmers claimed that he was too harsh in his judgement of the moral failings and the material needs of the poor. Yet he saw alternative strategies as doing greater damage to the poor as human beings, undermining their self-worth. Chalmers's communal ideal succumbed to a number of changes. It faded away in the face of the sheer scale of urbanization, with the extent of population turnover a major destabilizing factor. The overcrowded parishes in the city were just too dense. For Chalmers to have any hope of success he chose parishes which were not the very poorest, nor the largest or most overcrowded. St John's in Glasgow had about 10,000 to 11,000 parishioners, while the West Port in Edinburgh, where Chalmers returned to his social experiment in 1844, had only around 2,000. The West Port experiment was expensive too, overly dependent on contributions from the wealthy. It marked the last gasp of the parish community ideal, conducted within the wider confines of civil society, struggling against what were to become overwhelming odds.

Parish relief and private charity had been important well before our period. From the 1830s both were given new impetus by an evangelical movement within a Church of Scotland fearful of social unrest from a mobile and increasingly urbanized working class detached from established mechanisms of social control. Confidence to succeed through church and charitable structures alone, as Chalmers was finding out at this time, was not accepted by all. One instance of the undercurrent of change is that of a group of landed proprietors who came together in 1840 to form an association to deal with the problems of poverty identified by the writings of William Pulteney Alison, Professor of Medicine at Edinburgh University. Their aim was 'to obtain a full and searching inquiry into the extent of destitution, misery, and mortality, among the poor in Scotland (especially in the large towns, and in the highlands), their causes, and the most efficient remedy to be applied for its cure'. Their first act was to circulate Alison's *Observations on the Management of the Poor in Scotland* and then to send a questionnaire to each parish. They noted Alison's recommendation for the assimilation of the Scottish Poor Law into that prevailing in England, and the suggestion that poor health was the result of poverty from low wages, and not poor housing and sanitary conditions. Alison argued that something more had to be done by government in the towns and cities, but not to the detriment of municipal independence. The centralizing proposals embodied in the public health legislation from Edwin Chadwick – creating the Central Board of Health – were resisted. The medical profession was sceptical of giving such an influential role to a non-medical bureaucracy and thought the Scottish situation quite different in its problems. Their opposition helped ensure the rejection of the Public Health (Scotland) Bill of 1849, which would have forced the towns to establish a local public health board upon exceeding a death rate of over 23 per 1,000.

Surveys such as Chadwick's in 1842 suggested that poverty was especially bad in all of Scotland's four major cities. The tabular evidence he gathered was stark. When added to emotive case studies it had the power to shock reformers as much as middle-class sensibilities:

Asking some children in one of the rooms of the wynds in which they swarmed in Glasgow what were their names, they hesitated to answer, when one of the inmates said, they called them——, mentioning some nicknames. 'The fact is', observed Captain Miller, the superintendent of the police, 'they really have no names. Within this range of buildings I have no doubt I should be able to find a thousand children who have no names whatever, or only nicknames, like dogs.'

There was an acute paucity of housing that was secure from harsh winters, suitably ventilated, not overcrowded, with a safe and efficient water supply and refuse removal, and which was affordable. The poverty of the inhabitants of Scotland's towns was exacerbated when household income was interrupted. The trade depression in the years from 1841 to 1843 caused thousands of Paisley weavers to lose their wage, with no clear entitlement to relief. It gave the government a dangerous problem and provoked an unprecedented solution: it secretly raised private funds and organized their distribution. To achieve a more robust solution, Peel then set up a Royal Commission on the Scottish Poor Law, which reported in 1844. Some evidence presented to the inquiry put the cause of the creaking system upon the landowners' abuse of surplus labour, which forced many to look for work in the towns and cities; others blamed Irish immigrants, who were then in competition with the general labourer suffering during one of the periodic slumps in the building trades after 1826. All this put pressure on a system reeling from the devastation of cholera, influenza and typhus, which had all visited in the 1830s.

Further impetus for change in the old Scottish Poor Law came from continued unfavourable comparisons with England. Prior to reform, the Scots were not obliged to levy a compulsory rate for the relief of the poor except in the larger towns and cities; in the counties, the consent of the landowner was needed to make this compulsory. Instead, the kirk sessions raised a voluntary contribution, supplemented by legacies and fines. It was stated by opponents of such relief in the 1830s that the Scottish able-bodied poor had no legal right to support, and had never had that right, unlike in England. However, we have seen in previous chapters that the Scottish parliament of the seventeenth century had legislated for relief of the able-bodied, and that the redefinition of entitlement came only from the mid-eighteenth century. From 1845, under the management of the new parochial boards, parishes were compelled to raise money to relieve the poor, and could choose to levy compulsory rates: within a few decades nearly all did so. English parishes had long before the 1834 Act been required to provide workhouses – not so in Scotland, because of cost. While Edinburgh had three charitable workhouses by 1770, and poorhouses (Town's Hospitals) were long established features of life in Glasgow and Paisley, other towns that tried institutional solutions to the problem of poverty during the eighteenth century abandoned them after a short time. After the 1845 Act, Scottish parishes offered the poorhouse to the non-able-bodied poor, but outdoor relief remained the preferred and cheaper option.

Welfare management before reform was largely based on the kirk session of the Church of Scotland. By and large, those who controlled the kirk session in towns were the local shopkeepers and traders. The 1845 reform removed control from this body to a parochial board with a property qualification of £20, double that of the electoral franchise. It meant local urban Poor Law administration was in the hands of the large property-owner, no longer the more Whiggish commercial and industrial middle classes. The reform also brought in a central-government department – the Board of Supervision – to ensure that the intention of the Act was carried out. It was influenced by Highland paternalists with an emphasis on moral education and who advocated voluntary charity as the best form of funding relief. The poorhouse was directed to be nothing more than a safety-net and a deterrent to claiming relief. At all times, the Scottish system relied less on the poorhouse (indoor relief) than in England, where the workhouse was a compelling and threatening experience. In 1906, 14 per cent of the whole pauper population received indoor relief, compared with 32 per cent in England. Small amounts of financial and material help in the home (out-relief) were more prevalent, including special cases such as care for the mentally disabled. The Scottish system was less well funded and less generous in the amounts it distributed. Yet at the same time there was a less severe use of the law of settlement, the poorhouses were less harsh, and they catered for different medical and social needs in a way the English workhouses did not.

Throughout, the parish retained a significant role in relieving the poor, as did voluntary charitable activity. The churches combined their concern over the material welfare of their parishioners with their spiritual well-being. If they could not get the working classes through the church doors on a Sunday, then they had to create new means to convert the irreligious and to reach out to the masses. All sponsored a number of societies and clubs to spread their reach. The Broughton Place United Presbyterian Church set up day schools to teach the alphabet, appointed an evangelist to do their bidding, and established a savings bank which was handling 350 transactions a week in 1852: 'One of the lessons most needed by multitudes in that rank of life is, *to know the value of a penny* – how much of industry or of property that penny represents and can procure.' This was a way of imposing discipline on its parishioners, but it was also part of working-class involvement in the Christian act of charitable provision to the very poor.

Indeed, movements for moral and physical improvement were not always an imposition from above. For example, knowing the consequences of one's actions, showing restraint, and following a path of self-improvement and Enlightenment was imbued in the temperance movement. Its campaigning was an example of a powerful attempt to establish a pervasive and penetrating counter-culture which used the ethos of religion to press home its message. The first temperance society was set up in 1828, and various teetotal and abstinence societies grew up in the 1830s. Over the next decade it became a 'holy alliance' between the Established, Free and Dissenting Churches. Moderation versus total abstinence marked the two wings of the movement. There was a conscious attempt to provide an alternative life and leisure for those who wished to free themselves from a culture which so clearly revolved around the consumption of alcohol at all social levels. The temperance coffee-house catered for those who wished to display their respectability publicly. The temperance hotel, like the Christian hotel, was to offer the travelling salesman a place of refuge in an unknown town, secure in the knowledge that he would find there a healthy and respectable environment.

Bible and tract societies trumpeted their intent to shape the conduct of the lives of all classes of society. They were primarily money-collecting agencies run by church organizations in order to supply religious books to the poor, either free or at reduced prices. It was hoped that by reading the New Testament in particular, the word of Christ would effect spiritual redemption, carrying on the aims of the Reformation in 1560. Bible and tract societies aimed at a group who failed to attend church on a regular basis, and were never likely to rent pews. Their campaign was carried out interdenominationally to emphasize unity, despite the squabbling which existed amongst the participating churches. The British and Foreign Bible Society (founded in 1804) advocated education for the sole purpose of teaching men and women, boys and girls, to read, in order that they might understand the Holy Scriptures. The Scottish Board for Bible Circulation resolved in 1842 to secure the benefits of greatly reduced production costs to all who wished to purchase a Bible. Shocked by the loss of souls in the urban industrial slums, they sought to bring working people to the 'great Christian doctrine of sin, grace and redemption', although their reception was not often welcome, as Alexander Brown observed in 1858:

'Whilst thou have a tract?' says our *friend* to a woman somewhat more respectable than the others. 'We dinna want ony o' yer tracts here!' she replies in rather a petulant manner; and, with an offended air, withdraws from the group. 'It has nothing to do with religion,' we remark; 'it is simply a teetotal tract.' 'Weel, weel, whether or no, we ha'e owre muckle o' them here.' 'An' we're a' teetotal enough, an' obliged to be', ejaculates a smart little dame sitting on the third step of the staircase.

Some were determined to resist incorporation into the civility and structures of Scottish civil society, seeing it as unwarranted class-led instruction or, simply, as patronizing. Rarely daunted, Bible and tract societies used many techniques to include all in their mission: 'Religious Institution Rooms' were set up, while medical missions, which combined prayer with healing, were an innovative means of campaigning – evangelical doctors offered free medical treatment as an incentive to get people to attend prayer meetings in their dispensaries. Spiritual welfare was offered as a means of mastering material hardship.

Protection of the Sabbath was part of this package of religious subventions too. In 1839 the Committee for Promoting the Better Observance of the Sabbath, based on the Commandment to 'Remember the Sabbath day, to keep it holy', sought to stem what it perceived to be the tide of irreligion as it affected personal and family behaviour. It continued the work of Sabbatarians in the seventeenth and eighteenth centuries, and although the religiosity of the Scottish people remained high in this period, regulation of time in work and transportation seemed to epitomize the fears of many. High among Sabbatarians' targets were Sunday sailings. Seamen were involved in their campaigns against those ships which flouted the law on land, acting as floating bars serving alcohol. Resistance was mobilized in 1839 to the Dalkeith railway and to the stagecoach to London by the Scottish Society for Promoting the Due Observance of the Lord's Day: 'it is our desire to go hand in hand with the church courts, with the civil magistrates, and every lover of the divine commandment, with every man who desires to serve God himself, and who wishes in love to his neighbour, to protect him in the observance of the Lord's day'. The reminiscences of Sir Archibald Geikie, which he published in 1904, recall the story of the royal party visiting Ross-shire on a Sunday: 'tempted by the beauty of the day, [they] made an expedition by boat to one of the islands of the loch'. The local scandal was so great that the Free presbytery in the neighbourhood 'took the matter up with the Queen in a letter'. Dean Ramsay tells a similar story about an English traveller in a northern Scottish town on a Sunday, out for a walk. He asked a passer-by the name of the castle: 'It's no' the day to be speerin' (sic) things!' came the reply. Indicating that little had changed over the century, the writer R. H. Bruce Lockhart, in his memoirs of his youth in the 1890s, recalls: 'Games of any kind were forbidden, and, in spite of my father's devotion to cricket, one of the worst thrashings that Rufus and I received was for practising bowling on Sunday with a tennis ball against the garden wall.'

Religion was not just a cry of theology in the abstract, nor was Scottish presbyterianism just another variant of Protestantism within the United Kingdom. It gave volume to civil society. It was a means of organizing morality and self-reflection through non-state intervention in society, from what one did on a Sunday, through one's consumption of alcohol, to the extent of participation in the relief of the poor. The more overtly material underpinning of such religious argument was clearly seen in debates over the nature and extent of educational instruction and in the creation of leisure activities tinged with religion. Sunday Schools supplemented more than the educational diet of the poorest. Free meals would often go along with free education, although many paid their penny. Opportunities to attend physically and morally uplifting groups were both extensive and extensively used. In Glasgow in 1890, Protestant Sunday School scholars accounted for 65 per cent of all five- to fifteen-year-olds. Many young people were associated with youth organizations such as the Young Men's Christian Association (1841) and the Boys Brigade (founded in Glasgow in 1883), the Scouts, and – offering the virtues of temperance to the young – the Band of Hope. The editor of *Forward* and Scottish Secretary in 1941–5, Tom Johnston, tells of a picture show with the magic lantern graphically impressing on his young mind the folly of alcohol.

Sport was also used to promote the message of religion and morality in life, this among Catholics as much as Protestants. Hibernian Football Club (FC), in its first incarnation, was founded by Canon Edward Hannan in 1875. Its constitution stated that only practising Catholics could represent it; Celtic FC was founded by Brother Walfrid and the local Catholic priests in 1888, and the short-lived Dundee Harp was again Catholic led. The sense of common cause such clubs engendered saw Celtic Park built by voluntary labour from the local Catholic community. Until the advent of 'secular' sports and their commercialization under formal associations in the 1880s, organized 'respectable' recreation had been dominated by religious occasions like Sunday School excursions and temperance walks. The religious perception that idleness was sinful, and that free time should be used positively and systematically, was one taken up by the self-improvement Mechanics' Institutes and propagated in the best-selling fables from the Haddington-born Samuel Smiles. The early choirs and music societies offered companionship. The pieces sung were always morally uplifting – the popularity of the 'Messiah' was undiminished. The great benefits of muscular Christianity – Thomas Arnold's ideas on the benefits of sport to attract the young away from the many temptations of (urban) life – were loudly proclaimed. 'The dancing' and the music-hall were places of ritual as much as entertainment. Whereas the music-hall challenged the etiquette of the theatre, the dancing instructor David Anderson, who taught in Dundee from 1870 until 1907, was there to maintain social order: 'Gentlemen on entering the Ball-room, and after every dance, lead their partners to a seat by the right arm, bow and retire. Ladies are to sit with hands clasped; gentlemen with hands on knees.'

It was social order in the city which was uppermost in contemporary minds. The destitute, the unemployed and the poor were not just unfortunate in the sensibilities of middle-class society. Their plight was seen as a sign of failure, at times of political economy, or of Christianity, or both. The 'ragged school' movement which began in the early 1840s was a conscious attempt to mobilize society to look after its own through the virtues of education. Thomas Guthrie's original Ragged Schools were dominated by the Free Church, but by claiming to be motivated by 'securing that religion be taught, but not of itself teaching religion', he attracted support from the Church of Scotland and the United Presbyterians. The children were predominantly those of the Irish immigrants, generally the most disadvantaged in Scottish society, and those from Highland families. Guthrie's objective in 1849 was 'to give such children a position in the social scale', be it in Scotland or (more often) through migration overseas.

As in earlier times, a great deal of philanthropy was directed at the young (and improvable). The House of Refuge for the Destitute in Edinburgh provided for 1,003 individuals in the period from 22 February to 10 December 1832 (844 Scotch (*sic*), 107 Irish, 45 English, 7 foreigners). The children were placed under a master and taught reading and writing, with the girls instructed in sewing and knitting. Here was a society organized by ministers of a number of different denominations, and here too was an indicator of organized concern with the arrival of a large number of individuals and families from Ireland. By the 1830s, following the Catholic Emancipation Act of 1829, the fear of an influx of adherents to Catholicism was voiced. In 1835 Edinburgh hosted a meeting whose purpose was the formation of a Protestant Association for that city 'because Roman Catholics have taken advantage of their [Protestant] supineness to promote their own cause'. Dean Ramsay remarked around 1870 that 'English people, in speaking of the established Church of Scotland, seem to forget how much Episcopalians are mixed up with their Presbyterian fellow-countrymen in promoting common charitable and religious objects'. His 'Paterson and Pape fund' was 'vested jointly in the incumbent of St John's, Edinburgh [Episcopalian], and the two clergymen of St Cuthbert's [Established] Church'.

Adding weight to such interdenominational collaboration, a connection was often made linking the Irish migrant with crime, drunkenness and moral laxity. The association between crime and intemperance had long been clear to many contemporaries. Four-fifths of crime was attributed to intoxicating liquor in the tables presented by Sheriff Gordon to a gathering of the Apprentice Schools in 1846. Police Boards made similar claims. The link to lack of education was also an easy one to make: '. . . it is impossible to open a book of statistical returns to crime without seeing that out of ten criminals nine are either entirely ignorant of the commonest rudiments of education, or imperfectly acquainted with them', declared Charles Mackay in one of a series of letters to his Glasgow MP in 1846. An 1851 inquiry by a small number of ardent philanthropists, with assistance from the medical profession in Edinburgh, lamented the large proportion of the population who, they claimed, knew nothing of God or religion, and they put much of the blame on the 'considerable number of Irish descendants who have become prostitutes'. Strong polemic from associations dedicated to the Protestant cause, especially following the Irish migration to Scotland prompted by the potato blight of 1846–52, fed on such social investigations. The Scottish Reformation Society was instituted in 1850 to lecture and offer prizes (to all denominations), and to watch 'the aggressive movements of Romanism and Tractarianism at home and abroad, and resisting same by all constitutional means', including correspondence with government, MPs, electors and the press. It organized agitations against Maynooth and any 'other State encouragements to Popery, as well as against Nunneries, Monasteries, and other illegal Popish Establishments or Titles'. The society paid for a 'confidential' correspondent in London to attend parliament and engage in what it termed a 'Popish watch', collating signs of possible dangers to the Protestant cause, to be then passed on to the editor of their aptly named journal *Bulwark*. Both mid-century political electioneering and the debate over national education played on long-established and yet acute fears of a 'Popish menace', while highlighting an underlying tendency of secularism through, in their minds, Protestant apathy. By the 1870s the Orange Order was using the parade on 12 July as a vehicle for its active defence of Protestantism; while its political impact may have been relatively limited, it gained in prominence in opposition to the Irish Home Rule Bills of 1886 and 1893.

Franchise Reform

The intervention of religious and voluntary groups in the health and education of Scotland was organized within civil society; the role of the state was placed firmly in the background. The unwelcome judgement of the House of Lords at the time of the Disruption, the centralizing tendencies of Chadwick and the issue of non-denominational national education were all debates about the state *vis-à-vis* civil society. From another viewpoint, the nineteenth century witnessed the modern reform of the parliamentary process and of the electoral franchise. The first Reform Act in 1832 marked the breakthrough of the middle classes and the £10 property-holders of the towns into a world which the aristocratic and county élites had long established as their own.

Scotland's nineteenth-century political history was profoundly influenced by the Reform Bill of William IV's reign. Although somewhat lagging in terms of those who actually possessed the franchise (1 in 8 in Scotland compared with 1 in 5 in England), the 1832 reform produced greater proportional changes in Scotland. The electorate in England increased by 80 per cent from the pre-reform figure; in Scotland the change was 1,400 per cent. Despite three Reform Bills (the other two came in 1868 and 1884), by 1911 only 63 per cent of Scottish males were entitled to vote in the counties, a figure that reached nearly 70 per cent in England. The gap was less between the two nations in the burghs, but was still far from universal male suffrage: 57 per cent and 60 per cent respectively. Women had to wait until 1918 before they too could participate. Throughout, the list of voters was notoriously out-of-date in England and Wales, although less so in Scotland. Even following the franchise reform of 1884, it was all but impossible to keep up with a mobile population. Estimates made of the general election in 1910 suggest that the electoral register was eighteen months old. It was out of date for the county electorate, which probably changed by almost 5 per cent each year, and especially inadequate for a burgh rate of elector movement of 20 to 30 per cent.

Perhaps the most quoted of the nineteenth-century Whig commentators, Henry Cockburn, was convinced – or at least hoped he was – that Scottish politics had ended with the reform of 1832 and that now the Scots could take their prosperity to new levels attached ever more securely to the path of progress, which was British constitutionalism. However, we have seen that 1832 was not a reform for the people, although the role of the trades in supporting the cause and numbers involved in the processions in favour of reform are indicators of common cause across the ranks at this moment. In his 1848 *Autobiography of a Working Man*, Alexander Somerville sums up its welcome: 'Some people saw no good in the Reform Bill, but much evil; some saw no good in the railways, but much evil; others saw no evil in either, yet not much good; the greater number saw boundless good in both.' As many as 15,000 processed in Edinburgh to celebrate the passage of the 1832 Reform Act, and between five and six times that number took time off to spectate and to cheer. The procession included a model of Sir William Wallace paraded by the Caledonian Youth Society, yet the event was one of loyalty to the monarch and to the constitution, and one where order was demanded at all times from the crowds.

Whatever the shortcomings of the electoral system after 1832, and whatever remained to be achieved, the short- and long-term effects of a hugely increased adult male franchise can hardly be over-estimated. Resentment of their unsympathetic stance on parliamentary reform before 1832 did much to damage the non-Whig vote. Indeed, the Tories were effectively wiped out in the burgh constituencies from 1832, with sustained recovery only beginning from 1886. A similar initial crisis was found in the counties, but the surge in favour of the Whigs was not to last. At the general election of 1841, the Tories won 20 out of the available 30 seats in the counties, 16 without opposition. Comparable gains were obtained in England.

It was the Second Reform Act which offered enfranchisement to the trades. A public meeting of the inhabitants was held on 22 January 1866 in Dalkeith, for example. Their aim was to support the proposed Bill to extend the suffrage in both the counties and the burghs and to petition parliament to this end. The speeches made that night stressed how Scotland had gained from political representation in 1832, and how it had been governed effectively since then, but now, when a generation had passed, it was time to extend the suffrage to 'many who are at present denied that privilege, and in whose loyal attachment to the civil institutions of the country we have the fullest confidence'.

The passing of this Act in 1868 in Scotland seems to have been little commented upon, with events of the ensuing General Election taking precedence. The *Scotsman* commented that 'the scene upon the royal assent to the Reform Bill of 1832 was very different from the quiet and unimpressive spectacle of Thursday last'. Clearly the delay in this legislation after its successful and speedy passage in England in 1867 was partly to blame. The impact of the second Reform Act was to increase the electorate of Edinburgh by 176 per cent in the period from 1865 to 1880, although this only meant that 13 per cent of the population were enfranchised. The electorate of Edinburgh and Leith stood at 27,002 in 1868. The burgh electorate in Scotland had almost trebled, standing at 154,331.

It was before the passage of the 1867 Reform Act for England that the greatest public agitation was found in Scotland. Glasgow and Edinburgh held their pro-reform demonstrations a month apart in 1866. In Glasgow it was estimated that between 20,000 and 30,000 of the trades attended, with perhaps 60,000 to 70,000 spectating. The organization of the Scottish Reform League was such that they were able to secure workers' representation from all the major towns in Scotland and some of the larger manufacturing areas in England. And this monster rally dwarfed any comparable Chartist meeting in Scotland. Edinburgh was never able to compete in scale and had a tendency to follow Glasgow's lead, although the organizers claimed the issue 'had occupied the minds of all trades in Edinburgh for months'.

Between 10,000 and 11,000 took part in the procession in Edinburgh, with around 30,000 to 40,000 who took the day as a workman's holiday (or took 'French leave') to attend. Duncan McLaren was the only MP at the procession. The reports noted that in 1832 attempts were made to defend the demonstration from the working man but this time 'the processionists were artisans exclusively'. There were many flags which 'breathed the finest spirits of loyalty', many of which had flown in 1832. The usual terrible puns dominated the mottoes on the many banners. 'A sweeping measure of reform' was demanded by the brush-making trades, for instance. Many combined notions of Scottish nationalism and British patriotism with their claim on reform. The basket-makers displayed a basket cradle within which was the figure of 'Young Scotland awakening from sleep' with the cry of 'I was asleep but you've wakened me noo'. A bird of freedom was there to indicate 'Liberty to all'. The printers, bookbinders, type-founders and lithographers distributed copies of verses written by a printer, James Smith, and an engineer, Mr W. Wilson: 'While angel voices swell the cry, amid the rising storm – / Unfurl, once more, ye British hearts, the Banner of Reform!' The trades of rope-makers, sail-makers and ship carpenters also relied on rhyming verse: 'The State is our ship, / Her captain, Reform: / The Queen is our pilot, / A faction the storm.' The loyalty to Britain stated here was displayed by others too. A banner belonging to the coach-makers proclaimed that 'Labour is the wealth of [then pictures of the rose, the thistle and the shamrock]' and ought to have the suffrage. The brass-founders used a representation of the British lion 'resting not sleeping', and the sawyers re-used an older banner: 'Let the King [in 1832] be glorious and the People Free'.

Perhaps the most interesting banners came from the building trades. The Edinburgh branch of the Associated Carpenters and Joiners of Scotland had what was described as an immense banner dating from 1832 with a full-sized figure of a Highlander and the call, 'Turn the blue bonnets who can!'. They also carried three mottoes different enough to invite contemporary comment. The first was not too unusual: 'Loyalty to the Queen, our rights as men, and our privilege as citizens'; two others were 'No vote, no soldier' and 'Manhood suffrage, or no soldier'. Of these their bearers were asked to explain what they meant (the only participants to be so questioned), but no information was forthcoming other than the reply: 'Man, I'm a joiner', no doubt given with a shrug of the shoulders.

Yet it seems to fit one of the orthodox links between nationalism and the state, that the state uses patriotism to establish its own legitimacy and to engender loyalty to it. In the banners of 1866 there was a clear link between political reform and patriotism: not only that they were being loyal by demanding reform, but that this demand was the embodiment of their patriotism. It was the joiners who turned this around somewhat by statements that hit at the heart of state-sponsored patriotism. Loyalty to the state in its highest form (as soldiers fighting for queen and country) was not to be forthcoming unless in return for a widening of the franchise to include the trades.

The link between popular enfranchisement, a national identity that was Scottish, and a patriotism that was British, was revealed during the lead-up to the third Reform Act, 1884–5. A great procession and demonstration to support the County Franchise Bill took place in Queen's Park, Edinburgh, on 12 July 1884. A total of 15,570 people took part in the procession. A myriad of banners were on display with occasionally 'a piece of faded and tattered silk that did similar duty in 1832 and 1866; with many more of a less venerable age that could claim to at least have been carried in the latter demonstration'. Again, it is interesting to look at the printers' display. Theirs was an effigy of 'a demonstrative Highlander out in the '32' (copying the Jacobite nomenclature of 'the '15' and 'the '45') which they combined with a portrait of Gladstone and a declaration of their 'readiness to do all they could for the franchise bill and the grand old man'. The stonemasons also linked their demand for social reforms with distinct references to the structures of nationalism. They claimed to be 'pioneers of the nine hours movement' and that 'equal justice to all strengthens the constitution'. Joining the intellectual Whigs of the time, their reference was to the English constitutionalism of which the Treaty of 1707 was regarded as the guarantor. Loyalty to Queen Victoria was declared, along with the respectful claim for 'their rights as men and their privileges as citizens'. The whole event was described by the *Scotsman* as a 'spontaneous gathering' where there was no caucus, just working men and their trades societies 'animated by the spirit of sincere patriotism'. Yet little or no support was expressed here for extending the franchise to women. One woman caused what was described by the newspaper as 'great amusement' after 'gesticulating a demand' for women's franchise to be included with that of men. This was the only mention of the claim for women, and was one treated with the utmost derision by the crowd. Yet the activity of the women's movement in Scotland was strong, with a wide focus on the working conditions of women, the evils of workplace and domestic violence, and the importance of domestic duties. This derision at an overwhelmingly male gathering could not, however, arise from ignorance of the essential contribution of women to the family economy, particularly in the working class.

A wave of suffrage societies came into existence after 1868. The newly-formed Scottish Women's Suffragette Society met in Edinburgh with Priscilla Bright McLaren, wife of Edinburgh MP Duncan McLaren, as its president. Without a voice in parliament or a means of influencing the election of their town or county's representatives, the cause of women, and women's causes, were centred on civil society. An earlier impetus, stemming from rejection in the 1832 Act, achieved the formation of the Edinburgh Ladies' Emancipation Society whose constitution was passed in 1833. In 1854 the society asked: 'Can we behold, unheeding, / Life's holiest feelings crush'd; – / While Woman's heart is bleeding, / Shall woman's voice be crushed?'

Women's groups had been to the fore in the campaign to abolish slavery in the late eighteenth and early nineteenth century, and increasingly made plain the tension over emancipation for the male Negro in the West Indies, but not for the white female in Britain. The argument that even the Negro had a soul was not exactly new, but its increasing currency cemented the connection between anti-slavery and non-conformist religion in England. In Scotland the issue had exploded into a pamphlet war in 1846, when the Free Church came under heavy criticism for accepting donations towards its church-building programme from slave-owners and slave-holding churches in America's south. In both nations, anti-slavery societies were one of the earliest instances of women's group meetings which were separate from men's. The World's Anti-Slavery Convention was held in London at the behest of the British and Foreign Anti-Slavery Society in 1840. The event did much to raise the profile of the inequalities of the franchise. Acting upon resolutions of the Convention, the Glasgow Ladies Auxiliary Society was moderate in the connections it made to women's suffrage, while the Edinburgh Ladies Emancipation Society was more radical, especially in its reformulated New Edinburgh Anti-Slavery Society (from 1854). The slavery issue was a source of relative success for women's politics. In comparison with the male-dominated Chartists, who peddled the family wage as the proper (male) payment, this was particularly so. Suffrage campaigning took off after 1867 and two million signatures were obtained in Scotland in a decade of petitioning for the cause of women. Much hostility was faced, including forced feeding of women protesters in prison in the 1910s. Dundee opened a branch in 1911 of the Scottish League for Opposing Suffrage. There was also violence. Mrs Pankhurst came to Glasgow in 1914 and sparked a riot as the police rushed the platform to arrest her. Only in 1928 did women obtain the vote on the same basis as men.

Women and Work

Job opportunities were limited for young women and especially so in the smaller towns where industry was scarce. For the working classes throughout this period, the imperative was for paid employment to contribute to the household economy as soon as was practicable: deferring possible greater rewards through extended education was not an option for most. Nor were work aspirations necessarily high, but they were strong. Domestic service was the expected, or even the only, route to employment for young girls, although this later lost out to retail or textile work. In 1841 around 90 per cent of the female labour force was concentrated in textiles, clothing, agricultural work and domestic service, a figure which fell to 65 per cent in 1911. The often casual and intermittent nature of women's work made it unsuitable to be easily recorded by the national censuses (begun in 1801 and conducted every tenth year), although this problem can be exaggerated. Paid work could also take place in the home – by the women weavers of Paisley, for example. Yet domestic service was an experience for many, perhaps most, women for at least a short period of their working lives, before they went on to other employments offering more freedom and better wages.

The use of the domestic servant to clean and cook made it possible for the wealthier professional and commercial middle classes to develop a taste for the ornate clutter which came to dominate their household style in the latter part of the Victorian period. Domestic Service also had a profound effect on notions of privacy and on class relations. Control over the young female servant, her access to leisure and to boyfriends, offered what was one of the few opportunities the middle classes had to observe and to understand their social inferiors. In Glasgow in 1861 over three-quarters of all female servants were incomers, mostly from the Highlands and from Ireland, whereas in Edinburgh, where there were few female migrants looking for work in the newly-emerging industries, service was the preserve of local women and, to a lesser extent, men.

The precarious life in service for the young girl away from her family, and where her home and income were intertwined, was eased by help from voluntary organizations. That 80 per cent of the women applying for assistance from the Edinburgh Magdalene Institutes, in a five-year period in the mid-century, had once been employed as domestic servants highlights the role of this organization in helping vulnerable women avoid prostitution. The survey by the Edinburgh doctor William Tait in 1842 estimated that around 800 girls and women regularly, and perhaps half that number again occasionally, were employed in the oldest profession in the nation's capital. The Magdalene Institutes were formed to help those at risk of descending into prostitution rather than those already 'lost' to it; but, like the domestic worker and the female worker in industry, the Institutes were sites of male supervision and social control. After a probation period of a few months, the women who stayed were to experience a set of routines and order for two years before leaving.

Other sources of help for this class included the Scottish Register and Home Institution for Domestic Servants, but again male control was evident from its management by a 'Committee of Gentlemen'. The Edinburgh MP Charles Cowan, called to the chair at the fourth annual meeting of the Institution in 1859, declared that its remit was to 'elevate the moral character, and improve the temporal comfort of Domestic Servants, as well as to benefit employers'. The home had housed 565 servants in the previous year while receiving 8,795 requests from employers for servants, and directing 4,524 servants to those positions. Less instrumental was the Scottish Institution for the Education of Young Women, which had piano and singing lessons, as well as chemistry classes, for its day and boarding pupils in the 1830s. For those who were pregnant, and who lacked sufficient family or community support, a box containing every article deemed necessary for the mother and child would be lent for four or six weeks by the Society for the Relief of Poor Married Women, of Respectable Character, when in Childbirth. Each box contained a Bible as well as blankets and clothing and some food. Each subscriber of five shillings in 1854 could recommend a case for assistance, but help was conditional on the 'personal investigation of the ladies who undertake the important and often painful office of monthly visits': the activity and the ethos which lay behind Scotland's civil society could be distressing for those giving as well as for those receiving charity.

Charitable giving involved inequalities of power and wealth. Nineteenth-century recipients accommodated themselves to these realities. At the same time, there existed hierarchies of status among women in the factory and the mill. The women weavers in Dundee saw themselves as the social superiors of their sister spinners; the wearing or not wearing of a hat on leaving at the end of the day was an indicator of one's position. Paid employment, accompanied by class identity, was a reality of much significance to women in an age we remember for its (bourgeois) 'separate spheres': the domestic world of the woman and the public world of the man. The Dundee women were not limited to housework, with about a quarter of married women working, and more if widows are included. Nor was it a contradiction within the women's movement to place the domestic alongside paid employment, an argument of women's groups in the 1870s. The 1901 Exhibition in Glasgow saw the education stall of the women's section of the event dominated by the Schools of Cookery, Housewifery and Domestic Science. Furthermore, working was every bit as central to women's lives as men's. Oral historians have shown that when the elderly were asked to reflect on their early life experiences at the turn of the century, the world of work had a much clearer recall than the supposedly dominant domestic ideal. Yet male control over the workplace and through the voluntary organizations within civil society was firmly structured. Skills were guarded by men. The bespoke trade in tailoring was male, with women given work in carrying out minor alterations. Clerking remained male and its feminization had to wait until the twentieth century.

Education

Differences at work were a continuation and a reinforcement of gendered experiences at home and in school. In its report of 1866, the Argyll Commission – a committee set up by the government to examine the state of education in Scotland's schools – concluded that girls made up about 40 per cent of school pupils at the various burgh and independent secondary schools. This percentage dropped once the age of sixteen was passed, and girls were not to be found in the High Schools and Academies of Glasgow and Edinburgh. Instead they were mainly educated in the cheaper burgh schools, or in privileged single-sex schools. For boys and girls there was a great variety of schools: Sunday, industrial, factory and reformatory, as well as parochial and burgh schools and the endowed schools. It has been estimated by the historian Helen Corr that at least a dozen different types of school were brought under state control by the 1872 Education (Scotland) Act. Religion divided the provision for education, but it also provided much impetus for the promotion of learning, as it had for centuries. The Free Church took over Moray House in Edinburgh at a cost of £9,000 to train its teachers in 1848, and by 1865 it was estimated that there were around 570 Free Church schools in Scotland. The debate over the denominational teaching of education delayed the compromise on national education. This exacerbated the problem of the many who received but scant elementary education and ensured that Scottish educational policy tended to be derived from practices in England.

Much less attention was paid by campaigners to secondary education, and there was limited provision for the working classes. The higher-class schools, the technical and endowed 'hospital' schools, provided a varied curriculum of science and classical subjects. Post-elementary education made a route for the children of Scotland's middle classes to follow and make their mark in industry and empire, as well as in the arts and in society. The endowed schools were able to use the income from land investments within the boundaries of the growing cities to keep down the cost for the children of respectable, but not wealthy, families. The merchant companies established schools, such as George Watson's and Daniel Stewart's, to train the next generation in commerce. Their subsidies helped to broaden the blend of social classes who entered their orbit.

But it was an openness which was not to last long after the 1872 Act. A number of the endowed schools then became 'public schools' and the social class basis of the school roll narrowed as a consequence.

The range of educational establishments in Scotland, and the availability of a number of subsidized places, added to the long-held belief that Scotland was (and is) a place of educational opportunity. Scotland, for its size and especially in comparison with England, excelled at this time, with its five universities. In the 1860s, the tendency was for arts students at Edinburgh University to start their courses at the age of sixteen or seventeen. They were taught in the generalist tradition, open to intellect, not narrowed to specialism. Yet their course content was not always of a high standard. And the class openness of the universities and the secondary schools was never as far-reaching as it seemed, with parental self-selection of 'appropriate' schools, and the need for those from lower-income families to obtain a wage from their fourteen-year-old son or daughter, having much influence.

Meanwhile, the campaign to promote higher education for women was conducted chiefly by the various Ladies' Educational Associations which had been formed in the major cities of Scotland from the 1860s. The Scottish universities opened their doors to women in 1892, fifteen years after the University of London. This was made possible by the Universities (Scotland) Act, 1889, but it came after a struggle. In 1870 there had been a riot in Surgeon's Hall in Edinburgh when male students attempted to prevent women from attending an anatomy lecture. There was also resistance to women gaining admission to the Royal Infirmary, where they could receive practical medical instruction. At Edinburgh, medical women were only allowed to become full members of the university in 1916. The feminization of the teaching profession was slow, but this changed after 1872. In 1851 only 35 per cent of teachers in Scotland were female, a figure rising to over 62 per cent in 1881 and to 70 per cent by 1911. Women's earnings were about one half of those of their male colleagues in the last quarter of the nineteenth century. Until the First World War, when female teachers in Scotland were more highly qualified than their counterparts in England, they still received less pay. There was no national campaign for pay equality before 1914. Yet none of this stopped women teachers extolling the benefits of the Scottish education system: perhaps it was, after all, the reflection of an increasingly fluid and open society.

Reposed Capitals

What is clear is that increasing stability developed in Scottish society from the 1860s. An important aspect of this was the development of the big cities as a focus for that society. In most European national histories, the capital city plays a prominent part. Edinburgh held an equivocal status as a capital city without a national government, but it still retained many of the functions and features of a national capital: the principal law courts met there, as did the annual Assembly of the Church of Scotland; Scottish property was largely managed by the lawyers of the New Town and the property deeds and testamentary documents of Scotland were deposited in Register House; the National Gallery held Scotland's official store of visual art; the Scottish banks printed Scottish sterling banknotes; and the Advocates' Library (founded in the late seventeenth century and given copyright privileges by an Act of 1710) laid the foundations of the National Library of Scotland, formally constituted by Act of Parliament in 1925.

Despite this unusual history, Edinburgh retained and developed much of the economic and cultural character of a capital. The direct and indirect economic benefits of a parliament were absent, but there were other quasi-governmental bodies. Printers and stationers served the courts as well as the university and the Assembly. This was the basis of demand for a printing industry which grew to serve much wider markets. The brothers William and Robert Chambers made their fortune in the mass production of educational and popular periodicals. The Edinburgh engineering industry was based on the production of printing machinery for local and international markets. Edinburgh was at the centre of one of the richest and most technically advanced grain-growing areas in Europe. The result was a brewing industry supplying increasing areas in Scotland as well as a growing export trade. To the lawyers, the merchants and the small and growing number of university professors must be added the large rentier population: widows, landowners in town, retired military people and others who lived on rents, pensions and the income from government bonds, most notably in the New Town. They created a double demand typical of many capital cities, first for high-quality luxury crafts, requiring silversmiths, engravers, carriage-makers, furniture-makers and dress-makers, and second for low-income service occupations, for porters, seamstresses, washerwomen and above all domestic servants. Edinburgh had a bias towards wealth, towards the professions, services and high-quality craft industries, and towards finance and commerce, all typical of a metropolitan centre. In 1901 the most common male occupations were those of commercial clerk, printer, carter, messenger and porter, general labourer, painter and glazier. Domestic servants accounted for 42 per cent of the female labour force.

By the end of the century, the Edinburgh and Leith *Post Office Directory* showed just how important Edinburgh had become as a metropolitan centre, asserting and organizing power across Scotland in many guises. The *Directory* listed many organizations based in Edinburgh. They included:

> Board of Supervision for the Relief of the Poor
> Court of Session
> Crofters Commission
> Faculty of Actuaries in Scotland

Fishery Board for Scotland

General Record for Scotland (Register House)

Grand (Masonic) Lodge of Scotland

Grand Lodge of Scotland (Ancient Order of Free Gardeners)

Joint Stock Companies Registration Office

National Gallery of Scotland

Northern Lighthouse Commissioners

Pharmaceutical Society of Great Britain (North British Branch)

Register of Sasines (the property register)

Royal Scottish Academy

Royal Scottish Geographical Society

Royal Scottish Nursing Institution

Scottish Institute of Accountants

Scottish Trade Protection Society

Society of Antiquaries of Scotland

This list included agencies of the state, judicial, chartered and executive, as well as the voluntary associations of civil society. Most of the organizations in the list had been created as a result of the needs of an industrial commercial society and not because they were survivors from the Union of 1707. To these institutions must be added the banks, the insurance companies, the investment trusts and the university. These were the knowledge- and information-handling industries of the developed industrial and commercial society which was nineteenth-century Scotland. Edinburgh may not have been the seat of government for Scotland, but it was the metropolis for the governance of that polity created and bounded by the terms of the Union of 1707.

Edinburgh's position as a capital city was not simply a matter of history and functionality. During the nineteenth century, the city reconstructed itself as an elaborate symbol for Scotland. The Royal Scottish Academy building of 1822–6 and 1831–6, with its assertive Doric frontage, was initially the Royal Institution and housed the cultural leaders of civil society in Scotland, the Antiquaries, the Royal Society and the Society for the Encouragement of the Fine Arts. The National Gallery followed in 1848 with its cosier Ionic style and a Treasury grant. Both were powerful visual claims to cultural leadership by the 'Athens of the North'. Edinburgh Castle may well have had a pre-medieval origin but in its modern form it was a nineteenth-century creation. The gatehouse which provides the backdrop to so many modern tourist photographs was built in 1887–8 and is flanked by statues of Wallace and Bruce, unveiled in 1929. St Margaret's Chapel – a twelfth-century building – emerged from the restorations of 1851–2 and 1885 prompted by the Society of Antiquaries and a bequest from William Nelson, printer and publisher. New shopping streets, like Cockburn Street (1856–64), bristled with crow-stepped gables, baronial angle turrets, thistles and saltires, as did the tenements of new suburbs like Marchmont and Warrender, triumphs of respectability for the salaried and the profit-takers of prospering financial and commercial Edinburgh.

The reading of Edinburgh's streets revealed claims that were European as well as Scottish. The University Medical School, completed in 1888, was Renaissance Venice – if the money had not run out it would have included a copy of the campanile from St Mark's Square. Nearby Chambers Street was a product of the Improvement Act of 1867. It was one of the great institutional streets of Europe. The Royal Scottish Museum – its foundation stone laid by Prince Albert in 1861 – has an interior dominated by the new industrial materials of iron and glass, but the exterior is a Venetian Renaissance claim to wealth, taste and knowledge with busts of Watt, Darwin, Newton and Michelangelo, as well as a 'Bridge of Sighs' to link it to the university next door.

If Edinburgh was the first city in Scotland, Glasgow's claim was to be second city of the Empire, a claim based on a global commerce and the production of capital goods for a world market that went far beyond the formal limits of empire. Between 1841 and 1911, about 70 per cent of Glasgow's labour force, both male and female, was engaged in industry. Within that sector there was a move from the early dominance of textiles (38 per cent in 1841 falling to 17 per cent in 1911) and an increase in the importance of the engineering and metals trades (7 per cent in 1841 to 17 per cent in 1911). Despite the emphasis on industrial production, commerce remained central to Glasgow's income and culture. In 1911, commercial clerks still made up the most numerous male occupation (12,684), although they were closely followed by metal-related occupations: iron-founders (9,155), engine- and machine-makers (7,970), and fitters and turners (7,893). Glasgow was the most intensely urban of Scottish places. Between 1831 and 1911 it increased in population four times, to reach 784,000. In 1891, before the major boundary extensions, average population density had reached 93 per acre. Average figures masked the fact that the railway and rail station building in the central area had displaced some 20,000 people. Railway companies occupied around 8 per cent of this central area. At the same time, the Glasgow City Improvements Trust demolished 15,425 houses between 1871 and 1874. This, together with the piecemeal creation of shops, offices and warehouses, pushed low-income dwellers into surrounding areas.

In Glasgow, variety was not just a matter of production but also of people. In the 1890s, a quarter of the adult population had been born in Ireland and another quarter in the Highlands of Scotland. Despite the potential, the ethnic, religious and language differences involved did not lead to disruptive levels of conflict. Organization and leadership for anti-Catholic action were on offer in the form of anti-papist preachers and an active Orange Order. The Orange Order tended to be strongest in the iron and coal areas to the north and the shipyard burghs along the Clyde, but relatively weak in Glasgow itself. In the 1880s, Glasgow had some 7,000 Orangemen and mustered under 20,000 for large parades. This was very different from the 64,000 who marched in procession for the third Parliamentary Reform Bill, watched by crowds of over 200,000.

Glasgow was the skilled man's burgh. Less than a third of its male labour force were without any skill at all. Its working-class culture was dominated by the male Protestant liberal, proud of work and craft, but with little interest in sectarianism. Freemasonry and the Volunteer movement satisfied the need for hierarchy and patronage. The Masonic movement of mid-century Scotland attracted over 69,000 in 1879, with its mixture of ceremonial, lodge secrecy and public parades at events such as the laying of the foundation stone of Glasgow Municipal Buildings in 1885. The Volunteers had been formed by the government in 1859 during a French invasion scare. As a part-time military force it was an aspect of the state, but it depended on the time and effort of thousands of men, notably artisans and white-collar workers, as well as the support of employers and other patrons for equipment and uniforms. There was considerable collective funding in middle-class units such as those attached to the universities. The Volunteers formed a powerful link between Scottish civil society and the wider imperial identity, especially at events like the review in the Queen's Park in Edinburgh when units came from all over Scotland to be inspected by Queen Victoria.

For Glasgow people, insecurity in employment driven by the world trade cycle for capital goods together with shared, crowded and squalid housing conditions provided a basis of interest that bound all groups together. In the 1890s, over half of Glasgow households lived in 'single ends' (one-room houses). For many, memories of landlords in Ireland and in the Highlands provided common ground for support of the liberal doctrine. The Liberal Party under Gladstone, with its individualistic, free-market ideology, saw landlords as a potent barrier to economic and social advance and political tranquillity. This ideology was put into practice in land legislation in both Ireland and the 'crofting counties' of Highland Scotland.

Nineteenth-century Glasgow also produced an active and assertive middle-class culture which expressed itself in politics and lifestyle. Politics and much of public life was dominated by a liberalism that incorporated the radicalism of earlier years. This liberalism was led by an élite of the dominant Free Church and United Presbyterians. It was divided by religious and social issues such as evangelicalism, temperance and later Irish Home Rule. Even after the Home Rule divisions it was Liberal Unionists who challenged the Gladstonians.

From the High Street and George Square an irregular and open grid extended westwards, occupied first by shops and offices and then by middle-class housing. In the 1870s and 1880s, the residential choice of the middle classes was liberated by the horse-drawn and then the electric tram. The grid crossed the Kelvin river to form a series of distinctive residential suburbs. Home was separated from work and social class from social class. It was the world of the social parade and, in the larger villas, of the 'carpet dance':

In the morning two strong men came to the drawing-room and carried away all the furniture, except the piano, removed the door from its hinges, took down the heavy curtains, and stretched over every inch of the carpet a great white cloth with a sliding surface. The evening began at eight o'clock . . . the ladies' dresses were elaborately pretty, with voluminous frothy skirts but very décolleté . . . The programme included eighteen items – six quadrilles, two lancers, four waltzes, three polkas, two galops and one Highland schottische . . . For two hours the ceiling shook and the gasolier bobbed and jingled. Between dances most of the couples sought the coolness of the parlour and 'conservatory', while some who had absorbed advanced ideas from the South sat on the stairs. . . . after ten p.m. . . . in the dining-room . . . not only the gentlemen did themselves well but the ladies too. For plumpness was not a social handicap then . . . The most they had to drink was claret cup. Nobody dreamed of smoking. (C. A. Oakley, *The Second City* (Glasgow, 1946), 176)

This culture expressed itself in an especially intense and public way in the Glasgow Exhibitions of 1888, 1901 and 1911. The exhibitions displayed the universality to which a liberal middle class aspired. They were international exhibitions which set the world in order for commerce and industry. At the same time they were deeply competitive and particular. A wide range of local products was on display, from locomotives to porridge oats. Weir pumps and Coats thread were set alongside products from Germany, France, the United States and India. The works of the 'Glasgow boys' were displayed alongside selections from the art collections of local industrialists. Oriental style had been appropriated as a fashion item, beside themes incorporating Burns, Scott, thistles and St Mungo. The imperial theme grew stronger, especially in 1901 when a captured Boer gun was on display.

Middle-class Glasgow had an infinite capacity to shock itself. The story of Madeleine Smith was a morality tale with a live cast. She was the daughter of a respectable architect, James Smith, who lived in India Street and later in the even more prestigious Blythswood Square. In 1857, Sauchiehall Street was the venue for the social promenade and here she met the ten-shillings-a-week seedsman's clerk, Pierre Emile l'Angelier. Her letters to him, which were read at the subsequent trial, displayed in the words of *Notable British Trials* 'all the profound physical passion [of] the northern woman . . . a thing supposed at that date not to exist in a nice woman'. Parental pressure and the prospect of marriage to a £3,000-a-year member of Glasgow's merchant community led to a painful death for Pierre as a result of hot chocolate and arsenic, which all the evidence suggested was administered by Madeleine herself. Brilliant and expensive advocacy, and that particular Scottish verdict of 'not proven', enabled Madeleine to escape to England, where she made a small contribution to the socialist movement of George Bernard Shaw and William Morris.

Much more widespread was the distress caused in the same year by the collapse of the Western Bank. The world economic crisis exposed speculation and mismanagement by the directors. Worse followed in 1878. The collapse of the Glasgow City Bank was a result of criminal mismanagement. The directors were jailed and £2,500 was required from the holders of each £100 unlimited liability share. Liquidity and confidence were pulled from the Glasgow economy and the dominance of Edinburgh banking confirmed.

By the 1860s, engineering had replaced cotton textiles as the leading industry in Glasgow. The one-time handloom weaving village of Parkhead was the site of the forge purchased by Beardmore's in the 1860s. Under an aggressive paternalistic management characteristic of much of Scottish industry, the forge expanded to be one of the largest employers in Glasgow.

Parkhead Forge in the early eighties was controlled by the Beardmore family. It manufactured steel plates for all kinds of work, from quarter inch plates for tubes, to five inch and six inch plates and guns for warships; as well as locomotive types . . . The furnaces, foundry, rolling mill, steam hammers and press engaged a large staff of highly skilled labour – including bricklayers – and all under the patriarchal eye of old 'Bill' and 'Issac' Beardmore.

The plates, ingots of steel, propellers and keels for ships were hauled down to the Clydeside on a chariot-like conveyance which consisted of a car on two wheels at each end of a long pole – a 'monkey', as it was called. This 'monkey' was drawn by a team of ten, twelve or more horses, according to the load. To bring the load to the main road which led to the shipyards of Govan or Clydebank, there was a steep incline from the gate up the New Road (now Duke Street) to Parkhead Cross.

When as often happened, the horses got stuck, I have seen Issac Beardmore come up to Parkhead Cross, and call upon the workers who were to be found at the street corner to come and give assistance to the horses and haul at a rope. Once upon the straight road the men and Beardmore would adjourn to the corner public houses, and all engage in drinks at Issac's expense. (Tom Bell, *Pioneering Days* (London, 1941))

Although the business of supplying the shipyards in the Clydeside burghs created the demand for much of Glasgow's industry, it was in many ways the variety that was important. Templeton's, already established as a carpet manufacturer in the 1830s, expanded to build the Doge's Palace factory on the edge of Glasgow Green in the 1890s. By the end of the century, the Sarcen Foundry had a 2,000-page catalogue for its ornamental architectural ironwork. The skyline of the northern industrial suburbs was marked by the locomotive works of Springburn and the St Rollox 'stalk', the giant chimney of Tennant's bleach works. There were many hundreds of smaller establishments. Yet Glasgow remained a trading city. As early as the 1840s, James Finlay pulled capital out of cotton manufacturing and moved into commodity trading in the Far East. The Royal Exchange was the focus for, among other things, the 'iron ring', the Scottish Pig Iron Association, trading in the semi-finished products of the region, and the Stock Exchange in St Vincent Street mediated world and regional investments.

Above all, Glasgow was a municipal place. By the end of the century it was an object of praise and investigation by US visitors as one of the best-managed cities in the world. In one enterprise after another, municipal action was preferred over private. The Loch Katrine water scheme, opened in 1859, not only provided clean water but the prestige of a royal visit. The City Improvement Trust was created by an Act of Parliament in 1866. Initially the policy of using a combination of state authority to clear unhealthy property and private enterprise to redevelop the site was a success, but in the slump of the 1880s this policy faltered and some 1,362 houses were built directly by the Trust itself, thus involving the municipal authorities in the provision of working-class housing. Kelvingrove Park had been bought by the city in 1853 and in 1893 became the site for a new art gallery part financed by the profits of the exhibitions. This choice of a west-end site marked the park and gallery as a service for the middle classes, who were also moving west with the trams. Meanwhile Glasgow Green, which served the east end, was being levelled with soil excavated from the railway development.

The city provided police and fire services, baths and lodging-houses, markets and wash-houses, but the most commanding statement of Glasgow as the municipal city was the construction of the City Chambers in George Square in 1883–9. The building cost £520,000 and was designed in an Italian Renaissance style with pediment carvings ranging from 'Trust' and 'Liberty' to a list of the possessions of the British Empire. There was no clearer statement of a well-managed trading city of the British Empire. There were no dominant personalities in this process. The publisher-printer, evangelical-temperance Lord Provosts, Blackie and Collins, did play a part, as did the formidable town clerk, J. D. Marwick, and the statistician medical officer of health, J. B. Russell, but municipal Glasgow was a middle-class élite collective. Much of this activity was about control of health, public order and fire. The Improvement Acts of the 1860s initiated the practice of ticketing houses with a metal plate pinned to the outside wall, stating the cubic capacity of the dwelling and the number permitted to live there. It placed the authoritarian Scottish city at the sharp edge of class conflict. Police were able to visit working-class housing at any time of the day or night to check on overcrowding.

Glasgow University was not a municipal enterprise but it was deeply enmeshed in the city's identity. In the 1870s, the new building at Gilmorehill replaced ancient and scruffy city-centre premises. The flamboyant, prominent building was 'in the domestic Early English Style with Scoto-Flemish features' (1870) with a spot of 'domestic gothic' round the back for the Students' Union (1886–90). The university was bound into the city not only by some interesting property deals with the nearby Kelvingrove Park, but also by the public activities of those like Professor Smart who provided the intellectual muscle for the campaign against the extension of municipal power and spending in the 1900s.

Scottish cities, like those throughout the industrializing world, were places of consumption and the flow of information. They were places where newspapers were published and read, where periodicals and books were delivered and distributed. The central areas of cities became identified not only with offices and financial institutions, but also with the major shopping parades, like Argyle Street in Glasgow and Princes Street in Edinburgh. Nearby was an expanding range of theatres and clubs. By the 1890s, the eating-houses of Argyle Street offered 'automatic music' and sixpenny 'ashet pies', as well as more traditional sheep's head and pig's trotters (not ubiquitous – only on Wednesdays). Other customers were moving to the tea-shops, like Kate Cranston's in Ingram Street. The growing numbers of retail establishments were not just for buying, but also for learning about what was available. Products were local as well as imported. This function was even more important in smaller towns. In 1866, J. & H. Rutherford in Kelso offered the new photographic product, the *carte de visite*, together with a French-made album to keep them in. James Henderson had a selection of Yorkshire and West of England cloth as well as Scotch tweeds. The owners of the Commercial House promised that customers would keep up with fashion because 'themselves as well as their milliner visit London frequently'. London was the reference point for fashion, although tea and coffee came from Edinburgh. Fruit trees and turnip seeds were on offer from local sources. This local–international tension was very clear in the work and fortunes of Charles Rennie Mackintosh (1868–1928), designer and architect associated with the Glasgow style, which was a distinctive part of a wider European movement identified with Vienna. His flowing lines and sparing use of ornamentation was given free expression in Miss Cranston's Tea Rooms and the Glasgow Art College, but his totalitarian approach to domestic design (shown, for example, in Hill House at Helensburgh) attracted few customers from a Glasgow middle class that liked to select from the lavish and eclectic products around them.

The way in which the Scottish city operated as a market-place and information centre is demonstrated in the lives of two men, John Inglis and William Anderson, who lived in Edinburgh at the end of the century. Inglis was a clerk. He was a regular reader of the *Scotsman*. Here he learned about wars in India and read Gladstone's speeches. He also took Bradlaugh's sceptical and atheistical *National Reformer*, which provided him with ammunition for frequent arguments over religion, especially with his Aunty Bell. In the shops of Princes Street and the Bridges, his wife learned about domestic products, and he purchased *A Child's History of England* and a map of Europe from Bartholomew's, the engravers. Very different was the experience of William Anderson, a coalman who worked for the Co-op. He had to use the active and informal second-hand furniture market, but he profited from the informal and organized sociability of the city. The Young Men's Guild at the church and the concert at the Free Gardeners' Institute were as important as the books he borrowed from the library. In Edinburgh, he learned enough to make plans for his emigration to Toronto in 1903.

The big towns dominate any history of modern Scotland. Not only did a large proportion of the population live in those towns, but they represented Scotland to the world. Edinburgh as capital and national symbol, Glasgow as industrial and commercial metropolis. The smaller urban centres displayed great variety. As we saw earlier, Motherwell grew rapidly as an iron and coal boom town in the 1860s. Economy and politics were dominated by major employers like the Colvilles, who arrived in 1872, and the Caledonian Railway Company, which set up its workshops there in 1863. Burgh status was gained in 1865, but services were limited and fragmented: as late as 1901, the municipality of Motherwell spent £75 per head per year compared with Glasgow's £368. In the 1860s, two of the industrial companies had their own reservoirs and there was no town hall until 1887. Civic and mediating institutions were few and often fragmented by religious division. Labour relations were confrontational, and marked by evictions, violent picketing, police baton charges and, on two occasions (one being the railway company strike of 1891), by military intervention. Smooth and all-encompassing as it appeared, the fabric of civil society also had rents and tears.

Company housing and paternalism, both harsh and benign, marked social relationships in many other smaller Scottish towns. The textile economy of central Fife was based upon coarse linens. John Fergus attracted and dominated the labour force at his mills in Prinlaws by his total control of housing and by keeping the government of the village separate from the adjacent burgh of Leslie. The burgh of Kirkcaldy grew from the 1860s on linoleum manufacture. In the varied urban economy, the Nairns, owners of the largest firm, could not be as direct as Fergus. They sought a more cultural domination through patronage of the Free Church and YMCA, and the financing of a local hospital and library, as well as the occasional gathering on the lawns of the Nairn family mansion.

Nearby St Andrews was very different. In the 1830s, an economy based on the port and the university was in decline. By the end of the century, St Andrews was an expanding tourist and retirement burgh. The foundation for tourism had been laid by golf (the Royal and Ancient was founded in 1754), a mention in poetry by Sir Walter Scott, and separate bathing-places for men and women, but real success came with the railway in 1858. Much groundwork had been done by Major Hugh Playfair, who had returned home from service with the East India Company and was elected Provost in 1842. Paving, draining and cleaning streets followed. He was active in promoting the new town hall (1858), in the improvement of the harbour and in laying out walks around the town for visitors seeking health and recreation.

Scotland's urban places, large and small, had much in common, though one source of their variation was a dependence on local power and initiative. Even national legislation, like Lindsay's Act of 1862, encouraged variety. Large and small were dominated by the tenement building form. This was a result not only of the widespread availability of good stone, but was also related to feuing and the relatively low income of the people. The tenement itself was to be influenced by the increasingly extensive and strict building regulations of the burghs.

Challenging the State

The years around the end of the century were ones of multiple crises which formed the basis for challenges to existing national identities and power structures. The Scottish Labour Party had been founded in 1888 on the back of Keir Hardie's failed campaign in the Mid Lanark by-election. In 1894 it merged with the Scottish side of the Independent Labour Party (ILP). The ILP was at the centre of a network of socialist or, rather, 'labourist' organizations which grafted themselves on to Scottish skilled working-class and radical culture. For most, 'socialism' was not some complex intellectual and ideological system, but a simple will to use any means possible to combat poverty. The retail cooperative, the Socialist Sunday School and the Clarion Cycling Club were linked by overlapping memberships and enthusiasms. They fought for attention in a political culture dominated by liberalism, and by the vast range of self-help Friendly Societies, with their insurance and convivial functions. The insistent clamour of the Orange Order and the demands of the Catholic Church and Irish National League occupied many from the Irish sections of the working class. But it was the culture and morality of the skilled working-class Protestant male that remained central. Nascent trade-unionism in Scotland was weak. The famous Fabian socialists Sidney and Beatrice Webb calculated that in 1892 5 per cent of the population of England and Wales were members of trade unions, but only 4 per cent in Scotland. In Scotland the trade unions tended to be small, local and craft-based. The trades council, organized on a local basis to represent unions, was the most influential agency. The Scottish Trades Union Congress was formed in 1898. The Scottish preference was for the local and for a Scottish-based governance for the 'interests' within civil society. This was a labour movement and not a labour party. There were brief periods of influence – a series of regional trade unions among the miners, ten 'stalwarts' elected to Glasgow Council in the 1890s – but it was not until 1906 that a Labour MP was elected from Scotland.

The power of liberalism, the counter-attractions of imperial loyalty especially during the Boer War, the preoccupation with Irish Nationalism, and the fact that large sections of the potential support for any labour politics simply did not have the vote, were all factors in this. Two issues were to drive forward the influence of labour politics. The first was housing. The Board of Trade inquiry of 1908 confirmed that in general Scots paid less for their housing than the English, and in return received much less. In most of the large towns, 60 to 70 per cent of the population lived in one- or two-roomed houses. In the one-roomed houses over 90 per cent shared a stairhead water-closet. The figure was 60 per cent for the 'double ends'. One result may have been the growth of skills and values of collective living, together with a marked dislike of rent-taking landlords issuing eviction orders, but the effect on health and well-being was becoming increasingly recognized. In 1904, Glasgow children who lived in 'single ends' were four inches smaller than those who lived in four-roomed houses. Their weight was over ten pounds less. Housing was one issue that brought John Wheatley into the ILP in 1907. He was born in Ireland and grew up in a pit village near Baillieston. The experience of poverty and the dust and dirt of the pit led him to a study of tuberculosis and to his advocacy of housing reform – his *Eight Pound Cottages for Glasgow Citizens* was published in 1913. In the process he moved from the Catholic Young Men's Society and the United Irish League to the ILP and the Catholic Socialist Society. On the way he had public arguments with priests over the compatibility of his Christianity and his socialism. On one occasion he was burned in effigy as a crowd gathered outside his house. Election as a city councillor in 1910 was to lead to his becoming Minister of Health in the first Labour government at Westminster.

Many elements of discontent were drawn together in a wave of strikes which reached a peak in 1910–14. The skilled male worker, who played such a vital role in binding Scottish working-class culture into liberalism (with the occasional enthusiasms of imperialist loyalty), was increasingly threatened by the pressures on that workplace autonomy and pride which was so important to his material welfare and self-esteem. John Hill, boilermakers' leader, wrote in *Forward* in 1908:

With improved machinery our craft is at a discount, and a boy from school now tends a machine which does the work of three men . . . a line from some well known liberal or tory certifying that you are not an agitator or a Socialist, is the chief recommendation in the shipbuilding and engineering trades.

The turret lathe, the universal drilling machine and the grinding machine were part of a wider threat. The new styles of management had an impact right across the labour force. Scientific management of 'Taylorism', involving speed-ups and the use of bonus systems to increase the intensity of labour, lay behind strikes at Singer's in Clydebank, at the Argyll Motor Works and even the Glasgow Tramways. Old systems of paternalism were breaking down. The Paisley cotton-thread manufacturers Clarks and Coats had been conflict-free zones through the use of selective pensions, nursery schools, dining halls, annual excursions and the subordinations of gender in a mainly female labour force. By 1907, ten years after the merger of the two firms, this had gone. The ILP was holding meetings in the town hall to protest against deteriorating conditions and advising in strike after strike. Many strikes started at shop-floor level over the reorganization of work and payment systems. There was nothing tidy about the causes of these disputes; indeed in Scotland strikes were more likely to be spontaneous and free of formal union organization. Syndicalism, a faith in industrial action for political change, was much talked about and probably inspired some activists. The ILP and its members were influential, with their pragmatic 'socialism'. Full order books after a decade of falling real wages was an opportunity not to be missed. The majority of disputes were about wages and ended in compromise. This was no revolution or even a major change in class relationships, but many boundaries of authority were challenged and crossed in the years before 1914. The stability produced by industrial expansion and paternalism were replaced by the tensions of class and nation.

Scotland the Nation

The type of politics needed for the governance of Scotland after 1914 was so different from the confident liberalism which had grown out of 1832 and which developed its own cultural identity throughout the next five decades. Home Rule was an issue of class and nation, rooted in comparisons with Ireland. Catholic and Protestant marked this divide, whereas our story began with the Disruption within the Church of Scotland. This starting-point was important not for the lasting effect it had on the religious history of Scotland, but for its enduring impact on the nation's governance. The theological differences were small in comparison with the change that marked 1843 – a change from a godly commonwealth (albeit a varied one) to the beginnings of the bureaucratic state.

The 1830s until the 1860s were decades which witnessed urban and rural dislocation but also the beginnings of recovery and stability. By undermining the coherence of the kirk as the nation's church, and by adding to the pressure on the parish system, the creation of the Free Church was the midwife of change in the governance of Scotland's civil society. It shattered the old bargain before adding a new and more extensive range of voluntary and charitable societies to deal with the social and economic crises that were so evident. Its origin was opposition to outside interference in spiritual matters. Its activities in civil society were immense, its church-building programme problematic but active. Unrelenting strain on the old parish system was also coming from population growth, rural–urban migration and economic change. From these angles the role of the parish was diminished and civil society was buttressed, but this was not to last. As the 1860s turned into the 1870s, the state at Westminster and its developing bureaucracy was increasingly the focus of Scotland's governance. Welfare and the education system were to be negotiated between the Scottish Office at Dover House in London and the Westminster parliament.

Gladstone's speeches in his Midlothian campaign of 1879 epitomized liberalism as a long-held cultural statement in Scotland. From that time it was clear that this coherence had all but passed. Liberalism had become a party-based political choice and one suffering a secular disruption over Irish Home Rule. In the 1890s the Scottish body politic was still providing safe seats for Liberal cabinet ministers who might not have retained any Scottish identity, but the Liberal hegemony broke when the Conservatives took thirty-six out of seventy seats in the General Election of 1900. Liberalism regained its ground in 1906 and on until 1918, but unionism had temporarily taken hold and labourism, socialism and nationalism were to be added to the political mix in this century.

What then of Scotland as a nation? It was a fluid society experiencing immense population change; it was an industrializing society and an urbanizing one. Migration retained the role of safety-valve throughout our story. Scotland was a modernizing society, but was still clinging to its pre-modern past. On the proposed purchase of Balmoral by Queen Victoria and Albert, the *Scotsman* in 1846 wished to find 'a royal lodge in a romantic setting . . . which Wales and Ireland have nothing to rival', while suggesting that there were a number of impoverished lairds keen to find a buyer for their houses. Of Victoria's proposed third visit to the Highlands in that year, the newspaper anticipated the day when it would soon be possible with railway developments for the queen to 'breakfast in Buckingham Palace and to sup overlooking the Cairngorms'. In 1848 central Scotland was connected to London by two main railways, and by 1851 the tracks had reached Aberdeen. These were changes which restructured Scottish society; they were changes which forced reflections on Scotland's governance to be made. It was the source both for setting the parameters of Scottish civil society and for directing Scottish national consciousness. The removal of the stamp tax in 1855 and the spread of the electric telegraph in the 1860s gave the Westminster debates an immediacy beyond London that had hitherto been lacking, however mystifying the technology, as illustrated by Archibald Geikie, spinning once more the parochial Scot:

A West Highlander who had been to Glasgow and was consequently supposed to have got to the bottom of the mystery, was asked to explain it. 'Weel', said he, 'it's no easy to explain what you will no be understandin'. But I'll tell you what it's like. If you could stretch my collie dog frae Oban to Tobermory, an' if you wass to clap its head in Oban, an' it waggit its tail in Tobermory, or if I wass to tread on its tail in Oban an' it squaked in Tobermory – that's what the telegraph is like.'

The *Scotsman* (1855) and the *Glasgow Herald* (1859) moved to daily editions, others moved from weekly editions to publication on two or three days a week. A decade earlier twenty-five Scottish burghs had their own newspaper; five years later, the number had doubled. As the trend developed, still it was the village, the town and the city, the locality, which kept a close tie on Scotland's governance.

Scotland had a remarkably confident national identity. Duality and multiplicity have come to characterize the understanding of identity in Scotland today; are we guilty of historicism to suggest it was precisely such a duality which was then the essence of 'Scottishness' in the period 1832–1914? Evidence of coexistence is often stated: the Jacobite heart and the Unionist head of Sir Walter Scott; the order from the War Office in 1881 that it be appropriate for all the Lowland regiments to wear tartan trews. Often this is taken as evidence of the failure of Scottish people to untangle their identity from the Victorian 'economic miracle', which was British, from the British constitution, which was English, and a nationality that was underdeveloped or 'bought off'. What was stopping that nationality being either one or the other? Nothing and everything is our answer. The dual existence of Scottish and British national identities was not regarded as weakness by contemporaries.

Scotland in the 1830s had lost the radical tinge that had been there a decade before in the radical wars, although loyalty to English constitutionalism – to the Magna Carta – was part of the workers' demands then, as it was for the trades who campaigned for the franchise. English constitutional history was used as a new starting-point in Whig intellectual writings to explain Scotland's progress and the centrality of Protestantism within it. It also furnished an analysis whereby loyalty to the Hanoverian monarchy and to parliament could be accommodated and indeed celebrated in the discourse of Scottish national identity. Prince Albert was patron of the Waverley Ball in London to raise money for the construction of the Scott Monument (inaugurated in 1846). To free the debt under which Scott was burdened and to save Abbotsford from his creditors, 'it was an English suggestion' that a London committee be formed to raise the necessary subscriptions. Loyalty to the monarchy had been expressed at the meetings and celebrations of the National Association for the Vindication of Scottish Rights in the 1850s. Its petitions to Victoria were humbly sent and its secretary, James Grant, enlisted the support of the Prince of Wales in his application to become Lyon King-of-Arms. The speech by Dr Charles Rogers, secretary of the National Wallace Monument Movement, saw this monument's inauguration as a day for Britain, 'for we are celebrating the memory of a chief who made Scotland a nation, placed a new dynasty upon the English throne, and, under Providence, was the means of uniting these kingdoms together on equal terms, and with equal rights'. The Scottish Home Rule Association in the 1880s made the demand for a legislature an issue over purely Scottish questions, responsible to an executive government and the crown, and so it was hoped to maintain the integrity of the empire.

When profits from overseas trade waned, so a reassessment of Scottish national identity followed. The 1911 exhibition in Glasgow was a celebration of empire, but it was Scotland's past – and its future – which was its main preoccupation. The aim was to fund the endowment of the chair of Scottish history at Glasgow University: 'the time had fully arrived when Scottish history should be placed on a different plane from that which it had hitherto occupied in the education of the rising generations'. This move followed a range of more scholarly societies which had been formed in the 1880s to document Scotland's history: the Scottish History Society, the Historical Association of Scotland and the Scottish Text Society, along with a chair in Scottish history in Edinburgh, established in 1901. Nationalist writers followed this lead, but the stability of Britain was retained as an essential patriotic statement. Lewis Spence, who was to go on to form the breakaway Scottish National Movement in 1926, presented a biography of William Wallace to a series of 'Little Stories of Great Lives', published by Oxford

University Press in 1919. The series included biographies of Robert the Bruce, Joan of Arc, Francis Drake, Napoleon, Lord Nelson and Lord Kitchener. Spence could not ignore the context of his times: Britain at war – as an island – against a foreign foe. 'Never, perhaps, in the history of our island has the spirit of patriotism been so deeply aroused as during the years of the Great War.' This duality was Scottish national identity. Like all such declarations it was rooted in the governance of the nation. The extent and the vociferousness of the demands upon the Westminster state was a function of perceptions of freedom and prosperity (economic, social, political). The identity of the Scottish nation was formed at its point of governance – its civil society.

Bibliographical Essay

General

For many topics in this chapter, see W. H. Fraser and R. J. Morris (eds.), *People and Society in Scotland*, vol. 2: *1830–1914* (Edinburgh, 1990). The best single-authored social history for this period is T. C. Smout, *A Century of the Scottish People, 1830–1950* (London, 1986); a very accessible read is S. and O. Checkland. *Industry and Ethos: Scotland, 1832–1914* (London, 1984).

Civil Society

Ernest Gellner, *Conditions of Liberty* (London, 1994) and John A. Hall, *Civil Society: Theory, History and Comparison* (Cambridge, 1995) are the best introductions to the idea of civil society which pervades this chapter. A reading will show why the concept is so important to understanding nineteenth-century Scotland. On associations and voluntary societies, see R. J. Morris, 'Clubs, Societies and Associations', in F. M. L. Thompson (ed.), *The Cambridge Social History of Britain, 1750–1950*, vol. 3 (Cambridge, 1990), 395–443.

Religion

On the Disruption, the essays in S. J. Brown and M. Fry (eds.), *Scotland in the Age of the Disruption* (Edinburgh, 1993) provide the best analysis. For the religious history of nineteenth-century Scotland, with a strong emphasis on the social history, see C. G. Brown, 'Religion, Class and Church Growth', in Fraser and Morris (eds.), *People and Society in Scotland*, vol. 2, 310–35, and C. G. Brown, *Religion and Society in Scotland since 1707* (Edinburgh, 1997). A superb account of the life of Thomas Chalmers comes from S. J. Brown, *Thomas Chalmers and the Godly Commonwealth in Scotland* (Oxford, 1982). Still the best analysis of the Disruption in terms of the class dimension is A. Allan MacLaren, *Religion and Social Class: The Disruption Years in Aberdeen* (London, 1974).

National Identity

For the nation and nationalism in Scotland, see R. J. Morris and G. Morton, 'Where Was Nineteenth-Century Scotland?', *Scottish Historical Review* LXXIV, 1 (April 1994), 89–99; G. Morton, 'The Most Efficacious Patriot: the Heritage of William Wallace in Nineteenth-century Scotland', *Scottish Historical Review* LXXVII, 2 (November 1998), 224–51; G. Morton, *Unionist-Nationalism: Governing Urban Scotland, 1830–1860* (East Linton, 1999). C. Kidd, *Subverting Scotland's Past: Scottish Whig Historians and the Creation of an Anglo-British Identity, 1689–c. 1830* (Cambridge, 1993) explains the origins of the nineteenth-century interpretation of the Union. The best bridge from the nineteenth century to the twentieth century can be found in D. McCrone, *Understanding Scotland: The Sociology of a Stateless Nation* (London, 1992). A good source of ideas on the multiplicity of identities in a nation comes from T. C. Smout, 'Perspectives on the Scottish Identity', *Scottish Affairs* 6 (Winter, 1994), 101–13. On the activities of Scots overseas, see George Fraser Black, *Scotland's Mark on America* (New York, 1921).

Demography

For a discussion of population, see Michael Anderson and Donald Morse, 'High Fertility, High Emigration, Low Nuptiality: Adjustment Processes in Scotland's Demographic Experience, 1861–1914', *Population Studies* 47 (1993), 5–25 and 319–43; also M. Anderson, 'Population and Family Life', in A. Dickson and J. H. Treble (eds.), *People and Society in Scotland*, vol. 3: *1914–1990* (Edinburgh, 1992), 12–47; Anderson and Morse in Fraser and Morris (eds.), *People and Society in Scotland*, vol. 2, 8–45; R. A. Houston, 'The Demographic Regime, 1760–1830', in T. M. Devine and R. Mitchison (eds.), *People and Society in Scotland*, vol. 1: *1760–1830* (Edinburgh, 1988), 9–26; and R. I. Woods, 'The Population of Britain in the Nineteenth Century', in M. Anderson (ed.), *British Population History from the Black Death to the Present Day* (Cambridge, 1996), 281–357.

Towns and Governance

For towns, see R. J. Morris, 'Urbanisation in Scotland', in Fraser and Morris (eds.), *People and Society in Scotland*, vol. 2, 73–102. See also R. Duncan, *Steelopolis: The Making of Motherwell, c. 1750–1939* (Motherwell, 1991); W. H. Fraser and I. Maver (eds.), *Glasgow*, vol. 2: *1830–1912* (Manchester, 1996); J. M. Gilbert (ed.), *Flower of the Forest, Selkirk: A New History* (Selkirk, 1985); R. Rodger, 'The Law and Urban Change', *Urban History Yearbook* (1979), 77–91. Important for understanding Glasgow's self-image, and for a cultural translation of the ideals of empire, we recommend the work of P. and J. Kinchin, *Glasgow's Great Exhibitions, 1888–1988* (Glasgow, 1988). For an important part of the migration story, C. W. J. Withers, *Urban Highlanders: Highland–Lowland Migration and Urban Gaelic Culture, 1700–1900* (East Linton, 1998) is comprehensive.

To understand the mechanics behind the formation of local government in the towns and counties, and for the links to Westminster, the best introductions remain W. E. Whyte, *Local Government in Scotland, with complete statutory references* (2nd edn., London, 1936), and W. C. Dundas, *Development of Local Government in Counties in Scotland* (London, 1942). For useful case studies of urban government in action, and for giving a little colour to this often dry topic, see J. Cranna, *Fraserburgh: Past and Present* (Aberdeen, 1914); the essays contained in G.

Gordon and B. Dicks (eds.), *Scottish Urban History* (Aberdeen, 1988), especially Hume's work on transportation; J. S. Smith and D. Stevenson (eds.), *Aberdeen in the Nineteenth Century: The Making of the Modern City* (Aberdeen, 1988); N. Morgan and R. H. Trainor, 'The Dominant Classes', in Fraser and Morris (eds.), *People and Society in Scotland*, vol. 2, 103–37; G. K. Neville, *The Mother Town: Civic Ritual, Symbol and Experience in the Borders of Scotland* (Oxford, 1994); L. Miskell, C. A. Whatley, and R. Harris (eds.), *Victorian Dundee: Image and Realities* (East Linton, 2000); W. H. Fraser and C. H. Lee (eds.), *Aberdeen, 1800 to 2000: A New History* (East Linton, 2000).

Industry and Economy

On industry and social relationships, see Alan Campbell, *The Lanarkshire Miners* (Edinburgh, 1979); W. W. Knox, *Hanging by a Thread: The Scottish Cotton Industry, c. 1850–1914* (Preston, 1995); J. Smith, 'Class, Skill and Sectarianism in Glasgow and Liverpool', in R. J. Morris (ed.), *Class, Power and Social Structure in British Nineteenth-century Towns* (Leicester, 1986), 158–215; R. J. Morris and J. Smyth, 'Paternalism as an Employer Strategy, 1800–1960', in J. Rubery and F. Wilkinson (eds.), *Employer Strategy and the Labour Market* (Oxford, 1994), 195–225; W. H. Fraser, *A History of British Trade Unionism, 1700–1998* (Basingstoke, 1999).

For introductions to Scotland's economic history during the industrial period, see R. H. Campbell, *Scotland Since 1707: The Rise of an Industrial Society* (2nd edn. Edinburgh, 1985); S. and O. Checkland, *Industry and Ethos*; H. Hamilton, *The Economic Evolution of Scotland in the 18th and 19th Centuries* (London, 1933); C. A. Whatley, *The Industrial Revolution in Scotland* (Cambridge, 1997); William Knox, *Industrial Nation: Work, Culture and Society in Scotland, 1800 – present* (Edinburgh, 1999); and J. Scott and M. Hughes, *The Anatomy of Scottish Capital: Scottish Companies and Scottish Capital, 1900–1979* (London, 1980) offers persuasive evidence on networks among Scotland's business leaders. C. H. Lee, *Scotland and the United Kingdom: The Economy and the Union in the Twentieth Century* (Manchester, 1995) gives a very instructive analysis of Scotland's economic performance within the framework of Union.

The classic account of the Scottish coal industry in a United Kingdom context is by H. Stanley Jevons, *The British Coal Trade* (London, 1915), which should be used in conjunction with the National Coal Board's *A Short History of the Coal Mining Industry* (1958). Regional economic histories are found in, especially, G. Gordon, 'Industrial Development c. 1750–1980', and in G. Whittington and I. D. Whyte (eds.), *An Historical Geography of Scotland* (London, 1983), 165–90, but see also R. L. Mackie, 'Industry in Kirkcaldy: Mapping the Structure of Business in Twentieth-Century Scotland', *Scottish Economic and Social History* 18, 1 (1998), 61–84, along with other contributions to this issue of the journal; J. S. Marshall, *The Life and Times of Leith* (Edinburgh, 1986); R. E. Tyson, 'The Economy of Aberdeen', in J. S. Smith and D. Stevenson (eds.), *Aberdeen in the Nineteenth Century: The Making of the Modern City* (Aberdeen, 1988); and the short but useful introduction to an insightful contemporary diarist by C. A. Whatley (ed.), *Diary of John Sturrock, Millwright, Dundee 1864–65* (East Linton, 1996), is well worth visiting.

Agriculture and Rural Society

The considerable literature on agriculture and rural society includes: I. Carter, *Farm Life in Northeast Scotland, 1840–1914* (Edinburgh, 1979); E. Richards, *The Leviathan of Wealth: The Sutherland Fortune in the Industrial Revolution* (London, 1973); J. Hunter, *The Making of the Crofting Community* (Edinburgh, 1976); T. M. Devine (ed.), *Farm Servants and Labour in Lowland Scotland, 1770–1914* (Edinburgh, 1984); T. M. Devine, *The Great Highland Famine* (Edinburgh, 1988); T. M. Devine, *Clanship to Crofters' War: The Social Transformation of the Scottish Highlands* (Manchester, 1994); A. Fenton and B. Walker, *The Rural Architecture of Scotland* (Edinburgh, 1981); E. A. Cameron, *Land for the People? The British Government and the Scottish Highlands, c. 1880–1925* (East Linton, 1996); and for the importance of the Highlands to Scottish national identity, see C. W. J. Withers, 'The Historical Creation of the Scottish Highlands', in I. Donnachie and C. A. Whatley (eds.). *The Manufacture of Scottish History* (Edinburgh, 1992), 143–56.

Education

For an invaluable revision of the polemic on Scottish education, see R. D. Anderson, *Education and Opportunity in Victorian Scotland: Schools and Universities* (Oxford, 1983). A number of very useful contributions can be found in W. M. Humes and H. M. Paterson (eds.), *Scottish Culture and Scottish Education, 1800–1980* (Edinburgh, 1983); while important work on the gender dimension comes from Helen Corr, 'An Exploration into Scottish Education', in Fraser and Morris (eds.), *People and Society in Scotland*, vol. 2, 290–309. A contemporary analysis is to be found in C. Mackay, *The Education of the People, and the Necessity for the Establishment of a National System* (Glasgow, 1846).

Gender

The best histories of women in work and society in this period are: E. Gordon and E. Breitenbach (eds.), *The World is Ill-Divided: Women's Work in Scotland in the Nineteenth and Early Twentieth Centuries* (Edinburgh, 1990); E. Gordon, *Women and the Labour Movement in Scotland, 1850–1914* (Oxford, 1991); E. Breitenbach and E. Gordon (eds.), *Out of Bounds: Women in Scottish Society, 1800–1945* (Edinburgh, 1992); and E. Gordon, 'Women's spheres', in Fraser and Morris (eds.), *People and Society in Scotland*, vol. 2, 206–35.

Politics

A starting-point for the political history of this period remains I. G. C. Hutchison, *A Political History of Scotland 1832–1914: Parties, Elections and Issues* (Edinburgh, 1986). A useful contrast can be found in M. Fry, *Patronage and Principle: A Political History of Modern Scotland* (Aberdeen, 1987). Another political history, with a good focus on Aberdeen, comes from M. Dyer, *Men of Property and Intelligence: The Scottish Electoral System prior to 1884* (Aberdeen, 1996), and M. Dyer, *Capable Citizens and Improvident Democrats: The Scottish Electoral System, 1884–1929* (Aberdeen, 1996). Important analysis of the political system includes J. Brash, *Scottish Electoral Politics, 1832–1854* (Edinburgh, 1974); one of the most visited of contemporary sources is the *Journal of Henry Cockburn, being a continuation of the Memorials of his Time, 1831–1854*, 2 vols. (Edinburgh, 1874). The imperial dimension to Scottish politics and society is found in R. J. Finlay, 'The Rise and Fall of Popular Imperialism in Scotland, 1850–1950', *Scottish Geographical Magazine* 113, 1 (1997), 13–21; J. M. MacKenzie, *Propaganda and Empire: The Manipulation of British Public Opinion, 1880–1960* (Manchester, 1984). The Orange Order is best located in E. McFarland, *Protestants First: Orangism in Nineteenth-Century Scotland* (Edinburgh, 1990), and the essays collected in C. M. M. Macdonald (ed.), *Unionist Scotland, 1800–1997* (Edinburgh, 1998) and I. S. Wood (ed.), *Scotland and Ulster* (Edinburgh, 1994), which add to our understanding of the links between the politics of Scotland and Ireland. The Chartist movement can be located in two standard accounts: A. Wilson, *The Chartist Movement in Scotland* (Manchester, 1970) and L. C. Wright, *Scottish Chartism* (Edinburgh, 1953). For the end-of-century labour movement, see A. McKinlay and R. J. Morris (eds.), *The ILP on Clydeside, 1893–1932: from Foundation to Disintegration* (Manchester, 1991); William Kenefick and Arthur McIvor (eds.), *Roots of Red Clydeside 1910–1914: Labour Unrest and Industrial Relations in West Scotland* (Edinburgh, 1996).

Poverty and Welfare

Our understanding of poverty and welfare comes from R. A. Cage, *The Scottish Poor Law 1745–1845* (Edinburgh, 1981); M. A. Crowther, 'Poverty, health and welfare', in Fraser and Morris (eds.), *People and Society in Scotland*, vol. 2, 265–89; M. Flinn (ed.), *Report on the Sanitary Condition of the Labouring Population of Great Britain by Edwin Chadwick, 1842* (Edinburgh, 1965); M. J. Daunton, *Progress and Poverty: An Economic and Social History of Britain, 1700–1850* (Oxford, 1995); I. Levitt and T. C. Smout, *The State of the Scottish Working Class in 1843* (Edinburgh, 1979); L. Mahood, *The Magdalenes: Prostitution in the Nineteenth Century* (London, 1990). A classic contemporary account is William Tait, *Magdalenism: An Enquiry into the Extent, Causes and Consequences of Prostitution in Edinburgh* (2nd edn. Edinburgh, 1842).

Popular Culture

Aspects of Scottish society and culture are found in T. Cowan (ed.), *The People's Past* (Edinburgh, 1991); T. C. Smout and S. Wood, *Scottish Voices, 1745–1960* (London, 1990); W. Donaldson, *Popular Literature in Victorian Scotland* (Aberdeen, 1986); E. Casciani, *O! How we danced! The History of Ballroom Dancing in Scotland* (Edinburgh, 1994); J. H. Littlejohn, *The Scottish Music Hall, 1880–1990* (Wigtown, 1990); Bill Murray, *The Old Firm: Sectarianism, Sport and Society in Scotland* (Edinburgh, 1984); H. J. Crawford, *French Travellers in Scotland* (Stirling, 1939); M. D. Steuart, *The Romance of the Edinburgh Streets* (London, 4th edn., 1936, first published 1925).

Where possible we have made use of some wonderful reminiscences, autobiographies and biographies. We recommend: Alexander Somerville, *The Autobiography of a Working Man* (first published in 1848; London, 1951); The Shadow (Alexander Brown), *Glasgow's Midnight Scenes and Social Photographs* (1858), with an introduction by John F. McCaffrey (Glasgow, 1976); A. Smith, *A Summer in Skye* (London, 1865); Sir Archibald Geikie, *Scottish Reminiscences* (Glasgow, 1904); R. H. Bruce Lockhart, *My Scottish Youth* (London, 1937); and Ian MacDougall, *Mungo Mackay and the Green Table: Newtongrange Miners Remember* (East Linton, 1995).

7

The Twentieth Century, 1914–1979

JOHN FOSTER

I mich ha'e been contentit wi' the Rose
Gin I had ony reason to suppose
That what the English dae can e'er make guid
For what Scots dinna – and first and foremost should.
— Hugh MacDiarmid, 1926

Shortly after the outbreak of the First World War the Prime Minister, H. H. Asquith, received an urgent communication from two Scottish bankers. One was Lord Rosebery, Governor of the British Linen Bank and a former Liberal Prime Minister; the other was Lord Balfour of Burleigh, Governor of the Bank of Scotland and a previous Conservative Secretary of State for Scotland. They told him that if the London banks were given the right to expand their note issue, the Scottish banks must have this right too. The Prime Minister agreed. Asquith, as it happened, was married into the Tennant family, the owners of Scotland's biggest chemical firm and partners in the combine which held the British Empire patent rights for dynamite. He sat for a Scottish constituency. On the opposition benches the leader was Andrew Bonar Law. He was a director of another Scottish bank, the Clydesdale, and partner in a family steel-broking firm in Glasgow. The firm's principal business was the import of the steel plate used for the great armoured battleships built on the Clyde.

The first years of the twentieth century marked the zenith of power and influence for the owners of Scotland's capital. They controlled the biggest concentration of heavy industry in Britain and dominated world shipbuilding. Their wealth, and the existence of a separate Scottish banking system, enabled them to command their own vehicles for international investment. From Glasgow, Edinburgh and Dundee a network of control spread across the globe, covering shipping lines, railway companies, mining ventures and great tracts of farmland in North and South America, Australasia and South Africa. If, for an economy which comprised only 10 per cent of Britain's GDP, the Scots appear to have exercised disproportionate influence at Westminster, it was at least in part because they felt they had to. Scotland's exports depended on Britain's foreign and colonial policies. And it was the British state which consumed the most critical part of Scotland's domestic produce: materials of war.

The history of twentieth-century Scotland revolves around the question of how this tight integration into British power structures has changed – and why. At the end of the century the Prime Minister was also a Scot by origin and education. His principal ministers, in the Treasury, Foreign Office and Ministry of Defence, were Scots too. But their presence owed nothing to the influence of Scottish business. Scotland's productive resources were no longer owned from within the country. The capital required for the extraction of oil, the production of electronics and information technology equipment and even for the drinks industry, was controlled externally. Where Scotland once enjoyed industrial pre-eminence, there was either little left, as in steel, coal, or heavy engineering, or, as in the case of shipbuilding, what remained was controlled from outside.

Did it matter? Such shifts in ownership might be seen as the common condition of humanity in the age of a global economy: the fact that an industry was controlled from elsewhere might be of little concern compared with whether or not it existed at all. Moreover, other things had changed also. Previously, it was a minute élite which controlled the Scottish economy. By the end of the century it could be argued that the Scottish people as a whole had gained something far more important: the right collectively, in their own parliament, to form their views as a people. But was this really so? This question about the practical content of power will be the main focus of this chapter. Throughout most of the twentieth century there was a powerful sense of unfinished business in Scotland: that the country had not secured the political institutions it needed – and that such institutions were needed because of Scotland's deepening experience of economic and cultural dependence. As the century ended and Scotland's parliament took office, this tension between economic and political power, between power possessed and power needed, remained. Particular concern in the following sections will be with the kinds of power exercised in and over Scotland during the past century, how this exercise of power has changed and the way it has affected the lives, social organization and identities of the Scottish people. We will begin by looking at the period just before the First World War.

Prelude

Walk down Hope Street in Glasgow and look up six storeys to the roof of the Central Station Hotel. The spectacular skyline of towers, turrets and cornices was designed towards the end of the nineteenth century by Sir Rowand Anderson, then Scotland's premier architect. His work reflected the endeavour to create an architecture that was authentically Scottish yet also founded in the canons of European tradition. For Anderson, being Scottish meant being pre-modern. His designs flow from his own meticulous drawings of Scotland's medieval buildings later incorporated in the National Art Survey of Scotland. They reflect solidity, power, the richness of authentic materials, gothic splendour modified by the elegance of the early Renaissance. The designs from Anderson's architectural practice dominated the streets of Scotland's cities as they were rebuilt in the 1890s and 1900s. Edinburgh University's McEwan Hall, Dundee University's science buildings, the mock baronial houses of Colinton, the Conservative Club in Edinburgh's Princes Street and the Marquess of Bute's mansion at Mount Stewart all stood witness to the wealth that created them. The Central Station Hotel stood witness to something more. It was the place where the wealth was divided, the favoured meeting-place for Clydeside's company directors and shareholders.

Walk another 300 metres south and cross the Clyde and you will be on the site of what were some of the worst slums in Europe. These grey stone tenements, four storeys high, were endlessly subdivided. Families lived one to a room with limited access to water. Infectious diseases, especially tuberculosis, were rife. Still in 1900 one child in six died before its fifth birthday. Families lived here because they could afford no better. Such poverty could also be found in London and Manchester. What was different about Scotland was how many of its families lived like this. Well over a half of Scotland's families lived in one or two rooms, compared with less than a quarter in England.

This brings us to the central issue for the period before 1914: how far was Scotland's own indigenous industrial power already unsustainable – dependent on levels of internal and external exploitation that were unlikely to continue?

The 1907 census of production shows Scotland to have had a relatively diversified and mature economy. There were sophisticated niche markets in textiles: sewing thread, jute, carpets, rubberized fabrics and waterproofing. Printing did well too: school primers, novels, Bibles in particular. In food and drink Scotland had moved beyond whisky, beer and oatmeal to the export of jams and preserves from the fruit farms of the Clyde and Tay valleys, confectioneries from Dundee, herring from the east coast, cheese from the dairy farms of Galloway and the Borders. Specialist firms originally supplying medical and scientific equipment to Scotland's great teaching hospitals and universities now had markets across the empire. Scotland's working class itself had generated mass demands. Cheap white bread, margarine, soft drinks and mass-produced clothes were required for the second most urbanized population in the world.

Yet, despite all this, Scotland's economy remained inextricably tied up with heavy industry. Per head of population there were 13 per cent more coal miners than the British average, 15 per cent more engineers, 20 per cent more steel workers, 35 per cent more shipbuilders. Almost half a million workers across the central belt depended in some way on the manufacturing of iron and steel goods. When shipbuilding went into recession, and output fell by up to 40 per cent as it did between 1903 and 1905 and again between 1907 and 1910, the consequences were felt across Scotland. The tide of recession would roll back from the shipbuilding townships along the Clyde to the great iron and steel forges of east Glasgow and north Lanarkshire, and then on to the mining communities of rural Ayrshire, Stirlingshire and Fife. Conversely, when expansion returned, the consequences would be similarly comprehensive. Skilled workers no longer sought work outside Scotland, and new raw recruits streamed into central Scotland from the country's rural hinterland and from Ireland.

However, this does not really answer our question. A lot of heavy industry did not necessarily mean weakness. Concentration can also be a basis for growth. The question is: was it a vulnerable dependence – was Scotland's heavy industry inherently likely to be less robust and long-lasting than that of the Ruhr or Pennsylvania?

Overall the answer seems to be yes: not inevitably so, but likely in the circumstances. Three factors came together. One was the market. Scotland's heavy industry depended on a particularly narrow range of products, and the market for these products, ships, engines and locomotives, was highly cyclical and tied to fluctuations in export demand. In the minds of the owners this created a constant fear of over-capacity and over-investment. The second factor was labour. Unskilled workers were cheap and plentiful – thanks largely to the stream of immigrants. Reliance on labour-intensive production was therefore an ever-tempting alternative to investment and innovation. The third factor returns us to the issue of power: control over how to invest the often very high profits and, no less important, the locations where alternative investment might be made. Scotland's heavy industry was controlled by a relatively small group of families, no more than two or three dozen. Recent research has shown how tightly they were interlinked, already before 1914, with the Scottish banks and financial sector. Their privileged access to the British state and the externalized character of the Scottish economy gave them lucrative opportunities for investing overseas instead of at home. These opportunities were taken. The Dundee-based Fleming trusts and the Edinburgh trusts such as Scottish American Investment used monies in large part disinvested from industry and commerce in central Scotland and the east coast. By the end of the century the peculiarly Scottish institution of the investment trust had enabled Scotland to export more capital per head than any other part of Britain – £110 as against the English average of £90.

For the owners of Scotland's heavy industry such overseas investment made sound business sense. It avoided over-capacity in face of volatile markets, and enabled them to maximize short-term income both in their Scottish holdings and those abroad. For the industries themselves it was not necessarily the wisest strategy. Labour-intensive production ultimately meant relying on lower wages to compensate for less and worse technology. This tactic was no longer coupled, as it had been at an earlier stage of the industry's history, with innovation in *capital*-saving technology. Nor was investment

1. (*left*) Portrait of William Cumming, piper to the Laird of Grant, by Richard Waitt, 1714. Although raiding and warfare were a significant part of life in the Highlands, its lairds were patrons of the arts, encouraging a vivid Gaelic culture of poetry and song which spread despite the monarchy's attempts to suppress the influence of the Lordship of the Isles.

2. (*right*) Cast of a grave slab found at Finlaggan, dating from the mid sixteenth century. The stone bears an effigy of Donald McGill'easbuig, crown tenant of Finlaggan in Islay. Dressed in West Highland armour with a galley beneath his feet, he was probably a mercenary leader in Ireland. He holds a *claymore*, the fearsome Highland weapon of choice, a double-handed sword whose blade could exceed one and a half metres.

The Highlanders: Fighting Men

3. Highland dirks of the seventeenth and eighteenth centuries: all-purpose daggers which it was necessary to keep to hand at all times.

1. In the early seventeenth century, in the absence of patronage by the Presbyterian Church, only the nobility tended to commission art illustrating scenes from the Scriptures. Though kept behind closed doors, these images were as vibrant as anything to come out of the European Renaissance. This scene of Abraham's sacrifice of Isaac, *c.* 1605–27, was part of a painted ceiling at the great hall of Dean House in Edinburgh, home of the Lord Provost.

Spreading the Message of the Lord

2. (*right*) Humble pewter communion plate and beakers, 1671. Communion vessels that could accommodate the needs of the entire congregation were an essential requirement of post-Reformation services, but often the church was too poor to afford large quantities of silver, or items had had to be melted down for war funds.

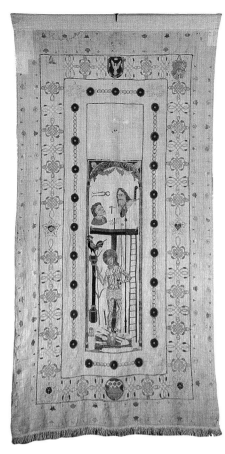

3. Pebble marked with a simple cross by a pilgrim to St Ninian's Cave, Wigtownshire. St Ninian, a bishop based at Whithorn in the fifth century, is claimed to have used the cave as a hermitage. His message, pre-dating that of St Columba, played a significant role in the spread of Christianity in southern and eastern Scotland. For centuries, pilgrims visiting the cave carved crosses into the rock-face and stones to record their visit.

4. (*left*) The Fetternear banner is the only known church banner to have survived from Medieval Scotland. Dating from *c.* 1520, it is thought that the Confraternity of the Holy Blood of St Giles' Collegiate Kirk, Edinburgh, may have used it in their church processions. The embroiderer has used graphic detail to illustrate Christ's Passion, bordering the image with Celtic knot-work patterns.

5. (*below*) Mask and wig of leather and hair used by the seventeenth-century Ayrshire minister Alexander Peden as a disguise when preaching at outdoor services for fellow Covenanters, which had been outlawed by King Charles I. When not preaching, Peden would travel undercover between sites, sleeping in caves and shelters to avoid capture.

6. (*left*) A Pictish cross slab of AD 700–900 found near the churchyard of Papil on the island of Burra, Shetland. The carvings reveal an intriguing fusion of old and new beliefs. A Celtic cross surmounts four monks with crosiers. However, at the bottom two sinister figures with birds' beaks peck at a human head, a device often seen in Pre-Christian art.

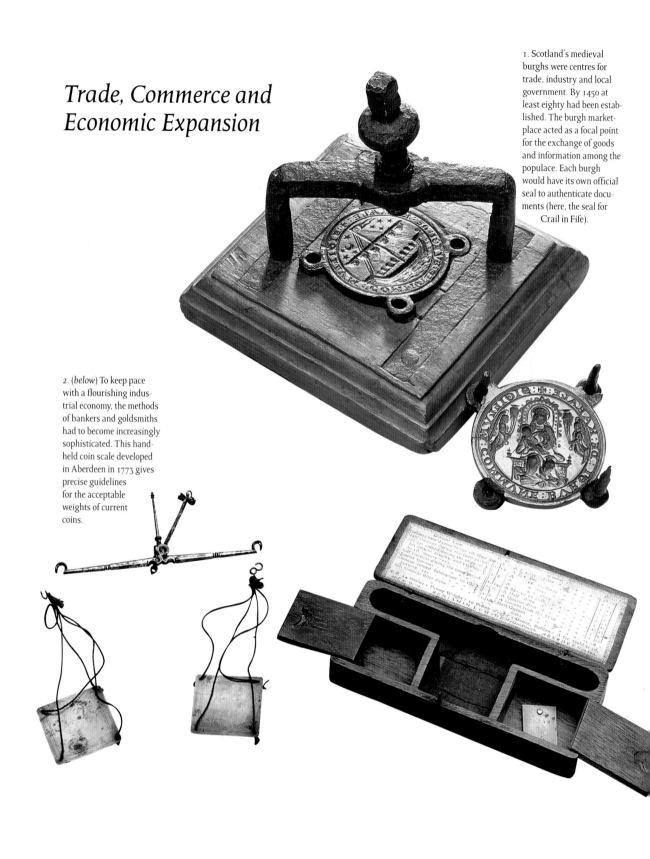

Trade, Commerce and Economic Expansion

1. Scotland's medieval burghs were centres for trade, industry and local government. By 1450 at least eighty had been established. The burgh marketplace acted as a focal point for the exchange of goods and information among the populace. Each burgh would have its own official seal to authenticate documents (here, the seal for Crail in Fife).

2. (*below*) To keep pace with a flourishing industrial economy, the methods of bankers and goldsmiths had to become increasingly sophisticated. This handheld coin scale developed in Aberdeen in 1773 gives precise guidelines for the acceptable weights of current coins.

3. Early banknotes: £12 (20 shillings sterling) notes issued by (*left above*) the Bank of Scotland in 1723, and (*left below*) the Royal Bank of Scotland in 1750. Eclipsing England, Scotland pioneered the concepts of branch banking, the wider acceptance of banknotes and the overdraft.

4. (*above*) The banner of St Cuthbert's Lodge of Free Gardeners. Started up in 1843, this was one of many national Friendly Societies popularized in the nineteenth century, with the intention of helping and insuring members within that trade and their families if they fell into financial need. Ritual and regalia borrowed some of the iconography of the Masonic Orders: note here the masonic eye alongside the ubiquitous thistle.

1. A Baird television receiver, or 30-line Model A 'televisor', of 1930. Television was invented by the Scot John Logie Baird in 1925, and demonstrated to the world at large the following year.

Signals and Connections

2. The physicist Sir William Thomson (later Lord Kelvin) was one of Scotland's ground-breaking scientific pion-eers, knighted in 1874 for his success in developing electric telegraphy to link Britain with America. His mirror galvanometer, shown here, measured the electric current passing through insulated marine cable.

THE FORTH BRIDGE

ON THE

LONDON AND NORTH EASTERN RAILWAY OF ENGLAND AND SCOTLAND

3. Railway poster of 1928 promoting the LNER's overnight service to north-eastern Scotland. The silhouette of the Forth Rail Bridge is one of the principal icons of Scotland. The immense project to span the Firth commenced in 1882, and provided jobs for many thousands of men. The radical steel cantilever construction, devised by the civil engineer Benjamin Baker, was designed to carry a double-track railway line and a road with the ultimate stability.

5. Medal struck to commemorate the grand opening of the Forth Bridge in 1890.

4. (*left*) A ticket for the Glasgow and Garnkirk railway, opened in 1831. The line provided a link to rapidly developing industrial centres such as Coatbridge to the east of the city. By the 1870s commuters began to build housing along the line in earnest, contributing to the accretion of the suburbs.

EMIGRATION

TO

CAPE OF GOOD HOPE AND NATAL,
NEW ZEALAND,
AUSTRALIAN COLONIES,
EAST INDIA AND CHINA,
UNITED STATES OF AMERICA,
CANADA,
MEDITERRANEAN PORTS.

PASSAGE TICKETS issued to any of the above Countries, and to other Parts of the World, by the *Best and Cheapest* Lines, and by the *Safest* Routes.

ALL INFORMATION given as to Dates of Sailing, Rates of Passage, and regarding Free and Assisted Emigration, on application to

JOHN HERALD, Auctioneer,
70 High Street, Arbroath.

2. A poster displayed in Arbroath in 1882, promoting emigration to the Colonies. The scale of migration from Angus was never on that of the Highlands, but even after the First World War the number of Scottish emigrants hoping to improve their lot by starting a new life overseas was statistically one of the highest of all European countries.

3. (*below*) A deerskin bag owned by the nineteenth-century explorer Dr John Rae of Orkney. Travelling among the North American Indian and Inuit peoples, he probably commissioned a Cree Indian craftswoman to stitch a thistle motif into the decoration of the band as a reminder of his homeland.

In a Foreign Land

1. (*below*) A silver snuff-box, presented to one of the Government agents partly responsible for supervising the emigration of thousands of Scottish crofters forced off their lands by the Highland Clearances. The box was presented in 1849, when the haemorrhage was at its height.

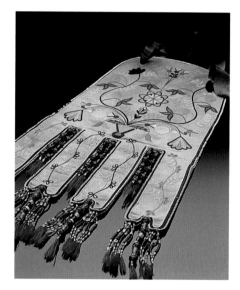

directed into product diversification which could have expanded the range of steel-using industries and hence produced the necessary economies of scale in steel production.

Had there been no options for external investment, the owners of Scottish industry might have faced up to these challenges. As it was, reliance on labour-intensive techniques and cheap labour was already exacting its toll by the new century. Scottish steel, produced on a smaller scale and using older technologies, was more expensive than that from Germany or England – creating lucrative business for steel brokers like Bonar Law. Shipbuilding itself was losing its technological lead. The Japanese now built their own ships. Perhaps symbolically, the engine that would revolutionize ship propulsion in the twentieth century, the steam turbine, was developed on the Tyne, although its inventor, Parsons, was trained on the Clyde.

All this made the control of labour particularly important. The high command of Scottish industry, the executive of the West of Scotland Shipbuilding and Engineering Employers Association, met in their lawyer's Glasgow offices just opposite Rowand Anderson's resplendent Central Station Hotel. Their main preoccupation was to prevent any further erosion of the critical wage differential between Scotland and the rest of Britain. This differential had been severely reduced in the early 1890s, retrieved in part during the middle years of the decade and then lost altogether for most areas of skilled work in the early 1900s – although still retained for some areas of labouring and unskilled jobs. Keeping a grip on wages was just one more reason for not over-expanding. The detailed implications of this mainly subterranean struggle bring us back to another and much more subtle aspect of power: the exercise of social and moral authority.

Scottish society in the years before 1914 had every appearance of being docile and well ordered. The 1900s saw many short-lived strikes and occasional longer and more bitter ones: in coal and steel in Lanarkshire, among the female mill-workers in Dundee, perhaps most notably in the giant, American-owned Singer sewing-machine factory in Clydebank. But there was no counterpart to the conflagrations in Liverpool or South Wales which brought the military into confrontation with entire communities. Per head Scotland had fewer trade-unionists, by a third, than England and Wales. In 1906 it elected only two Labour MPs as against thirty south of the border. At that point Scots divided their political support between fifty-eight Liberal MPs and twelve Conservative and Unionist.

All this could be seen as a tribute to the success, and perhaps acceptability, of the way the controllers of Scottish society exercised their authority. But first impressions are often misleading. While immediately effective, the tactics adopted also had long-term costs – in some ways as fundamental as those affecting the economy. Pre-1914 Scotland remained a society largely in a state of domination – not from outside but from within. Ministers of religion, lairds and employers still ruled local communities, their authority balanced on the poverty and insecurity of those they sought to control. Autocracy and paternalism went hand-in-hand. In this respect the Paisley cotton firm of Coats is not untypical. The firm was immensely successful. It had manufacturing plants spread across the globe. It dominated the world market for sewing-machine thread. Yet the formula for its success remained the composition and character of its home labour force in Paisley: young female labour. Trade unions were banned.

In heavy industry and engineering, on the other hand, employers had to accept the presence of trade unions by the 1900s. At the same time they strenuously resisted anything that might interfere with the prerogatives of management. Collective bargaining was not encouraged. Employers wanted the freedom to use the periods of unemployment to roll back wages and conditions. The collieries, which were Scotland's biggest employers of male labour, were the same. If Scotland had fewer trade-unionists it was at least in part because employers were far less tolerant of their presence than their counterparts in England. And if there were fewer Labour MPs, it was very largely because the Liberal Party had not, as in England, formed an electoral pact with Labour. The Coats, like many other employers, were Liberals. In terms of attitudes to social provision they were on the party's progressive wing. But their liberalism also gave primacy to the market and the rights of capital within it. Capital's special need to retain control over labour meant that the general response to the trade union movement was to marginalize it – rather than, as in England, embrace it. Scotland had no counterpart to Beatrice and Sidney Webb: moderate champions of organized labour centrally involved in the policy-making of both Liberal and Conservative Parties.

In face of this exclusion, Scotland's trade-unionists tended to give greater importance to their own independent social and political organization. Trades councils sought to assume a wider campaigning function on issues such as housing, and health and safety. The Scottish Trades Union Congress (STUC), formed just before the new century, attempted to do so at Scottish level – generally meeting with studied indifference from the press and government. Politically, there was more decisive support for independent Labour representation. The STUC's Scottish Workers Representation Committee managed to maintain an organizational unity on the electoral front between different ideological strands, from Marxist to Fabian and Catholic Socialist, in a way not found in England. In Glasgow, supporters of the Independent Labour Party (ILP) were able to sustain a newspaper, *Forward*, on a weekly basis from 1906. But generally the success was limited. Votes were small. There were no decisive struggles. Despite the environment, the abject poverty, the volatility of the regional economy and the aggressiveness of local employers, support for socialists remained small and even the influence of Marxist propagandists as talented as John Maclean was at this stage restricted.

Overall, therefore, pre-1914 Scotland gave every appearance of political stability and industrial success. It was a country secure in its position within the British state, yet proud of its separate national traditions. Even the espousal of Home Rule by the Liberal Party caused no great turbulence for this very reason. The country's élites – the learned professions, the landlords and the great owners of capital – were already presumed to rule in their own country as they effectively did as part of the British state. Scotland remained defined in most people's minds by this élite. It is perhaps only when we turn to the way this élite themselves defined their Scottishness that we become aware of what might be a deeper unease. Their Scotland drew its key symbols almost exclusively from outside the modern industrial world on which their wealth and power depended. Their favourite architecture was mock baronial. Their role models tended to come from the sixteenth and seventeenth centuries. The intellectual star of Scottish conservatism, John Buchan, chose as his exemplar the Marquis of Montrose. Buchan saw Montrose as a man of the Renaissance who still defended Scotland's feudal values of service to the poor and weak – a champion of Scotland's Presbyterian heritage who also saw the need to sustain the integrity of the British state. In literature, the élite's favourite author was James Matthew (J. M.) Barrie, earning £80,000 in a year from one West End play. The manse, the byre and the kailyard provided the backdrop to bittersweet tales of broken lives and unrequited rural love. Barrie's authenticity lay in the dialect and social simplicity of his youth in Angus. His success, which spawned a whole genre of kailyard imitators, seems to have sprung from his ability to conjure into reality a Scotland that was quite remote from the barbarity of the urban tenement where the great bulk of the population lived. In this Scotland, authority and social obedience were the natural order. In his play *The Admirable Crichton*, first performed in 1902, Barrie took up this theme explicitly. A social parable for the twentieth century, the play ostensibly deals with the effete ostentation of aristocratic life. Its social message is, however, spelt out sufficiently bluntly for even the most inattentive audience: whatever the circumstances, a natural order of ranks will reassert itself.

If there was an escape from the heavy Scottish baronial, the sombre never-never land of Barrie's rural Scotland and a still forbidding Church of Scotland (voting at its Assembly in 1914 to honour ties of 'race and religion' with their brethren in Ulster), it came from a quite different direction. It was that of cosmopolitan rejection. Although paradoxically it is today the products of this rejection which are seen to represent the Scotland of the 1900s, in the minds of their creators Scotland had very little to do with it – or, if it did, it was an earlier mysticized Scotland of Celtic art and religion. The raw blues and yellows of the French Impressionists glow through the palettes of the Scottish Colourists such as E. A. Hornel and J. D. Fergusson. Their paintings offer escape from the cities to the flowers and beaches of the Ayrshire coast. Charles Rennie Mackintosh's answer to oppressive gothic was the use of new materials in new ways: the construction of buildings out of glass, steel and open ironwork. White walls and elongated planes of space and light struggle to open out a hitherto closed architectural world. The originality of his contribution made late imperial Glasgow one of the world centres of art nouveau. The others? Perhaps not altogether uncoincidentally: Habsburg Vienna, Barcelona under the last of the Bourbons, and the Brussels of Leopold II.

The First World War and Social Change

James Bridie's play *A Sleeping Clergyman* opened in Glasgow in 1932. In his autobiography Bridie describes much of the audience as being in tears on the first night. The clergyman of the title is distinguished by his ability to sleep through the entire play and have altogether no part in it. The play itself is about the transcendent role of science, specifically medical science, as deployed by the dedicated professional. An old morality is banished. A new humanism takes its place. The closing scene of the play looks back to the days before the First World War: 'They lived at a time when what their neighbours thought and said could kill them utterly . . . we don't live in those times now.'

Bridie's play is a good measure of the gulf which separated the inter-war period from what went before. The hero, the driven, half-demented medical scientist, gives his war medals to a prostitute. The figure who attracts most opprobrium and derision is the titled Clydeside industrialist who did very well out of the war. The sixteen years from 1914 to 1932 saw something of the same transformation happen in real life. Politically the shift was far sharper than anything that occurred in England. By 1922 there were more Labour MPs in Scotland than Conservatives and Liberals: 30 Labour (including one Communist) against 16 Liberals, 15 Conservatives and 12 Liberal Unionists. In England there were 95 Labour against 312 Conservatives, 39 Liberals and 38 Liberal Unionists. The pre-war position had been reversed.

The cause? Mainly war and, above all, the change in the relative power of capital and labour wrought by the wartime employment conditions. The hidden collectivism of Scotland's working class became open and explicit – directly challenging the individualism of the old order. Overnight Scotland had become one of the British Empire's prime producers of munitions. Scotland was allocated two of the United Kingdom's twelve designated munitions centres. Workers poured into the crowded tenements of Clydeside: by 1915 250,000 were employed in munitions. In these circumstances trade-unionists gained the power to take on their employers and win.

In England war also brought full employment. What made Scotland different was the lack of any pre-existing accommodation between capital and labour. The government tried to make up for this. It imported structures of arbitration developed in England. It drew on officials from British trade unions – which had taken a pro-war position and surrendered their right to take industrial action for the duration. But its efforts proved counterproductive. As the war intensified and ever heavier pressures were brought to bear on real wages and working conditions, workers on the Clyde rejected the official union position and formed their own unofficial organizations at shop steward level. The leadership of these committees came by default from anti-war socialists in the ILP and the British Socialist Party (BSP). By December 1915, Clydeside was seen as the storm centre of opposition. Lloyd George was being shouted down by shop stewards. Left newspapers, including *Forward*, were being suppressed and the strike leaders arrested. A top civil servant, William Beveridge, was sent up to Scotland to find a compromise that could isolate the radical left. Such interventions by the state only tended to politicize industrial relations still further. The conflicts intensified as the war went on, surging to a new high in the autumn and winter of 1917–18 and culminating in the general strike of January 1919 and military occupation. Strike action continued at a high level through 1919 and into the early part of 1920, especially in steel and the coal industry. In 1919 and again in 1920 the Scottish conference of the ILP, very shortly to win twenty-two Scottish seats at Westminster, voted for affiliation to the Third (Communist) International.

This phenomenon, the 'Red Clyde', has long perplexed historians, for very soon the mood had changed. The Labour MPs who represented Scotland in parliament in the 1930s were generally on the right wing of the party, and the councillors who took control of Scotland's cities were even more so. This has tempted some historians to dismiss the whole episode as a myth, an attempt to claim socialist credentials for what was in fact a conservative defence of craft privilege: skilled male workers seeking to stop the wartime dilution of their jobs by women and labourers. For the origins of the revolt in 1915 there may be a grain of truth in this interpretation. However, it totally fails to explain what happened afterwards, in 1917, 1918 and 1919. Nor can it explain the reactions of those who ruled Scottish society.

In 1920 Sir Arthur Steel Maitland, coal-owner, Conservative MP and future Minister of Labour, returned to his estate in Stirlingshire. He wrote to a friend, as if it was a new discovery, that he was among 'savage folk'. 'His' miners were no longer respectful, but hostile, accusing, and capable of anything. The sudden loss of deference left members of the middle and upper classes deeply frightened. Would Glasgow become another Petrograd? A couple of hours after the January 1919 conflict in George Square, when some 50,000 strikers and ex-servicemen had overwhelmed a police cavalry charge, a hundred of Clydeside's biggest employers met to discuss tactics. As well as firing off demands for military intervention and calling on the civic authorities to stand firm, they also discussed contingency plans. One was to set up their own paramilitary forces, a civic guard. It did not happen. But at that moment they were not far off what fellow employers were to initiate a few months later in Belfast, where they armed their (Orange) workplace loyalists, or, in another type of uniform, in northern Italy.

The potency of Scotland's wartime industrial militancy stemmed from the way it penetrated the surrounding communities. Fear and insecurity no longer brought obedience, and class politics of a quite sophisticated kind flooded into the vacuum. The ideas were particularly worrying. Steel Maitland sought to persuade Edwin Cannan of the London School of Economics to write a popular text demolishing Marxism. The Glasgow correspondent of MI5 in 1919 saw the solution in a radical extension of the work of Glasgow University's extramural department. Four years later two of that institution's leading economists, W. R. Scott and J. Cunnison, commented in a survey of the regional economy that 'increasing numbers turned to Marx because they found in him convincing proof of their belief in the evils of capitalism and the reality of the class war'. It is important not to overestimate numbers. No more than a few thousand attended the economics classes of Marxist educators like John Maclean. What was important was the way they gave a voice, in terms of a new vocabulary, to a much wider population who had been drawn into activity by the wartime struggles on rents, pensions and food rationing – struggles which themselves involved the potent combination of workplace power and collective organization at street level. During the war the trade-union movement had doubled in size, radically redefined its objectives and transformed its composition – with a quarter of its members now being women.

Many years later the Red Clydesider Harry McShane recalled how the war impacted on the families at home. The slaughter across the sea was not remote. Each night the hospital ships would unload at Leith and Dundee. Ambulances, sirens screaming, would race through the night-time streets taking casualties across central Scotland to hospitals in Glasgow and the west. The noise and number would indicate to those listening the magnitude of slaughter over previous days. By the end of the war 74,000 Scots soldiers had been killed and 150,000 seriously wounded: in sum almost a fifth of the active male population. When war was declared in 1914, red, white and blue bunting was hung out in celebration in many working-class areas. On May Day 1918, 100,000 Glaswegians defied the law to stop work and demonstrate for a negotiated peace. The intervening years saw a transformation of attitudes and roles. In the community a key point in this change was the struggle on rent levels in 1915. Willie Gallacher, then chair of the Clyde Workers Committee, describes how 'in Govan Mrs Barbour, a typical working-class housewife, became the leader of a movement such as had been never seen before or since for that matter. Street meetings, back-court meetings, drums, bells, trumpets – every method was used to bring the women out and organize for the struggle.' It was eventually 'Mrs Barbour's army' which surrounded Glasgow's Sheriff Court and forced the suspension of the legal action against the rent strikers. These were mass actions: 25,000 households refused to pay rent – with more in Clydebank and other industrial centres. Tens of thousands of workers came out on strike. The collectivism of the factory for the first time merged with the collectivism of the street.

This was the depth of social change that faced the old political parties at the end of the war. Scotland's Conservatives tried to tackle the challenge head-on. At their Summer School in St Andrews in 1920, they defined their problem as a lack of any contact within this new reorganized type of working-class community. Unlike the English Tories they had never worked in the trade-union movement. No Scottish trade-union leader had ever stood as a Conservative candidate. Within a few months the party had established organizations for Conservative trade-unionists, a Workers' League and a People's League. These were lavishly funded, and supplemented by a weekly newspaper, *The*

People's Politics. As organizations, however, they gained little support and were disbanded by 1923. By then the Conservative Party had been overtaken by a more urgent priority: the need to maintain electoral mass by consolidating the middle-class vote. For the previous half-century the Liberal Party had dominated Scottish politics by maintaining a populist alliance of middle- and working-class voters. Now the Liberal Party had lost this ability. Its middle-class support was left frightened and isolated. Moves to field joint Liberal–Conservative candidates began in local government in 1919–20. By 1923 the Liberal Party's intellectual cadre force, the Free Church clergy, was deserting to the Conservatives. In 1924 the Liberals' main supporter in the Scottish press, the *Daily Record*, also switched its allegiance to the Tories. Across much of urban Scotland politics were now polarized. The middle class voted Tory. The bulk of the urban working class voted Labour.

Red Clyde and the Stalling of Scotland's Industrial Growth

How, then, did the owners of Scotland's industry react to this dramatic loss of authority and control? Was it the case, as has been suggested, that the phenomenon of the Red Clyde cost Scotland two decades of industrial investment?

The reality was somewhat more complex. There certainly were employers, such as Lithgow and Beardmore, who urged immediate dismissals in 1919 to restore discipline, but their colleagues failed to agree. The post-war boom was then in full flow, and few firms were willing to jeopardize their share of the market. Even when the boom collapsed in 1920–21 many employers struggled to keep their core workforces together in the hope that trade would improve. It never did. The demand for the products of Scottish heavy industry remained very weak till the end of the thirties. Was no one therefore responsible? Was it just market forces? This explanation is also too simple. These were the very years when, elsewhere in the world, the Swedish, French and American shipbuilding industries pulled ahead of Britain in terms of technology and fabrication techniques.

To find the answer we have to travel down from Scotland to the committee rooms of Whitehall and the Bank of England. Once there we would find them full of Scots — many complaining about the rigours of the overnight sleeper. We would quickly meet Lord Weir, wartime air minister and later government adviser on armaments, Sir James Lithgow, wartime controller of shipbuilding and later industrial adviser to the Governor of the Bank of England, Lords Maclay and Inverforth, wartime controllers of shipping, Allan Smith MP, leader of the Engineering Employers, Sir Andrew Duncan, wartime controller of steel and later adviser to the Bank of England, Sir Eric and Sir Auckland Geddes, directors of railway companies and tea and rubber plantations, both Cabinet ministers in the post-war government, and, not least, Andrew Bonar Law, Chancellor of the Exchequer and, by 1922, Prime Minister.

They were not there specifically as Scots, certainly not as any form of lobby. They were present as British business leaders and politicians helping to chart the way forward for the world's biggest (and recently victorious) imperial power. They did, however, generally share common perspectives which took them into close alliance with the bankers who dominated Treasury and Bank of England policy. In general they wanted deflation. In the key debates on post-war economic policy towards the end of 1919, most supported taking the pound back on to the gold standard, squeezing inflation out of the economy by hiking interest rates and drastically cutting public expenditure. They were well aware of the consequences. Their opponents, who included Lloyd George and Keynes, made sure of this. The outcome would be recession. Their counter-argument was that this would happen anyway. Best to get it over quickly and restore the pound as the world's banking currency. That way world trade could be re-established and the British economy take over from where it had left off in 1914. For Scots employers, so heavily dependent on export markets (and capital export), this policy made good sense – or so they thought. It also met another central concern: the degree to which wartime expansion had grossly over-extended industrial capacity. Still in the immediate post-war period the English banks were lending massive sums of cheap money. The banker R. H. Brand estimated that cotton and shipbuilding had received £500 million in loans in the space of a year. One Scots firm, Beardmore's, expanded from steel, ships and tanks to aircraft, submarines and motor vehicles. Little of this was likely to be sustainable (unless it was at someone else's expense), and would seriously undermine the profitability of the whole sector.

Then between November 1919 and April 1920 the financial markets and the Bank of England moved. The Treasury bill rate was almost doubled from 3.5 per cent to 6.5 per cent and Lloyd George was forced to cut back the government's lavish spending on housing and welfare. The Cabinet chose Sir Eric Geddes to draw up the programme of cuts. As demand dropped throughout the economy, whole sections of industry, particularly those producing capital goods, became technically insolvent. On Clyderside shipbuilding employment fell from 60,000 to 25,000 in eighteen months. The rise in unemployment quickly changed the balance of power in industry. By 1921 the government and coal-owners felt able to take on the biggest single group of male employees, the one million miners. The following year the engineering employers locked out their members. It was one of the Scots we met earlier, Allan Smith MP, who led the operation. Smith was chair of the general purposes committee of the British Empire Union (which sponsored fifty MPs), member of the 1919 Royal Commission on Coal and, later, the Balfour Commission on Trade and Industry, and secretary of the Engineering Employers Federation. All the Federation's leading staff, including Smith and Sir Andrew Duncan, were lawyers from the Glasgow firm of Lumsden, Biggart and Company, which acted for Scotland's biggest industrial companies and also operated Scotland's largest single group of investment trusts.

In other words we get a qualified answer to our question. The leaders of Scottish industry did have an indirect hand in the timing and character of the post-war recession and actively used the resulting unemployment in an endeavour to defeat the shop stewards movement and regain industrial control. But this was not their main objective. Their ultimate goal was the restoration of sterling as the world banking currency and a return to their pre-1914 predominance in world trade. The problem was that this never happened.

The reasons take us once more to Whitehall. A key part of the strategy was wage reduction. Politically, however, this proved far more difficult than was originally thought. It involved not just Britain. American bankers now dominated the international economy. If American investment was to be retained and currency stabilization continued, parallel policies of wage reduction had to be pushed forward across the continent. Without this the gold standard could not be held. At each stage in this process, governments, bankers and employers had to consider politically just how far they could go. In 1920, for instance, Bonar Law, leader of the Unionists but also a Glasgow MP, still wanted to maintain the government's housing programme and was very anxious about the long-term political consequences of deflation and the gold standard. In 1923 Allan Smith was urging Stanley Baldwin, the new Prime Minister, to take action on unemployment. Despite the apparent victory in the 1926 general strike the prevalent opinion in the Cabinet was that wage reduction should be taken off the agenda. Political stabilization had to take precedence.

In consequence wages did not come down – or at least not enough. The Clydeside shipbuilders James Lithgow and Murray Stephen lamented this failure each year in the *Glasgow Herald*'s review of trade. This problem interlocked with another. The amount of capital tied up in Scottish industry, grossly expanded during the war, was now far more concentrated and much of it was controlled by the banks. The level of bank indebtedness meant that the profits crisis was not going to be automatically resolved in the old way – by the bankruptcy of marginal firms. The banks stood in the way. Any reduction in capacity required a long, complicated game of financial diplomacy.

In short, the Scots in Whitehall were not altogether free agents. They knew that if they were going to maintain their industrial power, it would be on terms set in London, and particularly by the Bank of England. This is the background to the strange alliance that was to dominate Scotland's economy – and much of England's – during the inter-war years. On the one side there was the Governor of the Bank of England, Lord Norman, holding office for twenty years, responsible to the inner core of London merchant banks, remote, reclusive, yet dominating international finance and the key figure in virtually every government economic decision up to the Second World War. On the other side, there were the practical men of business from Clydeside. Their support gave Norman his answer to the accusations by Keynes and others that he was sacrificing industry to finance. Weren't these men Britain's real industrialists? No less than the bankers, they saw the need to balance the books, squeeze inflation out of the system and get rid of excess capacity.

It took fifteen years to complete the process of rationalization. By 1936 Colville's was the most profitable steel firm in Britain and controlled virtually all Scottish steel production and much of the coal. Lithgow's had a controlling interest in Colville's and had taken over Beardmore's to become the main producer of heavy munitions. In shipbuilding Lithgow was easily dominant – launching twice the tonnage of any other shipbuilder. None of this would have been possible without the support of the Bank of England. Sir James Lithgow headed the National Shipbuilders Security Scheme that was funded by the Bank of England to rationalize British shipbuilding capacity. In the five years after 1930 Lithgow bought up and closed a third of the industry. Jarrow on Tyneside had both its yards closed – becoming, in the phrase of its Labour MP Ellen Wilkinson, 'the town that was murdered'. Sir Archie Duncan was given a somewhat similar job to do as chair of the British Iron and Steel Federation. Every move required complex negotiations with creditors and shareholders, the Bank of England and the Treasury. All of it was conducted behind closed doors.

Long-term objectives depended on informal personal understandings between a few key players: Norman, his deputy Sir Henry Clay, Duncan and Lithgow. Their economic assumptions, cautious and conservative, penetrated deep into the Scottish business community. The Scottish banks, which had far more credit out to heavy industry than their English counterparts, also lent much less to other sectors of industry and particularly new industries. Lithgow himself denounced the dangers of 'safeguarding' industries such as aircraft and cars by imposing import tariffs. Special treatment of this type, he argued, would put pressure on wage levels in Scotland's staple industries and put off even further the day when profitability was restored. Even calls for the structural re-equipment of heavy industry fell on deaf ears. In 1929 the leading Scottish steel firms commissioned, with Bank of England support, an inquiry into ways of further cutting production costs. The resulting Brassert Report proposed the replacement of Scotland's small-scale and obsolete steel technology by building a giant integrated steel complex with deep-water access on the Clyde estuary. Most of the owners of the steel industry were horrified at this apparently bizarre proposal to spend money on creating new capacity.

'The Unemployed Regard the Promised Land'

Scotland's tragedy was that it bore the brunt of policies which were doomed from the start. Sterling was never going to resume its pre-1914 role. Nor was it likely, across Europe, that sufficient wage flexibility could be achieved to keep the American bankers on board. Britain's bid to sustain an overvalued currency turned the 1920s into a decade of stagnation. And if England did badly compared with America, Germany and France, Scotland fared even worse. For an economy so dependent on exports and heavy industry, an overvalued pound meant death. By 1931, when sterling went off the gold standard, the damage had been done. Over the previous decade 550,000 Scots had left their country to find work elsewhere. The scale of the losses dwarfed the Highland clearances of the early nineteenth century. Most of the emigrants were young and with industrial experience. They represented over a fifth of the total working population. In the coalfields of South Yorkshire, Leicestershire and Kent the density of resettlement was such that whole communities retained their Scottish links. From 1928 the government funded a relocation scheme for young women to go down to London and the home counties to ease the shortage of domestic servants. Overseas, Canada, the United States and Australia were the main destinations. Barnardo's sent boatloads of orphan children to Canada for adoption and employment.

These economic refugees were fleeing levels of unemployment double those in England. Their flight in turn intensified the crisis of Scotland's domestic economy. In 1920s Britain the only real prospect lay in the domestic market. In these circumstances Scotland found itself deprived of both skilled workers and potential consumers. South of the border new industries did develop around London and in the Midlands. In Scotland the disproportionate contraction stalled consumer demand. Housing construction provides a good index of these differences. In England the number of new houses built between the wars was equal to over half the existing stock. In Scotland it was only a quarter. Fewer new houses meant less household goods and less substitution of electricity for gas. Scotland's infant car industry was not inherently weaker than that in England, but it did not survive the 1920s. John Logie Baird's television failed to make it to the starting line. It was not that Scotland lacked the scientific knowledge and skills needed to take its economy forward to the next generation of industrial products. In some ways it was uniquely positioned to do so. What stopped development was the wider economic environment – one which was politically based on that strange alliance between Scottish heavy industry and the City of London.

What were the consequences for ordinary people? By 1932 average male unemployment was just under 30 per cent for Scotland as a whole, and over 50 per cent for many mining and shipbuilding areas. When John Boyd Orr was commissioned to undertake research on levels of nutrition and health in the late 1930s, he found in

Scotland the worst infant mortality rates in Europe outside Portugal and Spain – 30 per cent higher than those in England and Wales. Looking at nutrition he found that 20 per cent of Scottish families suffered vitamin deficiency in all areas of diet – twice the number in England. In housing, where Scotland had always done badly, the pre-war differential had widened. 23 per cent of Scots lived in overcrowded housing as against 4 per cent in England. These statistics gain more power when related to the experiences of individuals. One unemployed youngster from north Glasgow, Tommy Ferns, was interviewed in old age by one of the pioneers of oral history in Scotland, Ian MacDougall. His testimony is one of many in *Voices from the Hunger Marches* (Edinburgh, 1990):

I was more or less unemployed from leavin' school in 1927 until 1937 . . . I had short periods as a message boy and I got a job in a chemical work – one or two jobs which lasted short periods, including workin' wi' the farmers, liftin' potatoes and workin' on the fruit farms – and then no work . . . Under the Means Test every single penny that came intae a household was taken into account and they stated a figure and if that figure was exceeded you got nothing . . . I was a victim of that for two years because my brother was working – he was a moulder – and receiving a reasonable wage. They considered his wage sufficient to keep me. So I got nothing at all . . . for two years. What it resulted in of course was the wholesale breaking up of families . . . ye felt ye were being a burden on the person who was working in the family . . .

For the young, fit and unattached, unemployment could provide the opportunity to explore the world and roam the wildernesses of the Scottish Highlands. The 1920s and '30s saw a rediscovery of rural Scotland by urban youngsters fishing, poaching and living rough over the summer months. But the majority had no such opportunities. For many families it was a period of profound dislocation: moving from place to place, enduring periods of separation, the loss of sons and daughters and often break-up. Survival was an achievement. Adult males were those worst hit by unemployment, particularly those in the staple trades of mining and shipbuilding. Unlike the cyclical unemployment before 1914 these older workers found themselves permanently unemployed. Divisions in working-class communities now cut across the previously prosperous skilled trades. In *Major Operation* the novelist James Barke describes the tramlines of Dumbarton Road in Glasgow as the social equivalent of 'barbed wire entanglements'. To the north were the relatively well-repaired red sandstone tenements housing families lucky enough to retain employment. To the south were the grey sandstone slums, even more overcrowded and run-down than before 1914. Of the four Scottish cities, Dundee undoubtedly came off worst. Previously its jute industry had provided employment for large numbers of women, and made Dundee something of an exception to the heavy patriarchalism which dominated the rest of industrial Scotland. Now unemployment rose from 30 per cent in the twenties to over 50 per cent in the thirties. The journalist James Cameron, then working for the D. C. Thomson group, recalled the town's 'singular desolation'. Hugh MacDiarmid described the city as a 'monument to man's inhumanity to man'.

In terms of damage to communities it is probably the remote and rural West Highlands that tell the bleakest tale. In the twenties the population actually shrank by 10 per cent. Those who left were young people of working age. The semi-communal systems of tillage and fishing required minimum numbers in each crofting township to function. Many areas began to slip below the margins of viability. Then in the 1930s a reverse process occurred. As employment collapsed elsewhere, the emigrants returned. The already damaged agricultural base was stretched to the limit. Crofters found themselves unable to keep enough marketable produce to pay the rents. Often it was only casual summer work on the sporting estates that could provide a money income. In his *Scottish Journey*, undertaken in the summer of 1934, the Orcadian poet Edwin Muir describes the feeling of despair and degradation. 'A great part of the Highland population now depend for their living on their obsequious skill in rendering the slaughter of wild animals more easy or convenient for the foreign owners of shooting lodges.' He continues: '. . . they have kept through all these changes their courtesy, their dignity, one might almost say their freedom. But these qualities are bought at the expense of a disdainful resignation which a proud people feels in acknowledging defeat.' Two years later the Gaelic poet Sorley MacLean spoke to the Gaelic Society of Inverness. He speculated on how it was that the clearances, one of the 'most astounding successes of landlord capitalism in Western Europe', should have been achieved with 'such ease, cruelty and cynicism'. Was it mistaken loyalty to clan chiefs? Or was it the Free Church? MacLean suggested that the people had turned to the Free Church in reaction to the treachery of the established order. But, he argued, its ministers served that order equally well. The lack of resistance into the twentieth century was because the church itself had introduced and disseminated the ideology of 'private property and *laissez-faire*'.

Why so passive?

Historians have since posed very similar questions about Scotland as a whole. Given the scale of poverty in inter-war Scotland and the scale of militancy at the end of the war, why was there ultimately so little resistance? Was the passivity primarily a product of the same sort of intervention? Let us start at the level of everyday life. One historian of Scottish culture, Dr Callum Brown, has suggested that state agencies did at least seek to channel popular activity into safe and approved forms. What he describes as 'rough' culture came under systematic legal attack. It is important to note, however, that the real push for this assault came at local level. It also had a definite political edge to it. The main manifestations of rough culture, drinking and gambling, had always been subject to strict regulation. The 1920s saw this control became a major obsession.

433

Some 500 ward-level plebiscites were organized under the Temperance (Scotland) Act of 1913, of which forty resulted in the creation of 'dry' (pub-free) localities. Billiard halls were subject to new controls. The police came under intense pressure to enforce the Street Betting Act – with prosecutions running into thousands by the early 1930s. In general the driving force was the Protestant churches. Often there were overtly sectarian overtones. In 1923 the General Assembly of the Church of Scotland had issued its notorious report accusing Irish and Catholic immigrants of 'subverting' the Scottish national identity. Particularly at risk were the 'Scottish' values of sobriety, commitment to work and Sunday observance. The local campaigns against drinking and gambling followed. In public discussion it was general practice to dwell on the allegedly non-Scots – usually Irish or Italian – origin of publicans, street bookmakers and the owners of ice-cream parlours.

Looked at historically, these local crusades coincide very closely with the moment when the urban middle class felt most isolated and vulnerable. The Labour Party was making its parliamentary breakthrough. Its new ally was the Catholic church. The rallying cry of law and order – with an Orange tinge – held out the prospect of reassembling some sort of wider mass support for the new middle-class alliance. If this was the intention, the outcome was somewhat different. Sectarian conflict did increase sharply in inter-war Scotland. Yet it was not to the benefit of any middle-class alliance. One of the remarkable features of the post-war period is the degree to which the resurgent forces of Protestant and Orange politics sought to distance themselves from the Conservatives and to mimic the class rhetoric of the Labour Party. In 1922 the Orange Order in Scotland formally broke with the Conservatives and established a separate Orange and Protestant Party – primarily in protest at the Conservatives' support for the 1918 Act giving state maintenance to Catholic secondary schools. A few years later, as unemployment intensified, Protestant populism emerged as a major force in both Glasgow and Edinburgh. In Glasgow the Scottish Protestant League's main venom was reserved for the middle-class alliance party, the Moderates, which controlled the council. This party was accused of betraying working-class Scots. It had not just failed to give preference to Protestants, but had not delivered on social welfare and employment in general. The Protestant League at the height of its influence in 1933 polled 67,000 votes across twenty-two mainly working-class wards in Glasgow – against 63,000 for Labour and 53,000 for the Moderates in the same wards. The net result was to split the Moderate vote and give Labour its first overall majority. The Conservative *Glasgow Herald* hinted darkly of a tacit alliance between the League and Labour, and pointed to common voting patterns in the previous council. Even though Orange politics split the working class, their proponents now had to use anti-middle-class rhetoric to do so. This itself was a measure of the profound reorientation of working-class attitudes over the previous decade. Mass unemployment may have broken the shop stewards movement, but there was no simple return to the old ways.

This cultural assertiveness within the working population was a feature of inter-war Scotland. It was not necessarily political. But it did mark a transformation of attitudes to authority. Working people now felt able to go out at the weekend and spend their leisure time as they wanted. The ministers and priests would not stop them. It was this shift in behaviour rather than any big jump in purchasing power that produced the new mass market for working-class leisure. At the height of the depression in the early 1930s Glasgow had 156 dance halls. On a typical Saturday night up to 30,000 people, mostly young, would be dancing. A further 40,000 would be in the city's one hundred cinemas. And anything up to 100,000 would attend 'old firm' matches between Celtic and Rangers. Edwin Muir noted the cultural gulf in his *Scottish Journey*. Tea-rooms were the preserve of the lower middle class. Workers never entered. 'There is a clear majority of women and among them a surprising number of old ladies. The men, I fancy, belong chiefly to the class of clerical workers who do not know very clearly where they stand in the economic hierarchy, who yearn, almost legitimately, for the luxury of the wealthy.' At the end of Princes Street in Edinburgh, the place where the fashionable wanted to be seen, the road continued into Leith Walk, a preserve of the working class. 'One suddenly finds oneself among ice-cream and fish and chip bars and pubs. At one point the two different streams of promenaders are brought within a few metres of one another; yet they scarcely ever mingle, so strong is the sense of social distinction bred in city life.'

If, then, the local élites failed in their attempts to create new cross-class alliances, did the state itself intervene in the local structuring of Scottish society? Central government undoubtedly did expand the scope of its local involvement, and some of the motives were political, but again the results were somewhat mixed. Prior to the 1920s central government had remarkably little presence at local level. When, in preparation for the 1926 general strike, government ministers were looking for personnel to staff the emergency apparatus, they had to rely on the local officers of the Ministry of Health – then responsible for running the national insurance scheme. It was deeply troubling to the government that some of the smaller units of directly elected local government were falling into unreliable hands. Although there was no counterpart in Scotland to what happened in London (where the entire leadership of Poplar council was imprisoned for exceeding the legal rates of unemployment relief), parish councils in the Vale of Leven and some semi-rural mining areas did defy the government over parochial relief levels. No doubt partly in consequence, parish councils were abolished in 1929. So also were directly elected local education boards, which controlled aspects of child welfare in addition to schools. Poor relief eventually ended up with the Ministry of Health, and education either with county councils, which were all Tory, or city councils, which were mainly so. Yet, again, there were less welcome consequences. The removal of poor relief from local control tended to focus anger more directly on the government. The abolition of parish councils also removed an important forum for local élite intervention in the many areas of rural Scotland where working-class politics were still weak.

Our original question asked: if the First World War did mark something of a breakdown of the old cultural subservience, how was it that any subsequent challenge to the old order was so muted? There are probably two answers. The first is that the inherited cultures of the working class, though now more assertive, were not necessarily progressive. As carried forward from the pre-war period, they were essentially cultures of survival. They reproduced within the working class the divisions and hierarchies of a radically unequal society. One acute social observer of the time was the Conservative politician and writer, John Buchan. He had been a government propaganda adviser during the war, insisting that effective propaganda had to be exercised through 'normal' channels, especially novels and newspapers; it should use well-known and trusted authors; and it needed to work with the grain of existing attitudes. His own post-war novels carefully built up the stereotype of the loyal Scottish working man. In *Mr Standfast* (1919), Andrew Amos, the skilled shipyard worker, comments on his colleagues: 'I don't say that there's not plenty of riff-raff – the pint and dram gentry and the saft heads that are aye reading bits of newspapers and muddlin their head with foreign whigmaleeries. But the average man on the Clyde, like the average man in ither places, hates just three things, and that's the Germans, the profiteers, as they call them, and the Irish.' It was a comforting stereotype for Buchan's socially apprehensive middle-class readers. Treason and subversion was identified with foreigners. Jews and the Irish were the usual suspects. The native stock was sound.

Buchan's picture did involve a degree of exaggeration. Yet there was also an element of truth. Old prejudices survived. As Callum Brown notes, the Scottish Office had no coordinated master plan for social control. It did encourage 'safe' activities, defined as the Boys Brigade and the Scouts, as against less safe activities. Similarly in local communities, middle-class responses to working-class attitudes would usually be informal and often almost unconscious. But the middle class still controlled the resources – including the most precious of all, employment. Their deployment could powerfully reinforce existing stereotypes. The status of women would be a case in point.

Before the war Scotland was distinctly patriarchal. It had fewer women in work than in England, bigger wage differentials between the sexes and sharper divisions in terms of domestic roles. This was mainly the product of the industrial predominance of mining, steel and engineering in Scotland. None the less it left its mark on Scottish culture as a whole. During the war, as we have seen, there was a powerful tide of change. Married women, who previously almost never had paid jobs, moved into employment, and women in general entered engineering and other areas from which they had been hitherto excluded. Traditionally female-employing areas such as printing and laundry work saw major struggles on wages and conditions. The female agitator joined Buchan's pantheon of unpatriotic types. But pre-existing attitudes quickly reasserted themselves. Proposals put at the STUC for a radical campaign to end the segregation of men and women at work were opposed at its 1918 Congress on the grounds that 'a women's natural sphere is the home' and that female employment 'had a depressing effect on public morality'. The resurgence of these attitudes – in face of growing male unemployment – created circumstances where employers could easily reinstate the old divisions. The Restoration of Pre-War Practices Act provided the legal basis.

By 1931 the proportion of married women in paid employment was scarcely different from that in 1901. It was different for unmarried women. In absolute numbers many more unmarried women were working – 667,000 as against 590,000 in 1901 – even though male employment had fallen. But this was because there were now more unmarried women. The age of marriage had risen sharply. In 1929 there were 200,000 less males than females in Scotland – the combined result of war deaths and emigration. The jobs done by these women remained overwhelmingly menial: 127,000 worked in shops and 138,000 were domestic servants, an increase of 15,000 on 1921. Only 26,000 worked in teaching, the main profession open to women. And reflecting this casual and vulnerable employment was the decline in trade union membership. By 1938 women made up less than a seventh of a much smaller total. All but a minute number of married women had returned to the home. There they had to bring up families that were on average considerably larger than those in England. Of Glasgow babies born in 1932, fully half were to grow up in families with five or more children. For most working-class women housework had to be done without the assistance of hot water, electricity, fridge or washing-machine. Laundering clothes alone could take up to two days a week. Both Catholic and Protestant Churches offered strenuous opposition to any form of birth control. Women were once more subordinate: sexually, occupationally and socially. The subtle combination of working-class prejudice, religious endorsement and, not least, employer sanction ensured that Scottish patriarchalism survived alive and well into the second half of the twentieth century.

So if that is one explanation for the strength of social conservativism, what of the other? When it came to anything considered directly hostile to the existing order, much more focused intervention took place. In 1927 Walter Elliot, Conservative MP for Kelvingrove and junior minister at the Scottish Office, wanted to convince his ministerial colleagues of the educational power of film. He organized a special showing of what he considered the best available. They were features by the Soviet director Sergei Eisenstein. Yet the very same films could not be seen by the general public. Along with all other Soviet material they were banned by the film censor. Private film clubs in Glasgow and Edinburgh, specifically established to circumvent the ban, were subject to police harassment well into the 1930s. Government agencies made it quite clear that the ideas of revolutionary socialism were not acceptable. Those who sought to promote them were subject to detailed surveillance, frequent imprisonment and fairly systematic exclusion from employment. Sentences for sedition were frequent. In 1926 alone they ran into hundreds.

For those in authority the most worrying organization was the Labour Party. Even more in Scotland than in England, Labour emerged from the war as an unpredictable amalgam: industrial militants, members of the cooperative movement, Marxists in both the ILP and the Communist Party, community housing activists and trade union leaders. Constitutionally, power was largely vested in the trade union affiliates. The big question was whether the newly-expanded forces on the left of the trade union movement would set the agenda. The Labour Party's support for industrial direct action in 1920, in 1921 and again in 1926 highlighted the dangers.

The Transformation of the Labour Party

The story of how the Labour Party was transformed into a constitutionally safe parliamentary party has to be told at British level. It involved the leaders of both the Liberal and Conservative Parties. Stanley Baldwin claimed it as his biggest achievement as Prime Minister. Yet the process had very particular implications for Scotland, where the left had always been stronger than in England. The centralization of power in the hands of the parliamentary leadership and the National Executive Committee, the subsequent lurch to the right and the exclusion from membership of Communists and allied left-wingers represented a special challenge to the broad, federal tradition of Labour politics in Scotland.

One consequence was a much higher level of haemorrhage out of the Labour Party in Scotland. The Communists were expelled between 1925 and 1927. In 1928 the Home Rule wing of the ILP left to form the National Party of Scotland. The ILP as a whole disaffiliated in 1932. At that point, after Ramsay MacDonald's defection to the Tories and the subsequent elections, the Labour Party had only seven MPs left in Scotland. The ILP now took three of the seven seats and many of the party's activists at branch level. The new Scottish party secretary, Arthur Woodburn, appointed directly by the NEC in London, described his task as 'rebuilding the party from scratch'. What materials did he have to work with? Not very much. Most of the industrial activists had gone. The party's centre of gravity had already shifted from the trades councils to local council wards. Often the only active members were the immediate family of the councillor. Local structures of patronage became increasingly important. So did the alliance with the Catholic Church which had been forged in the early twenties. At that point the Catholic Church had been looking for an alternative to the disintegrating Liberal Party as guardian of its separate state-maintained system of education. Labour in return gained clerical support in the poorest areas of the cities. During the fierce battles for ideological dominance in the 1920s, the church played an active role. Catholic Action in particular was important in reconsolidating the base of the right wing in the trade union movement. The result was a Labour Party which by the 1930s was quite different from what it had been at the end of the war. In some ways it was now much closer to the very poor and to the hitherto excluded Irish community and far more involved in detailed social amelioration. But it was no longer a party which challenged the social system.

Hence, if we want an explanation for the apparent passivity and conservatism of inter-war Scotland, we have to look in two directions. One is the almost unconscious reassertion of the old ideas of hierarchy and division – even if in a form in keeping with a more assertive working class. The other is a very conscious and targeted transformation of the bodies on which working people had relied for leadership. And, where these bodies could not be transformed, their fairly brutal destruction. The fate of the shop stewards movement after the 1922 engineering lock-out would be one example. The disintegration of the miners' union after the 1926 general strike would be another. The miners were by far the largest contingent within the Scottish trade union movement. Their union's defeat and fragmentation marked a turning-point very similar to that after the miners' strike of 1985–6. On the positive side, it could be argued that the restructuring of the Labour Party did eventually enable it to play the central role in Scotland's social modernization. Labour became the central vehicle for that peculiarly British system of moderate class politics which emerged at the end of the Second World War. As such, it was able to deliver policies which materially transformed the lives of working people in Scotland, but at a high cost. Far more than in England and Wales the party was ideologically fractured by the interwar struggles. When the Labour MP Jennie Lee came back to Fife in the mid-1930s, she found the party in 'a spiritual paralysis' and asked, 'where was all the vigour, the belligerency and the robust certainties of the Labour movement as I remembered it . . . ?' And this itself had direct implications in the way Scots defined themselves. The Labour Party in Scotland had emerged from a specifically Scottish experience and had its own traditions and organization. At the end of the First World War it appeared strong enough to impose its own radical solutions. There was hope of a new life won and defined in Scotland. Its transformation meant that this was no longer so.

In terms of national identity the change was a fundamental one. It was also so at a personal level. Consider the cases of John Wheatley, Patrick Dollan and Helen Crawfurd – in 1915 close friends, all members of the ILP and involved in anti-war campaigning. We met John Wheatley in the previous chapter. Of Catholic Irish descent and a key figure in the electoral rise of the ILP, he was among those who chose to oppose the First World War. He backed the rent strikers in 1915 and gave organizational support to the Clyde Workers Committee in their conflicts with the government in 1916. The Clyde Workers Committee chair, and later Communist MP, Willie Gallacher, describes him at this stage as an unlikely rebel: rotund, avuncular, wearing thick glasses and carefully cut suits, and twenty years older than the rest of them. However, within two months of the Bolshevik revolution in Russia, in January 1918, Wheatley again redefined his position. In the pages of *Forward* he argued that Britain's constitutional and parliamentary traditions rendered new systems of direct democracy dangerous and inappropriate. By 1922 he had been elected as an MP. In 1924 he was the only Clydesider to become a member of the new Labour Cabinet. As Minister for Health he piloted through parliament the Act which provided the basis for council house building for the following decade. Then he changed course again. Wheatley was dismayed at the economic conservatism of MacDonald's first administration and by 1925 had moved into opposition. In 1926 he denounced what he saw as the Labour Party's betrayal of the miners in the general strike, and worked with fellow ILP MP James Maxton and the miners' leader Arthur Cook to draft the Cook–Maxton Manifesto of 1928, calling for a return to socialist policies. In 1929 he refused to join the second minority Labour government. By 1930, shortly before his death, Beatrice Webb describes him as disillusioned with parliamentary socialism and stating that if he were not a practising Catholic he would become a Communist.

Patrick Dollan came from a very similar background, but was sixteen years younger. Both his parents came from Ireland. He attended the same school as Wheatley and also worked for eight years in the mines. He joined the ILP one year after Wheatley in 1908, and for fifteen years worked very closely with him, as a journalist, as a town councillor from 1913, and after 1914 as a fellow opponent of the war. Dollan and his wife Agnes were much more directly involved than Wheatley in organizing the struggles on housing and rents in 1915, and in 1916 Dollan was sentenced to three months' hard labour for taking part in what was construed as anti-war activity while registered as a conscientious objector. Dollan worked closely with the Clyde Workers Committee and edited the strike bulletin during the general strike in 1919. Agnes Dollan had particularly close relations with those who were campaigning to bring the ILP out in support of the Third International, and it might have seemed likely at this stage that the pair would have broken their links with Wheatley. But they did not. Instead Dollan became the leading organizer for the pro-Macdonald grouping in the West of Scotland ILP and laid the basis for an organizational grip on the branch structure he would retain for the following decades. In 1925 Wheatley's revolt faced him with another choice. Surprisingly, Dollan now ended his lifetime association with Wheatley and spent the next seven years opposing both Maxton and Wheatley in the Scottish ILP. When Maxton led the ILP out of the Labour Party in 1932, Dollan managed to hold on to a section of the membership for the Labour Party. He titled the new organization, almost entirely misleadingly, the Scottish Socialist Party. It was on this basis that Dollan led the Labour Party to its first victory in the Glasgow council elections in 1933.

Helen Crawfurd came from a somewhat different background. Her parents, who were born in the Gorbals, were members of the Church of Scotland; her father was a master baker. She was well educated and her upbringing relatively prosperous. At twenty-one she married a Church of Scotland minister who was an anti-militarist opponent of the Boer War. Her mid- and later twenties brought involvement with the suffragist movement and the radical culture of the Glasgow Repertory Theatre, then performing Ibsen, Shaw and Gorky. She joined the ILP in 1914. Already a leading suffragette, several times imprisoned and a colleague of the Pankhursts, she took a stance on the left of that movement before the war. When war broke out, she opposed it. In 1915 Crawfurd became secretary of the key organizing group behind the rent strikes, the Glasgow Women's Housing Association, and in November 1915 established the Glasgow branch of the Women's International League along with Agnes Dollan. By 1916 she was closely associated with Gallacher and Maclean and the shop stewards movement. In June 1917 Helen Crawfurd and Agnes Dollan launched the Women's Peace Crusade, designed to build a movement for peace along class lines among working-class women. By 1918 Crawfurd was vice-president of the Scottish ILP. At this point she might have moved in the same direction as the Dollans. Instead she became a leader of those in the Scottish ILP, then the majority, pressing for affiliation to the Third International and the formation of a Communist Party in Britain. In 1920 she was one of three Scots who made the illegal journey across British military lines in north Russia to the Second Congress of the Third International in Moscow. In 1921 Crawfurd, with others in the ILP, joined the Communist Party and was elected to the executive soon afterwards. She continued to work with those who remained in the ILP, and in 1925 was a member of the joint committee which, with Maxton, published the *Sunday Worker*.

Similar stories could be told for many others who took part in that tidal wave of political activity that did so much to transform Scotland during and immediately after the First World War. The years that followed brought disappointment and retreat. Individuals came to terms with these realities in different ways. Wheatley, Dollan and Crawfurd were not perhaps fully representative. A couple of industrial activists would have been needed for that. But the intertwining of their lives illustrates the breadth of the ideological spectrum that existed within the Labour Party in 1920. By 1933 this was no longer the case. The Labour Party was represented by Dollan alone, but Dollan's Scottish Socialist Party was neither socialist nor Scottish. Like the Labour Party as a whole it was organizationally dependent on London, and its main political thrust was against organizations to its left. The pages of *Forward* illustrate the change. In 1920 *Forward* had been filled with reports and advertisements reflecting an amazing density of local political activity covering all shades of working-class opinion. In 1936 the weekly was still owned and controlled by Tom Johnston – previous Clydeside MP and future Secretary of State. But its pages have virtually no local reportage. They are dominated instead by tabloid features from Herbert Morrison, Hugh Dalton and Dollan. Johnston himself, like the rest, polemicized against ILP extremism, the Popular Front and Soviet dictatorship.

Through the 1920s Scotland's towns and cities remained, perhaps surprisingly, almost entirely under the control of the Conservative Party – sometimes disguised under the title Moderates. It was in the mid-1930s that the refashioned Labour Party eventually began to take over. In Glasgow it was the Protestant League split in the Moderate vote in 1933 that let Labour in. Motherwell and Clydebank followed in 1934, Dundee in 1935 and Falkirk in 1936. When Glasgow went Labour in 1933, the pro-Tory *Glasgow Herald* warned that 'left-wing government will mean prejudiced class administration and an orgy of extravagance'. Its concerns were quite unfounded. Dollan was the new city treasurer, and introduced a regime of extreme fiscal prudence. When Dollan presented the city accounts in 1936 he was able to claim that since 1933 the city's debt had not been increased by one penny after steadily rising every year since 1920 from £15 to £45 million. Dollan did this by slashing the council house building programme undertaken by the Tories, a reduction which continued into 1937.

Dollan presided over Glasgow into the 1940s. He liked to compare his city with New York and to project New-Deal America as the democratic future to which he aspired. In the summer of 1939 he and Agnes Dollan led a deputation of civic and business leaders on a six-week trip to New York. Their host was Fiorelli LaGuardia, also the son of Catholic immigrants, whose election as mayor of New York marked a similar political watershed. 'Can America teach us anything about working-class homes?' ran the heading in the commemorative brochure. 'Yes, indeed!' But the text reads more like advertising copy than a political manifesto. The glittering gods of the labour-saving American home mock the impoverished citizens of Dollan's home city. Little remained of the high hopes of radical social transformation which once galvanized the new leaders of Scottish society.

The Scottish Renaissance

Hugh MacDiarmid's great poem, 'A Drunk Man Looks at the Thistle', was a kind of riposte to this transformation.

> Glesca's a gless whaur Magdalene's
> Discovered in a million crimes . . .
> Hard faces prate o' their success
> And pickle-makers awn the hills
> There is no life in a' the land
> But this infernal Thistle kills.

MacDiarmid published the poem just after the failure of the General Strike in 1926. Although not capturing anything like popular attention for another twenty years, it was quickly accepted by the new generation of Scottish writers as a defining moment for Scottish literature. Its subject was national failure. It attacked the client status of Scottish culture. It was written in a Scots so broad as to be a foreign language to the English – and perhaps some Scots. It sought literary reference in French, Italian, Spanish, Russian and German. When it spoke of failure it did so in unflinchingly modern terms, addressing precisely the inability of the Scots to carry through a social revolution for themselves. Against all the odds, Scotland had produced a socialist movement with a genuinely mass base, one of the strongest in Europe. Yet, as so often before, Scotland had failed to complete what it had started.

> I never saw sae braw a floo'er
> As yon thrawn stick became
> And still it grew till it seemed
> The hail braid earth had turned
> A reid reid rose that in the lift
> Like a ball o' fire burned . . .
> Was it the ancient vicious sway
> Imposed itsel' again
> Or verve o'er weak for new emprise
> That made the effort vain? . . .
> The vices that defeat the dream
> Are in the plant itsel'
> Until they're purged its virtues maun
> In pain and misery dwell.

Not all of those associated with MacDiarmid in the Scottish Renaissance of the 1920s would have defined either the dream or the failure in exactly the same terms. But all participated in MacDiarmid's anger. The old forces had returned. These forces did not rule with the same directness as before. But they still determined the basic terms of Scotland's economic existence – and did so in a form which both underlined their external dependence and the costs which this dependence now exacted.

The Scottish Renaissance was therefore something quite different from the Scottish tradition of Stevenson, Barrie or Buchan. Neil Gunn, Edwin Muir, Eric Linklater, Grassic Gibbon, Naomi Mitchison – all identified themselves in some form or other with movements seeking to change the political relationship which defined that tradition: the union between Scotland and England. Some supported Home Rule; others independence. Some sought formal links with working-class politics – like MacDiarmid, who sat as an independent socialist councillor in Montrose in the twenties. Others saw their role more in terms of the literary renaissance of 1900s Dublin in preparing the way for political transformation. All, however, wished to break with a past in which Scottish literature existed as a sub-species of English. They also saw this as involving a rejection of its real-life basis: Scotland as a product of the continuing complicity between

Scotland's ruling élite and British state power. For Edwin Muir it meant a sweeping clean.

> Now smoke and dearth and money everywhere
> Mean heirlooms of each fainter generation
> And mummied housegods in their musty niches
> Burns and Scott, sham bards of a sham nation
> And spiritual defeat wrapped warm in riches
> No pride but pride of pelf.

The new mood demanded iconoclasm. It pointed the finger at the economic roots of national defeat. Mitchison sought in her historical novels to create a new realist Scottish tradition that exposed these roots. The baroque romanticism of Scott and Stevenson was to give way to a new approach that allowed a reasoned understanding of self-interest and calculation.

The question, however, was what model of Scottishness to substitute. No member of the Scottish renaissance gave an altogether convincing answer. Neil Gunn went back to the communalism of the croft. With compelling power, if some romanticism, he described the sentient, conscious labour of those who also controlled and organized their own lives. His portraits of working people were from the inside, direct, unpatronizing. Yet this society was, as he recognized, dying, 'dying like an old person'. The remembered Sutherland of his youth faced the economic power of the 'real Scotland'. In *Morning Tide* the mother laments the degradation of industrial labour: 'to think this fine fellow Alan, this Hugh in his sensitive boyhood, should become common . . . No! It was alright here where everybody was the same.' Grassic Gibbon also started with the croft. The central character of *A Scots Quair* was Chris Guthrie, symbol of the anchoring role of women within small-scale rural production. Like MacDiarmid, Gibbon sought to write Scots in a new form. In his case it was not an archaic Scots, but the raw language as it was then spoken with a diversity of class inflections. In contrast to Gunn, Gibbon did not stop in the croft. His focus was on change. *A Scots Quair* moves from the early lyrical portrayal of the wholeness of life in rural Kincardine to the destruction of war and then the jagged, broken society of the industrial city. *Grey Granite*, the final novel in the series, published in 1934, describes arrogant, corrupt employers, police brutality, craven journalists and marching workers with a sharpness which left contemporary literary critics mumbling about 'coarseness' and 'unworthy ending'. Even more directly than MacDiarmid, Gibbon challenged the dead parochialism of a Scotland defined in terms of its past alone. Scottishness was also what Scotland was becoming.

Eric Linklater's *The Lion and the Unicorn*, published the following year and dedicated to Gibbon, sums up all the uncertainties of the literary movement for Scottish independence. Was it possible to define a new Scottish patriotism in terms that were not simply negative – about hatred for the English? Would a small-scale economy be viable – and would not an independent Scotland just collapse into its ancient practices of internal feuding? The inter-war politics of nationalism were no less confused. On paper neither the Liberal nor the Labour Party had revoked their pre-1914 support for Home Rule, but they did nothing actively to promote it. By 1928 this had led its most determined supporters to form the National Party of Scotland (NPS) – drawing together nationalists from different backgrounds, but primarily from the ILP. The NPS gained the support of the key figures in the literary Renaissance, but secured very little public backing. In 1929 its two candidates, the very able party secretary John MacCormick and its chairman Roland Muirhead, both ex-ILP, got fewer than 3,000 votes. In 1931 a rival group, the Scottish Party, was formed by the Duke of Montrose and Sir John MacEwen to provide a home for nationalists of a more right-wing hue. Although MacCormick managed to secure a union between the two in 1934, creating the Scottish National Party (SNP), he lost those like MacDiarmid who resented the conservatism of the new body. Electorally, the SNP was little more successful than its predecessors. In 1935 it lost all but three deposits.

The Popular Front, Planners and the Politics of Order

At the same time, it would be wrong to write off the nationalist challenge. Intellectually, its influence was important. Many younger writers and poets had repudiated Unionism, and their ideas increasingly suffused the wider movements of opposition developing in Scotland in the 1930s. By 1935 the Popular Front had brought together the SNP, the ILP and the Communists and, in combination, they created a quite distinct political climate in Scotland. In general, anti-establishment forces were much more to the fore than in England. The rump of the Labour Party was weaker and the ILP was proportionately stronger.

In terms of creating a special political climate in inter-war Scotland, probably the most important force was organization among the unemployed. Activity by the National Unemployed Workers Movement (NUWM) had declined in the mid- and later twenties. It was revived in 1928 by a bizarre mistake, or perhaps a display of over-confidence, by the government. Employment Exchanges were instructed to recruit 10,000 unemployed males to take temporary work in Canada. Refusal to respond led to loss of benefit for 'not genuinely seeking work'. Thousands succumbed. When they reached Canada they found there was no work directly available, hostility from the local trade union movement and wages so low that they did not cover the return fare. Mass mutinies occurred. Ships were forced to return, and once back in Scotland the NUWM took up hundreds of individual cases. Marches from Lanarkshire, Stirlingshire and Fife temporarily compelled the Scottish Board of Health to recognize the NUWM. In 1931 the imposition of the means test brought a further upsurge. Thousands came out in demonstrations – some, including those in Glasgow, meeting considerable police violence. The national hunger march of 1932 started from Scotland, as did that in 1934. There were also a number of specifically Scottish marches. In 1933 Harry McShane led 2,000 unemployed from Glasgow to Edinburgh, and in 1935 3,500 marchers tackled the 300 kilometres from Aberdeen to Glasgow. Only a fraction of those unemployed were ever actively involved in these actions, but many more relied on the NUWM to represent them at tribunals. To this extent the NUWM revived and sustained the type of community activism experienced during the war. This was particularly so for women. Under the leadership of Isobel Brown women developed their own sections. The first such contingent appeared on the 1928 march in Edinburgh, and between 1932 and 1936 the number of women's contingents on the national hunger marches doubled. The NUWM also provided many of the recruits for the International Brigade. Over 500 young Scots, almost all from the working class, went off between 1936 and 1938 to defend the Spanish Republic. Proportionately to population, the Scots formed by far the biggest contingent within the 2,200 who joined the British battalion.

In Scotland therefore the challenge represented from 1935 by the Popular Front was somewhat different from that in England. By then the ILP had four MPs and the Communists one. The SNP were without MPs, but could call on a range of well-known figures such as Eric Linklater and Compton Mackenzie – who won the rectorship of Glasgow University on a nationalist ticket in 1932. And, as the national government conspicuously failed to take any effective action on the economy and appeared to give passive acceptance to the spread of fascism in Europe, so the arguments of the left gained greater credibility. Compared with England, opposition ideology tended to be more explicitly socialist. Maxton, MacCormick and Gallacher all took it for granted that capitalism had failed as a system. And their advocacy was, in general, framed in terms that drew on Scottish national sentiment. The object of planning, 'people's planning' from below as the Communists stressed, was to rescue Scotland's economy and rebuild the country's towns and villages. This was why a Scottish parliament was needed.

What, then, was the response of those people, a relatively small group, who actually controlled Scotland's economy and government? The answer to this question is of no small consequence. It has been persuasively argued, notably by Professors Christopher Harvie and David McCrone, that it was precisely this period which saw the victory of those *within* Scotland's élite who advocated state intervention. This victory, they argue, had profound and long-lasting consequences. Over previous centuries individualism had been the hallmark of the Scottish ruling élite, and as a result Scotland's social institutions had developed in a way that was quite distinct from that of England. Now, it is claimed, this balance was reversed. Those ruling Scotland concluded that market forces had to be controlled. The collective good depended on the visible hand of the state. Harvie and McCrone claim that the new ethos, once articulated in policy, penetrated Scotland's large professional middle class and gave direction to the new cadre of administrators gathered together for the first time in St Andrew's House in Edinburgh. It was this belief in the necessity of state intervention that united Scottish politicians through the 1950s and '60s, and eventually brought Scottish society as a whole into conflict with the neo-liberal policies of the Thatcher years. To this extent, they argue, the 1920s and '30s were the cradle of a new beginning. These decades saw the emergence of a 'principled society' in Scotland – whose values, in their conflict with neo-liberalism, were to define the need for a Scottish parliament in the 1990s.

This perspective is highly appealing and contains large fragments of truth. Nevertheless, there is also an element of simplification. The argument assumes continuities when the reality was much more fraught and problematic. Just how fraught can be seen by looking at the career of Walter Elliot, probably the key figure in the development of the 1930s 'planning movement'. He was an upper-middle-class Tory, educated at Glasgow Academy and Glasgow University, who married into the Tennant family. Under-Secretary of State for Scotland for most of the 1920s and Secretary of State from 1936 to 1938, he was also a member of the Fabian Society while at university, and qualified as a doctor with experience of practice in working-class Glasgow. Despite his roots, he possessed a healthy contempt for the penny-pinching hypocrisy of the old order. In the 1920s Elliot was largely responsible for bringing the bulk of the Scottish civil service from London to Edinburgh and reorganizing it in coherent departments for health, education and home affairs. In 1936 he helped develop the Scottish Economic Committee (SEC) with responsibilities for industrial redevelopment planning, and initiated a whole series of state-subsidized ventures for transforming Scotland's infrastructure, health and education.

His ideas were very similar to those of his close friend James Bridie, the playwright. He believed in science and scientists. Or perhaps more specifically Scottish scientists – of the kind found among his own friends within Scotland's professional élite. In his *Toryism and the Twentieth Century* he outlined his commitment to an ordered society, developing organically from the past, motivated by older ideas of social responsibility yet able to draw upon the achievements of science to resolve the problems facing human society. In the vacuum created by the collapse of the old morality and the authority of Scotland's men of property, he offered the classless, scientifically validated achievements of a beneficent élite. He backed the work on nutrition of his friend John Boyd Orr, at the Rowett Institute. He himself undertook research to expose the physical stunting of working-class children and used his position in government to experiment with the supply of subsidized milk to schools. As we have seen, he was an admirer of Eisenstein's use of the documentary and sponsored John Grierson's pioneering Scottish productions while Under-Secretary of State in the twenties. Subsequently, in 1936, he helped establish the state-sponsored Films of Scotland.

Yet within it all there was an element of naivety – or perhaps just unavoidable contradiction. Who was to set the values of the scientific élite? To whose agenda were they to work? Elliot, with fatal consequences for his own career, had ultimately to follow an agenda that was not of his making. The Scottish planning movement which Elliot did so much to encourage was very diverse. The Scottish National Development Council (SNDC) derived from attempts by the 1929 Labour government to stimulate thinking on regional development. It was formally convened by the Convention of Royal Burghs in 1930. By 1931 its leading figures were James Lithgow and Stephen Bilsland, a cousin of the Colville steel family. It was essentially a promotional body with a remit to stimulate industrial development and assist diversification from heavy industry. In 1934 it was the national government in London which took the initiative. In response to criticism on unemployment it established a commissioner with responsibility for four of the worst unemployment black spots, the 'special areas'. In each, deputy commissioners were given limited budgets for developing infrastructure. In Scotland the new organization won autonomy from Treasury control and came under the authority of the Scottish Office, and in 1937 – again in response to agitation on unemployment – gained powers to subsidize new or struggling firms. Parallel to these developments came the establishment of the National Trust for Scotland in 1931 and the Saltire Society in 1936, which were respectively dedicated to preserving Scotland's physical heritage and promoting town planning.

These organizations drew on a diversity of traditions. Town planning took forward the legacy of Patrick Geddes. His ideas were rooted, rather like Elliot's, in positivism and the French philosopher Bergson's belief in biological processes, and sought to mould the urban landscape to the organic life of their populations. It stressed the link between good housing, health and efficiency, but in a somewhat paternalist fashion. Geddes himself had been strongly influenced by the Charity Organisation Society and the early Scottish pioneers of social work. The Scottish Economic Committee, formally responsible to the SNDC but paid for by the Scottish Office, developed perspectives which gave a central place to state direction within the economy. Its submission to the Royal Commission on the Distribution of the Industrial Population called for the establishment of a 'central planning authority' with 'full cognisance of everything necessary to overcome the difficulties of Scotland in the full sense'. It saw this body as having a corporate character, including representatives of industry, finance and labour, and modelled on the Special Area Commissions. Yet planning did not necessarily mean planning on behalf of the working class. On the contrary, as implemented in the 1930s it was autocratic rather than democratic and its agenda was ultimately set by the most powerful of business interests. It was not entirely accidental that the first Scottish Commissioner was an Edinburgh manufacturer, Sir Michael Rose, who had been the government's Controller for Scotland during the general strike.

This was the ambiguity at the heart of governmental economic intervention in 1930s

Scotland. It involved a range of people of left-wing sympathies: Boyd Orr, John Grierson, Tom Johnston and James Bowie, the pro-Keynesian economist and principal at Dundee College. Yet the real levers were controlled by others. James Lithgow may have supported the introduction of light industry, but he did so within limits. It must not interfere with the wider drive to reduce capacity in heavy industry or affect the labour market. Although diversification was the objective of the SNDC, it had to make do without modern steel production, any significant subsidies, or much of a local consumer market. Lord Weir, who like Lithgow remembered the militancy of 1914–20, spelt out his terms even more starkly. Weir represented heavy industry on the government's Defence Requirements Committee. Full-scale rearmament was, he argued, incompatible with the government's other aim of restoring the profitability of basic industries. The only condition on which it would be acceptable to the industry was wartime-style direction of labour. Even in Elliot's case, his belief in corporate-style planning drew him in directions he would have preferred to avoid. As Minister for Agriculture and Fisheries between 1932 and 1934, he went a long way to rescue home producers from the effects of the world slump. He did so by establishing quotas for imports and home production and creating marketing boards to enforce them. However, this policy in turn depended on protectionist policies, ratified in the Ottawa agreement, that converted the British Empire into a closed trading bloc.

Empire has never been very far from the history of modern Scotland. It was particularly important economically in the 1930s – as it was for Britain as a whole – because it provided a controlled market, supplied cheap raw materials, and gave the luxury of an economic cushion, an uncomfortable one for those under it, not possessed by either America or Germany. In sharp contrast with the profit collapse in those countries, British profits rose. By the late thirties oil alone contributed 5 per cent of total profit income. The many Scottish shareholders in Burmah Oil and Anglo-Persian Oil enjoyed investments yielding up to 20 per cent a year in the mid- to late 1930s. For the well-off who invested wisely, the 1930s were very good years and the national government was determined to keep it that way.

This international dimension to prosperity provided very strong arguments for coming to terms with Nazi Germany. On the industrial front British recovery policies depended largely on European quota arrangements on steel, coal and chemicals. These were negotiated with Germany – directly or indirectly by the man who bankrolled Lithgow, the governor of the Bank of England, Lord Norman. On the military front, the only alternative to appeasement was rearmament. Again, as Weir argued, this would destroy the delicate balance on which profits depended. Worse still, it would require alliance with the United States, the cost of which, as the Americans made clear, was the end of empire preference. Elliot did not like the policy of appeasement. His private letters show that he thought it was a gamble that would probably lead to disaster. Yet he could not disentangle himself from the policies that sustained it. Other Scots in the government were less anguished. The two aristocrats, Lord Dunglass (Alec Douglas-Home) and Philip Kerr, Marquis of Lothian, were enthusiastic supporters of an anti-Soviet alliance. The new Secretary of State for Scotland, ex-steel magnate Sir John Colville, who replaced Elliot in 1938, steadily supported Chamberlain to the end. To all appearances, so too did Elliot and the entire Scottish political and economic élite. It was the depth of this involvement which was soon to cause irreversible damage to the political influence of Scotland's ruling élite – and, in Elliot's case, terminate his political career.

However, we can pause at a happier moment in Elliot's life: the Empire Exhibition of 1938. This formed the climax of his period as Secretary of State and drew on all his enthusiasms. The exhibition was sited in Bellahouston Park in Glasgow. It displayed Scotland's achievements in science, engineering, arts and film, and was housed in an array of modernist buildings which rivalled the Paris exhibition of 1937. Its lead architect was Thomas Tait, the doyen of the new school of Scottish architects. Tait had placed himself in the mainstream of the modern movement – drawing on the work of the German Walter Gropius, the French Robert Mallet-Stephens and the Dutch Willem Dudok. He had already designed the new seat of government in Scotland, St Andrew's House. Now Tait's soaring white tower dominated the exhibition with the brilliant simplicity of international modernism. Tait's team included all the younger experimental modernists in Scotland: Basil Spence, Jack Coia, Mervyn Noad, Margaret Brodie. Their ambition was to show what a new, reconstructed Scotland might physically look like.

As soon as the exhibition opened, the realities of 1938 supervened. The procession which drove through the gates on 3 May emphatically represented the old Scotland. Robed royals, feathered politicians, industrialists and bankers posed incongruously before the stark white buildings. The royal party provided an exact grading of importance. Behind the landau of the king-emperor came the tenth Earl of Elgin, educated at Eton and Balliol, owner of a large part of Fife, decorated in the war, Grand Master Mason for Scotland in the twenties, president of the SNDC since 1931. In the second royal car came Walter Elliot. In the first processional car was Sir Ian Colquhoun, thirteenth baronet, decorated in the war, Grand Master Mason in 1934, owning much of Dumbartonshire, previously rector of Glasgow University and Lord High Commissioner of the Church of Scotland. Joining him was the Dominion Secretary, the Rt Hon. Malcolm MacDonald, Ramsay's son. In the second processional car came Sir James Lithgow together with the man who actually organized the exhibition, Sir Cecil Weir, vice-president of Glasgow Chamber of Commerce. In the third processional car came Lady Lithgow and two government ministers (for Labour and Transport). In the fourth car was the general manager of the Union Bank, Mr Norman Hird, and his wife, together with Captain Salvesen (educated at Fettes and Edinburgh, shipowner and landowner, vice-convener of the exhibition) and Mrs Salvesen. The first person in any way associated with the Labour movement came in the eleventh car: Sir John Stewart, Lord Provost of Glasgow (the City Treasurer, Patrick Dollan, was later presented to the king). Then came the prime ministers and high commissioners of the white dominions, a number with Scottish names, starting with Vincent Massey.

Others, of course, took no part in the proceedings. Helen Crawfurd was organizing a separate Peace and Empire Congress, also held in Glasgow. She had urgent issues of her own. Two days before the exhibition's royal opening His Majesty's forces had opened fire on an illegal demonstration in Jamaica. Three trade-unionists had been killed and many others injured. The Empire Exhibition ran through the summer of Munich. The buildings were then dismantled. They had been constructed using the latest prefabrication techniques and clad in the new wonder material, asbestos sheeting. Twelve months later Britain was at war.

War and the Eclipse of the Old Order

What the war had to do with them the people of the village did not know. It came on them as an alien plague, taking their sons away and then killing them meaninglessly, randomly. They watched the road often for telegrams.

Iain Crichton Smith captures the eerie, apprehensive uncertainty of wartime Scotland. Rumours abounded. Trust was limited. Why had the Germans not bombed Clydeside? In March 1941, a week before the raids started, the pioneering social survey organization, Mass Observation, found that over 40 per cent of the population were 'vague or indifferent' when asked this question. Almost a third believed the Germans would never bomb. Those from the working class gave matter-of-fact reasons, like distance or their proximity to high ground. Those from the upper and middle class tended to be more suspicious. They believed the Germans were allowing time for social unrest to develop within the working population. This fear of the unknown reached deep into government.

Tom Harrison, the director of Mass Observation, was in Scotland in the late winter of 1941 because he had been sent there to probe opinions. As soon as the big raids began, the Home Office separately commissioned a confidential civil service report on Clydebank. The Germans had dropped 500 tons of high explosives, killed 538 people and damaged or destroyed all but a handful of the town's closely packed tenements. The town's emergency services had been overwhelmed. But the investigator found that the population reacted with spontaneous practicality: they rescued each other and set off for the hills above the town till the raids subsided. Although the Home Office correspondent noted that the town had a 'reputation for social unrest', he reported that one consequence of the raids had been a return to work by strikers in John Brown's shipyard. The Mass Observation report, which was completed before the raids started, also discounted the view held 'by a number of important Glasgow people' about 'gathering social unrest':

It is not that the Clydeside workers are against the war or for peace. They want to win it as much as anyone, though there is a considerable Maxtonish minority. It is rather that Clydeside workers are *also* having a war of their own, that they . . . cannot overcome the bitter memories of industrial insecurity in the past ten years . . .

The more general findings of Mass Observation were that large sections of the population had little knowledge of the purposes of the war. Many displayed an exhausted resentment at the twelve-hour shifts and the bureaucratic confusions of industrial conscription – policed by the same employment offices that a year before had been administering the means test.

This new war had none of the predictability of its predecessor. Its politics were complex and shifting – its violence totally erratic, often far distant, sometimes terrifyingly near. Aberdeen was geographically the most exposed of Scottish cities and eventually experienced more air raids than any other. For the first eight months of Chamberlain's 'phoney war' very little happened. In September 1939, 30,000 children from the west of Scotland were evacuated to rural Aberdeenshire. By November 1939 most had returned home. In January 1940 an Aberdeen trawler was dive-bombed off the coast. Further such attacks followed in spring 1940. The first big blow to the city only came in June 1940 with news from France that the Gordon Highlanders had been decimated at St Valéry. In June 1940 the first bomb landed – demolishing a bungalow at Nigg on the outskirts of the city. The following month a lone bomber dropped a string of bombs across the city itself, killing thirty-four people. Aberdeen never suffered mass bombing like Clydebank. But thirty-two further air raids occurred intermittently across the following four years. The terror came from not knowing when or how the enemy might strike. The biggest raid came in April 1943, when twenty-five bombers attacked the city. The last wave of planes swept low to machine-gun the streets – by then full of women and children. Of the 40,000 Scottish war dead, 6,000 were civilians.

The new war was also quite different from its predecessor in terms of the way production was organized. This time war work was initially steered away from Scotland: 90 per cent of the Scottish factories re-designated for war work were still being used for storage in 1941. Scottish arms production remained largely restricted to the existing shipyard and engineering facilities. Consequently Scots still had to move south to where the work was. At one point 500 girls a week were being conscripted for war work in English factories. Why? No doubt it was in part because the new industries were mainly located in the English Midlands, but issues of social control were never far away. Scottish employers well remembered the effects of full employment twenty years before – as did government advisers like Beveridge. Even during the tepid rearmament of 1937, Clydeside engineering factories had been hit by an unprecedented strike wave from apprentices demanding minimum wages and improved conditions.

However, the biggest contrast with 1914 concerned the role of Scotland's traditional élite. In the first war its influence had been all-pervasive. In the second its public role largely ceased in May 1940. It was then that Chamberlain's efforts to broker peace with Germany finally collapsed. Over the previous months Colville, Douglas-Home, Lothian and Elliot continued as loyal members of Chamberlain's government. Elliot himself had maintained particularly close links with the Italian ambassador, who was acting as an intermediary between the powers.

On 10 May 1940 Churchill took office as prime minister. He had scores to settle. Within twelve days the police had arrested and interned one of the better-known sons of the Scottish aristocracy, Captain A. H. M. Ramsay, Tory MP for Peebles and nephew of the Earl of Dalhousie. Ramsay had been a member of a number of pro-Franco and pro-Nazi organizations – but then in 1930s upper-class Scotland so had many others. Rudoph Hess was not entirely bereft of intelligence when he made his parachute jump over the Duke of Hamilton's estate in 1941. Quite apart from the politicians who supported appeasement, a significant number of aristocrats and Tory MPs had actively supported fascism. Sir Thomas Moore, MP for Ayr burghs, had been particularly outspoken in his support for the blackshirts and an anti-Soviet alliance: 'from my personal knowledge of Herr Hitler, peace and justice are the key words of his policy'. When Churchill talked about the 'malignity in our midst', it was not just innocent Italian shopkeepers, interned in their hundreds, who watched apprehensively for policemen at the end of the street. In the event, all the Scots in government lost their positions. Elliot was put in charge of air raid shelters in Chester. Colville was sent to India. Sir Thomas Moore joined the Home Guard. In an unprecedented snub, an English MP, Ernest Brown, was appointed Secretary of State for Scotland in the new Cabinet.

Brown faced an almost impossible task and failed. The political environment in Scotland was quite different from that in England. The ILP under Maxton actively opposed the war. So did a majority with the SNP. And up to June 1941 the Communists also characterized the war as inter-imperialist. These groupings were relatively small. But the government was unsure how far their influence might spread – particularly in view of the sudden displacement of many of the traditional leaders of Scottish society. It was this concern that led Churchill, in March 1941, to recruit as Secretary of State the man who had edited *Forward* during the previous war and was now a bastion of the refashioned Labour Party, Tom Johnston.

Johnston met the challenge with vigour and imagination. The Scottish Office planned as it had never planned before. Johnston sought to revive a Scottish legitimacy. He got Churchill's agreement to create a Scottish Council of State made up of all previous Scottish Secretaries. This gave him an active all-party consensus for Scottish legislation. He convened a meeting of Scottish MPs in Edinburgh – the first, he noted, for 234 years. He set up a Scottish Council for Industry which brought together trade union and business leaders as well as Scottish Office administrators. This Scottish Council was then used as a vehicle to pressure the government into shifting significant amounts of war production back into Scotland. By the end of 1942 over a hundred new industrial units had opened with a labour force of 20,000. By 1945 the number had increased to 700 with a labour force of 90,000. In 1943 the Scottish Council of State gave Johnston backing to create a state-run Scottish Hydro-Electric Board. This he saw, in the same light as Roosevelt's Tennessee Valley Authority, as an engine for regenerating the whole of the Highland region. He turned the government-controlled civil defence hospitals into a shadow national health service which provided the prompt and professional medical attention previously denied to the bulk of the population. He ensured that the state control of food distribution was used to benefit the slum-dwellers of the cities and towns. At least partly in consequence, infant mortality in Scotland actually fell by 27 per cent during the war years – the biggest fall anywhere in Europe – and the average height of Glasgow children increased by 5 centimetres. As John Boyd Orr commented in his autobiography, this was despite worse overcrowding and less food overall. What changed was the distribution – in favour of those Scots, probably a near majority, previously denied adequate nutrition. In a final act of masterly symbolism, Johnston converted the luxury hotel at Gleneagles into a health centre for miners.

There can be no doubt that these policies did have immediate political objectives. In 1940 the SNP secured 37 per cent of the vote in the Argyll by-election. By 1944 it was scoring 41 per cent in urban Kirkcaldy. When Johnston made comparisons with the rise of Sinn Fein twenty years before, he may have been trying to frighten Whitehall into concessions. He certainly viewed the SNP as a threat. The war also produced a renewed challenge from the left. By 1943 full employment had restored the influence of the shop stewards movement and given Communist activists a dominant position in many of the large industrial workplaces. The Ministry of Information estimated that one Scot in ten was now reading the *Daily Worker* and by the end of the war the party's Scottish membership had reached a peak of 10,000. In face of these challenges Johnston's high-profile projection of Scottish-based planning was ultimately very successful. Government in Scotland was seen as distinct from that in London. Legitimacy was given to a post-war settlement which made the Labour Party the natural heir of previous aspirations for a planned and rationally organized society in Scotland.

However, this still leaves us asking: was the continuity real? Professors Harvie and McCrone see Johnston's wartime and post-war planning as a progression – a further step in the development of a 'principled society'. But this is to make big assumptions about the character of pre-war Scottish planning. As we saw earlier, it was not particularly principled in terms of any commitment to its people. What really determined the shape of the Scottish economy in the 1930s was not the deliberations of the SNDC but the informal decision-making within the Bank of England. Lithgow wanted to control implementation in Scotland and in consequence strongly supported administrative devolution – at the same time as defending the Union. Lithgow was happy to work within a British state system in which Scottish big business still enjoyed great influence. After 1945 the centralization of effective economic decision-making in London remained. What changed was that Scottish big business had virtually no part in it. The Labour Party now held political power – but economic power was another matter.

1945 – a New Beginning?

Perhaps the best way of gauging the new situation is to look at the fate of the two great planning exercises initiated by the Scottish Office in 1943. One was the East of Scotland Plan, the other the Clyde Valley Regional Plan under Patrick Abercrombie. They were intended to provide the blueprints for the economic and industrial reconstruction of the new post-war Scotland. Teams of planners were brought together from local authorities. The best expertise was sought from architectural schools – already partly collated in *Building Scotland*, published under the sponsorship of the Saltire Society in 1944. The exercise shared the assumptions of the minority report of the Barlow Commission signed by Abercrombie. This had argued that regional development could not be left to market forces. The state had to direct industry and, if necessary, run it. The emphasis of the planners was on comprehensive development. The grimy, soulless conurbations had to be rebuilt. New communities were to be established in the countryside alongside new or relocated industries. Throughout, as Geddes had argued, the link between economic and social life was to be respected. Comprehensive development meant building on the strengths that already existed, in steel, coal and heavy engineering, and supplementing them with new industries producing cars, aircraft and electrical goods which could reap economies of scale from local suppliers and cheap energy and materials.

Had such comprehensive planning been adopted in 1945 it is likely that many of the subsequent difficulties of the Scottish economy would have been avoided. The problem with the consumer-durable branch plants established in the 1950s and '60s was that they did not form part of comprehensive development. They were, in the words of economist George Kerevan, 'cathedrals in the desert'. They imported ready-made parts. And, as branch plants, they were very vulnerable when economic recession returned precisely because they had not been integrated into a wider Scottish economy in the way envisaged by the planners of 1945.

Yet by the time these plans were published in 1946–7 their moment had already passed. As in the 1930s, the imperatives of state policy at British level intervened – though in a totally different international environment. Now it was the United States that was dominant. The price which had to be paid for wartime aid was the end of a protected British Empire market and free access to empire resources. In the eyes of Scotland's business élite this was bad enough. Far worse was the way Whitehall strategists sought to deal with the new environment. Keynes's ideas now ruled the

Treasury. For him and his colleagues full employment and fast industrial growth were Britain's only hope. The firms producing the new generation of export goods, motors, chemicals and electricals, had to grow to the point where they could meet the competition of the giant American corporations. A profitable internal market was needed. Externally, ways had to be found to make the output of Britain's firms as cheap and competitive as possible. The method adopted struck directly at Scottish big business. It involved the nationalization of coal, power and steel. The conditions attached to post-war American aid prohibited direct export subsidies. The hidden subsidies concealed through government control over prices and investment in nationalized industry were essential if cheap transport, power and basic materials were to fuel export growth in the private corporate sector.

The City of London gave these modernization policies its full support. Scotland's industrial élite did not. The nationalization of coal, transport, power and steel broke the backs of the great integrated empires of the 1930s. Only shipbuilding remained in private hands – and in circumstances where limited steel quotas and restricted markets made it a poor prospect for long-term investment. In terms of the industrial economy Scotland's traditional élite faced marginalization. Walter Elliot, now a backbencher representing the Scottish universities, complained in the Commons that nationalization was a total misnomer. In Scotland it meant 'denationalization', the loss of national control – a comment which also nicely exposes all the élitist assumptions of Scottish planning as it actually took place in the thirties.

What happened to the plans of 1945? Bits were implemented, but it was more by chance than design. The Scottish Office had powers to propose, but it could not implement. This depended on ministries in London – and there the Keynesian supporters of national demand management had by and large won out over those like Dalton who favoured a greater measure of direction.

Initially in 1945–6 the Board of Trade and Stafford Cripps's Ministry of Economic Affairs did make an attempt to begin comprehensive development. It used the 1945 Town and Country Planning Act to direct a significant proportion of new industrial investment to the development areas, particularly Scotland, and to prevent the return south of war factories, such as the Rolls-Royce works at Hillington. It also made a determined effort to initiate car production at the giant Linwood heavy pressings plant owned by the Beardmore-Lithgow group and used for tank production during the war. But the Lithgow group resisted – long enough to ensure that no major development took place. During the war similar obstruction had occurred. In 1943 Johnston proposed the creation of an Industrial and Commercial Finance Corporation to finance new industries. The two banks with closest links to Clydeside big business, the Union and the Clydesdale, intervened. They demanded direct representation for steel and heavy engineering interests to ensure there was no unfair competition. This preoccupation remained. The old order may have been sidelined in terms of national policy. But its battle to protect its access to skilled labour and steel was to colour Scottish economic development for another two decades.

The year 1947 largely saw the end of concerted central government action to develop the Scottish economy. The sterling crisis of that year made exports the overriding concern. Housing finance was cut – leaving the physical reconstruction of urban Scotland largely unrealized for another two decades. Plans for industrial renewal were shelved. At British level the proportion of new factories relocated to development areas fell from 51 per cent before 1947 to 19 per cent thereafter.

This left Labour policies in Scotland dangerously exposed. The result was a bizarre marriage of convenience. The Labour heirs of Tom Johnston found common cause with American multinationals looking for a bridgehead into European markets. These companies sought politically stable environments and non-union labour forces. The Board of Trade did not particularly want American companies bringing inflationary pressures to the English Midlands, and Scotland was the obvious alternative. Over the five years to 1951 Scotland attracted over 70 per cent of all American investment into Britain. By the mid-fifties the volume of American investment exceeded the rest of Europe combined and gave Scotland the highest level per head of population outside Canada. NCR in Dundee, IBM in Greenock, Burroughs in Cumbernauld and General Motors in Lanarkshire were some of the early names. In general these firms chose greenfield sites away from the heavily unionized major conurbations. Many were steered to the New Towns – East Kilbride, initiated in 1947, Glenrothes in 1949 and Cumbernauld in 1957. Sir Patrick Dollan became the first chairman of East Kilbride Development Corporation, perhaps fittingly in view of his New York venture ten years before. It was a strange end for a Clydeside militant.

It was also a strange outcome for the Scottish planning movement. The New Towns, as they actually took shape, did not represent comprehensive development. They were inhabited by branch plants. Their industrial relations practices were quite different from those elsewhere in Scotland. Even their architecture and road systems seemed to emphasize their separateness. Just twenty kilometres away from their new brethren, old conurbations continued much as before. The shipbuilding and heavy engineering industries still employed upwards of 100,000 – producing for a post-war sellers' market that was to last into the mid-fifties. The old mining areas gained a renewed vigour after the war. Coal was a strategic industry: the main source of energy and a key part of the export drive. Some 80,000 miners, scarcely fewer than in 1914, worked in an industry which, while now publicly owned, retained many of the management structures of the old mining companies.

So, to return to our earlier discussion, the development of twentieth-century Scotland as a society with a particularly large public sector and a commitment to state intervention cannot be seen to issue smoothly from plans and ideas laid down in the 1920s and '30s. The actuality of planning in the thirties was private, informal, élitist – powerful precisely because it represented the interests of regional big business. In the 1940s and '50s, by contrast, the driving force was external, dependent on the demand-management assumptions of central government and ultimately responding to the interests of big business at British level. In neither case did it have a democratic basis within Scotland and in neither case did it lead to development that was either coherent or sustainable.

This sense of fracture and discontinuity is no less strong when we turn from economic to social reconstruction. One of the biggest achievements of the 1940s was the establishment of the National Health Service. In time this did create a strong constituency within Scotland's professional strata which supported the concept of state provision, but this was not the case in 1946. April 1946 saw one of the biggest ever meetings of general practitioners held in Glasgow. The 400 doctors who gathered in St Andrew's Hall denounced the Labour government proposals. They rejected any idea that they were to become 'servants of the state'. Nine months later a reconvened meeting overwhelmingly voted for non-cooperation unless general practitioners were allowed to keep full ownership of their practices. Private ownership was 'a point of most fundamental importance to secure professional unity as well as freedom'. Scottish doctors voted against the government proposals just as heavily as those in England in the BMA's January 1947 plebiscite.

There was a similarly rough-edged feel to the other great achievement of the 1940s: the maintenance of post-war full employment. This did transform lives by giving security and confidence. Yet many aspects of the old occupational order continued. The Nuffield Foundation financed research on male entrants to the Glasgow labour market in 1947 – youngsters who had been born in 1932. It found these young men were much less exposed to unemployment compared with their counterparts in the early 1930s. Then the average period of unemployment was just over five months at the age of sixteen. For the youngsters of 1947 the total experience of unemployment over three years did not amount to more than three weeks. Yet in other respects life had not changed so much. The report concluded on the situation as it was in 1950:

. . . there can be but small cause for complacency in a community where, at age 17, three years after leaving school, 1 in 4 of the boys is still in a stop-gap job with no clear idea of what his life work is to be; where less than half of them have undergone sustained training for work demanding skill or responsibility; where aimless shifting about from job to job is still characteristic of 1 boy in 4; where 3 in 4 have never made use of the most obvious facilities for continued education . . . The Welfare State should mean not only medical services but healthy men, women and young people; not only a housing programme but sufficient houses to accommodate every family in decency, free from overcrowding, and in good surroundings. These are not the conditions in which the youths of today are growing up. Nor does such a new society appear overnight. The conditions bearing on the character and performance of youth are always a mixture of the old and new; and, despite the rapidity of the changes of recent years, there is more of the past than of the present that goes to their moulding.

None of this is meant to deny a sense of a new beginning in 1945. It is, however, to stress its problematic character. While there was a strong feeling that the old order had received a blow from which it would not recover, no one was certain how secure the future was. The diaries of Naomi Mitchison capture this uncertainty. Mitchison was very well connected, moved regularly between rural Argyll, Glasgow, Edinburgh and London, lectured to the Army Bureau for Current Affairs and kept a diary for Mass Observation. In 1945 she was a member of one of Tom Johnston's reconstruction advisory committees, her husband was a Labour parliamentary candidate and she herself was involved in the Scottish Convention set up by John MacCormick to bring together a cross-party coalition in favour of Home Rule. Her assessments of post-war developments shift sharply. At moments she had premonitions of sweeping political change. She reported the scale of support for the Soviet Union from her army lectures and even from the fishermen of Carradale. She noted the popular backing for the Beveridge report, the detestation of the old Voluntary Hospital system and the conviction that the end of the war must bring something better. Yet she was very unsure how it would come about. The Scottish Convention was poorly organized and marginal. The Labour Party was unreliable. The old order was 'entrenching itself in government offices'. Bevin and Morrison were so reactionary she 'felt ashamed to be in the same party'. International events also impinged. In the final months of the war there were the political changes in America: the death of Roosevelt, the displacement of his vice-president Henry Wallace and the succession of Truman. Furthermore, there was the use of the atomic bomb: 'wondering if this meant another war and felt deeply depressed'. Even as a feminist, Mitchison was constantly disappointed at the persistence of the old attitudes. Men gave lip service to equality, but failed to understand its economic preconditions. Women looked forward to the return of normal home life with its old division of labour, 'and I could not blame them given their historical conditioning and this god-awful church which considers sex as a sin'.

Was there, then, no counterpart to the radicalism of 1919? Ideologically, the answer is probably yes. Mitchison found that support for a planned economy and social ownership was now extending beyond the working class to farmers and some other sectors of small business who 'hate the big monopolies'. Within the working class in large-scale industry there was considerably greater sophistication than before. During the war the workplace Joint Production Committees (JPCs) had played an important role in refining ideas. Established by the government to expedite production, they became mass organizations for debating reconstruction and the post-war order. Clydeside employers complained to the Ministry of Production that the JPCs were turning themselves into 'little soviets'. On the other hand, as Mitchison noted, these ideas of radical social change had nowhere to go. The Labour movement was run by social democrats, committed to Beveridge and Keynes, but ultimately aligned to the *status quo* – with all that this brought in its train. The Communists and their allies had significant strength at shop steward level, but it did not extend much further. Efforts were made, unsuccessfully, to push Labour towards a more radical form of nationalization. In 1946 homeless families occupied vacant properties in Glasgow's west end and in other cities such as Aberdeen, in a bid to force the government's hand on re-housing. As the rearmament drive got under way, resistance developed to the government's mandatory wage freeze – which by 1949 had cut real wages by up to 5 per cent. In 1950 the STUC became the first major trade union organization in Britain to reject continued cooperation. Nevertheless, any wider radical impetus had been lost.

By 1951 Britain was involved in another war. The Highland Division was now fighting in Korea. In the previous conflict, Hamish Henderson had written his *Elegies for the Dead in Cyrenaica*. The lines are stoical, purged of sentiment or condemnation. Henderson wrote for both the Scottish dead and the German: 'that wronged proletariat of levelling death in which all the fallen are comrades'. Yet there is also a certainty. The war had a purpose. In 'The Interlude', written during the artillery barrage before El-Alamein, 'Mak siccar' (make sure) is repeated and then repeated again.

> Mak siccar against the leaching lies
> against the worked out systems of sick perversion
> *mak siccar*
> against the executioner
> against the tyrannous myth and the real terror
> *mak siccar.*

No elegies were written for the dead of the Korean war. But from the television sets of the 1950s, 500,000 of them in Scotland by 1958, came the songs of Andy Stewart: 'There was a soldier, a Scottish soldier, Who wandered far away, and soldiered far away . . .' – in Indonesia, Indo-China, Malaya, Kenya, Suez, Cyprus and Aden.

A Strange Normality

When the Conservatives returned to power in 1951, the shift in votes was, as in the rest of Britain, small. In 1945 Labour had secured 49 per cent of the Scottish vote and forty seats. The Conservatives had taken 41 per cent and thirty seats. In 1951 Labour slipped to 47 per cent and lost four seats. The Conservatives gained almost 48 per cent with thirty-five seats – an advance at least partly explained by the fall in the Liberal vote from 5 per cent to less than 2 per cent. The SNP scored negligibly in both 1945 and 1951.

Electorally, therefore, Scotland was very similar to the rest of Britain. Votes were divided almost equally between two parties. In addition, allegiances were largely determined by occupational status. The Conservatives held their rural fiefdoms and affluent suburbs. Labour controlled the industrial towns and most mining areas. The main difference was the Orange vote within the manual working class. Combined with support from supervisory and white-collar staff, this enabled the Conservatives to score well in a number of industrial constituencies. In 1955, for instance, Craigton, Pollok and Cathcart, largely working-class areas of Glasgow, were represented by Tory MPs.

In some ways this political conservatism matched the social and political attitudes within Scottish society in the 1950s. In the short term Naomi Mitchison's premonitions proved accurate. Across much of Scotland it was as if the turmoil and hopes of the 1940s had never been. The great landowners were still entrenched in the county councils. The ancient professions ruled the residual institutions of Scottish society. The old industrial élite, maybe a little apprehensive and embattled, dominated large sectors of the economy. Even in parliament there was a limited return of the old political order. The new Conservative government appointed as Secretary of State Chamberlain's chief whip from the 1930s, the aristocrat James Stuart. A rising star was Alec Douglas-Home. Although the Conservative administration maintained much the same economic and social policies as its Labour predecessor, it also gave a renewed emphasis to the defence of empire. The nationalization of steel was reversed. Shipbuilding maintained its post-war levels of output. The big engineering and textile firms remained largely under Scottish control. Birth and place still visibly mattered – even if it was in somewhat camouflaged form. When Lord Weir retired as chair of the family firm in 1998, he recalled his apprenticeship in the early 1950s. Each morning his grandfather's butler brought in a neatly pressed boiler suit along with the morning tea. The Lord Weir we met in the 1920s was still in command.

For those in a less exalted social position, these post-war years represented an era of unfamiliar security. Work existed for almost everyone. Unemployment was as low as 2·5 per cent through most of the fifties. While this was double the rate in England – and in some areas of the Highlands and Islands the rate remained stubbornly higher – it meant that for most people a job was available more or less where they lived. The constant upheavals of previous generations were at an end. Emigration, which continued, was now more a reflection of the better living conditions and higher wage rates elsewhere: skilled workers were 10 per cent better off in the English Midlands. Health in Scotland also became dramatically better. The transformation of Scotland's vital statistics had begun during the war itself. The introduction of free milk and vitamins for children cut the mortality rate among under-fives by 40 per cent within three years. This improvement continued after the war as full employment brought higher incomes and improved nutrition. The long-term divergence between mortality rates in Scotland and England ended in the late forties. By the fifties the killer diseases of childhood had been all but wiped out and tuberculosis among young adults was making its final stand.

In part these developments also reflected better housing conditions. In the immediate post-war years, progress had been slow. Still in 1951 a third of Scottish households shared a WC: 42 per cent in Dundee and 46 per cent in Motherwell. Under the Tories the level of council house building in Scotland accelerated. At the peak of Macmillan's housing drive in 1954, 40,000 council houses were being built each year. The specifications of these houses were lower than those built previously and the use of new building techniques left them vulnerable to damp and dilapidation. None the less, the 1950s were the years that saw the populations of Scotland's big cities at last escaping from the tenements. New estates took shape with back-and-front-door houses, gardens and modern amenities: for example, in Glasgow's Pollok and Knightshood, Edinburgh's Sighthill and the Inch in Liberton, and Dundee's Whitfield and Menzieshill. For those moving into these homes it finally seemed that the demands of the pre-1914 socialists had been answered.

This new sense of security and geographical stability may also explain another feature of Scotland in the post-war years: the revival of its churches. From the beginning of the century about half the Scottish population had maintained some form of church involvement. This had always fluctuated somewhat. It was dipping a little before 1914. It rose somewhat between 1918 and 1929 when the Church of Scotland and the United Free Church reunited. It fell a little in the late thirties. Throughout, it maintained itself at roughly 50 per cent. The remarkable feature of the period between 1941 and the late fifties is that church involvement increased significantly. This was most marked in the Protestant denominations, above all the Church of Scotland. Research carried out in the sixties found no particular link to social class. In Falkirk and Alloa a large number of skilled manual workers attended church – although proportionately the professions and supervisory and white-collar occupations attended best. The most significant finding was the link with stability of residence – highest among owner-occupiers and council house tenants and lowest among those in the private rented sector.

This picture of an increasingly stable home-centred family unit is confirmed when we look at the role of women. During the war women had been mobilized for employment and, as in the First World War, levels of female unionization had increased sharply. The biggest single strike in wartime Scotland was over equal pay for women. It was initiated by women workers in the giant Rolls-Royce factory in Hillington and had been successful. Predictably, once the war was over, previous practices were resumed. Married women returned to the home. In addition, women now married much earlier. By the early 1960s the *average* age at first marriage had come down to twenty-one – lower by three years than in the 1930s. These young wives were correspondingly fertile and the number of children born within marriage rose to an all-time high in the early 1960s. In many ways the early 1960s can be seen as the golden age of the two-parent nuclear family in Scotland. The proportion of children born outside marriage declined to its lowest level at any point in the twentieth century. The number of divorces fell over a ten-year period. And once women had started to bear children, they remained in the home. The characteristic pattern of the later twentieth century, of women working in their thirties and forties, did not get under way till the end of the 1960s – awaiting the decline in male employment, the expansion of part-time work and the introduction of the contraceptive pill. The new housing schemes of the early 1960s were full of children.

Yet if this was the golden age of the family, it was a strange and often contorted family. New freedoms existed alongside old attitudes. The journalist Meg Henderson tells the story of her family moving, between the late 1940s and the late 1950s, from inner-city Glasgow, via Blackhill, to the new housing scheme of Drumchapel, then situated in the open country between the city and Clydebank. The children could wander through the bluebell woods, catch sticklebacks in the burn and then walk on to the bombed-out ruins of Clydebank: 'Arum lilies grew all through the ruins; probably seeds had blown over from the nearby graveyard.' Yet that was all. Government housing finance did not extend to shopping centres, schools or community halls. The van was the shop. As the daughter of a Catholic father, Meg Henderson had to travel back to a Catholic school in the city centre. Protestants did the same. The houses had baths, gas fires and enough space to end any hint of overcrowding. Those who saved could afford fitted carpets and their own terrazzo door steps. The television made up for the geographical isolation. For Meg's mother the new house was the 'palace of her dreams', but it was also a prison. Meg's father made it so. The family brought with them age-old convictions about the mutual duties of husband and wife. The husband had the right to spend the money, to drink and use physical violence. The wife had the duty to accept this and keep up external appearances. Not a word of what happened left the house. For this two-parent family, like many others, it was the silence that was golden.

These were the Scots of the late 1950s: geographically settled and church-attending, voting for British parties, seeking outward respectability, and providing a new and diversified consumer market. The Clyde had apparently become safe enough, in 1960, to be chosen as the base for the United States' nuclear missile submarines. Yet Scotland, as we will see, was also on the brink of very fast social and political change. How, then, do we explain this strange interlude?

Political commentators of the time, such as David Butler and Richard Rose, saw the new attitudes as permanent rather than temporary. They argued that they marked the maturity of a *British* industrial society. Steadily rising living standards were making workers more middle class in their tastes and more British in their allegiances. A common consensus limited divisions of party and class. No less important, the new unifying values, embodying support for a mixed economy, full employment and a welfare state, were conceived in the essentially British terms of the 1945 political settlement. More recently, Scottish historians have tended to see the stability of the

1950s as an end rather than a beginning: the product of the powerful forces of social inertia in Scottish society. In these terms the fifties are portrayed as the final expression of an old and authentically Scottish civil society – framed retrospectively in the secure and predictable world of 'Dr Finlay's Case Book'. Both explanations have some truth, but they also miss the point.

For the apparent stability was, in reality, much more of an equipoise and thus inherently unstable. It might be objected that this was nothing new. Did not class also divide pre-war Scotland? But there was a new factor. It was the sheer depth of confidence now felt by ordinary people. Full employment gave it them. And they knew it. Even in the remotest parts of the country its effects were felt. In the early fifties an Edinburgh sociologist, James Littlejohn, conducted field work in the sparsely populated sheep-farming border country north-west of Lockerbie, to which he gave the fictitious name 'Westrigg'. There was no industry. The sole areas of gainful employment were in agriculture. For centuries the area had been ruled by the dukes of Buccleuch. This family had owned the land and let it out to large commercial sheep farmers. By the fifties the Buccleuchs had sold off their local estates to the big farmers. Although there were a few small 'working' farmers, the social structure was fairly polarized between an upper middle class of big farmers and the hired farm hands. Any contact with the wider world was as difficult as it had been before the war for those who had no motor transport. Yet attitudes changed decisively. What had previously been a subterranean and usually unspoken resistance became public. The agricultural workers now had their union and were open in their complaints. One shepherd commented: 'Farmers are mean, you know, they are always good at finding excuses for not paying you more than the minimum wage.' Another responded to the farmers' claim that their employees no longer worked hard: 'They have only themselves to blame. Before the war they made us work hard enough for them . . .' Another added: 'It's not so bad now but before the war you daren't say a word or out you'd go.' These men were not radicals. Littlejohn calculated that politically quite a number probably still voted Unionist. Nevertheless they knew their worth and were not to be put down. Previously the minister and schoolmaster had been effective agents of social discipline. Now, because of these pre-war associations, the farm-worker families treated them with ill-concealed contempt. In Littlejohn's Westrigg the tide of secularization was already strong in the early fifties – particularly among the women. They did not want the minister coming into their homes, a practice which smacked too much of the inspection visits of the past. Therefore they stopped attending church.

In the Highlands there were parallel changes that are evocatively described by Naomi Mitchison in her novel *Lobsters on the Agenda*, written in the early 1950s. By then Mitchison was a member of the Advisory Panel on the Highlands established by the Scottish Office at the end of the war as a roving commission to highlight issues of concern. Her subject was 'Port Sonas', a small town in western Argyll. Poor road transport made the weekly visit by the steamer the main link with the outside world. Crofting and fishing provided the basic occupations, and the ministers, Free Church and Free Presbyterian, ruled. Yet they did so against a strong undercurrent of change. New full-time jobs existed in the Forestry Commission. Motorcycles took young men up to the aluminium smelters, many still wearing their wartime 'battledress or parts of it' as their badge of independence. For women unemployment benefit removed the necessity for servile part-time jobs. Cleaners could not be got. 'You would get more unemployment money from the Buroo. If you'll ask for a whole-time job, they'll not stop it if you'll no' take the school.' The novel's plot is superficially humdrum. It is about the building of a village hall. The ministers opposed the hall because they saw it as a secular threat to their power. But no one is willing to say so out loud. The tension comes from the novel's penetration into the ambiguities of Highland life: the demeaning of personal worth in a closed community where no one dares speak the truth. Opinions depend on who is listening. 'Is there such a thing as a Highland weighing machine that shows the weight right?' asks the expatriate Lowland doctor at the beginning. Everyone dissembles. Eventually opposition crystallizes and the ministers fail — rebuffed in part by breakdown of the old sexual mores within their own flock and the public exposure of the overly respectable.

Across the Highlands this decay of the old ways ran parallel to the decline of the crofting economy. Population levels stabilized in the 1940s, but fell away again in the fifties. The 1953 Report of the Commission of Enquiry into Crofting Conditions noted that the croft 'by itself had never been able to provide a reasonable living'. Its survival depended on auxiliary industries, weaving, fishing and knitting, that were also now in decline. What new employment there was tended to be concentrated at a few sites. The construction of the hydro-electric system from the 1940s and then the Dounreay nuclear reactor in Caithness in the 1950s tended to pull labour away and intensify the dislocation. It was precisely this period, between 1931 and 1961, that saw the biggest fall in the number of Gaelic speakers in the century: from 33 to 17 per cent in Argyll, 44 to 18 per cent in Sutherland and 57 to 41 per cent in Ross. At the same time the latent radicalism of Highland society began to find expression. The Western Isles, Gaelic's strongest base, returned a Labour MP in 1945 and continued to do so through the fifties and sixties.

In more industrial areas these years saw Scotland become one of the most strike-prone parts of Britain. Employers in shipbuilding and engineering were intent on holding the wage differential against England. In shipbuilding the resulting conflicts were particularly intense. The owners did not invest in new construction techniques. Yet to meet their competitors, they did have to adopt new materials and designs. The result was an explosion of demarcation disputes. The different crafts struggled to capture new types of work. The finishing trades in particular expanded at the expense of the traditionally dominant black squad of metal trades and boilermakers. Like the farm hands of

Westrigg, these workers were not radicals. Sectarian allegiances were still present. A significant number would vote Conservative or Progressive, the slightly more Orange-tinted local government equivalent of the Tories. The yards and engineering still sustained a strongly male-oriented culture that was carried back into the home. But, despite all this, there was a new combativeness. These were the years that saw the redevelopment of the shop stewards movement and the spread of militant trade-unionism among draughtsmen and other staff grades in manufacturing industry. The biggest strike in post-war shipbuilding was in 1956. Its object was to introduce a guaranteed weekly wage for all grades of metal-worker and to replace piece rates. It was in essence about power over the production process and was won by the workers.

Perhaps the most telling evocation of this period of uneasy equipoise comes in the semi-autobiographical work of John Byrne. His play 'The Slab Boys' is located in the design offices of a Paisley carpet manufacturer – among the marble slabs where the apprentices ground the colours with a view to becoming designers themselves. There is no reference to a union or organized labour. The dialogue is a pastiche of the intensely local and the worldwide – the cultural imports flooding into Scotland through films and the newly-installed television: Elvis, 'white jacket . . . Yankee . . . finger-tip drape . . . roll collar . . .', jujitsu, Brylcreem. 'Rebel without a Cause' is the password. When the youngsters want to lampoon management, they adopt the fake English public school dialogue of Billy Bunter. Byrne plays the anarchic energy of the slab boys against the tatty conventionality of the fifties: the office hierarchy in their cavalry twills, the plastic and plywood furnishings, the naff designs, 'a bunch of no-talent, no hopers, arse-licking . . . up the turkey runner to Barton's office', the managing director driving home in his British-made Jag. In this sense the play is about youth against age, but it is also a very specific youth. The teenagers in the slab room come from a section of society that was previously excluded – the despised Irish labourers of Ferguslie – but which now possessed a new power to get another job, enter art college and say whatever it wanted:

HECTOR: How come if everybody's a mason you and Phil's working here . . . eh? Tell us that . . .

SPANKY: I lied about my age and Phil there swore to Waldo Bathtubs he'd flush his Nine Friday's down the pan if only we could get to be slab boys. Aw, no . . ., when Mr Bathtub took me into his office, grasped my hand . . . strangely but firmly . . . and offered me one pound, two and nine a week . . . I went straight home and set fire to my scapulas . . .

PHIL: And don't think it wasn't sore – I was there when he done it. Soon as Father Durkin heard we were working here . . .

SPANKY: Phil's Auntie Fay got beat up by the Children of Mary

PHIL: Gave her a right doing . . .

SPANKY: She had to go to Lourdes

PHIL: And the whole family were refused entry to Carfin Grotto . . .

Byrne's work was not published till the 1970s and the density of local reference was, as we will see, much more typical of that decade. The 1950s themselves were marked by the sharply increased dominance of external culture. The BBC initiated television in Scotland in 1952 with almost all its production coming up from London. The commercial station, STV, opened in 1955, but again most production was taken from south of the border. The station was owned by the Canadian Roy Thomson, who three years before had bought the *Scotsman* newspaper. In film, still the staple fare of the majority of the population, little remained of Grierson's hopes of a Scottish industry. One of the last Scottish films to be produced, Alexander MacKendrick's 'The Maggie' in 1953, described a duel of wills between the captain of a Scottish puffer and an American millionaire. The Edinburgh Festival was similarly international in its focus. Its initiation in 1947 was largely accidental – the result of a search by the organizers of the Glyndebourne Festival for a temporary new venue at a time when Munich and Salzburg were out of action. While it was given strong establishment backing, James Bridie promoting it as an antidote to Scottish parochialism, it was always seen as distinctly un-Scottish. This feeling was well expressed by the Very Reverend Charles Warr, Dean of the Thistle and Chapel Royal, at the service organized by the citizens of Edinburgh to mark, or perhaps exorcize, the Festival's inauguration: 'for centuries owing to causes located in political and ecclesiastical controversies, we neglected the place of the arts and emotions . . . until comparatively recent days the aesthetic was regarded with coldness and suspicion . . . Today, Scotland is awakening to the full significance of art and beauty.'

By 1947 the radical objectives of the Scottish renaissance were long forgotten. MacDiarmid and some of his colleagues were beginning to achieve academic acceptance. Their works would soon be available in critical editions. For all this, there was no artistic movement. The political and social iconoclasm of the 1930s had vanished and left its artistic proponents without bearings. Eric Linklater's *The House of Gair*, published in 1953, sums up the feeling of bewildered impotence. A deeply pessimistic novel, it explores the failure of the writer in post-war Scotland – unable to escape, except by futile and ineffective gesture, from the magnetism of English literature and the black-mailing power of its commercial machine.

The Roots of Radicalization

What was it, then, that brought about the dramatic changes of the 1960s and 1970s – the sudden upsurge of the SNP and, even more surprising, the emergence of a radicalized and left-wing Labour Party? First and foremost, it was the country's economic base. Effectively Scotland now had two economies. There was Scottish-owned heavy industry and manufacturing, and there was the external sector: British and American plants producing consumer durables and electrical goods. These two economies could co-exist as long as neither side placed too much pressure on supplies of labour, steel and energy. Any expansion, however, was a problem. The Americans had long been unhappy that Scotland's steel industry did not produce strip steel, the staple material for their consumer goods. The Organization for European Economic Co-operation, the overseer for American investment in Europe, highlighted this as early as 1954. Then in 1956 came the Suez débâcle. The Eden government collapsed after its empire-based policies had brought it into conflict with the United States. The new government of Harold Macmillan sought to work much more closely with America and set the British economy on a course of fast industrial modernization.

This, however, exposed another problem. Britain's new industries were unduly concentrated in the south-east and fast expansion quickly brought overheating and financial crisis. The policy response was the introduction of a new type of macro-economic regulation which was to dominate the British economy throughout the 1960s and into the 1970s. At its heart was regional policy. Scotland, Northern Ireland, Tyneside, Merseyside and South Wales were brought into the forefront of economic planning. What was their secret? Unemployed labour. It was not a vast amount by historic standards. But in percentage terms it was double what existed in the south-east. This, it was felt, was enough to enable Britain to escape inflationary pressures on profits and achieve the steady rates of economic growth seen in Germany and Japan. The mechanism was the progressive dispersal of new industrial capacity to areas where unemployment was highest. At the British level these policies were adopted between 1960 and 1963. The Federation of British Industries (later the CBI) adopted 'indicative planning' in 1960 and from 1963 the Conservative government's National Economic Development Council (NEDC) began publishing a series of reports highlighting the growth potential of labour reserves within both regions and 'declining industries'.

In Scotland, on the other hand, the process began earlier. Later in the sixties Scottish Office civil servants sought to claim responsibility for the whole idea and suggest, probably without too much real basis, continuity back to the 1930s and 1940s. What is certain is that policies were given their first test run in Scotland and that they caused deep and long-lasting divisions within the country's political élite.

The two words 'Ravenscraig' and 'Linwood' are etched in Scottish industrial history. Ravenscraig was the site of Scotland's first and only strip-steel mill, constructed between 1959 and 1963 and closed in 1990. Linwood was the location of Scotland's only venture into the mass production of cars – begun in 1959 and closed in 1981. The two projects were meant to work together. Cars needed strip steel. Ravenscraig required a local strip market to make it viable. Both projects involved personal interventions by the Prime Minister, Harold Macmillan. The political battle began in 1957–8. On one side an alliance was brought together by the Scottish Council (Development and Industry) which had been the main channel for American investment in Scotland since 1948. It was composed of American firms (like George Perry's General Motors division in East

Kilbride), the STUC and a number of smaller Scottish firms, largely suppliers to American or British firms or with interests in property development. They fought under the banner of modernization and full employment and had the tacit support of Macmillan's new Scottish Secretary, John Maclay. On the other side were the owners of heavy industry. These included the Colville family (who had re-established control of steel after denationalization), the Lithgow interests and the other shipbuilders, and the financial groupings with which they were interlocked, primarily the Bank of Scotland. The first group had the backing of Roy Thomson's American-financed *Scotsman* and STV, the second of the *Glasgow Herald*.

The Colvilles did not want a strip mill, certainly not of the size proposed by the government. Nor did those who used steel plate and structural steel. Three essential ingredients of steel-making, scrap, anthracite and skilled labour, were already in short supply in Scotland and expansion would seriously inflate costs. If the market for the strip steel failed, then the unit cost for all steel would go up even further. To get compliance Macmillan had to threaten to finance a rival English steel company, RTB, to build a Scottish plant. Similar strong-arm tactics were used to persuade Lord Rootes, who headed the weakest and most vulnerable of UK car producers, to site his new factory at Linwood.

The divisions within the Scottish élite were quite complex. They extended inside the Conservative Party and even into the traditional business élite. Sir Stephen Bilsland, a Colville cousin and still head of the Scottish Council, was the front man for the modernizers. Those Conservatives most directly concerned with the party's electoral fortunes also tended in this direction – especially after the loss of five Scottish seats in the 1959 election. And so did a number of leading figures in the universities. The most sophisticated presentation of the modernizers' case came in the Toothill report. The secretary was Tom Burns, later Professor of Sociology at Edinburgh University and one of the seminal minds of mid-twentieth-century Scotland. The chair was Sir John Toothill, Scottish-based director of the English electronics giant, Ferranti. The committee started work in 1959 under the non-governmental auspices of the Scottish Council, but with assessors from the Scottish Office, the Ministry of Labour and the Board of Trade. The committee included two other representatives of large UK firms – and no representative of Scottish heavy industry.

Like the Abercrombie report before it, Toothill stressed the need for comprehensive modernization. It noted the danger of what it called the branch plant syndrome: plants with their headquarters abroad and without control over markets or technologies. It advocated the root-and-branch renewal of Scotland's infrastructure: the road and rail systems, airports and especially the transport links to the south. Unlike Abercrombie, however, its definition of comprehensive did not extend to Scotland's existing industrial strengths. Scotland's renewal was to be founded on new science-based industries, using mass production methods and located in new industrial districts which would form growth poles for the future. Heavy industry tended to be presented as an obstacle: identified with combative industrial relations, poor management and antique production methods.

The report was implemented badly. Had the same level of state direction and control been used as in France, one of the models of modernization adopted by Toothill, the outcome might have been different. It was not. Instead, implementation was hit by political conflict, undue reliance on market forces and mistaken assumptions. The Scottish Office duly published its White Paper on Central Scotland in 1963. The problem was that, apart from atomic energy, the state did not control any science-based industries. It had to rely on persuasion. Companies located as it suited them, and the companies that were most susceptible to financial pressure tended to be, like Rootes, the least competitive. When big companies, such as GEC, came to Scotland as part of government-brokered mergers, they tended to take away the high-quality jobs and use Scottish plants for routine engineering. When UK companies were lacking, American branch plants were once more used to fill the gap.

Worse still from the point of view of the employers, the assumptions about surplus labour turned out to be misconceived. Although the percentage of unemployed was higher than in the English Midlands, the absolute number of skilled workers was smaller – especially where they were needed. Shortages soon appeared. American firms in particular had a tendency to pay over the rate to avoid unionization. The 10 per cent average wage differential with England quickly came under pressure and was wiped out within ten years by labour shortages in Scotland. The response of government planners was twofold. One was to broaden and deepen labour markets. The 1966 White Paper examined how to ensure the operation of travel-to-work areas which encompassed the whole of the Clyde and Forth valleys. New road bridges were to be built across the estuaries and fast rail services introduced. The 'blue trains' were to run right along the Clyde from Motherwell to Greenock and Dumbarton. Motorways were to be further extended – with the Kingston bridge and the M8 motorway ultimately opening in 1971. New technologically-based universities in Glasgow and Edinburgh expanded the output of scientists and engineers. A new generation of further education colleges were to train and retrain technically equipped workers. More money was to go into urban redevelopment. The close-knit inner-city communities, the heart of the old localized labour markets, were now themselves to be demolished. Bulldozers began moving among the tenements of Gorbals and Anderston.

The other approach was still more brutal. Labour was to be 'released' from the old industries. The 1966 White Paper estimated that Scotland contained a potential 60,000 new workers out of an estimated British deficit of 400,000. Realizing this potential depended on recycling workers from declining industries and releasing women from the home. Back in 1963 the NEDC had put the number of workers who could be shed from 'old' industries as 200,000 across Britain. This designation of 'old' and 'declining' was of course almost entirely political. The industries in question, coal, iron and steel, shipbuilding and railways, were not so designated in America, Germany or Japan. In Britain, on the other hand, these industries were largely under state control and the release of labour could be brought about by political decision. In coal and railways the closures started in 1961. The rural pit villages of Ayrshire, Lanarkshire, the Lothians and Stirlingshire were one by one deprived of their employment and transport links. By 1967, 119 of Scotland's 166 coal pits had been closed and 40,000 jobs lost.

In shipbuilding the key policy change came somewhat earlier. Within a few months of Macmillan taking office, at the same time as pressure was being put on Colvilles, the government changed the rules on government credits for British ship-owners. In a quite astonishing act of reverse subsidization, credits were only to be available for purchases made outside Britain. That year, 1957, marked the beginning of the end for shipbuilding on the Clyde. The owners lobbied in vain. Eventually they were reduced to organizing their own credit scheme, through the Bank of Scotland, the one major bank they controlled. Scottish Tory MPs vented their anger in parliament. The MP for East Dumbartonshire, who included at least two of the shipbuilding dynasties among his constituents, attacked the Americans in particular for 'tragically unfair competition': 'the Russians would not go so far in the subsidizing and patronage of a particular industry as the Americans have done'. Within ten years the shipbuilding workforce had fallen from 60,000 to 20,000.

These changes were momentous. By the end of the sixties government expenditure on regional modernization constituted up to 20 per cent of all its outlays on industry. A third of this was spent on Scotland. All aspects of society were affected, and if we want an explanation for the big shifts in family and social life that took place in the later sixties, it is here that we must start.

What were these changes? There was a decline in the number of children born to married women – a trend starting in the mid-sixties and continuing through the seventies. There was a very big increase in the number of women working in the age group 30–50. There was a doubling in the number of divorces through the 1960s. The number doubled again in the first five years of the seventies. The number of children born outside marriage started to increase. There was a precipitate decline in levels of church adherence – starting in the late fifties, and a sure sign of major geographical relocation. No doubt part of the explanation lies in technical factors. Divorce became legally easier. More reliable forms of oral contraceptive made it possible for women to choose to postpone having a family – or, more typically, to limit the number of children after a certain age. However, the circumstances cannot be detached from the massive process of economic reconstruction. Removing up to 70,000 male workers from coal, railways and engineering within seven or eight years meant that many men would not secure employment at the same level of pay – or even at all. This was particularly so for the older workers. The decision of married women in their thirties and forties to go

out to work was as much to make up family income as to find fulfilment. The jobs were
overwhelmingly part-time and low-paid: in office cleaning, catering, distribution or
repetitive jobs on the twilight shift in one of the new American factories. Similarly,
the process of physical reconstruction now involved an element of compulsion. The
construction of the new schemes in the fifties was not accompanied by inner-city
demolition. Home, with the grannies and uncles, still remained back in the city. Now
the familiar landmarks disappeared. Networks of families and friends went with the
closes and tenements, the miners' welfare and the lodge. 'On the wrecker's ball the rains
of greeting cities drop and drink their fill', wrote Edwin Morgan.

Morgan and the novelist and artist Alasdair Gray pick the suddenness aspect of
these changes. They came from outside. They happened. They were not explained.

> You know the old pawnshop by the yard
> It's closed now. It's all to be demolished
> for the motorway, POLONSKY'S PAWN, remember?

Morgan captures the surreal dislocation, Alasdair Gray the subjection. His novel *Lanark*
portrays Glasgow as a twentieth-century version of hell. It is ostensibly ruled by a
bureaucracy of welfare offices and an overweening but pathetic council. Physically the
city is subsiding, sunless, without time. Its residents are progressively diseased. As they
inexplicably disappear, their bodies are recycled – to provide heat and food for 'The
Institute' located somewhere else, possibly near New Cumbernauld. 'Cannibalism has
always been the main human problem . . . [The Institute] could easily be destroyed if it
were simply a murder machine. But it is like all machines, it profits those who own it
and nowadays many sections are owned by gentle, powerless people who don't know
they are cannibals.' The two writers offer an interesting contrast with the thirties. Both
present a social critique, but it is a critique without resolution. They have none of the
certainty of cause and effect, friend or enemy, found in Gibbon, Bridie or MacDiarmid.
What was the 1965 National Plan? Who wrote it? Who did it benefit? The modernization
it proposed seemed to have the support of both Labour and Conservatives. The local
professional élite loved it.

Class Politics Return

Quite unexpectedly, in the later sixties the inevitability of this process was disrupted.
Two revolts happened in quick succession. One was raised by the owners of Scottish
industrial capital; the other by the industrial working class. Both identified causes,
enemies and solutions. Class politics returned.

This moment of politicization arose directly from the National Plan. As social engineering it did not work. The labour market was never sufficiently freed up, wage pressures continued and, even worse for the planners, trade union organization began to spread. The American plants, bastions of non-unionism, fell one by one: Caterpillar, General Motors, Timex, NCR. Their managers found themselves under pressure to join the same structures of 'inflexible' national bargaining as their Scottish and British counterparts. By 1965, with a Labour government once more in office, the focus of attention settled on industrial relations. Why, asked Americans like George Perry of General Motors, could Clydeside not learn to make industrial peace? Models were already there. Esso's Fawley agreements had, they argued, shown how it could be done. Localized plant bargaining would link wages to productivity, and that way managerial control could be restored.

The result was a bizarre episode, a mixture of farce and tragedy, which exposed all the conflicts and hostilities within Scotland's economic and political élite: the Fairfield experiment. In 1965 the Fairfield shipyard, the largest on the Clyde, was placed in receivership by its owners, a consortium of banks led by the Bank of Scotland. The expectation among the other shipbuilders was that the closure of this yard would take much of the heat out of the Clyde labour market – even if it inflicted some hardship on the local shipyard supply firms. To their consternation the yard was rescued. A strange alliance came together with the object of transforming it into a model of modern American-style industrial relations practice. Who were these allies? There was George Brown, Minister of Economic Affairs, an ambitious but frequently drunk right-winger, who had inherited the regional planning strategies of the Tories and was now being held responsible for the rising job losses. There was Sir Iain Stewart, owner of a major shipyard supply firm, but also a close associate of Roy Thomson, chairman of STV and a convert to the American-financed sect Moral Rearmament (MRA). There was Derek Palmar, a director of Hill Samuel, the City of London merchant bank which handled the bulk of government-brokered industrial amalgamations. There were the right-wing leaders of the Electricians and General Workers Unions, both signatories to Moral Rearmament's Marlow Declaration on industrial peace, who became directors of the new firm. The personnel staff handling industrial and public relations were transferred wholesale from STV. Shop stewards were treated to daily briefing meetings and flown down to the Electricians' palatial training school in Surrey for sessions on partnership and productivity. The earliest big order was for the American navy, the first ever placed on Clydeside by the US government. The outcome was that shop stewards sat through the MRA lectures, enjoyed the lunches, bargained up the wage rates and used the opportunity to consolidate the authority of a joint shop stewards' committee which eventually represented all unions and all staff, including junior management. By 1966–7 all other Clyde yards were subject to similar demands.

It seems to have been this episode that was the final spur to a concerted fight-back by Scottish capital. This counter-offensive had a level of ambition and self-consciousness

473

not seen since the 1930s. Its beginnings probably go back somewhat earlier: to the 1963 defence of the last major newspaper remaining in Scottish hands, the *Glasgow Herald*. Over the previous two decades the bulk of the popular press in Scotland had come under the control of English publishers, the *Express, Mirror* and *Mail* being the major groupings. The other quality paper, the *Scotsman*, had gone to Roy Thomson in 1952. Now Thomson moved to take over Outrams, the publishing firm which controlled both the *Herald* and a big slice of the local press. This produced a sustained and public resistance. The man who fronted the campaign was Sir Hugh Fraser, the owner of Glasgow's biggest department store, who had been buying up English properties, including Harrods, with money from the Scottish financial sector. He now used the same funds to rescue Outrams in a campaign that explicitly highlighted the need to retain Scottish ownership and control.

In 1966 Scottish capital made a much more daring bid. It reclaimed control of the Scottish Council (Development and Industry), the semi-official body which had overseen economic strategy in Scotland since the thirties and had acted as the main conduit for modernization policy in the fifties and early sixties. Ronald Colville, second Baron Clydesmuir, took over the chairmanship from the ageing Bilsland – who was seen as having been taken prisoner by the modernizers. At the same time William Lithgow, son of Sir James, came on to the board with special responsibility for research. The Scottish Council now attacked on two fronts. It produced a stream of research reports which highlighted the loss of Scottish control and the dangers of the branch plant syndrome. 'The question', it stated in a document of 1969,

is how to stem the stampede of decision-making centres . . . to the South . . . Pressures of international competition, particularly from America, draw companies together in amalgamations . . . The increasing involvement of government in industry, both publicly and privately owned, adds to the forces which lead companies to locate their headquarters in London.

The other front was to advance a radical plan to rescue Scotland's metal-based heavy industries, 'Oceanspan'. This plan had been in preparation under the personal supervision of William Lithgow since 1967. At its heart was a direct challenge to the City of London and the process of industrial centralization. The plan sought to redevelop a cost-efficient Scottish steel industry, based at Hunterston, using electric arc smelting technology. The shipbuilding industry would be relocated to the mouth of the Clyde so that it had the capability to build very large ships and tankers. The new flow of cheap, high-quality steel would be used to create a corridor of advanced metal-using plants between the two 'oceans' from the Clyde to the Forth. Scotland would become the trans-shipment and manufacturing depot for trade between Europe and America.

In themselves these plans had much to recommend them. In practice they amounted to a declaration of war on London-based industrial rationalization. Steel had been re-nationalized in 1967. Before Lord Melchett and the new London British Steel Corporation managers had a chance to move in, the old Colville's management issued plans for a £300 million investment at Hunterston. Within a matter of months BSC liquidated its entire regional management. According to the *Three Banks Review*, controlled by Lloyds Bank, this was to prevent any further promotion of schemes which were 'highly dangerous to rational planning'. The Hunterston plan, it claimed, represented a bid to 'harness national and political pressures, by no means new on the Scottish steel scene, to ensure the idea could not be quietly dropped'. The plan for shipbuilding was equally defiant. Under the government's Geddes report, shipbuilding was regrouped in 1968 into two big companies in ways that significantly diluted the control of the existing owners but did not reduce capacity. The 'Oceanspan' proposals assumed radical surgery of the existing yards and the reinforcement of Scottish ownership.

The confidence with which these plans were advanced was no doubt in part because their architects believed that they had secured a new understanding with the leadership of the Conservative Party. Teddy Taylor, Tom Galbraith and Jock Bruce Gardyne, MPs with close links to Scottish industry, began to move into policy positions. Direct discussions took place over industrial policy with Keith Joseph's deputy, Nicholas Ridley. In the Commons, Scottish Tory MPs became much more explicit in their attacks on regional aid and its use to give unfair advantages to American companies. In February 1970 the Conservatives unveiled their election programme. This promised an end to such regional aid and the adoption of a much tougher monetary policy. At the same time the Scottish Council of the CBI came into unprecedented conflict with its British parent body by demanding that the Scottish Office take powers to decide the location of government-aided and externally owned factories. As if in preparation for the new era, a Scottish Stock Exchange was opened in 1969. Its aim was to provide capital for 'the many Scottish-owned private companies involved in home-based business which can grow at least as fast as imported industries'. Simultaneously, the Bank of Scotland, with its close associations with shipbuilding and steel, negotiated an alliance with Barclays' subsidiary, the British Linen Bank, to broaden its capital base.

The outcome brought bitter disappointment. The new Tory government of Edward Heath came to power in 1970. It did cut the regional wage subsidy – but only for existing firms in Scotland. It ran the economy at a significantly higher level of unemployment – but pushed ahead with mergers and industrial centralization. It failed to deliver Hunterston – but at the same time put Upper Clyde Shipbuilders (UCS) into receivership. To make matters worse, the minister concerned, Nicholas Ridley, let his briefing notes fall into the hands of the press. These notes recorded conversations with Clydeside industrialists, including Sir Eric Yarrow and 'someone' at the Lithgow yard, which urged the incoming government to 'butcher' the yards on the upper Clyde. They were, it was said, a 'cancer eating into the whole of Clydeside industrial life'. Naturally, these revelations infuriated the workers, but the most damaging impact was elsewhere. The UCS bankruptcy meant that hundreds of subcontract and supply firms, hitherto loyal supporters of regional capital, found their own businesses placed in danger by the deliberate act of a Tory government. The Progressive (Conservative) Lord Provost of Glasgow publicly attacked the government. Splits emerged throughout the Conservatives' Scottish base. The traditional leaders of Scottish capital fell suddenly silent. Within a few months, and at the hands of a Conservative government, the revolt of Scottish capital was at an end. Then, equally unpredictably and quite unforeseen by the government, another revolt took place. Scotland's industrial working class took on the Tories and beat them. In July 1971, 8,000 shipyard workers occupied the yards on the Upper Clyde and held them for fifteen months. By March 1972 they had won almost all their demands and rescued shipbuilding on the Upper Clyde.

In 1976 key figures in Edward Heath's 1970–74 government were asked why they had capitulated and, more generally, performed a U-turn on industrial policy. Nicholas Ridley claimed it was because the Cabinet feared civil violence would spread from Belfast to Glasgow. Peter Walker remembered a 'genuine feeling that unless some action was taken social disorder of a kind not seen in this country could have taken place in the city'. J. Bruce Gardyne, PPS to the Scottish Secretary, claimed the key moment came when the Chief Constable said he would need an extra 15,000 men if he was asked to clear the yards.

This was almost certainly not their real fear. The 8,000 shipyard workers who occupied the UCS yards never threatened to use force. Nor did the workers in the dozens of other factory occupations which followed. The picket lines outside pits and power stations in 1972 and 1974 were very peaceable affairs compared with what happened under different policing policies in 1984–5. Yet the government was undoubtedly alarmed, and it did retreat. The real reasons were different and did not bear too much public discussion. One was the need to rescue the Conservative Party's disintegrating Scottish base among small and medium businesses. The other was the politicization of the trade union movement – most significantly in Scotland. By 1971 this had reached a level which was endangering the government's longer-term goals.

Within a very short period, between 1968 and 1972, three landmark changes had occurred within the Scottish labour and trade union movement. Each amounted to a small earthquake. The STUC swung round to support a devolved Scottish parliament – after three decades of opposition. Most major unions returned to the pre-1926 position of endorsing strike action for political ends. Finally, the language of class struggle returned to everyday speech. By 1974 such language even found modified reflection in the Labour Party's election manifesto. Not all of these shifts were specifically Scottish. Devolution obviously was, and at the time had no counterpart in Wales. The political strikes were more general. London, Yorkshire and the West Midlands all figured prominently in the one-day protest strikes, against state regulation of trade union activity, which had gathered momentum since 1969.

Yet even here Scotland can be said to have made a very specific contribution. In the early summer of 1971 the outlook for continued resistance to the Tories' Industrial Relations Act was decidedly bleak. Once the Act had become law it seemed that the movement's official leadership would step back from illegality. But by summer 1971 the UCS occupation had transformed the situation. The shop stewards had won STUC backing for the use of industrial action to compel government intervention. By August the TUC General Secretary and the Labour ex-Cabinet minister Tony Benn were walking through the streets of Glasgow arm-in-arm with Communist shop stewards at the head of 50,000 striking workers. The STUC had given its backing to a regional general strike on the same terms as in 1919: to demand political action against unemployment.

Three main factors gave the Scottish left this unexpected power. The first was the rift in the country's political élite. Nowhere else in Europe had the issue of economic control been so publicly debated. Economically Scotland had not done badly in the 1960s. Relative to the rest of Britain it had in fact improved its position. Yet there was now an acute awareness of the power of big business and the loss of local control and accountability. The second factor was the weakness of the Labour Party as an ideological force in Scottish society. The scars of the 1930s remained. The post-war Labour Party had proved a very successful electoral machine. As long as it was able to deliver housing, welfare and full employment, it gained votes. Nevertheless the Scottish electorate remained fickle. In the fifties it could switch to the Conservatives and the Progressives on the delivery of similar promises. In the sixties, as unemployment increased across Britain, the Scottish National Party finally emerged as a major challenge in urban Scotland – most notably in the Hamilton by-election victory of 1967. In Scotland the Labour Party had no national champion to compare with Bevan in Wales – or Maxton or Keir Hardie in the old ILP. Jimmy Allison, later secretary of the Scottish Labour Party, remembers the party in the 1960s as an organizational shell. Branches were usually run by a handful of individuals, often relatives of the local councillor. There was no political discussion. The job losses and population shifts of the 1960s were given no detailed political justification – within a working class in which the traditions of past struggles were still alive. When it all went wrong in 1970–71 and unemployment began to soar towards pre-war levels, the third factor could come into play.

This was the continuing strength of the Scottish left – now composed mainly of the Communist Party and those Labour Party members, particularly in the trade union movement, who rejected policies of partnership with big business. The strength of this alliance lay principally in the trade unions. Communists now led all the key industrial unions in Scotland: the miners, the transport workers, the main district committees of the engineering union and the draughtsmen. A Communist, Jimmy Milne, was about to become General Secretary of the STUC. No less important was the strength of left-wing leadership within the shop stewards movement, then at the peak of its post-war power. Few major workplaces did not have joint shop stewards' committees able to mobilize united action among different grades and unions. Still more critical, however, was the left's ability to put forward a coherent case for an alternative, in face of the collapse of Scottish industrial capital and the inability of right-wing Labour to say anything new. The proposal for a Scottish parliament with democratic powers of industrial intervention and public ownership seized the moment. In the autumn and winter of 1971–2 the STUC, local authorities, the churches and organizations representing Scottish business came together to convene the first Scottish Assembly. It sat in the cold magnificence of Edinburgh's Usher Hall – cold because of the power cuts imposed by the first miners' strike. The Progressive Lord Provost of Glasgow proclaimed that 'Scotland could not wait and would not accept that 150,000 persons should be denied the right to work'. Any comments critical of the miners were shouted down. The Scottish chairman of the CBI noted afterwards: 'The intensity of feeling for devolution came across in a way I have never experienced before.' However, it was devolution set in strongly class terms. James Jack, then STUC General Secretary, emphasized this in his summing-up: 'I am all for a Scottish parliament because – wait for it – there is not the slightest doubt that it will be a workers' parliament.' There was no coherent response from either the Labour Party or the spokespersons of Scottish business. Within five weeks, at the end of March 1972, Edward Heath's government had conceded a rescue package for the shipyards, taken Rolls-Royce into public ownership, and reversed its entire industrial and regional policy.

The accelerating loss of control by the trade union movement's right-wing leaderships represented a major problem for Heath's government. Its whole industrial relations strategy was based on strengthening the authority of these leaderships against shop stewards and unofficial action. But there was also another more immediate Scottish concern that was by no means unrelated: oil.

The Black, Black Oil

Oil had first been discovered off the coast of Scotland in 1969. The discovery of the two mammoth fields, Brent and Forties, came in 1971. These were big enough to transform Britain into a major oil exporting power, to end concerns about the balance of payments and re-launch the City of London as a world banking centre. This potential was known by autumn 1971. The problem was extraction. The two oil companies holding the licences for Forties and Brent were BP and Shell. They were already two of the biggest British multinationals on the basis of their overseas holdings and were closely linked to the banking sector. But they did not possess the technology for deep-water offshore extraction. Nor did they have the sheer scale of capital necessary for offshore infrastructure. The best guess at the cost, later found to be a serious underestimate, was up to 15 per cent of the country's entire manufacturing investment for ten years. There was also the problem of labour supply and inflation. The platforms, oil pipeline systems and terminals would have to be built in Scotland and draw on labour from the heavily unionized central belt. These problems were being discussed intensively by BP, Shell, the London banks and the government in October–November 1971. The man in charge, John Davies, Minister for Trade and Industry and an ex-BP executive, was also responsible for negotiations over the future of UCS.

The outcome determined much of the future development of both Scotland and Britain for the rest of the century. The path chosen was in strong contrast with that adopted by Norway. It locked Britain into a strategic alliance with the United States – then determined to find new, politically safe sources of oil which could liberate them from dependence on OPEC. The alliance committed Britain to the fastest possible extraction. The Americans wanted it. So did the British oil companies and bankers – even if this meant turning the pound into a petro-currency and drastically shrinking Britain's existing industrial base. For the Scottish economy it meant that there would be no breathing space, as in Norway, to enforce technology transfer and the development of a locally controlled supply industry. Fast extraction meant that technology would have to be imported even if it was to be manufactured locally by American-owned companies.

For the Highlands, oil marked the final twist of the screw away from indigenous, locally-based economic development. The Highlands and Islands Development Board (HIDB) had been established in 1965 with exceptionally wide powers to promote regional development, including the compulsory purchase of land. Hopes existed for a radical agenda. The Board could have ended the stranglehold of the great landlords – with just 140 individuals then owning over half the total land surface of the Highlands and Islands. It could have provided support for the type of small-scale local industry needed to complement the ailing crofting economy. In the event, it did neither of these things. The HIDB was wedded to the same vision of modernization as the planners of the central belt. It went for a few big projects. Massive grants were used to attract externally owned manufacturing plants. The Fort William pulp mill was followed by the Invergordon aluminium smelter. Both pulled labour out of the crofting areas, but themselves failed to survive for more than two decades.

Once oil arrived the same policies were writ large. The multinational oil contract companies like Brown and Root or Taylor Woodrow saw Highland locations as very desirable for rig-building. They had deep water and green labour. In negotiations with the National Trust for Scotland in 1972, one confidential minute stated that the company did not want 'to work near major conurbations because of possible labour disputes which could not be tolerated because of the tight schedule'. On both east and west coasts key areas were earmarked for development. Gordon Campbell, the Secretary of State, overruled opposition to one site with the statement: 'I am certain it is necessary to have one site on Loch Carron if we are to have oil as quickly as possible, whether the people like it or not.' Cherished areas of the Highland coastline were quickly subjected to a slash and burn economy which brought together massive concentrations of workers for short periods of time. There was little concern for the future of the locale itself. By 1973 Brown and Root had assembled 3,000 workers at Nigg on the Cromarty Firth, many housed on two derelict cruise liners. Of these, a thousand had been paid off within eighteen months as work came to an end.

The strategy of fast development made this type of external implantation inevitable. The 1971–2 licensing round set the mould. In this the government allocated mineral rights of the oil-bearing areas of the North Sea for the next thirty years. It did so on extremely generous terms. The licences went for £27 million with the obligation to pay no more than a 12 per cent royalty on the value of the oil. It enabled the oil companies to set capital costs against future revenue and gave a commitment that there would be no future depletion controls for these blocks. It also set the terms of the bidding in a way that was designed to lock American capital into the North Sea and to ensure the firms worked with UK companies. The individual blocks were very small and demanded partnerships between different licence-holders for effective extraction. The outcome was to give about 60 per cent of the oil assets to American companies and most of the rest to BP and Shell. External finance was negotiated with American banks for BP, with additional guarantees from the American government, on condition that American equipment was used.

Little of either the magnitude or the strategic implications of these developments was known publicly at the time in Scotland. Realization only came slowly in the course of 1972.

TEXAS JIM

Take your oil rigs by the score
Drill a little well just a little offshore
Pipe that oil in from the sea
Pipe those profits – home to me
Your union men just cut no ice
You work for me – I name the price . . .
All you folks are off your head
I'm getting rich from your sea bed
I'll go home when I see fit
All I'll leave is a heap of shit.

The play from which these lines come, John McGrath's 'The Cheviot, the Stag and the Black, Black Oil', was first performed in Edinburgh in March 1973. The play was closely researched. It named the companies involved. It exposed the role of the City of

London. It pilloried the Scottish investment trusts and property-owners now scrambling to get a share of the action. It portrayed the Tory ministers, Campbell and Polwarth, as the bumbling puppets of external interests. The play was directly, even didactically, political. It spoke to a new audience, the working-class generation educated in the 1950s and '60s, having the confidence of full employment and now increasingly mobilized in the struggles of the seventies.

McGrath's 7:84 theatre company, so named to illustrate the percentage of wealth held by just 7 per cent of the population, was one of a number playing in miners' welfares and community centres across Scotland. McGrath later wrote of the liberating effect of these audiences. There was now no need to play to the anglicized expectations of a literate middle class. The new audiences carried with them the raw, mongrel roots of a directly Scottish experience: the bitter memories of Highland parents, the closed culture of Catholic survival and the self-mocking dignity of the industrial worker. *The Cheviot* was probably the first play to fuse these elements together – rescuing, for instance, the Gaelic laments of Sorley Maclean and framing them, in Gaelic, within a production that focused on the pillage of Scotland in the 1970s. 'The families of well over half the working class of those areas settled there from the Highlands for precisely the reasons given in the play. They responded . . . with recognition and pleasure.' John Byrne was another product of this dialogue – less didactically, but with the same angry power of recognition. Billy Connolly's mocking of working-class life, its demeaning embarrassments, its sexual repression and religious obsessions, was acceptable precisely because Connolly carried with him the new confidence of a shipyard worker who had occupied the UCS.

It was, however, the writer William McIlvanney who produced the most considered response. His novel *Docherty* was written during the second miners' strike of 1974 and published in 1975. It was set in the 1910s and 1920s among the mining families of Kilmarnock. Its dialogue was on their terms, as they themselves spoke, not in the archaic Scots of MacDiarmid. *Docherty* describes the long battle to create and defend a culture of collectivism and self-confident secularism amid defeat and self-doubt. The novel sought to prise open the hard surface of working-class life and comprehend the everyday reality of McIlvanney's own inheritance and that of the majority of Scots. 'It wasn't only, as the socially conscious were inclined to say, the pathetic desire to escape from their condition. They were, much more profoundly, the expression of the condition. They gambled to gamble . . . they drank to drink . . . The mystique of the habits they practised . . . came closer to primitive rites for exorcizing the bastard god, economy . . .' The novel ends with the death of the father. McIlvanney makes him the embodiment of the historic will to organize and transform. His language echoes that of the miners' leader Mick McGahey as he rallied support in the pit villages in 1974. Three sons are left alive. One has become a contractor's man. Two remain loyal: one a Communist injured in the war, the other defending a less precise legacy of defensive struggle. 'You and me, whit's left of ma feyther . . . it's between you and me. Me wi' wan airm and you in twa minds, eh?'

While the industrial struggles of the 1970s lasted no more than four years, they profoundly changed identities. In a way working people now became the nation. In 1972 and in 1973 it was the STUC which convened Scottish Assemblies. The churches, the royal burghs, local authorities, business organizations and political parties attended. Those who spelt out the issues were those who had led the struggles on jobs, wages and trade union rights. Perhaps this was simply because no one else wanted to take the initiative on such controversial issues. Yet this very fact marked a critical turning-point. These Scottish Assemblies represented the first practical attempt in the modern era to bring together all the institutions of Scottish life. The Assemblies debated the general state of Scotland, but they did not do so in a vacuum. The discussion was framed by what was happening on the streets. Jimmy Reid, in his defining speeches during the Upper Clyde work-in, always hyphenated his two key forces for change: the Scottish people and the British working class. The struggles of the miners, dockers and engineers demonstrated this.

How deep-seated was this shift in identities? Like industrial struggle itself, it was in part contingent. But it was also rooted. It was a product of long-term changes in Scottish society and its embodiment in the Scottish Assemblies gave it a more permanent symbolism. Take the issue of religious sectarianism. The 1970s saw communal conflict in Northern Ireland at its worst. Yet in Scotland sectarian hostility did not increase – despite its ugly history and a level of unemployment that had once more passed the 100,000 mark. On 12 July 1971 Orange marchers in George Square queued up to sign their names at the UCS petition stands. Apart from one or two isolated incendiary attacks on Catholic pubs and chapels, there was no communal violence.

The shortest explanation for this is the long preceeding period of full employment. The three decades since 1945 had opened up new occupations and made many of the old exclusions irrelevant. Furthermore, re-housing had dispersed the inner-city communities where sectarian prejudices were most entrenched. The growth in the public sector, especially in Labour-controlled local authorities, opened up white-collar employment. The traditional Catholic focus on education produced a generation that was able to take advantage of the new post-1944 opportunities. Glasgow University saw the number of Catholic students treble between 1956 and 1972. Not least, the trade union movement now encompassed the great majority of manual workers among whom sectarian conflict had previously been most marked. Politically and economically, the Labour Party and the trade union movement demanded a common identity. As the struggles of the early seventies unfolded, the rhetoric of unity became explicit. The contrast with the 1920s could not have been greater. Then the Church of Scotland could still present itself as the custodian of a Protestant national identity. The new identity, emerging from the struggles of the 1970s, celebrated the unity and collective power of a diverse nation. Perhaps to mark this, in 1975 Archbishop Thomas Winning became the first Catholic to address the General Assembly of the Church of Scotland.

This new pluralism also framed the political emergence of the Asian community in Scotland, even if only to an extent. An Indian community of about 300, largely traders and shopkeepers, had been established in the Gorbals since the 1930s. In the late 1950s and '60s a new generation arrived, in the main young and well educated. They had been recruited to meet labour shortages which were particularly severe in transport and public services. The new workers, mostly from the Punjab, entered occupations that were already highly unionized. By the early 1970s the banner of the Indian Workers Association was beginning to appear on trade union demonstrations. By that time also a majority of shop stewards in some of the Glasgow Corporation bus garages were black. Yet acceptance tended to be on these terms. It required a degree of correspondence to the norms of trade union unity. A pamphlet of the Scottish International Labour Council, established with the support of Glasgow Trades Council (GTC) during the struggle against the 1973 Immigration Act, shows two black workers on the cover. The man and woman are dressed in the uniform of Glasgow Corporation transport department. The title is 'Working for a Multi-Racial Scotland'. The man, a Sikh, does not wear a turban.

In 1976 the National Front made its first attempt to intervene. It contested a Glasgow council seat in Kingston, an area of significant Asian settlement. Their candidate went down to ignominious defeat. The Labour movement, led by the General Secretary of the STUC, took steps physically to prevent the National Front holding its one public meeting. Among the dozens of trade-unionists charged with riotous assembly were the secretary of GTC and the Scottish regional secretary of the Transport Workers. This was the strength – but also the limit. The trade union movement could build on its earlier support for colonial liberation movements and against apartheid. It would itself fight any open attempt to split its unity on racist lines. However, it was itself less than understanding of separate cultures. Within a few years this was to become an even bigger issue for Scottish society as a whole. Rising unemployment forced the black community back into its own shops and restaurants. The strength of the trade union movement declined. The bridgehead established in the early seventies was not consolidated.

Socialism and Nationalism

The Tories were ejected from office in 1974. In their assessments of what went wrong, Scotland figured prominently. The combined challenge of coal, oil and class mobilization soon called up new plans for social engineering. Some of these, like Keith Joseph's proposals for monetarist shock treatment, were of general application. Others had a more specifically Scottish focus. A Tory policy document of June 1974 commented, 'simply by visiting Glasgow one can see life as it will be throughout the country if the trend of council housing continues. Housing in industrial Scotland has much in common with many Iron Curtain countries . . . Scotland is sharply divided into middle-class and working-class housing areas . . . housing has frozen class divisions.' Scotland could not be ignored. It guarded access to a prize of critical importance for British capital: North Sea oil. Just how important can be judged from an incident in the final days of the Tory government. With industrial power supplies cut to three days a week and the front line of industrial revolt moving ever closer, Edward Heath received a special communication each morning in his Downing Street office. It came from the Offshore Supplies Office and listed those firms working on assignments for the North Sea. These companies alone were given authority to receive power supplies seven days a week.

Were class politics really transformed in these years? In terms of unionization the late seventies did represent the high point of the twentieth century. In 1970, 40 per cent of the workforce were union members. By 1981 the number had jumped to over 48 per cent, and included a very significant portion of white-collar and junior-professional occupations. This movement was not just bigger; it was also more politicized. Between 1969 and 1983 Scotland saw twenty-two separate one-day strikes described by the Ministry of Labour as political. Their scale was not dissimilar to those of 1918–21. Initially these political strikes were mostly against industrial relations legislation, but increasingly broader social issues, such as employment and the welfare state, were raised. By the mid-1970s their scope went even further. The Rolls-Royce workers in the previously non-union town of East Kilbride took industrial action in defence of fellow workers overseas: halting the repair of jet engines for the Pinochet regime in Chile. So also did the workers in Rosyth dockyard.

Yet at the same time the base of this action was quite narrow. As the *Sunday Telegraph* pointed out in an analysis in 1977, the focus of this industrial militancy was industrially concentrated and hence vulnerable. It was largely limited to the biggest workplaces, and was restricted to certain industries: mining, car manufacturing, ship-building, the docks, transport and engineering. In Scotland the one-day strikes found only a proportion of the total workforce willing to sacrifice a day's pay, and risk management hostility, in order to show solidarity with other workers. The biggest, in 1973, saw almost half of all trade-unionists coming out in protest against the government's incomes policy. In 1980 one in five trade union members came out against government spending cuts. In 1982 a similar proportion struck in support of the NHS workers. Generally the number striking was less than one in ten. While key sections of the workforce were sufficiently committed to take significant risks, the majority were not.

McIlvanney's closing judgement was therefore probably near the mark. Scotland's workers were in two minds. There was a powerful trend of socialist analysis. It held sway among many shop stewards and dominated the conference policies of most industrial unions. Many more were willing to wait and see what a Labour government would bring. And a significant number, more than ever before, felt the Scottish Nationalists might provide a solution.

In the February 1974 election Labour gained 36 per cent of the Scottish vote, the Tories 32 per cent and the SNP 22 per cent. In the October 1974 election the SNP vote had risen to 30 per cent, the Tories fallen to 24 per cent and Labour held steady at 36 per cent. In terms of seats, Labour gained the lion's share: 41 per cent in October 1974. In the same election the SNP picked up 11 per cent, its highest ever. The Labour Party's 1974 election programme had been particularly radical. It promised an extension of public ownership, a dismantling of anti-trade union legislation and 'public control' of the oil industry. For Scotland it promised a Scottish Development Agency with active powers of industrial intervention of the kind urged at the two STUC-sponsored Scottish Assemblies. For the second 1974 election, after much prodding from London and in response to the SNP challenge, the Labour Party finally committed itself to a measure of devolution.

Gordon Brown, a future Labour chancellor, captured Labour's ambivalence towards the national question in the introduction to his *Red Paper on Scotland*, published in 1975.

The long-standing paradox of Scottish politics has been the surging forward of working-class industrial and political pressure (and in particular the loyal support given to Labour) and its containment through the accumulated failures of successive Labour governments . . . We suggest that the rise of modern Scottish nationalism is less an assertion of Scotland's permanence as a nation than a response to Scotland's uneven development . . . the discontent is a measure of the failure of both Scottish and British socialists to advance far and fast enough in shifting the balance of wealth and power to working people.

In a section headed 'A Planned Economy', Brown continued: 'It is the erosion of the market – and of the multinationals who manipulate the market – to determine social priorities that is the forging ground for socialist progress.'

Labour was in government for five years. It established the Scottish Development Agency in 1975. It nationalized shipbuilding and aircraft production in 1977. Its National Enterprise Board extended state finance and accountability into many areas of industry, including car production. It also sought to implement some form of public intervention in the oil industry. The British National Oil Corporation (BNOC) was established in 1976 after Tony Benn had become Minister for Energy. Benn did succeed in subjecting the oil companies to some element of public control. The 1975 Petroleum and Submarine Pipelines Act provided the government with future powers, after 1982, to impose partial depletion controls. The establishment of BNOC, together with the 1976–7 licensing round, gave Benn just enough power to negotiate a buy-back agreement with the oil companies by which BNOC marketed 51 per cent of the oil produced. By forming a tactical alliance with some of the British industrial conglomerates, particularly ICI, Benn also managed to create a series of partnerships through which BNOC and British Gas were able to enter the field of oil production. None of this, however, seriously challenged the grip of the American oil majors and their British partners, BP and Shell. On matters of health and safety and trade union recognition, the production regime established by the American companies and their contractors continued virtually unchallenged. The North Sea, even though it was then absorbing over a fifth of all British capital investment, was specifically exempted from the 1978 provisions whereby health and safety representatives were appointed by trade unions.

None the less, the fight to establish BNOC did much to confirm American corporate opinion that the Labour Party was no longer a safe vehicle. During negotiations in 1975 the US Department of Commerce threatened to pull back US-owned drilling rigs. Further pressures were applied during the sterling crisis of 1976. There was also acute concern about trade union influence. In 1973 the United States had appointed a very senior diplomat as its consul in Edinburgh: twenty years before Richard Funkhouser had headed the State Department's Middle East oil section. Funkhouser's telegrams from Edinburgh display increasing concern about trade union power. From the American point of view, there was little benefit in investing $10 billion to outflank OPEC just to give the same power to a few thousand Scottish trade-unionists.

How far this influenced American support for the SNP will never be known, nor just how important such support was. The Thomson press had backed the SNP since 1967. In the early 1970s a new group of intermediaries appeared. These were the Edinburgh merchant banks. They drew their money from Scottish investment trusts and used it to put together consortia to bid for North Sea licences. The inclusion of local with overseas capital generally assisted selection. In 1974 the directors of the most active of these, Noble Grossart, declared for the SNP. They included Sir Hugh Fraser, son of the buccaneering draper of the 1950s, who brought with him control of the *Glasgow Herald* and a big slab of the Scottish local press.

In the short run this type of business and press backing was important for the electoral rise of the SNP – and conversely for the Conservative decline. In the longer run it was not. One of the most remarkable features of the 1970s was the failure of the SNP to consolidate its electoral base – in face of an incumbent Labour government which had been considerably less than successful in delivering its electoral promises. The problem for the SNP was the social diversity of its support. In rural areas it was small business. In the central belt it was both ex-Tories and a large segment of working-class voters – attracted by promises of jobs and welfare on the basis of the slogan 'It's Scotland's Oil'. The SNP leader, Gordon Wilson, had issued the slogan in 1973 after a series of meetings with the oil companies. In 1974 this slogan, plus support from small business, proved a winning combination. Thereafter the party found itself immobilized by a struggle between those who wanted to move in a leftward direction and consolidate the working-class vote, and those who did not. By and large the latter won.

Professor Christopher Harvie, writing in 1978, revealed his exasperation: 'despite its claims, the policy-making dynamic within the SNP is corporate rather than radical, directed by middle-class activists in the interests of their professions ... there is no "radical" questioning of the role of doctors or teachers. So far political success has inhibited any exposure of these contradictions, but for how long can this last?' On defence the party adopted an Atlanticist position and failed to support nuclear disarmament. On public ownership the party was unenthusiastic. The SNP's whip in the Commons, Hamish Watt, publicly tore up a telegram from Scottish trade-unionists urging the party to vote for shipbuilding and aircraft nationalization. Finally, after the devolution referendum, the SNP joined the Conservatives in a successful no-confidence motion. In the ensuing election the SNP was reduced to two seats and 18 per cent of the vote. Its biggest losses were among manual workers. The converse of this was the success of the Labour Party. This was also remarkable. In the 1979 election Labour fared very badly in England and Wales. Its vote dropped 3 per cent to 36 per cent. In Scotland the Labour vote increased by 6 per cent to 42 per cent, and the party gained forty-four seats – more even than in 1945. The big increase was among working-class voters – both blue- and white-collar. This was despite the cuts in public spending imposed by the International Monetary Fund in 1976–7, an incomes policy that actually cut real wages and the débâcle of the devolution referendum. It is at this point that the divergence of voting patterns between England and Scotland, so marked in the 1980s, begins.

Part of the explanation is the disintegration of the Conservatives as a Scottish party. After 1972 the party never regained a coherent base. Before the war, Scottish capital had ruled both by virtue of its economic dominance in Scotland and its political alignments in Whitehall and Westminster. For the three post-war decades it retained a limited authority based on its industrial and financial power in Scotland. After 1972 this was lost. 'Oceanspan' was abandoned. Clydeside industrialists withdrew from active politics. In one last salvo in 1973 the journal of the Scottish Council condemned the whole direction of Labour and Conservative government planning since the 1960s. The creation of the new towns, the bleeding away of Glasgow's skilled labour force and the subsidies to external multinationals were, it was claimed, directly responsible for the problems of Scotland's indigenous industries. Indeed it was in just this period that their decline was at its fastest. Between 1968 and 1977 the proportion of manufacturing employment in Scottish-owned plants fell by a quarter: from just under 46 per cent to 36 per cent. The money went mainly into investment trusts – and much of it into bidding for licences for North Sea exploration, where Scottish capital could only figure as junior partners for American or City of London interests. The process left the remaining leaders of Scottish business fatally divided over devolution. Some went with the SNP. Others, like McEwen Younger, would have preferred devolution. But British business in

Scotland, like BP, Ferranti and GEC, did not want this. Nor did the new leadership of the Conservative Party around Margaret Thatcher.

Labour was also divided on devolution, but by no means so fatally. In Scotland some Labour supporters, such as Tam Dalyell, remained sceptical. In class terms they saw devolution as dividing the Labour movement's organizational strength at British level. The fear of competing regional and national lobbies was also strong in England, and it was George Cunningham, born in Dunfermline but MP for Islington, who amended the Scotland Bill in 1978 to make it much more difficult to gain assent. The referendum now required 40 per cent of the total electorate, and not just voters, for a parliament to be created. Hence although a narrow majority of Scots did vote yes on 1 March 1979 it was not enough.

Yet despite this self-inflicted wound, the Labour Party did particularly well in the general election two months later. There are perhaps three explanations. We have already noted the Conservatives' disarray in Scotland. We have also seen the SNP's loss of face with the working-class voter, but there was, it would seem, another more positive factor. This was the new and quasi-independent role taken by organized labour in Scotland. In the vacuum created by the demise of Scottish business, the STUC was increasingly projected as the representative of the nation as a whole. In the struggles of the early seventies in particular it had come to be seen as a campaigning body in its own right and one which was able to unite loyalties of both class and nation. By 1978 its membership had topped a million and its new standing had been given somewhat startling confirmation the previous year. Harold Wilson, accompanied by seven senior ministers, spent two days at STUC seminars in Glasgow on the problems of the Scottish economy. The STUC had no inhibitions about speaking out against the aspects of Labour policy it disliked – such as incomes policy and spending cuts. It also began to project its own left alternatives. Public ownership figured prominently as Scottish manufacturing moved into precipitate decline. Even the election of Margaret Thatcher did not initially dim this confidence in a non-capitalist future. Six weeks after the Tory victory, two Soviet airliners waited on the tarmac at Glasgow airport. They had been chartered by the STUC to enable 324 Scottish trade-unionists, including many of the movement's leaders, to study how a centrally planned economy might work.

Conclusion

Muriel Spark's novel *The Prime of Miss Jean Brodie*, published in 1961, looks back to an Edinburgh childhood in the 1930s. The superficial tragedies of schoolgirl life are interspersed with the blacker comedy of Scottish existence. At one point Spark describes the anglicized insulation of the Edinburgh middle classes:

She had no experience of social class at all. In its outward forms her fifteen years might have been spent in any suburb of any city in the British isles; her school, with its alien house system, might have been in Ealing. All she was conscious of now was that some quality of life peculiar to Edinburgh and nowhere else had been going on unbeknown to her all the time, and however undesirable it might be, she felt deprived of it; however undesirable, she desired to know what it was, and cease to be protected from it by enlightened people.

It was the resulting contact with this undesirable, submerged world, real or imagined, that brings the denouement of the novel and the betrayal of Miss Brodie. For Spark the elemental Scotland was now represented by those beyond and beneath the middle class: 'she walked round the forbidden quarters of Edinburgh to look at the blackened monuments and hear the unbelievable curses of the drunken men and women'. If Scotland had an élite, its Scottishness had gone.

This narrative has sought to show how. Scotland always had its élites – though they have changed sharply in composition and character. Each tried to make their chosen identities those of the nation. Each proposed a history. Each demanded continuity. Here we have sought to stress the opposite: the contingent, passing character of the way authority has been exercised. The industrial and financial élite of 1914 held virtually absolute economic and political power over Scotland. They dressed the interests of property in the morality of a Protestant nation – and found themselves shipwrecked in the class turmoil of the First World War. Walter Elliot and his Conservative colleagues came from very much the same background, but they represented it differently. Property did not figure. Their chosen identity was that of the professional élite: the men of the Scottish medical schools and scientific laboratories, fount of a neutral, classless, benevolent science that of itself could transform life. The 'unbelievable curses' of drunken men and women were not heard – at least not till May 1940, when the political universe of the old élite fell apart.

Thereafter authority was exercised in a decidedly different way. British politics entered. Was this new? As *mass* politics, yes. The Union had always been central to the identity of the old élite. For the Lithgows, Weirs and Colvilles it was scarcely separable from their Scottishness, the guarantee of a privileged place at the centre of empire. By contrast, the settlement of the 1940s was the outcome of political struggle. Ordinary people saw themselves as participants. Tom Johnston and his Labour successors were their agents. Support for '45 combined the symbols of Red Clydeside with policies which at last delivered something like full employment.

These were Scottish politics as well as British – but also in a new way. The new identity had nothing to do with that of a Protestant nation. In theory at least, it was inclusive. It encompassed the diversity of traditions within Scottish labour. And it drew its credibility from the way Scots were seen to exercise power, jointly with others, at British level. Yet this was also its problem. The post-war settlement was exactly that.

It had two sides. There was the need to appease a mobilized working class while at the same time meeting the requirements of large-scale capital now concentrated at British level. Ultimately the question would be posed about who was exercising the real power: was it Scottish power exercised at British level, or power exercised over Scotland? The balance of perception was critical. The potency of the revolt of the early seventies was precisely because this new Scottish identity was challenged by the apparent withdrawal of the post-war settlement. The shop stewards of 1972 could in the same breath appeal to the Scottish people and the British working class. By 1974 only a reaffirmation of the 1945 settlement, now explicitly defined as a Social Contract, could stabilize the situation.

We began with a riddle. If in 1914 the influence of Scots in government was secured by dint of their property and capital, why were Scots similarly so influential in government at the end of the century – when Scotland's capital was externally controlled? The events of the 1970s provide much of the answer. It was from this point that the Labour Party began to develop such a disproportionate role in Scottish life, and in turn to become very heavily dependent on its Scottish support. The new Social Contract settlement lasted only five years. The extension of public ownership to shipbuilding, aircraft and oil was never consolidated. Nor were the new worker rights in terms of health and safety and trade union recognition. Yet the victories of 1974 powerfully reinforced the shift in national identity. Scots began to consider their collectivity in a new way. Their success in winning their objectives in the 1970s, actively and on the basis of relatively mass participation, was seen to come both from its own internal organization, principally in terms of the trade union movement, and the *joint exercise* of this strength within the British state. It was this identity which the SNP so fatally misunderstood in 1979. The Conservatives were ultimately to challenge it at their peril.

Bibliographical Essay

General Histories

The best general history of twentieth-century Scotland remains Christopher Harvie's *No Gods and Precious Few Heroes: Scotland, 1914–1980* (London, 1981; 2nd edn., 1998): excellent on culture, the Scottish élites and the fast-changing periodization. Use the latest edition. The second volume of T. C. Smout's magisterial history of Scotland since the sixteenth century, *A Century of the Scottish People, 1830–1950* (London, 1986), is strong on social history and stresses continuities between nineteenth- and twentieth-century Scotland. Michael Fry's *Patronage and Principle* (Aberdeen, 1987) provides a high Tory introduction to Scotland's political history and should be complemented by Michael Lynch's *Scotland: A New History* (London, 1991). Tony Dickson, *Scottish Capitalism: Class, State and Nation from before the Union to the Present*

(London, 1981) provides a more left-wing perspective. Also useful are three collections of specialist essays produced over the past decade: Ian Donnachie and Christopher Whatley (eds.), *Modern Scottish History, 1707 to the Present* (East Linton, 1998); T. M. Devine and R. Finlay (eds.), *Scotland in the Twentieth Century* (Edinburgh, 1996); and A. Dickson and J. Treble (eds.), *People and Society in Scotland*, vol. 3: *1914–1990* (Edinburgh, 1992). These provide particularly helpful introductions to issues of gender relations, education, demography, religion and leisure. In terms of the wider theoretical perspectives which have informed this chapter, J. Foster, 'Nationality, Social Change and Class', in D. McCrone, S. Kendrick and P. Straw (eds.), *The Making of Scotland: Nation, Culture and Social Change* (Edinburgh, 1989), provides a review of texts.

Political Economy

Peter Payne's *Colvilles and the Scottish Steel Industry* (Oxford, 1979) and Richard Saville's *The Bank of Scotland: A History, 1695–1995* (Edinburgh, 1997) provide introductions to the two key institutions of twentieth-century Scottish capital. John Scott and Michael Hughes, *The Anatomy of Scottish Capital* (London, 1981) examines changes in the overall patterns of ownership and interlocking directorships through the twentieth century. C. Woolfson, *The Politics of the Upper Clyde Shipbuilders Work-In* (London, 1986) focuses on the three post-1945 decades, while Christopher Harvie, *Fool's Gold* (London, 1994) provides a background to the exploitation of North Sea oil. More general histories are provided by R. H. Campbell, *The Rise and Fall of Scottish Industry, 1707–1939* (Edinburgh, 1980); Richard Saville (ed.), *The Economic History of Modern Scotland 1950–1980* (Edinburgh, 1985); and A. Slaven, *The Development of the West of Scotland, 1750–1960* (London, 1975). C. H. Lee, *Scotland and the United Kingdom in the Twentieth Century* (Manchester, 1995) examines the changing relations between the Scottish and British economies. His *British Regional Employment Statistics, 1841–1971* (Cambridge, 1979) is an invaluable collection of statistical material.

Politics and Institutions

James Kellas, *The Scottish Political System* (Cambridge, 1989) provides the most comprehensive introduction and can be supplemented by Lindsay Patterson's *The Autonomy of Scotland* (Edinburgh, 1994). I. G. C. Hutchison, *A Political History of Modern Scotland, 1832–1924* (Edinburgh, 1986) is particularly useful on the decline of the Liberal Party, and Alan McKinlay and R. J. Morris (eds.), *The ILP on Clydeside, 1893–1932* (Manchester, 1991) on the rise of Labour. James Mitchell, *Conservatives and the Union* (Edinburgh, 1990) charts the changing fortunes of Scottish Conservativism, and Christopher Harvie, *Scotland and Nationalism: Scottish Society and Politics, 1707–1994* (London, 1994) the uncertain rise of nationalism. Jack Brand's *The National Movement in Scotland* (London, 1978) includes invaluable research on the origins of the SNP and its social milieu in the 1950s and '60s. Much can be learnt from biographies and autobiographies. Some of the most interesting are J. Adam-Smith, *John Buchan* (London, 1965); Robert Blake, *Andrew Bonar Law* (London, 1955); John Boyd Orr, *As I Remember* (London, 1966); J. Bruce Gardyne, *Whatever Happened to the Quiet Revolution* (London, 1974); Colin Coote, *Walter Elliot* (London, 1965); W. Gallacher, *Revolt on the Clyde* (London, 1936); Tom Johnston, *Memories* (London, 1965); W. W. Knox, *James Maxton* (Manchester, 1987); Naomi Mitchison, *Among You Taking Notes: War Diaries* (London, 1985); G. Pottinger, *Hugh Fraser*

(London, 1971); and Graham Walker, *Tom Johnston* (Manchester, 1988). Business histories also provide important insights. Some of the most revealing are Sam McKinstrey, *Albion Motor* (Edinburgh, 1997); and W. J. Reader, *Imperial Chemical Industries* (Oxford, 1970) and *The Weir Group* (London, 1971). W. W. Knox, *Scottish Labour Leaders, 1918–1939: A Biographical Dictionary* (Edinburgh, 1984) is an authoritative source for a spectrum of Labour politicians and trade union leaders.

People and Movements

Angela Tuckett, *The Scottish Trades Union Congress, 1897–1977* (Edinburgh, 1986) provides a detailed and documented history, and Keith Aitken, *Bairns o'Adam* (Edinburgh, 1997) a more impressionistic assessment of the wider political role of the STUC. W. W. Knox's *Industrial Scotland: Work, Culture and Society* (Edinburgh, 1999) is so far the only comprehensive treatment of labour in its wider social context. James Hinton, *The First Shop Stewards Movement* (London, 1973) provided the first scholarly reconstruction of Clydeside industrial militancy during the First World War. R. K. Middlemas, *The Clydesiders* (London, 1965) examines the politics and personalities, and Iain McLean, *The Legend of the Red Clydeside* (London, 1983) attempts a revisionist interpretation. Robin Page Arnot, *The Scottish Miners* (London, 1955) remains an indispensable account of what was Scotland's dominant trade union through most of the twentieth century. It is to be supplemented by Alan Campbell, 'The Social History of Political Conflict in the Scottish Coalfield, 1910–1939', in A. Campbell *et al.* (eds.), *Miners, Unions and Politics, 1910–1939* (Aldershot, 1997). Ian MacDougall (ed.), *Essays in Scottish Labour History* (Edinburgh, 1979) is the starting-point for the critical analysis of Scottish labour history. His oral history collections provide essential materials for the study of the inter-war unemployed workers' movement (*Voices from the Hunger Marches*, vols. 1 and 2, Edinburgh, 1990–91; and for the Scottish contribution to the International Brigade in Spain: *Voices from the Spanish Civil War*, Edinburgh, 1986). Alan Troup, 'Paisley Engineers', in T. Clarke, J. Foster, W. Knox, C. Madigan, G. Nair and A. Troup, *Essays in the Social and Labour History of Renfrewshire* (Paisley, 1999) documents the scale of activity generated by the shop stewards movement in the 1970s. Mary Docherty, *A Miner's Lass* (Cowdenbeath, 1994) describes the life of a female trade union activist. Eleanor Gordon, *Women and the Labour Movement, 1850–1914* (Oxford, 1991) and Esther Breitenbach, *Women Workers in Scotland* (Edinburgh, 1982) both provide more general appraisals. Helen Corr and Arthur MacIvor, 'Women and Gender Relations', in Ian Donnachie and Christopher Whatley (eds.), *Modern Scottish History* (East Linton, 1997) is the best starting-point for a study of the changing place of women in Scottish society. Religious movements are well covered by Callum Brown's contribution to the same volume. Tom Gallacher, *Glasgow: The Uneasy Peace* (Manchester, 1987) and *Edinburgh Divided* (Edinburgh, 1987) examine religious sectarianism in Scotland's two biggest cities. P. Sissons, *The Social Significance of Church Membership in the Burgh of Falkirk* (Edinburgh, 1973) is an important case study.

Ideas, Identities and Cultures

Ian Donnachie and Christopher Whatley (eds.), *Manufacturing Scottish History* (Edinburgh, 1992) and D. Brown, R. Finlay and M. Lynch (eds.), *Image and Identity: The Making and Remaking of Scotland* (Edinburgh, 1998) examine the different ways in which Scotland's history and identity have been expressed across the century. Novelists, poets and dramatists provide the key texts and invariably speak better for themselves. They have been referred to directly in the text. However, particularly useful commentaries are provided by David Craig, 'The Radical Literary Tradition', in Gordon Brown (ed.), *Red Paper on Scotland* (Edinburgh, 1975) and Jack Mitchell, 'Hamish Henderson and the Folk Song Revival', in P. M. Kemp-Asraf, *Essays in Honour of William Gallacher* (Berlin, 1966). W. Eadie, *Movement of Modernity: The Case of Glasgow and Art Nouveau* (London, 1990) is a fascinating attempt to develop a sociology of Glasgow at the zenith of its artistic influence. Sam McKinstrey, *Rowand Anderson* (Edinburgh, 1991) examines the architectural counterpoint to the early modernist movement. Alan Reiach and Robert Hurd, *Building Scotland* (Glasgow, 1944) provide a contemporary manifesto for modernism.

Social Structures

Scotland's social diversity is quite remarkable for a small nation. Frank Fraser Darling, *West Highland Survey* (Oxford, 1957) provides a massively researched study of the West Highlands as they were in the 1940s. Naomi Mitchison, *Lobsters on the Agenda* (Edinburgh, 1952) is a vivid reconstruction of the social and religious tensions. James Littlejohn, *Westrigg: The Sociology of a Cheviot Parish* (London, 1963) does the same for the Borders. Scotland's cities are still only partially researched. Sean Damer, *Glasgow Going for a Song* (London, 1990) and Michael Pacione, *Glasgow* (Chichester, 1995) are supplemented by Christopher Whatley, David Swinfen and Annette Smith, *The Life and Times of Dundee* (Edinburgh, 1993) and John Holford, *Reshaping Labour: Edinburgh after the Great War* (Edinburgh, 1988). Billy Kay, *The Complete Odessey: Voices from Scotland's Recent Past* (Edinburgh, 1996) covers a massive range of local experience. The history of Scotland's black population is so far poorly researched. Useful starting-points are Mary Edwards, *Who Belongs to Glasgow: 200 Years of Migration* (Glasgow, 1993) and Ann Dunlop, 'Lascars and Labourers: Reactions to the Indian Presence in the West of Scotland during the 1920s and 1930s', *Scottish Labour History Society Journal* 25 (1990), 40–57.

8

Scotland after 1978: from Referendum to Millennium

CHRISTOPHER HARVIE

The Road to Parliament Square

On the morning of 1 July 1999 the members of the Scottish parliament convened beneath the hammer-beam roof of the Parliament House off Edinburgh's High Street. There, 292 years before, their predecessors had voted themselves out of existence, to begin the bold experiment of the British Empire, whose technology, administration and culture had revolutionized the world. The day was an odd but somehow satisfactory mixture of the traditional and the informal. There were few kilts among the MSPs, though the Kings at Arms and Royal Company of Archers still strutted medievally. The Queen, there as an honoured guest rather than as a monarch, seemed to enjoy herself, even when confronted with the republican internationalism of Burns's 'For a' That'. The gangling, witty figure of First Minister Donald Dewar was in his element. The sun shone, field-guns banged and trumpeters blared, and later on fireworks whooshed above the most beautiful city in Europe singing and dancing into the night, and into what Dewar called 'a journey without an end'.

It was a ceremony private to the Scots. The rest of Europe scarcely noticed. With similar ceremony, the Germans were also inaugurating a new parliament and a new president. There was a sullen peace in Kosovo, where those to whom evil had been done were doing evil in return. The Ulster peace process was deadlocked, and Orangemen restive in their 'marching season'. Those with a taste for historical parallels remembered the last time a Serbian and an Ulster crisis had coincided, in August 1914, and the more ingenuous among them consulted Nostradamus, who had prophesied the Apocalypse for the beginning of July. That apart, the event of the week for British newspaper readers was the wedding of a Spice Girl to a Manchester United footballer. In this salad of ingenuity and bravery, viciousness and downright idiocy, the Scots were involved – nervously driving trucks in the Balkans, building Berlin, stamping impatiently on the Garvaghy Road, managing Manchester United. And other Scots – the bewigged literati who had written and drunk claret and talked around Parliament Square 250 years before – had been in great part responsible for creating the whole busy, crazy world structure. How had their descendants got here, to a destination which, on 2 March 1979, had seemed impossibly remote?

One person, of course, was absent from Edinburgh, whom many considered the parliament's 'onlie begetter': Lady Thatcher. She may supply a means of structuring this chapter. Did she create the conditions for the loosening of the Union, or was she more an instrument of the blind forces of international capitalism and technological progress which she commended, though only fitfully understood? I have placed politics late in my account. Thatcher's impact on Scotland in the early part of her government was mainly the result of her economic policy. Few in the Labour Party could really object to her ditching of devolution, which they were unenthusiastic about. But the impact of economic changes, relatively unmediated by government action, was to create an altogether different and less reassuring future for traditional Unionist politics. Hence my route will begin by interrogating the sense of being Scottish in the 1980s and 1990s, and move from that to the economic background and political geography, before homing in on the political world. Through this – with its traditional influence on education, housing and health – Scottish society is best approached, while a final section on culture returns to some of the questions posed in the introduction. But, first, what sort of a country faced the grey days of May 1979?

Scotland: Virtual and Virtuous?

In 1983 the telephone box at Pennan, Aberdeenshire, became briefly the most famous in the world, with a starring role in 'Local Hero'. Bill Forsyth's comedy about Big Oil meeting Brigadoon became a cult both in Europe and in Anglo-America, emphasizing a 'geo-poetical' poise – the phrase was that of Kenneth White, the Scots poet whom the French had raised to bardic status – between the two ideologies which were competing for the world's future. Forsyth had started as an ironic observer of youth in housing schemes and new towns, moved on via oil in 'Local Hero' to Glasgow's 'ice-cream wars' in 'Comfort and Joy'. He failed when he tried to use his Hollywood chance to be profound about the human condition.

By 1999 the phone box was as relevant as a megalith. The mobile and the satellite had wrecked Local Hero's plot. The ice-cream wars were no longer comic. Glasgow's drug habit, of which they were part, was costing the country over half a billion pounds a year. Yet Hollywood's part in reviving Scotland was not just Sean Connery – clad, on that July day, like a revenant from the '45. It dramatized the matter of Scotland in 'Braveheart' and 'Rob Roy', in which the country became the man of honour suffering at the hands of Englishmen or Scottish aristocrats. If, as the Welsh historian Gwyn A.

Williams wrote, 'Small nations develop in the interstices of other nations' histories', then the gap throughout Europe between the traditional politics of the nation-state, with its framework of defence-based, legal, welfare and cultural functions, and the dynamism of the market, associated with American-driven global capitalism, was where Scottish nationality thrived. This much is clear, but at the cusp of the millennium, and in the new constitutional dispensation, towards which pattern did the Scots incline?

In 1989–91 Hollywood had won. The Communist alternative, which had entranced so many Scots writers, trade-unionists and political activists, died in Beijing's Tiananmen Square and decomposed in Yeltsin's Russia. Would this spell the end of the nation or would collectivism regroup at a European, and subordinately at a regional, level? Had the Scots gone ahead of the game in rebuffing Thatcher, in combining 'civic' nationalism and socialism, even in transforming footballing belligerence into the heart-warming drollery of the Tartan Army? Did 'post-nationalism' mean inclining towards Labour for Westminster and towards the SNP for Holyrood? Or were they as baffled as everyone else as a century rich in innovation and barbarism slumped towards its close?

The victors included outsize characters who were, or appeared to be, Scots. Iain Robert Maxwell (formerly Jan Ludwig Hoch) owned – besides much else – Aberdeen University Press. Before his fall he subsidized the scholarly editing of Walter Scott and the *Sunday Mail History of Scotland*. His rival Rupert Murdoch was from a line of Australian Free Kirkers, married to a Lithuanian Catholic from Kirkintilloch. Donald Trump, the flamboyant New York property tycoon, had a Lewis mother. John Calder went from the *Daily Record* to the United States' leading 'junk newspaper', the *National Enquirer*. Its owners, the Barclay brothers, of a Kilmarnock Catholic family, who built a gothic Xanadu on a Channel Island, took over the *Scotsman*. A Scot fleeced Europe's most loathsome élite in Moscow's biggest casino. For Russian hangovers there was Moscow-manufactured Irn-Bru. Doubts might be expressed about Anglo-Saxon capitalism, but plenty of Scots *savants* were well paid to defend it: Norman Stone and Niall Ferguson, Andrew Neil and Madsen Pirie.

Hollywood did not appeal much to the Europeans, who looked for Scots templates of a more elevated sort: Alasdair MacIntyre's revival of the Aristotelian collective; Kenneth White's 'geo-poetics'; Emmanuel Todd's links between family structures and economic development; Tom Nairn's restructuring of the nation state. This was a reprise of the eighteenth-century Enlightenment: but works about Scotland and society of a seriousness rivalling anything printed in the place came from all the arts, as did scholars, artists and epicures. Wolfram Siebeck, the hanging judge of German food critics, was in 1998 bowled over by the consistent high quality of the food in small country hotels. 'People come from all over to shoot here. But also, I'm sure, to eat well.'

Why was it possible for all these to treasure, in however scholarly or sentimental a way, a rather complex Scots connection, while most rarely advanced beyond stereotypes? 'Scotland the Brand', Scotland as signifier – the 'Glen Garry, Glen Ross' of David

Mamet's Jewish advertising salesmen, plus golf, tweeds, whisky and the Edinburgh Festival – had fitted itself into a consumerist niche. The worry was that the Scots themselves were becoming like native Americans on a reserve: their distinctiveness compounded of low income, immobility, short life and addiction or ill-health, distinctive because no one wanted to share their lifestyle.

In July 1996 a young journalist, Deborah Orr, watched Ravenscraig steelworks being blown up:

The big blue gas holders spouted a pretty fringe of white puffs round their tops, bellied out like drops of water, and crashed backwards to the ground like flattened tin cans. The cooling towers disappeared in neat little plumes of dust. Nothing was left of them but circular marks on the ground, and a fluffy beige mist that drifted away in minutes.

The theme of disappearance recurred in a bestseller of 1995, Andrew O'Hagan's *The Missing*, a sensitive recollection of a childhood spent in Glasgow and the new town of Irvine, site (in its older incarnation) of John Galt's *Annals of the Parish* and Gordon Williams's bitter picture of a failing industrial Scotland, *From Scenes like These* (1968). With the end of a manufacturing order and its institutions, self-created and inherited, came new social barriers, not just those of the poverty in which 30 per cent of Scots children grew up – the German figure was 9 per cent – but a form of mental exclusion, as the sociologist Professor Bob Holman wrote of the accounts he collected of Easterhouse life: 'In terms of public communication it is the words and voices of the top 40 per cent – supplemented by the middle 30 per cent – that are read and heard. Those of the bottom 30 per cent are silenced.' O'Hagan spoke for many among them; but one angle of his inquiry seemed to invoke another person associated, albeit briefly, with Irvine: Edgar Allan Poe. Those who became detached from society faced, often, an end which was horrific, the down-and-outs dying on urine-soaked cardboard, the girls raped and butchered in Gloucester by Fred West.

Culture mattered because it was tradeable, hence subject to economic analysis and market research. The literary skills of O'Hagan, Kelman and, to some extent, the younger 'chemical generation', could use it to open out society. However, sociology – the investigative arm of the welfare state – largely migrated to the private sector or to contracting university departments. Who would then comprehend, let alone speak for, the legion of the victims?

Speak of the Place: the Scots' Image of Themselves

The Scots were keen on Europe. They had not been so in the 1970s, but hostility dwindled by the Common Market referendum of 1975, and then dropped to below the UK level, although secondary identification in the late 1990s still remained 'British'. Visitors, and their number practically doubled over our period, marvelled at the bleak desolation they flew over, motored through, or saw, like the American Paul Theroux, from a train:

Most of this western coastline in Scotland looked elemental in that way — as if it had been whipped clean . . . It was hard and plain, most of it. It was very cold. I stared at it and decided that it was ferocious rather than pretty, with a size and a texture that was surprisingly unfinished. It changed with the light as coastal cliffs always did; it was always massive, but in certain pale lights it seemed murderous.

'Murderous' also applied to the traffic gulch of the A74, between England and the central belt. This led to a jumbled country: the glossy guides (Germany had thirteen) promised staggering scenery and the restrained architecture of kirk, tower-house, farm steading and town square. This was not false. In 1997 Strathclyde University assessed 189 towns and cities on the criteria of crime, cost of living, pollution, shopping, education, scenery, transport, jobs and housing. Dumfries came top, followed by Livingston New Town and Kendal in the Lake District (Hull was bottom). On the other hand, what were visitors to make of recent accretions: the point blocks, the pastel-coloured slabs of factories — far more elegant than the surrounding estates of poky private houses — the subtopian sprawl of superstores, car dealers, McDonalds franchises, the often clogged roads and endless car parks, and behind them, grim, grey, 'multiply-deprived' housing schemes?

If anything, the Scots seemed anxious to get out of the place. The consistent growth of travel agents catered for a trebling of passengers at Scottish airports between 1975 and 1996. The Scots spent 5 per cent more on foreign holidays than the more affluent English, and about as much money — around £2 billion — left the country as came to it through foreign tourists. This meant, as another Strathclyde study, this time of teenagers, found, that 21 per cent of Scots had visited England, while only 3 per cent of West Midlanders in the same age-group had come to Scotland. The writer Hans-Magnus Enzensberger hypothesized, about the ever-travelling Germans, that identity itself was diffused. At least the Germans tried to speak other languages, while the number of Scots pupils studying European languages fell by two-thirds between 1980 and 1995; a sobering thought for those buoyed up by a TV and playgroup-assisted revival in Gaelic. Possibly language itself was fracturing; those who found TV's *lumpenprole* Rab C.

Nesbitt hard going had also to cope with a strange 'offshore English' on the oil rigs, as remote from received pronunciation as the 'cyberbabble' which contended with Japanese in Silicon Glen.

In 1998 Livingston workers were making chips and wafers and eating tempura. Other workers were ripping down the Aviemore centre, Lord Fraser's 1964 St Moritz decayed into a steak bar. Had Scotland moved on from the other, universal, chips which christened Glasgow's most fashionable restaurant? Perhaps, for Glasgow and Edinburgh seemed more cosmopolitan than London or most English cities. Because they were smaller, their immigrants tended to become integrated and were not segregated by suburb; it took some mental effort for Scots to realize that there *were* substantial immigrant ghettos in Glasgow in particular, and public commitments to liberalism had done little for them. Multi-culturalism delighted incomers, whether tourists or professionals – the Edinburgh Festival, at last accepted by the citizens, was a world-class salute to it. However, it did not explain the nexus of problems denoted by the deep-fried Mars Bar: that Scotland had a very big minority who were not doing very well at all.

By 1998 political activists could reflect, rather gloomily, on a tripartite pattern highlighted in a Scottish Council Foundation report. Most of them would be 'settled Scots', roughly the baby-boomers of 1944–50. For them, books and museums, party activity and local societies were ways of ordering their experience of unending change. 'Insecure' Scots grasped at stability: through re-orientating the country's institutions, or commercial ventures aimed at survival in a world of tourism, the media, property dealing and financial services. However, and this was a major difference from England, this did not totally occur outside a public sector which, in Glasgow in 1996 at least, furnished a third of jobs, and sustained many more.

Where was the proletariat in all this, those appealed to by two young Scottish politicians, Gordon Brown and Robin Cook, in 1982, seven years after the idealistic *Red Paper on Scotland*? Some 42 per cent of the workforce in 1978, maybe 30 per cent by 1990, it straddled these sectors, divided between the unionized and secure, largely in the public service; the employees of the new high-technology and service concerns, often part-time female workers. Those lastingly penalized by redundancy, social breakdown and ill-health fell into the Scottish Council Foundation's third group, the 'excluded Scots'. Such people were more likely to be single parents, council tenants, and crime victims; reported crimes almost doubled to 600,000 between 1977 and 1992. Crime then fell by a quarter, but not in problem areas where it was fuelled by drugs and cost perhaps as much as 2 per cent of Scottish GNP. The tripartite division, of course, concealed variations: households and families could combine all three – the settled, insecure and excluded – an indeterminacy which led to a search for other means of communal expression.

Scotland: The Real Divide was a clarion call for redistribution to replace what Brown and Cook saw as the false conflict of home rule. Two decades later they were in charge, but tackled a different question: 'British' economic management in the global market. Instead the home rule issue, far from going away, marked the election of 1997 and the referendum on the Scots parliament, while 'the divide', too, had changed. Scottish trade-unionists fell in numbers, from 46 to 35 per cent of the workforce. They became more middle class, while manual workers in manufacturing (particularly in local supplier companies to the largest multinationals) became less organized, subject to lean, tough/tender American-style management – 'Unions? What have they to worry about, the quality of the lemons in the iced-water machines?' was how one Motorola manufacturing associate summed it up.

In another offering of 1982, 'The Body in the Kitbag' published in *Cencrastus*, the critic Cairns Craig reckoned that explaining Scottish society had been made more difficult by a sort of national amnesia. History had been so turbulent, particularly since 1914, that the past became 'buried', 'disappeared'. Yet the frustration of 1979 worked its leaven, and the 1980s saw the completion of 'national' intellectual projects cognate with those of the European 'historical nationalities'. Eight volumes of the *New History of Scotland* (1981–4), four of the *History of Scottish Literature* (1987–8) and three of *People and Society in Scotland* (1988–92) filled the lacunae of the industrialized country, the first real outpouring of monumental historical writing since the high Victorian period. It is less clear that this history-writing impinged on ordinary schoolchildren. Indeed, information technology, theoretically connecting them with an infinity of facts, was seemingly drowning rather than sustaining them. Vocationally oriented courses had caused two-thirds to abandon history in the 1980s: Sydney Wood, the historian and educationalist, found that of a sample of sixteen-year-olds, 50 per cent had heard of Wallace and Bruce, 10 per cent of Tom Johnston, 3 per cent of Ramsay MacDonald.

Yet if 'the kids' were in contact with a literary canon, it would be Scots, not English literature. Neo- rather than post-modernism marked the work of Alasdair Gray, whose *Lanark*, composed between the late 1950s and 1982, melded a particularly harrowing didactic novel with themes out of Scots literature since the eighteenth century, something he shared with other urban writers like James Kelman and Tom Leonard. The renaissance had been rural or small-town: Neil Gunn, Sorley MacLean, George Bruce, George Mackay Brown and Norman MacCaig voiced a rural elementalism to salve the wounds of industrialism, migration and urban alienation probed by Edwin Muir in *The Story and the Fable*. The approach of Robin Jenkins, who dissected the Scottish renaissance stereotype in his timely *Fergus Lamont* (1979), took a different angle; it analysed and historicized, thus connecting with the Victorians – James George Frazer, George Douglas Brown and above all Thomas Carlyle – as well as the younger writers.

The Scots debated Joyce's 'long words that make us sad'. Non-alcohol-propelled hedonism was rare, though the 1960s had produced the Glasgow-Italian Alexander Trocchi, whose narcotic confessional *Cain's Book* (1963) was taken up by the chemical generation after 1988. Alan Warner, Duncan MacLean and above all Irvine Welsh became the voices of an under-employed, low-paid graduate labour force, recording both what they regarded as the communality of Ecstasy and dance culture, and the impact of hard drugs among the 'schemies' (those who lived in council housing schemes). The talents involved were variable, but the new Scottish novel was as lucrative as the kailyard: Welsh was quite truly a Master in Business Administration. Could this be classed as 'enlightened'? Would a tenth of the 'people who do not read books' get as far as Kelman and Gray? Was the on-lining of Scots newspapers, something achieved by Bobby Campbell on the *Scotsman* and Pat Kane on the *Herald*, and made both papers far superior to London broadsheets, enough to coax Scotland abreast of contemporary European social and political philosophy?

Let us leave the last word with an official from the Scottish Development Agency, the body which, in the absence of a parliament, incorporated the nation's attempt to manage change, from its foundation in 1975 to reconstitution in 1991 as Scottish Enterprise: 'There is constant tension within the organization over, for want of a better description, its soul. Basically, the division is between those who believe effort and money is best skewed towards seizing opportunities and those who believe that meeting needs should be high on the agenda.' This was not resolved by Great Britain PLC – even when modified after 1997 by Brown and Cook into Cool Britannia. In Scotland 'needs' prevailed, but this response owed to cumulative cultural changes: more collective, but also more tentative and confused.

Patterns of Industry: Unthank

In the course of extracting oil in the frequently hellish conditions of the northern North Sea, technologists found that, by linking satellite signals to computers which controlled a rig's electric thruster motors, the rig could maintain position to within a few square centimetres: enough to enable it to drill. Absolute positioning at sea – allowing exploitation of the ocean seabed – had never before been achieved in man's thousands of years of struggle with the element, and is the result of information technologies almost inconceivable two decades earlier. The same sort of technology was also on hand to revolutionize huge areas of society as well as industry. Whoever won the general election in 1979 would inherit much more than the bounty of North Sea oil. Labour's failure to deliver on devolution, and the SNP's impatience to dismiss the government, were political setbacks; but as nothing compared with the chances and catastrophes that technical and economic change would bring. At Honeywell in Newmains they had been building computers the size of cupboards for industry and local government since 1973. No one could imagine that within a decade a score of factories in what called itself Silicon Glen would put machines a tenth the size, and a thousand times the capacity, into a third of the offices and studies of Europe.

In *Lanark*, given life by the caesarean of referendum, Alasdair Gray juxtaposed Unthank, the victim-city of the old industrial order, with the futuristic underground society of the Institute: smooth and manipulative, but not alien to a Scottish tradition which had practised enlightenment only hundreds of yards from the slums. The oil and computer businesses, and their social and speculative entourage, had almost caught up with Gray by the time his novel came out. Oil certainly aided the Unthank world of Scottish engineering and supply concerns, though only two – the Wood Group of Aberdeen, and Weir Pumps – became important independent players. Yet even these were second fiddlers to suppliers in Spain or Singapore, who were used to delivering equipment to the other side of the world. The supply bases and production-platform yards were essentially depots for American expertise. Aggregate growth increased, but these were as isolated on land as the rigs at sea. For one thing, the higher wages on- and off-shore actually drove many local firms in the north-east out of business. For another, the health of the industry was tied to the volatility of oil prices. The Norwegians, with slow depletion of reserves and state control, enjoyed success, but by the time the British government developed an analogous but milder policy by setting up the British National Oil Corporation in 1975, the multinationals had the whip-hand.

James Callaghan had warned his squabbling followers that whoever won the 1979 election, oil would keep them in power for a generation. Mrs Thatcher scooped this advantage. By 1986 oil production, at 127 million tonnes, made up 5 per cent of British GNP, and by 1995 – when production was headed for a second peak – a net £27 billion had been paid in petroleum revenue tax to Whitehall. However, oil's economic implications were more ambiguous; it checked the move to nuclear power – except, ironically, in Scotland – and further undermined the coal industry; in 1979–81 the hike in oil prices caused by the Iranian revolution and the Gulf War strengthened the pound sterling, just when Mrs Thatcher's monetarist policies kicked in. With interest rates boosted to check the money supply, the petro-pound rose to nearly five Deutschmarks, throttling exports and wiping out a fifth of British manufacturing jobs.

In Scotland this included once-great concerns like the Singer factory at Clydebank and the Carron ironworks, and a fledgling automotive industry which never flew the nest. Chrysler-Peugeot pulled out of Linwood and British Leyland out of Bathgate. The Corpach pulp mill and the Invergordon aluminium smelter closed down. Unions and workers reacted with anger, bewilderment, and latterly fatalism: a lengthy steelworkers' strike in 1981 simply emphasized how hard Ravenscraig had been hit by the fall in local demand. This would worsen after the Gartcosh cold rolling mill closed in 1985, but Ravenscraig took another seven years to die. Remarkable improvements in productivity meant that it then employed only 1,800 men; in 1980 it had been 7,000. The suspicion with which workers regarded productivity had some grounds to it. Numbers gave political clout: an efficient works could also be a vulnerable works. The same could be said of the last of the Clyde shipyards. Ailsa at Troon and Ferguson's at Port Glasgow produced small specialized ships that sold well, but Yarrow's kept to defence contracts and Scott Lithgow and Fairfield's specialized in tankers and liquid-gas ships. A huge and disastrous oil rig contract finished Scott Lithgow in 1990, and Fairfield's, now owned by the Norwegian Kvaerner, built its last passenger boat, the 'Norsea', in 1988 – just before a new boom in cruise ships, the Clyde's speciality only three decades before.

The staples of agriculture, fisheries, mining, steel, engineering and textiles had been 53 per cent of Scottish industrial production in 1907. Even in 1960 they were 30 per cent, but by 1976 this was down to 20 per cent. Their last struggles were to dominate the early 1980s. Thatcher tried in 1981 to rationalize the mines and failed. Then she moved the hammer of the steelmen, an aggressive Scots-American called Ian Kinloch MacGregor, brought up in the aluminium 'company town' of Kinlochleven, to the Coal Board. What did she actually want: to force through closures *per se*? Or to provoke a confrontation in an industry already in a weak position, which would break the trade union élite? It was in a way the 1915 Red Clyde confrontation all over again, with MacGregor as the reincarnation of the 'Americanizing' Willie Weir. The miners' leader Arthur Scargill relished the confrontation; his Scottish Communist deputy, Mick Mac-Gahey, did not, and for a time it looked as if he would prevail. The capitulation, when it came, was near total. Of eighteen deep mines in 1979, only the Longannet complex, serving its power station near Alloa, survived. The tonnage of coal extracted declined from 11 million in 1979 to 6 million in 1997, of which only 1.5 million was deep-mined. This proved that the upper classes had still the upper hand, accelerating the proscription of 'political' strikes and the decline of union membership – but this did not remove power as a political issue.

Scottish electricity was privatized in 1987, but in fact remained state-provided because it was disproportionately generated by nuclear power. About 55 per cent (compared with a UK level of 27 per cent) came from Scottish Nuclear's stations at Hunterston, Chapelcross and Torness. Its privatization and amalgamation in 1995 with the UK Nuclear Electric provoked a substantial nationalist (with a small 'n') backlash. Both the private utilities proved acquisitive in their turn. In 1995 Scottish Power bought the Wales and north of England ManWeb. In 1998 Scottish Hydro amalgamated with Southern Electricity and moved the joint headquarters to Perth. In contrast with England, where American firms had virtually run off with the regional companies, the Scots had their eyes on American acquisitions.

Conservatives liked to claim that, once shot of heavy industry, the country could really catch up. The reality was a sequence of jolting advances and retreats. If we compare Scots gross domestic product *per capita* and that of the United Kingdom as a whole, then Scotland's product went up from 94.4 per cent of that of the UK in 1980 to 97.5 per cent in 1983, but fell to 92.6 per cent in 1990. Growth then increased from a low of 0.3 per cent in 1991 to 1.7 per cent in 1996, while the UK went negative by 2.2

per cent in 1991, so that by 1995 GDP was about level. Part of this 'success' was due to population decline (by 4.3 per cent over the period 1987–95), but Scotland was still wealthier than, say, north-east England (static at 86 per cent) or Wales (actually falling from 86.4 to 83.3 per cent). No longer a laggard, its exporting bias meant that it often reacted more rapidly than the rest of the UK to global stimuli like oil prices, changes in computer technology – or the wealth of the bosses in newly-industrializing countries.

'Facts are chiels that winnae ding' was the old line, but their reliability depended on who was stating them and when. In 1995 foreign-owned manufacturing was 22 per cent of Scottish employment, although this was down by three percentage points on its 1981 level. American firms, once paternalist in a Fordist sense but now shareholder-driven, had cut back in oil-related industry and engineering – the big Caterpillar works went in 1987 – and in analogue-based electronics. European, Far Eastern and English employers increased. The 'merger mania' which gripped the City of London in 1985–7, just before the 'Big Bang', reduced the amount of capital controlled by Scottish commercial and industrial firms from £4.7 to £2.3 billion. Bells and Distillers in whisky, and Coats Patons in textiles, went south. The Conservative industrialist Sir Norman MacFarlane had complained in 1982 that takeovers made for 'remote decision-making and a constant drain of quality management and technical talent to the south and overseas', but four years later he found himself chairman of London-based Guinness after its takeover of Distillers turned into the financial scandal of the century.

Patterns of Industry: the Institute

Takeovers diminished Scots' presence in high-value 'headquarters operations' – marketing, advertising, audit, research – but such developments also affected English firms caught in the global current. In this Scotland found a place, with the banks contradicting the long complaint by politicians about their detachment from industry. Charlotte Square became salient; oil enterprise had energized it and drawn in a multitude of foreign banks (most of which departed after production started). The reliable management of life insurance funds, in contrast with the flamboyance of the City, created confidence, just as information technology was revolutionizing the world financial system. By 1992, 11 per cent of the country's labour force was in financial services; its contribution to GNP went from 5 per cent in 1979 to 15 per cent in 1990.

Finance was political, and its crises were more important for Scotland than most parliamentary issues. The first, in some ways an equalizer to the 'own goal' of 1979, was the attempt in 1981 of the Standard Chartered Bank to take over the Royal Bank of Scotland. After pressure from George Younger as Secretary of State, the Monopolies and Mergers Commission ruled in favour of the Royal Bank's autonomy. This seems to have proved crucial: banking independence, buttressed by executive experience in bodies like the SDA, helped create aggressive privatized Scots utilities, assisting management buy-outs and subsequent takeovers. These cooperated with state and local authorities in attracting inward investment, while maintaining an informal ring-fence against southern predators.

The second financial earthquake was the Guinness takeover of Distillers in 1986. Guinness's aggressive chairman, 'Deadly Ernest' Saunders, persuaded the Scottish financial élite to turn down a bid from the Scottish industrialist and Tory adviser James Gulliver. The merged company was supposed to settle in Edinburgh. Then he reneged, and Charlotte Square, with a furious premier on its side, took its vengeance. The story of illegal share support schemes leaked out and the principals on the Guinness side went to jail. This had further consequences: Mrs Thatcher discovered an interest in Scotland which was, ultimately, bad for her political health.

Takeovers did not come to an end. The City still swallowed the Trustee Savings Bank in 1983 and Scottish Nuclear in 1995 – after bitter resistance. Ford took over Tom Farmer's Kwik-Fit car repair business for one billion pounds in 1999, and in that year the relative marginalization of the City from the European financial scene caused by the introduction of the Euro led to further 'consolidating' pressure on Edinburgh. The colossi of the life companies began to crumble towards demutualization, and the Bank of Scotland made a fool of itself through its dalliance with the American gospel preacher Pat Robertson.

Scotland's entry into the 'real time' world was a mixture of the planned and the random – and the IT scene itself was similarly complex, as Scottish executives discovered when they visited Japan and found systems of thought among managers and researchers inscrutable to the West. Yet history still counted. In the 1960s, Sir William Lithgow, whose father had the economic say in inter-war Scotland, shifted his investments to South Korea, where super-tankers could be built on green-field sites instead of on the congested and restricted Clyde, and governments were utterly pragmatic and indeed ruthless in forcing the pace of industrialization. By 1998 the leading sector of Scots manufacturing was an electronics industry, partly dominated by South Korea and other former low-wage countries turned 'Little Tigers'. With billions in Far Eastern funds, Scotland was simultaneously high-finance agent and artisan patient; what was lacking was the orthodox native entrepreneur.

Much enterprise depended on combinations of the sophisticated and the primitive. In 1984 an ingenious insurance man, Peter Wood, working with the Royal Bank, set up Direct Line car insurance. Within four years he was on a million-a-year salary and by 1996 Direct Line was Scotland's fastest-growing industry: 130 call centres employed 16,000, mainly women. British Telecom's Dundee centre cost £6 million for 800 jobs (£7,500 a job, compared with perhaps ten times that in the oil industry). The call centre was intermediate between counter-service and full computerization. Using satellite communications, it enabled information and booking to be provided world-wide. Virgin

Rail and BSkyB were thus served from central Scotland by the mid-1990s. However, such jobs were stressful and isolated, vulnerable to further technological advance and low-wage competition.

The same was said of the country's major exporter: Silicon Glen. Its ancestry lay in American firms – notably IBM at Greenock – which sited branches in Scotland after the war in order to access European markets. Many pulled out in the 1970s, when semiconductors and digital programmes came in, but there was a boom when, following the tailing-off of oil investment in the mid-1980s, Scottish authorities started luring computer firms. They believed that they could achieve a critical mass which would transform 'screwdriver' operations into high-value-added software and research. It took only a few months to ship in and erect a state-of-the-art factory, and the victory of the autoteller and the PC over the cashier and the typewriter was completed by a further boom in 1990–93. Nevertheless, critical mass stayed away. Turnover in 1990–93 increased by 26 per cent to £9.3 billion, but components from Scotland declined from 12 per cent to only 5 per cent, against imported supplies of £5.3 billion: 37 per cent from the Far East, 27 per cent from the USA, 20 per cent from Europe and 10 per cent from the rest of the UK.

Silicon Glen employers wanted government aid, docile labour, specialized training and higher education for local management, product testing and communications, and such research as came to hand. Ireland was moving in on software – riskier but more rewarding – when the SDA had scarcely a handful of staff devoted to this. Native entrepreneurs like Spider Systems, Edinburgh computer networkers, were swallowed up by American competitors. Only in 1997 was a major software concern, Cadence, hooked – and at that moment chip prices began to slump.

Ill fares the land?

'That is the Land out there.' Alasdair Gray's Institute, like the chip plant or call centre, was windowless. An epiphany in his novel comes when Lanark climbs up a hill, and sees himself and Scotland whole. In late-twentieth-century Scotland land had perhaps assumed mystic qualities previously attributable to God. Most secondary school children managed to read *Sunset Song*, and if raised at a party conference, 'the land issue' guaranteed applause. To two-thirds of Scots, this meant changing either its ownership or its owners' use of it. In 1975 the veteran socialist and land reformer John McEwen found that 1,400 families owned 60 per cent of Scotland. The pattern stayed, but the Lloyd's insurance underwriting crash in the mid-1980s accelerated the buying and selling of huge tracts; the 41,000 acres of Glenavon went to a Malaysian, the 48,000 acres of Corrour to a Swedish packaging heiress. In 1986 the Scottish Crofters' Union was formed to publicize the issue. The founder was Dr James Hunter – historians had their practical uses. By 1993 the land issue was becoming critical. An American millionaire bought Mar Lodge on Deeside for a new wife, who promptly left him. After much agitation, its 77,500 acres went to the National Trust. Assynt went to its crofters. Eigg, sold by a rally driver to an eccentric German artist, also ended in the public domain, and Knoydart, passed from one City shark to another, looked likely to do so.

The newspapers watched each deal like hawks, but the money would not have bought a middling centre-forward, and the number of people involved was small – there were perhaps 14,000 mainly part-time crofters. Yet this sort of life, combined with horticulture, tourism, the caring services and crafts, seemed to have more flexibility and job-creating potential than much inward investment and, indeed, than the traditional larger-scale tenant farm. In the lowland counties mechanization had reduced the agricultural labour force to under 10 per cent. In the 1980s Borders Region had Scotland's largest proportion of *manufacturing* workers, at 37 per cent, but by the mid-1990s a combination of changes to the Common Agricultural Policy, which provided a third of the sector's income, the beef crisis and the high pound was crushing the family farms. A hill farm income of £11,000 attracted few sons. Conditions were little better in fishing, where Scots accounted for 73 per cent of a dwindling British catch. This meant that sea-fishing income was on the same level – around £350 million – as the fish farming that had grown up since 1970, and just as precarious. The latter was threatened by cheap imports and infectious disease. The former suffered, almost uniquely, from a drug problem produced by affluence. In 1999 not Easterhouse but Fraserburgh had Scotland's highest percentage of heroin addicts.

The countryside was the base of high-value-added manufacturing – £2.4 billions' worth of whisky from 110 distilleries in 1994, tweed and knitwear, cheese and preserves. If a native Scottish capitalism could thrive – and Baxter's of Fochabers showed that it could – then here would be the place to start. But traditional quality products could be affected by bureaucratic interference and the fashionable preferences of a small, well-off market. Strathclyde Region made a determined effort to kill off the promising farm cheese industry; though this hygiene obsession overlooked the Wishaw butcher who spread e-coli poisoning. Tweed might be 'in' one year, and 'out' the next, and celebrating Scots would have to drink an awful lot to compensate the distilleries for the loss of duty-free sales from 1 July 1999.

Scottish GNP may have been level with the UK in 1997, but wages were 5 per cent below the national average. This might be thought to have helped small companies, but it did not. New company formations were 30 per cent below UK level and in depression declined faster. Politicians said the Scots were unenterprising (their own business connections, never robust, had all but vanished by 1997). The Scots market was smaller and poorer, the state sector larger, and takeovers meant that London headquarters attracted ancillary enterprises. Certainly, when questioned in the British Social Attitudes survey, Scots put job security as their highest priority, at 71 per cent, followed by the interest of the job. Younger workers were more flexible — twice as many expected to change jobs soon, 16 per cent against 8 per cent — but they wanted more money more quickly, and were critical of big business, though union membership was not seen as a remedy.

Yet who should appear as the friend of the unions at the STUC's annual conference in 1998 but Brian Souter of the Stagecoach transport conglomerate? Directing one of that group of Scottish companies capitalized at over a billion pounds and dominated by financial services, transport, and power, Souter and his sister Anne Gloag made their pile by swallowing the tiddlers released by the sell-off of the National Bus Group in 1986 and its Scottish counterpart in 1990. John Major's inept privatization of the railways handed them South West Trains in 1992, and later on two rolling stock leasing companies. The Royal Bank did very well out of this, too, and one lucky former British Rail manager, Sandy Anderson, turned a £100,000 investment into a £36 million windfall. By 1998 Stagecoach effectively controlled the west coast main line, bailing out the beleaguered Richard Branson. Souter (a timely supporter of devolution, on good terms with the SNP leadership) certainly snatched Scottish advantage out of what looked like a suicide attempt by the British state. Did Stagecoach also represent the phenomenon of the regional corporation, seen in some post-industrial areas of North America, where externally earned profits were balanced by local paternalism and public subsidy? Or would it, further along the line, succumb to an offer it could not refuse?

Trying to safeguard competition, the Conservatives franchised Scotrail to the National Express Group shortly before the election of 1997, with an annual subsidy of £280 million; it also kept going the sleeper services to the south, while the American-owned English, Welsh and Scottish Railway restored freight services over many lines that had lost them. As usage rose by 10 to 15 per cent a year, there was even the prospect of trains returning to St Andrews and Galashiels, but there were also doubts about too great a variety of technologies and the political power exerted by the new transport barons. The Labour government and the new parliament made coordination a priority, but in 1999 baffled foreigners were still being asked for 'exact fares, please' on Edinburgh routes and Stagecoach's buses still left Leuchars Station for St Andrews five minutes before the Scotrail train got in.

By 1998 Souter had also taken over Prestwick Airport, once the great hope of Scottish transport and by the mid-1990s a huge white elephant, when Glasgow airport was allowed to take on long-distance flights. Freight transport by air admittedly rose, but British Aerospace closed down its aircraft factory in 1997 and then shifted pilot training to Spain. The approach of autonomy raised nagging transport issues. Should Scotland have had three medium-sized airports, when a large-scale hub, handling long-distance flights, was not just a possibility but a necessity where logistics were organized supranationally? Should it not have retained an Atlantic seaport? The freight conference system, a transport untouched by market competition, meant that it was as economic to send goods from Liverpool or Southampton as from the Clyde ports, despite the hazards of an A74 slowly being brought up to motorway standard. The Clyde ports suffered while the east coast ports did better, with the privatized Forth Ports Authority moving strongly into English dock ownership. By way of a trophy, the old Clydebank-built royal yacht 'Britannia' was moored to Leith's new ocean terminal.

Scott of the Antarctic's 'Discovery' was a similar focus on the waterside of Dundee, and the town boasted, thanks to the National Lottery, Britain's most modern arts centre. Could a Dennis the Menace Experience be far behind? The Thomsons, Britain's second most reclusive press barons, were recognizing their and the city's prime piece of social capital. Anyone who was winning, travelled. Tourism in Scotland was at £2 billion annually, 10 per cent of the British total. Overseas visitors, mostly European, rose by two-thirds between 1988 and 1995. The weather was always against beach holidays, and global warming conspired against the attempt to develop winter sports. Traditional resorts like Arbroath, Rothesay and Ayr made little recovery, but museums and houses open to the public grew mightily, from 100 in the 1960s to over 500 in the 1990s. This lay behind ideas of culture-led development: the 'Scotland the Brand' formula of exploiting heritage, environment and cultural endowment corporately. Conferences and colloquia, expertly housed and serviced, would become a sort of timeshare approach to capturing industrial headquarters. In 1985 Glasgow at last realized Sir William Burrell's project for a great arts museum and, on the basis of this and four other world-class collections, the town remade itself as a City of Culture in 1988. Edinburgh fought back with the opening in Chambers Street of the National Museum of Scotland in the autumn of 1998. Enrico Miralles's bold design for parliament was yet to come. However, this servitor capitalism — so close to the peripatetic wealth and power of Gray's Institute — had risky economics. In 1995 Scottish Enterprise's flagship scheme, a private-enterprise hospital at Clydebank, collapsed. Only £40 million was recovered from an investment of £120 million. By 1998 Glasgow was miles more insecure; Edinburgh had yet to see its Conference Centre break even.

Privatization (despite the institution of Britain-wide structures of control) produced more than 'the politics of noisy inaction'; in certain key areas a Scots interest was skilfully advanced and defended. The loser was the 'British' dimension. Scotland was increasingly compared with Ireland, where GDP went from 56 per cent of the UK level in 1976 to equality by 1997, though because of foreign firms and low corporate taxation GNP was only 92 per cent of the UK average. This acted as an argument for Scottish nationalists, but there were differences. Ireland's industrialization, after the Whitaker report in 1957, coincided with a still dominant Catholic church, and the result was a birth rate which stayed high until the 1980s. Educational adaptation, however, turned this into a well-trained labour force, and 'picked winners' in software and pharmaceuticals. The *dirigiste* role of the state was proportionate to the authority it enjoyed as a full member of the European Union. In 1994–5, by being sharp in Brussels politics, Ireland got 11 billion ECUs (3,000 *per capita*) out of the structural funds (three times more than the Greeks, who were theoretically better entitled), while Scotland got 2.4 billion (500 *per capita*). In the competitive business of financial services, Dublin was already overtaking Glasgow.

Politics: Thatcherism Rebuffed?

In retrospect the political drive towards statehood seemed to dominate the years 1979–2000. This was not how matters seemed at the time. Until 1987 the national issue lay fallow, mentioned little by the parties formally pledged to home rule, the Liberals and Labour, and marked by a fall in support for the SNP from 18 per cent in 1979 to 11 per cent in 1983, rising only to 14 per cent in 1987. Arguably, what marked Scottish politics under the first half of Mrs Thatcher's rule was that they represented a collectivist Britishness that was otherwise in abeyance: the 'soft leftist' Labour leadership – in retrospect incredible – of Michael Foot.

In the UK, the polls of the 1980s were characterized by Conservative persistence around the 42 per cent level, while Labour was lucky if it made it out of the lower thirties. In Scotland the relationship was reversed. Only in 1983 did Labour fall to 35 per cent (when the Liberal Democrats had a brief and unsustainable revival to 25 per cent) while by 1997 it was back to 46 per cent. The Tory vote slumped almost relentlessly, from 30 per cent in 1979 to 24 per cent in 1987 and 17.5 per cent in 1997. Worse still was the deployment against them of tactical voting; if much of their command of Scots rural constituencies from the 1930s to the 1960s came from a divided opposition, they suffered from the reverse in the 1980s. Their 22 seats in 1979 had fallen to 10 in 1987, and vanished altogether in 1997. The Liberal Democrats, paradoxically, benefited from the first-past-the-post system they were supposed to hate. Their 13 per cent of the vote gave them 10 seats in 1997, up from 3 in 1979; the SNP suffered from it. An 18 per cent share in 1979 gave them only 2 seats; 22 per cent in 1997 only 6. By now Scots politics was definitely a four-party race.

The nation-state paradigm still survived in Norway's social-democratic use of North Sea oil, affecting the doctrines of home rulers and Labour's 'alternative economic strategy'. There was strong local support for such publications as *Manifesto* (1981) – in the preparation of which Jimmy Reid and Robin Cook were involved – and *Scotland: the Real Divide*, edited by Robin Cook and Gordon Brown (1982). Yet, despite the secession of only two MPs to the Social Democrats and no great enthusiasm for the Falklands War in 1982, it was in Scotland that 'Bennism' failed. The disciplining by Malcolm Rifkind of 'radical' local authorities ended any parallels with Ken Livingstone (Scots, but agnostic about it) and his mobilization of the Greater London Council as a resistance movement. In 1983 the new Labour leader Neil Kinnock moved against the hard left by attacking Militant Tendency, its most sectarian and thus least defensible salient. In Scotland, left-wing socialism had already shot its bolt.

Advances on several fronts – council house sales, parental choice, securing Ravenscraig and the Royal Bank – characterized a confident Conservatism run by George Younger, who played the 'soft cop' to Rifkind's 'hard cop'. To his leader, on the other hand, he was a marked man: 'for all his decisiveness and common sense . . . very much part of the paternalist school of Scottish Tory politicians'. Mrs Thatcher was routinely compared with Edward I, and did her country even less service in Scotland. Her traits were far from alien in a country more bourgeois, nationalistic and ideological than England; Neil Kinnock was no more popular. Yet hers was not simply a presentational failure. A politics which was closer to French Gaullism than to a free enterprise crusade unravelled in Scotland because the alliance of forces she depended on was not there.

Thatcher was misunderstood, not least by herself. In fact she was most of the time orthodox and cautious, dependent for advice on Willie Whitelaw, a paternalist Scottish Tory of the old school. She opposed selling council houses and privatizing the Hydro Board. She held on to Benn's BNOC until 1984. Her one 'radical' trait was her monetarism, and that was dropped in 1981 after its appalling consequences had become patent. The Scottish element of these dogged her, and a marginal decline in the 1983 election (1.6 per cent of the vote and one seat) contrasted with her triumph in the south. Two things then converted, in her eyes, the economic upswing into a Scottish problem. The takeover binge of 1984–6, and the oil price decline after 1986. She realized the alienating effect of the takeovers for her 'people's capitalism'; her reaction to the Guinness affair was as venomous as that of any Scot. In addition she could see that in harder times Scottish issues could again take on their own dynamic. She could build on the relative success of one Scots-based privatization, council house sales (Younger's policy, not hers), but her assault, wrapped up in a half-comprehended economic classicism and an increasingly unbalanced judgement (not least about her subordinates) proved disastrous. The poll tax was an incalculable blunder, unpopular and unworkable. It was not her policy, but went from the Adam Smith Institute's Douglas Mason to Kenneth Baker and from him to Younger. What she did was to make it British.

This process was watched, lizard-eyed, by Scotland's real rulers: no longer west coast industrialists and Edinburgh bankers, but the civil servants ensconced in Edinburgh's various administrative slabs, commanding an army of some 10,000 which did not notably diminish during the 1980s and 1990s. Their commitment to devolution in abeyance, they watched as Younger excised the other threat of the 1970s: decentralization to the regions. At the same time they shielded themselves from the winds of market capitalism sweeping Whitehall. They failed to gain control of privatized utilities, but picked up on environmental and training powers. There were fewer players in their ring: a declining number of trade-unionists, less than 100,000 political party members

(40,000 elderly Tories, 25,000 Labour, perhaps 12,000 Nationalists and 4,000 Liberals). They could afford to wait.

The years 1986–90 were Thatcher's 'rough wooing' of Scotland, born not out of Longshanks determination, but ignorance amounting to frivolity. They ended in catastrophe. Much of the blame must rest with Younger's successor, Malcolm Rifkind: intelligent, principled and fatally insensitive. The *Herald* nailed a speech of his in 1988: 'No one was enthused, no one was dismayed. He is deliberately distancing himself from the mainstream of Scottish life. He listens only to his friends, and they are few.' Rifkind gave Scottish policy a new ideological edge – justifying huge cuts in regional aid and electricity privatization as well as the poll tax – only to run into the disaster of the 1987 election, when tactical voters converted the Tories' 4.4 per cent loss of votes into a 50 per cent loss of seats. There then followed Thatcher's own assault: in 1988 the Sermon on the Mount, which annoyed the kirk and accelerated the Constitutional Convention movement; in 1990 the attack on Rifkind and appointment of Michael Forsyth as chairman of the Scottish Conservatives. This signalled the implosion of the party – in a way anticipating the British events of 1997–8 – and dramatized her failings: notably the lack of a strategic sense in selecting opponents. Between 1986 and 1990 Thatcher took on all comers, and they beat her senseless.

What followed was more conciliatory, but by 1990 the nationalist genie was out of the lamp. If the Tory triumph in the 1987 election had surfed on the Lawson boom, what would happen after the looming slump? Thatcher was right to express an element of urgency, but Scotland was not 'marginal' territory which had to be won. It was marginal in the sense of Alfred Marshall's economic theory: where the demand for a commodity ran out. Thatcherism was cultural as well as economic, framed by image creation and the affluent opportunism of the south-east (though English voters were not, when polled, much keener about most of its details than the Scots). Yet conditions for it were weak in Scotland in 1988. It was the wrong time, and the wrong place, and events were happening elsewhere, not unconnected with Thatcher (though less due to her than she imagined) which led her to take her eye off the game.

Society: Unsettled Scotland

The end of Communism in Eastern Europe focused attention on liberal notions of civil society, and on the legacy of the Scots Enlightenment. Ernest Gellner, once of Edinburgh University and director of George Soros's Central European University in Prague, stressed it as the antithesis of Communist *dirigisme*. Tom Nairn, who was in Prague for a time, was less sure: the Scots' stress on intermediate bodies, the traditional 'estates' of land, church, law, education and local politics, made for something more coercive. Instability in these in the 1960s and 1970s had aided the rise of nationalism; was it not being reawakened by the disruptive effect of the 'universal pander' of the market?

Distinctiveness started in the home and it is possible to make a shot at explaining it by analysing household expenditure. Although the population fell slightly, from 5.18 million in 1981 to 5.13 in 1997, the number of household dwellings increased by 27 per cent, from 1.96 million in 1979 to 2.7 million by 1995, with more second homes and an increase in single-adult households thanks to more divorces and to children moving away from home earlier. Expenditure had changed dramatically in twenty years. Though 1997 GDP *per capita* was level with the rest of the UK, family income, at £287 a week, was about 3 per cent below, which suggested fairly extensive variations across households. The old 'essentials' – food, rent, clothing – were falling as a proportion of the family budget at the same rate as the UK average, from about 60 to 50 per cent. What, then, was new? Motoring took 14.6 per cent, more than the UK's 13.3 per cent, though fares for public transport at 2.4 per cent were the same: the Scots had fewer cars, but spent more on them. They spent about the same on leisure and household items and services, respectively 15.5 per cent and 13.6 per cent.

The devil lay in the details of the old staples. The Scots spent 50 per cent less on lamb than the English and a quarter more on beef, a quarter less on vegetables, a fifth less on beer, a quarter less on pets, a quarter more on newspapers. 'We drink 50 per cent more carbonated drinks than the national average,' said a market researcher, 'eat 48 per cent more chocolate biscuits, 60 per cent more canned soup and consume 33 per cent more alcohol and tobacco.' Pasta might be catching up on chips, 'Diet Irn Bru' might exist, but they did little to help Scottish health. Professor Philip James of the Rowett Institute, Aberdeen, commissioned to examine Scottish diet in 1992, was appalled at what he found: Britain's lowest levels for greens, roughage and breast feeding, coupled with levels of obesity, heart disease and alcoholism which were fighting it out with some east European states for the prize of least healthy nation. The badly-off were most at risk, but even the middle classes still had 'a poor medical history'. In general the problem stemmed from historic shifts in Scottish agriculture from arable to pastoral: fewer oats, more beef, milk and fat. Cows were a problem, long before they went mad.

The fulcrum statistic was the 14 per cent increase in expenditure on housing. This went to the private sector, and the sell-off of council housing meant that a revolution was carried through, with owner-occupiers rising from under a third to nearly two-thirds, and renting from councils declining commensurately. Ownership was popular, though it did not help the Tories one whit. However, if the 426,000 houses that changed hands are seen as an economic factor, this meant that (assuming an average price of £35,000) something like £14 billion had been injected into finance in the form of mortgages and linked insurance schemes. This was not replicated in England, where council houses were fewer. As much as the oil business, it may help to explain the health of the Scottish financial sector.

These averages concealed dramatic and widening social divisions. In the 1980s the great American economist (Canadian-Scots in origin), J. K. Galbraith, wrote of how a 'culture of contentment' differed from traditional 'Fordism' (the mass production of goods for those working in welfare-capitalist societies). The well-doing no longer had to be a majority, just articulate and coordinated enough to manipulate the political process. In Europe this would be constrained by the formal barriers erected by social democracy or social 'marketism'; not so in Thatcher's Britain. The Scots believed they still had a community ethic, but the 'mutual' network – trade unions, churches, youth bodies – was in decline. This made it difficult to map social pathology, and a sociology, much of which had cashed in on market research, did not help.

The wealth was largely in London. According to the *Sunday Times* computations of the super rich, over 50 per cent lived there and only 6 per cent in Scotland. Souter and Gloag topped the Scots list, with half a billion each. They had bought Ochtertyre from the Murrays and Beaufort from the Frasers. In John Buchan's *Huntingtower*, the huge empty Dalquharter House served as a *memento mori* of the upper classes' pre-1914 prosperity, and between then and 1980 some Dalquharters survived by housing the 'excluded', or becoming hotels or schools; others were unroofed or demolished. However, the desires of more modest 'settled' and 'settlers' meant a boom in their reconstruction as flats, enhanced after 1981 by timeshare schemes. These were Galbraith's winners: the Scottish Council Foundation's 'settled Scotland': a group with sufficient power and leisure to access the financial services industry on advantageous terms. A teacher who had bought his house for £3,000 in the 1960s and could sell it in 1990 for £130,000 might be more of a winner than someone starting in financial services at twice a teacher's salary who had to buy it. Teachers, or others of a relatively privileged, non-employed class, the retired or early-retired, as David McCrone and his colleagues found, tended to dominate 'winners' organizations' like the National Trust for Scotland.

The same would not go for a younger colleague, who might be on a short contract rather than enjoying tenure, but still had to fork out for pricey housing. Increasing insecurity – privatization, automation, rationalizing and downsizing – meant that the settled were being sustained by the increased labour of the insecure, or by establishing free markets within the caring services which disadvantaged their employees. Political activism was one response to this; the two-income family was another, more frequent one.

The third category were the real victims. Between 1979 and 1993 families on or below half the national average income rose from 9 per cent to 24 per cent. Lacking property and suffering from a dwindling social security system, they were trapped by a vicious circle of unemployment *and* overwork, ill-health, relationship breakdown and addiction. Age mattered, and aided the settled. In 1995 the social security income of a single parent caring for a ten-year-old daughter in Edinburgh was £125.10; of a 71-year-old partly disabled Glasgow pensioner, £181. An inquiry reported in the autumn of 1998 that the suicide level in Scotland among adult males was 25 per cent higher than the English level. This reflected a situation where, in Glasgow, 60 per cent of council tenants were on income support, and where the damage inflicted by drugs, petty crime and pervasive ill-health were cumulatively that much greater. People did not have to be poor to have troubles. The rise in expenditure on the car, on television and videos meant a growth in family expenditure. At the same time the family as an institution declined. A third of marriages ended in divorce, and these only fell in the mid-1990s (from 12,500 in 1992 to 12,000 in 1995) because more couples cohabited without getting married; the number of single-parent households rose tenfold. This may have meant that people were living less emotionally painful lives, but among the poor it compounded social problems.

Lawyers were kept busy with matters other than divorce. Excluded Scotland was not alone in its vulnerability to the disturbed, as investigation of the world of Thomas Hamilton disclosed in the aftermath of the Dunblane horror of March 1996. The gloss of the big cities had a seamy rest-and-recreation subculture of prostitution, gambling and drugs. Multinational corporations frequently behaved badly. Exploring this labyrinthine ensemble produced some remarkable crime fiction, accurately described by Ian Rankin, who wrote much of it, as 'post-imperial'. Following the retreat of the British state from interventionism, law rather than policy became instrumental – 'If you can't beat them, sue them'; so real judges as well as fictional detectives gained new importance. Lord Cullen tackled Piper Alpha and Dunblane. Two working-class Highlanders went to the Woolsack, though Lord MacKay of Clashfern, Calvinist and Unionist, represented the Scottish juridical-philosophical tradition better than Lord Irvine of Lairg. The Lockerbie suspects were tried in a Dutch air force base under Scots law, and when European jurisprudence sought conventions to govern a diffused sovereignty, it found them in the work of Lord Rodger and Judge David Edward in Luxembourg.

Law was, in any case, big business: solicitors as house and insurance agents were a major part of the financial services constellation. If Silicon Glen broke through to high-value systems chips it would be because Scots intellectual property law was cheaper than that of the United States. Scots communities could excel and embarrass in legal issues, though women, now on the bench for the first time, managed a tough fight with credit. The people of Dunblane, led by local housewives, mounted a passionate amateur assault on the influential handgun lobby, and shattered it. The Teries of Hawick tried to ban women from the Common Riding and made asses of themselves. 'Why is there no Nativity Play in Hawick? Cos they wouldnae let Mary ride on a donkey, an' they couldnae find three wise men in the place.'

Religion was a paradox: shrinking churches were politically influential as never before. There were still 700,000 in the kirk and a religious census in 1994 (the first since 1851) found 14 per cent of Scots adults in church. The spread of faith varied, from over eight members in ten present in Thurso, to only one in ten in Angus. The problem was that for every three members lost by death, only one was acceding to the roll. Some lively churches had gone charismatic, using the emotional 'Toronto blessing' of 1994. Otherwise a complex sacralization affected politics. Embarrassed at its inept contribution to the 1979 referendum, the kirk promoted an agreed constitutional settlement. Canon Kenyon Wright, an ecumenical Episcopalian, mediated in the Constitutional Convention, keeping its various participants on speaking terms. This development had links with Presbyterian traditions. Popular theology still flourished in figures like William Barclay in the 1970s. Would it go autistically evangelical, or be swallowed by politics? Without the application of figures like Maxwell Craig, Will Storrar and Wright the Convention movement might have slowed and stopped, but, as Storrar's own *Christian Vision* indicated, its theology remained inchoate. Worryingly for some, the Labour leadership in 1997 was largely Scots and overtly Christian, but not much affected by the fact. The global ethic of liberal-Catholic theologian Hans Küng still remained remote; indeed those seeking the globally diabolic – including Dennis Potter, last of the nonconformists – looked no further than the Born Again, Free Kirk, New Labour-supporting Rupert Murdoch.

Into this vacuum moved the Scottishness of a dynamic, though no longer cohesive, Catholic community. When Pope John Paul II – the first non-Italian pope since 1495, and no slouch at recognizing nationalism – visited Scotland in 1982, he kissed the soil of a separate country. It may have been because of the mixing of Irish and Italian leaven and experiences, and a leftish though theologically conservative hierarchy, that the community and austerity of an earlier Presbyterianism marked the best Catholic schools. A perceptive and increasingly ecumenical lay intelligentsia expressed itself in literature, music, history-writing, feminism and the media – with talents from William McIlvanney to Tom Devine, Kay Carmichael to James MacMillan. The SNP's Mr Scotland was Sean Connery, but even the SNP was surprised in September 1998 to find that Catholics, traditionally Labour, now backed independence by 58 per cent, against 51 per cent of Protestant voters. The downside was a dwindling vocation to the clergy, a trend already in place in the 1980s but further hit by the scandals of 1996 surrounding Bishop Wright of Argyll, and worsened by the ethical vacuity of his self-defence. Would home rule be Rome rule or – in a period when half of Catholic marriages were mixed – a retreat from a papal authoritarianism which had lasted too long?

One teacher sat in the Commons in 1910, 11 in 1979, 21 in 1997, a trajectory which matched the decline of MPs from a business background (25:10:5). The voice of the dominie was heard in the land, but was he or she being heard in the school? Secondary education involved 96 per cent of pupils going to state comprehensives, yet their pattern was altered and some idealism lapsed when in 1981 parents were given the right to send children to a school of choice instead of a neighbourhood one. By 1992 they accounted for 50 per cent of entries to good schools and a league table of results showed enormous divergences, from 62 per cent of pupils at Dunblane High getting three or more Highers to seventeen Strathclyde schools whose Highers were too few to register. From Braidfield

High School, built in Clydebank in 1972, an old girl recollected that in the late 1970s 'most of us went on to higher education', but by 1998, after two decades of steady economic decline in the town, only 14 per cent were taking this route – half the Scottish average. Yet when Michael Forsyth, as Under-Secretary in 1988, attempted to undermine local authority control with school boards, these met with little enthusiasm and only a handful of opt-outs were recorded. Attempts to create 'national' curricula stopped at the Tweed, but attempts to secure greater teaching of Scottish studies were also frustrated. One worry was that, given the aggressive competition of the media, lower levels of literacy would encroach; another that government aggression and parental choice were alienating the teachers. Following a bitter strike in 1986–7 many withdrew from unpaid work: loss of cooperation and cynicism were still evident a decade later.

In the 1980s and 1990s the number of students in higher education doubled, as did the number of universities. New foundations were adapted from higher education colleges or 'central institutions': Napier in Edinburgh, Glasgow Caledonian, Dundee's Abertay, Aberdeen's Robert Gordon and the University of Paisley. Forsyth used his secretaryship in 1995 to set in motion the long-considered project for a multi-campus, distance-learning University of the Highlands and Islands. Was all this, some academics argued, not a question of resources being spread very thin, with the traditional research–teaching relationship breaking down, and a major shift in the vocational subjects being taught (the 25 per cent who studied business administration, for example) that fulfilled few of the criteria of 'increasing human knowledge'? The writer George Rosie – whose forte ran from economics to drama – noticed among the youngsters a facility for fashion, pop, food, music, with no inclination towards hard social or science themes or, for that matter, towards accurate spelling and grammar.

The Slippery Slope?

The 1987 election was a blow the Tories could have parried by adroit use of the devolution issue. Sir Alec Douglas-Home had become surprisingly popular two decades earlier by backing a scheme which was in retrospect no more than a third-level chamber, a sort of beefed-up Scottish Grand Committee. Why was this not persisted with? There were plenty of *sotto voce* rumblings that it might reappear sometime, somewhere. These did not reach Thatcher. Instead the poll tax issue in November 1988 carried Jim Sillars into Govan, against a trade union dullard whom he briskly destroyed in a television debate. Asked what 'additionality' (the regional funds released by Brussels to match local initiatives) could do for his prospective constituents, the poor man had not a clue.

Sillars having turned SNP European policy round 180 degrees, Labour reinforced its lukewarm embrace of the Constitutional Convention, which the dogged Campaign for a Scottish Assembly demanded through a committee of leading figures in *A Claim of*

Right for Scotland (mid-1988). MPs 'might have to live a little dangerously', said Donald Dewar with all the menace of a dowager on her second sherry. The Nationalists had called for the Convention, but withdrew after its first session: dominated by existing MPs, it would not offer independence as a referendum option. The rank-and-file, and even some father figures like Dr Robert MacIntyre, had doubts; but constitutional bodies are not sexy, by-elections are. The SNP, unbound, still had this possibility to hand.

With the poll tax revolt (a rarity in a country which was historically so law-abiding – or just apathetic), the revived SNP, and Rifkind mud-wrestling with Forsyth and Thatcher, the Convention had a low profile: only 17 per cent of voters were aware of it. The Tories went centre stage as Forsyth's initiatives, jejune publicity campaigns and Reaganite policy advisers tore them apart. In summer 1990, Rifkind insisted that he should go. Reluctantly, Thatcher had to agree. Within two months her increasingly rigid opposition to Europe led to her own dismissal. A premier in command of a large Commons majority was removed, a first in British politics.

The new premier, John Major, was *tabula rasa*, but reassuring in a turbulent time. With Germany uniting, *perestroika* collapsing and Yugoslavia breaking up, his Foreign Secretary Douglas Hurd had more exciting things than Scotland to deal with. The Tory vote held up in two by-elections, and the Gulf War, in which Britain soon became involved, proved far more popular with the Scots (who had many workers in the region, as well as service personnel) than the Falklands crusade. As inept in Kincardineshire in their choice of candidates as Labour had been in Govan, the Tories lost a by-election in November 1991, but to the Liberal Democrats. On top of this came – inevitable, but sooner than expected – the final closure of Ravenscraig. The result was a moment of Tory hysteria in early 1992, as the prospect of annihilation loomed.

Murdoch ratted, pledging the *Sun* to the SNP on 23 January – in retrospect an adroit move aimed at countering tactical voting. The success of this tactic became clear on 9 April. The 1992 election saw a rise from 14 to 20 per cent for the SNP, but the loss of Govan. Labour and the Liberal Democrats lost two seats to the Conservatives, who managed to push their vote up a little. Ian McLean of Nuffield attributed this to the poll tax knocking 2 per cent of the electors off the register. So too did Lady Thatcher, congratulating herself. This gave the government a sense of security which turned out to be disastrously false. Again, some concession towards home rule might have been made to good effect, but Major remained rigid – in fact, he rarely thought about Scotland at all. Under his premiership, decentralization meant a little more authority to Scottish committees (schoolrooms of grievance on account of their press-ganged English-manufactured majorities) and the administrative devolution of the arts and higher education.

The initiative was back with Labour, under the well-regarded John Smith. Kinnock had only been tolerated, and handled the Scottish comrades crassly. Smith could practically do no wrong (although, given his shadow budget in 1992, Middle England would disagree) and headed a powerful and disproportionately Scottish team, including Robin Cook and Gordon Brown. 'John Major looks like a bank clerk,' the German *Die Zeit* commented, 'while John Smith looks like a bank director.'

The ball was again in Labour's court, although Labour's shadow Scottish Secretary, Tom Clarke, did not shine even against the indolence of Iain Lang. Then in April 1994 Smith suddenly died in London. The grief went to the point of irrationality. Political scientists have commented, specifically in connection with the death of Diana, Princess of Wales, on the emotionalizing of politics by those with a dwindling stake or hope in them. Almost instantly Labour's local command began to unravel. When Major, cornered by Eurosceptic Tories, counter-attacked in mid-1994, Michael Forsyth unexpectedly rode to his rescue. His reward was the Scottish Office, and he lost no time in launching a three-pronged attack on Labour: conciliating the unions and local government, backing a series of 'cultural nationalist' initiatives, the most intriguing of which was the return of the Stone of Scone after 700 years down south, and assaulting the increased 'tartan taxes' that would accompany devolution.

Scandals in the town councils within Smith's old constituency, Monklands, almost gave the SNP the seat and exposed the problem of the Scottish local authorities. Monklands was only the tip of an unlovely iceberg of nepotism, fiddled expenses, back-handers to get council tenders and tenancies, expensive foreign trips. The Tories made a lot of this, but only because they had not controlled much since 1980 and their own record had been none too savoury in places like Edinburgh. In fact the Wheatley two-tier experiment of 1974 had worked. The regions were not loved, but their administrations had a strong economic and European presence, and they were innovative in areas like transport planning and education. For them to be closed down in 1994–5 in favour of single-tier authorities which were smaller, less powerful, and above all unable to tap the resources in the suburbs that the regions (especially Strathclyde) had managed, was pure gerrymander, designed to keep Tory control of a few local authorities. The new councils failed even to do this, but their inadequacies were still making themselves patent in 1998.

Monklands was a foretaste of this theme. It also put the SNP back in contention. But by this time Labour had a new leadership, born in, but doubtfully of, Scotland. Gordon Brown had somehow (the details are still vague) been persuaded to give way to Tony Blair. How Blair remodelled the Labour Party remains unclear: beneath the formal business of ditching Clause IV and the hard-edged identification of 'swing' voters (those who could be won over rather than those who needed help) was an update of the secret MacDonald–Gladstone pact of 1903, settling with big private donors who had had enough of the Tories, and whose influence only became apparent *after* the election. The team which thrashed the battered and discredited Major Cabinet was impressive, but its grasp of Scots policy was uncertain. Blair's shadow Secretary, George Robertson, never a home rule enthusiast, coped incompetently with his boss's decision, in July 1996, to require a preliminary two-question referendum (on the parliament and on tax-varying powers) before the home rule bill was tabled. Blair had Middle England in mind and the deadly effect that Smith's planned tax rises had had in 1992. However, his finesse deserted him in the north – a line about the Scottish press corps being 'unreconstructed wankers' was repaid with interest. Had he realized that the two-question referendum both confirmed Scotland's separateness and demanded rapid legislation? Happily for him, his problems were obscured by Scottish Conservative scandals which voided themselves on an already harrowed Major.

The Tory defeat on 1 May 1997 was the greatest, in terms of seats lost, since 1832, although the subsequent paralysis of the party made it more like 1846, when it split over free trade and lost power for a generation. However, the Scottish result appeared more ambiguous. Tactical voting, which had slipped in 1992, came back, and although the Tory vote only fell by eight percentage points, the annihilation of MPs was total. The SNP slightly increased its vote, but took two new seats – Tayside North, and Dumfries and Galloway. The party now had two women MPs, Labour nine and the Liberal Democrats one.

The referendum came faster than anticipated. The sense was that the Scottish Labour vote was soft, something that subsequent poll statistics more than confirmed. This was coupled with impending problems in Paisley and Govan. Blair replaced Robertson by Donald Dewar: clever, likeable and flexible. Lacking MPs, the Conservatives could not answer him, and the 'Think Twice' group opposing devolution was worse than ineffectual. The Conservatives had at last started to co-opt the Catholic middle class, so the choice of Donald Finlay, QC, an unreconstructed 'bluenose' (Orange Protestant) to head their campaign was imbecilic. The swing to home rule was 43 per cent. This probably saved the companion Welsh assembly, which needed 30 per cent and only just got it, and eased further elements of regional devolution, Northern Ireland included.

The Scotland Act, passed by mid-1998, stipulated exclusions to the parliament's powers. All else was possible: economics, education, planning, crime, transport. The two big exceptions were media and social security; as time went on these seemed dubiously tenable. Yet few Labour MPs joined in the debates; fewer still seemed interested in going to Holyrood. Instead, with scandals in the western burghs, two suspended MPs, one suicide, and the failure of New Labour as a concept to take off in Scotland, troubles were coming in battalions.

A Country the Poets Have Imagined?

In the 1970s, commentators such as Neal Ascherson had regretted the low profile of culture, as distinct from politics. This was perhaps overdoing it. As we saw in the previous chapter, John McGrath's *The Cheviot, the Stag and the Black, Black Oil* (1973) was the most important political drama in Scotland since *The Three Estates*; Norman MacCaig, Edwin Morgan and George Mackay Brown were at their most creative. Hugh MacDiarmid died in 1978: he had said that he would have voted no to devolution, hoping for a bigger confrontation, but his volcanic poetic had burned itself out three decades earlier. What remained could have been, as in Ireland after the poet W. B. Yeats, a huge upas-tree effect. The German critic Ursula Kimpel claimed that MacDiarmid's ambition of 'seeing Scotland whole' isolated talents which drew their power from regional roots, and individual or philosophical concerns. Against this, the quality and skill of cross-cultural interpretation invoked by Edwin Morgan or Iain Crichton Smith, Robert Garioch or Kenneth White, suggested a latent power. The initiative of the early 1980s to establish a Scottish Poetry Library was as significant in its way as the founding of the Irish Literary Theatre in the 1900s. Its premises in Edinburgh's Royal Mile became a focal point for singers and scholars from Europe and beyond, and its work for poetry – perhaps, because of its 'guid gear in sma' buik', the most convenient of the disciplines – travelled far. It did not just gain friends; it helped propel the Scottish constitutional movement.

Poets look for metaphors to express social and behavioural realities as they impinge on the actions of 'ordinary' individuals, and they settled on that peculiar disruption – antisyzygy, MacDiarmid had termed it – of the Scottish intellect whereby concerns which had been common to the national debate for three centuries resumed in exotic and unpredictable environments. Not just Connery and Bill Forsyth, but also Alan Sharp and Allan Schiach ended up in Hollywood, that mart of the banal and the occasionally significant. In 1985 the Commonwealth Writers' Conference, eluding a Commonwealth Games annexed with characteristic brutality by Robert Maxwell, showed many delegates just how fissile Britain had become.

'The music of things happening' was Seamus Heaney's line, but Scotland's relation to music was odd. It seemed to qualify so easily as 'das Land ohne Musik' ('the land without music'), yet even in the apparently barren Victorian years it had produced Sir William MacEwen, Eugene D'Albert, and the soloists Frederic Lamond and Mary Garden, whose work was now being reassessed. It was something on which 50 per cent of the Arts Council budget was spent, for the benefit of 15 per cent of the public – perhaps an even smaller percentage, as music provision in schools deteriorated. What remained was curiously disarticulated: symphonic music and opera continued successful, with the Scottish Chamber Orchestra and Cantilena reaching rural areas, although in

1996 the country lost Sir Alexander Gibson, burnt out in the cause. Scottish Ballet was less successful and its future was clouded, but classical music won a new audience. The atonality of an earlier generation – Thea Musgrave and Iain Hamilton – was replaced by a new lyricism and links with folk music in the work of James MacMillan, which drew on his own radical Catholicism; radical Protestantism was no less present in Donny Munro and Runrig. Folk, country and western, and rock seemed on parallel, non-communicating courses. This was, tragicomically, brought out by John Byrne in 'Tutti Frutti' (1987) in which the Majestics, retarded rockers from the 1960s, roam a Scotland that had moved on a lot faster than their clapped-out minibus, settling on Methil in Fife to begin their comeback tour.

The visual arts were similarly eclectic; they remained representational but the subject-matter changed, in ways parallel to the novel. The painting of William Gillies or Anne Redpath had looked towards the France of Cézanne, Matisse and Bonnard: restrained, formal, almost unpeopled. In the 1970s and 1980s, with John Bellany, Alexander Moffat, Ken Currie and Peter Howson a tumult of urban figures – famous, notorious, imaginative, thuggish – poured in, as if from the Weimar days of Grosz, Dix and Beckmann, or the murals of Diego Rivera. Howson went to Bosnia as a war artist, an experience which, he said, nearly destroyed him. There was another flight out, into cool political indifference, in the enigmatic figures of Stephen Conroy; and an undoubted MBA in marketing for Jack Vettriano's high-testosterone kitsch.

Theatre was a contested space. The Festival had an uneasy relationship with the rest of Scotland, but its synergic Europeanism – like that of the unreconstructed Tom Nairn of 'The Three Dreams of Scottish Nationalism' – radiated out from Edinburgh's Traverse and Glasgow's Citizens theatres. The project for a National Theatre lured like a *fata Morgana*, and Ewan Hooper and Tom Fleming struggled between 1981 and 1987 to keep the Scottish Theatre Company going, with some fine productions. Under-funded and homeless, it went under. Others argued that a guerrilla theatre of smaller, community-based or travelling companies was a better bet. Both sides could have called on a wide range of dramatic talent – from John McGrath (now equally adept in film) to Iain Heggie, Liz Lochhead, John Byrne and Stephen MacDonald. However, there was no Scottish equivalent to Ireland's Field Day Company, which linked theatre, poetry, philosophy and intellectual history, and generated the talents of Brian Friel and Seamus Heaney.

Cinema was even more poignant: artistically acclaimed and financially disastrous. Its flops included John Byrne's 'Slab Boys' trilogy and Stephen MacDonald's 'Not about Heroes'. The renaissance of cinema-going did not seem to help at all. The new multiplexes outside towns vomited Hollywood, whose taste for the Scots film, prominent in the mid-1990s, from 'Shallow Grave' to 'Braveheart', was probably no more stable than London publishers' taste for the Scots novel. The attempt to film Jeff Torrington's crackling Gorbals novel *Swing, Hammer, Swing* with a script by Peter MacDougall never even got the chance to fail.

There was an economics of culture, and culture industries, demanding high returns. The Edinburgh Festival cost around £3 million in the early 1990s, but injected £60 million into the local economy. Yet most of the big profits went to London's network of agents and largely multinational publishers. Culture was pluralistic for the mature-to-elderly, and substantially Scottish; for youth it was subordinate to an unrelenting American pressure for conformity in food, clothes and entertainment, in which a Scottish dimension counted for nothing when compared with profit. The weird tartans of Bay City Rollers fans in the 1970s were touchingly hand-crafted by mothers. Their offspring in turn were cloned in Adidas gear and daft trainers churned out by third-world, near slave labour; cool to their peers, they damned themselves in the eyes of teachers and employers. On the other hand, youth was more likely to get back to some relationship with European culture via Scotland than anywhere else.

In this the press, rather than formal literature, remained influential and Scots. Though more English titles circulated, they now printed north of the border, with quite different content. In the 1970s Scotland had been dominated by the *Daily Record* and the *Sunday Post*. Now there was a partial shift away from tabloid banality, as proprietors found they could lose money by underestimating the intelligence of the public: some brows were so low they had given up reading altogether. The revived *Scottish Daily Mail* provoked the *Record* (circulation 760,000 in 1992) and its competitor the *Sun* to move up-market and the *Scotsman* (bought in 1996 for £90 million by the Barclay brothers) down-market. The *Herald* passed from Lonrho to the Scottish Media Group, where the former far-left Gus MacDonald, recruited by Sir William Brown in 1985, and managing director from 1990, carried through a drastic reconstruction and fired more than half the staff. As for the Howard Hugheses of Dundee, the Thomson family, they saw circulation of the *Weekly News* halve between 1985 and 1995, and even the *Sunday Post* fall by 400,000. But since they printed many of their rivals, and franchised the *Beano* and *Dandy* heroes enthusiastically, they did not have too much to worry about. Colour was commonplace, and (by 1997) internet editions. The progress of Scottish politics towards home rule could be observed on-line, from anywhere.

The span of fame shortened. In 1994 Scot FM, a talk-and-music radio station, was saved, rather as TV-AM had been by Roland Rat, by an actor posing as Scotty McClue, a loudmouthed Shock-Jock. After a few months, he vanished. The BBC turned Radio Scotland from a joke into something that could take on Radio Four. Radio Clyde cultivated a local, folksy idiom, and succeeded. Otherwise the accountants imposed their rigidities. If idealism made its peace with them, it could go far, though not necessarily in the direction of enlightenment. One runaway success was the National Lottery: Scots were the biggest gamblers in this updating of Adam Smith's 'tax on all the fools in creation', though rather less than their proportionate contribution came back to them.

The paradox was that this remarkably lively and critical public culture occurred in a physical environment which more and more aped the rest of the West. In *1982*

Janine and *Our Fathers*, Alasdair Gray and Andrew O'Hagan respectively had caught something of the utopianism of the 1960s; it was the likes of Jock McLeish who had raised the high-rise blocks which now loomed like grim ghosts over the central belt – akin to the satellite towns of Eastern Europe, but lacking their trams or supermarkets. In Motherwell or Dumbarton the new order – the culture of Barratt and Miller Homes, McDonalds and the shopping mall – might have been in Watford or Birmingham. The conservative English architectural critic Gavin Stamp rightly slammed the mediocrity of Scottish public architecture, and the destruction of some of the country's best modern work by Basil Spence and Jack Coia.

On his eightieth, Norman MacCaig lit up two fags: 'One for each lung!' He lasted another five years, movingly saying his farewells to Lochinver and his friends:

> He went through a company
> as himself. But now he's one
> of the multitudinous company of the dead,
> where are no individuals.
> The beneficent lights dim
> but don't vanish. The razory edges
> dull, but still cut. He's gone: but you can see
> his tracks still, in the snow of the world.

Many of his contemporaries soon followed him – George Mackay Brown, Sorley MacLean, Iain Crichton Smith. But in Scotland, themes from a younger world, ideals and decencies were still alive. Rumoured huge advances from some London publishers may mean another modish phase for the Scotch novel. Local literary workshops, writers in residence, oral historians and women's groups ensured that the novel and short story were troubled, because their authors were involved in, and reflected, a troubled world. The result was not catatonia: more a ransacking of memory, tradition and history – think of titles like O'Hagan's *The Missing*, Meg Henderson's *Finding Peggy*, A. L. Kennedy's *Looking for the Possible Dance*, not to speak of the literary detectives – and in the protean case of Alasdair Gray the construction and destruction of history after the 'conjectural history' of the Enlightenment. Perhaps the mark of nationalism on all this was that it could only be properly comprehended, and its writers ordered, from within. A figure like James Kelman, in London notorious only for his expletives, registered a grieving humanism close to that encountered in the German culture of Käthe Kollwitz, Frank Wedekind or Franz Kafka, a mixture of solidarity and desperate pessimism. Daily life – 'It will be horror' – was not a pose, as the working people of Holman's Easterhouse could confirm.

Culture had been radical. Now the great enemies dissolved. In 1994 the American missile subs left the Holy Loch, taking with them part of the scenario of what would happen if the Scots went anti-nuke while Britain did not. Adjusting to this was complex for those who had the compulsion or leisure to involve themselves: an ageing, articulate population. Small publishers – Canongate, Argyll, Richard Drew, B and W – brought Scottish writers like Willa Muir and Catherine Carswell, many of them out of print for decades, back into the canon; the Open University allowed many more mature folk to undertake serious academic work; the dialogue and density of literary effort increased. One minor issue caught the drifting apart of the cultures. In 1999 Blair did not appoint Carol Ann Duffy as Poet Laureate: a Glaswegian lesbian would not suit Middle England. His nominee, Andrew Motion, wanted the job, but held his silence during the 1 July occasion. He was wise to do so.

For youngsters, the English canon simply fell away. Their generation was insecure. Getting away – anywhere – mattered, and low salaries led to a culture of clubbing and recreational drugs, which gripped in 1988 and – unexpectedly – held on. This was articulated in the novels, plays and films of Irvine Welsh, whose impact paralleled *No Mean City* in the 1930s. Dance became rhythm and sound-mixing and drugs. Already in the 1970s, Scots rockers were earning more in a week than their engineer fathers made in a year. Twenty years on and the fathers' jobs would have vanished, while the rockers, headed by the grand old hooligan Rod Stewart, were box office on both sides of the Atlantic. Annie Lennox, Sheena Easton, Deacon Blue and Wet, Wet, Wet would be denounced by the purists. The Proclaimers and Hue and Cry had their parallels in the remarkable renaissance of rock groups in Wales – particularly Welsh-speaking Wales. On the other side they overlapped with folkies such as the Battlefield Band and the Tannahill Weavers, and individual performers like Brian McNeill, Bobby Campbell and Dick Gaughan, who were the heirs to Hamish Henderson's brew of history and radicalism.

By its fiftieth anniversary in 1997 the Edinburgh Festival had become the biggest arts bash in Europe, possibly in the world. The official festival had always been a rather exotic transplant; Edinburgh folk preferred the Tattoo on the Castle Esplanade. The Tattoo continued, but in the 1990s the Festival was swamped by the Fringe, with upwards of 700 shows, and TV-led marketing routines for recruiting new young comedians. Television came to dominate the Film Festival, and its MacTaggart Lecture, named after the country's best director of the 1970s, became a firing-off point for manifestos concerning the rapid technological development, and as rapid commercialization, of broadcasting.

Whatever solidarity Scotland displayed – and the high profile of arts-sensitive bodies like the STUC was undermined by a fast-falling membership – there was still a question mark over the future of a country whose élite had so often looked beyond its boundaries and, in the Blair government, continued to do so. Scotland came over as surreal. The superstructure seemed to have become the base. Most unskilled manual workers were women. A sum of £400 million per annum was invested in Scottish football – 40 per cent of the English level; yet almost two-thirds of attendances were at the grounds of the Old Firm: Celtic and Rangers. So far had both drifted from the old religious stand-off that their pool of players contained thirty foreigners. However, sport had become a subsection of media, no longer the great democratic game. With pay-as-you-view TV, the original supporters and participants, the folk on low incomes of the big cities, found themselves further excluded.

That hath such creatures in it

If people in 1997 worried about the Roslin Institute's Dolly, the cloned sheep, various past episodes gave them reason. The innocuous phrase 'mechanically recovered meat' actually meant mincing up dead animals to feed to live ones, a reprise of Alasdair Gray's horror in *Lanark*, with even nastier consequences, as infections entered the food chain, among them the lethal Creutzfeld-Jacob disease. In 1991 pressure groups around Agriculture and Fisheries, as with the Ministry of Agriculture in England, quashed an attempt to monitor disease-free cattle, although such a scheme was set up in Northern Ireland. Scottish herds were thus included in the EU's ban in 1996, still in place in 1998. In 1996, e-coli bacteria killed twelve elderly people in Wishaw after infection hit a local butcher's shop. There were rumours that BSE had spread to sheep, of lice and anaemia in farmed salmon, salmonella in chickens. Ravenscraig's empty site was not empty. It was filled with pollutants which would take years to clean up. Easy, compared with that other centre of glamorous 1960s technology, the experimental nuclear reactor at Dounreay, where nuclear waste dumped in a shaft was found to be dangerous, while more of the stuff was being shipped in from Eastern Europe, sometimes in passenger planes. Blair tried to retain the plant, then suddenly pulled the plug on it. It came out that the cost of securing the waste could run to £10 billion (or two-thirds of the Scottish government's annual grant).

Semi-independence hove in view to a creaky chorus of chickens coming home to roost. In 1998 Far Eastern depression and relative calm in the Middle East meant that oil prices fell to $10 a barrel, the point where North Sea production became financially questionable. Despite the tight budgeting of the oil companies in their 'Cost Reduction in the New Era' programme (CRINE), redundancies were unavoidable. The yen for malt whisky and woollens in Japan shrivelled, with ominous consequences for the Highlands and the Borders. Mass-produced microchips tumbled further into the cellar, falling from $45 to under $2 a unit. In financial services, the City began to grasp at the Edinburgh Life offices. The massive Hyundai plant at Dunfermline was mothballed before being completed, and the closure of Via Systems' Selkirk factories brought further misery to a region already hit by the high pound.

Despite Charlotte Square's forebodings about home rule, none of the above could be attributed to it. Labour believed that devolution would 'kill the SNP stone dead'. This was contradicted by opinion polls and local by-elections, which showed a tendency to vote Labour in UK elections and for the SNP in Scotland. Alex Salmond, the SNP's able and canny leader, positioned himself to the left of Labour (not difficult) and was assisted by four factors: sleaze in Labour's one-party states in west-central Scotland; the limited powers of the Edinburgh parliament; tension over the level of its block grant, the level of which attracted hostility in the English regions; and a fundamental disjunction between New Labour's marketism and the more redistributive Scots left.

Yet a positive sense of being British was poorly developed, and the Tory party was a squalling bunch of sectaries. In his capture of the centre Blair had been too successful; his constitutional project had taken on a life of its own, just as the pillar of the unwritten constitution, the opposition as alternative government, had crumbled. Defeated in most Scottish council by-elections, and with two uncomfortable cases (Tommy Graham and Mohammed Sarwar) on hand, Labour worried about a mid-term reaction coinciding with the Scottish parliament election in May 1999: with the Conservatives out of the running, the SNP looked truly menacing. The election for Holyrood (which replaced Royal High as the favoured site, with a radical design by the Catalan Enrico Miralles) would be by proportional representation. There were seventy-three constituency MSPs, plus fifty-six from lists based on the old European constituencies. The selection procedures did not inspire confidence, with awkward figures being sidelined and a suspicion that the drive towards women's equality by twinning seats in fact meant a new sort of cronyism.

Yet the SNP lost support after mid-1998 – down from about 40 per cent to around 26 per cent in the polls. Labour in early April was being put as high as 48 per cent, within striking distance of an absolute majority. In the Holyrood contest, Gordon Brown's role was more crucial than that of Dewar, and depended greatly on his personal popularity, and also on the links he shared with the lost leader, John Smith. The general situation made the economics of independence unfavourable – even the SNP had to admit that – and Salmond's critique of the intervention in Yugoslavia, though well-grounded, clashed with enthusiasm for a 'righteous war'.

A week before the poll the SNP vote began to recover and the Labour vote to fall, something perhaps influenced by events in Bremen on 28 April. Anticipating yet another Scottish defeat – they had not won against Germany since 1959 – Blair's sports minister suggested that a Great Britain team should replace the separate nations in international competitions. This heresy was broken when a (totally unexpected) Scots victory was announced.

In fact the polls were less accurate than usual. On 7 May, the SNP saw its first vote increase from 24 per cent to 29 per cent, but its attempts to carry target seats failed in every case but one. Compared with 1997, Labour's first vote fell by 7 per cent and its second vote by 13 per cent, but the modified D'Hondt system used in Scotland favoured the constituency seats by about 3 to 4 per cent over the list; this denied the SNP the forty seats it had hoped for. Nevertheless the Nationalists got thirty-five MSPs and made substantial percentage gains in the Labour fortresses of west-central Scotland, evidence of a longer-term trend which was worrying for Labour. Labour, at fifty-six seats, was well short of the sixty-five it needed for an absolute majority, and had to go into coalition with the Liberal Democrats. The one Liberal Democrat sticking-point, opposition to university tuition fees, was fudged by being referred to a Committee of Enquiry.

Female representation went up from under 10 per cent of Westminster MPs to over 37 per cent of MSPs. Both Labour and the SNP were assiduous in promoting something close to parity, but the Conservative (3:18) and particularly the Liberal Democrat (2:15) outcomes were disappointing. There were three women in a Cabinet of ten, and a high proportion of dual MP/MSPs, though not much evidence of New Labour. Confidence in that was not altogether helped by Tony Blair's post-election reshuffle; he moved the high-profile Dr John Reid to the post of Secretary of State, thought by many to be up for abolition – highlighting future Anglo-Scottish relations, which had featured not at all in the contest. Would this calm last? Gordon Brown's Unionism could not guarantee Scots public finances against English MPs demanding cuts in 'subsidy' to Scotland, coupled with restrictions on what Scots MPs at Westminster could vote on. Oil staged a price revival, by up to 70 per cent over two months, as OPEC restrictions on output were made to stick: evidence of just how fast the global economic climate could change.

Parliament convened in the kirk's Assembly Hall in May, and powers were formally handed over on 1 July. Originally it was to have been January 2000 but Dewar, fearful of too much hype riding on the millennium, chose the earlier date. Observing the first sessions, journalists were merciless to many new MSPs, but Holyrood's Demosthenes would take time to learn, and orators like Dewar and Salmond needed some recuperation. More ominous were the European elections on 10 June; a Strasbourg parliament which had actually made things very rough for European bureaucracy received only the insult of a 25 per cent poll (returning three Labour MEPs, two SNP, two Tory and one Liberal Democrat). Professor Neil MacCormick would go to Brussels as an SNP representative, to sit in a parliament first proposed by his predecessor in his Edinburgh chair, James Lorimer, in 1885. Could his father, founding the National Party seventy-one years before, ever have imagined this?

Was Scotland 'a dark land', in the words of the Reverend Pat Robertson, appalled at its toleration of homosexuals? Or was it a welcome flame on the otherwise darkling plain of war, pollution and chaotic capitalism? The Bank of Scotland repeatedly worried about the effect of home rule on business and the Union. Would they hold out until 2007? Yet it was prepared to commit millions to the Reverend Robertson, who believed the world would end in that year. In the first months of the new millennium, Scotland's richest man, Brian Souter, resumed the Robertsonian vein, attacking the Dewar ministry's opposition to the anti-gay Clause 28 and — purely coincidentally, as speculators' cash was flooding into internet stocks — his Stagecoach concern lost half its share value. Amid all of this, the Royal Bank swallowed the National Westminster, and the Norwich Union and Commercial and General insurance companies merged, with thousands of redundancies forecast.

On 8 June 2001, Tony Blair became the first Labour leader to be assured of a second term, though on a pitifully low poll of 58 per cent. The Scottish results showed little change from 1997: the SNP lost Galloway to the Conservatives. But the political leadership was very different. Alex Salmond left Holyrood for Westminster, and in October 2000 Donald Dewar died. The piety of the tabloids was stomach-turning, but the man — eccentric, witty, erudite — was missed. Only days after the election, death claimed his sometime ally, sometime opponent, Cardinal Thomas Winning. In an early summer when the pyres of burning cows and sheep, victims of foot and mouth disease, marked the southern counties, and folk fretted about global warming, the gloom of William Dunbar seemed apposite:

> On to the ded gois all Estaitis,
> Princes, Prelotis and Potestatis,
> Baith riche and pur of al degre;
> *Timor mortis conturbat me.*

The architect of the parliament, Enrico Miralles, was already dead at 45. His project absorbed cash like quicksand. Yet for 57 per cent of the electors, Holyrood *was* politics; Westminster got the trust of only 31 per cent (an ominous inversion of the pattern of loyalty in federal Germany). Labour was ahead, so far, but when Scotland voted again, in May 2003, would it return the SNP as the main party, in time to imperil the tercentenary of the Union in 2007?

Bibliographical Essay

Anyone writing on contemporary Scotland is going to find it hard to deal with his or her sources as political revolution and communications revolution coincide. The rubric 'further reading' raises unprecedented problems, made mountainous as the computer shrinks to a tiny laptop. It is certainly convenient having parliament, Scottish Office and MSPs on-line, and reading the the *Scotsman* or the *Glasgow Herald* without getting your fingers dirty — but where are the press cuttings that have formed much of the feedstock of this chapter? Not there: newspaper on-line archives, where they exist, are generally unreliable because they are incomplete. More, so much of the 'stored' evidence is now in obsolete programmes, or found on discs readable only on old machines, that a cyber-cerebral haemorrhage is all too possible. The *Abstract of Scottish Statistics*, one of my basic sources, simply did not appear in 1999.

When we look at the sources available, it is clear that this has been a politically framed period whose shape can be gauged, reliably enough, through the last part of many a recent book whose 'brief bibliography' can run to forty titles, mostly recent and published in Scotland. The 'General Histories' section of the bibliographical essay for the previous chapter is an essential starting-point. Between the prematurely elegiac William L. Miller, *The End of British Politics: Scots and English Political Behaviour in the Seventies* (Oxford, 1981) and Tom Nairn's *After Britain* (London, 2000), is Lindsay Paterson, *The Autonomy of Modern Scotland* (Edinburgh, 1994), to be read with Tom Gallagher's *Nationalism in the Nineties* (Edinburgh, 1991) and James Mitchell's *Strategies for Self-Government* (Edinburgh, 1996). An insider's view of the Convention is Kenyon Wright's *The People Say Yes!* (Colintraive, Argyll, 1998), and a near insider's view of parliament came from Brian Taylor, *The Scottish Parliament* (Edinburgh, 1999). There are essays on politics in Christopher Harvie, *Travelling Scot* (Colintraive, Argyll, 1999). For a guide to the New Labour response, Paul Anderson and Nyta Mann, *Safety First: The Making of New Labour* (London, 1997) is surprisingly non-London centred. The same cannot be said for Philip Gould's *Unfinished Revolution: How the Modernisers Saved the Labour Party* (London, 1998), in which Scottish affairs are mentioned once. Gould also goes for a plethora of *ad hominem* biographies of Blair, Brown, Cook and others: an approach which passes these days for political history. Peter Lynch's *Minority Nationalism and European Integration* (Cardiff, 1996) is valuable in surveying an evolving overseas presence.

For a more panoramic view of the estate, Ken Cargill (ed.), *Scotland 2000: Eight Views on the State of the Nation* (Glasgow, 1987) disastrously failed to coincide with the BBC series, but is still useful; as is Magnus Linklater and Robin Denniston (eds.), *Anatomy of Scotland Today* (Edinburgh, 1992). Tom Devine and Richard Finlay (eds.), *Scotland in the Twentieth Century* (Edinburgh, 1996) is uneven for this period; Peter Payne would probably want to forget an essay prophesying the clearing of much of Silicon Glen by 1997. Otherwise, for the economy, besides the *Herald*, *Scotsman* and *Scottish Business Insider*, see the bulletin of the Fraser of Allander Institute, the government's *Scottish Economic Bulletin*, and the publications of the Scottish Council Institute. Jeremy Peat and Bill Jamieson, *An Illustrated Guide to the Scottish Economy* (London, 1999), along with Christopher Harvie, *Fool's Gold: The Story of North Sea Oil* (London, 1994) and Clive Lee, *Scotland and the United Kingdom* (Manchester, 1995), tackle (among other issues) the vexed question of the country's balance of payments. Ausland Cramb, *Who Owns Scotland Now? The Use and Abuse of Private Land* (Edinburgh, 1996) updates John McEwen's *Who Owns Scotland? A Study in Land Ownership* (Edinburgh, 1977; 2nd edn., 1981). 'Glasgow Redux' comes under the eye of Ian Spring in *Phantom Village* (Edinburgh, 1989), and of Michael Keating, *The City that Refused to Die: Glasgow* (Aberdeen, 1988), but there's no equivalent for dynamic Edinburgh.

Searching for social background, we encounter the once-reliable *Abstract*, reinforced by *Social Trends*. Edinburgh University's *Yearbook of Scottish Politics* and its more gallus *doppelgänger*, *Radical Scotland* lasted until 1993 and 1992 respectively, and the quarterly *Scottish Affairs* thereafter has a wealth of well-researched pieces on politics and policy – but, alas, no cartoons, diatribes or insults. Along with Christopher Harvie, *No Gods and Precious Few Heroes: Scotland, 1914–1980* (London, 1981; 2nd edn., 1998), Cairns Craig, *The History of Scottish Literature*, vol. 4 (Aberdeen, 1987), A. Dickson and J. Treble (eds.), *People and Society in Scotland*, vol. 3, *1914–1990* (Edinburgh, 1992), the quarterlies the *Edinburgh Review*, *Cencrastus* and *Chapman* offer valuable comment on cultural affairs.

In analyses of society, the national question won out over the 'real divide'. David McCrone's *Understanding Scotland: The Sociology of a Stateless Nation* (London, 1992) and D. McCrone, Stephen Kendrick and Pat Straw (eds.), *The Making of Scotland: Nation, Culture and Social Change* (Edinburgh, 1989) overtook the Bennism of Gordon Brown and Robin Cook (eds.), *Scotland: The Real Divide. Poverty and Deprivation in Scotland* (Edinburgh, 1982). The latter's solicitousness about the fate of the 30 per cent who were on the other side of the divide did not outlast the 1980s; the 1990s poor were more dependent on the Christian socialism of Bob Holman, *Faith in the Poor* (Oxford, 1998) and the marxism of Tommy Sheridan, *A Time to Rage* (Edinburgh, 1994). For minorities and the under-represented, see Bashir Maan, *The New Scots: The Story of Asians in Scotland* (Edinburgh, 1992); Raymond Boyle and Peter Lynch (eds.), *Out of the Ghetto? The Catholic Community in Modern Scotland* (Edinburgh, 1998); Woman's Claim of Right Group, *A Woman's Claim of Right in Scotland* (Edinburgh, 1991); and Edinburgh University Centre for the Study of Theology and Politics, *Churches and the Political Process in Scotland Today* (Edinburgh, 1989).

As to coverage of culture, there are the relevant parts of Craig Beveridge and Ronald Turnbull, *The Eclipse of Scottish Culture: Inferiorism and the Intellectuals* (Edinburgh, 1989) and their *Scotland after Enlightenment: Image and Tradition in Modern Scottish Culture* (Edinburgh, 1997). See also Duncan MacMillan, *Scottish Art, 1460–1990* (Edinburgh, 1990); John Purser, *Scotland's Music: A History of the Traditional and Classical Music of Scotland from Earliest Times to the Present Day* (Edinburgh, 1990); Ian S. Wood (ed.), *Scotland and Ulster* (Edinburgh, 1994), a pioneer probe in a sensitive area; Gavin Wallace and Randall Stevenson (eds.), *The Scottish Novel since the Seventies: New Visions, Old Dreams* (Edinburgh, 1993); Cairns Craig, *The Modern Scottish Novel: Narrative and the National Imagination* (Edinburgh, 1999); and Grant Jarvie and Graham Walker (eds.), *Scottish Sport in the Making of the Nation: Ninety-Minute Patriots?* (Leicester, 1994). For political rock and much else, see Pat Kane, *Tinsel Show: Pop, Politics, Scotland* (Edinburgh, 1992).

About the Authors

Dr Ian Armit is a Senior Lecturer in Archaeology at the Queen's University of Belfast. He gained his first degree and doctorate at Edinburgh University, where he also managed the Centre for Field Archaeology from 1990 to 1992, and edited his first book, *Beyond the Brochs* (1990). From 1992 to 1999 he worked as an Inspector of Ancient Monuments with Historic Scotland. His research focused initially on the archaeology of the Western Isles and the study of brochs, and his doctorate on this subject was published as *The Later Prehistory of the Western Isles of Scotland* (1992). Latterly he has worked more in southern Scotland, notably undertaking the first modern research excavation programme on the major Iron Age hill fort of Traprain Law in East Lothian. Dr Armit has published numerous books on Scottish archaeology, most recently *The Archaeology of Skye and the Western Isles* (1996), *Celtic Scotland* (1997), and *Scotland's Hidden History* (1998). He has also published more than fifty academic papers relating to various aspects of Scottish and north-west European prehistory. He is a Fellow of the Society of Antiquaries of both London and Scotland, and a member of the Institute of Field Archaeologists.

Keith Brown has been Professor of Scottish History at the University of St Andrews since 1995. A graduate of Glasgow University, where he also completed his Ph.D. in 1983, he held a succession of post-doctoral positions at St Andrews until he was appointed Lecturer in History at the University of Stirling in 1990. His main research interests are the early modern Scottish nobility and issues of Scottish and British identity in the seventeenth century. In addition to essays and articles on these themes, he has published *Bloodfeud in Scotland, 1573–1625: Violence, Justice and Politics in an Early Modern Society* (1986); *Kingdom or Province: Scotland and the Regal Union, 1603–1715* (1992); and *Noble Society in Scotland: Wealth, Family and Culture from Reformation to Revolution* (2000).

Dr Thomas Clancy is a Lecturer in Celtic at the University of Glasgow, where he teaches medieval Celtic languages and literatures, as well as history, religion and culture. He holds a B.A. in Medieval Studies from New York University, and a Ph.D. from the University of Edinburgh, where he was initially a Fulbright Scholar. His doctorate was on folly and sanctity in early Irish literature, and portions of this have since been published in article form. From 1993 to 1995, he was a British Academy Postdoctoral Research Fellow, before taking up his current post. His published work is wide-ranging, with articles on early Gaelic literature; on the development of the early church in Scotland; on the cult of St Columba, and the writings of Adomnán; and on modern Scottish Gaelic poetry. With Gilbert Márkus, he published *Iona: The Earliest Poetry of a Celtic Monastery* (1995). More recently, he edited *The Triumph Tree: Scotland's Earliest Poetry AD 550–1350* (1998), in which a team of translators made accessible the poetic remains of early medieval Scotland. He has also edited, with Dauvit Broun, *Spes Scotorum – Hope of Scots: St Columba, Iona and Scotland* (1999); and with Richard Welander and David Breeze, *The Stone of Destiny* (2000). He edits the *Innes Review*, the journal of the Scottish Catholic Historical Association.

Dr Barbara Crawford is Lecturer in Medieval History at the University of St Andrews. Her doctoral research was about the Earls of Orkney-Caithness from the late Norse period until 1468. An interest in archaeology from undergraduate days was then developed as part of an inter-disciplinary approach to Norse studies, and she conducted her own excavation of a Norse farm site on the island of Papa Stour in Shetland. The report has been published: *The History and Excavation of a Royal Norwegian Farm at the Biggings, Papa Stour, Shetland* (1999). The same multi-disciplinary approach underlies her textbook *Scandinavian Scotland* (1987), and a book of essays on the place-names of Norse settlement edited by her: *Scandinavian Settlement in Northern Britain* (1995). Other works she has edited include *Scotland in Dark-Age Europe* (1994), *Scotland in Dark-Age Britain* (1996) and *Conversion and Christianity in the North Sea World* (1998). Her main research programme focuses on the links across the North Sea in the Viking and medieval periods. She is a member of the Norwegian Academy and, as a member of the Royal Commission on Ancient and Historical Monuments of Scotland, chair of the Treasure Trove Advisory Panel for Scotland and chair of the Conference of Scottish Medievalists, she is deeply involved in the protection and advancement of Scotland's cultural heritage.

Dr David Ditchburn is a graduate of the University of Edinburgh, where he completed his doctoral thesis on the Scottish connections with Germany and the Baltic in the later medieval period. He was appointed a Research Fellow in History at the University of Aberdeen in 1989 and has been a Lecturer in History there since 1993. The author of *Scotland and Europe: The Medieval Kingdom and its Contact with Christendom c. 1215–1542* (2001), he has also published several articles on commercial and diplomatic aspects of Scotland's overseas contacts in the later medieval period and on the economy of the Isle of Man in the Middle Ages. He is co-editor (with Angus MacKay) of an *Atlas of Medieval Europe* (1997) and (with Terry Brotherstone) of *Freedom and Authority: Scotland c. 1050–1650. Historical and Historiographical Essays presented to Grant G. Simpson* (2000). He is currently co-editing a volume on the history of Aberdeen before 1800. Possessing British-Swiss dual nationality, he is an unashamed Lusophile and long-suffering Dunfermline Athletic supporter.

Professor John Foster was born in Hertford in 1940 and has lived in Scotland since 1968. He is currently Professor of Applied Social Studies at Paisley University. He previously taught politics at Strathclyde University and history at Cambridge, where he was a Research Fellow at

St Catharine's College. In the 1960s and 1970s he researched and wrote on English social history in the nineteenth and twentieth centuries, his main work being *Class Struggle and the Industrial Revolution: Early Industrial Capitalism in Three English Towns*. In Scotland he contributed 'Scottish Capitalism' to Gordon Brown's *Red Paper on Scotland* (1975) and the section on medieval Scotland to *Scottish Capitalism*, edited by Tony Dickson (1981). He has written a number of research articles on the Red Clyde and has collaborated with Charles Woolfson in a series of books on the modern Scottish working class: *The Politics of the UCS Work-In* (1986), *Track Record, the Story of the Caterpillar Occupation* (1988) and *Paying for the Piper: Capital and Labour in the Offshore Oil Industry* (1996). In the 1960s and 1970s he was on the editorial boards of *Marxism Today* and *Scottish Marxist* and was editor of *Our History* from 1969 to 1985. Today he is on the editorial board of *Communist Review*. In 1989 he helped produce *Claiming the Future: Scotland's Economy* for the Scottish Trades Union Congress. His current research focus is on ethnicity and industrial relations in late nineteenth-century Scotland.

Professor Christopher Harvie is a graduate of Edinburgh University. He lectured in history at the Open University and is now Professor of British and Irish Studies at the University of Tübingen in Germany, and an Honorary Professor at Aberystwyth and Strathclyde. His publications include *The Centre of Things*, on political fiction in Britain, the textbook *No Gods and Precious Few Heroes: Scotland, 1914–1980* (1981), *Scotland and Nationalism* (1977; 1998), *The Rise of Regional Europe* and *Fool's Gold: The Story of North Sea Oil* (both 1994). A prolific writer of both academic and popular works, he is also a well-known figure on the international lecture circuit. He is currently engaged on a study of the society and culture of the Atlantic coast, 1860–1920.

Rab Houston was born in Hamilton and went to school in Edinburgh. He graduated M.A. in Modern History at St Andrews in 1977. He then spent six years at Cambridge as a research student at Peterhouse and a Research Fellow at Clare College before returning to St Andrews as a lecturer in 1983. He became Reader in Modern History in 1993 and Professor of Early Modern History in 1995. In 1994 he held a visiting professorship at the Faculteit der Historische en Kunstwetenschappen, Erasmus University, Rotterdam, and was a 'Distinguished Visiting Scholar' at the Department of History, University of Adelaide, for a semester in 1996. He has published extensively (nine books and seventy articles and book chapters) in the social history of early modern Britain and Europe, including the fields of literacy and education, urbanization, historical demography and social relationships. His most recent work has been on the history of mental disability, including *Madness and Society in Eighteenth-century Scotland* (2000) and *Autism in History: The Case of Hugh Blair* (2000). He is a Fellow of the Royal Historical Society and of Academia Europea. He is married and lives in St Andrews.

Dr William Knox was born and raised in Edinburgh, where he gained his first degree and doctorate at the city's University. After a period of lecturing at Heriot-Watt University, Dr Knox moved to the University of St Andrews in 1989, where he is a Senior Lecturer in, and Head of the Department of, Scottish History. His published work has focused on social and labour history, and includes four books and numerous articles spanning the last sixteen years. His work encompasses biographical studies – *Scottish Labour Leaders, 1918–1939* (1984), and industrial histories – *Hanging by a Thread: The Scottish Cotton Industry, c. 1850–1914* (1996). More recently he published a major work on the Scottish working class: *Industrial Nation: Work, Culture and Society in Scotland, 1800–present* (1999). He is currently studying the impact of US multinational companies on Scotland's economy in the period 1945–1970.

Bruce Lenman is Professor of Modern History in the University of St Andrews. He was born in Aberdeen and educated at Aberdeen Grammar School, Aberdeen University and St John's College, Cambridge. He was trained as an imperial historian, started working in a Canadian university, and published first on colonial warfare in India. A job in Dundee University led to an interest in the jute industry, a Scoto-Indian topic, and to publication on that industry and on Scottish east coast ports, followed by a short economic history of modern Scotland. He is also a retired Jacobite historian, having written three books on the Jacobite rebellions and co-authored another. His recent publication has been in his original field and includes a two-volume work on colonial wars and English identities in the early modern period. He has held visiting professorships in the College of William and Mary in Virginia and in Emory University in Atlanta, Georgia, as well as fellowships in the Newberry Library in Chicago, the John Carter Brown Library in Providence, Rhode Island, the Huntington Library in Pasadena, California, and the Virginia Historical Society in Richmond. He is a Fellow of the Royal Historical Society. His current research interest is in Spanish colonial port cities and the history of attacks on them by other maritime powers.

Dr Alastair MacDonald was brought up near Dunfermline and in the United States. He obtained a degree in English and History at the University of Aberdeen and completed his doctoral thesis on Anglo-Scottish relations in the later fourteenth century at the same university in 1995. His thesis has been revised for publication as *Border Bloodshed: England and Scotland at War, 1369–1403* (2000). He has published several other articles (on topics such as the nobility and warfare, and the historiography of the later medieval Anglo-Scottish frontier) and is currently writing a new monograph on war and society in later medieval Scotland. He was appointed Mackie Lecturer in History at the University of Aberdeen in 1997. He is a keen amateur footballer.

Bob Morris has been Professor of Economic and Social History at the University of Edinburgh since 1992. Born in Sheffield, he has worked all his tax-paying life in Scotland. Professor Morris's major research interests include the development of the British middle class in the nineteenth century, focusing on patterns of association and the family as an economic unit, and on urban social structure in Britain, Ireland and Canada. His major publications include: *Class and Class Consciousness in the Industrial Revolution* (1979); 'Voluntary Societies and British Urban Elites, 1780–1870', *Historical Journal* (1982); *Atlas of Industrializing Britain, 1780–1914*, edited with John Langton (1986); *Class, Sect and Party* (1990); 'Middle Class and British Towns and Cities in the Industrial Revolution, 1780–1870', in D. Fraser and A. Sutcliffe (eds.), *The Pursuit of Urban History* (1983); *People and Society in Scotland*, vol. 2: *1830–1914*, edited with W. Hamish Fraser (1990); 'Associations', in F. M. L. Thompson (ed.), *The Cambridge Social History of*

Britain, vol. 3: *1750–1950* (1990); *The Victorian City. A Reader in British Urban History, 1820–1914*, edited with Richard Rodger (1993). He was a founding editor of *History and Computing* for the Association for History and Computing.

Graeme Morton, MA, Ph.D., is Lecturer in Economic and Social History at the University of Edinburgh. Born and bred in Fife, he was appointed to his present post in 1992. His current interest in civil society and local/central government developed from themes identified during a research fellowship (1994–8) awarded by the Economic and Social Research Council; their support is gratefully acknowledged. Dr Morton's special area of interest remains Scottish national identity. His major publications include *Unionist-Nationalism: Governing Urban Scotland, 1830–1860* (1999) and *Locality, Community and Nation*, with Angela Morris (1998). He is currently completing a book on the myth of William Wallace. Recent articles include: 'Civil Society, Municipal Government and the State: enshrinement, empowerment and legitimacy, Scotland, 1800–1929', *Urban History* 25, 3 (1998); 'The Most Efficacious Patriot: the heritage of William Wallace in nineteenth-century Scotland', *Scottish Historical Review* LXXVII, 2: 204 (1998); and 'What if? The significance of Scotland's missing nationalism in the nineteenth century', in D. Broun, R. Finlay and M. Lynch (eds.), *Image and Identity: The Making and Re-making of Scotland through the Ages* (1998).

Index